D0850353

THE PSYCHOPHYSIOLOGY
OF THINKING

Studies of Covert Processes

Jacobson

Stoyva

Sperry

From left, standing: Osgood, Rechtschaffen, Paivio, MacNeilage, Hefferline, and Black, *seated*: Chapman, McGuigan, Grings, Mulholland.

THE PSYCHOPHYSIOLOGY OF THINKING

STUDIES OF COVERT PROCESSES

Edited by

F. J. McGUIGAN and R. A. SCHOONOVER

Department of Psychology
Hollins College
Roanoke, Virginia

 ACADEMIC PRESS   New York and London   1973

ACADEMIC PRESS, INC.
111 Fifth Avenue, New York, New York 10003

United Kingdom Edition published by
ACADEMIC PRESS, INC. (LONDON) LTD.
24/28 Oval Road, London NW1

LIBRARY OF CONGRESS CATALOG CARD NUMBER: 72-82658

PRINTED IN THE UNITED STATES OF AMERICA

TO DR. EDMUND JACOBSON

In recognition of his pioneering research
in the psychophysiology of higher mental processes.

Contents

Emphasis on
Central Nervous System—Primarily Surgical Approaches

Emphasis on Peripheral Measures—Primarily Autonomic Behavior

Integrative Approaches

List of Contributors

Numbers in parentheses indicate the pages on which the authors' contributions begin.

A. H. BLACK (35), Department of Psychology, McMaster University, Hamilton, Ontario, Canada

LOUIS J. J. BRUNO (299), Department of Psychology, Columbia University, New York, New York

JANET A. CAMP (299), Department of Psychology, Columbia University, New York, New York

ROBERT M. CHAPMAN (69), Eye Research Foundation of Bethesda, Bethesda, Maryland and Walter Reed Army Institute of Research, Washington, D.C.

WILLIAM W. GRINGS (233), Department of Psychology, University of Southern California, Los Angeles, California

RALPH F. HEFFERLINE (299), Department of Psychology, Columbia University, New York, New York

EDMUND JACOBSON (3), Laboratory for Clinical Physiology, Chicago, Illinois

F. J. MCGUIGAN (343, 449), Department of Psychology, Hollins College, Roanoke, Virginia

LINDA A. MACNEILAGE (417), Department of Lingustics and Psychology, University of Texas at Austin, Austin Texas

PETER F. MACNEILAGE (417), Department of Lingustics and Psychology, University of Texas at Austin, Austin, Texas

THOMAS MULHOLLAND (109), Massachusetts Perception Laboratory, Veterans Administration Hospital, Bedford, Massachusetts

CHARLES E. OSGOOD (449), Department of Psychology, University of Illinois, Urbana-Champaign, Illinois

ALLAN PAIVIO (263), Department of Psychology, University of Western Ontario, Ontario, Canada

ALLAN RECHTSCHAFFEN (153), Department of Psychology, University of Chicago, Chicago, Illinois

R. W. SPERRY (209), Division of Biology, California Institute of Technology, Pasadena, California

JOHANN STOYVA (387), Department of Psychiatry, University of Colorado Medical Center, Denver, Colorado

Preface

Within the last decade, sizable advances have been made in the physiology, psychology, and psychophysiology of what has traditionally been called "thinking." In more contemporary language it may be said that we are considerably increasing our knowledge about internal information processing. To mention but a few such advances, we may note successful research on the contingent negative variation, unique evoked brain potentials as a function of meaning of stimuli, established relationships between parameters of eye activity and cognitive content both in dreams and while awake, impressive phenomena and theories in the areas of semantics, verbal mediation, speech perception, and so forth.

The purpose of the conference upon which this book is based—that of integrating such disparate knowledge about thinking—was thus most timely. The strategy employed was to bring together experts from a variety of areas so that they could exchange information on problems of common interest, though the approaches are from different points of view and with different measures. The fruits of this week of pooling of knowledge should allow us to better relate brain events with peripheral bodily phenomena in the context of psychological theory, and thus not only to facilitate research in specific areas but to advance our general level of scientific understanding of "thought." The outstanding qualifications of these distinguished participants, and the high level of their interchange guarantees successful accomplishment of this goal.

The approach taken in this conference thus stands in some contrast to related ones, like the Hixon Symposium (Jeffress—*Cerebral Mechanisms in Behavior*), the Laurentian Conference (Delafresnaye—*Brain Mechanisms and Behavior*), or the Pontifical Academy Study Week (Eccles—*Brain and Conscious Experience*), in that its scope was more extensive. Both approaches—that of concentrating on cerebral phenomena and that of integrating different bodily processes have virtue. The integrative approach is, however, the more unusual. While the present proceedings also include some concentration on *cerebral mechanisms* (see especially Black, Chapman, Mulholland, and Sperry) they should also have appeal for those whose principal concern is with the involvement of other bodily (behavioral) mechanisms in thought. The range of specific topics covered, while centering on the "higher mental processes," is therefore necessarily broad. For example, a number of participants made impressive contributions to *conditioning* (for conditioning of central states see Black, and also Mulholland; for the skeletal musculature see Hefferline, Stoyva, Osgood and McGuigan; for autonomic activity see Grings). Others made important contributions to the study of *hallucinations* (Hefferline, Stoyva), to *sleep and dreaming* (Rechtschaffen, MacNeilage), to *imagery* (Paivio), to *biofeedback* (Stoyva, Mulholland, McGuigan), to *evoked potentials during thought* (Chapman), to *meaning* (Osgood, Paivio), to the *generalized study of thought with concomitant measures* (Black, Jacobson, McGuigan), etc. It is indeed difficult to find many important topics in the scientific study of thought that do not appear somewhere in these proceedings. Only an extension of the week would have allowed greater emphasis on some, such as cardiac and vasomotor involvement, computer analogies, salivary measures, hypnosis, or sensory deprivation.

The conference itself was attended by some 300 visitors who made noticeable contributions during the discussion following each major presentation, and during the final period of open discussion. We appreciated this enthusiastic attendance, and are also grateful to the National Science Foundation and to Hollins College for financial support.

Informality was the theme throughout, a factor that contributed to the success of the conference by encouraging vigorous discussion, usually until the early hours of the morning. However, though the major presentations were informally spoken at the conference, the written versions here were later reworked by the authors. The discussions, but not the papers, were edited, in cooperation with the authors, for the benefit of the reader.

Finally, it should be noted that Dr. Jacobson's paper clearly fits under the category of Peripheral Electromyographic Measures, where it *was* presented eleventh in order. However, his paper serves as such an impressive introduction, with its historical development of electrical measures of covert processes, that it was moved forward to the first position. This change should be kept in mind when reading the discussion following Dr. Jacobson's paper.

INTRODUCTION

CHAPTER ONE

Electrophysiology of Mental Activities and Introduction to The Psychological Process of Thinking[1]

EDMUND JACOBSON

Laboratory for Clinical Physiology, Chicago

People differ. They differ in their thumbprints, as the F.B.I. knows, so that they can be identified individually. They differ in their cardiograms, as the cardiologist knows, although those differences often are rather hard to point out. They differ in their anatomy tremendously— much more than the textbooks give you reason to believe. In my personal experience the most thorough textbooks in anatomy are really only diagrammatic in their description of nerves and muscles. People have a lot of muscles. Their use is commonly called "behavior," although when I read the literature of behaviorists I often wonder whether the writers clearly realize that what they are largely describing are the overt manifestations of the neuromuscular configurations of approximately 1030 individual skeletal muscles.

People differ tremendously and uniquely in their blood picture and in their every cell, tissue and organ. However, the common characteristics are equally striking. Difference in thinking would seem to be greater than the differences in the various other respects mentioned. Thinking depends upon certain elements that have been discussed and will be discussed in this conference by others. I had planned originally to discuss conceptual thinking in addition to "Electrophysiology of Mental Activities," but upon hearing your excellent papers, discretion got the better part of

---

[1] Recordings by Richard E. Lange.

3

valor. The problems of "thinking" are hard to subject to laboratory techniques, although we have a good understanding in the clinic, from daily investigation tested by clinical results.

In 1910, I left Harvard to go to Cornell with the express purpose of studying thinking, but found that perception had been so little studied that there was scarcely a general understanding of this function. I do not refer to the extensive studies of psychologists and physiologists on vision, hearing, and other sensory responses. But perception—just what happens when an object is perceived, not merely sensed, had not been studied. I went to Cornell also, if I may be forgiven reminiscence, hoping that the students would be experts in self-observation; unfortunately, finding to my disappointment that they had to be taught from scratch, largely because they did not know the difference between *meaning* and *signals*. In a year they became quite skilled.

In electrophysiology, of course, we record signalization, not meaning. As one knows, some physiologists and some of you likewise have joined in the complex study of "information processing in the nervous system." I think the term is not quite accurate, but attending the meetings proves rewarding. A tremendous amount of information has been developed since the first meeting at Leiden some years ago. Nevertheless, information is not what is processed in the nervous system. I continually use a figure of speech when comparing the human organism with the telegraph system— Morse Code. There you brought the message to the receiving operator and he used a telegraph key to transmit your words in signals. These were conveyed with the speed of light along wires (dc) to the end operator who interpreted them and gave the message. This illustrates essentially the structure and function of the human mind, excepting that in the place of one such communications system you have 20—at least 20. I do not know how many; nobody but ourselves would be interested in determining how many there are. As yet we lack the facilities to determine how many there are. It is a problem for at least the next 50 years. At any rate, here is your human organism, provided with 20 or more different forms of signals and meanings intertwined and integrated, called "the human mind."

Now to come back to differences: There are differences among students on any subject. We should not expect an identity of concept—not even in the same person from time-to-time. He differs. He differs in many respects even from himself. The concept of mental activity is something that has come down to us historically—come down to us in what many psychologists have regarded as philosophic confusion, as, e.g., the doctrine of parallelism and interaction, which are simply signs of the confusion of former days about the nature of the so-called human mind. I believe that present-day students inevitably carry a great deal of their conceptions quite often from the past and have not really faced modern technology. For today, you could not pick a better example than Charles Sherrington, a magnificent physiologist, who introduced the conception of integration by the nervous system. Yet he was certainly anything but clear about the human mind when he argued for the doctrine of interaction.

What I am trying to indicate in this prelude is that we cannot expect students generally to share an identical concept of mental activity. Some will carry over concepts from the past without knowing it and be utterly confident that what they say is unchallengeable. In our institute we have a custom of buying almost all the books that come out on brain research and these are for the most part by capable physiologists with occasionally some psychologists joining in the symposium. The conception of physiologists of mental activity is *not your* conception. There are some, without question, who have part of your training, but in general, when a physiologist speaks about mental activity to the experienced psychologist, he is talking in a foreign language. This difference in conception is quite interesting.

Now, after listening with great enjoyment to the magnificent paper on measurements of yesterday afternoon, in contrast what I have to say will be more or less elemental. If I am permitted to indulge in a reminiscence, answering a question from Dr. McGuigan—how I first happened to measure mental activity peripherally. I had for many, many years been hoping to get started at it and had cultivated a sort of internal observation which seemed to indicate to me that whenever I engaged in any type of mental activity—no matter how abstract, I would simultaneously—not successively or previously, but simultaneously be engaging the muscle groups in various portions of the body, many of them ocular, many of them speech, but apparently any muscle group could engage so far as this type of observation indicated. Now, this is what you call introspective observation, excepting that it is nothing like the introspection of Professor Titchner. He felt that meanings didn't belong in psychology. Psychology was to Titchner exemplified by Ebbinghaus' nonsense syllables. Any process associated with meanings he called "logic" and therefore he acquitted his students from having any studies on meaning. He never realized that all thinking is concerned with meanings. He never visited the laboratory in the days when I was there. Neverthelesss, at the end of the year, suddenly he called me to his home and said, "Cornell has been criticized for the neglect of meaning, but you haven't neglected meaning!" and so he wanted a paper published at once, namely, my paper on "Meaning and Understanding" (Jacobson, 1911). Meanings are part of thinking. It was amazing that Titchner did not share this view and after I left, he engaged in efforts still further to prove that meanings did not belong in psychology.

William James, of course, had no such views of introspection nor did Wilhelm Wundt. Both of these great men included meanings in their introspection. However, neither of them differentiated meanings from signals, the modern imperative distinction introduced by the article on Meaning and Understanding mentioned above (Jacobson, 1911). Furthermore psychologists of a former day misunderstood elementary mental processes, mistaking abstractions such as sensation and association for mental activities (Jacobson, 1970). During the 1920s, I asked how could one bring basic psychology into the laboratory clearly and definitely? With regard to measurement, I tried to get started as early as 1920. I remember visiting Dr. H. S. Gasser (who later became head of the Rockefeller Institute) and saying "I shall need to measure certain physiological occurrences in terms of microvolts" and Dr. Gasser said "Isn't that a millionth of a volt?" To my affirmative reply he said "I take my hat off to a microvolt!"

I relate this to indicate that in early years voltage measurement was not yet in the physiological literature. Recording microvoltage on your records was not yet in vogue and had to be introduced to physiologists. At any rate, how to measure minute muscular contractions became an acute problem until the intervention of that providence which undertakes to help psychologists. The chairman of physiology at Columbia University introduced me to two very great engineers of Bell Telephone Laboratories, and this led to an association of their laboratories with my own laboratory then at the University of Chicago. This was unique. In deference to Bell Laboratories, I might say it was the greatest honor that can come to a biologist. They never have collaborated with any individual or university in the thorough manner of our association, and thanks to their public service contribution, I was able to invent some measuring instruments capable of evaluating what I needed measured. I nearly lost out on that, recalling the first conference and relating to the engineers that the job would be to measure in terms of a fraction of 1 μV, the engineers all agreed that this was, of course, impossible. Now, if I had said it was possible, they might have quit at once. So I agreed. We went on, and after I showed them early circuit designs they got started, and thanks to their continuous efforts, I was able to develop the integrating neurovoltmeter which will be introduced in the pictures that we have here on the slides. I should add that today we have vastly refined the exactitude of this instrument. Let me say briefly that, in biology, rectification and integration had never been known; I had to introduce these methodologies via this instrument. What was required, which we did not realize until later, was that we had to narrow our bandwidth. By the way, somebody has said here that the muscle potentials go up to 50. Wachholder early said that they were sometimes as infrequent as 1/sec. But Oliver Buckley (President of the Laboratories) and I in a study made at his home found that there are harmonics that you could record up to 6000/sec. I do not think we have ever published that. However, you can narrow your bandwidth as you choose for your purposes if you avoid 60-cycle interference.

Today, we have it down to an accuracy of one ten-millionth of a volt, that is 1/10 of a microvolt. On short circuit of our amplifier input the recording line is straight, approximately, at 1/10 of 1 μV above zero which is an amazing performance. Originally, at the University of Chicago, I could not even permit the technician alone in the room for fear that he might insert some switch into the circuit. Now we have any number of switches in the circuit with no difficulty whatsoever. However, let me emphasize that we have not yet been able to supply inexpensive models of these instruments for laboratories of psychology and physiology and general education (for which there is considerable demand). Our foundation plans to do this but as yet we have not succeeded in getting a corporation that would manufacture them at a reasonable price. This leads me to emphasize that the electromyographs that you buy commercially in Europe or this country are not adequate for studies of electrophysiology of mental activity.

Now, as to "concepts": Many physiologists seem to write as if the brain is a man who receives messages and issues orders. (Permit me a little latitude of speech here, because one would not say it in that form. I am writing a little parody on their use of the term "brain.") Our work, our results, not only in the laboratory but in the clinic, rather encourage the use that psychologists long ago introduced—that of comparing the human mind with the telephone system—central and the telephone. The analogy can be carried too far. The brain has been compared with central. The comparison is good insofar as central is indispensable to telephoning. (Whether central is personal operators or automatic central makes no difference.) Without central, you cannot phone from here to New York.

On the other hand, I do believe that this figure of speech enables us to point out the common failure of proper conception of the human mind; namely, central is indispensable and the brain is indispensable, but nobody has ever proved that the brain does all the thinking. As a matter of fact, the measurements such as I shall show you were considered by physiologists of the University to indicate that by no means does the brain alone do the thinking. Ralph Lilly, a venerable physiologist, said that my studies made in 1930–1934 proved that the brain had no closed circuits when it came to mental activity. I would abide by that. And A. J. Carlson, head of the department—the world-renowned skeptic in physiology, commented in a dialect that I am not able to imitate—"Well, what you have proved is that mental activities are physical acts." He meant, of course, miniature, not overt acts. If these are the correct conceptions of the human mind, we should not expect them to get over quickly to the scientific public, because concepts take a long time to die when they are traditional. Suffice it to say, in any event, that what we show, I believe beyond any doubt (what Dr. McGuigan, illustrated beyond any doubt) is that if you are going to study thinking, imagination and memory from the standpoint of electrical measurements, you must differentiate the peripheral aspects from the central. Central aspects are important, of course. Unfortunately, and it is a terrible misfortune, the human brain is in the skull, which you don't like to open up for your psychological study. It is too bad! And the brain circuits are just endless! I can not do better than to ask you to refer to the conditioning studies of M. N. Livanof of the Soviet Republic, where you see evidence that in the learning processes studied any portion of the brain is found to be active at the moment of learning. Imagine the complexity of anything like that—far more complex than your central telephone system! But on the peripheral side, there is fortunately a much greater clarity, in the skeletal system at least. Thinking, likewise, involves the emotional system, but we do not have the facilities for direct study as we do in the skeletal muscle system. For example, in emotions there are specific relationships too, e.g., fear. Now fear is an odd experience, preeminently an activity of the gastrointestinal tract, especially the esophagus. I once said to a physiologist (who wanted me to read some paper) that the esophagus is always involved in fear. As a scientist, he did not like the word "always." I did not argue else I could have said, "The eyes are always involved in vision." I don't think he could have debated that too far, but it seemed better not to debate. However, in our experience, the esophagus *is* always involved, as indicated by fluoroscopic studies of one who is fearful and anxious. We give a spoonful of thick barium paste and the esophagus will not expel this into the stomach of the fearful person as it does in the person without fear. We took 100 students at the University of Chicago and gave them such a spoonful of paste and it almost all passed into the stomach under a minute. If, in a fearful person, you take a film of the esophagus, you will find much of the barium is still there after 5 min, often 10 min, 20 min, even an hour. Now nobody, I think, would be inclined to state that the experience of the esophagus is really in the brain. I might explain that I am not an adherent of the James Lange emotional theory. I am not following any theory; *I have never advocated the motor theory of consciousness.* I am just discussing the straight facts of mental experience. Well, with that long introduction, maybe I had better have Slide 1, please.

The study here is with the integrating neurovoltmeter, and the subject was fairly thoroughly trained in relaxation. Now why the training in relaxation? What does that have to do with it? Well, if you are going to study mental activity, you must take into account that the normal healthy individual is extremely noisy inside (using the term "noise" in the sense of the electronic engineer). Every individual has continual interplay of 1030 skeletal muscles; many of them—or most of them are doing something all of the time. How do we know this? Well, we make measurements of normals, and patients before treatment, also, from time-to-time during treatment and afterward. The measurements are simultaneously recorded from forehead, brow, lids, eye movement, EOG, jaws, tongue (sometimes), larynx (sometimes), arms, and legs, or at least one arm and one leg. We take a 30-min reading with our integrating neurovoltmeter while a digital computer listens in so that we have typical recordings of normals, as well as patients and compare them from time-to-time. Accordingly, we know from daily measurements that the average person is pretty noisy in the sense of various tensions of his muscles and if we are going to isolate the particular phenomenon like this one—imagine saying the first three letters of the alphabet—if we are going to bring that out, we can not have him just tensing all of his musculature. Like the average untrained person, we must show him first how to be muscularly relaxed. But that is a long procedure and will not be discussed here. Among the teaching procedures I have used is one that today would be called "feedback." Many years ago I used the oscilloscope, while the patient or the normal person learning to relax would watch the movements (which you see here) on the oscilloscope and then we would show him how to begin to relax the muscles, and he would have the oscilloscope tracings there to watch as he learned. This was widely published (not only in scientific journals, but also in *Newsweek*, Feb. 1, 1954, p. 39). I did not call that feedback, in fact, the term feedback is misused in psychology and physiology and I think Dr. McGuigan seemed to indicate something of that point. In feedback, the output of an amplifier or other instrument is connected directly with the input. This connection conveys current or voltage (electrical pressure) with the speed of light. The information is not first expelled from the output and later fed back into

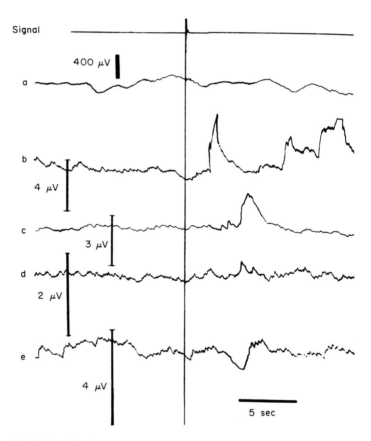

Fig. 1.1. Subject P. A., male, 57 years old, trained to relax. Instruction "Imagine saying first three letters of alphabet." Signal line at top. Trace a is EOG, left = upward movement of eyes, right = downward. Trace b is tongue, c is lips, d is jaw muscles, e is mylohyoid region. Imagining is registered chiefly in traces b and c.

the input. Engineering feedback is instantaneous. I believe that we had better avoid the term feedback as too much of an inaccuracy and too much of a publicity stunt besides. At any rate (see Fig. 1.1) this man relaxes here fairly well. The top line is the signal line, and the one below is the EOG eye movement up and down: up is left and down is right. There is not too much of interest in the EOG here. In trace b you have

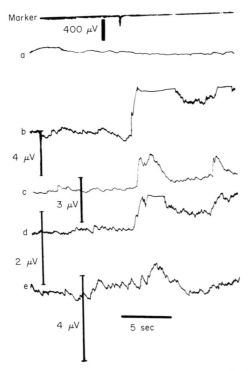

Fig. 1.2. Control test is same subject instructed to say same aloud. Tracings similar except higher microvoltages. Jaw muscle voltages pronounced.

the tongue, in c, the lips. We assume that the activities recorded here in the tongue and lips are the imaginative activities. In c the peak thus represents the labial action upon imagining saying the second letter of the alphabet; d is the jaw, which does not show too much and e is from the mylohyoid region. You can see the voltages that are involved here.

Figure 1.2 is a control test where the individual is asked to say the same "A, B, C" out loud. Voltage in imagination is far less.

Figure 1.3 indicates the individual reading silently. We want to know what takes place in this individual. Notice trace g here at the bottom, a record of the pneumograph of breathing. Breathing takes into account the general tension of the organism. Muscular tension, the contraction of the muscle, as we know, depends upon the burning of foodstuffs like carbohydrates and fats. But we are now able to be more specific, namely,

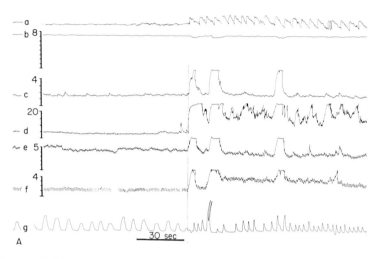

Fig. 1.3. Subject J. R., 67 years old, trained to relax, silently reading magazine. Section 1, control test, following instruction to relax. Trace g, from pneumograph, indicates respiration reduced from normal of 18 to 9/min showing relaxed state; a is EOG, left = up, right = down; b, brow muscles; c, jaw muscles; d, tongue muscles; e, mylohyoid; f, larynx. Eyes quiet but brow is tense, offscale above 8 μV; jaw quiet, tongue and floor steady tension at about 5 μV, larynx steady at about 1 μV. Section 2, silent reading: a, regular left to right repeated pattern, about. 10/min; b, brow still offscale; c, jaw muscles irregular hills and valleys, peaking about 4 μV; d, tongue irregular hills and valleys averaging about 20 μV, peaks at about 25; e, floor, similarly with peaks about 7 μV; f, similarly with averages about 4 and peaks about 5 μV; g, 17–21/min (compare with g of first section and with g of Fig. 4).

that the real fuel that corresponds with the use of gasoline in your car, the fuel of human muscle, is adenosine triphosphate, which is responsible not only for the energy of muscle contraction, but also for the energy of the nerve impulse and largely of the passage of impulses in the brain itself. Now that is *not* exclusive, but adenosine triphosphate seems to be the chief factor. Muscle contraction requires energy; it requires a burning of something, mainly adenosine triphosphate, or dextrose, or fats.

Burning requires oxygen as a rule (we are not discussing anaerobic function just now) whether it is in your furnace or your grate or your muscle, and the oxygen in the muscle comes ultimately from the air—from breathing. We find then, that, if the individual is relaxed toward zero—and nobody gets to a perfect zero and holds it in the skeletal musculature—nobody does that—but when the individual acquires skill, he uses less oxygen and you can easily identify this in your tracings with the pneumograph. If the individual becomes well-relaxed, as shown by the integrating neurovoltmeter, the breathing rate undergoes a remarkable change. It is no longer irregular, like normal breathing, but is quite regular and quite slow. Why does the breathing rate become very regular during general relaxation like clockwork, and quite shallow? Why? Because the reflex mechanism, whatever it is in the human organism, which is activated when you contract your muscles, leading to the supply by the bloodstream and blood pressure of oxygen to the muscle, needs it. That system then no longer has interference from the voluntary musculature as when you take a deep breath, but becomes automatic, and the rate and depth of the breathing then becomes automatically determined by the oxygen tension in the plasma which bathes the center of respiration in the medulla. This has been a rather long but necessary preamble.

Here the pneumograph shows you that while the trained subject relaxes, the respiratory volume is shallow and the rate is reduced to 9/min. It will increase to 17–21/min when she reads. In Fig. 1.3 the top tracing is the signal line. Trace a is EOG, showing eye movement from left to right as before—left is up, right is down, b is brow, but she does not relax in the brow; in other words, she is not completely relaxed by any means—the brow, as a matter of fact, is at a high mark there and remains steadily so. Later on, let us see if she relaxes; c records jaw muscles, d, tongue, e, the floor of the mouth—that is, the tongue again, externally measured—f is the larynx, and as I said, g is the pneumograph. Now, here is your control period in which she is asked to relax, and here is your period in which she is asked to read. You notice particularly, of course, the eye goes left to right, left to right, left to right, etc.; and you see the difference from the control period; the jaw also shows some changes. The tongue, however, gets very busy. This tongue is recorded not as Dr. McGuigan showed you yesterday in a very excellent method of recording, but in a way that we have been inclined to use, more or less like a thermometer is used, under the tongue on both sides. Formerly I inserted a fine platinum wire into the tongue, but this requires a highly skilled subject. With a wire in your tongue, to relax to the point of no salivation requires a certain dedication, which not everybody has; d, then, is the tongue, which is very busy, and e, is the tongue measured from the floor but you donot get it so much; f is the larynx. When these measurements first came out in the early 1930s, I am told that Professor Watson, with his behaviorism, said that my findings proved his point that thinking is laryngeal behavior. The larynx is not so busy as the tongue—a very busy member of our internal society. It is an organ, all muscle (with a little covering) that can go in every direction. No wonder there are so many quips and jokes made about restless tongues! At any rate, we do not by

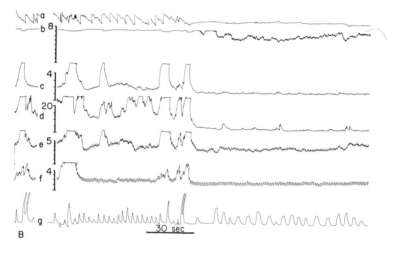

Fig. 1.4. Subject same, instructed to cease reading and relax. Control record similar to first section of Fig. 3, except brow is less tense, down to about 6 μV; g, breathing rate slows to 12/min.

any means feel that Watson was correct that thinking was chiefly a laryngeal phenomenon, but that, of course, the larynx apparently is involved in the peripheral examination of thinking. A rather amusing comment was made by his colleague Karl Lashley, who was at the University of Chicago and my very close friend although we did no work together; Lashley told me with a chuckle that when he and Watson would spend an evening together, working out principles of behaviorism, much of the time would be devoted to introspection.

In Fig. 1.4 we have much the same kind of story. The individual is asked to relax as a control test. As you see, for the first time she does relax the brow a little. Our average patient would not give as good a performance as you see here from a subject not a patient.

In Fig. 1.5 she reads aloud as a kind of control test. As you observe, in traces c and d, the tongue and jaw, reading aloud, overload the amplifier above 20 μV. Obviously, reading aloud requires much less sensitivity than reading silently.

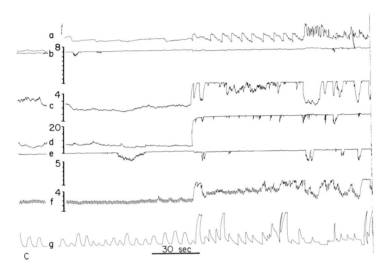

Fig. 1.5. Control test, same conditions. Section 1: subject requested to relax, eyes closed, sitting, holding book open on pillow resting on lap. Section 2: to read aloud. Section 1: a, eyes quiet; b, brow above 7 μV, offscale; c, jaws about 2 μV; d, tongue about 7 μV fairly steadily; e, floor above 7 μV, offscale; f, larynx, fairly steady about 2 μV; g, 11/min, showing moderate relaxation. Section 2: a, EOG, left to right reading pattern; b, brow as previously; c, jaw varying from 5 μV to offscale above 6; d, tongue, mostly offscale about 25 μV; e, floor, as previously; f, larynx varying up to about 4 μV; g, 15/min.

In Fig. 1.6 we especially used the measurements of the eyes (EOG) which affords a clean and simple recording of eye movements. Recording eye movement was originally as easy as it sounds today, because it is so generally done. To learn how, I had to work in the laboratory many a night and the first study was published from the University on eye imagination–visual imagination. These recordings were first accomplished with a direct current amplifier as we had to do in those days, and it was very hard to determine just what you were measuring. But you get a very

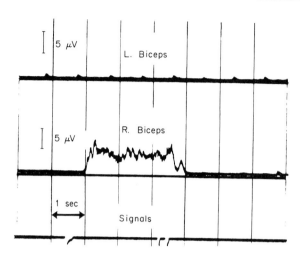

Fig. 1.6. Subject quiet, eyes closed, supine, trained to relax, instructed on one click to bend right arm at elbow, on double-click to relax same. Right arm flexor contractions show about 5 μV, while left arm shows zero values (excluding EKG interruptions).

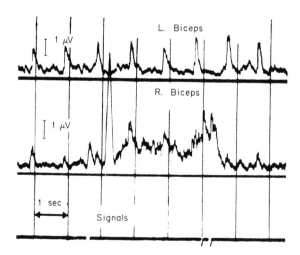

Fig. 1.7. Subject and conditions same, except instructed to imagine bending right arm at elbow. Results similar to Fig. 6, except microvoltage of right flexor muscles about one-fifth. Left arm control test, negative.

definite curve of eye direction as the individual imagines, as we shall see here. First, however, a more simple story: This is a study of bending the right arm. You see the individual is asked to bend the right arm; EMG of the right arm is positive and the left one is negative. Signals are shown on the bottom and the microvoltage is stated.

In Fig. 1.7 is imagining bending the right arm. The microvoltage is much less here, as you can see. Negative on the left. Please ignore the cardiographs which you cannot always avoid. This illustrates the imagining curves as faint repetition of the actual act.

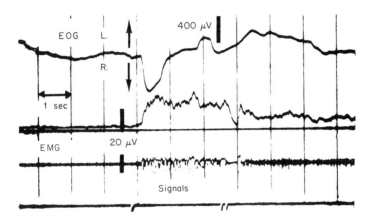

Fig. 1.8. Subject somewhat trained to relax. Conditions and instructions same as for Fig. 6. Upper trace, EOG, up = left, down = right. After signal to bend right arm, eye is shown to move to right practically simultaneously with EMG of right flexor muscle action, about 25 μV. Trace 2, amplified EMG from right arm flexors integrated. Trace 3, same, unintegrated. Traces 2 and 3, before signal to bend, show residual tension (failure to relax well) about 2–3 μV. Trace 4, signal line.

In Fig. 1.8 instruction is the same—he is again requested to bend his right arm (he is supine). The EOG is used here to illustrate that many people actually, in bending the arm, tend to look in that direction—part of the total act. Left is up; right is down. The individual bends the right arm, as you see, and also looks to the right, simultaneously, to do it. Now notice the lower sensitivity. This is a recording without integration of the same phenomenon.

In Fig. 1.9 the individual is asked to imagine bending the right arm at the elbow. Again, you notice the eye movement is as if to look toward the bending arm, but this occurs more frequently in subjects tested than it does in the actual bending. Possibly we might interpret this as if to watch what he is doing. Now, of course, you could always ask him if you want, but it is a leading question and you have to be careful with a leading question. Some subjects asked to imagine bending an arm respond with EOG activities left or right but without arm muscle contraction. They imagine visually only.

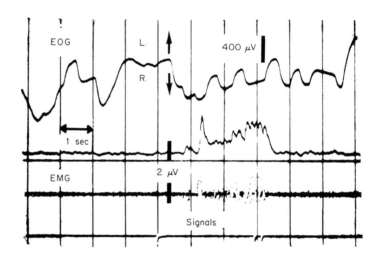

Fig. 1.9. Subject and conditions, same. Instruction to imagine bending right arm. Results similar to actual bending, as in Fig. 8, except (1) microvoltage much less, namely, 2–4 μV (in contrast with 25); (2) eye movement (EOG) precedes EMG by about 1/3 sec. (Some subjects imagine same visually only.)

In Fig. 1.10 imagine a motorcar coming from left to right and here you get the same left to right, of the eyes; that is, the EOG shows a first turning to the left. The neck muscles were shown to act in vision by the physiologist, Magnus, about 1890. Part of their function is to be accessory eye muscles; they move the eyes by moving the head; a shows muscles on the left side of the neck, just a little active here on the right shown in b. The brow, shown in c, is becoming active.

In Fig. 1.11 instruction is to imagine the Eiffel Tower in Paris. As you see, the EOG shows a gradual looking up.

In Fig. 1.12 are control tests which would take a long time to go into.

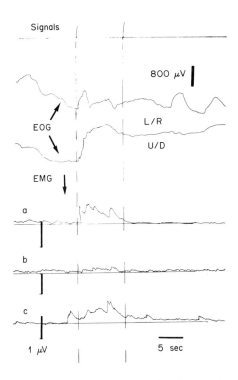

Fig. 1.10. Subject slightly trained to relax, supine. Instruction "Imagine an automobile passing from left to right." Signal line at top. Trace 2, EOG, up = left, down = right. Trace 3, EOG, up = up, down = down. Trace 4, a, EMG from muscles on left lateral side of neck. Trace 5, b, similarly on right. Trace 6, c, brow EMG. After the instruction to imagine, EOG shows eye movement to left and up, followed by rapid eye movement to right; persisting there 20 sec to end of record (N.B., this subject not well-trained to relax). Simultaneously with onset of eye movement to left, EMG of left neck muscles increases .5 μV, persisting until about 1 sec after signal to cease to imagine, while right neck muscles do not increase significantly. Brow increases before signal to imagine, continuing until about 2 sec after signal to cease.

In Fig. 1.13 a slide of the individual when the instructions are to imagine rowing a boat. Notice the beautiful rhythmicity which is shown in c and d, the hand flexors and hand extensors of the right side and here similarly on the left side.

We can discuss the EOG: Recording of EOG is, of course, relatively gross as compared with a recording of imagination from tongue, lips, and arms. The EOG does not, by any means, require the same voltage sensitivity of apparatus. The history of the finding is interesting. Six years after I had described a way to measure eye movement and record it, a psychologist, Mowrer, at Yale at that time, repeated my study and stated that he confirmed every statement that I had made about the recording, but disagreed on one point. Namely, he said that I had claimed that I

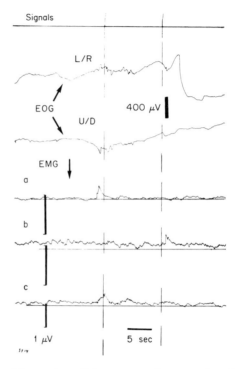

Fig. 1.11. Same subject and conditions. Instruction "Imagine Eiffel Tower in Paris." After signal to imagine, EOG shows slow upward eye movement initially, with slight, rapid lateral movement but without accompanying change of EMG of laterally situated neck muscles and none in brow.

was measuring action potentials of muscles but really what I was measuring was the movement of the retina. Now he did not question the method of the recording but confirmed all my findings. Nevertheless after the publication of his paper, subsequent writers called EOG recording "Mowrer's Method" which is an example of how investigators may neglect to read original findings. Now, as for Mowrer, a very eminent and excellent student and laboratory man—I do not know if Mowrer ever read

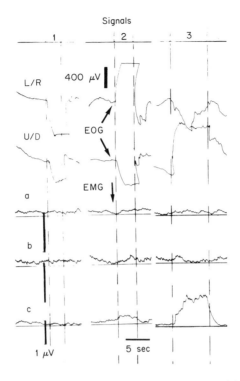

Fig. 1.12. Control test for previous two figures, with same subject and conditions. Instructions: Part 1. Look straight ahead. At first signal click actually look right; at second signal look straight ahead. Part 2 same as part 1 except look left at first signal click. Part 3 same as part 1 except look up. As indicated, relatively slight EOG changes on looking straight ahead, but marked direction changes corresponding to looking right, left and up. No marked EMG changes in lateral neck muscles and brow, except upon looking up, microvoltage in brow increases from 1 to 2.

the subsequent studies on apes where the retina was removed. (Then you could not get an EOG, according to Mowrer.) Well, you could not for the first 2 days while the wound was healing. But after recovery, with no retina, you got the same EOG as in unoperated animals (Pasik, Pasik, & Bender, 1965). Today, we can say, "Here's the way to record eye movement." But certainly Mowrer's view is not the correct one, and it is not quite correct to state that this EOG is measurement of the recti muscles. In one very excellent paper that you heard here, there was a measurement of the recti musculature reported to you by electrodes placed under the eye; of course, in eye movement, the recti muscles do play a recordable

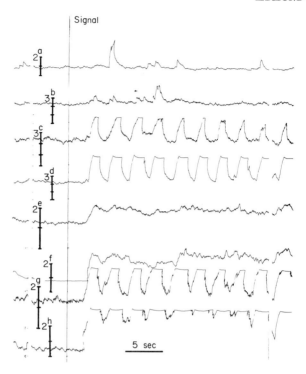

Fig. 1.13. Same subject and conditions. EMG leads: a, biceps–brachial muscle group; b, r. extensor muscle group; c, r. hand flexors; d, r. hand extensors; e–g, same muscle groups on left side. Instruction: "Upon first signal, imagine that you are rowing a boat. Upon second signal, discontinue imagining." The illustration does not include the discontinuance of muscle potentials (EMG) which ensued after the second signal. Strikingly positive rhythmical results are notable chiefly in tracings c, d, g, and h, namely from extensors and flexors of both hands.

part. The importance of eye movements in imagination, of course, suggests the same sort of thing that we heard discussed so systematically here the other day—the dreaming. In the 1930s my use of this EOG in daytime imagining, waking imagining, naturally led to my using it in sleep, likewise, and finally, I was able to apparently get some response from N. Kleitman who had never been interested in any of these questions in the laboratory; he said my discussions were for electrical engineers only. But finally he came up and visited and then he sent his graduate student Aserinsky to learn how to do it. I was happy to have this opportunity; I had written about the measurement in dreams in a book on sleep (published in 1938). This account of EOG measurements in dreams was the first to be published (Lufkin, 1969). Kleitman had reviewed the book so followed up these eye movements (measurements) and developed a tremendous interest, as you know. Recently, I am informed, Kleitman told an audience in California that I was the first to study fast and slow eye movements during sleep. I did not use the term, REM, but I think their term is a very good one.

We report here also on a total of 18 subjects recorded during silent reading. All but three had received more or less drill at relaxing muscles, including those of speech. However, among these the best example of effective relaxation was presented in Figs. 1.3–1.5.

One of the 18 had been diagnosed as chronic hebephrenia, another as a pathological personality. These two will be discussed afterward herein. A third subject, about 20 years old, back from college on brief vacation, evidently in an emotional state, exhibited much activity of speech parts during the control tests, evidently being in a highly generally tense state at the time. Accordingly there was little contrast between EMG values of speech parts before and during silent reading.

There remain here to be considered the recordings with 15 subjects. During silent reading all showed patterns marked by EOG rhythmicity and by irregular EMG rises and falls in some of the speech muscle groups recorded. However, in every subject individual uniqueness was clearly indicated. Obviously, individuals are thus found to differ in their psychological processes of getting the meaning of what they read.

In Table I is shown the relative frequency in which each speech muscle group increases or decreases in activity as compared with control period values for each of the 15 subjects. All subjects showed increased steady and intermittent voltages in at least one speech region. Eighty percent of all showed such increase in three or more speech regions.

The two mentally disturbed patients mentioned above evidently had shown marked, if slow, general improvement in their work and daily lives. One no longer showed the initial symptoms of irrelevant snickering. Both continued at daily work.

Unlike the 15 subjects free from marked mental disturbance, these two showed rhythmic eye motion only part of the time when requested to read silently. This suggests a general, simple EOG test that could prove useful in the diagnosis and treatment of chronic mental retardation in its various forms.

Much said above baffles brief summary. However, we have confirmed our original findings of the 1930s on the electrophysiology of mental activities. We have shown that these activities can be measured peripherally clearly and definitely, although central brain measurements of

TABLE I

Neuromuscular Activities during Silent Reading Compared with Previous and
Subsequent Control Tests (Sitting Quietly with Eyelids Closed)

	Increase (%)[a]	Decrease (%)[a]	No change (%)[a]
EOG reading pattern	100	0	0
Brow	80	7	13
Jaw	80	7	13
Tongue	60	7	33
Lips	67	8	25
Mylohyoid	73	7	20
Larynx	60	0	40
Breathing rate and depth	80	0	20

[a] Percentage of subjects showing increase, decrease, no change in the various regions.

equally specific imagining and recall still remain vague and dubious. EOG
measurements apply to dreams as well as to waking states as set forth
in my volume on sleep (1938) and as confirmed by Aserinsky and Kleitman
(REM) upon use of, the methods which, when consulted, I recommended
to them.

We have reported likewise on silent reading by 15 subjects showing
that all engaged in activities of speech muscles, although with striking
individual differences. This group included silent reading by a nationally
known teacher of speed reading. Her EMG patterns followed the general
principles related above. Detailed accounts of EMG and EOG findings
will be published later by E. Jacobson and R. E. Lange, to whom I am
indebted for invaluable help in the presentations.

The Discussion of Dr. Jacobson's Paper

LED BY DR. JOHANN STOYVA
University of Colorado

Stoyva: I want to thank Hollins College for giving me the opportunity
to meet Dr. Jacobson for the first time yesterday morning, although I do
feel that I have known him for some years. When I first went to graduate

school at Chicago, I had a somewhat checkered undergraduate background in psychology, and they told me that I would have to take a course in learning. And I was hit, in that course, with Professor Osgood's treatise in experimental psychology. When I recovered from my first fear reaction, I pulled myself together and drew a lot of nourishment from that book. One of its most engrossing parts is the section where Dr. Jacobson's work is described, around p. 650.

Until recently, I had thought that Dr. Jacobson's classic work, *Progressive Relaxation*, had been first published in 1938; but the first edition was actually in 1929, and as Dr. McGuigan mentioned yesterday, he began working on progressive relaxation in 1920. However, this was by no means, his first work. In 1911, he published a philosophical paper on meaning and understanding; and the year before that, in 1910, he published a paper on symbolic logic.

I think we have to be amazed at Dr. Jacobson's sustained interest and productivity over the years. He is a pioneer in the use of electronic instrumentation for investigating psychophysiological questions; for example, the use of the integrating neurovoltmeter in quantifying EMG activity, and the use of the EOG recording technique for eye movements, and even use of the feedback principle with some of his patients who, many years ago, monitored their own oscillograms.

What we did not discuss today, and I think it ought to be mentioned, is Dr. Jacobson's long series of notable clinical contributions. Many years ago, he developed his progressive relaxation technique, or "cultivated relaxation," and he applied that technique to a variety of disorders, including insomnia, anxiety disorders, gastrointestinal disorders, and certain cardiovascular disorders. An important idea embodied in this work is that patients who suffer from stress-related disorders can learn to modify their response to stress—a concept of far-reaching implications. Even though many people are interested in, and support his work such as psychologists and psychiatrists, I think in the 1930s the mental health profession supported it less than one might have expected on the basis of his contributions. Maybe mental health professionals were all engrossed in psychoanalysis at that time. His comments on this would be of historical interest.

Dr. Jacobson's distinguished work and productivity in the clinical area, in innovations in instrumentation, and in innovations in the field of "thinking" is remarkable. He is a very good recommendation for his own training in progressive relaxation.

Open Discussion

Dr. T. H. Bhatti (University of Virginia): The relationship between muscles and the brain (as a central processor) suggest that oxygen consumption may be a useful physiological measure. The oxygen consumption of skeletal muscle varies depending on amount of activity, from a peak during violent physical exercise to a low during rest. In contrast, the brain (only about 2% of the body weight) consumes about 20% of the oxygen being consumed at any one moment, and without much difference between waking and sleep. Would Dr. Jacobson comment on that?

Jacobson: We are beginning such a study, with partly theoretical interests. There is much agreement in the physiological literature that you can measure energy in terms of oxygen consumption. Many of these studies are magnificent, especially the classic one by Benedict and Benedict, showing what a small amount of oxygen is used in the process of thinking. The studies in exercise have paved the way for our work in thinking in which we use the integrating neurovoltmeter to obtain a measure of energy expenditures; we also use electrodes in similar placements to those described by Dr. McGuigan—on the forehead, the brow, the right leg, the trunk, at the eye, and also the pneumograph. We are hoping, through our studies of such combined measures, to introduce into medicine and physiology a theoretical measure, like in theoretical physics, of expenditure.

By good fortune, we have subjective and objective evidence suggesting that we can diminish mental activity; we can then compare the oxygen usage during that period of general relaxation, and diminished mental activity, with amount during a slight state of tension, namely, that which is sufficient to permit mental activity, in the sense of the original Benedict and Benedict study.

Dr. Richard Blanton (Vanderbilt University): The area of breathing, and the respiratory response, is fascinating, especially in relation to the problem of activation, thinking, and arousal. Even before Dr. Jacobson began his work, in the 1880s, two people in Italy and France pointed out the important relationship between activation and respiratory rate. The discovery of the CO_2 mechanism actually diverted physiologist's attention from the very important fact that amount and rate of gas respired is often unrelated to motor work, e.g., emotionally disturbed people often hyperventilate—a very important clinical phenomenon of which the behavior therapists are only now beginning to be aware.

Dr. Larry Rust (State University of New York, Potsdam): My question to Dr. Jacobson and Dr. McGuigan concerns EOGs and the tongue mechanisms during reading. Do high-speed readers (those who use a two-spot or three-spot structure across a sentence, instead of the normal seven-spot structure) really read at the rate of 1800 words a minute? Do their tongues move at a relatively fast rate? Is there a change in their EOGs?

McGuigan: This was the intent of our "Reading Improvement" experiment that I present on page 361, and you can note the suggestion that amplitude of tongue EMG increased when we increased reading rate. Frequency of end of line eye movements ("EOGs") increased, too. However, very fast "readers" are probably not reading in the sense in which we normally think of reading—eye movements of "speed readers" are supposed to go down the page in a vertical dimension, but some such "readers" apparently produced U-shaped eye movements. So, whereas the intent in the speed reading courses is to develop hand–eye coordination to increase the reading rate, apparently the eyes don't do what the reading trainer says they should be doing; and apparently, the tongue is not doing what they say it should be doing, either.

Audience: At some point, might there be a changeover (shift) from tongue movements to movements in neck muscles, in the jaw, etc.?

McGuigan: You remind me of one thing I should say about Peter Mac-Neilage's reaction to my paper on p. 378. MacNeilage said while reading that there is only a tonic rise. A. N. Sokolov has emphasized that there is *phasic* activity from the speech mechanism, and phasic activity is critical in carrying a verbal code, as we hypothesized. During silent reading, there is a tonic rise with phasic bursts; and I see it in our laboratory, too, exactly as with Sokolov. In some such way, the neck, jaw, etc., muscles perhaps phasically participate in the internal information processing loops. You know, you can "hypnotize" yourself by hours of watching such bursts on your scope, so you get to "see" the information rising from the tongue, going to the brain—you know about then that it is time to get out of your laboratory and back into the real world.

Audience: In defense of the neck muscle, your neck gets stiff after hours of steadily reading.

McGuigan: We suspect that's part of the complex loop, and the neck may be directly connected internally with the ear.

Dr. William Jennings (Randolph-Macon College): I don't want to defend the centralist position against the adversaries that are present here, but you must have some information on time sequences in order to say that these electrophysiological measures are actually components of thought. The electrophysiological events may be merely the results (products) of the thought process. For example, the thought may actually precede the tongue and eye movement.

Jacobson: There is a rather widely held concept, due to our general tradition, that thought is more or less indescribable, and exists in the sphere called the human mind. We record what takes place peripherally in the human organism during what is called "thinking," during "hearing," "listening," "perceiving," "reflecting," and also the trained report, for what it is worth. The report is very accurate, in the same sense as your description of a slide of histopathology, for example, your description, your words, are no real translation, but call attention to specific points of the slide.

Now the point that bears upon your question is that it is typically not difficult to rid a patient of his complaints of poor concentration or poor thinking. We do not say this is the way to think, or give him books to read. We show him how to control his musculature, and then let him solve the problem of concentration himself—it works out very, very prettily.

The actual procedure of thinking is too vast for our minds to conceive. The configurations of the whole brain–muscle mechanism vary at every instant—as you make your point, and mine as I answer it. The complexities are so great that we can do no more than designate them. Accordingly, we would do well to determine the facts by precise measurements, whether we use oxygen determinants, or other approaches. Find them! Determine them! Then apply them, not as in psychiatric interviews, not as in psychoanalysis, but by straight physiological methods.

Stovya: I want to thank Dr. Jacobson again for the memorable experience.

REFERENCES AND SUPPORTING PUBLICATIONS

Aserinsky, E., & Kleitman, N. Eye movements during sleep. *Fed. Proc.*, 1953, **12**, 13.

Aserinsky, E., & Kleitman, N. Two types of ocular motility occurring in sleep. *Journal of Applied Physiology*, 1955, **8**, 1–18.

Aserinsky E., & Kleitman, N. A motility cycle in sleeping infants as manifested by ocular and gross bodily activity. *Journal of Applied Physiology*, 1955, **8**, 11–18.

Aserinsky, E., & Kleitman, N. Regularly occurring periods of eye motility and concomitant phenomena, during sleep. *Science*, 1953, **118**, 273–274.

Bailey, P. The academic lecture. *American Journal of Psychiatry*, 1956, **113**, 387–406.

Berger, R. Tonus of extrinsic laryngeal muscles during sleep and dreaming. *Science*, 1961, **134**, 840.

Courts, F. A. Relations between muscular tension and performance. *Psychiatry Bulletin*, 1942, **39**, 347–367.

Davis, R. C. Patterns of muscular activity during "mental" work and their constancy. *Journal of Experimental Psychology*, 1939, **24**, 451–465.

Dement, W. Dream recall and eye movements during sleep in schizophrenics and normals. *Journal of Nervous and Mental Disease*, 1955, **122**, 263.

Dement, W., & Kleitman, N. Cyclic variations in EEG during sleep and their relation to eye movements, body motility and dreaming. *Electroencephography and Clinical Neurophysiology*, 1957, **9**, 673–690. (a)

Dement, W., & Kleitman, N. The relation of eye movements during sleep to dream activity: An objective method for the study of dreaming. *Journal of Experimental Psychology*, 1957, **53**, 339–346. (b)

Dement, W., & Wolpert, E. A. The relation of eye movements, body motility, and external stimuli to dream constant. *Journal of Experimental Psychology*, 1958, **55**, 543.

Freeman, G. L. Mental activity and the muscular processes. *Psychological Review*, 1931, **38**, 428–449. (a)

Freeman, G. L. Spread of neuromuscular activity during mental work. *Journal of General Psychology*, 1931, **5**, 479–494. (b)

Gould, L. N. Verbal hallucinations and activity of vocal musculature, an electromyographic study. *American Journal of Psychiatry*, 1948, **105**, 367–372.

Jacobson, E. On meaning and understanding. *American Journal of Psychology*, 1911, **22**, 553–577.

Jacobson, E. The use of relaxation in hypertensive states. *New York Medical Journal* 1920 (March). (a)

Jacobson, E. The reduction of nervous irritability and excitement by progressive relaxation. *Trans. Soc. of Nervous Mental Disease, AMA*, 1920. (b)

Jacobson, E. Progressive relaxation. *American Journal of Psychology*, 1925, **36**, 73–87.

Jacobson, E. Voluntary relaxation of the esophagus. *American Journal of Physiology* 1925, **72**, 387–394.

Jacobson, E. Response to a sudden unexpected stimulus. *Journal of Experimental Psychology*, 1926, **9**, 19–25.

Jacobson, E. Spastic esophagus and mucous colitis. *Archives of International Medicine*, 1926, **39**, 433–435.

Jacobson, E. Action currents from muscular contractions during conscious processes. *Science*, 1926, **66**, 403.

Jacobson, E. Differential relaxation during reading, writing, and other activities as tested by the knee-jerk. *American Journal of Physiology*, 1928, 86, 675–693.

Jacobson, E. *Progressive relaxation*. Chicago: University of Chicago Press, 1929. (Rev ed., 1938).

Jacobson, E. Imagination of movement involving skeletal muscle. *American Journal of Physiology*, 1930, **91**, 567–608.

Jacobson, E. Imagination and recollection of various muscular acts. *American Journal of Physiology*, 1930, **94**, 22–34. (a)

Jacobson, E. Visual imagination and recollection. *American Journal of Physiology*, 1930, **95**, 694–702. (b)

Jacobson, E. Evidence of contraction of specific muscles during imagination, *American Journal of Physiology*, 1930, **95**, 703–712. (c)

Jacobson, E. Variation of specific muscles contracting during imagination. *American Journal of Physiology*, 1931, **96**, 115–121. (a)

Jacobson, E. A note on mental activities concerning an amputated limb. *American Journal of Physiology*, 1931, **96**, 122–125. (b)

Jacobson, E. Imagination, recollection and abstract thinking involving the speech musculature. *American Journal of Physiology*, 1931, **97**, 200–209. (c)

Jacobson, E. Electrophysiology of mental activities. *American Journal of Psychology*, 1932, 44, 677–694.

Jacobson, E. Measurement of the action potentials in the peripheral nerves of man without anesthetic. *Proc. Society Biol. Med.*, 1933, 30, 713–715.

Jacobson, E. *Electrical measurements of activities in nerve and muscle in the problem of mental disorder*. New York: McGraw-Hill, 1934. Pp. 133–145.

Jacobson, E. Electrical measurements concerning muscular contractions (tonus) and the cultivation of relaxation in man—studies on arm flexors. *American Journal of Physiology*, 1934, 107, 230–248.

Jacobson, E. *You can sleep well*. New York: McGraw-Hill, 1938. Pp. 144ff.

Jacobson, E. The neurovoltmeter. *American Journal of Psychology*, 1939, 52, 620–624.

Jacobson, E. An integrating voltmeter for the study of nerve and muscle potentials. *Rev. Scient. Instruments*, 1940, 11, 415–418. (a)

Jacobson, E. The direct measurement of nervous and muscular states with the integrating neurovoltmeter (action-potential integrator). *American Journal of Psychiatry*, 1940, 97, 513–523. (b)

Jacobson, E. The physiological conception and treatment of certain common psychoneuroses. *American Journal of Psychiatry*, 1941, 98, 219–226.

Jacobson, E. The effect of daily rest without training to relax on muscular tonus. *American Journal of Psychology*, 1942, 55, 248–254.

Jacobson, E. The cultivation of physiological relaxation. *Annals of International Medicine*, 1943, 19, 965–972.

Jacobson, E. Direct measurements of the effects of bromides, sodium amytal and of caffeine in man. *Annals of International Medicine*, 1944, 21, 455–468.

Jacobson, E. Electrical measurements of mental activities in man. *Trans. New York Acad. Soc.*, 1946, 2, 272–273.

Jacobson, E. Neuromuscular controls in man: Methods of self-direction in health and in disease. *American Journal of Psychology*, 1955, 68, 549–561.

Jacobson, E. Les principes soulingant les méthodes de la relaxation. *Revue Scientifiques de Medecine Psychosomatiques*, 1961, 3, 49–56.

Jacobson, E. Psychology and the integrative action of the nervous system. *Acta Symbolica*, 1970, 2, 31–35.

Jacobson, E. *Physiological psychiatry: Introducing of science based on action potential measurement and multidisciplinary approach*. To be published.

Lorens, S. A., Jr., and Darrow, C. W. Eye movements, EEF, GSR and EKG during mental multiplication. *Electroencephography and Clinicial Neurophysiology*, 1962, 14, 739–746.

Lufkin, B. Letter to the editor. *Psychophysiology*, 1969, 5, 4, 449–450.

Max, L. W. An experimental study of the motor theory of consciousness. 1. Critique of earlier studies. *Journal of General Psychology*, 1934, 11, 112–125.

Max, L. W. An experimental study of the motor theory of consciousness. 3. Action current responses in deaf mutes during sleep, sensory stimulation and dreams. *Journal of Comp. Psychology*, 1935, 19, 469–486.

Max, L. W. Action current responses in deaf mutes during sleep, sensory stimulation and dreams. *Journal of Comp. Psychology*, 1935, 19, 469–486. (a)

Max, L. W. An experimental study of the motor theory of consciousness. 4. Action-current responses in the deaf during awakening, kinesthetic imagery and abstract thinking. *Journal of Comp. Psychology*, 1937, 24, 301–344. (b)

Pasik, P., Pasik, T., & Bender, M. B. Recovery of the electrooculogram after total ablation of the retina in monkeys. *Electroencephography and Clinical Neurophysiology,* 1965, **19,** 291–297.

Roffwarg, H. P., Dement, W. C., Muzio, J. N., & Fisher, C. Dream imagery: Relationship to rapid eye movements of sleep. *Archives of General Psychiatry,* 1962, **7,** 27–50.

Schiff, S. K., Bunney, W. E., Jr., & Freedman, D. X. A study of ocular movements in hypnotically induced dreams. *Journal of Nervous and Mental Disease,* 1961, **133,** 59–68.

Shaw, W. A. The distribution of muscular action-potentials during imagining. *Psychological Record,* 1938.

Shaw, W. A. Relation of muscular action-potentials to imaginal weight lifting. *Archives of Psychology,* 1940, **35,** 50.

Snyder, F. The new biology of dreaming. *Archives of General Psychiatry,* 1963, **8,** 381–391.

Wolpert, E. A. Studies in the psychophysiology of dreams. 2. An electromyographic study of dreaming. *Archives of General Psychiatry,* 1960, **2,** 231.

EMPHASIS ON CENTRAL NERVOUS SYSTEM—PRIMARILY ELECTROENCEPHALOGRAM

CHAPTER TWO

The Operant Conditioning of the Electrical Activity of the Brain as a Method for Controlling Neural and Mental Processes[1]

A. H. BLACK

McMaster University

I. INTRODUCTION

Recent research has demonstrated that central nervous system (CNS) electrical activity can be operantly conditioned (see Table I for references).

[1] The preparation of this paper and the research from my laboratory described in it, were supported by Research Grant 258 from the Ontario Mental Health Foundation, Research Grant 70–476 from the Foundations' Fund for Research in Psychiatry, and by Research Grant APA-0042 from the National Research Council of Canada. I thank G. Young, L. Grupp, and F. Brandemark who collaborated in the research. This paper was completed in the autumn of 1971, and is derived in large part from a more extensive review of the literature that was completed recently (Black, 1972).

The applications of this procedure have aroused a great deal of interest. The claim has been made that the operant conditioning of CNS electrical activity will permit us to obtain more powerful control over the minds of others, and also to increase voluntary or self-control over our internal neural and psychological processes. The same claims have been made about the operant conditioning of autonomic responses. The apparent power of such internal control was, of course, well-known long before the current research was published.

> It may be of interest to you to know that some years since a gentleman—Colonel Townsend, lived who possessed the power of controlling the actions of his heart and lungs. You will tell me this is quite simple—you can do it yourself. Not so fast. It is quite impossible, at all events improbable, that you have any such ability. Draw in your breath now, and you are, bloated like the frog in the fable, undergoing your torture with heroic fortitude. The gallant gentleman I have mentioned, however, could really influence his heart in much the same way as you can control the action of your forefinger, which I fancy I see elevated in an attitude of sceptiscism; as the Ingoldsby legend goes:
>
> > "The sacristan, he says no word, to indicate a doubt,
> > But he puts his thumb unto his nose, and draws his fingers out."
>
> Colonel Townsend performed the experiment once in the presence of his physician, who cautioned him strongly against its repetition. Nevertheless, he did again exhibit the control he had over his circulatory organs, and this time more triumphantly than ever, for he so completely suppressed the heart's action that it never throbbed again. The unlucky individual added another name to the list of scientific martyrs . . . [Lawson, 1873, p. 64].[2]

The use of operant conditioning procedures to control internal processes produces optimistic and pessimistic reactions whose only common feature seems to be the intensity with which they are expressed. On the one hand, we have the hope that they will help to create a better future. "The children of the future may look back on us as little more than Neanderthal men, crude creatures who were unable to control our feelings, our physiology— and unable to play upon the instrument of the brain [Luce & Peper, 1971, p. 139]." On the other hand, there is fear that the method will lead to a worse future in which it will provide a powerful technique for thought control and the like. Krutch (1953), for example, has labeled future societies in which we have "the scientific ability to control men's thoughts with precision" as "ignoble utopias."

The purpose of this paper is to evaluate the claims that operant neural conditioning produces powerful and far-reaching control over internal processes. In order to do so, we must deal with two problems.

[2] This example was brought to my attention by Mr. P. Croskerry.

First, those who claim that the operant conditioning of CNS electrical activity is a powerful control procedure must assume that obtaining control over the electrical activity of the brain gives us control over important internal neural and psychological processes. Suppose that one operantly conditions two electroencephalographic (EEG) patterns recorded from the same location over the cortex, employing the same reinforcer and schedule of reinforcement. During the performance of the first EEG pattern, the subject is angry, tense, agitated; during the performance of the second pattern, he is serene, calm, relaxed. The conclusion usually drawn from such data is that control over these specific EEG patterns also gives control over the related mood states. So, the first question that we must answer in order to evaluate operant neural conditioning as a method of control is the following: *Over what neural and psychological processes, if any, do we obtain control when we operantly condition a particular pattern of CNS electrical activity?*

One might infer from the discussion so far that the control of CNS electrical activity by operant conditioning is a new achievement. But this inference is not necessarily true; we have always been able to bring neural activity under operant control. For example, whenever we operantly condition the ubiquitous bar-pressing response, we bring under operant control processes in neural systems which control the reinforced movements as well as processes in related CNS systems. Furthermore, a variety of other techniques are already available for controlling internal neural and psychological processes—drugs, electrical stimulation of the brain, etc. Questions naturally arise, therefore, about the differences between operant neural conditioning and other methods for controlling internal processes. If the operant conditioning of CNS electrical activity is not different from, and in some sense "better" than other methods of control, there would be little point to its use. Therefore, we must also answer the following question: *Does the control provided by the operant conditioning of CNS electrical activity differ from that obtained by other methods for controlling internal neural and psychological processes, and if so, how?*

Often, just as I am about to launch into an attempt to answer these two questions, I am stopped short by an interjection that goes something like this.

"Just a minute. How do we know that you really have operantly conditioned some pattern of CNS activity? Perhaps the changes in CNS electrical activity were produced not by operant conditioning, but by some other variable or procedure. Or, even if one did operantly condition a response, perhaps the operantly conditioned response was not CNS electrical activity but some other response such as skeletal movement, and this other response mediated the change in CNS electrical activity."

Let me comment briefly on these two issues. (See Black, 1972, for a more extended discussion.)

The essential feature of the operant conditioning procedure is usually assumed to be the contingency between response and reinforcer. We can ask, therefore, whether the probability of the reinforced response increased because of this contingency, or because of some other variable such as the noncontingent presentations of the reinforcer, the contingency between a discriminative stimulus (S^D) and reinforcer, and so on. Only when the first of these alternatives is correct, can we conclude that we have operantly conditioned neural activity.

The most commonly employed method for distinguishing between these alternatives is the *bidirectional procedure* (see Black, 1967; 1971b, for a discussion of such procedures). In it, we operantly condition two groups in which all the relevant procedural variables (noncontingent presentations of the reinforcer, etc.) have the same value in both groups, except for the response that is reinforced. The reinforced response in one group is usually mutually exclusive of the reinforced response in the other group. For example, one group of subjects might be operantly reinforced for increasing the rate of a given response, while another group might be reinforced for decreasing the rate of that response. If a difference was found between the two groups in the rate of reinforced response, it could be attributed to the effects of the contingency between response and reinforcer, provided, of course, that other relevant variables were constant in the two groups.

In Table 2-1, the experiments on CNS operant conditioning are classified according to type of CNS electrical activity, location of the recording electrodes, and type of subject. In addition, experiments which have employed bidirectional controls or some equivalent procedure, are indicated. This table reveals that for each type of electrical activity, at least one experiment employed bidirectional or equivalent controls.[3] Therefore, we can conclude that all the types of CNS electrical activity that have been studied so far can be modified by response–reinforcer contingencies.

As far as the mediation issue is concerned, the demonstration that we can operantly condition CNS electrical activity in subjects whose skeletal musculature has been paralyzed by curare-like drugs, makes it clear that peripheral mediation by skeletal responses does not occur, at least for a

---

[3] Two further points that are revealed by this table should be mentioned. First, the major concentration of research effort has been on spontaneous EEG patterns; second, fewer types of CNS electrical activity in fewer brain locations have been operantly conditioned in human subjects than in infrahuman subjects. This is understandable since it is difficult to study single cell activity and to record from subcortical structures in human subjects.

few of the CNS patterns that have been studied (Black, Young, & Batenchuk, 1970). One might, of course, argue that central mediation takes place. That is, one might say that one has really operantly conditioned some other pattern of CNS electrical activity inadvertently, and that this pattern mediated the change in CNS electrical activity that one had reinforced. But, this argument is really irrelevant. Our purpose is to demonstrate that we can operantly condition the electrical activity of the central nervous system. If we demonstrate that we have operantly conditioned a mediating central response, we will have achieved our goal just as surely as if we demonstrate that we have operantly conditioned the reinforced pattern of CNS electrical activity directly.[4]

Having established that at least some of the changes in reinforced patterns of CNS electrical activity can be attributed to the direct effects of the response–reinforcer contingency, we can now return to the two questions in which we are primarily interested—the questions concerned with the control over internal processes that is exerted by operant neural conditioning. Each of these questions will be discussed separately in the next two sections.

II. THE PROCESSES CONTROLLED BY OPERANT NEURAL CONDITIONING

The question that we shall consider in this section is over what neural and psychological processes, if any, do we obtain control when we operantly condition a particular pattern of CNS electrical activity?

Now it is obvious that the successful operant conditioning of a pattern of CNS electrical activity, by itself, will not provide the answer to this question. It does not tell us what these related processes are; it tells us only that the reinforced pattern is part of some neural system that can be operantly conditioned. How do we find out, therefore, which internal neural and psychological processes are controlled, when we control a particular pattern of CNS electrical activity? One can refer to the literature on the neural and behavioral processes that are related to such patterns of electrical activity in order to obtain the required information, or, if it is not available there, try to provide the information by employing traditional methods for studying brain–behavior relationships—correlating neural activity with behavior in natural situations, analyzing the effects of brain stimulation and lesions on these relations, and so on.

---

[4] The mediation issue has also received a great deal of attention on operant autonomic conditioning (Black, 1971b; Crider, Schwartz, & Shnidman, 1969; Katkin & Murray, 1968; Katkin, Murray, & Lachman, 1969; Miller, 1969).

TABLE 2-1

Classification of Experiments on Operant Neural Conditioning

Subject	Electrode location	Type of conditioned neural activity		
		Single cell	"Spontaneous" EEG	Evoked potentials
		Motor cortex	*High- and low-voltage EEG*	*Elicited by visual stimuli*
		Fetz, 1969[a]	Carmona, 1967[a,b]	Fox & Rudell, 1968[a]
		Fetz & Finocchio, 1971[a,b]		Fox & Rudell, 1970[a]
			Sensorimotor rhythm, postreinforcement synchronization, desynchronization[a]	*Elicited by movement*
	Cortex		Chase & Harper, 1971	Rosenfeld, 1970[a]
			Sterman, Wyrwicka, & Roth, 1969[a]	
			Sterman, Lopresti, & Fairchild, 1969	
			Sterman, Howe, & MacDonald, 1970	
			Wyrwicka & Sterman, 1968[a]	
Infrahuman		*Limbic system*	*Hippocampal RSA and non-RSA*	
		Olds & Olds, 1961[a]	Black, 1971a[a,b]	
		Olds, 1965, 1967, 1969	Black, Young, & Batenchuk, 1970[a,b]	
			Dalton, 1969	
	Subcortical Structures		*Amygdala spindling*	
			Delgado, Johnston, Wallace, & Bradley, 1970[a]	

		Alpha, beta, theta waves	*Elicited by auditory stimuli*
Human	Scalp	Beatty, 1971[a] Brown, 1970, 1971[a] Dewan, 1967[a] Green, Green, & Walters, 1970a,b Kamiya, 1968[a], 1969[a] Lynch & Paskewitz, 1971[c] Mulholland, 1968[c], 1969[c], 1971[c] Nowlis & Kamiya, 1970[a] Paskewitz & Orne, 1971 Paskewitz, Lynch, Orne, & Costello, 1970[a] Peper, 1970[a] Peper & Mulholland, 1970[a] Spilker, Kamiya, Callaway, & Yeager, 1969	Rosenfeld, Rudell, & Fox, 1969[a]

[a] These experiments employed bidirectional control procedures or their equivalent.
[b] These experiments employed curare-like drugs or dissociative conditioning procedures to rule out peripheral mediation.
[c] These are theoretical or review articles in which no new data are presented.

We cannot be sure, however, that processes which are related to a pattern of CNS electrical activity in natural situations will also be related to the pattern in operant conditioning situations. It would seem necessary, therefore, to examine the relationship among the reinforced pattern of CNS electrical activity, other measures of neural activity, and behavior in the operant conditioning situation. Methods for doing so are discussed in Section V.

The data on certain neural patterns that have been obtained by these methods are too limited to permit us to guess their functional significance with any accuracy (see Table 2-1). The electrical activity of the amygdala was studied in only one subject by Delgado *et al.* (1970). Olds (1965, 1969) reported no clear correlations between the reinforced firing of single units and concomitant measures of neural activity and behavior, nor did Carmona (1967) in his work on EEG amplitude. As one begins to classify the remaining patterns, the outcome is rather surprising. Most of the reinforced neural events seem to be related to motor control systems. There are two neural patterns whose involvement in motor control systems would be expected: single unit activity of the motor cortex (Fetz, 1969), and sensory-evoked potentials resulting from movement (Rosenfeld, 1970). Also, high frequency hippocampal rhythmic slow activity (RSA) (Black, 1971a), pontine single units (Olds, 1967), and the cortical sensorimotor rhythm (Chase & Harper, 1971) seem to be related to motor processes— RSA and unit firing to certain types of movement, and the sensorimotor rhythm to the inhibition of movement. The CNS patterns that have been studied most extensively in humans are alpha production and blocking. The processes related to these CNS patterns are difficult to specify, although alpha blocking also seems to be related to motor processes. A typical experiment (Kamiya, 1969) showed that human subjects can be operantly conditioned to change the density of alpha waves (i.e., the number of alpha waves that occurred during a fixed period of time). The data are presented in Fig. 2.1. Because different mechanisms might be involved in alpha blocking and production, I shall discuss these two responses separately. One proposal suggests that the blocking of alpha waves is produced by processes which lead to cortical desynchronization, and that these processes involve the activation of visual motor systems (Dewan, 1967; Mulholland, 1968, 1969, 1971, 1972). The subject may focus his eyes, track some object, or even imagine some visual object, and this results in alpha blocking. A more general hypothesis of the same type has been proposed by Lynch and Paskewitz (1971). They suggest that decreases in alpha wave density are produced by paying attention to any stimulus. Another possible mechanism is that one can produce decreases in the density of alpha waves

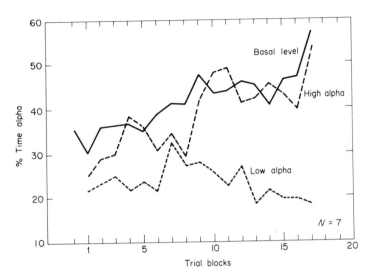

Fig. 2.1. Data for seven human subjects each of which was studied under three conditions. (1) Reinforced for increasing alpha density (high alpha). (2) Reinforced for decreasing alpha density (low alpha). (3) Resting. [From Kamiya, 1969.]

by becoming drowsy and producing slow wave activity (Mulholland, 1971). Much of the data are consistent with the visual motor hypothesis. For example, alpha control is better in subjects whose eyes are open when it would be easier, presumably, to control the visual system (Nowlis & Kamiya, 1970). Also, subjects who are paying attention to stimuli but are not employing the visual motor apparatus do not show alpha blocking (Mulholland, 1972). This visual motor hypothesis has, however, received some criticism. Chapman, Cavonius, and Ernest (1971), for example, suggested that the occurrence of alpha and alpha blocking in eyeless subjects is inconsistent with the hypothesis.

While there is some agreement about the neural and psychological processes that may be related to alpha blocking, there is less agreement about the processes that occur when the density of cortical alpha waves is increased. As is indicated in Fig. 2.1, the subjects displayed a gradual increase in the relative frequency of alpha waves during the rest period that were very similar to the changes that occurred during the period in which the subjects were trained to increase alpha wave density. This similarity in performance during training and rest periods has raised questions about what was learned during training to increase alpha wave density in this experiment.

A variety of hypotheses have been proposed to account for this result.

According to Mulholland (1972), refraining from visual motor activity
is a necessary but not sufficient condition for the occurrence of alpha
activity, since alpha activity does not necessarily begin for some time
after a subject begins to refrain from visual motor activity. It may be,
nevertheless, that the subjects learn to refrain from employing the visual
motor system when they are being trained to increase the density of
alpha waves, and this permits alpha wave density to gradually increase
during this experimental period. If the subjects were also gradually decreasing visual motor activity during the rest period, we would see a
similar increase in alpha density. Lynch and Paskewitz (1971), and Paskewitz, et al. (1970) have presented a similar hypothesis in which they
suggest that subjects learn to refrain from paying attention to features of
the experimental situation, and this permits the alpha density to increase
during both training and rest periods. A third proposal is that cortical
alpha activity is related to a psychological state very similar to that
which occurs during Zen or Yoga meditation, and that subjects learn to
produce this state (Brown, 1970, 1971; Kamiya, 1968, 1969). Kamiya
(1969) accounted for the gradual increase in alpha wave density during
the rest period in the following manner. The psychological state related to
alpha activity is pleasant for some subjects. Once such a subject learns to
produce this state efficiently, he enters it both during the rest period and
during the training period because it is preferred to the nonalpha state. A
fourth explanation of the production of alpha waves is that the alpha
state is produced by self-induced anoxia (Watanabe, Shapiro, & Schwartz,
1971). The subject might decrease the level of oxygen content by controlling respiration, and this could produce both the pleasant state associated with alpha and the increase in alpha density.

It would seem that the processes related to the production and blocking
of human cortical alpha waves in operant conditioning situations is still
not well-understood. Similar problems of interpretation are found when
we consider other human cortical EEG patterns (Brown, 1970, 1971).

There are two examples of operantly conditioned CNS patterns that do
not seem to be related to motor processes; one is the postreinforcement
synchronization which seems to be related to reinforcement and motivational processes (Sterman, Wyrwicka, & Roth, 1969), and the other is
the visual-evoked potential (Fox & Rudell, 1968).

One might be tempted to speculate further, as was suggested by Olds
(1965), that success has been achieved with patterns of neural activity
that are related to motor processes because they are easier to condition
than patterns that are related to nonmotor processes. There is one bit of
evidence that could provide some support for the hypothesis that motor-

related processes are easier to condition. Fox and Rudell (1970) operantly conditioned changes in late components of the visual cortical-evoked potential in cats. Rosenfeld (1970) operantly conditioned changes in components of a sensory-evoked potential in the primary somatosensory cortex of cats that was elicited by feedback from movement. When cats were trained to make the visual-evoked potential more positive, they required from 6 to 10 days to depart from baseline. When cats were trained to make the evoked potential elicited by feedback from movement more positive, they began to depart from baseline in the first session (Rosenfeld, 1971). Therefore, it could be easier to operantly condition sensory-evoked potentials elicited by movement than sensory-evoked potentials elicited by visual stimulation. Such an interpretation must be treated with caution, however, because the experiments did differ procedurally. For example, the cats in the Rosenfeld experiment received extensive pretraining in which they were reinforced for movement, and the cats in the Fox and Rudell experiment did not.

In summary, it would seem that most of the CNS patterns of electrical activity over which we have obtained control by means of operant conditioning are related to motor processes. It may be that so many motor-related patterns have been conditioned because they are prewired for easy learning, or because transfer from previous motor learning makes them easy to learn. But the alternative is equally, if not more likely, that motor-related neural patterns have been conditioned frequently simply because the experimenters chose to study such patterns.

III. OPERANT NEURAL CONDITIONING AS A METHOD OF CONTROL

The question that we must consider is this: Does the control provided by the operant conditioning of CNS electrical activity differ from that obtained by other methods for controlling internal neural and psychological processes, and if so, how? In order to answer this question, we must deal with differences in the *types of neural processes than can be controlled* by each method, as well as differences in the *type of control* exerted by each method. I shall discuss each of these issues separately.

A. DIFFERENCES IN THE TYPES OF PROCESSES THAT ARE CONTROLLED

The simplest approach to this topic is to ask whether we have been able to control patterns of CNS electrical activity by operant conditioning that we had not been able to control by other methods. The data seem to indicate that we have not reinforced novel patterns of electrical activity with the possible exception of certain components of the evoked potential (Fox & Rudell, 1970). This outcome, however, may be a function of the behavior of the experimenters rather than a property of reinforceable patterns of CNS electrical activity. The patterns that have been studied so far, obviously were not chosen at random; they were probably chosen because the experimenter had information that led him to believe that they were related to important psychological or neural processes. It may very well be that one might be able to reinforce patterns of CNS electrical activity that have never been observed before by shaping, but to my knowledge, this has not been done, with the exception noted above (Fox & Rudell, 1970).

A number of examples can be cited in which the operant conditioning procedure, rather than producing novel patterns of electrical activity, seems to have resulted in apparently novel relationships among neural and behavioral events. Effects of this sort very often play a prominent role in discussions of the specificity of operant neural conditioning. Before conditioning, the reinforced event was observed to be correlated with a number of other responses. After conditioning, the correlation is no longer observed. The reinforced response occurs without accompanying changes in the other responses. Examples are provided by research on the relationship of components of the average evoked potential (Fox & Rudell, 1970), and on the relationship of a single unit activity in the motor cortex to electromyographic (EMG) activity (Fetz & Finocchio, 1971).

One must interpret results such as these with caution. One could infer that the operant conditioning procedure *revealed* the presence of certain relationships that had not been seen before. One might say, for example, that the interconnections of the elements of a given neural system were not changed; rather, the operant conditioning procedure simply produced a normal mode of functioning in this system that no one had bothered to elicit before. Alternatively, one could infer that the operant conditioning procedure *produced* new relationships that had not been seen before. For example, one might say the operant conditioning procedure produced a fundamental change in the relationships among elements of a given neural system so that components which were related before are no longer related, and vice versa.

The latter interpretation attributes greater power to the control achieved by operant conditioning than does the former. At the same time, we know so little about the circuits that relate many of the neural events and processes in which we are interested that we have little support for either interpretation. Perhaps it is wiser to avoid taking any position on this issue until more evidence is available.

B. DIFFERENCES IN THE TYPE OF CONTROL

There is a possibility that we might obtain control over neural and psychological processes by the operant conditioning of patterns of CNS electrical activity that is more efficient, more powerful, or has fewer side effects than we have been able to obtain by other methods of control. In order to deal with this possibility, one has to compare neural operant conditioning with these other methods of control. The most obvious comparison is with the operant conditioning of observable behavior. It might be that some patterns of electrical activity that are related to overt skeletal responding might be controlled better by reinforcing skeletal responding than by reinforcing the neural patterns. Another comparison is control achieved by drugs, electrical stimulation, etc.

The question is unsettled at the moment because explicit comparisons between the reinforcement of neural events and other methods of control have not been made. For example, in research on the mood states associated with alpha rhythm, could the same effect have been obtained by training subjects to lower their respiratory rate, to refrain from visual motor activity, or, perhaps, to relax?

One especially important claim about the advantage of the control achieved by the operant conditioning of CNS electrical activity over other methods for controlling internal processes is that it leads to voluntary or self-control of internal processes. The term "voluntary control" is difficult to define operationally. While the reinforcement of the response, and feedback about the response may be necessary for establishing voluntary or self-control, they do not seem to be enough. In fact, certain types of operant conditioning seem to decrease voluntary control when, for example, they lead to compulsive behavior, as is illustrated in the work of Solomon, Kamin, and Wynne (1953) on the difficulty of extinguishing certain types of operantly conditioned avoidance responses.

A set of minimum requirements for recognizing voluntary control might be the following: To achieve effective voluntary control over some behavior, we must demonstrate not only that we can operantly condition subjects to make the response to stimuli which normally do not elicit it, but also that we can condition them to refrain from making the response to stimuli which normally elicit it. (We must, of course, employ the same reinforcers and schedules of reinforcement in both cases.) We would be loath to say that we have voluntary control if the subject could not refrain from performing a response as well as perform it or could not switch easily back and forth from one to the other. Furthermore, this stimulus control must be conditional on the behavior of the subject. That is, if required to, he should be able to perform a response when his own behavior produces the S^D for the response, and refrain from performing the response when the S^D is presented by some external agent. Also, we usually assess the precision of voluntary control, which could range from the awkward initiation or inhibition of a response at one extreme, to skilled control over the amplitude and direction of the response at the other. Finally, the fewer the constraints on the conditioning and performance of the response, the more voluntary control we would judge a subject to have (see Section IV A).

All of the neural patterns that have been operantly conditioned in experiments employing a bidirectional procedure meet the first criterion. It is only in the operant conditioning of cortical EEG patterns in human subjects that some of the other criteria have been met, and the data is still sketchy. Dewan's (1967) attempt to train subjects to send Morse Code messages by varying the duration of bursts of alpha activity indicates that considerable voluntary control can be achieved, but more work must be done on precision of control and on constraints.

Furthermore, it is not clear that the operant conditioning of patterns of CNS electrical activity is the better procedure for establishing voluntary control. Although there are many ways of defining voluntary control, the view seems to be accepted in research on operant neural conditioning that voluntary control in human subjects implies a conscious and deliberate decision to perform a response and an awareness of the response as it occurs. Given this view, one essential step for achieving voluntary control is to make the subject aware of the response when normally he is not aware of it.

There are at least two distinct conditioning methods that might be employed to make a subject "aware" of his internal responses. One is to employ the internal response as an S^D in an operant conditioning situation. An experiment on human subjects that was described by Kamiya (1969) illustrates this approach. In this experiment, the presence and absence of alpha waves served as discriminative stimuli. When alpha waves were occurring, the subjects were reinforced only if they made the appropriate identifying response—A. When alpha waves were not occurring, the subjects were reinforced only if they made the correct identifying response—B. After subjects had learned this discrimination, they were asked to produce or refrain from producing alpha, and they could do so. It would seem, then, that employing an internal pattern of electrical activity as an S^D led to voluntary control over that pattern. It would be interesting to see whether classical discriminative conditioning procedures, such as those in which internal autonomic states were employed as conditioned stimuli (Adam, 1967; Bykov, 1959; Razran, 1961), would lead to the same sort of voluntary control.

The second method for making a subject aware of his own internal responses is to add feedback following the response. I shall discuss this procedure in Section IV. The point of the present discussion is that it is still not clear which of the procedures for establishing voluntary control in human subjects is the more effective.

C. SUMMARY

In comparing operant neural conditioning with other methods of control, one can look for differences in the types of processes that can be controlled by each method, and for differences in the type of control that can be exerted by each method. With respect to the types of processes that are controlled, there is little evidence that operant neural conditioning produces control over novel patterns of CNS electrical activity. Operant conditioning procedures do seem to result in new relationships between the reinforced pattern of electrical activity and other responses. It is not clear, however, whether the procedure produces such relationships or simply reveals their presences. With respect to the type of control achieved, operant neural conditioning seems to differ from other control procedures in that it establishes voluntary or self-control in human subjects. The data on this question, however, are inadequate, and we still cannot assess accurately the extent to which control by operant conditioning is different from control achieved by other methods.

IV. EFFICIENCY OF CONDITIONING: FEEDBACK AND CONSTRAINTS ON CONDITIONING

It is clear from the attempt to answer these questions that we need more research on the types of CNS processes that can be operantly conditioned and on the comparison of different control procedures. As one examines the literature it becomes apparent that we need more research on another topic—the variables that control the rate of CNS conditioning. There are no experiments in which parametric analyses of the conditioning procedure have been carried out. The research on infrahuman subjects provides no relevant data, and the research on human subjects provides only what could best be described as a few hints. Nowlis and Kamiya (1970) have shown that more subjects could be conditioned to increase and decrease the number of alpha waves per unit time when they were trained with eyes open than with eyes closed. Peper (1970) indicated that the same differences were found when his results were compared to those of Waitzkin (1970). Also, once subjects have learned to increase and decrease the density of alpha waves, they can maintain the response for a brief period of time after feedback and reinforcement have been omitted (Peper and Mulholland, 1970).

It is somewhat surprising that so little formal research has been carried out on variables related to the efficiency of CNS conditioning. There are two classes of variables that are especially noteworthy in this respect. The first, which concerns the effects of feedback about response state, is important because there seems to be some question about its role in the operant neural conditioning of human subjects.[5] The second, which concerns variables which provide limitations on the operant conditioning of neural events, is important for practical applications. If the situations in which a subject can be conditioned or can perform a previously conditioned response are very limited, practical applications of the technique will be correspondingly few. I shall discuss each of these issues briefly.

A. Feedback about Response State and Reinforcement

The main question concerning the addition of feedback following a response is whether it is a sufficient condition for reinforcement. Consider a standard experiment in which a rat must press a lever in the presence of an auditory S^D in order to obtain a food reinforcement. The S^D is presented, and the rat presses the lever. This is followed by added feedback (e.g., the noise of a switch that is operated when the lever is depressed). The operation of the switch is followed by a second noise that is produced by the food magazine. The rat then leaves the vicinity of the lever, and approaches the food cup. Finally, it picks up the food and eats.

The stimuli in this sequence can have a variety of functions. First, they can act as reinforcers; they can increase the probability of responses which they follow. Second, they can act as discriminative stimuli; their presentation can lead to the occurrence of a response. Third, they can provide information about the state of the response. Two types of feedback about response state can be distinguished—naturally occurring feedback (e.g., proprioceptive feedback from movement), and feedback added by the experimenter (e.g., the switch noise that follows a lever press).

While it is difficult to specify the conditions that must be met for a stimulus to be a reinforcer, we can do so roughly in at least some cases.

---

[5] Much has been done on feedback from cortical EEG activity in nonoperant conditioning procedures (Mulholland, 1968, 1969, 1972; Peper, 1970). Also, considerable research has been carried out on the role of feedback produced by EMG and autonomic responses in operant conditioning experiments (e.g., Basmajian & Simard, 1967; Brener, Kleinman, & Goesling, 1969; Green, Green, & Walters, 1970a,b).

Stimuli which provide some consequence that is important for the internal economy of the organism are reinforcers (e.g., food in the aforementioned example). Also, stimuli which originally did not have reinforcing powers can acquire them by being paired with other stimuli that are reinforcers. They can become "conditioned reinforcers" (e.g., the noise of the switch and of the magazine in the aforementioned example). Arranging to have a stimulus provide feedback about response state, however, does not seem to be a sufficient condition for making it a reinforcer. If, in the example described, one had simply added the noise of the switch after each lever press without arranging to have food follow it, there would have been no increase in the probability of the lever press. It might be, of course, that added feedback will only act as a reinforcer for internal responses which have no naturally occurring feedback. But this does not seem to work either. We have added clicks and tones following the occurrence of hippocampal theta waves in rats, and this, by itself, has not produced any apparent learning.

One might argue that human subjects are different from infrahuman subjects, and that for human subjects, added feedback is a sufficient condition for reinforcement. This seems to be the implicit assumption in much of the human research where the training procedure is described as "feedback control" or "biofeedback" as often as "operant conditioning." Clear-cut evidence on this point is not available. Nevertheless, it seems to me that the most likely explanation of the operant conditioning of neural activities in human subjects when the only apparent reinforcer is feedback about response state, is that other subtle reinforcers are established by instructions and by the previous history of the subject. Human subjects are usually motivated to cooperate with the requirements of the experimenter (Orne, 1962), and therefore, feedback could be a reinforcer, not so much because it provides information about response state, but because it indicates successful performance. Obviously, it would be extremely useful to have more data on this point.

That feedback about response state may not be sufficient in itself to produce learning does not, of course, rule out the possibility that it plays an important ancillary role in operant conditioning. The unwritten lore of operant conditioning laboratories passes the dictum on from generation to generation, that added feedback about the response facilitates operant conditioning in certain situations. Such feedback is also considered very important in the training of complex motor skills (Bilodeau, 1969). While it is clear that the ancillary role of such added feedback is to facilitate operant conditioning, this need not always be the case. Rosenfeld, Rudell, and Fox (1969) employed money to reinforce increases and decreases in the voltage of late components of an auditory-evoked potential in human subjects. One group of subjects received further information about their responses by watching the evoked potential on an oscilloscope, while a second group did not receive such additional information. They found no obvious differences in performance between the two groups. In fact, some of the subjects complained that feedback from the oscilloscope distracted them from the task.

It would seem that many assumptions concerning the role of feedback, especially in human research on operant neural conditioning, are on shaky grounds. We require more data in order to determine whether added feedback about response state is a sufficient condition for reinforcement in human subjects. Also, we require more data on the ancillary function of such feedback in the training of complex responses. When does it facilitate, and when does it hinder conditioning?

B. CONSTRAINTS ON THE OPERANT CONDITIONING OF NEURAL EVENTS

The second area in which more parametric research is needed concerns the constraints or limitations on the operant conditioning of neural events. The assumption has often been made that, if we can condition a given response in one situation, we can condition any other response in that situation. As has been emphasized in a number of recent papers (Black & Young, 1972; Bolles, 1970; Seligman, 1970; Shettleworth, in press), this assumption concerning the interchangeability of elements of the conditioning situation is not correct for certain observable responses. For example, rats that were deprived of water, were trained to press a lever to avoid shock in the presence of one S^D and to drink water to avoid shock in the presence of a second S^D (Black & Young, 1972). The rats were trained until they were avoiding shock regularly, both by lever pressing and drinking. Then they were satiated. The rats continued to press the lever to avoid shock, but the performance of the drinking response deteriorated. In this case, the drinking response was more constrained than the lever pressing response with respect to conditions under which successful performance could occur.

Similar constraints on the operant conditioning and performance of CNS electrical activity have been observed. Paskewitz and Orne (1971), for example, first operantly conditioned subjects to produce cortical alpha waves. They then required the subjects to continue performing the conditioned alpha wave response while counting backward by sevens. This produced a deterioration in alpha wave performance. If other operantly conditioned neural patterns do not show the same deterioration under the same conditions, one might conclude that the performance of operantly conditioned alpha waves is constrained by the concurrent behavior of the subjects. Similar constraints have been shown for hippocampal EEG (Black, 1971a). Rats could be operantly conditioned to make high frequency RSA waves while moving, but not while holding still.

Without further knowledge of such constraints, we will not be able to assess accurately the extent to which the operant conditioning of particular neural responses can be used in practical situations. If an operantly conditioned neural response, for example, could be performed only under laboratory conditions, it would be of little use in practice.

C. Summary

It would seem, then, that there is a surprising lack of parametric research on the variables that control the conditioning procedure, especially with respect to the role of feedback about response state, and constraints on operant neural conditioning. Perhaps a concern with the response–reinforcer contingency and with mediation (see Section I), while understandable during the early stages of development of this research area, has captured our attention for too long, and has prevented us from progressing as rapidly as we should have on this issue. At this stage, we should know more about the learning process and about efficient training procedures.

V. OPERANT NEURAL CONDITIONING AS A METHOD FOR STUDYING FUNCTIONAL SIGNIFICANCE

The results of our discussion so far have not been particularly encouraging. We do not have a large number of demonstrations that operant neural conditioning provides control over thought processes, internal motivational states, mood states, and other equally exotic internal processes. In all but two cases, the available data suggests that the reinforced CNS patterns are related to motor processes in one way or another. Also, much more research is needed on the comparison of operant neural conditioning with other methods of control and on the factors that might facilitate and hinder conditioning before we can say much about the usefulness of the technique. Therefore, its contributions as a method of control, if any, lie in the future. I do not want, however, to give a completely dark picture of past accomplishments because it would be incorrect to do so. This method has been put to another use, and in this case, the results have been impressive. The other use of operant neural conditioning procedures is to study the functional significance of the reinforced pattern of CNS electrical activity.

As was pointed out in Section II, we require information beyond the fact that we have operantly conditioned a pattern of CNS electrical activity in order to deal with its functional significance. Several modifications of the basic operant conditioning procedure have been employed to provide the required information. I shall describe one of these, the concomitant measures procedure, in order to illustrate this use of operant neural conditioning.

In the concomitant measures procedure, we analyze the relationships between the reinforced pattern of electrical activity and other concomitantly measured patterns of neural activity and behavior. The steps in this approach are first, to identify the concomitantly measured patterns of neural activity and behavior that are highly correlated with the reinforced patterns of CNS electrical activity; second, to study the nature of the relationship among these events; and third, to make inferences from these and other available data, about the functional significance of the reinforced pattern of electrical activity.

One example that illustrates this method is our research on hippocampal EEG patterns (Black, 1971a; Black, Young, & Batenchuk, 1970; Dalton, 1969). In these experiments, electrodes were chronically implanted in the dorsal hippocampus of dogs. After recovery from surgery, each dog was reinforced for a given pattern of hippocampal EEG activity. Both food and positive brain stimulation were employed as reinforcers. We reinforced hippocampal RSA (rhythmic slow activity). This is relatively high amplitude almost sinusoidal waveform between 4 and 7 Hz in the dog. In order to identify some of the concomitant measures that might be related to reinforced patterns of hippocampal electrical activity, we videotaped overt skeletal behavior, and recorded heart rate and cortical EEG. During the occurrence of operantly conditioned hippocampal RSA, cortical desynchronization was observed, heart rate was high, and the dogs moved about a great deal (turning their heads, lifting their legs, etc.). One might be tempted to conclude that all of these changes were related to the RSA response. But this conclusion could be wrong as the following discussion will make clear.

Figure 2.2 presents schematic diagrams which illustrate in an extremely oversimplified manner the types of changes that might occur after different responses had been reinforced in the presence of an S^D. In Fig. 2.2a, the reinforced response is some skeletal movement. The S^D is presented; circuits involved in the reception of the S^D are activated; central integrating circuits process the input; then the motor system controlling the response is activated. In Fig. 2.2b, the reinforced response is some

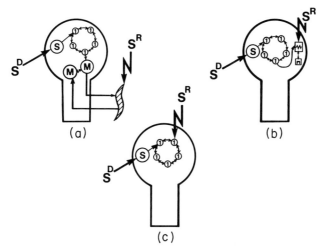

Fig. 2.2. Schematic diagrams illustrating the possible connections between the discriminative stimulus (S^D) and the response that was followed by reinforcement (S^R) after operant conditioning has taken place. The keyslot form represents the central nervous system; the small squares and circles within it represent structures of the central nervous system that might be involved in the stimulus–response connection. Figure 2a illustrates the situation that might exist if some observable skeletal response had been reinforced. Figures 2b and 2c illustrate the situation that might exist if some patterns of central nervous activity had been reinforced. S-circuits involved in the input of information. I-circuits involved in central processing. M-circuits involved in the control of movement. [From Black, 1972.]

pattern of CNS electrical activity. The same circuits are activated after the presentation of the S^D except for the final one which is a circuit of which the reinforced pattern is a component. (The situation in Fig. 2.2c, where the reinforced event is a component of the integrative system involved in the learning process, provides some interesting complexities, but, fortunately, the data have not yet compelled us to deal with this alternative.) Certain neural processes which occur during the performance of the operantly conditioned response are the same when both observable responses and neural events are reinforced; others are different because they are associated with a particular response that is reinforced. It is the latter in which we are interested. If we were interested in the former, there would be little point to the use of operant neural conditioning; we could study the former just as well by reinforcing more familiar observable responses.

The problem, of course, is to distinguish between those changes to the S^D in concurrently measured events that are uniquely related to the reinforced response, and those that are not. One way of making this distinction is to reinforce two different patterns of CNS electrical activity, and to compare the concomitant measures in the presence of the two patterns of electrical activity. Presumably, only those concomitant measures which are related to the type of response would be different.

We have carried out several experiments in which two different hippocampal EEG patterns were reinforced, RSA and non-RSA (Black, 1971a; Black, Young, & Batenchuk, 1970; Black & Young, 1972; Black & de Toledo, 1972).

Non-RSA could include a variety of different patterns such as the LIA (large amplitude irregular activity) and SIA (small amplitude irregular

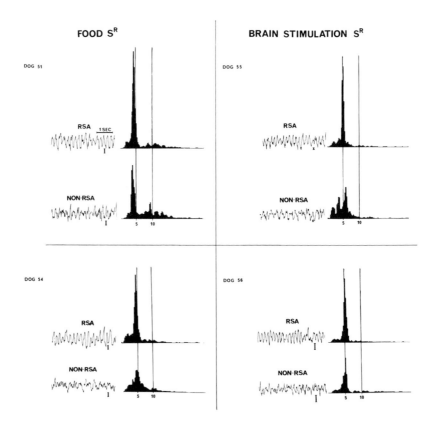

Fig. 2.3. Sample EEG records and power spectra for two dogs reinforced with food, and two dogs reinforced with brain stimulation. A sample of the EEG recorded for a 5-sec test trial during the phase of the experiment in which RSA was being reinforced, and for a 5-sec test trial during the phase of the experiment in which non-RSA was being reinforced, is shown for each dog. Power spectra taken over the last three to five test trials on the final training session for RSA and non-RSA are also shown. [From Black, 1972.]

activity) described by Stumpf (1965). Examples of RSA and non-RSA are shown in Fig. 2.3. Overt behavior differed in the presence of the two responses. RSA was accompanied by skeletal movements such as head turning, struggling, and so on, and non-RSA was associated with either holding still or licking. Heart rate increased during the S^D for the RSA response and remained the same or decreased during the S^D for the non-RSA response when non-RSA was accompanied by holding still. But when non-RSA was accompanied by consummatory and instinctive responses, such as licking, heart rate tended to be higher. There were no apparent differences in cortical electrical activity; desynchronization was observed during both RSA and non-RSA. It would seem, then, that the cortical EEG and heart rate changes were not closely related to the reinforced CNS response, while overt behavior was.

Our next step was to attempt to analyze the relationships between these concomitant measures of overt behavior and the reinforced patterns of CNS electrical activity. One question which we considered was whether the relationship is symmetrical with respect to the administration of reinforcement. The reinforcement of hippocampal EEG patterns led to correlated changes in observable behavior. Would the reinforcement of overt behavior of the appropriate type lead to correlated changes in hippocampal electrical activity? The answer is yes. Reinforcement of pedal pressing and lever pressing was accompanied by high frequency RSA, and reinforcement of holding still or drinking was not.

The symmetry of these results suggests that the patterns of hippocampal electrical activity are closely related to overt behavior; it does not tell us, however, whether one is necessary for the occurrence of the other. One method for determining whether they are necessarily related in the operant conditioning situation is to carry out what may be called *dissociative* conditioning—i.e., to block or hold constant one of the related responses while operantly conditioning the other.[6] One example of this method is provided by research that employed curare-like drugs to paralyze the skeletal musculature (Black, Young, & Batenchuk, 1970). RSA was conditioned while overt skeletal responding was blocked by a curare-like drug, Gallamine. Therefore, we can conclude that the occurrence of overt behavior is not necessary for the operant conditioning of the hippocampal RSA pattern.

The possibility still remains that the central components of the neural circuits controlling overt skeletal movements are necessarily related to

---

[6] Schwartz (1971) in research on operant autonomic conditioning, has discussed similar procedures. He refers to the operant conditioning of increases in one response and no change or decreases in another, as *differentiation*, and to the simultaneous operant conditioning of changes in the same direction in the two responses as *integration*.

the RSA patterns because curare-like drugs do not block activity in these central circuits. Another dissociative conditioning procedure is based on the assumption that holding still keeps at least some central components of the system controlling skeletal movement in a steady state. If a subject can learn to make hippocampal RSA responses while simultaneously holding still, then hippocampal RSA and central movement control systems would not be necessarily related. We have attempted to operantly condition rats to hold still and make hippocampal RSA. The reinforcement was water. The results indicate that we can operantly condition rats to make low-range frequency RSA while holding still, but not high-range frequency RSA. Figure 2.4 presents examples of EEG records for one rat. Examples are shown of RSA responses which occurred during the final stage of training when the rat was reinforced for making RSA responses while holding still, and when it was reinforced for making RSA responses while moving. In each condition a shaping procedure was employed to increase the frequency of the RSA response. Four reinforced RSA responses during each phase of training are shown. The form of the RSA wave is less regular and the frequency of RSA lower when the rat is required to hold still while making RSA than when it is required to move

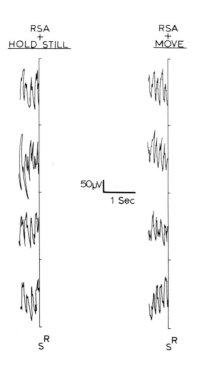

RSA
+
HOLD STILL

RSA
+
MOVE

50μV

1 Sec

S^R

S^R

Fig. 2.4. Examples of reinforced RSA responses. The four examples on the left are from a session in which a rat was required to simultaneously hold still and produce three consecutive RSA waves in order to obtain water reinforcement (S^R); and the four examples on the right are from a session in which the rat was required to simultaneously move and produce three consecutive RSA waves in order to obtain water reinforcement. The rats were shaped to make higher frequency RSA under each condition by increasing a criterion level above which the frequency of RSA had to be for reinforcements to be administered. The criterion level was increased during each session until fewer than six reinforcements per 100 sec occurred. The first four responses are shown for the period of each session during which the criterion level was at its highest. The criterion was 6.0 Hz in the hold still condition, and 7.6 Hz in the move condition. [From Black, 1972.]

while making RSA. This result, then, suggests that certain types of skeletal movement are necessarily related to high frequency RSA, at least in the very limited situations that we have explored so far.

The next step in this approach is to attempt to make some inferences about the functional significance of the reinforced pattern of electrical activity. We should, of course, discuss data in addition to that obtained in the operant conditioning experiments described previously. Space limitations do not permit us to deal with this extensive literature which has been reviewed recently by Bennett (1971), Gray (1970), and Vanderwolf (1969, 1971). It is worth mentioning, however, some examples of apparent exceptions to the relationship between high frequency RSA and skeletal responses such as lever pressing. Gray reported hippocampal RSA in the 7.5–8.5 Hz range in rats that were holding still. Bennett also reported that trains of relatively high frequency hippocampal RSA waves occur during periods in which animals were holding still. Still other exceptions could be described. Whether these are related to species differences, differences in the function of different parts of the hippocampus, problems in recording behavior, or are actual exceptions to the hypothesis, has yet to be determined.

The relationship between higher frequency RSA and skeletal responses such as bar pressing, if it is confirmed by further research, is consistent with two types of hypotheses. The first is the hypothesis that the neural processes represented by both RSA and skeletal behavior belong to the same system. Vanderwolf (1969, 1971), for example, has suggested that RSA represents processes in a motor system that controls voluntary behavior, and Klemm (1970) has suggested that RSA represents processes in the system that produces EMG changes in skeletal muscles. The second hypothesis is that high frequency RSA belongs to a neural system that is different from the system that controls skeletal responses such as bar pressing, and that the two systems are necessarily related. For example, hippocampal RSA may represent some event in a neural system controlling attention or orientation to external stimuli, and this system is activated only during certain types of movement. Another possibility is that RSA may be involved in producing corollary discharge for certain skeletal movements. The present results, then, are consistent with hypotheses that suggest that high frequency hippocampal RSA represents processes in neural systems controlling certain types of skeletal movement, or in other neural systems that are congruent with the systems that control these types of skeletal movement.

Other examples (Chase & Harper, 1971; Fetz & Finocchio, 1971; Fox & Rudell, 1970; Sterman, Wyrwicka, & Roth, 1969) could have been used to illustrate the method. In each case, some contribution was made to our understanding of the functional significance of the reinforced pattern of CNS electrical activity, especially by the use of dissociative conditioning techniques.

VI. CONCLUSION

Two questions with which we began concerned the use of operant conditioning procedures to obtain control over internal neural and psychological processes, and the comparison between operant neural conditioning and other methods of control. There is no doubt that one could employ the operant conditioning procedure to obtain control over psychological processes related to the reinforced pattern of CNS electrical activity. It was somewhat surprising, however, to find that most of the reinforced patterns were related to motor processes. Furthermore, it is not well-established that the control achieved by reinforcing patterns of CNS electrical activity is significantly different from that which would be achieved by other methods of control such as the reinforcement of observable behavior, drugs, direct stimulation, etc. Some results indicate that the relationships between the reinforced neural event and other events are different after operant conditioning. But it is not clear whether these differences were produced by the operant conditioning procedure. Also, there is evidence that operant neural conditioning will provide control that we could not achieve by other means, especially with respect to voluntary or self-control.

Further research on the use of the operant conditioning of CNS electrical activity to obtain control over neural and psychological processes is especially important for practical applications. We need more information on the operant conditioning of neural patterns that are related to non-motor processes. We need more information on the range of patterns of neural activity that can be operantly conditioned; it is incorrect to assume that we can condition all patterns because we can condition some of them. We need more information on the variables that influence the rate of conditioning because no parametric studies on this topic have been carried out. We need more information on the constraints on the operant conditioning of particular patterns of neural electrical activity, especially about the conditions under which the operantly conditioned brain wave patterns will generalize beyond the training laboratory. Finally we need more information on the nature of voluntary control and on the optimal procedures for producing it.

Perhaps we should wait until more of this information is available before we permit ourselves to be carried away by the passionately expressed hopes and fears for the future that were mentioned at the beginning of this paper. In this respect, it is somewhat ironic that many discussions of operant neural conditioning have focused on its role in the control of neural and psychological processes in real life situations, when the literature reveals that its main contribution so far has been as an analytic tool for studying neural function.

The Discussion of Dr. Black's Presentation

LED BY DR. RALPH HEFFERLINE
Columbia University

Hefferline: I regret that Dr. Black ran out of time. I could have listened much longer. What he was talking about at the end—the quick enthusiasms for and the attempt to make practical application of findings not too well-understood—stand in direct contrast to his own careful experimental method and to his need to know at all times just what he is doing.

The timeliness of this conference is underscored by the fact that there now exists a sudden, widespread interest in "biofeedback." Black did not use this term, but I think it will be heard repeatedly during this conference. It has come to designate the enhanced information about one's own functioning that can be made available by means of instrumentation. By electrically recording from particular parts of the body, some kind of analog, visible or audible, can be obtained of what is going on in those parts. For Black in his present paper, the region involved is a portion of the brain or, more specifically, the hippocampus. Other investigators may record in similar fashion various autonomic activities. My own major concern lies with the detection and experimental manipulation of very small skeletal responses.

Most sensational in biofeedback work to date has been Joe Kamiya's finding that one can be trained to control one's own alpha waves. Commercial exploitation of the technique is already well-underway. For instance, just before I left New York, I read an advertisement for Alphagenics, Inc. For a fee, one can be taught, it was claimed, to increase one's alpha waves and, as a consequence, to have one's psychosomatic ills clear up, including tension headaches and spastic colon. Psychological hangups also were reported to fade away in the process. I am sure you will agree that Dr. Black's approach is somewhat more conservative and certainly more appropriate to the present state of our knowledge in these matters.

Black has demonstrated, using dogs with electrodes implanted in the dorsal hippocampus, that operant conditioning procedures can provide bidirectional control of theta waves—i.e., theta waves can be increased by reinforcement or decreased by reinforcement of nontheta frequencies. Further, the use of concomitant measures revealed that theta seems related to overt behavior and cardiac changes, but to be independent of electrical activity recorded by scalp electrodes.

I am particularly interested in Black's additional refinement of the relationship between theta activity and reinforced holding still. Immobility is the opposite of overt behavior. However, electromyographic recording sometimes indicates that holding still is a rather violent sort of doing nothing—i.e., there may be a high degree of tension in antagonistic muscles. Thus, there is nothing contradictory in Black's finding that theta frequencies may be conditioned without the animal being overtly active.

Dr. Black goes along with the view that the operant conditioning procedure may very well provide control not otherwise achievable, particularly with respect to voluntary or self-control, but also that it is most important that more formal experimentation on this question be carried out. This is a prerequisite for sound practical applications. Meantime, the hopes and fears expressed for the future of biofeedback research may be excessive and are certainly premature.

Open Discussion

Dr. Larry Thompson (Duke University): Would Dr. Black talk about any similarities between his work and Adey's work, and others regarding theta activity and learning.

Black: I can't comment on much of Adey's data because he does not present the kinds of detailed observations on the behavior of his subjects that I need in order to relate his data to ours. For example, he has observed that theta frequency differs on correct and incorrect trials in a discrimination problem. It is possible that differences in theta frequency could be correlated with differences in motor activity on correct and incorrect trials rather than the "degree of correctness" itself.

There *are* data, however, which do not seem to be consistent with hypotheses that relate theta to movement. The data obtained by Gray (1970) and Bennett (1971) were mentioned in the paper. First, Gray, at Oxford, says that he can get animals to produce theta between 7.5 and 8.5 Hz when they are holding still, if they are frustrated. Bennett reports theta when an animal holds still during an S^Δ.

Dr. Allen Rechtschaffen (University of Chicago): I would like to address myself to the major thrust of what you have said, rather than to what you have specifically said. The major thrust has to do with the question of what is being reinforced, viz., is it specifically the EEG pattern that is being reinforced, or is the EEG pattern epiphenomenal to some mediating link, such as motor activity? Now, in a sense, it is necessarily so that you are right about this mediator; and in another sense, you can never prove yourself right. First, in the sense that you have to be right, you have to admit that there are mediating processes between your reinforcement contingencies, and your discriminative stimuli, and the EEG response. Nobody would believe that there is an immediate direct causal link between your reinforcement contingencies and your discriminative stimulus to the EEG. There must be a mediating response in the nervous system to which the EEG must be epiphenomenal and, under some circumstance that we don't know about yet, the EEG can be eliminated. So what you say in principle *has* to be right. It has to be right anytime we approach any question of this sort between stimulus and response. If you fail to find a mediating process, it's an accident of the limitations of your technology, of your inability to see the mediating process. There definitely has to be some mediating process—whatever it is. What you have shown is that you have not been able to destroy the correlation between fast theta and motor activity. Now, that does not necessarily mean that the motor activity may not be epiphenomenal to the theta. You have a correlation, and maybe you should study the motor response because the EEG is perhaps epiphenomenal to that. You do not show that the motor response is perhaps epiphenomenal to the processes which are most intimately related to the EEG. Finally, in the sense in which you can never be proven right, your failure to find a dissociation may be a product of the limitations of our technology at the moment. That is, under other circumstances, they may be dissociable. For example, the time when you find the fastest theta occurring most regularly in the nervous system is during paradoxical sleep, where you get a regular 8-cycle/sec theta sustained for long periods of time with very intermittent motor twitching. In those cases, there is a massive descending inhibition of motor output.

Black: One comment about this notion of mediation and epiphenomenon: I didn't use the word "mediation," I guess for the reasons that you've stated. Obviously, something else is also going on in the CNS in addition to the reinforced event. The question of interest then, from my point of view, is to specify just what that "something" might be. The simplest approach is to try to determine the various central circuits that might be activated when the reinforced response occurs (though there are problems in that). We once made up a series of simple-minded excitatory models and simple-minded inhibitory models which relate hippocampal EEG and skeletal movement. The most obvious one is a peripheral mediation model; the animal performs a skeletal response and feedback from that response produces theta. In a series of experiments with curarized animals we have ruled out this possibility. You can condition both theta and nontheta in animals where there has been a block at the neuromuscular junction so that there is no skeletal movement and no feedback from it. So, you can to some extent delimit the types of neural circuits that are involved when you reinforce a particular CNS event.

With reference to your point about paradoxical sleep, Vanderwolf argued that during paradoxical sleep there is a block at a lower level of the CNS. In a sense, the hippocampus acts as though the animal were awake, but the output is blocked lower down. If you could break that block, you'd obtain movement when theta was occurring.

Rechtschaffen: The block of the muscle inhibition is produced by a lesion of the locus coeruleus nuclei (apparently responsible for the descending inhibition). The thrust of what you are saying now is that you do produce a dissociation. Perhaps there is an origin of motor output which is being blocked or masked, so that in paradoxical sleep, there is an additional element. So, of course, that destroys one model. What you have done is to still permit the possibility of the common generator, at least so that there might be a motor outflow which is blocked before it gets to the effector organ. The conditioning of alpha (or theta in this case) may be no more unique than the conditioning of a neural motor outflow that doesn't hit the periphery because it was blocked. But if you follow that kind of assumption, you can ask, "why should you do your experiments," because once you are willing to admit that kind of assumption, then you can always invoke it for any condition in which you block the correlation between the EEG and the motor activity.

Black: It depends on how you produce the block and at what level. The block at the neuromuscular junction is just one of many possibilities. Each can give you a clue as to the way the things are organized.

Rechtschaffen: That is like the joke about William James. He went up to see this very wise man in the Himalayas, and asked the wise man to tell him what holds up the earth. The wise man answered that it was an elephant. So James asked what it was that held up that elephant, and the sage told him that it was another elephant. Then James asked, "Then perhaps you can tell me . . .," and the wise man said, "Please, Mr. James, I know your next question. And the answer is that there are elephants all the way down."

That is, you can always hypothesize a block which is closer and closer to a common generator.

Dr. T. H. Bhatti (University of Virginia): When you record EEG from electrodes at the hippocampus, we all understand that the EEG originates in the hippocampus. When you talk of cortical EEG, terms become confusing. In fact, what you are getting is scalp recordings. Secondly, you assume that, although you are recording from the scalp, the waves originate in the cortex; I don't know if we really have enough evidence to assume that.

Black: I don't want to make that assumption.

Bhatti: In that case, I wonder if we should avoid using the term "cortical patterns."

Black: Right. We'll call them scalp recordings.

Dr. Johann Stoyva (University of Colorado): Since Dr. Rechtschaffen mentioned paradoxical sleep, is there any relationship between the conditioning of hippocampal theta during wakefulness and the hippocampal theta which occurs in sleep? The reason I ask is because Sterman has found that, by conditioning sensorimotor rhythms in waking cats, changes occur in the ensuing sleep—that there is quieter sleep with a lower heart rate.

Black: Sterman obtains two changes. One is that there are more long periods of quiet sleep; the other is that EEG patterns similar to the sensorimotor rhythm occur more frequently. You are suggesting a transfer study—condition an animal to the normal state in the presence of a discriminative stimulus, and then let him sleep in the presence of that stimulus. I suspect that an animal which was conditioned to make theta in the presence of an S^D would sleep less when allowed to sleep with that discriminative stimulus present. We don't have the data, unfortunately.

REFERENCES

Adam, G. *Interoception and behaviour: An experimental study.* Budapest: Publishing House of the Hungarian Academy of Sciences, 1967.

Basmajian, J. V., & Simard, T. G. Effects of distracting movements on the control of trained motor units. *American Journal of Physical Medicine,* 1967, **46,** 1427.

Beatty, J. Effects of initial alpha wave abundance and operant training procedures on occipital alpha and beta wave activity. *Psychonomic Science,* 1971, **23,** 197–199.

Bennett, T. L. Hippocampal theta activity and behaviour—a review. *Communications in Behavioural Biology,* 1971, Part A, **6,** 1–12.

Bilodeau, E. A. (Ed.) *Principles of skill acquisition.* New York: Academic Press, 1969.

Black, A. H. A comment on yoked control designs. Technical Report No. 11, September 1967, McMaster University, Department of Psychology.

Black, A. H. The direct control of neural processes by reward and punishment. *American Scientist,* 1971, **59,** 236–245. (a)

Black, A. H. Autonomic conditioning in infrahuman subjects. In R. F. Brush (Ed.), *The aversive control of behaviour.* New York: Academic Press, 1971. (b)

Black, A. H. The operant conditioning of central nervous system electrical activity. In G. H. Bower (Ed.), *The psychology of learning and motivation, Vol. 6.* New York: Academic Press, 1972.

Black, A. H., & de Toledo, L. The relationship among classically conditioned responses. In A. H. Black & W. F. Prokasy (Eds.), *Classical conditioning II: Current research and theory.* New York: Appleton, 1972.

Black, A. H., & Young, G. A. Constraints on the operant conditioning of drinking. In R. M. Gilbert & J. R. Millenson (Eds.), *Reinforcement: Behaviour analyses.* New York: Academic Press, 1972.

Black, A. H., Young, G. A., & Batenchuk, C. The avoidance training of hippocampal theta waves and its relation to skeletal movement. *Journal of Comparative and Physiological Psychology,* 1970, **70,** 15–24.

Bolles, R. C. Species-specific defense reactions and avoidance learning. *Psychological Review,* 1970, **77,** 32–48.

Brener, J., Kleinman, R. A., & Goesling, W. J. The effect of different exposures to augmented sensory feedback on the control of heart rate. *Psychophysiology,* 1969, **5,** 510–516.

Brown, B. Recognition of aspects of consciousness through association with EEG alpha activity represented by a light signal. *Psychophysiology,* 1970, **6,** 442–452.

Brown, B. Awareness of EEG-subjective activity relationships detected within a closed feedback system. *Psychophysiology,* 1971, **7,** 541–464.

Bykov, K. *The cerebral cortex and the internal organs.* Moscow: Foreign Languages Publishing House, 1959.

Carmona, A. Trial and error learning of the voltage of the cortical EEG activity. *Dissertation Abstracts,* 1967, **28,** 1157B–1158B.

Chapman, R. M., Cavonius, C. R., & Ernest, J. T. Alpha and kappa electroencephalogram activity in eyeless subjects. *Science,* 1971, **171,** 1159–1161.

Chase, M. H., & Harper, R. M. Somatomotor and visceromotor correlates of operantly conditioned 12–14 c/sec. sensorimotor cortical activity. *Electroencephalography and Clincial Neurophysiology,* 1971, **31,** 85–92.

Crider, A., Schwartz, G. E., & Shnidman, S. On the criteria for instrumental autonomic conditioning. *Psychological Bulletin,* 1969, **71,** 455–461.

Dalton, A. J. Discriminative conditioning of hippocampal electrical activity in curarized dots. *Communications in Behavioral Biology,* 1969, **3,** 283–287.

Delgado, J. M. R., Johnston, V. S., Wallace, J. D., & Bradley, R. J. Operant conditioning of amygdala spindling in the free chimpanzee. *Brain Research,* 1970, **22,** 347–362.

Dewan, E. M. Occipital alpha rhythm, eye position and lens accommodation. *Nature,* 1967, **214,** 975–977.

Fetz, E. E. Operant conditioning of cortical unit activity. *Science,* 1969, **163,** 955–957.

Fetz, E. E., & Finocchio, D. V. Operant conditioning of specific patterns of neural and muscular activity. *Science,* 1971, **174,** 431–435.

Fox, S. S., & Rudell, A. P. Operant controlled neural event: Formal and systematic approach to electrical coding of behavior in brain. *Science,* 1968, **162,** 1299–1302.

Fox, S. S., & Rudell, A. P. Operant controlled neural event: Functional independence in behavioral coding by early and late components of visual cortical evoked response in cats. *Journal of Neurophysiology,* 1970, **33,** 548–561.

Gray, J. A. Sodium amobarbital, the hippocampal theta rhythm, and the partial reinforcement extinction effect. *Psychological Review,* 1970, **77,** 465–480.

Green, E. E., Green, A. M., & Walters, E. D. Self-regulation of internal states. In J. Rose (Ed.), *Progress of cybernetics: Proceedings of the International Congress of cybernetics, London, 1969.* London: Gordon & Breach, 1970. (a)

Green, E. E., Green, A. M., & Walters, E. D. Voluntary control of internal states: Psychological and physiological. *Journal of Transpersonal Psychology,* 1970, **2,** 1–26. (b)

Kamiya, J. Conscious control of brain waves. *Psychology Today,* 1968, **1,** 57–60.

Kamiya, J. Operant control of the EEG alpha rhythm and some of its reported effects on conciousness. In C. Tart (Ed.), *Altered states of consciousness: A book of readings.* New York: Wiley, 1969.

Katkin, E. S., & Murray, E. N. Instrumental conditioning of autonomically mediated behavior: Theoretical and methodological issues. *Psychological Bulletin,* 1968, **70,** 52–68.

Katkin, E. S., Murray, E. N., & Lachman, R. Concerning instrumental autonomic conditioning: A rejoinder. *Psychological Bulletin,* 1969, **71,** 462–466.

Klemm, W. R. Correlation of hippocampal theta rhythm, muscle activity, and brain stem reticular formation activity. *Communications in Behavioural Biology,* 1970, Part A, **3,** 147–151.

Krutch, J. W. *The measure of man.* New York: Grosset, 1953.

Lawson, H. *A manual of popular physiology.* New York: Putnam, 1873.

Luce, G., & Peper, E. Mind over body, mind over mind. *New York Times Magazine,* Sept. 12, 1971.

Lynch, J. J., & Paskewitz, D. A. On the mechanisms of the feedback control of human brain wave activity. *Journal of Nervous and Mental Diseases,* 1971, **153,** 205–217.

Miller, N. E. Learning of visceral and glandular responses. *Science,* 1969, **163,** 434–445.

Mulholland, T. B. Feedback electroencephalography. *Prehledy a Oiskuse,* 1968, **4,** 410–438.

Mulholland, T. B. Problems and prospects for feedback electroencephalography. Presented at the meetings of the Feedback Society, Los Angeles, California, 1969.

Mulholland, T. B. Can you really turn on with alpha? Paper presented at the meetings of the Massachusetts Psychological Association, Boston College, May 7, 1971.

Mulholland, T. B. Occipital alpha revisited. *Psychological Bulletin,* 1972, **78,** 176–182.

Nowlis, D. P., & Kamiya, J. The control of electroencephalographic alpha rhythms through auditory feedback and the associated mental activity. *Psychophysiology,* 1970, **6,** 476–484.

Olds, J. Operant conditioning of single unit responses. *Excerpta Medica International Congress,* 1965, **87,** 372–380.

Olds, J. The limbic system and behavioral reinforcement. In W. R. Adey & T. Tokizane (Eds.), *Progress in brain research. Structure and function of the limbic system.* Vol. 27. Amsterdam: Elsevier, 1967.

Olds, J. The central nervous system and the reinforcement of behaviour. *American Psychologist,* 1969, **24,** 114–132.

Olds, J., & Olds, M. E. Interference and learning in paleocortical systems. In J. F. Delafresnaye (Ed.), *Brain mechanisms and learning.* Oxford: Blackwell's, 1961.

Orne, M. T. On the social psychology of the psychological experiment: With particular reference to demand characteristics and their implications. *American Psychologist,* 1962, **17,** 776–783.

Paskewitz, D. A., Lynch, J. J., Orne, M. T., & Costello, J. The feedback control of alpha activity: Conditioning or disinhibition? *Psychophysiology*, 1970, **6**, 637–638.

Paskewitz, D. A., & Orne, M. T. Cognitive effects during alpha feedback training. Paper presented at the annual meeting of the Eastern Psychological Association, New York City, April., 1971.

Peper, E. Feedback regulation of the alpha electroencephalogram activity through control of the internal and external parameter. *Kybernetik*, 1970, **7**, 107–112.

Peper, E., & Mulholland, T. Methodological and theoretical problems in the voluntary control of electroencephalographic occipital alpha by the subject. *Kybernetik*, 1970, **7**, 10–13.

Razran, G., The observable unconscious and the inferable conscious in current Soviet psychophysiology: Interoceptive conditioning, semantic conditioning and the orienting reflex. *Psychological Review*, 1961, **68**, 81–147.

Rosenfeld, J. P. Operant control of a neural event evoked by a stereotyped behavior. Unpublished Ph.D. thesis, University of Iowa, September, 1970.

Rosenfeld, J. P. Personal communication, 1971.

Rosenfeld, J. P., Rudell, A. P., & Fox, S. S. Operant control of neural events in humans. *Science*, 1969, **165**, 821–823.

Schwartz, G. E. Operant conditioning of human cardiovascular integration and differentiation. Unpublished Ph.D. thesis, Harvard University, 1971.

Seligman, M. E. P. On the generality of the laws of learning. *Psychological Review*, 1970, **77**, 406–418.

Shettleworth, S. J. Constraints on learning. In D. S. Lehrman, R. A. Hinde & E. Shaw (Eds.), *Advances in the study of behavior, 4.* New York: Academic Press, (in press).

Solomon, R. L., Kamin, L. J., & Wynne, L. C. Traumatic avoidance learning: The outcomes of several extinction procedures with dogs. *Journal of Abnormal and Social Psychology*, 1953, **48**, 291–302.

Spilker, B., Kamiya, J., Callaway, E., & Yeager, C. R. Visual evoked responses in subjects trained to control alpha rhythms. *Psychophysiology*, 1969, **5**, 683–695.

Sterman, M. B., Howe, R. C., & MacDonald, L. R. Facilitation of spindleburst sleep by conditioning of electroencephalographic activity while awake. *Science*, 1970, **167**, 1146–1148.

Sterman, M. B., Lopresti, R. W., & Fairchild, M. D. Electroencephalographic and behavioral studies of monomethylhydrazine toxicity in the cat. Aerospace Medical Research Laboratory Report TR-69-3, 1969.

Sterman, M. B., Wyrwicka, W., & Roth, S. Electrophysiological correlates and neural substrates of alimentary behavior in the cat. *Annals of the New York Academy of Sciences*, 1969, **157**, 723–739.

Stumpf, Ch. Drug action on the electrical activity of the hippocampus. *International Review of Neurobiology*, 1965, **8**, 77–138.

Vanderwolf, C. H. Hippocampal electrical activity and voluntary movement in the rat. *Electroencephalography and Clinical Neurophysiology*, 1969, **26**, 407–418.

Vanderwolf, C. H. Limbic-diencephalic mechanisms of voluntary movement. *Psychological Review*, 1971, **78**, 83–113.

Waitzkin, B. Brandeis University. Personal communication referred to by Peper (1970).

Watanabe, T., Shapiro, D., & Schwartz, G. E. Meditation as an anoxic state: A critical review and theory. Paper presented at the Psychophysiology Society Meetings, St. Louis, 1971.

Wyrwicka, W., & Sterman, M. B. Instrumental conditioning of sensorimotor cortex EEG spindles in the waking cat. *Physiology and Behavior*, 1968, **3**, 703–707.

CHAPTER THREE

Evoked Potentials of the Brain Related to Thinking[1]

ROBERT M. CHAPMAN

Eye Research Foundation of Bethesda

and

Walter Reed Army Institute of Research

Averaged evoked potentials (AEP) can be obtained from human electro-encephalographic recording by averaging the time-varying voltages obtained from scalp electrodes in response to a number of similar stimuli. Since these electrical responses are recorded from the brain, we expect them to be affected by a wide variety of influences, including the physical characteristics of the stimulus and the psychological characteristics of the stimulus, such as the history of the individual and the meaning of the stimuli to him. There is a growing body of literature supporting both kinds of influences on these evoked responses (e.g., Donchin & Lindsley, 1969).

For those interested in the psychophysiology of thinking, the averaged evoked potential represents one of the few techniques now available for

[1] This work was partially supported by Public Health Service Research Grant NIH–NEI–5–R01–EY00490.

69

looking at brain functioning in normal man. The overall experimental question, I think, is how specific are these effects? We know that thinking is complicated and evoked responses appear complicated; is it possible to find specific aspects of thinking that may be related to specific aspects of the evoked response?

One part of the overall question of how specific are the relationships is the distinction between prestimulus and poststimulus effects. In considering effects of the physical parameters of stimuli, it has been necessary to deal not just with the discrete stimulus, and its effects, but also to be concerned with the recent history of the system. For example, in the visual system, not only the characteristics of the light flash influence the response, but also the adaptation level which has resulted from the recent history. A well-known example is Weber's law. In a similar way the psychological state of the organism may be important to the psychological response to stimulation. In considering brain processing of stimuli, what the brain does with stimulus information may depend on the task that the brain is performing, i.e., on the relevance of this information to the task. If differences in brain processes are found in two situations are the differences related more fundamentally to poststimulus processes or to the states existing prior to the stimulus presentation?

From the standpoint of studying the psychophysiology of thinking, it would seem to be advantageous to control *what* thinking takes place and *when* it takes place. If we can unleash the thinking by a discrete stimulus which requires the subject to perform some particular, defined task, then we may be able to relate it to physiological processes. Averaged evoked potential experiments often appear to have these two characteristics, but unfortunately, both the *what* and the *when* in many experiments have lacked precision. *What* thinking has sometimes been "controlled" by presenting "meaningful" stimuli, e.g., pictures, words, etc., by asking the subject to pay attention, to count the stimuli, to guess the next stimulus, etc. (e.g., Sutton, 1969). *When* the thinking takes place has presumably been controlled by presenting a discrete stimulus. The time of stimulation and averaging may be precise, but the time of thinking may be in doubt. Because the averaged evoked potential depends on averaging, the *same* stimulus has often been repeated throughout a run. This procedure makes it unnecessary to even "perceive" the stimuli. If the stimuli are presented rhythmically, a counting task can successfully tolerate large gaps of not sensing the stimuli. Presenting "meaningful" stimuli without designating a task, does not seem like a good way to control *what* thinking, if any, results from the stimulus. Nor does asking the subject to guess which stimulus will appear next exercise much control over what the subject does when the stimulus does appear, since the guess is occurring prior to the stimulus.

In view of the foregoing discussion, I would like to suggest that experimental designs attempting to relate physiology to thinking should strive to:

1. assure that each and every stimulus is processed in a defined way;

2. separate effects due to general states of the organism, such as level of arousal;

3. separate effects due to recent history from poststimulus effects;

4. have adequate controls for the physical stimulus reaching the receptors.

I. EXPERIMENTAL DESIGN

I here now present some data that has been obtained with Sam Shelburne and Hank Bragdon at Walter Reed. The experimental design is an extension of a relatively simple design that we first published in 1964 (Chapman & Bragdon, 1964; Chapman, 1965; Chapman, 1967; Chapman, 1969a,b; Sheatz & Chapman, 1969). The subject was given a set of problems to solve that involve comparing two numbers and indicating which of the two was numerically larger. For comparison, on each trial two letters were also presented which were irrelevant to the task. On other runs, the same physical stimuli were presented, but the problems were solved on the basis of comparing the alphabetical order of the letters while the numbers were irrelevant. Figure 3.1 illustrates the type of stimuli used. They were presented sequentially at retinal fixation as brief flashes (approx 10 μsec) spaced $\frac{3}{4}$ sec apart. On each trial six light stimuli were given: two numbers and two letters in random order sandwiched between blank flashes at the beginning and end of the trial. On each trial after the light stimuli were given, the subject gave his answer by moving a switch to one side or the other depending on which of the two numbers was larger (if numbers were relevant). A correct answer produced a tone and an incorrect answer a buzz. The blank flashes at the beginning and end of each trial were intended to reduce "first stimulus" effects and postpone muscular activity associated with giving answers, respectively. After the second blank flash, a 1.5 sec time-slot was available in which the subject could answer. The performance accuracy was better than 99%. Since the numbers and letters were randomly selected (1–6, A–F), nearly every stimulus was being processed by the subject in order to achieve this high performance level. One hundred and two trials constituted a run and ten runs of each type were obtained over five sessions from each of 12 subjects

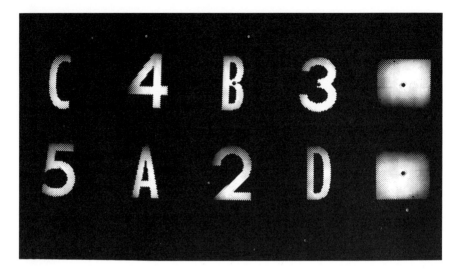

Fig. 3.1. Examples of stimuli. Each row represents stimulus sequence of a sample trial with first blank stimulus not shown. The sequence of letters and numbers and the particular letters and numbers were randomized from trial to trial. Each stimulus presented at the same locus as a brief flash of approximately .1 fL (about 2.0 log units of luminance above threshold for stimulus recognition).

(Subject JA had only eight runs from four sessions.) While a subject was solving these problems his EEG was being recorded from standard scalp electrodes, so that the brain response evoked by each type of stimulus could be averaged by computer.

The randomization of the stimuli is important not only for assuring that each stimulus be processed, but also for controlling the effects of many confounding variables such as eye movements, EEG activity, activation level, differential expectancies, etc. This procedure tends to eliminate the differential effects of all processes occurring before the stimulus. It is the possibility of prestimulus differences that has clouded interpretations attempting to relate evoked response differences to post-stimulus processes. We want to synchronize the perceptual–cognitive processes to the stimuli, in order to study their effects in the averaged evoked potential.

The experimental design permits examining the effects of post-stimulus processes both with and without different prestimulus conditions, as is summarized in Table 3-1. There are four positions in each trial where the numbers and letters may appear. The EEG activity at each of these positions was averaged separately for numbers and letters. The computer programs which were used to average the evoked potentials in these within trial positions were arbitrarily designated as Programs G, H, J, and K. Since these programs do not average all of the brain responses that occur in each of these positions, as will be explained further, the data will be described in terms of the programs rather than the trial positions. The additional meaning of "programs" here is that these partitions of the data may correspond to various mental programs or thinking within the subject. Only two of the visual stimuli presented on each trial were relevant to the problem-solving task. When the numbers were designated relevant (subject informed before runs), the letters were irrelevant. Conversely, when the letters were designated relevant, the numbers were irrelevant. Considering the task the subject is performing, the mental programs or thinking may be different for the two relevant stimuli in each trial. For the first relevant stimulus the subject has to perceive the stimulus and store the information in his memory. As indicated in Table 3-1, Programs G and H compute the AEPs to the first relevant stimuli (on various trials the first relevant stimulus occurs at various trial positions). For the second relevant stimulus the subject has to perceive the stimulus and compare it with the memory of the first in order to solve the problem. The AEPs to the second relevant stimulus are computed by Programs J and K. Since the subject may be performing different cognitive poststimulus processes to the second as compared with the first relevant stimulus, we are raising the question whether their AEPs will be different. Another aspect of the experimental design is prestimulus bias. For each of the programs one can ask whether a prestimulus difference might exist between relevant and irrelevant stimuli. The answers are summarized in Table 3-1 and more explicitly described later by reference to the insets in Figs. 3.2–3.5. For

TABLE 3-1

Summary of Experimental Design

Position in trial	1	2	3	4
Program	G	H	J	K
Relevant stimulus	# 1	# 1	# 2	# 2
Poststim. process	Store		Comp. and solve	
Prestim. diff?	No	$\frac{2}{3}$ No		Yes

Program G no prestimulus differences exist because the randomization procedure meant that the first stimulus was equally likely to be a number or a letter and therefore, equally likely to be relevant or irrelevant. Nor was there a prestimulus difference for Program J. However, there is a prestimulus difference for Program K. This arises because on each trial exactly two numbers and two letters are given, making it possible for the subject to anticipate the category of the fourth stimulus (not the particular letter or number). For Program H there is a partial bias, since for two-thirds of the time the stimulus for Program H is the opposite category than the immediately preceding stimulus. In short, there are prestimulus differences between relevant and irrelevant stimuli for Programs H and K, but not for Programs G and J. And the poststimulus processing may be different for the first relevant stimulus (Programs G and H) than for the second relevant stimulus (Programs J and K). Thus, the possible effects of poststimulus processes both with and without different prestimulus conditions may be examined.

II. AVERAGE EVOKED POTENTIALS FROM ONE SUBJECT

Data from one of the subjects are shown for Programs G, H, J, and K in Figs. 3.2–3.5 to illustrate the experimental design and the kind of results. In the upper right of Figs. 3.2–3.5 the six possible sequences of two numbers and two letters are depicted. These six stimulus sequences were randomized within a run. In each of these figures the circled stimuli are the classes whose responses were collected by a particular program. For example, Fig. 3.2 indicates that all of the stimuli in the first position are used by Program G. Four different AEPs are obtained within Program G representing number and letter stimuli when each is relevant and irrelevant. The AEPs shown represent the average brain activity for approximately a half-second period after each kind of stimulus. Each is made of 102 points spaced 5 msec apart, the points starting slightly before the stimulus occurred (30 msec). The 102 time points in each AEP were connected automatically by an $X-Y$ plotter to form the continuous curves. Each of the AEPs in Figs. 3.2–3.5 is the average of AEPs from eight runs obtained from four sessions (the runs from the fifth session were lost for technical reasons). Thus, the number of individual EEG traces averaged was 408 (51×8) for each AEP in Fig. 3.2.

The four rows of AEPs in Figs. 3.2–3.5 show different kinds of bioelectrical activity. In the top row (C_z^P) the electrical activity was recorded monopolar from an electrode near the top of the head on the midline between central and parietal areas. Although the waveforms are

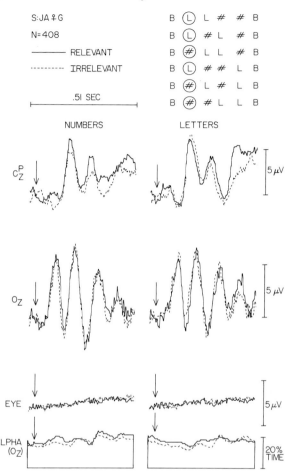

Fig. 3.2. Averaged evoked potentials (AEP) for Program G from one subject. The six stimulus sequences, which were randomized in the runs, are represented by L for letters, # for numbers, and B for blank stimuli. Circles indicate the stimuli whose responses were collected by a particular Program. For Program G there were no pre-stimulus differences and the relevant stimuli must be stored in subject's memory. Solid lines (AEPs to relevant stimuli) are X–Y plotter traces and dotted lines (AEPs to irrelevant stimuli) are hand copies of plotter traces with AEPs adjusted vertically to superimpose at the beginning. Arrows indicate time of stimulus flashes. The electrical activity, except eye, was recorded monopolar relative to linked earlobe reference electrodes with positive at the active electrode shown as up. Electrode locations based on the International 10–20 system (Jasper, 1958). Frequency response of system: .3–70 Hz. N is number of individual EEG traces averaged in each AEP shown. Top row: midline central-pariental electrode site. Second row: midline occipital electrode site. Third row: EOG from electrodes near one eye; bipolar recording. Bottom row: alpha EEG index obtained by electronic scorer (Kropfl, Chapman, & Armington, 1962) from occipital recording.

similar, the solid and dotted lines show that the AEPs are slightly different when the stimuli are relevant than when the identical physical stimuli are irrelevant to the problem-solving task. Since the subject could not anticipate whether the stimuli used in Program G would be relevant or not, she must perceive both classes of stimuli after the stimulus is presented and the AEP differences are not due to prestimulus differences. The AEPs from O_Z (electrode on the midline over the occipital area, which presumably is more exclusively concerned with vision) have a different waveform than those from the central-parietal electrode. Furthermore, the differences between relevant and irrelevant responses are smaller. (Measurement and statistics will be considered later.)

One of the important concerns in interpreting AEP studies is the possibility of artifacts, especially from the eye (Chapman, 1969a,b). The eye acts as a battery; its movement produces a differential field which can be detected by electrodes on the surface of the head. A second, more subtle way in which eye movements can produce artifacts is when the eyes move across a visual field, producing visual-evoked responses from the changing retinal image due to the relatively strong transient on- and off-responses (Gaarder et al., 1964).

If a stimulus display is maintained, or even if there is an experimentally unrelated visual image available to the view of the subject, the eyes may scan the visual field differently depending on the relevance of the experimental stimulus and thereby produce some secondary difference in AEPs which is dependent on differential eye movement, rather than more directly on differential neural processing. To combat this problem we have presented our visual stimuli as very brief flashes in a dark room, thus removing the possibility of retinal movement relative to the stimulus. However, we still must be concerned with direct electrooculogram (EOG) effects. Eye data (EOG) were obtained from bipolar recording from electrodes near one eye (scalp electrodes placed in the external canthus and directly below the center of the eye). The EOG was averaged in the same way, using the same amplification and filtering, as the brain evoked potentials. The eye traces in Fig. 3.2 are not horizontal, indicating that this subject's eyes did tend to move slightly in synchrony with the stimulus. However, the movement appears to be similar for the relevant and irrelevant stimuli, since the eye traces superimpose rather nicely.

In relation to the general question of the specificity of effects it was indicated previously that one should be concerned with general states of the organism, such as level of arousal. The main control for these variables in this experimental design is by randomizing the stimuli. In addition we have measured one index of level of arousal, namely the amount of alpha activity in the EEG. An automatic on-line scorer was used (Kropfl,

Chapman, & Armington, 1962) which indicates by a voltage step when alpha activity (about 7–12 Hz above 15 μV) is present. This voltage was averaged in the same way as the AEPs, which yields an index of alpha EEG in percentage of time. In Fig. 3.2 alpha was present about 20% of the time and was approximately the same for relevant and irrelevant stimuli.

Figure 3.3 shows data obtained by Program H from the same runs on the same subject. The physical stimuli and the cognitive aspects of the task were the same for Program H as for Program G. Program H is re-

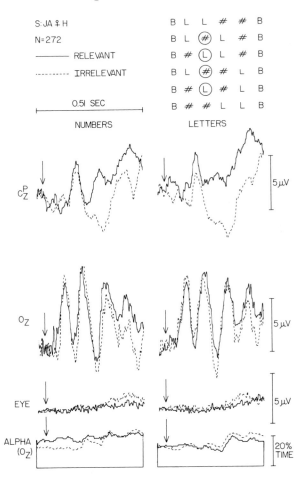

Fig. 3.3. AEPs for Program H from same subject as in Fig. 2. Poststimulus process: store relevant stimulus in memory; prestimulus differences of two-thirds bias. Other details as for Fig. 2.

stricted to averaging only "first" relevant stimuli where the subject may
be storing the information in his memory; stimuli preceded by like stimuli
(i.e., LL and ✻ ✻) were not used. Unlike Program G, however, Program H
has a possible prestimulus bias. After Program G (first position) stimulus
had occurred, the subject could predict with two-thirds accuracy that the
next stimulus (second position) would belong to the other class (Fig. 3.3
top). For example, if the first stimulus was a letter, then the probability
was two-thirds that the next stimulus would be a number; the particular
number could not be predicted better than chance. It appears that this
prestimulus bias does have an effect, since the AEP differences between
relevant and irrelevant stimuli for Program H (Fig. 3.3) appear to be
larger than they were for Program G.

Program J deals with responses to some of the stimuli in the third intratrial position (Fig. 3.4). For the relevant stimuli, the cognitive task may
be different than for Programs G and H because Program J deals with
the "second" relevant stimuli. "First" relevant stimuli, which sometimes
occurred in intratrial position three (top and bottom rows of Fig. 3.4
inset), were not used by Program J in order to isolate the effects of the
different kind of thinking which might follow the "second" relevant
stimulus. When the stimulus occurred, if it was relevant, the subject had
to compare it with the memory of the "first" relevant stimulus in order
to solve the problem. Due to the randomization procedure, there were no
prestimulus differences for Program J stimuli, since there was a 50–50
chance that the previous stimulus was a letter or a number and consequently, a 50–50 chance that the previous stimulus was relevant or irrelevant. The differences in AEPs between relevant and irrelevant stimuli
in Fig. 3.4 may be related to the different thinking processes after the
stimulus is presented. The physical stimuli whose responses are being
compared were identical and the subject could not anticipate which
stimulus would occur. In a logical sense it is necessary to discriminate
the stimuli (both relevant and irrelevant) before different mental processing
can take place. In this sense the AEP differences may be postperceptual
for Programs G and J.

Program K (Fig. 3.5) involves the stimuli which require the same
mental processing as Program J; in addition, however, there is a prestimulus difference for Program K. Since there are exactly two numbers
and two letters presented within each trial, by the time for Program K
stimuli (fourth intratrial position) the subject could predict which class
of stimuli is going to occur. That is, he could know whether the stimulus
will be relevant or not, although he could not know which particular
letter or number will occur. Thus, although he can anticipate when a
relevant stimulus will occur, he must still await its occurrence before

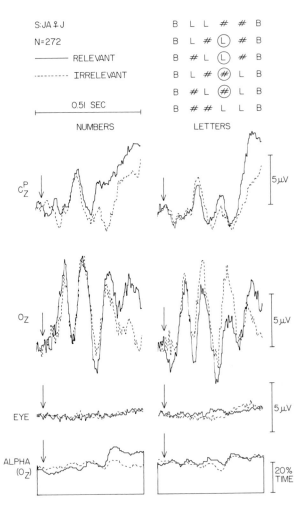

Fig. 3.4. AEPs for Program J from same subject as in Fig. 2. Poststimulus process: compare relevant stimulus with memory of earlier stimulus and solve problem; no prestimulus differences. Other details as for Fig. 2.

comparing it with the memory of the "first" relevant stimulus. Some of the stimuli in the fourth intratrial position are not used by Program K (Fig. 3.5 inset) in order to equalize the frequency of occurrence of the category of the preceding stimuli, i.e., so both numbers and letters are preceded equally often by numbers and letters. The large AEP differences seen in Fig. 3.5, compared with those of Fig. 3.4, show the importance of prestimulus effects.

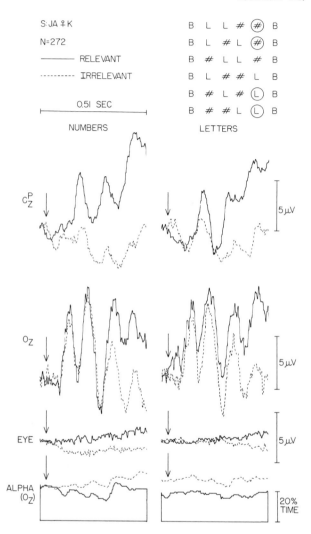

Fig. 3.5. AEPs for Program K from same subject as in Fig. 2. Poststimulus process: compare relevant stimulus with memory of earlier stimulus and solve problem; prestimulus difference: can predict which stimulus class will occur. Other details as for Fig. 2.

III. ANALYSIS OF GROUP DATA

Illustrative data from one of the subjects were presented above. In this section a quantitative analysis based on a nonselected group of 12 subjects is presented. Each of the subjects was run with the same experimental design, explained above. Each run contained 102 trials (problems). Each subject had ten runs of each type (i.e., number-relevant and letter-relevant runs) distributed over five sessions (intrasession order randomized). Eight separate AEPs were computed for each run by using Programs G, H, J, and K on numbers and letters (4 × 2). The number of responses contributing to each run-AEP was 51 for Program G and 34 for Programs H, J, and K. Statistical analyses were run separately for each subject using the ten runs of each type as the basis of estimating the variability; these analyses will not be discussed here. In order to assess the results which more generally hold, analyses of effects across the entire group of subjects are discussed. For this purpose the data for each subject were collapsed across runs by averaging the ten run-AEPs of each type (subject JA, Figs. 3.2–3.5, had only eight runs available). The group statistical analyses used the replication across 12 subjects as the basis for estimating the variability; the alpha EEG was available for only 11 subjects. For each measure a three-way factorial analysis of variance was made using Programs (G, H, J, K) × Relevance (relevant, irrelevant) × Stimuli (numbers, letters). Each effect (main effects and interactions) was tested against its subject × effect error term, e.g., Program by Relevance (P × R) was tested against Subject × P × R.

Consider, first, a global measure of the responses, namely the area under the response. The inset in Fig. 3.6 graphically shows this measure applied to the grand average AEP from the central-parietal midline electrode. The measures are made by a computer program which first establishes a baseline for each AEP by averaging the amplitude at seven time points near the beginning of the AEP (four before the stimulus and three after). The area (mean amplitude) is then obtained by computing the average amplitude of AEP deviations from this baseline during the 480 msec after the light flash. This response area measure has the virtues of (1) being objective, (2) representing the entire response (tendency for the AEP to go positive or negative from its start), and (3) averaging out fluctuations which may in part be noise (high frequencies removed by integration and low frequencies by resetting baseline for each AEP), and (4) being sensitive to the experimental variables of interest.

The group mean amplitudes of the central-parietal AEPs for the various conditions as well as a summary of the analysis of variance are shown in Fig. 3.6. As indicated above, for Programs G and H the subjects must be perceiving the stimuli and if the stimulus belongs to the relevant class, storing the information. For Programs J and K relevant stimuli must be perceived and compared with the memory of the earlier relevant stimulus in order to solve the problem. The AEP area was reliably affected by the Program factor ($p < .01$). Also, AEP area was significantly more positive

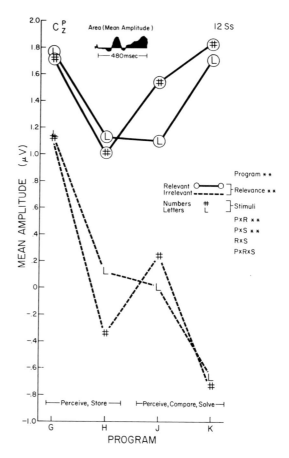

Fig. 3.6. Average area (mean amplitude) of midline central-parietal AEP for 12 subjects. Response measure which is relative to level at beginning of response, is illustrated on AEP which is actual average for all subjects and conditions shown. Subject's poststimulus mental operations for relevant stimuli summarized above appropriate Programs; prestimulus differences exist for Programs H and K, but not for G and J. Three-way factorial analysis of variance summarized in inset; statistically significant effects indicated by * for $p < .05$ and ** for $p < .01$.

when the stimuli were relevant than when the same stimuli were irrelevant ($p < .01$). The statistically significant interaction between Programs and Relevance ($p < .01$) is especially interesting because such an interaction would be expected if the various aspects of thinking in this task are related to these brain-evoked responses. Tests of the simple effects in this interaction showed statistically reliable differences between relevant and irrelevant responses for each of the four programs ($p < .01$). Thus, the AEPs were reliably different even in the cases where there were not pre-stimulus differences (Programs G and J). The response area was not consistently different for numbers than for letters (Stimulus factor). There was a significant interaction between Stimuli and Program ($p < .01$), the breakdown indicating that letters gave larger responses for Program H, numbers gave larger responses for Program J, and no reliable differences between letters and numbers for Programs G and K. Thus, the physical characteristics of these two stimulus classes, numbers and letters, did not have a consistent effect on the area measure of the central-parietal AEP, whereas the psychological characteristic of stimulus relevance did have a consistent, reliable effect.

A similar analysis of the occipital AEP yielded similar results although the waveform of the AEP was quite different (Fig. 3.7). The mean area of the occipital AEPs was significantly more positive when the stimuli were relevant ($p < .01$). The magnitude of this effect varied significantly with Program ($p < .01$), being largest for Programs H and K where

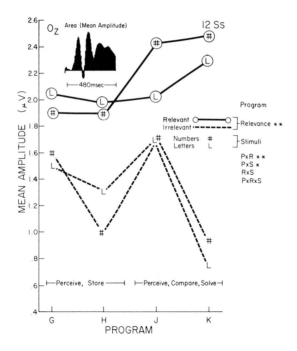

Fig. 3.7. Average area (mean amplitude) of midline occipital AEP for 12 subjects. Other details as for Fig. 6.

prestimulus differences existed in addition to poststimulus cognitive requirements. At this electrode position also letters did not have consistently different responses than numbers.

As indicated above one of the greatest sources of artefact in AEP experiments is eye movements. They were assessed by averaging electro-oculograms and measuring response areas (Fig. 3.8). The major effect is the difference in eye activity for various Programs ($p < .01$) with the greatest eye movement occurring during Program G (first intratrial position). The eye measure unlike the brain AEPs, did not show an overall relevance effect. There was, however, a significant interaction between Program and Relevance ($p < .01$). Interestingly enough, looking at the components in this interaction showed no differences in eye movement between relevant and irrelevant stimuli for Programs G and J where there were no prestimulus biases and opposite effects where there were prestimulus differences, namely, more eye movements for irrelevant

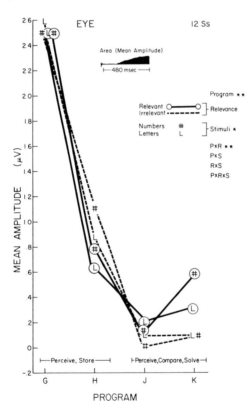

Fig. 3.8. Average area (mean amplitude) of eye movement (EOG) for 12 subjects. Other details as for Fig. 6.

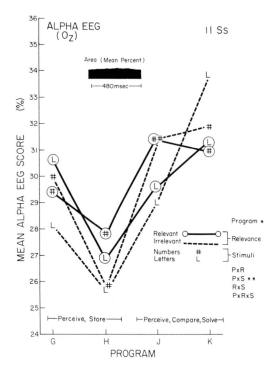

Fig. 3.9. Average area (mean percent) of alpha EEG activity for 11 subjects. Other details as for Fig. 6.

stimuli in Program H and for relevant stimuli in Program K. So it does not look like these eye movements could explain the relevance differences found at the central-parietal or occipital sites (Figs. 3.6 and 3.7).

In pursuing the question of the specificity of the relation between AEP effects and cognitive processes, we have suggested that it is important to separate effects due to general states of the organism, such as level of arousal. We have measured alpha EEG as an index of arousal (Fig. 3.9). There was not a great deal of change in percent alpha among the various conditions; the mean alpha scores lay between 26 and 34%. There was a significant Program effect ($p < .05$) and a significant interaction between Program and Stimuli ($p < .01$). However, Relevance did not have a significant effect, either by itself or in interaction with any of the other factors. On these grounds the differences between relevant and irrelevant AEPs may not be explained by differences in percentage of alpha activity.

Now the measure used in the data analyses above was a rather global one, the area under the response for 480 msec after the stimulus. You might ask what is going on inside the response at various points in time.

One of the measures we have used is the amplitude of the AEP at a particular latency, for example at 225 msec. This method avoids the problem of identifying particular AEP components in advance; the problem of identifying particular positive and negative peaks is well-known. The amplitudes were measured by a computer program relative to the baseline established near the beginning of the AEP (same baseline used for area measure).

The analysis of the amplitude of the central-parietal AEP at 225 msec is summarized in Fig. 3.10. In general, the results were similar to, but not identical with, those obtained by the more global measure of response area (Fig. 3.6). There was a significant main effect of Relevance and none of the interactions with Relevance were significant. This means that post-

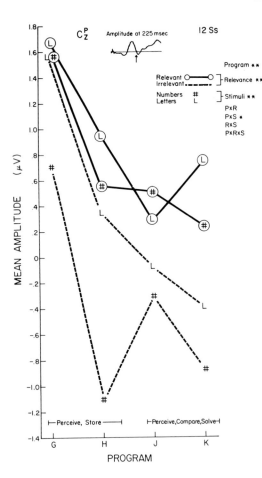

Fig. 3.10. Average amplitude of midline central-parietal AEP at 225 msec for 12 subjects. Other details as for Fig. 6.

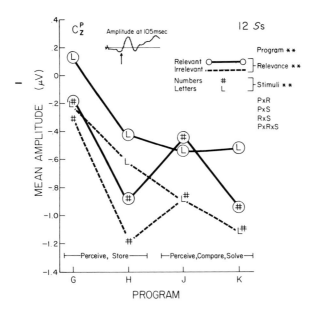

Fig. 3.11. Average amplitude of midline central-parietal AEP at 105 msec for 12 subjects. Other details as for Fig. 6.

stimulus differences between relevant and irrelevant AEPs may be found as early as 225 msec after the stimulus has occurred.

One might get bolder and go earlier, making measures at 105 msec (Fig. 3.11). Again the measure does not necessarily correspond to a peak or a trough, although perhaps it corresponds often to a negative deflection in the central-parietal AEP. Basically, the same kind of results were obtained. The significant Relevance effect and lack of significant interactions indicates that even as early as 105 msec after the stimulus the AEP is sensitive to whether the stimulus turns out to be relevant or not.

IV. CNV AND AEP

A part of the AEP has been dignified by its own name, the CNV (contingent negative variation), and often has been studied as a separate phenomenon (e.g., review by Cohen, 1969). The CNV is a negative wave which occurs in anticipation of a critical stimulus. If this kind of concept is applied to our experiment, the critical stimuli may be identified as the relevant stimuli and we might expect to find a negative potential occurring in anticipation or expectancy of those relevant stimuli. Previously, it was reported that CNVs could be seen in AEP data obtained when the sequence of stimulus classes was fixed throughout a run (Chapman, 1969b). It was suggested that the differences in AEPs could not be completely explained as merely terminations of anticipatory negative waves which were different.

To assess the possible role of CNV-like potentials in the present experiment, the amplitude of the AEP was measured at 0 msec (time at which stimulus occurred). The amplitude at 0 msec was measured relative to an arbitrary voltage level which was common to all the AEPs and may be thought of as extending across the entire trial. (The measure at 0 msec was actually the baseline established near the beginning of the AEP, which was used as the reference for all the other amplitude measures, as described previously.) Figure 3.12 is a summary of the CNV effects. There was a significant interaction between Program and Relevance ($p < .01$). Within this interaction there was not a significant difference between relevant and irrelevant stimuli for Programs G and J, where

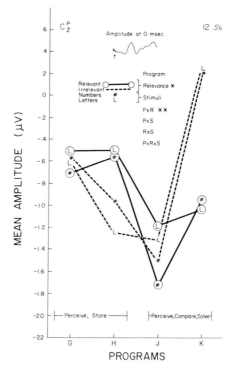

Fig. 3.12. Average CNV measured as amplitude of midline central-parietal AEP at 0 msec relative to an arbitrary voltage level which was the same for all responses. Other details as for Fig. 6.

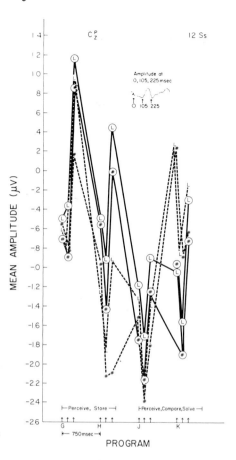

Fig. 3.13. Average amplitudes of midline central-parietal AEP at 0, 105, and 225 msec for 12 subjects. All measures relative to same arbitrary voltage level. Other details as for Fig. 6.

there are no prestimulus differences and where consequently CNV differences would not be expected. However, for Programs H and K, where the subject can anticipate something about what is going to occur, the amplitude is different at the point in time at which the stimulus is delivered. Especially interesting about these data is that they go in opposite directions. For Program K the direction is in accord with the usual CNV prediction in that the amplitude is more negative when a relevant stimulus is expected, whereas for Program H the amplitude was more negative when an irrelevant stimulus was more likely.

Thus, it does not appear that CNV differences measured at 0 msec can explain the relevant differences found later in the responses at 105 and 225 msec. The relationships among the amplitude measures at 0, 105, and 225 msec are shown in Fig. 3.13, where they have all been plotted relative to a common, arbitrary voltage level.

Another way to look at the relationship between the CNV and the AEP is to compute correlations between them, using the measure at 0 msec relative to the common voltage level and the measures at 105 and 225 msec relative to the beginning of each AEP. Correlations were computed for each subject using measures on 16 average responses (4 programs $\times$ 2 stimuli $\times$ 2 relevances); using z transforms these correlations were then averaged over the 12 subjects. The average correlations between the CNV and AEP measures were $-.08$ and $-.02$ (0 with 105 msec and 0 with 225 msec, respectively).

Thus, within this experimental paradigm the CNV measure predicts nothing about the AEP measures, although as shown above each type of measure is systematically related to the experimental variables. The average correlation between the AEP measures at 105 and 225 msec was .65 (significantly different from 0).

V. AEP CHANGES WITH LEARNING

The data presented above were gathered when the subject already knew how to solve the problems and was merely applying the mental operations he already knew. Here we present an example showing how these AEPs change as the subject learns the problem-solving principle. The responses in Fig. 3.14 were all evoked by the same physical stimuli and were collected by Program G, which selected the stimuli in the first intratrial position where randomization prevented prestimulus differences. The subject knew to watch the stimuli and respond after the blank flash at the end of each trial by moving a switch one way or the other; if he guessed correctly he would hear a tone, if not, a buzz. By chance he would be correct on 50% of the trials. In this case the problem-solving principle was based on comparing the number stimuli, while the letter stimuli were irrelevant. On the basis of the subject's performance we have divided the learning trials into presolution, solution, and postsolution phases during which the accuracy was 49, 72, and 100%, respectively. During the presolution trials the AEPs to the numbers and to the letters were relatively similar (Fig. 3.14, top left). Later on as the subject begins to use a problem-solving principle that works part of the time (72% correct), the responses begin to pull apart. By the time the subject has found the completely correct principle, a larger difference between the AEPs to the relevant numbers and irrelevant letters has emerged (Fig. 3.14, top right).

The question can be raised whether the AEP differences which emerged are due to changes in the AEPs to the relevant stimuli or to changes in the AEPs to the irrelevant stimuli. The AEPs in the top row of Fig. 3.14 have been rearranged in the bottom row to facilitate these comparisons.

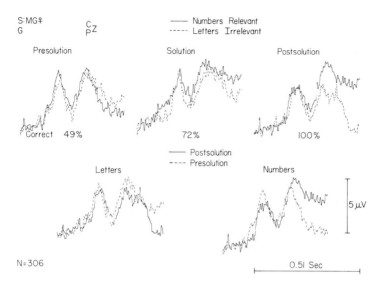

Fig. 3.14 AEP changes with learning. Data collected by Program G on three sequential blocks of trials during learning of the number comparison problem by one of the subjects. AEPs from central-parietal electrode, positive up. Top row: responses to numbers and letters compared as learning progressses from left to right. Bottom row: responses to identical stimuli compared before and after learning.

The AEPs to both letters and numbers appeared to change as the subject moved from presolution to postsolution trials. The later parts of the responses appeared to be less positive for the letters when they were found to be irrelevant (lower left) and to be more positive for the numbers when their relevance to the problem solution was secured (lower right). It is to be noted again that poststimulus processing is required for both kinds of stimuli, since the subject cannot anticipate which class of stimuli will occur. These data suggest that when a person learns something about the situation, his brain activity does not change to only the relevant stimuli or to only the irrelevant stimuli, but rather to both. These AEP changes with learning provide further support for the specificity of their relationship to aspects of thinking.

VI. DISCUSSION

Can these data be explained by *attention?* Part of the data can, but not all of it unless attention is given some rather subtle nuances, which perhaps convert the construct into what is more equivalent to mental operations. The following discussion of attention is based on a recent paper by Posner and Boies (1971). They consider three aspects of attention: (1) alertness, (2) selectivity, and (3) limited central processing capacity.

(a) The alertness aspect of attention (sensitivity to stimuli), is in general related to prestimulus preparation, such as might vary in vigilance tasks, foreperiods, etc. In our experiment, randomization held alertness constant for Programs G and J and yet differences in the evoked responses were found. Two kinds of measures which have been used as indices of alertness support the lack of arousal bias for the stimuli in our Programs G and J: neither alpha EEG percentage nor evoked response amplitude at 0 msec were related to relevance.

(b) Another aspect of attention is selectivity, i.e., sensitivity to some stimuli more than others. The selectivity required in our experiment is of a high degree, since both the attended and unattended stimuli were in the same sensory modality (vision), of the same luminance, and used the same parts of the receptor surface (retinal fovea). Selectivity by matched spatial filtering would be complicated, since six different stimuli were randomly used as the "attended" ones. Thus, the attention would have to be tuned to a class of stimuli (letters or numbers), not to a fixed physical configuration. Furthermore, since the AEPs were different for Program G ("storage stimulus") than to Program J ("compare and solve stimulus"), the amount of attention would have to vary accordingly. Therefore, for selective attention to explain these data, it would have to have the properties of (1) discriminating between two classes of stimuli which are not very different (visual letters vs. numbers), (2) reacting to these small sensory differences rapidly (within 105 msec), and (3) reacting differently to "attended" stimuli which have different functional roles in the task. These properties indicate a lability which is strangely similar to what some would call thinking, rather than attention. More important than the name, these properties seem interesting enough to study in their own right. For example, discriminating between stimulus classes can be viewed as encoding operations which may have their own signs in the AEP, and reacting differently to physically identical stimuli can be viewed as mental operations of various kinds depending on the task requirements (memory retrieval, addition, comparison, response preparation, etc.).

(c) The third aspect of attention discussed by Posner and Boies is limited central processing capacity. Limited capacity may have contributed to the differences found since the stimuli occurred at a fairly short interval ($\frac{3}{4}$ sec). This procedure may have placed a premium on rapidly processing the stimuli. However, even the irrelevant stimuli had to be attended to the extent of determining that they belonged to the irrelevant class. The comments above about selective attention would also apply to the limited central processing capacity aspect.

There are a number of unidimensional constructs, such as attention, which have been proposed to account for the psychological effects on evoked responses. Although such constructs as attention, task relevance, significance, information, or preparation, etc., begin at different starting points, when any one of them is enlarged sufficiently to handle some variety of AEP data, the simple construct tends to have adduced additional properties which are similar no matter which starting point was used, as I have discussed elsewhere (Chapman, 1969b). Other discussions of such matters have been made by Uttal (1965), by Sutton (1969), and others. I would like to discuss one other such unidimensional explanatory attempt (Karlin, 1970), especially since our kind of data was considered.

In considering evoked potential experiments which might be related to cognitive processes, Karlin (1970) has attempted a reinterpretation with hypotheses that are not cognitive, but rather based on *preparation* or *readiness*. Karlin hypothesizes two kinds of preparation: "development of preparation before, and reactive change in preparation after presentation of critical stimuli." The first hypothesis is similar to interpretations that others have proposed in terms of attention, arousal, expectancy, etc. The hypothesis is that the relevant stimulus occurs when the subject is in a different state of readiness and for this reason the AEP is modified. This explanation requires that the sequence of stimuli make possible differential advance preparation prior to stimulus presentation [a point we have previously emphasized (Chapman, 1966; Sheatz & Chapman, 1969; Chapman, 1969a)]. This prestimulus preparation hypothesis was eliminated by randomizing the sequence of relevant and irrelevant stimuli in some of our work (Chapman, 1966; Chapman, 1969a). This is not to say that this hypothesis cannot account for part of the results, because it can, for example, account for the differences we find on Programs H and K. However, it cannot account for the differences we obtained on Programs G and J, for which the appearance of a relevant or irrelevant stimulus cannot be predicted. For these kinds of data Karlin has invoked a related hypothesis which is a reactive change in preparation occurring after certain stimuli. This hypothesis is concerned with the inverse of preparation, that is the turning off of readiness after a relevant stimulus occurs. The reactive nature of this hypothesis makes it difficult to distinguish from other poststimulus operations, such as cognitive processes. Further, he associates the prestimulus preparation with a slow, negative wave (CNV) and the reactive preparation with a positive-going termination of the CNV.

Karlin is proposing that the termination of a state of expectant readiness occurs *after* the information-processing activity itself, which is assumed by him not to be indexed by the obtained changes in AEP. He suggests that his reactive hypothesis "probably could not explain enhancement of components with latencies shorter than the magnitude expected from RT studies." We have found such enhancement at latencies as short as 105 msec (Programs G and J), which presumably would be too soon for the reactive readiness hypothesis. We can adduce further evidence against this hypothesis by considering the conditions under which it should occur, namely, when the occurrence of the relevant stimulus reduces the probability that the next relevant stimulus will occur soon, and when the subject starts to relax as a result of task completing in response to the relevant stimulus. In our experiment in considering the data where prestimulus differences are absent, the conditional probability of another relevant stimulus is higher after a relevant stimulus in Program G than after a relevant stimulus in Program J ($\frac{1}{3}$ versus $\frac{0}{2}$). The first condition of Karlin's reactive hypothesis would predict more reactive readiness and therefore less positive return for CNV for our G response than our J response. However, we found that the amplitude of the G response was more positive than that of the J response. Furthermore, relevant stimuli in Program J were directly associated with termination of the task whereas Program G stimuli were not. The second condition of Karlin's reactive hypothesis would predict more reactive response (more positive return of CNV) for J than for G. So both aspects of the reactive hypothesis predict greater positive responses for J than for G relevant stimuli. Since our data gave opposite results, we conclude that neither the usual preparation state hypothesis, nor the reactive preparation hypotheses are sufficient to account for evoked potential differences found with our design. Perhaps by adding a few *ad hoc* conditions related to the particular conditions of our experiment, the reactive preparation hypothesis could be stretched sufficiently to cover our data. However, such additions would probably look more and more similar to the conditions which could be called cognitive operations.

This leads us to an important point. A well-reasoned attempt to explain evoked response effects by a relatively simple hypothesis based on prestimulus effects, lead rather quickly to additions which involved poststimulus processes. In order to preserve the simplicity of a unidimensional explanation, such as readiness, arousal, alertness, or expectancy, etc., the poststimulus changes in *any* such hypothetical construct must occur *after* the perceptual and/or cognitive processes which specify the change. This suggests that the acceptance of any of these unidimensional explanatory constructs permits bracketing the time required for the perceptual and/or cognitive processes, which must occur after the stimulus and before the evoked potential change attributable to the construct. For example, if a stimulus has an equal chance of being some number or letter and the task requires a different mental operation for one of these classes of stimuli and the averaged evoked response with appropriate controls is different by 105 msec when one operation is performed rather than another, it would indicate that the mental operation must be performed within that time span. This kind of model, then, sets time restraints on the physiological mechanisms involved. The neural or glandular or muscular mechanisms that are necessary for those mental operations must occur within 105 msec in our example. This sets rather severe limits for muscular or glandular involvement in this kind of thinking. In fact, it is even taxing for neural codes based on impulse frequency, where spike frequency has generally been measured over longer time spans.

On the other hand, if we consider the hypothesis that the AEP is associated with the perceptual and/or cognitive processes themselves, rather than some afterproduct like relaxing alertness, then the time restraints may be loosened, and, further, we may be able to determine something about the times at which various of these component mental operations occur. From this standpoint the early differences in the AEPs may be associated with the early mental operations and subsequent components of the response with subsequent mental operations. This kind of model gives hope of examining a finer grain anatomy of thinking by correlating various components of the evoked response with various task requirements. This approach depends on the various mental operations being synchronized with the stimulus and not overlapping each other completely in time. The assumption that the effects are fixed in time relative to the stimulus is essentially the same as the basis for averaging evoked brain potentials from the EEG. The assumption that various mental operations occur at different points in time is supported by various models of information processing which use serial stages, in keeping with logical arguments that some stages cannot begin their work until previous stages have completed their jobs.

For us to entertain seriously the possibility of examining a fine grain anatomy of thinking by dissecting the components of the averaged evoked potential, we must determine whether these responses have a number of separable components. The presence of a number of peaks and troughs in the responses does not necessarily mean that they are different processes. We have taken a multivariate statistical approach to this question. The averaged evoked potentials were subjected to a principal components analysis, using the responses from the experimental design we have been discussing. By applying statistical tests to the resulting eigenvalues, which are variances associated with the various response components, we have found that there are about 15 orthogonal components. Figure 3.15 shows

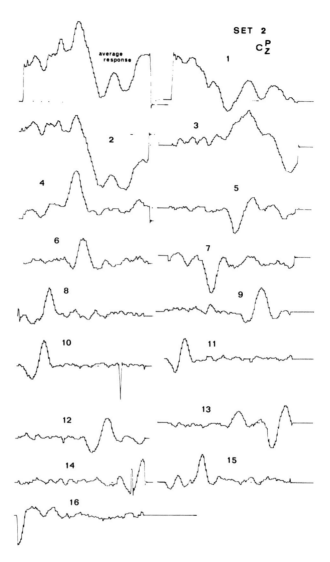

Fig. 3.15. Average AEP decomposed into 16 components by multivariate statistical techniques. Data entering analysis were 160 AEPs, each with 102 time points, from central-parietal electrode of one of the subjects.

these components after a varimax rotation for the data from one of the subjects. At the upper left is the evoked response averaged across all the conditions; it was decomposed into the independent components shown in the rest of the figure. Each trace covers a half-second of poststimulus time and the physical stimuli were relatively constant, being the number and letter flashes. It appears from data such as these that the averaged evoked potential has sufficient complexity to be a reasonable candidate for relating to perceptual/cognitive operations.

VII. CONCLUSIONS

In summary, sensitivity to the details of mental behavior and correspondence in time, recommend the averaged evoked potential as a good candidate for studying the psychophysiology of thinking. Rather subtle changes in task requirements are correlated with AEP changes. These changes occur within a fraction of a second. Furthermore, the AEP is composed of a rich number of components, about 15 orthogonal ones in our relatively simple experimental situation. The AEP effects may be related not only to prestimulus processes, but also to poststimulus processes. Consequently, simple hypotheses such as attention or arousal are not sufficient to explain the AEP effects. It is necessary to consider more refined operators which have properties of discrimination of stimulus classes within a sensory modality, quick change, and response differentiation.

The Discussion of Dr. Chapman's Paper

LED BY DR. THOMAS MULHOLLAND
VA Hospital, Bedford, Massachusetts Perception Laboratory

Mulholland: The experimental design was ingenious, and is a step forward in better articulating the hypothetical mental operations that influence evoked potential studies. The problems in evoked potential recording, even before one gets to the correlation with inferred or expected psychological processes, are not completely resolved. I would like to present some questions to form a framework for audience reaction to this paper, rather than going point by point—a compliment-and-rebuttal kind of thing—which is fantastically boring.

One overriding question concerns the variance of evoked potentials; and I don't think that problem is solved by comparing different evoked potentials on the basis of integrated functions which are measures of the area under a curve. A comprehensive analysis should involve a comparison of corresponding peaks and valleys ("components") which requires a variance estimate to tell us how reproducible is the waveform. This is not just a problem for Dr. Chapman's paper, but for many evoked potential studies.

I wondered, too, about the dichotomy between pre- and postprocesses (events before and after each stimulus presentation). Behind the clearly dichotomous way of prearranging stimuli (into the conceptual categories of words, letters, etc.) is the real possibility that the different processes have different time constants that produce variations in the evoked potential. If the subject detects a stimulus as being relevant, then—no matter what that complex cognitive process is—the decay of that process and the emergence of another process with the next stimulus may or may not be in different time domains than the 5-sec interval that was taken for analysis, or the three-fourths of a second interval between stimuli. Related to this is the question of eye movements, which someone brought up from the floor. An eye movement process could be initiated, and in turn could trigger the processes which have a longer time constant; these processes could be in the cortex, or in regions from which these evoked potentials are derived. Moreover, the time constant of the underlying processes may be so much slower that they have effects, which in turn could be picked up and manifested in the signal averaging. I thought that problem needed some further comment.

I wondered, regarding the measurements, was there equal optimization of the filter characteristics for the eye movement recording, for the alpha recording, and for the evoked potential recording; and was the comparison on the basis of the amplitude or power density? I know that alpha is a big problem in evoked potential studies. I was impressed with the big alpha-like frequencies in the evoked potential but not picked up in the average evoked potential. As I went along with this very interesting talk, I thought about afterimages. Do afterimages intrude in the poststimulus process? I know there is that possibility with pattern stimuli, especially with a very bright flash.

I felt myself in complete agreement with Dr. Chapman when he emphasized that an analysis of a physiological process, such as an evoked potential, in terms of a squashy concept like attention, is pretty fruitless. We have seen the same problems in many other kinds of neurophysiological measurements. I think that neurophysiology acted as a storehouse, in a way, for psychological concepts such as attention, when they were being kicked out of psychology. Every now and then psychology has reached into the neurophysiological storehouse and found those concepts still alive and felt kind of good about it. Now we recognize the difficulties of trying to postulate a psychological cause, if you will, to explain a physiological effect. I think it diverts us away from looking for the mediational process. What are the analogs of psychological processes in the physiological domain, that may be modifying an evoked potential in *its* physiological domain? I think Dr. Chapman's analysis of the ineffectiveness of the attentional construct as an explanatory principle was valuable.

Open Discussion

Chapman: The eye movement records, as well as the evoked potentials, were obtained with a time constant which passed frequencies down to .3 cycles/sec. This was sufficiently slow to span the time between points in the experimental paradigm where randomization would remove pre-stimulus differences. Any differences in waveform between evoked responses obtained from the occipital and central-parietal electrodes may not be attributed to filter characteristics of the recording system, which were the same for all electrode locations. The alpha EEG score, of course, was based on a system which filtered out nonalpha frequencies and had a band-pass of about 7–12 Hz.

Concerning afterimages, the stimulus intensities used were not very bright. If afterimages were present, they could not contribute to AEP differences associated with thinking in this design since comparisons were made among responses to identical physical stimuli. This assumes that afterimages are a product only of more primary action in the visual system. An interesting possibility is that thinking tied to visual stimuli could be elaboration of afterimage processes.

Dr. Ralph Hefferline (Columbia University): Did you say that the peaks and troughs do not necessarily indicate separate processes? What about the work of people like Vaughn, or Samuel Sutton, in which peaks are counted ("Peak 3," etc.), and the amplitude and shapes of peaks are interpreted?

Chapman: We are all searching around for how to handle a complicated phenomenon that we don't know how to measure. Different people take different approaches, and I guess any measurement approach in science is legitimate, if it makes sense out of the relevant realm. In this case, we correlate measures of the evoked response with some aspect of behavior. It is very important to ask whether or not our measures are independent. With 102 time points in each channel, we could make 102 measurements of the response. Are there really 102 separate things going on? Multivariate analysis tells us how many different things are going on. A peak or trough seen in the response may represent several components which overlap in time.

Dr. Abe Black (McMaster University): When you operantly condition an animal to increase or decrease the voltage in an evoked potential, and examine fixed times after the stimulus is presented, the changes at those poststimulus times are sometimes independent of what is going on at other times in the evoked potential. Does that create any difficulty in interpretation?

Chapman: I think so. Your approach is to see if you can split things, take them apart, and thus experimentally find out what a component is; mine is a correlational approach which sets various tasks for the subject and looks to see what parts of the neural response change. The two approaches may not give the same answers—different models are involved. Perhaps we could take a unitary component obtained by my approach (i.e., a particular set of operations that the subject is performing with his brain) and fractionate it by a change in the experimental situation. We might expect that the neural components that are found are relative to the experimental situation, since behavior is often situation-dependent.

Dr. Richard Carney (Eastern Kentucky University): Did you have a particular reason for concentrating on the first 250 msec? The clearest differentiation between your conditions occurred later, particularly for eye movements.

Chapman: Yes, because the earlier that we can find differences, the more it pushes certain kinds of models.

Dr. Charles Osgood (University of Illinois): I am deeply interested in your use of factor analysis, i.e., multivariate analysis. You said there were about 15 orthogonal factors. Usually, one finds there are a few factors, perhaps three or four, which account for a large part of the variance—in your case, a portion of your curves or traces; and then the amount of variance accounted for by additional factors drops off very rapidly. Can you tell us something about the relative proportion of the variances? How many really important factors are operating?

Chapman: Your description is accurate in this case, also; that is, the first factor accounts for a huge proportion of the variance. But I don't think we want to confuse significance with size. Small differences could very well be important: cognitive operations may be revealed in the evoked potential, superimposed on the sensory response as very small changes in magnitude.

Osgood: Did you make any attempt to identify these factors?

Chapman: We are just into this business, and it is very elaborate, as you know.

Dr. Robert Eason (University of North Carolina, Greensboro): In going from the irrelevant to the relevant condition, it looked to me as if your entire function rotated in a counterclockwise direction; that is, as if the ac components of the evoked potential were riding on a kind of dc wave that was relatively more positive for the relevant than for the irrelevant condition. It appears to me that you have confounded this dc component in your amplitude measures of particular ac components of the evoked potential. Your measure of the amount of area falling underneath the horizontal zero voltage line should be less for the relevant than for the irrelevant condition if the entire evoked response did in fact contain a dc wave which was relatively more positive for the relevant condition. The same point applies to the two measures you made at 105 and 225 msec. The voltage level of the ac components of the evoked potential at these latencies would be more positive under the relevant than under the irrelevant condition due to the dc change. It seems to me that all of the measures you talked about changed in a similar manner as a function of the relevant and irrelevant condition. This is to be expected if all of them were similarly affected by the change in slope of a dc component.

Regarding the CNV, I was surprised, in view of what appeared to me to be a very marked negative dc change in your data under certain conditions, that you later stated the CNV was not present; but I didn't quite understand what the reference point was for measuring the CNV. Would you comment on that?

Chapman: The measurement is always relative to something, and most of the measures I talked about were relative to what the potential was at the time the stimulus came in. In other words, measurements of the area under the curve were made relative to the value of the potential at the time *each* stimulus was presented (time zero). This turns out to be a different voltage for Program G than it is for Program H, for example. So in trying to measure the CNV amplitude at time zero, we take as a reference some point that is common across the entire trial. There is no real true zero in this system; but that does not matter. All our measurements are relative. When we do that, we find that the correlation essentially is zero between those two classes of measures; the CNV measure at zero, relative to the trial, is not correlated with the measures in the response, relative to the point at zero.

Eason: The dc shift occurring prior to the stimulus is not correlated with the dc shift following it. How can you explain the dc shift following the particular stimuli that you are talking about; why is there a greater

dc shift in the positive direction—and maybe you do not agree with this—
when the stimulus is relevant than when at zero?

Chapman: There are various ways of describing what is essentially a
time series. It sounds as if what you would prefer to see is a measure in
terms of frequency, to identify what is going on at various frequencies,
slow versus fast frequencies. This is an alternative measurement approach
that could be taken. But I think that alternative is not as easy to relate
to mental operations, in the sense of using models that might be built on
a temporal sequence of analysis. I should make one thing clear about the
CNV. I am not saying that the CNV is not present; I think it is. What
I am saying is that the CNV level for Program G is the same for relevant
and irrelevant conditions.

Eason: One more point, if I may. Where you compare components of
your waveforms, between the relevant and the irrelevant stimuli, at given
points in time: to me they look highly similar, though not identical. So if
you look at the analysis in terms of a short period of time, comparing
components, there did not seem to be any difference; the difference seemed
to be due to the fact that these ac oscillations were riding on a slow changing
function that was different under the irrelevant condition than under the
relevant.

Chapman: I am actually proposing to utilize components found by
multivariate statistical techniques (see Fig. 3.15). There may be 15 different things going on. Some could be classified as slow waves, and others
faster. We might also consider what Dr. Mulholland said about variance,
which is a very nasty problem indeed. We only get these responses by
averaging across many, hopefully similar, conditions; now the question
is whether those conditions are really similar. It has been often suggested
that if you express the variance as well as the mean for the evoked potential, you would really have an advance of information about this. But I
am not at all sure that is true. It depends on the model you take. You
assume that you have a signal, the real response, and you have noise,
which is the background EEG that is not synchronized with the stimulus;
what we see in the raw record is the sum of those two. Both the signal
and the noise have variance. But if you permit the signal to have variance, then what do you have when you average the sum of the two?
You have a sum of the variances. So part of that variance estimate is
associated with the response variability, and part of it is associated with
the background variability. That makes for quite a problem when analyzing the data.

Dr. Russell Harter (University of North Carolina, Greensboro): There are
a number of factors in your data that suggest the importance of motor

processes. One of them is that you got greater differences, over the vertex between relevant and irrelevant stimuli, near motor centers. Second, the effects of relevant versus irrelevant conditions increased as a function of time after stimulation; this means that there was a greater possibility of a person making an implicit (covert) response. When the numbers were relevant, I am sure subjects rehearsed them and not the letters. Do you think that motor processes were involved, and that they possibly affected your data?

Chapman: By saying that rehearsal is a motor component, you would predict that there would be more motor components involved late in the series. Is that right? It is very interesting, what you call motor. You can push the "motor" more and more central, as you can push the sensory side more and more central.

Harter: It could be central. But after the specific stimulus, the changes that occurred would make the probability of a covert motor response more plausible—you have time to rehearse.

Chapman: We have tried to push these psychophysiological events around by using other kinds of tasks; one task yields larger differences on the first relevant stimulus, presumably by increasing the mental operations that are occurring.

Audience: Regarding the CNV, consider the reversal that you see between points H and K. How about the possibility of distractibility, and how might this affect the CNV? If you have introduced some type of mental activity that results in a distraction from the task, momentarily, so that the focus of attention is changed, the amplitude of the CNV is reduced. Note the reduced amplitude of the CNV at points H, and then note the reverse at points K, in relation to the relevant and irrelevant stimuli. Do you think that, at point H, the person is busy storing the relevant stimulus, whereas at point K, he is in the process of preparing to respond?

Chapman: I would go along with some analysis of that sort. We should now relate it to what we think the mental operations are. The CNV data cannot be explained in a simple way. We should relate the CNV to behavior, because we know more about the behavior than we know about the physiology.

Audience: What is going on at point H, as opposed to point K?

Chapman: At H, for the relevant stimulus, the subject has to perceive it and remember it; at K, he has to perceive it, compare it with the memory of the first, and solve the problem. The subject does not make the muscle response until after the blank stimulus that occurs after K. We postponed the motor response to get it out of the way.

Dr. Allen Paivio (University of Western Ontario): Would you comment further on the direction of your thinking on the psychological side. You have uncertainty, it seems to me, on both sides of this psychophysiological problem. You have something like 15 different components in your evoked potential data, but on the psychological side you have not conceptualized that many processes. Presumably, you need to pin the psychological side down; you have to have an anchor on one side or the other before you can interpret this relationship. As I see it, you have only a few behavioral (psychological) anchors to which you can relate the evoked potential data. I do not see any possibility of using the evoked potential data as an anchor. What kind of differentiation of psychological units do you hope to be able to make?

Chapman: I think that it *is* possible to use these evoked potential components as the anchor. Having obtained a set of components, we should seek them in other situations. Then, ascertain what is common in situations that yield a lot of any given component. And what are the situations that yield very little of that component? Then you know something about the behavioral side of the component. It is thus possible to turn the direction of the research around the other way. Incidentally, we really have 16 conditions. We have four programs × two stimuli × two relevances; so there are 16 different things going on in this task, though they are not separate or discrete processes. The question is—and I wish I could give you the answer to this—how those 15 evoked potential components, for example, map onto those 16 different situations.

Dr. Allen Rechtschaffen (University of Chicago): You might get your psychological anchor by employing psychological averaging. By using "cognitive" input, you obtained a separation in your evoked potential, depending on the kind of that stimulus input. But you do not know that "cognition" occurred at the moment of separation, merely that there was separation as a function of the stimulus. Certainly cognition, or awareness, must begin somewhere, and you may have the *beginning* of such a process; but it is not part of the process that is *intimately* associated with the cognition. What you could do is to ask subjects whether or not the first stimulus is relevant; then you could see how the detection of relevance is associated, timewise, with which change in the evoked response.

Chapman: I had thought some about this possibility; what concerns me is whether or not the addition of this aspect of the experiment would interfere with the processes that are going on. It is the old question of whether the measurements would interfere with that which is being measured.

Rechtschaffen: But that would be a separate experiment.

Chapman: Problem-solving and thinking have been studied extensively in psychology, and there are a variety of strategies that subjects can use in solving the same problem. You are suggesting that we look at the particular strategies, as revealed by the verbal report. That is one way of going about it.

Rechtschaffen: What I am asking is, with which part of that separation is the cognitive aspect associated?

Chapman: I was trying to discuss that point toward the end of my talk, where two alternatives were considered. If you take a unidimensional construct to explain these data, then the cognitive processes are completed by the time the separation occurs. If you accept an alternative view that the differences are associated with perceptual–cognitive processes, then you are entirely correct that we may be looking at only the beginning, middle, or the end. So we must find other techniques to pinpoint the times at which relevant events occur.

Rechtschaffen: If you do not extend your time scope, then there is a danger; you may be studying purely neural events that *eventuate* in cognitive processes, but not the neural events most intimately associated with cognitive processes.

Chapman: Operationally, of course, that is a difficult thing to handle. To the extent the neural components correlate with various successful performances one builds confidence that those components are intimately associated with perceptual cognitive processes. The relatively rapid rate of stimulus presentation (every $\frac{3}{4}$ sec) puts a temporal constraint on when the processing can occur. All we can do is look for correlations in space and time and then test the relations by trying to fractionate or dissociate them.

Dr. Peter MacNeilage (University of Texas at Austin): You might cut into this cognitive question on the psychological side by having, instead of two types of linguistic stimuli, one type of linguistic stimulus and one nonlinguistic. The nonlinguistic stimuli could be pairs of geometrical figures that vary in their degree of completion and the subject would indicate which is more complete. Do you think there would be any profit in that? We suspect, on a number of grounds, that the processing of linguistic material is a process with very distinctive features about it; that is not true of the nonlinguistic material.

Chapman: I think there is a rich field for a lot of experiments; it is hard to know which ones to do first. Part of the rationale is to do one where hopefully you know something about both sides of the equation. But I am not sure how your geometrical experiment has an advantage.

MacNeilage: The advantage is that in processing linguistic material one makes absolute judgments about what item it is, e.g., whether the item is a number or a letter. That is a distinctive process, and may involve tapping into a speech-related function. On the other hand, no such processing stage could be postulated for geometric stimuli.

Chapman: I think it could—any stimulus can tap verbal mediation!

MacNeilage: Yes. But figures with various degrees of completion, would involve the same verbal mediation, e.g., "squares."

Chapman: I am not sure. Perhaps using the concept "sides," and presenting only three, the subject might wonder where the fourth one is. There may be various responses to any nonlinguistic stimulus. We have argued that it is best, whenever possible, to have a very well-defined task.

MacNeilage: As long as you are going to have two, as you do here, why not vary the two more than you have?

Black: With respect to Dr. MacNeilage's point, data indicated that people show such differences in the processing of visual and verbal materials. They seem to be in different channels.

Chapman: There is also the possibility of using lateral (hemispheric) differences here. Dr. Sperry will be talking about this later.

Dr. William Conner (Vanderbilt): Another person raised the point that the dc shift (the slow-wave phenomenon) was important. The slow wave *is* important, then your time constant of .3 sec would clearly distort the waveform.

Chapman: Any time constant, in a sense, distorts the waveform; the question is whether or not we are looking, within sufficiently short times, to see the effects. The question is how much the voltage changes within the time period that we examine. The most time that we have to span is 1.5 sec between the two points in the trial where randomization brings the average potentials to the same values. Our time constant passes frequencies down to .3 Hz.

Dr. Henry Edwards (University of Ottawa): Dealing with averaged data, and with individual differences, you could conduct your analysis either with an N of one, or with a three factors by subjects design. Would your findings cross-validate with either design?

Chapman: I showed a statistical analysis across 12 subjects. There *are* individual differences, but because of time limitations, I have presented only group data.

Edwards: Correct, but what could you say about another group of 12 subjects? Have you split that group in some way?

Chapman: That is what inferential statistics tells us. If the probability of a particular effect is less than .01 in one sample, then you expect the same in others.

Edwards: I am sorry to pursue that a little more. The statistics are also based on the assumption that you have a representative sample from the population to which you extrapolate. Otherwise, we are only able to generalize to the 12 subjects whom we have studied. Can you generalize beyond this? Would you get the same findings with another group of 12 subjects?

Chapman: There was no systematic selection of subjects and we did not eliminate anybody on the basis of their data, provided it was technically free of artefacts.

Dr. Fritz Klein (Duke University): The title of that attention paper?

Chapman: It is "Components of Attention," by Posner and Boies, in *Psychological Review*, September, 1971.

Dr. Alec Dale (Allegheny College): With regard to individual differences, how many subjects showed the effects you are talking about?

Chapman: Group data are characteristic of individuals, with some differences among subjects.

Dale: Did some subjects not show differentiation?

Chapman: No, all subjects showed some relevance effect.

Dr. Michael Seitz (University of Pittsburgh): Some people define the evoked potential as a particular waveform, such as a negative wave or a positive wave.

Chapman: I would not so define it—it is an averaging operation performed on the EEGs. Now we can raise questions about its composition— it is not just one thing, and hence it is not very secure to talk about *the* evoked response.

Dr. F. J. McGuigan (Hollins College): I appreciate you examining events as close to stimulus impingement as you can, and your thoughts about Karlin's work. If you will perseverate on this, may we push you even closer to the stimulus? Think about the very rapid muscle responses with a latency of 8 msec, and the relevance of such rapid responses to your model. I will not ask you to answer that right now.

REFERENCES

Chapman, R. M. Evoked responses to relevant and irrelevant visual stimuli while problem solving. *Proceedings of the 73rd Annual Convention of the American Psychological Association*, 1965, 177–178.

Chapman, R. M. Human evoked responses to meaningful stimuli. *18th International Congress of Psychology*, 1966, **6**, 53–59.

Chapman, R. M. Human evoked responses to meaningful stimuli. *Acta Psychologica*, 1967, **27**, 53–59.

Chapman, R. M. Discussion of the definition and measurement of "psychological" independent variables in an average evoked experiment. In E. Donchin, and D. B. Lindsley (Eds.), *Averaged evoked potentials: Methods, results, and evaluations.* NASA SP–191, Washington, D.C., Government Printing Office, 1969. Pp. 262–275. (a)

Chapman, R. M. Discussion of eye movements, CNV, and AEP. In E. Donchin, and D. B. Lindsley (Eds.), *Averaged evoked potentials: Methods, results, and evaluations.* NASA SP–191. Washington, D.C., Government Printing Office, 1969. Pp. 177–180. (b)

Chapman, R. M., & Bragdon, H. R. Evoked responses to numerical and non-numerical visual stimuli while problem solving. *Nature (London)*, 1964, **203**, 1155–1157.

Cohen, J. Very slow brain potentials relating to expectancy: The CNV. In E. Donchin, and D. B. Lindsley (Eds.), *Averaged evoked Potentials: Methods, results, and evaluations.* NASA SP–191. Washington, D.C., Government Printing Office, 1969. Pp. 143–198.

Donchin, E. & Lindsley, D. B. (Eds.), *Averaged evoked potentials: Methods, results, and evaluations.* NASA SP–191. Washington, D.C., Government Printing Office, 1969.

Gaarder, K., Krauskopf, J., Graf, V., Kropfl, W., & Armington, J. C. Averaged brain activity following saccadic eye movement. *Science*, 1964, **146**, 1481–1483.

Jasper, H. H. Report of the Committee of Clinical Examination in Electroencephalography. *Electroencephography and Clinical Neurophysiology*, 1958, **10**, 370–375.

Karlin, L. Cognition, preparation, and sensory-evoked potentials. *Psychological Bulletin*, 1970, **73**, 122–135.

Kropfl, W. J., Chapman, R. M. & Armington, J. C. Apparatus for scoring selected electroencephalographic rhythms. *Electroencephography and Clinical Neurophysiology*, 1962, **14**, 921–923.

Posner, M. I. & Boies, S. Components of attention. *Psychological Review*, 1971, **78**, 391–408.

Sheatz, G. C., & Chapman, R. M. Task relevance and auditory evoked responses. *Electroencephography and Clinical Neurophysiology*, 1969, **26**, 468–475.

Sutton, S. The specification of psychological variables in an average evoked potential experiment. In E. Donchin and D. B. Lindsley (Eds.) *Averaged evoked potentials: Methods, results, and evaluations.* NASA SP–191. Washington, D.C., Government Printing Office, 1969. Pp. 237–298.

Uttal, W. R. Do compound evoked potentials reflect psychological codes? *Psychological Bulletin*, 1965, **64**, 377–392.

CHAPTER FOUR

Objective EEG Methods for Studying Covert Shifts of Visual Attention[1]

THOMAS MULHOLLAND

Psychophysiology Laboratory
Veterans Administration Hospital

I. INTRODUCTION

Clinical neurophysiology, emphasizing studies of humans, managed to preserve many mentalistic concepts during the purge of those ideas from psychology by the arch-behaviorists. However, preservation is not development and old-fashioned concepts such as attention, volition, and mental imagery lagged behind the development of the main body of ideas in neurophysiology and behavioristic psychology.

More recently, mentalistic concepts have become respectable in contemporary psychology. With this new acceptance has come a new criticism of the use of those concepts as explanatory principles in neurophysiology and neuropsychology. The history of the concept of attention in electro-

[1] The work in this paper was supported in its entirety by the Veteran's Administration, RCS 15-4, Program 01/5890.1/69-09.

encephalography is a good example of these trends (Evans & Mulholland, 1969).

Attention has been an important concept in EEG since the early work of Berger (1930). Though researchers in the 1930s and 1940s, especially Adrian (Adrian & Matthews, 1934; Adrian, 1943) linked changes in the EEG occipital alpha to vision and visual control processes, this emphasis gave way to the concept of "visual attention" or simply "attention" (Mulholland, 1969). Attention in EEG was never clearly defined, yet it proved to be a remarkably durable explanatory concept.

For many researchers the outcome was a disenchantment with *any* psychological concept in neurophysiology, and a rejection of the EEG as an index of anything psychological except as a consequence of gross brain pathology or epilepsy. This contrasts with the current wave of enthusiastic faddism and exorbitant claims for alpha in relation to states of mind and alleged mental powers by nonscientific "alpha" pop groups (Mulholland, 1971). My attitude toward the alpha rhythms is between such extremes of scientific pessimism and popular optimism.

I will begin with a brief statement of the classical assumptions about the response of the occipital alpha rhythms to visual stimulation, then a description of how we define and measure alpha will follow. After presenting the experimental results of our studies of attention and alpha, I will review my hypothesis that visual attention and the suppression of occipital alpha are mediated by visual control process, especially efferent processes in cortex associated with the adjustment of the eye. At the end, a criticism of the classical assumptions about the response of the alpha rhythms to visual stimulation is presented and some new kinds of experiments proposed.

A. THE RESPONSE OF THE OCCIPITAL ALPHA RHYTHMS

The classical concepts of the response of the alpha rhythm emphasized the *singularity* of the response—the single alpha "block" after stimulation, *functional equivalence* of all alpha "blocks," and the *functional identity* of all stages of the single alpha block. In all the studies of "attention" and alpha, these assumptions played their role influencing the methods of stimulus presentation, the collection and analysis of data, and the theoretical treatment of the results. In my view all three assumptions of singularity, functional equivalence and functional identity are either contrary to experimental and clinical evidence or simply unnecessary and superfluous. I shall discuss each of them in the context of our work at Bedford. Before I do, it is necessary to review the kind of definition of alpha that we use.

B. DEFINITION OF ALPHA

When the EEG is used as an index of behavioral and psychological processes, the requirements of EEG analysis are different from those of an analysis of the EEG as a complex signal per se. In the latter a rapid, finely differentiated description is required such as fast spectral analysis. In the former the degree of differentiation of the index is related to that of the associated behavioral and psychological processes. Features of the EEG must be so described that they match the features of the behavioral process, in the time domain. In the case of fairly slow behavioral changes which are also large-scale a fast, highly differentiated EEG analysis may in fact be an impediment because fast, transitory and finely differentiated changes will occur in the EEG which have no necessary relation to behavior. Here a method for defining and detecting EEG occipital alpha is described which meets the requirements for an index of visual attention.

The occipital EEG is defined as a series of events. An event is either alpha or it is not. This does not mean that the response of the EEG is either/or, only that the EEG meets criteria for our definition or it does not. The series formed by the alternation between alpha and no-alpha events is called the alpha-attenuation series. There is no mechanism implied by the term; it is a name for a familiar phenomenon.

The alpha detection and control system described here is currently in use.[2] Consideration in its design were accuracy, reliability, and convenience. Occipital alpha is easy to detect but because of its low frequency, the minimum detection time is about .1 sec. A band-pass filter with rectification and integration was chosen on the basis of overall performance. Other detection systems offer quicker response times or sharper frequency discrimination but the filter–rectifier–integrator combination has a time constant which best approximates the time constant of the biological system that it is measuring, neither too fast nor too slow. The feedback control system is designed to control visual and auditory displays, to perform routine housekeeping such as controlling clocks, markers, and counters, and to provide maximum flexibility in experiment design.

1. Definition of Alpha for Each Individual

The classical definition of alpha is an 8–12 Hz, nearly sinusoidal signal at a voltage level of between 5 and 150 μV. These are statistical limits and say nothing about an individual's alpha. Individual amplitude and frequency parameters must be determined and used as criteria for setting

---

[2] The system described here was designed and built by R. Boudrot. Complete description will be published elsewhere.

the alpha detection system. The alpha frequency counted manually over several seconds is used to set the center of a 2-Hz passband. The "static maximum alpha" (eyes closed in the dark after a period of 1 or 2 min) is attenuated or increased at the preamplifier to produce full-scale deflection of the meter in the detection circuit. The threshold amplitude for "dynamic alpha" (alpha under operating conditions) is standardized with the threshold set control. When the filtered signal is equal to or greater than 25% of the static alpha amplitude, response of the relay to an above-threshold alpha in the EEG is between .25–.35 sec.

Raw data is collected in the normal fashion on a Grass Model 7 Polygraph. The amplified but unfiltered raw data appears at a high level output jack (J7) with a potential of 2 V (peak-to-peak) corresponding to a 1-cm pen deflection. This output is processed by a tunable RC-type bandpass filter which has a 24 dB/octave roll off filter function. The output of the filter is bridge rectified then integrated by a critically damped, variable threshold, optical meter relay. The meter is protected from overload with a Zener diode which also serves to limit the "OFF" time delay when an exceptionally high-amplitude alpha period is detected. This easily assembled system offers a settable passband, a settable threshold, repeatability and linearity within 2%, .25-sec response time, ease of calibration and operation, durability, and low cost (see Fig. 4.1).

2. Choice of Parameter Values

Filter. For most subjects, the probability for the occurrence of alpha is higher when the probability for the occurrence of competing brain rhythms is lower. When alpha is present it is usually prominent and dominant. Conversely when the probability of other rhythms is higher, the probability of alpha is lower (Cobb, 1963; Lindsley, 1960). Occipital alpha, which is the most prominent brain rhythm has a frequency stability of ±1 Hz and is usually an order of magnitude greater than the noise (signal–noise >10) and 2–10 times the amplitude of other rhythms which are usually 20 μV or less (Cobb, 1963). Our variable passband RC filter has been superseded by newer types with better performance characteristics but it performs adequately in distinguishing the nearly noise-free, nearly coherent alpha signals. With our filter, the shape of the attenuation frequency curve does not change significantly as the passband indicator on the filter is narrowed from 4 Hz down to 1 Hz. There is a large increase in attenuation of the band-pass frequencies with the narrowing of the passband indicator. We have standardized pass indicator settings at 1 Hz above and 1 Hz below the resting alpha frequency.

Threshold. An alpha sensitivity function was obtained using two matched

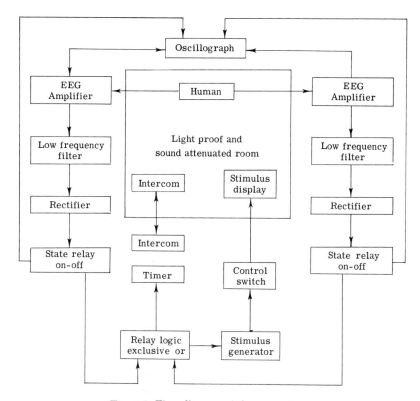

Fig. 4.1. Flow diagram of the apparatus.

recording channels each receiving the same EEG input. One channel was maintained at 25% threshold, the other was varied in successive trials. Data was then collected from a subject and the percentage of time the alpha state relays were ON was computed.

The percentage of alpha on both the constant and variable threshold channel changed over the experiment due to habituation. To correct for this and to express the values relative to the constant threshold, the percentage of alpha with the variable threshold at 25% were averaged with the values on the constant threshold which were the lowest values occurring early in the trial. This number was used to adjust the value obtained with the variable threshold for a particular trial. In this way a correction for habituation was made and the corrected value made relative to the average value at 25%.

The "dynamic alpha" threshold was determined from the inflection in the percentage of alpha-threshold function. The slope between threshold values of 20 and 40% is nearly -1. At threshold which is 25% of the value of the maximum resting value the alpha patterns on the polygraph are sufficiently large and coherent to be recognizable, there is a nearly linear relation between percentage of alpha and detection threshold, and the on and off delays of the detection system are about equal shifting the stimulus in time but maintaining a stimulus duration equal to an alpha duration.

Response time. Since the EEG is used as a *gross* index of relatively *slow* psychological and behavioral processes, we require an EEG index of *large* changes which have a relatively *long* time constant. Note that we are not analyzing the EEG signal per se, but using it as an index of something else. Consequently fast signal detection is not necessary. In fact if the alpha detector has a response time of $<.2$ sec it may hinder the utility of the alpha feedback method in the study of visual attention, because of the increased rate of detecting transients which are not correlated with behavioral change.

Typical examples of behavioral and psychological times related to attention and orienting are (1) latency (.2 sec) for saccadic eye movements (Stark, Michael, & Zuber, 1969); (2) shifts of attention vary from .1 to 5.0 sec with most shifts greater than .2 sec (Woodworth & Schlossberg, 1954); (3) latency for alpha blocking is .2 sec or greater (Cruickshank, 1937; Cobb, 1963). Most intervals of alpha and alpha blocking are greater than .5 sec (Mulholland, 1972). A response time of .25–.35 sec seems to be a reasonable compromise between matching the system and biological time constants, avoiding noisy response to transients and having the feedback stimulus occur without too much delay. With faster detection, the system is excessively noisy, exhibiting responses which are faster than changes in the behavioral processes we are studying. With longer delays feedback stimulation occurs less often and the variance of alpha intervals increases.

Calibration. The detection system is calibrated by adjusting the gain of the metering circuit to a full-scale deflection corresponding to a 1-cm polygraph pen deflection using a train of simulated alpha waves produced by a variable frequency sine wave oscillator. The frequency of the sine wave (simulated alpha) should be the same as that of the subject's alpha with a passband set at 1 Hz and 1 Hz below the alpha frequency. Normalization between hemispheres or between subjects is accomplished by adjusting the "static alpha" amplitude with the polygraph preamplifier gain control to produce a 1-cm pen deflection. This 1-cm pen deflection at the calibration frequency causes a full-scale deflection in the metering circuit. Normalization reduces the individual or interhemispheric differences in alpha amplitudes. If differences then occur under experimental conditions they are likely to be reliable differences. The time required to calibrate and normalize the two channel detection system is 3–5 min.

3. Feedback Control System

The basic requirement for the feedback control system is to cause a feedback stimulus to occur in response to an alpha–no-alpha event. Additional requirements are event counting, timing, and marking, and flexibility and expandability to encompass a wide range of experiments. In keeping with these basic requirements, the control system allows up to four separate stimuli in any combination of EEG event and stimulus and controlled from either left or right sides. It has a 70-terminal connector panel externalizing key circuit points permitting patching to accomplish experimental goals plus a way of "adding on" functions that are not part of the system. The quantification of alpha–no-alpha events is to the nearest .1 sec. Data acquisition and processing is done by the PDP-12. The various events and data sampling time are marked on the polygraph[3] (see Fig. 4.2).

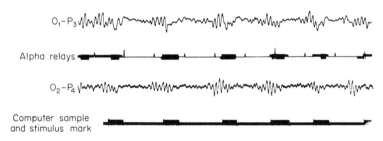

Fig. 4.2. Polygraph record.

C. Experiments on Alpha and Attention

1. Distribution of Alpha and No-Alpha Durations

The event series of alpha and no-alpha events are measured to the nearest .1 sec. The distribution of percentage of cases as a function of duration shows clearly that different conditions involving "visual attention" produce large changes in the alpha-attenuation series.

The following are from a study of 24 children[4] (see Fig. 4.3). Condition

---

[3] Programs for acquisition, measurement, display and analysis of alpha and no-alpha events were developed by Brad Cox and David Goodman. They will be published elsewhere.

[4] This study was in collaboration with Dr. Constance Murray, Lexington, Massachusetts School Department, and Dr. Generoso Gascon, Seizure Unit, Childrens Hospital Medical Center, Boston, Massachusetts.

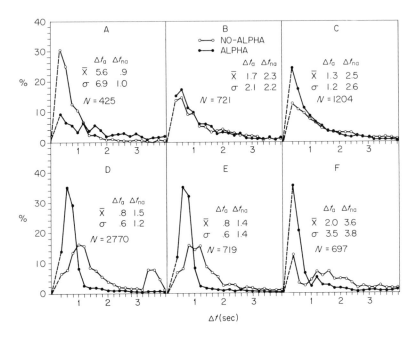

Fig. 4.3. Distributions of Δt_a, Δt_{na} for 24 children. (A) Eyes closed in the dark. (B) Eyes open in the dark. (C) Eyes open, steady light. (D) Eyes open, feedback stimulation (Loop 1). (E) Eyes open, Loop 1 feedback. (F) Eyes open, Loop 2 feedback.

A is eyes closed in the dark. Alpha events range from very brief to 14 sec duration (events greater than 4 sec are not shown). There is no definite central tendency. The intervals of no-alpha are brief with most being less than 1 sec. In condition B, eyes were open in the dark. The change in the distribution functions is clear—alpha durations become briefer, no-alpha longer. Again, most values are 1 sec or less. The distribution functions are quite similar for alpha and no-alpha. In condition C, a steady spot of light was turned on in front of the child. The alpha duration is decreased, no-alpha increased and the distributions are less alike.

In conditions D and E alpha controlled the occurrence of a visual stimulus. When alpha occurred a colored picture was turned on, for no-alpha it was turned off (Loop 1). The distribution functions are changed compared to the steady light condition. Alpha durations are briefer and the central tendency more pronounced. No-alphas are longer still varying over a wider range.

In condition F, alpha feedback was reversed. Alpha caused the picture to be off, no-alpha turned it on (Loop 2). The distribution functions are different from Loop 1 conditions. There are more longer durations (>4 sec) for both alpha and no-alpha (Mulholland, 1968). It is clear that shifts in seeing and looking at visual stimuli produce definite changes in the distribution functions of the durations of alpha and no-alpha events. A feedback path between the alpha and stimulus reduces the variance of alpha and no-alpha intervals (Loop 1).

2. Time Series of Alpha and No-Alpha Durations

Alpha and no-alpha durations show a *temporal* variation in relation to the onset of a stimulus, an ocular maneuver or both. The systematic and reproducible variation over time can be estimated by averaging to obtain an average series or by fitting functions to individual series. The values of $\bar{\Delta}t_a$ and $\bar{\Delta}t_{na}$ are functions of the number (N) of events in the series.

Earlier work showed that repeated stimulation was followed by a *disturbance* and a *recovery* of the alpha-attenuation cycle (see Fig. 4.4) (Mulholland & Runnals, 1964b). From the terminology of classical EEG these are average habituation functions. Average durations of no-alpha

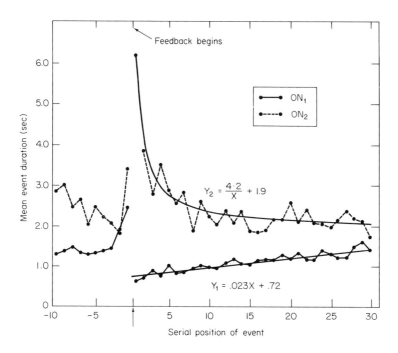

Fig. 4.4. Disturbance and recovery of the alpha-attenuation cycle with feedback stimulation. ON_1 is alpha; ON_2 is no-alpha. [From Mulholland & Runnals, 1964b.]

are initially increased with the onset of stimulation, then decreased; alpha durations are initially decreased then gradually increased.

Similar functions are obtained when eyes are opened in the dark without visual stimuli or when a steady light is turned on or when the subject starts an ocular maneuver such as focusing on a target (Mulholland & Runnals, 1964b; Mulholland, 1968).

Figure 4.5 shows results from the study of children described before. Average alpha and no-alpha series are shown beginning with the onset of various conditions. With eyes closed in the dark alpha durations are generally long and no-alpha brief. When eyes are opened in the dark the typical *disturbance* and *recovery* for the event series are seen. When a steady light is turned on, there is again a disturbance followed by recovery. For the onset of feedback, again a disturbance followed by a recovery.

Similar results from a study of alpha and no-alpha events during various tracking tasks are presented in Fig. 4.6. The subjects were tracking a target $\frac{1}{2}$-in. in diameter about 5 in. in front of them, moving back and forth at regular or irregular motion. They either tracked it accurately with clear focus (focus–track, FT) or blurred tracking with relaxed accommodation (blur–track, BT) or not tracking, simply viewing the target (blur–no-track, BNT). The average alpha and no-alpha series beginning with the onset of the ocular maneuvers are shown in Fig. 4.6. The same kind of disturbance and recovery functions can be seen (Mulholland, 1972).

I hypothesize from these data that a shift of attention from a lower to higher level, induced by stimulation, or by opening the eyes in the dark, or by ocular maneuver is mediated by visual control processes which produce a characteristic disturbance and recovery of the occipital EEG

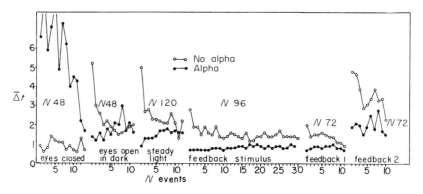

Fig. 4.5. Disturbance and recovery functions of the average alpha-actuation cycle (24 children).

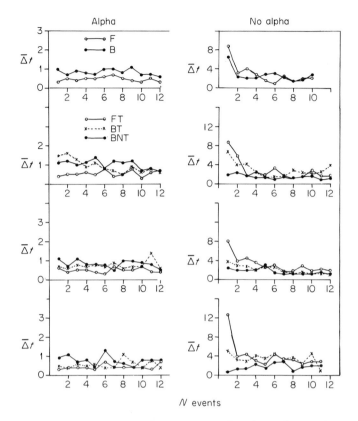

Fig. 4.6. Average disturbance and recovery functions for various ocular maneuvers. The top of the graph is for a stationary target. The lower graphs are for a moving target. See text.

alpha-attenuation cycle. For this process a stimulus is a sufficient but not a necessary condition as evidenced by the disturbance and recovery after the opening of the eyes in the dark. A quantitative approximation to the disturbance and recovery function is

$$\bar{\Delta}t_{a} = AN + B \tag{1}$$

$$\bar{\Delta}t_{na} = C/N + D \tag{2}$$

When N is the number (less than 50) of the event starting from the onset of stimulus or ocular maneuver.

In the study of 24 children (see Fig. 4.5), the average hyperbolic and linear functions for the conditions (1) eyes open in the dark, (2) steady light on, and (3) Loop 1 feedback are shown on the right side of Table 4-1.

The individual data were also fitted with these functions and for the majority of 24 subjects the best fit was statistically significant. The individual best fit functions for in single trial are useful for comparing the similarity of the functional response of the EEG from left and right sides. In Fig. 4.7 an example of computer-derived functions is shown for the no-alpha series and the alpha series during visual feedback stimulation. The functions are for a single trial, from a 6-year-old boy. In this case the functions fitted the data well. In other cases the individual functions do not fit the data as well. For this reason, the hyperbolic and linear functions described before apply only to average data, though they are representative of the majority of cases.

Average disturbance–recovery functions for each various experimental conditions were separately estimated by fitting a linear function to the alpha series and a linearized hyperbolic function to the no-alpha series with the method of least squares. Each serial event was associated with a mean and σ based on 24 children. The standard error of the estimate (SE) and the correlation coefficient indicate how well the functions fit the actual data. The functions ± 1 SE include about 68% of the data. For eyes open in the dark and steady light conditions $r = .53$ is significant at the .5 level; $r = .66$ significant at the .01 level. For Loop 1, $r = .35$ is significant at .05 level; .45 at the .01 level. For both alpha and no-alpha the functions of the means, and the standard error of the estimate are least for Loop 1 feedback.

In the feedback conditions, Δt_a includes the average latency: $\bar{\Delta} t_a =$ latency $(\bar{l}) + \bar{L}_2$. Here, $\bar{L}_2$ is the average time between recorded alpha

TABLE 4-1

Estimate of the Statistics of Regression Functions of Δt_a, Δt_{na} on N

$\Delta t_a = AN + B$	Average of regressions			Regression of the average			
	A	B	$r_{y \cdot x}$	A	B	SE	$r_{y \cdot x}$
Eyes open, dark	.07	1.3	$+.44$	.07	1.3	.4	$+.54$
Steady light	.02	1.2	$+.31$	.06	1.1	.2	$+.78$
Loop 1 feedback	.01	.7	$+.44$	.01	.7	.1	$+.76$
$\bar{\Delta} t_{na} = (1/N)C + D$	C	D	$r_{y \cdot f(x)}$	C	D	SE	$r_{y \cdot f(x)}$
Eyes open, dark	3.8	1.2	$+.67$	3.7	1.3	.2	$+.98$
Steady light	3.1	1.6	$+.78$	3.1	1.7	.3	$+.93$
Loop 1 feedback	1.4	1.3	$+.68$	1.4	1.3	.1	$+.87$

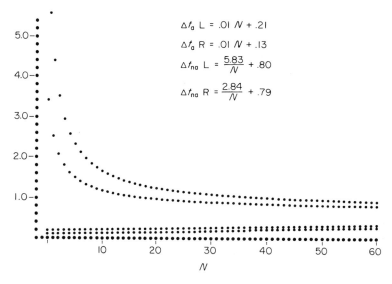

$$\Delta t_a \; L = .01 \; N + .21$$

$$\Delta t_a \; R = .01 \; N + .13$$

$$\Delta t_{na} \; L = \frac{5.83}{N} + .80$$

$$\Delta t_{na} \; R = \frac{2.84}{N} + .79$$

Fig. 4.7. Computer-calculated disturbance and recovery functions for $\Delta t_a \Delta t_{na}$ on right and left sides. Data from a single trial with a 6-year-old child. The best fit correlation coefficients (r) for the four functions are Δt_a, left (.26); Δt_a, right (.24); Δt_{na}, left (.74); Δt_{na}, right (.38).

blocking and state relay off. In this study $\bar{L}_2$ was .3–.4 sec. Systematic changes in the $\bar{\Delta} t_a$ are due to systematic changes in the latency.

For the regression of the average feedback condition (Table 4-1).

$$AN + B = \bar{l} + \bar{L}_2$$

$$.01N + 0.7 - .35 = \bar{l}$$

$$\bar{l} = .01N + .35 \text{ (sec)}.$$

The recorded duration of EEG attenuation after stimulation can be estimated

$$\bar{\Delta} t_{rna} = \bar{\Delta} t_{na} + \bar{L}_2 - \bar{L}_1.$$

$\bar{L}_1$ is the delay between recorded alpha and state relay on (alpha). $\bar{L}_2$ is as before.

$$\bar{\Delta} t_{rna} = (C/N) + D + \bar{L}_2 - \bar{L}_1$$

$$C = 1.40, \qquad D = 1.30, \qquad \bar{L}_1 = 0.25 \text{ sec}$$

$$\bar{\Delta} t_{rna} = (1.4/N) + 1.3 + .1 = 1.4/N + 1.4 \text{ (sec)}.$$

The habituation function is described as a change in the latency and duration of the EEG attenuation after stimulation. In Loop 1 the initial response to the first stimulus had an average latency of .36 sec; average duration of 2.80 sec. After 30 stimulations the average latency was .65 sec; average duration, 1.44 sec. The ratio duration/latency is called the *index of orienting* (IO). After the first Loop 1 stimulus, IO was 7.8, after 30 stimulations it was 2.2. An approximation to IO is the ratio of $\Delta t_{na}/\Delta t_a$ which is sufficient for most experiments.

3. Instructional Set and Voluntary Attention

The time series of alpha and no-alpha events can be influenced by voluntary attention and cognitive tasks. The simplest attention task is to have the subject "pay attention" for a series of flashes or to simply view them. With instructions to "pay attention" the subject usually shows longer no-alpha and briefer alpha durations (see Fig. 4.8; Mulholland & Runnals, 1962b). Similar results are obtained when the subject is instructed to be "alert" or to be "relaxed" (see Fig. 4.9; Mulholland, 1968). Counting the stimuli also produce similar changes in the alpha attenuation series (see Fig. 4.10; Mulholland & Runnals, 1962b). There are the expected

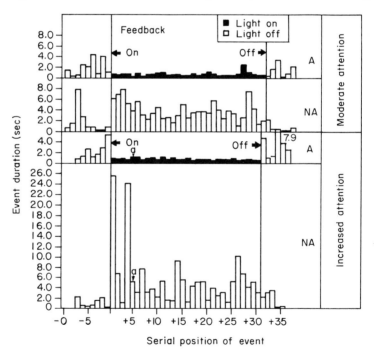

Fig. 4.8. The Δt_a (A) decreases, and Δt_{na} (NA) increases when subject pays attention. [From Mulholland & Runnals, 1962b.]

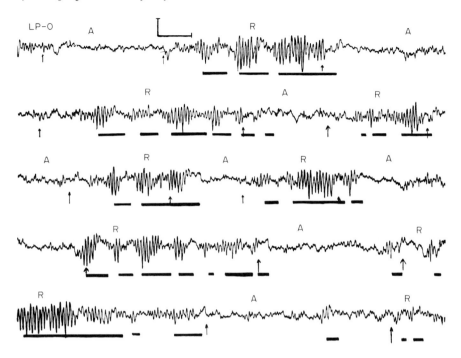

Fig. 4.9. Subject reports he is alert (A) or relaxed (R). The EEG is prominent during the "relax" intervals. [From Mulholland & Evans, 1966.]

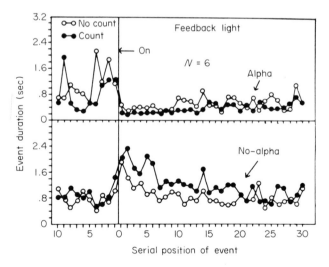

Fig. 4.10. Average Δt_a, Δt_{na} while counting or not counting feedback stimuli. [From Mulholland & Runnals, 1962b.]

individual differences. Some subjects do not show large changes; a few
show none at all.

More complex attentional tasks require the subject to "pay attention"
or to count the feedback stimuli flashes according to a prearranged schedule,
e.g., instructions to "pay particular attention to a particular flash." Using
feedback method the series of alpha and no-alpha bursts associated with
the "target" stimuli were different from the others compared to control
conditions (see Fig. 4.11; Mulholland & Runnals, 1963).

In Fig. 4.12 results for a single subject on a single run are shown. He
was instructed to "pay attention" to the 10th, 20th, 30th, and 40th flashes.

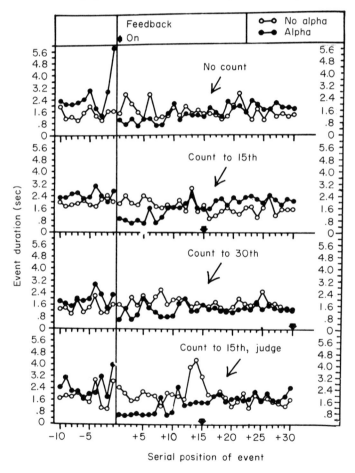

Fig. 4.11. Average Δt_a, Δt_{na} while counting specific feedback stimuli. The bottom
graph is for instructions to pay particular attention to the 15th flash and judge its
brightness. [From Mulholland & Runnals, 1963.]

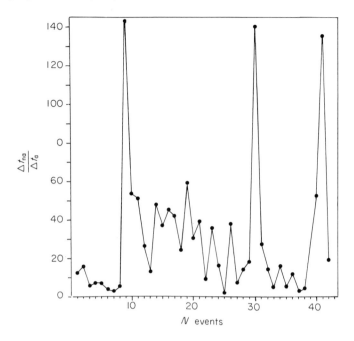

Fig. 4.12. Index of orienting for a single trial with prior instructions to pay attention to the 10th, 20th, 30th, and 40th stimulus (12-year-old boy). [From Mulholland, 1970.]

The number used here was the ratio of (Δt no-alpha)/(Δt alpha). The response series was changed as scheduled by instructions, with greater orienting at the 10th, 20th, 30th, and 40th response (Mulholland, 1970). In experiments like this we have found that the alpha-attenuation series can be reliably modified by subjects according to a prearranged schedule. There are individual differences. Some show much greater effects than others.

My interpretation of these results is that the subject, using a memory scheme of the instructions, "counts down" using inner speech to the proper stimulus in the series. This is associated with activation and intensification of visual control processes as expectancy increases and the occipital alpha is suppressed for a longer time. The term *internal attention gradient* is used to describe those still-hidden, complicated cognitive and perceptual operations that result in occipital EEG changes on schedule following instructions (Mulholland, 1962).

4. Shifts of Attention and Emotional Stimuli

It is well-known that emotional or evocative stimuli such as pictures of nudes compared to pictures of flowers (Peper, 1970), pictures of sexual activity compared to nonsexual activity (Mander, 1971), emotional words compared to neutral words (Mulholland & Davis, 1966), elicit different degrees of attention and longer durations of alpha blocking. I believe that when they look, people spend a longer time looking at such pictures compared to neutral ones, and the intervals of no-alpha are longer. These changes occur reliably with the feedback method yielding characteristic shifts in disturbance and recovery functions to such stimuli. See Figs. 4.13 and 4.14. The response to the various kind of stimuli can be analyzed in terms of the initial effect, rate of habituation to determine whether the alpha function, no-alpha function, or both are affected.

5. Shifts of Attention from One Stimulus to Another

Ordinarily the disturbance and recovery of the occipital EEG alpha-attenuation cycle is interpreted as a shift in the *level* of attention. In studies where the subject shifts his attention from one stimulus to another, there is no clear evidence in the EEG which permits one to know which

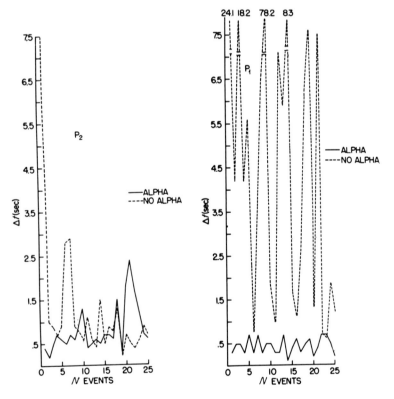

Fig. 4.13. Disturbance and recovery of Δt_a, Δt_{na} for a single trial with a picture of a flower (left) and with a picture of a nude (right). [From Peper, 1970.]

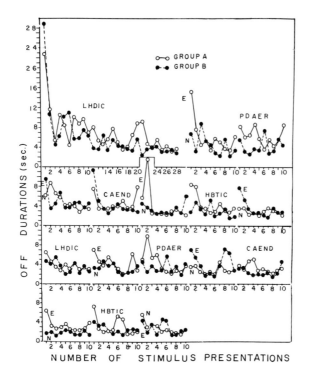

Fig. 4.14. Disturbance and recovery of Δt_{na} with neutral (N), emotional (E), and scrambled words. [From Mulholland, T. & Davis, E. Electroencephalographic activation: Nonspecific habituation by verbal stimuli. *Science,* **152,** 1966, 1104–1106, Fig. 1. Copyright 1966 by the American Association for the Advancement of Science.]

stimulus is being attended to. The next studies demonstrate that feedback EEG can be used to show which stimulus the subject is attending to and looking at.

Previous studies have shown that the length of alpha "bursts" during feedback can be increased by increasing the stimulus delay during feedback (Mulholland, 1968; see Fig. 4.15). The results for the three time delays is clear. The longer the delay the longer the alpha bursts. This effect is a statistical one. As delay increases the number of longer alpha bursts increases. If the delay is too long, the alpha will be episodically and unpredictably attenuated and the stimulus will occur infrequently. Figure 4.16 summarizes the statistical relation between alpha-stimulus delay and alpha durations, latency and the number of alpha events associated with stimulation based on experimental results from five subjects.

This result can be applied to the study of orienting to *one* stimulus when *two* stimuli are linked to alpha. If two stimuli are presented, one with a *brief* time delay, the other with a *longer* time delay, the question is—can

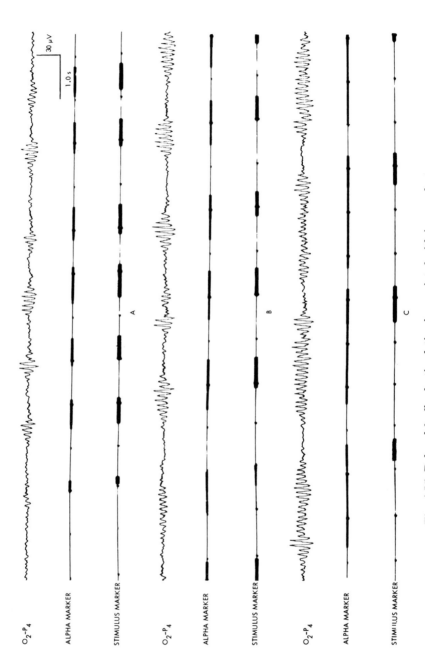

Fig. 4.15. Delayed feedback stimulation is associated with increased Δt_a.

Fig. 4.16. Statistical summary of the relationship between Δt_a and feedback delay. From five normals. At delays <.25 sec almost all intervals of alpha are associated with stimulation.

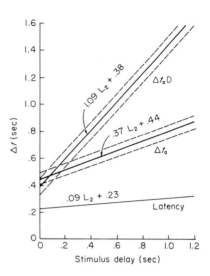

the subject, by selective attention, by selective looking, respond to the feedback stimulus having the long time delay and not to the one having the brief time delay? If he can shift from one stimulus to the other, the EEG should shift from longer to briefer alpha bursts and vice-versa.

Recent results from our laboratory show that some subjects can voluntarily shift from one loop to the other so that the EEG can show which stimulus is "in the loop" and when the shift occurs from one loop to the other. The subject must have well-defined alpha and a definite response to stimulation.

The subject is seated in a simple perimeter. A chin rest is used. On each side, 25° from straightahead are small lights, about 12 in. from the eye. Both lights are controlled by alpha and both are clearly seen by the subject. One light has a long time delay (LTD), the other has a brief time delay (BTD) (.2 sec). In practice sessions the subject is tested with the BTD light, and the LTD light separately. Then the LTD light is connected in the feedback path until about 15–40 alpha-light events have occurred. Then the BTD light is turned on. The result is a change in the EEG from longer to shorter alpha bursts which is often apparent from visual inspection of the record. An abrupt shift of both alpha and no-alpha durations occurs. The computer display of the successive alpha, no-alpha intervals shows the change in the alpha-attenuation series with the presentation of the brief time-delay stimulus though the effects on the alpha durations are most evident (see Figs. 4.17 and 4.18).

In the next conditions both lights are connected in the loop together. The experimenter instructs the subject "I want you to pay attention to the light on the left." Thirty alpha-light events are collected. Then he says "pay attention to the lights on the right." These conditions are practiced until the subject gives predominantly long alpha bursts in association with the light having the long time delay when "paying attention" to it or short alpha bursts when "paying attention" to the light having a brief time delay, taking care that complete habituation to the stimulus does not occur.

In test trials the subject voluntarily shifts attention from one side to the other side while viewing the lights. Subjective attention to the right is indicated by pushing a hand switch which marks the ink record. When paying attention to the left the button is not pushed. The EEG results from three subjects are shown in Figs. 4.19–4.21. One subject who did not exhibit good control stated that she could not ignore the brief time delay light. The results of these preliminary studies were

(1) For most subjects there is a definite change in the EEG alpha bursts in association with the stimulus that the subject reported he was attending to.

(2) For some subjects the EEG changes are not consistent.

(3) Some subjects do not show any effect after a brief training period.

We have also found that if the subject is told to look at the lights he attends to or is not told that he cannot look, the results are like those described above. If the subject is instructed to look straightahead, (both

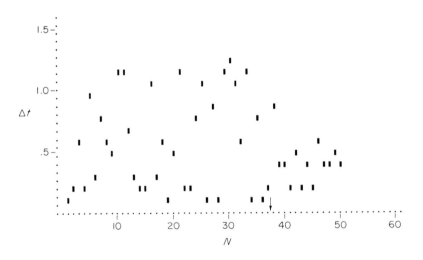

Fig. 4.17. Computer display of Δt_a during feedback stimulation with long time delay and adding a second stimulus with a brief time delay.

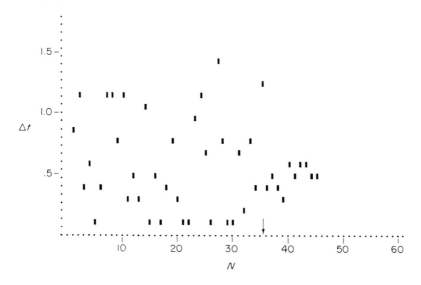

Fig. 4.18. Same as 17. Different subject.

lights can be clearly seen), to shift his attention but *not* his eyes, no differential effect of the attentional variable set has been seen yet. Although much more work is needed, this new method will extend the use of EEG in the study of human orienting, and permit closer correlation of the EEG with changes in looking behavior and subjective reports of attention.

The results shown in Figs. 4.17 and 4.18 indicate that the method of delayed feedback may be employed to study the shift of orienting from a suprathreshold stimulus to another which is just at threshold. First the subject would be habituated to a visual stimulus having a long time delay. Another stimulus connected in the feedback loop would be well below threshold with a short time delay. This stimulus is then increased in graded steps. As the stimulus having a brief time delay enters the threshold range of magnitudes, and the subject reacts to it, there would be a shift from predominantly longer to briefer alpha durations, a decreased variance of alpha durations and increase in durations of no-alpha, i.e., the subject would show EEG changes associated with orienting to a near threshold stimulus. Sokolov has shown that orienting to a threshold stimulus is greater and more prolonged compared to suprathreshold stimuli (Sokolov, 1963). The effect may be transitory as a weak stimulus will rapidly habituate. These methodological suggestions following from preliminary, promising results must be tested further before their usefulness can be fully appreciated.

The remainder of this paper reviews my current hypotheses linking the suppression of alpha to visual control processes. This is followed by a

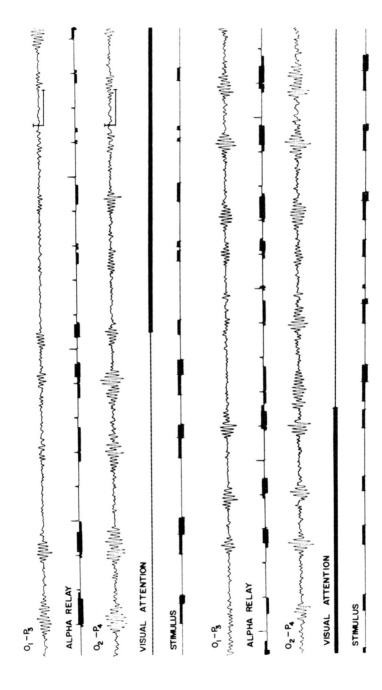

Fig. 4.19. The EEG record of subject voluntarily paying attention to either a stimulus having a long time delay (L) or a brief time delay (R). When paying attention to the stimulus on the right subject pressed a hand switch causing a mark on the polygraph tracing labeled voluntary attention. See text.

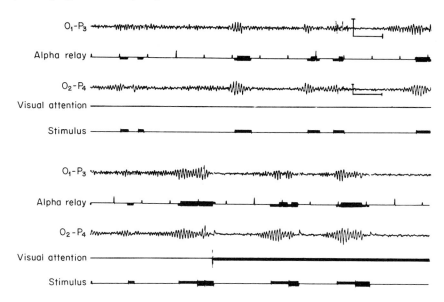

Fig. 4.20. Same as 19. Different subject. BTD on left stimulus.

critical evaluation of three assumptions often made in EEG studies: (1) *singularity* of the responses of the occipital alpha rhythm to visual stimulation; (2) *functional equivalence* of EEG events; (3) *functional identity* during the temporal interval of alpha suppression. Some new kinds of experiments are suggested which may extend the study of visual attention with objective EEG and behavioral methods.

II. NEUROPHYSIOLOGICAL BASIS FOR CHANGES IN THE EEG RELATED TO VISUAL ATTENTION

A. VISUAL CONTROL AND THE OCCIPITAL ALPHA RHYTHMS

Visual control processes refer to the ongoing adjustment of the visual receptor on the basis of information about the target fed back from the retina. It includes processes involved in fixation, lens accommodation, tracking, saccadic and vergence movements, and control of pupillary diameter. A visual stimulus is both *seen* and *looked* at. Visual control does not occur as separate units, e.g., afferent, integrative, and efferent processes. Visual control involves the whole of the visual apparatus and the study of alpha suppression in relation to visual attention requires a consideration of the whole visual processes otherwise a one-sided interpretation will result. This has been the case for the familiar interpretation of

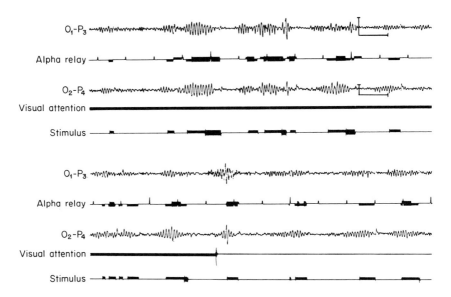

Fig. 4.21. Same as 19. Different subject. BTD on left stimulus.

alpha suppression after visual stimulation, an interpretation which emphasizes the afferent processes, neglecting the receptor adjustment processes.

When Moruzzi and Magoun (1949) introduced the concept of the
reticular activating system they laid the groundwork for an interpretation
of the desynchronization or "activation" of the electrocorticogram and
EEG which has persisted until now. Their discovery that afferent excitation passed along collaterals into the midbrain up to the thalamus and
then to extensive regions in the cortex is known to every student of brain
research. The emphasis was on *afferent* processes, and the extent and
complexity of those processes were shown to be much greater than previously thought. Moreover, they drew an analogy between EEG changes
which occur naturally when an animal "alerts to attention" (Magoun,
1954) and the changes after stimulation of the reticular formation. There
was no consideration of the possibility that efferent processes occurring in
cortex subsequent to the arrival of afferent excitation could also produce
cortical activation and EEG desynchronization. This possibility was there
even in the anesthetized animal because of the difficulty of suppressing
eye movements, i.e., of stopping visual processes. Subsequent research on
the oculomotor system with stimulation and lesion techniques, showed
that processes involved in eye movement were located in the same zone
of the midbrain tegmentum as the reticular activating system (Bender &
Shanzer, 1964).

Moreover, visual processes related to pursuit tracking, fixation and lens accommodation are occurring in cortical regions *17*, *18*, and *19* which are the regions from which the parietal–occipital EEG is derived (Robinson, 1968; Wagman, 1964). These visual functions are also involved in the orienting to visual stimuli. Studies of the occipital EEG and accommodative vergence, pursuit tracking and fast eye movements confirm the hypothesis that the occurrence of alpha is linked not to visual attention but to visual control processes (Mulholland & Peper, 1971). A representative experiment from those studies is presented here.

Adult humans with normal corrected vision and who had recordable occipital alpha with eyes open were studied. Recordings were made in a quiet audiometric test room. Three kinds of recordings were obtained: EEG, EOG, and a report of the apparent clearness or subjective clarity (SC) of the target. EEGs were obtained from parietal–occipital electrodes, $Pi–O_1$, $Pi–O_2$, or occipital $O_1–O_2$ in the international nomenclature. The EEG electrodes were attached to the scalp with electrolytic paste and connected to a Grass Model 5 polygraph. An electrode over the mastoid was ground.

The EEG was automatically classified into intervals of alpha and no-alpha (Mulholland, 1968). The definition of alpha was accomplished by means of a band-pass filter, amplifier, and state relay circuit as described before.

The target moved laterally at eye level in the frontal plane through a distance of 5–6 in. Movement of the target was controlled by two variable-speed motors. These were connected by cams to rigid levers which were linked to the target holder. The levers and motors were noisy when the target was moving. By varying the speed of the motors with a manual control, simple and complex movements could be generated. Target motion was recorded from a potentiometer linked to the movement of the target holder. As the target moved, it turned the potentiometer through a small angle. The change of resistance was recorded as a voltage deflection by connecting the potentiometer between the polygraph driver amplifier and ground. The beginning, direction, and end of target motion was recorded, which was sufficient for these studies.

The EOG was recorded with nonpolarizing AgCl (Beckman) electrodes from the inner and outer canthi for each eye. The EOG showed the beginning, direction, and end of eye movements. At the beginning and end of each trial the EOG for extreme left, right, upward, and downward ocular deviation was recorded. A head or jaw support was used for all subjects. When necessary a bite board was used.

Three kinds of eye movements were recorded: a slow accommodative vergence, slow tracking movements, and fast movements. To record accommodative vergence the target was viewed monocularly, one eye being occluded. Then the target was brought near the viewing eye, the occluded eye moved inward (convergence) while the viewing eye moved outward (divergence). For other subjects the target was viewed binocularly and both eyes showed the symmetrical movements of binocular convergence. Change in vergence was usually associated with a change in subjective clearness of the target. The subject was instructed to press a telegraph key whenever the target appeared clear and focused. The key position was marked on the EEG record. Sometimes the report of subjective clarity (SC) lagged behind the recorded change of vergence.

Pursuit tracking movements were distinguished from fast movements by a slower velocity and close correspondence with target motion. They were distinguished from vergence movements by their velocity. Vergence movements were slower and each eye moved in opposite directions.

The EEG, EOG, and subjective clarity (SC) report were recorded while viewing a target moving laterally in a complex, unpredictable trajectory.

Tracking tasks and instructions were focus and track the target (focus–track, FT); relax accommodation until the target is subjectively blurred and continue tracking (blur–track, BT); or relax accommodation and not track (blur–no-track, BNT). The number of experimental trials sometimes varied from subject to subject. For this reason, data for each subject are presented separately. Fourteen subjects were tested. Two subjects showed no alpha under any of the conditions; three did not monitor target clearness reliably. The EEG results for the last three were similar to those obtained by the majority of the remaining nine subjects whose results are presented here.

The quantification of the EEG was based on measures made on the ink tracing:

Alpha index. State relay ON defined alpha; OFF defined no-alpha. From these the series of durations of alpha and no-alpha events were obtained and an estimate of percentage of time alpha.

Maximum alpha amplitude. In each trial the maximum peak-to-peak amplitude of alpha associated with state relay ON was measured in millimeters.

Alpha delay. The delay between the beginning of an experiment trial and the first state relay ON (alpha) was measured.

Total time. The total time (in seconds) for each trial was measured. The beginning of a trial was defined as the ON or OFF interval during which the brief instructions were given over the intercom as prearranged with the subject. These were "focus–track," "blur–track," and "blur–no-track." The total time in each trial was also measured. The mean of total time, percent time "alpha," maximum "alpha" amplitude, and "alpha" delay were analyzed by analysis of variance.

With divergence and a report of a "blurred" target and no pursuit tracking, "alpha" occurs more often, with greater maximum amplitude and sooner (see Table 4-2). For percentage of time alpha the average for FT < BNT for nine subjects; FT < BT < BNT, six subjects. For maximum alpha amplitude FT < BNT, six; FT < BT < BNT, two subjects. For alpha delay FT > BNT, eight subjects; BT > BNT, seven subjects; FT > BT > BNT, four subjects. For total time FT < BNT, four subjects; FT < BT < BNT, no subjects.

Analysis of variance for the differences among conditions FT, BT, and BNT yielded F significant ($p < .05$) for maximum alpha amplitude; F significant ($p < .001$) for percentage of time alpha. The F ratios for total time and alpha delay were not significant. Figure 4.22 illustrates these results. Saccadic eye movements were not reliably associated with a decrease of alpha occurrence.

It is true of control systems using negative feedback that good control

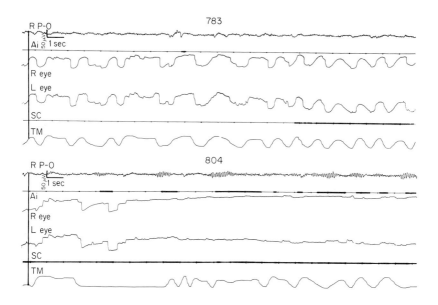

Fig. 4.22. Tracings are: R P-O right parietal-occipital EEG; Ai, alpha index, R eye, L eye, right and left EOG; SC, subjective clarity of target; TM, target motion. The EEG and EOG for a subject tracking with focused vision, defocusing, then not tracking and still defocused. Alpha increases when tracking ceases. [From Mulholland & Peper, 1971.]

TABLE 4-2

Unpredictably Moving Target[a]

Subject	N trials			Total time			X̄ percent-time alpha			X̄ maximum alpha amplitude (mm)			X̄ alpha delay (sec)		
	FT	BT	BNT	FT	BT	BNT	FT	BT	BNT	FT	BT	BNT	FT	BT	BNT
P.W.	3	3	3	117	114	102	23.3	16.2	28.9	10.6	9.0	10.0	1.6	3.3	1.4
W.C.	4	3	3	65	98	80	10.8	17.1	38.8	4.8	4.3	7.0	3.8	2.3	2.0
S.F.	3	3	3	68	64	86	3.8	5.2	34.3	6.3	4.6	10.3	7.7	2.1	1.8
S.L.	3	3	3	112	85	107	1.8	3.4	20.5	4.0	8.0	11.5	9.9	9.2	3.8
R.H.	2	2	2	51	68	41	48.7	80.7	75.4	11.0	8.2	8.0	1.6	.6	.5
R.D.	2	2	2	91	71	79	6.6	9.9	46.3	8.0	7.5	9.5	8.5	1.1	4.4
W.P.	3	3	3	132	171	132	15.1	41.9	44.7	12.0	15.0	16.5	7.6	3.9	1.3
R.G.	3	3	3	180	149	258	9.4	15.1	12.2	10.0	7.5	10.0	3.1	5.2	4.6
A.M.	3	3	3	106	59	70	2.1	13.9	41.1	7.3	11.6	10.6	4.7	6.3	2.6
X̄				102.4	97.6	106.1	13.5	22.6	38.2	8.2	8.4	10.4	5.4	3.8	2.5

[a] From Mulholland and Peper (1971).

in terms of frequency response and stability can result even if the components of the system are somewhat noisy, i.e., have an imperfect reliability. The characteristics of a feedback system can be identified even though there is "loose" causal coupling among the component operators. This empirical fact has a methodological counterpart—feedback configurations can be used to detect causal links among variables even though the functional relationship includes noise or unpredictable variation. Thus, if one hypothesizes A causes B or, if A, then B, etc., then connecting B back to A through an external path should produce different effects depending on the sign of feedback from B, i.e., whether feedback is positive or negative. The contrast between these two kinds of feedback effects is an index of the reliability of the link A to B (Mulholland, 1968). For instance, if it were true that a visual stimulus decreased alpha to some minimum and that absence of visual stimulation increased it to a maximum, then connecting the EEG alpha back to the stimulus with negative feedback should produce a stable oscillation between alpha and no-alpha whose frequency would depend on the transfer function of the system. With positive feedback it should go to a limit of maximum or minimum alpha or swing erratically between these limits. Of course, this does not happen because in fact the hypothesis is incorrect—absence of visual stimulus does not increase alpha to a maximum, nor does increasing a visual stimulus decrease it to a minimum. This is already known. There are other variables which must be identified. As these variables are introduced into the feedback system the difference between positive and negative feedback should increase and provide evidence that the variables are, in fact, relevant. In the following experiment, hypothesized variables are connected into the system until the maximum difference between negative and positive delayed feedback was achieved.

The basic feedback connection was between the alpha-attenuation cycle and the visibility of the target which can be stationary or moving. The variables which were introduced were target visibility, target motion, and modes of oculomotor response. The changes of the alpha activation cycle were compared among the various feedback configurations for the time series of duration of alpha events, the duration of no-alpha events and the period (Δt alpha $+$ Δt no-alpha) of the alpha-attenuation cycle. If the experimental variables loaded on the system are causally linked to the EEG response, they should exhibit minimum variation under negative feedback and swing erratically and unpredictably between limits with positive feedback.

In one experiment in my laboratory, E. Peper connected the EEG by an external path to the visibility of the moving target by an external path. Eye-tracking functions were linked to target visibility by instruction to the subject. The experimental set-up was that described previously. When in view the target was always moving in a quasi-sinusoidal path. The subject was instructed to view the target and track it whenever it was visible. Peper found in all cases where alpha was present with eyes open that the EEG showed a very stable alternation between Δt alpha and Δt no-alpha with Loop 1 (alpha → target ON, no-alpha → OFF). With the reverse configuration Loop 2 (alpha → target OFF and no-alpha → target ON), a runaway system with erratic swinging between long periods of alpha and no tracking and no-alpha and tracking was observed. The contrast between negative and positive feedback was clearly greater than what we had observed previously with stationary targets (see Fig. 4.23). It was concluded that the tracking process was linked to the EEG occipital alpha-activation cycle and that Loop 1 was a negative feedback, and Loop 2 a positive feedback configuration.

One can therefore hypothesize quite reasonably that both efferent visual control processes and afferent processes and their integration occurring in cortex are involved in the suppression of alpha after stimulation. Moreover this hypothesis permits an interpretation of transitory suppression of alpha when eyes are opened in the dark or when one "attempts to see" in the dark, without resorting to a demon called "attention." The interpretation of older and recent studies of alpha and attention in terms of visual control processes have been summarized elsewhere (Mulholland, 1968, 1969, 1972; Mulholland & Peper, 1971).

B. A NEW EXPERIMENTAL APPROACH TO THE CLASSICAL THEORY

The response of the occipital EEG after visual stimulation is not singular, it is a disturbance followed by a recovery of the alpha-attenuation cycle; as shown before. The alternation is not invariant but changes with the availability of visual information. Though looking can be initiated voluntarily it does not continue in the absence of visual stimulation. To start looking again a new command must be given to the visual apparatus. Intervals of alpha and little or no-alpha may reflect in a gross way a "not-look"–"look," a "not-scan"–"scan" system. Such a system would be related to a schedule of the sampling of visual information. When information was high look (no-alpha) samples would be long and no-look (alpha) times briefer. As information became redundant or not relevant, look samples would be briefer and not-look times would be longer. Also, one may see or be aware of stimuli yet not look at them. In this sense, one could be attending to a stimulus, but without *looking* there would be little or no effect on the alpha rhythm.

The habituation of the response to stimulation may be a change in the visual field sampling function in response to an increasingly redundant

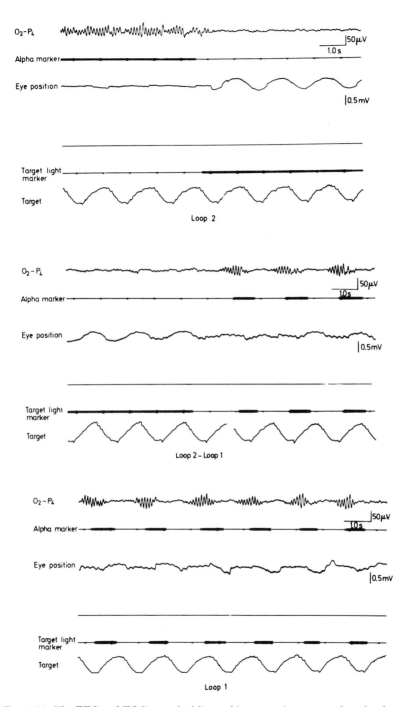

Fig. 4.23. The EEG and EOG record while tracking a moving target whose luminance is controlled by the occurrence of alpha. Transition from Loop 2 feedback to Loop 1. [From Peper, 1970.]

stimulus. This approach lends naturally to a time-series analysis of alpha and no-alpha events during habituation rather than an overemphasis on the singular, no-alpha intervals after successive stimulations.

A second classical assumption was that all alpha events reflect the same level of behavioral or psychological function. For instance all alpha intervals were assumed to indicate a *low* level of visual attention, all no-alpha, low amplitude–fast activity were assumed to indicate a *high* level of visual attention. This assumption of *functional equivalence* is seen in those statistical procedures whereby all alpha events are pooled to get percent-time alpha or where all intervals of no-alpha are lumped together as an index of orienting.

Although direct experimental evidence is lacking, it is worthwhile to consider an alternative hypothesis that all alpha and all no-alpha events are not functionally equivalent. For instance, when habituation to a recurring visual stimulus, as described before, the changes in $\bar{\Delta}t_a$ and $\bar{\Delta}t_{na}$ can be approximated by the function where N is equal to or less than 50.

$$\bar{\Delta}t_a = AN + B$$

$$\bar{\Delta}t_{na} = C/N + D.$$

Behavioral performance, attention, alertness, etc., may not necessarily be functions of alpha versus no-alpha but functions of the habituation functions. It is possible that an interval of alpha occurring just after stimulation is associated with a higher level of visual attention or behavioral alertness than is an interval of little or no-alpha occurring after 30 alpha events. If the stimuli are say, words to be memorized or learned, perhaps learning is complete when habituation reaches an asymptote, etc.

The assumption of functional equivalence is related to the assumption of response singularity because then the initial, singular no-alpha is also at the beginning of the habituation process. The behavioral changes which are observed during that initial, single no-alpha interval may not be true of other intervals of no-alpha, i.e., they may be functions of the habituation function.

A third classical assumption is that all parts of an interval of no-alpha, low amplitude–fast activity, are associated with an identical psychological or behavioral state. For instance, the "blocking" of alpha after visual stimulation is said to reflect a state of arousal, alertness, activation, or increased attention. By means of such concepts the disappearance or suppression of alpha is explained. However, after awhile alpha returns. How is the recurrence of alpha explained? There must be a return to a *lower* level of arousal, alertness, activation, or attention. Obviously the sequence of changes from alpha to no-alpha back to alpha implies a dynamic cycle, another kind of disturbance and recovery *within* the no-alpha interval.

The idea that the EEG activation or desynchronization was composed of different processes was expressed by Sharpless and Jasper (1956). In their terms there are two components to the response of the EEG to stimulation—a *phasic* response and a *tonic* response. Phasic responses have a short latency, brief duration, and do not habituate. Tonic responses have a longer latency, a longer duration, and habituate readily. Sharpless and Jasper showed that different brain processes were involved for phasic compared to tonic responses.

The blocking of alpha to stimulation includes both phasic and tonic components. The latency of an alpha block has to be the phasic latency as it always occurs and is briefer than the tonic latency. The phasic activation may end quickly and, the tonic process, already begun, will continue and alpha will not occur. In this way the processes at the beginning of an alpha block would be phasic while those at the end after the phasic process has subsided would include the tonic process. The longer the duration of desynchronization or alpha suppression the greater the difference between early phasic and late tonic parts of a no-alpha interval. After habituation has occurred, the no-alpha may be due to phasic processes, since Sharpless and Jasper showed that the tonic component became habituated, but not the phasic.

These considerations point to some new kinds of experiments, which test the hypothesis that electrophysiological and behavioral changes may be occurring within the interval of low-amplitude–fast activity. For instance, if a stimulus were systematically delayed so that it was made to occur near the beginning, near the middle, or near the end of an interval of no-alpha would the average evoked response be the same for these three delays? Would the latency of fast eye movement to a new target be the same if the movement occurred just after an interval of no-alpha began compared to a longer delay so that it occurred just before alpha returned? From this paradigm one can imagine studies of stimulus thresholds, pattern recognition using tachistoscopic method, learning and remembering as a function of the amount of delay between the start of the no-alpha interval and the stimulus. By means of such studies, some estimate of the functional changes within the no-alpha interval can be made.

All of these ideas are summarized in the schema of the alpha-attenuation series, presented in Fig. 4.24 (Mulholland, 1969). Some process which is associated with alpha gives way to a suppression of alpha if a critical value is reached. However, after a time the processes reverse moving toward the value favorable for alpha. The series alternates in a complex

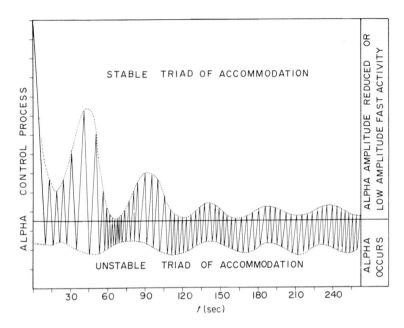

Fig. 4.24. Hypothetical schema of the alpha-attenuation series. [From Mulholland, 1969.]

way. The schema points up the difference between the older and the newer hypotheses. The response is a series, all intervals of all alpha and all intervals of no-alpha may not be functionally equivalent and all parts of a given interval may not be functionally identical. This schema is only a guide to experimentation and may be quite incomplete or incorrect. Nature has an endless capacity to outwit theorists.

The fundamental question of the alpha process is of course still obscure and functional experiments cannot provide an answer. However, when neurophysiology provides the necessary evidence and alpha *is* explained, we shall understand the neurophysiological basis for the observations and the empirical findings already made and verified during the brief history of research on the occipital alpha rhythm in relation to human attention.

1. Practical Applications

In conclusion, I would like to speculate on some applications of feedback EEG in relation to visual control as I see them. Some of these are already close at hand, others require considerable development (Mulholland, 1970). The following groups of applications are intended as an outline.

Alertometers. This would be a system for comparing one visual display with another in terms of the alertness of the viewers. With the aid of a computer, the attentional-looking response of brain rhythms could be averaged and printed out on a graph, an alertograph. Such a system could be mobile, that is, a specially equipped vehicle could be used to sample alertographs in various areas permitting regional and market comparisons. With modern radio telemetry techniques people need not be connected to the brain wave machine by a cable. This would permit study of attentive looking in more natural settings. Such a system would also have application in research on the many variables linked to attentive looking, for instance the ontogenesis or development of attention, and changes due aging.

Attention controllers. In this application a computer is used. It looks at the response of the brain rhythms to the visual stimulus and compares the response against a rule that has been programmed. If the brain response is too little, it changes the visual display according to its program until the proper brain response is achieved. This feature could be incorporated into a teaching machine which would present a warning or alerting signal or change the display to keep the subject paying attention.

A more complex system would require a large variety of visual displays. The rule of the game would be to present visual displays which produced the most brain rhythm reaction. The computer would store the reactions and use this past experience in selecting a visual display. After awhile the computer would make selections which in fact produced the most attentive looking for the longest time. It would be most interesting to find out what this set of "alerting" visual displays was like.

Display controllers. Here the characteristics of a display could be controlled by attentive looking, which is also under voluntary control. For instance, when alpha was suppressed by attentive looking a series of visual displays could be presented at a rapid rate. A much slower rate plus a warning could be given when alpha occurred. In the case where there is a continuing inspection of stimuli required, then the rate of presentation of the various objects would be so regulated by attentive looking that the best inspection would occur. One can imagine a vehicle or machine which is unsafe if the operator is not attentive or alert. Such a machine could be automatically shut down if attentive looking flagged below a critical level.

Attention compensators. This is a special case of display controller. Here the display would magnify or exaggerate the visual display effect of attention to make up for an attention defect. For instance, when a person was not attentively looking at a visual display it would get brighter or clearer or larger, permitting a better reception of it.

Attention trainers. Here the goal would be to use feedback to tell a person when his brain rhythms indicated that he was alert. He would practice until he could voluntarily change the display indicating that attentive looking, or not, was achieved. Such training might help people to improve their attentive-looking behavior. They may learn an improved self-control of attention. Experimental studies show that by feedback training, control of the brain rhythms is improved (Nowlis & Kamiya, 1970; Peper & Mulholland, 1970).

In these applications I have talked about brain wave responses. It would be important also to study eye movement and pupillary changes to make displays controlled by eye behavior. In these ways we may improve the evaluation and automatic control of visual displays in terms of their effect on the orienting response of the viewer.

The Discussion of Dr. Mulholland's Paper

LED BY DR. WILLIAM GRINGS

University of Southern California

Grings: The papers which we have heard thus far have impressed me by the extent to which they give clarity to one of the terms in our program title, namely "psychophysiology." In all cases the presentations have attended to both sides of the definition of that field, that is, to both the psyche and the physiology. Our past discussion questions have been similarly oriented. I expect that the questions for this paper will be divided between the matters of achieving an adequate psychological definition of attention and the deciding among available physiological measures. It takes ingenuity to work on both sides of a concept like attention, and the present paper provides novel integrating material.

The variable of time delay feedback poses a number of questions. One was raised with reference to the auditory detection problem. During the paper there was no mention of work with acoustic stimuli. Have the time delay feedback manipulations been checked out with auditory stimuli in a fashion similar to that used with lights?

Another question concerns the role that specific instructions to the subjects about the time delay variable may have on the variable's efficacy. Such information to the subject will clearly determine his sensorimotor adjustment to the performance task.

For persons interested in conditioning behavior, there is a clear parallel between the operation of the feedback manipulation where two stimuli are involved and other situations involving discrimination among stimuli. The question arises about the resemblance of the feedback manipulation to instances in learning where various forms of differential reinforcement are applied to accomplish discrimination behavior.

Which brings up questions concerning the generality of the gross shift manipulation and the extent to which it can be elaborated or extended. This probably leads to specific procedural matters regarding manipulation of the on–off variable and the extent to which these procedural parameters are critical to the appearance of the phenomena. One question relates to criteria for cut-off and criteria for various kinds of triggering operations.

Open Discussion

Mulholland: With regard to auditory stimulation as feedback, there is a very brief effect. The disturbance of the system does not occur with the same magnitude as with visual stimuli, and it very rapidly habituates. This can be attributed to the role the oculomotor system plays in the orienting of response to any stimulus. In a dark homogenous field, listening to sound stimuli, there will be a brief orienting response, which includes the looking response. This response very rapidly habituates because it is not followed-up by any target feedback. If you use the method for auditory detection, you would have to be observing "on-line," because it would rapidly habituate.

I have to agree that the question of the arbitrary definition of alpha due to the cut-offs and the triggering functions is difficult. We have tried various criteria. We wanted to detect alpha as quickly as we could, but this did not work. Even though we could detect alpha within half a cycle, the system was very noisy, relative to the orienting response. The criterion for the threshold is determined by taking the maximum output, during resting, over a 2–5-min interval. We then examined the probability of making an alpha detection in a series of records with various threshold settings. We got an approximation to a sensitivity function, which was fairly flat when the threshold was high; when the threshold was lowered, the function increased rapidly. The probability of an alpha detection increased very rapidly as threshold went below 20% of the maximum. We set the threshold at the point of inflection of that function where the rate of change of threshold and percent detection attained a slope of -1. If you use that threshold, the stimulus on–off delays tend to be equal. This was a good feature for us, but it is arbitrary. You would get different results if you lowered the threshold.

Dr. Robert Chapman (Eye Research Foundation of Bethesda): You are saying that there are three major things that control alpha: visual input, something about efferent output, and attention? That may be wrong, but I just want to talk about one of them—all your data could be explained by dropping out the efferent aspect of the explanation. In the two-light case, where the subject is supposed to pay attention to one light or the other, he might be shifting his gaze. We know that there is an amplification of the visual input when the visual stimulus falls on the fovea, so we might expect that kind of change; such is a visual input, even though it is brought about by an efferent change that shifted the eyes. The question is whether it is the intent to shift the eye, or whether it is really the change in the afferent (visual) input consequent to that light.

Mulholland: In the two-light experiments there would be all three, input, output, and "attention." I would like to drop attention. Attention, as far as the EEG goes, can be reduced to the input functions and ongoing adjustments of the receptor. That is why I talked about *seeing* and *looking*. When you look at a visible target, you cannot unravel the two, except at the initiation of the process, and if there is a measure of when the efferent process started.

When the subject's eyes are open in the dark, or when the subject intends to look in a certain direction, there may be some kind of relevant attention process. But terms such as "directed attention," "focusing one's attention," are really metaphors for visual control.

Chapman: The specific experiment in which you manipulated the efferent aspect, concerned learning and not learning, that is, tracking and not tracking; this was an instructional procedure. To the extent that the subject defocuses to the point that he blurs, that means the visual input is different. So, again, we have confusion as to what the afferent input is and what the control is; now that can be divorced by a different technique. If you put ancillary lenses in, such that the subject's accommodation cannot overcome it, then you can manipulate what the accommodative response actually is, and separate it from the visual input.

Mulholland: My experiment was not intended to separate input functions from eye movement control functions; it was to test the hypothesis about ongoing monitoring of the target, that is, to determine if the visual attention hypothesis were incorrect. We had the subject monitor the clarity of the target, and then showed, by these complicated ocular exercises, that the alpha shifted as a function of whether or not he was tracking with relaxed accommodation. Monitoring the target has to include what we mean by "visual attention."

The key problem is that when the subject directs his gaze in the dark, you will always confound the attentional, and output variables. My study provides circumstantial evidence in support of the efferent oculomotor hypothesis, and it points to some neurophysiological studies. One might look at the outflow down to the extrinsic ocular muscles and evaluate the EEG desynchronization in terms of what is involved there. I don't think the EEG studies can answer your question. Also looking in the dark blocks the alpha rhythms. This cannot be explained on the basis of change in stimulation.

Chapman: Would you predict that looking in the dark would produce accommodative changes? That would suggest an experiment in which one actually determines what such oculomotor changes are.

Mulholland: If you give a person a task, say "look straightahead in the dark," the eyes will fixate momentarily, then they will drift from that position, since there is no target feedback. If there were not oculomotor changes in the dark, associated with the alpha blocking, then we would have to say that our hypothesis is incorrect. We already know that eyes move when you do this in the dark, but the experiment combining the oculomotor and EEG has not been done. Also, when the subject clenches one fist, then there is a blocking of central alpha in the recording from the opposite hemisphere, followed by blocking on the same side but a little later. If he clenches both fists, alpha blocks on both sides at the same time. If motor responses block the central alpha, then may not oculomotor responses block the posterior alpha?

Dr. Johann Stoyva (University of Colorado): What happens to alpha if the oculomotor system is inactivated, and also if an animal is enucleated?

Mulholland: With regard to a case of binocular enucleation, the alpha was irregular and not well defined; but it did block to auditory stimuli. That really poked a hole in our thinking. Such cases might have muscle remnants that can still receive efferent impulses; there could be cortical processes which would ordinarily eventuate in movement. I asked Dr. Bender, who is an expert on oculomotor systems, if that could happen, but his experience would not permit him to say whether that would be enough to desynchronize the EEG.

There is also a problem with blind subjects. If a person is blind from birth, his alpha is absent; a person who loses his sight later in life may have some alpha. So there seems to be an intimate relationship between the appearance of alpha and the integrity of vision.

All of our work has been concerned with the blocking of alpha, and we can identify conditions that are very likely to block alpha; but we don't have any good explanation for why, when these conditions are not present, the alpha returns. The genesis of the alpha rhythm is still an enigma and constitutes an obstacle for our kind of functional investigation.

Dr. Paul Woods (Hollins College): Your puzzlement regarding the response when the eyes are open in the dark might be answered by considering the past history of the organism. In evolutionary situations, the eyes have been opened *many* times to visual stimuli, perhaps producing conditioning—perhaps a sensory-preparatory hookup allows the brain to respond to the opening of the eyes prior to the onset of the visual input.

Mulholland: Would it be the looking response that we conditioned so that the subject starts to look as soon as he opens his eyes?

Woods: Maybe a conditional central preparatory reaction to the expectation of the stimuli following the output.

Mulholland: Dr. Black comments that "conditioning" of an EEG wave exclusively of something else is increasingly difficult to demonstrate. The suspicion is growing that the conditioning of brain waves involves the conditioning of motor processes. When you open your eyes in the dark, learned responses associated with looking occur, and these could be associated with the transitory blocking of alpha.

REFERENCES

Adrian, E. D. The dominance of vision. *Opthalmological Society, U.K.*, 1943, **63**, 194–207.

Adrain, E. D., & Matthews, B. H. C. The Berger rhythm: Potential changes from the occipital lobes in man. *Brain*, 1934, **57**, 354–385.

Berger, H. On the electroencephalogram of man. In P. Gloor, (Ed.), Hans Berger on the electroencephalogram of man. (Trans.) *Electroencephalography and Clinical Neurophysiology, Suppl.*, 1969, **28**, 75–93. Original published in *Journal fur Psychologie und Neurologie*, 1930, **40**, 160–179.

Bender, M., & Shanzer, S. Oculomotor pathways defined by electric stimulation and lesions in the brainstem of monkey. In M. Bender, (Ed.), *The oculomotor system*. New York: Harper, 1964. Pp. 81–140.

Cobb, W. A. The normal adult EEG. In D. H. Hill, & G. Parr, (Eds.), *Electroencephalography: A symposium on its various aspects*. New York: Macmillan, 1963. Pp. 232–239.

Cruikshank, R. M. Human occipital brain potentials as affected by intensity-duration variables of visual stimulation. *Journal of Experimental Psychology*, 1937, **21**, 625–641.

Evans, C. R., & Mulholland, T. B. *Attention in neurophysiology*. London: Butterworths, 1969.

Lindsley, D. B. Attention, consciousness, sleep and wakefulness. In J. Field, H. W. Magoun, & V. E. Hall, (Eds.), *Handbook of physiology*, Vol. III. Washington, D.C.: American Physiological Society, 1960. Pg. 1553.

Mander, J. Arousal to neutral and sexual stimuli as a function of repressor and intellectualized defense styles and stress. Proposal for Ph.D. thesis, Boston University Graduate School, 1971.

Magoun, H. W. The ascending reticular system and wakefulness. In E. D. Adrian, F. Bremer, & H. H. Jasper, (Eds.), *Brain mechanisms and consciousness*. Oxford: Blackwell, 1954. Pg. 1.

Moruzzi, G., & Magoun, H. W. Brain stem reticular formation and activation of the EEG. *Electroencephalography and Clinical Neurophysiology*, 1949, **1**, 455–473.

Mulholland, T. The electroencephalogram as an experimental tool in the study of internal attention gradients. *Transactions of the New York Academy of Science*, 1962. **24**, No. 6., 664–669.

Mulholland, T. Feedback electroencephalography. *Activitas Nervosa Superior, Prague,* 1968, 10, 410–438.

Mulholland, T. B. The concept of attention and the electroencephalographic alpha rhythm. In C. R. Evans, & T. B. Mulholland, (Eds.), *Attention in neurophysiology.* London, Butterworths: 1969. Pp. 100–127.

Mulholland, T. Automatic control of visual displays by the attention of the human viewer. In C. M. Williams, & J. L. Debes (Eds.), *1st National Conference on Visual, Literacy.* New York: Pitman, 1970. Pp. 70–80.

Mulholland, T. Can you really turn on with alpha? Paper presented to the Masschusetts Psychological Association, Boston College, May 7, 1971.

Mulholland, T. Occipital alpha revisited. *Psychological Bulletin,* 1972, (in press).

Mulholland, T., & Davis, E. Electroencephalographic activation non-specific habituation by verbal stimuli. *Science,* 1966, **152,** 1104–1106.

Mulholland, T., & Evans, C. R. Oculomotor function and the alpha-activation cycle. *Nature,* 1966, **211,** 1278–1279.

Mulholland, T., & Peper, E. Occipital alpha and accommodative vergence, pursuit tracking and fast eye movements. *Psychophysiology,* 1971, **8,** 556–575.

Mulholland, T., & Runnals, S. Evaluation of attention and alertness with a stimulus-brain feedback loop. *Electroencephalography and Clinical Neurophysiology,* 1962, **14,** 847–852. (a)

Mulholland, T., & Runnals, S. A stimulus-brain feedback system for evaluation of alertness. *Journal Psychology,* 1962, **54,** 69–83. (b)

Mulholland, T., & Runnals, S. The effect of voluntarily directed attention on successive cortical activation responses. *Journal Psychology,* 1963, **55,** 427–436.

Mulholland, T., & Runnals, S. Cortical activation during steady and changing stimulation. *Electroencephalography and Clinical Neurophysiology,* 1964, **17,** 371–375. (a)

Mulholland, T., & Runnals, S. Cortical activation by alternate visual and auditory stimuli. *Cortex,* 1964, **1,** 225–232. (b)

Nowlis, D. P., & Kamiya, J. The control of electroencephalographic alpha rhythms through auditory feedback and the associated mental activity. *Psychophysiology,* 1970, **6,** 476–484.

Peper, E. Feedback regulation of the alpha electroencephalogram activity through control of the internal and external parameters. *Kybernetic,* 1970, 7, 107–112.

Peper, E., & Mulholland, T. Methodological and theoretical problems in the voluntary control of electroencephalographic occipital alpha by the subject. *Kybernetic,* 1970, **7,** 10–13.

Robinson, D. A. Eye movement control in primates. *Science,* 1968, **161,** 1219–1224.

Sharpless, S., & Jasper, H. H. Habituation of the arousal reaction. *Brain,* 1956, **79,** 655–680.

Sokolov, Y. N. *Perception and the conditioned reflex.* Oxford: Pergamon Press, 1963.

Stark, L., Michael, J. A., & Zuber, B. L. Saccadic suppression: A product of the saccadic anticipatory signal. In C. R. Evans, & T. B. Mulholland (Eds.), *Attention in neurophysiology.* London: Butterworths, 1969. Pg. 291.

Wagman, I. H. Eye momvenents induced by electric stimulation of cerebrum in monkeys and their relationship to bodily movements. In M. Bender (Ed.), *The oculomotor system.* New York: Harper, 1964. Pp. 18–39.

Woodworth, R., & Schlossberg, H. *Experimental psychology.* New York: Holt, 1954.

CHAPTER FIVE

The Psychophysiology of Mental Activity during Sleep[1]

ALLAN RECHTSCHAFFEN
University of Chicago

Why might sleep research have some special contribution to make to the psychophysiology of thinking?

1. Sleep studies permit examination of the generality of psychophysiological relationships determined during wakefulness. Do the relationships of wakefulness reflect necessary links between physiological measures and

[1] Preparation of this paper was supported by Grants M-4151 and K5-MH-18,428 from the National Institute of Mental Health, U.S. Public Health Service, and Grant 148-13-RD from the Department of Mental Health, State of Illinois.

153

the kinds of responses which are generally taken to reflect mental activity? If they do, we would expect the relationships to obtain during sleep as well. If, on the other hand, the relationships of wakefulness reflect only one specific kind of psychophysiological organization rather than necessary causal or isomorphic relationships, then we would not necessarily expect to find the same psychophysiological relationships during sleep.

2. Any search for correlations is enhanced by variability in the parameters studied. Although there are exceptions, notably in autonomic measures such as heart and respiratory rates, there is generally greater physiological and psychological variability during sleep than during wakefulness. For example, the EEG of wakefulness is fairly uniform in amplitude and fluctuates mostly between alpha and low voltage fast activity. The EEG of sleep, by contrast, can range from less than 10 μV to over 200 μV, and from less than .5 Hz to over 25 Hz. Between these limits there is a rich display of distinctive waveforms during sleep, such as 2–3 Hz "sawtooth" waves, 4–6 Hz "theta" activity, biparietal humps, K-complexes, and 12–14 Hz sleep spindles. During wakefulness the eyes move intermittently throughout the day, depending on the task at hand. During sleep there are well-defined long periods with little or no rapid eye movement and well-defined periods with a wealth of eye movement activity.

The enhanced variability of mental activity during sleep is even more apparent. Certainly wakefulness has its ups and downs—its more emotional moments and its less emotional moments—its more attentive moments and its less attentive moments. On most days, however, there is a fairly stable level of consciousness with few or no extended periods that we would describe either as completely blank or fantastically stimulating and exciting. By contrast, during each night of sleep we fluctuate many times between apparent mental voids and a sort of low-keyed mental idling on the one hand, and the vivid, highly emotional, absorbing material of vivid dreams on the other. Thus sleep provides the pronounced variability of physiological and psychological activity that should be opportune for revealing correlations between the two.

3. Sleep permits evaluation of psychological–physiological correlations under conditions of reduced responsivity to external stimuli. Where the focus of study is on the "spontaneous" covariation of psychological and physiological parameters, the lower responsivity of sleep aids the cause by reducing the error variance contributed by nonexperimental stimuli. Where the focus of interest is a comparison of physiological and psychological responses to given stimuli, then sleep studies suffer from the limited range and intensity of stimuli that can be introduced.

4. Finally, as with any new area of investigation, the study of sleep permits the discovery of new relationships and phenomena which could not have been anticipated from studies of wakefulness. It has been almost 20 years since Aserinsky and Kleitman (1953) first reported on the eye movement–dreaming relationship that started the boom in psychophysiological sleep research; it may be mostly verbal habit that still makes us refer to this sleep research as a new area. Nevertheless, the past two decades have provided a flow of stimulating discoveries that were not anticipated by the psychophysiology of wakefulness.

This paper will review research on relationships between physiological and psychological measures during sleep to see how well the potentials listed above have been realized. Reliance will be placed on reports elicited on awakenings as the indicators of mental activity during sleep. Several variables other than sleep mentation can influence waking reports including verbal style, memory, and alertness upon awakening. But the verbal report is probably the best available indicator of sleep mentation so researchers stay with it and try to hold the nonexperiential factors which influence reports relatively stable with respect to the physiological measures. Even with an attempt to achieve this kind of control, correlations between a report and a physiological variable could result from a relationship of the physiological variable to the *recall* process rather than to the sleep mentation. Therefore, the terms "recall" or "sleep mentation" in this review, strictly speaking, refer to the verbal production. In spite of all controls, there is always a residue of uncertainty about how much of verbal production was determined by sleep mentation. For example, some studies aim at the physiological correlates of how much mental activity there was during sleep. But we cannot be certain whether the amount reported reveals the amount of mental activity that was present or the amount that could be remembered. The problem of using awakening reports as indicators of sleep mentation has been reviewed in greater detail in another paper (Rechtschaffen, 1967).

I. DESCRIPTION OF THE STAGES OF SLEEP

As a subject passes from wakefulness to sleep, there is a gradual slowing of EEG activity. The waking EEG, be it alpha or low voltage–fast activity, gradually subsides and is replaced by a relatively low voltage, mixed frequency pattern with increased activity in the 2–7 Hz band. This pattern is called Stage 1. After 5–10 min of Stage 1, bursts of 12–14 Hz sinusoidal waves called sleep spindles and isolated higher voltage biphasic waves called K-complexes appear and define the presence of Stage 2. After varying amounts of Stage 2, high voltage, slow "delta waves" signal the appearance of Stage 3. This delta activity increases gradually so that it dominates the record, which is then called Stage 4. Stages 1–4 collectively are called NREM, or *no* rapid eye movement sleep, because it was once believed that there were no rapid eye movements during these periods. Recently, more refined recording techniques have revealed the intermittent occurrence of small rapid eye movements during NREM sleep, and more will be said about that later. For the moment we need note only that these eye movements are much less plentiful than in the now well-known REM, or rapid eye movement periods of sleep. Sometime during the second hour of sleep, large amplitude eye movements occur episodically during periods when EEG activity is very similar to the Stage 1 observed at sleep onset. These REM periods may last from a few minutes to over a half-hour. They reappear at about 90-min intervals during sleep so that typically there are about four REM periods a night, comprising altogether about one-fourth of total sleep.

The EEG stages of sleep and their associated eye movement patterns are shown in Fig. 5.1. These stages should not be construed to represent a

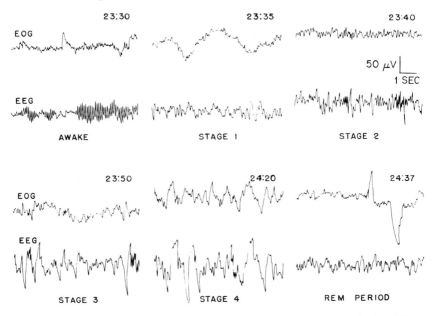

Fig. 5.1. Illustration of the eye movement (EOG) and EEG patterns in the different stages of sleep. The potentials in the EOG tracings of Stages 2, 3, and 4 represent EEG activity in prefrontal areas rather than eye movements.

continuum of light to deep in the general sense that the brain, body, or nervous system is more active in one stage than another—as common sense or our wish for order might dictate. Rather, the stages represent different neurophysiological organizations of activity. As we shall see, some measures may be elevated and others depressed within a stage. For example, it is usually most difficult to awaken a subject from Stage 4 (Rechtschaffen, Hauri, & Zeitlin, 1966), yet heart rate and spontaneous GSR activity may be at their highest levels of the night during this stage.

Figure 5.2 illustrates the progression of stages through the night during the last 7 of 15 consecutive nights which one subject (the author) spent sleeping in the laboratory. As is true of most subjects who are relatively

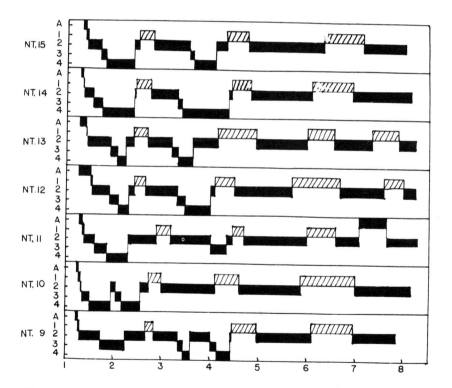

Fig. 5.2. Progression of sleep stages during seven consecutive nights in one subject. Designations of 1–4 along the ordinate indicate the respective sleep stages; "A" indicates awake. REM periods are shown by the bars with diagonal markings. Very brief stage changes were omitted for purposes of schematic clarity.

good sleepers and accustomed to the laboratory, the sleep pattern remains relatively stable from night to night, e.g., the first REM period occurs at about the same time each night, as does the second and third. Note that Stages 3 and 4 appear mostly during the early part of the night.

II. RELATIONSHIP OF MENTAL ACTIVITY TO SLEEP STAGES

To venture an historical interpretation, it now seems fortunate that some of the earliest work on this area suffered from a certain crudeness of data collection, data analysis, and, very likely, a very fortuitous selection of subjects. Were it not for the overly simplified but attractive generalizations which resulted, sleep research might not have gained the popularity that it did during the next 15 years, and most of the substantial discoveries which resulted from this research might not have been made.

The great interest in psychophysiological dream research started with the report by Aserinsky and Kleitman (1953) that 74% of awakenings from REM sleep produced dream recall, as compared to 9% of awakenings from NREM sleep. The next published study in this area (Dement & Kleitman, 1957) reported similar results: 80% dream recall on REM awakenings and only 7% dream recall on NREM awakenings. Dement and Kleitman suggested that the dream reports elicited on NREM awakenings probably represented the recall of dreams experienced earlier in the night.

These early findings and the interpretations that were attached to them encouraged general acceptance of the view that dreaming occurred in all REM periods and that NREM sleep was a mental void. Indeed, it was my own initial belief in this view that attracted me to this field of research. When I first arrived at the University of Chicago 14 years ago, I chanced to be introduced to Edward Wolpert, then a medical student at the University. Wolpert had learned the REM research techniques from William Dement who had just completed his graduate and medical studies at Chicago. Wolpert told me a bit about this field of research—which I had not heard about until then—and invited me to observe an experiment of his own which he was conducting in Dr. Kleitman's laboratory. My first evening of observing Wolpert's experiment decided my choice of work from that time to the present. I remember Wolpert poised over an old 4-channel Grass Model III EEG. (This historic machine was used by Aserinsky, Kleitman, Dement, Wolpert, Kamiya, Foulkes, and myself— in short, the whole first generation of Chicago REM researchers. The same machine is still in use in Chicago.) Wolpert showed me the rapid eye movements as they were traced on the moving paper and told me that when he awoke the subject we would hear a vivid dream report; that is exactly what happened. About a half-hour later, Wolpert pointed out the spindles and lack of eye movements of Stage 2. He said that this time the subject would have nothing to report upon awakening, and that is just what happened. At that point, I said to myself something like, "My God, here is the mind turning on and off during sleep, and we actually have a physiological indicator of when it is happening. What better opportunity is there to study how the mind and body are related?"

As it turned out, my initial impressions and the interpretations of the early REM researchers were, as we might expect in the early phases of almost any research, overly simplified. Most of the sleep studies which followed revealed more recall on NREM awakenings than was reported in the first wave of this research. The first of the reports in the "second wave" came from Goodenough, Shapiro, Holden, and Steinschriber (1959) who found that 35% of NREM awakenings led to the report of a dream. These authors were inclined to follow the earlier interpretation that the NREM reports might represent the recall of dreams experienced earlier in the night. Encouraged by a popular press which did not even try to explain inconsistent observations the way the original researchers had, the lay public as well as scientists began to refer to REM and NREM as "dreaming" and "nondreaming" sleep, respectively.

The first to seriously question the exclusive assignment of dreams to REM sleep was Foulkes (1962). Foulkes found that 74% of NREM awakenings produced recall of some mental activity and that 54% produced "dreams" by the criteria that the reported mental experiences contained some sensory imagery, or that in the experiences the subject assumed an identity other than his own or felt that he was in a physical setting other than the laboratory. Five years later, in a review of research on NREM mental activity, Foulkes (1967) would report on nine studies subsequent to the original reports of Aserinsky and Kleitman and Dement and Kleitman. The incidence of NREM recall in these studies ranged from 23 to 74. Obviously, the numbers were now too large to permit dismissal of NREM recall as infrequent products of faulty memory.

Although Foulkes (1966, 1967) has reviewed many of the reasons why NREM reports had not been recognized and accepted as indicative of mental activity during sleep, the reasons are worth a brief review here, since much of our discussion will concern NREM mental activity.

One reason relates to qualitative differences between REM and NREM reports. Foulkes (1962) first reported on these differences as follows: "Reports obtained in periods of REM activity showed more organismic involvement in affective, visual, and muscular dimensions and were more highly elaborated than non-REMP reports. REMP reports showed less correspondence to the waking life of the subject than did reports from spindle and delta sleep. The relatively frequent occurrence of thinking and memory processes in spindle and delta sleep was an especially striking result." Rechtschaffen, Verdone, and Wheaton (1963) reached similar conclusions: ". . . as compared with REM mentation, subjects report NREM mentation as more poorly recalled, more like thinking and less like dreaming, less vivid, less visual, more conceptual, under greater volitional control, more plausible, more concerned with their contemporary lives, occurring in lighter sleep, less emotional, and more pleasant. Our impression is that NREM mentation resembles that large portion of our waking thought which wanders in seemingly disorganized, drifting, nondirected fashion whenever we are not attending to external stimuli or actively working out a problem or a daydream."

Two reports from consecutive awakenings—the first NREM, the second REM—from a subject studied by Rechtschaffen, Vogel, and Shaikun (1963) illustrate the most typical differences between REM and NREM reports.

NREM report: "I had been dreaming about getting ready to take some type of an exam. It had been a very short dream. That's just about all that it contained. I don't think I was worried about them."

REM report: "I was dreaming about exams. In the early part of the dream I was dreaming I had just finished taking an exam, and it was a very sunny day outside. I was walking with a boy who's in some of my classes with me. There was a sort of a, a break, and someone mentioned a grade they had gotten in a social science exam. And I asked them if the social science marks had come in. They said yes. I didn't get it, because I had been away for a day."

Clearly, the second report contains much more of the perceptual vividness and thematic organization that is ordinarily associated with dreaming but the decision about how much of such vividness and thematic coherence a report should contain before it is labeled a dream is arbitrary. Most important, the discovery of wide-variations in mental activity during sleep with widely varying degrees of "dreaminess," underlines the importance of specifying reproducible operations by which the distinction between dream and nondream is made. For example, Dement and Kleitman indicated only that, "The Ss were considered to have been dreaming only if they could relate a coherent, fairly detailed description of dream content." It is doubtful that reliabilities of dream–nondream discriminations would be very high given that criterion alone. Thus, it is very possible that Dement and Kleitman found much less NREM dreaming than the vast majority of subsequent investigators largely because they required more dreaminess[2] of a report before they were willing to call a report a dream. By the criteria imposed by the majority of subsequent investigators, there is much more dreaming in NREM sleep than one would have imagined from the early papers in this area.

Another variable which could have caused different results in different studies is the subject variable. Whereas young adults, the favorite subject of REM type dream content studies, report dreams (by almost any criterion) with high frequency on REM awakenings, the incidence and quality of NREM reports varies widely from subject to subject (Foulkes & Rechtschaffen, 1964). Thus any study with few subjects is susceptible to a sampling error which might bias the results against NREM mentation. (The bulk of data from the original Dement and Kleitman study came from five subjects.)

It did not take very long for sleep researchers generally to accept that NREM reports were more frequent than they had believed. Now the focus of skepticism shifted to how accurate the NREM reports reflected the mental activity of the subject while he was asleep. Foulkes (1966, 1967) has reviewed the major arguments against the acceptance of NREM reports and has effectively, we believe, countered them, therefore we need review this issue only briefly here.

The argument that NREM dream reports might represent dreams experienced in earlier REM periods is countered by several studies which showed that NREM reports, including NREM dream reports, may be elicited on awakenings made before any REM periods have occurred. Another argument has been that NREM reports may refer to mental activity elicited in the process of waking up, i.e., hypnopompic mentation, rather than to what was happening during sleep. Goodenough *et al.* (1965) compared the content elicited after abrupt awakenings with the content elicited after awakenings which were induced gradually, thus increasing the length of the awakening process. More reports of "thinking" were

---

[2] A factor analysis of dream reports elicited on REM awakenings (Hauri, Sawyer, & Rechtschaffen, 1967) revealed a "vivid fantasy" factor which reflected primarily three correlated variables: (a) unreality—imagination, distortion; (b) intensity of experience—dramatization, clarity, emotion; (c) productivity—length of dream report. As these authors put it, "These three elements—the extent of a dream, its unreality and intensity—are central to what is commonly referred to as a 'good dream' (a lot of strange and wonderful things seem really to be happening). It is the combination of these components—with the unreal seeming real—that most distinguishes dreams. . . ." We use the term "dreamy" in the present paper as a conversational and shorthand way of referring to these qualities.

elicited on the gradual NREM awakenings, which lends credence to the argument that some NREM reports of thinking may represent hypno-pompic rather than sleep experiences. However, many NREM thinking reports were elicited on abrupt awakenings, and these are not so easily explained as products of the awakening process. Furthermore, there was no relationship between the incidence of NREM dream reports and the abruptness of the awakening.

Another argument against the acceptance of NREM reports has been that many of them might represent confabulations designed to meet the presumed expectations of the experimenter. Foulkes and Rechtschaffen (1964) found virtually no correlation between the MMPI L scale, which has been used to measure the tendency toward such confabulation, and the amount of recall on NREM awakenings. Rechtschaffen, Verdone, and Wheaton (1963) and Foulkes (1967) have recorded several instances in which NREM awakening reports indicated an apparent incorporation of external stimuli into an ongoing stream of NREM mental activity. Evidence of a similar significance comes from the studies of sleep talking. Arkin *et al.* (1970) and Rechtschaffen, Goodenough, and Shapiro (1962) found that the content of NREM sleep-talking incidents frequently corresponded with the content of reports elicited on awakening shortly after the talking. These two types of evidence—the incorporations and the sleep talking—provide temporal landmarks to which the content elicited on subsequent awakenings can be reasonably assigned. Thus these lines of evidence indicate that NREM reports cannot be completely dismissed as confabulations, hypnopompic reveries, or memories of mental activity experienced at a much earlier time.

It now appears that the early research underestimated the absolute amount of NREM mental activity and too quickly rejected the evidence for NREM dreaming. But as it turns out, this early work did not over-estimate the degree of relationship between mental activity and sleep stages. Dreaming does seem to occur in NREM as well as in REM sleep, and individual subjects may report mental activity on as many as 70% or more of their NREM awakenings. However, fewer reports of mental activity are elicited on NREM awakenings, the proportion of reports which are labeled thinking rather than dreaming is higher for NREM, and even the NREM reports which are labeled dreams tend to be less dreamy than REM reports. The net result is that REM and NREM are highly discriminable on the basis of the amount and quality of mental activity that they yield.

The degree of discriminability between REM and NREM was shown in a study by Monroe *et al.* (1965) who asked two judges to postdict whether reports had been elicited on REM or NREM awakenings on the basis of the amount and quality of the content reported. A postdiction made simply on the basis of whether any mental content had been elicited on the awakening yielded 70% correct identifications of sleep phase (assuming that REM awakenings would yield recalled content and NREM awakenings would not). When judges were asked to consider both the amount and quality of content, postdiction accuracy rose to 80% (average of two judges). When REM and NREM reports were matched for other variables which are associated with sleep mentation (subjects, night, and time of night) discriminability rose to 89%. These figures—discriminability ranging from about 70 to 90%—probably represent one of the best correlations ever discovered between psychological and physiological variables.[3]

To what extent the association between sleep stage and mental activity was enhanced by the variability in psychological and physiological activity during sleep, by the reduction of responsivity to external stimuli, or by the emergence of distinctive psychological and/or physiological phenomena during sleep cannot be determined here. But in general, at least some of the potential promise of sleep research for yielding correlations between psychological and physiological responses has certainly been realized.

Sleep researchers have not rested content with the wonderful correlations that have been established between sleep stages and mental activity. At least two major problems have remained. Perhaps encouraged by earlier successes, sleep researchers have pursued these problems with vigor. The first problem is that considerable variance in sleep mentation

---

[3] The high discriminability of REM and NREM reports does not premit the convenient generalization that the mental activity of REM sleep is dreaming and the mental activity of NREM sleep is thinking. Subjects describe their NREM mentation more often as dreamlike (see review by Pivik & Foulkes, 1968), and extremely vivid, bizarre, emotional, highly organized reports which would qualify as dreams by almost anyone's definition may be elicited on NREM awakenings. In fact, if there is any question about the validity of NREM awakening reports as indicators of sleep mentation, that question has to be asked more seriously about the NREM thinking reports than about the NREM dreaming reports. As noted earlier, Goodenough *et al.* (1965) found that gradual awakenings produced more NREM thinking reports than abrupt awakenings, which supported the possibility that some NREM thinking reports reflect hypnopompic rather than sleep mentation. The evidence on temporal landmarks for NREM mentation simply indicates that *not all* NREM thinking reports can be so explained; an unknown number of NREM thinking reports may actually represent hypnopompic activity rather than thoughts experienced *during* the NREM sleep. By contrast, the NREM dream reports do not appear related to abruptness of awakening; apparently, they are much less likely to represent hypnopompic artifacts. In our own experience, subjects appear to be much more certain about what had been going on in their NREM dreams than in their NREM thoughts.

remains unrelated to sleep stages. But this is the relatively smaller problem. Even if all of the variance in sleep mentation could have been related to sleep stages, the second problem would have still remained. This second problem is the determination of the most "intimate" physiological correlates of sleep mentation. A sleep stage is a complex organization of several physiological variables. To this point, we have attended only to the EEG and eye movement patterns which are the defining characteristics of sleep stage. But the stages have other physiological correlates as well—including muscle tone, cardiorespiratory, and metabolic variations. Which of the defining characteristics and correlates of stages are most intimately correlated with sleep mentation?[4]

In reviewing this question, several strategies can be used. Most important, is to examine within-stage empirical correlations between physiological measures during a period of sleep and reports of mental activity which presumably occurred during the same period. For some physiological measures, evidence on the relationship between the measures and reports is either absent, sparse, or conflicting. In these cases, one might gain some impression of the likelihood of a correlation between the report and the psychological variable by observing how each is related to a third variable. For example, given the known relationships of awakening reports to stage, one might expect a good physiological correlate of reports to vary with stage as the reports do. (Although it is possible that each stage has its own best physiological correlates of reports, a first parsimonious guess would be that the most intimate correlates of the mentation remain stable across stages.) Also, there are certain temporal correlates of reported sleep mentation independent of stage (see next section) and one might expect good correlates of sleep mentation to vary with time parameters in the same manner that reports do.

---

[4] Hidden behind this relatively humble question is a more pretentious hope. Might it be possible eventually to find such a precise psychophysiological correlation that we can feel either that the perfect mirror-image ideal of isomorphism has been achieved or that we are knocking on the door of causality. Even if such a glorious correlation were achieved, however, empirical proof of causality might not be demonstrable. The empirical demonstration of causality is usually defined by the effect of an *experimentally* introduced stimulus. Naturally occurring responses certainly act as stimuli and may be reasonably *interpreted* as such, but one could not be certain of their causal role. Even when such responses precede and are highly correlated with presumed effects, the possibility exists that an undetected stimulus causes both the initial response and its presumed effect. One can speak of the causal effect of experimentally manipulated *external* stimuli on responses which are defined as psychological or physiological. But the causality now in question is between *internal* psychological and physiological responses, which cannot, by virtue of being internal, be directly manipulated themselves.

III. TEMPORAL CORRELATES

In the search for the best physiological correlates of amount and quality of mental activity during sleep, certain temporal correlates of this mental activity may be of assistance. Reports tend to be more detailed and more emotional (but not more bizarre) on awakenings made late in a REM period than on awakenings early in a REM period. There is a similar increase in detail and emotionality on REM awakenings made later in the night than on REM awakenings made early in the night, with most of the variance accounted for by the relatively mundane quality of the first REM report of the night (Foulkes, 1960; Verdone, 1963).

The data on temporal correlates of NREM mentation are more equivocal. Hauri and Rechtschaffen (1963) found no substantial difference in amount of recall on NREM awakenings made 15 min after sleep onset as compared to NREM awakenings made 45 min after sleep onset. However, only two points in NREM sleep were sampled and only three subjects were studied, so the possibility of some yet undetected within-cycle temporal correlate of NREM mentation cannot be firmly excluded. Pivik and Foulkes (1968) reported that NREM mentation became more dreamlike later in the night. However, their time-of-night variable was partially confounded with NREM stage differences, and their conclusion was based largely on the results of only seven reports from the first Stage 2 awakening of the night. Therefore, time-of-night effects for NREM mentation are not so firmly established as one might wish.

IV. EEG CORRELATES

Since EEG is one of the defining characteristics of sleep stage, the opportunities for correlating EEG with sleep mentation independent of stage are limited. Nevertheless, there are enough data to indicate that EEG-mentation correlations during sleep are not particularly strong. Within NREM sleep, the EEG patterns of Stages 2 and 3 appear quite different. Stage 2 has a relatively low voltage, mixed frequency pattern with periodic sleep spindles and K-complexes. During Stage 3 there is a marked increment in high amplitude, slow wave activity along with the sleep spindles and K-complexes. Yet the amount and quality of recall elicited on Stage 2 and Stage 3 awakenings are quite similar (Pivik & Foulkes, 1968). The EEG of Stage 4 differs even more dramatically from the EEG of Stage 2, but Stage 4 is so strongly related to time of night that uncontaminated comparisons of mental activity in Stages 2 and 4 are difficult to make.

It is doubtful that the EEG pattern of Stage REM is most responsible for the quality of mental activity in that stage. The EEG of Stage REM and the Stage 1 EEG pattern which occurs at sleep onset are very similar. Both consist of relatively low voltage, mixed frequency activity. There are some differences. In Stage REM, distinctively notched 2–3 Hz sawtooth waves tend to occur in conjunction with bursts of rapid eye movement; activity resembling sawtooth waves may appear in Stage 1, but the waves are not so clearly formed nor nearly so plentiful as in Stage REM. High voltage vertex sharp waves are more abundant in Stage 1 and sometimes do not appear at all in Stage REM. Although there are differences in episodic EEG events as noted, the tonic, background EEG activity of Stage 1 and Stage REM are virtually indistinguishable. Vogel, Barrowclough, and Giesler (1970) asked judges to postdict whether reports had been elicited on REM awakenings or on awakenings from sleep onset Stage 1. They found that the judges could do this with much better than change accuracy. Therefore, stages with very similar EEG patterns seem to yield discriminable reports.

Finally, there is the obvious point that within stages there is much variation in the amount and quality of mental activity reported on awakenings. For example, Pivik and Foulkes (1968) found that 71.6% of awakenings from Stage 2 produced recall, which means that 28.4% of awakenings from the same stage—with the same EEG—did not.

To summarize: stages with different EEG patterns may produce similar awakening reports; stages with similar EEG patterns may produce discriminable awakening reports; and within a single stage—with a single EEG pattern—there is marked variation in the reported content. Evidently, the EEG alone is not a very good indicator of sleep mentation. But all of the studies cited above refer to "tonic" EEG patterns, i.e., gross patterns which persist over extended periods of at least several minutes. Perhaps more productive of correlations with mental activity would be a focus on specific EEG waveforms—especially where hypotheses for such specific relationships exist. Later we will review some studies of this type in relation to phasic events during sleep.

V. MOTOR ACTIVITY

That mental activity during sleep may have motor correlates is dramatically demonstrated by the correspondences between sleep talking and sleep mentation noted earlier. But sleep talking does not occur very frequently. Therefore, the question progresses to whether there are any less overt motor correlates which regularly accompany sleep mentation.

There is very conclusive evidence from the work of Wolpert (1960) and Stoyva (1965) that there are many more fine movements of the extremities in REM than in NREM sleep. In this crude sense there is definitely a relationship between fine motor twitches and dreaming. However, these fine motor twitches might represent some expression of stage physiology which is not specifically related to the mental activity of the stage. To attack this question, one must consider the relationship between the twitches and mental activity within stages. Wolpert (1960) found a relationship between the specific electromyographic activity recorded just before REM awakenings and specific dream content which was reported to have occurred just prior to the awakening, e.g., dreams of using the hand associated with EMG potentials at the wrist, but the relationship obtained only for some subjects. A recent report by Grossman, Gardner, Roffwarg, Fekete, Beers, and Weiner (1971) also offers evidence that twitches of the extremities may be associated with REM dream content. McGuigan and Tanner (1970), in a study of one subject, found a relationship between conversation in REM dreams and lip and chin EMG potentials.

Thus there is little doubt that the psychological events of the dream may be reflected in motor discharges. But it is also clear from the data of the reports cited above that not all of the fine muscle twitches are accompanied by dreams of correlated motor activity, nor are all the hallucinated motor acts in dreams reflected in the recorded EMG potentials. Stoyva (1965) found that deaf subjects, who presumably would dream of moving their fingers more often than normals, had no more frequent finger twitches in REM sleep than control subjects—contrary to the historic report of Max (1935).

Apart from the relationship of the EMG twitches to specific dream content, are the twitches diagnostic of dream activity per se? There is not very much data on this question, but the report of Stoyva that the finger twitches of his deaf subjects were not correlated with reports of NREM dreaming would argue against such a possibility.

Apart from discrete motor responses, are higher levels of psychological activity during sleep accompanied by higher tonic levels of muscle activity? Here there is a clear answer which illustrates a dramatic departure from waking psychophysiological correlations. During REM sleep, when psychological activity is at a peak, tonic electromyographic activity in the head and neck region is drastically reduced (Berger, 1961; Jacobson *et al.*, 1964). Trunk and limb muscles do not show the same decrease in tonic activity during Stage REM. Except for increases in tonic activity associated with occasional body movements, the tonic activity of the limb and trunk muscles remains stable in the transition from NREM to REM sleep. Thus the increased fine muscle twitches of REM sleep discussed above occur against a background of stable tonic EMG activity of limb and trunk muscles and a decreased level of tonic EMG activity in the head and neck region.

In the cat it has been shown that the decrease in tonic EMG activity in the neck muscles during REM sleep results from an active supraspinal inhibitory control, since this decrease is not seen in Stage REM after prebulbar transections of the brain stem (Jouvet, 1967). In fact, the structure responsible for the inhibition of neck muscle tone has been localized by Jouvet to the area of the nucleus locus coeruleus.

In view of the evidence in the cat for a cerebral structure which actively participates in the inhibition of muscle tone during REM, it becomes reasonable to ask whether the decreased muscle tone also signals the emergence of active processes responsible for dreaming. Larson and Foulkes (1968) took advantage of the fact that the chin EMG frequently decreases just prior to Stage REM to investigate the relationship between EMG suppression and reported content in NREM sleep. (Since the tonic EMG suppression is maintained throughout most of REM sleep, the association with mental activity has to be studied during NREM sleep where the suppression occurs only occasionally.) Contrary to the expectation that the NREM EMG suppression might be a positive dream indicator, Larson and Foulkes found a trend toward fewer and less dreamlike reports on awakenings made from periods of EMG suppression than on control awakenings.

To summarize, apart from the increased muscle twitches of Stage REM and the relationship of some of these twitches to specific mental content, muscle activity during sleep does not appear to be a very promising indicator of mental activity. There are two additional aspects of muscle activity during sleep which are of potential importance, phasic EMG inhibitions and the activity of the extraocular muscles. These two topics can be more meaningfully discussed in a later section on phasic events during sleep.

VI. CARDIAC AND RESPIRATORY ACTIVITY

Heart rate per se does not appear to be related to sleep mentation. Several investigators have failed to detect significant relationships between heart rate during Stage REM and emotionality of the subsequent awakening dream reports (Fahrion, Davison, & Breger, 1967; Hauri & Van de Castle, 1970; Knopf, 1962; Verdone, 1963). Shapiro, Goodenough, Biederman, and Sleser (1964) found no relationship between REM period heart rate and whether dreaming, thinking, or no content reports were elicited on the awakening. There are some indications, however, of a relationship between heart rate variability and the content of REM dreams. Fahrion *et al.* found that heart rate variability was significantly related to REM dream emotionality in one subject but not in another. Hauri and Van de Castle (1970) found that heart rate variability prior to a REM awakening was significantly related to emotionality and other content parameters in the subsequently reported dreams.

The data on respiration show mixed results. Knopf (1962) found no significant relationships between respiratory rate in REM sleep and several parameters of dream content. Hauri and Van de Castle (1970) found that the respiratory rate during the last minute of REM sleep just prior to awakening was related to emotionality of the whole REM dream reported on awakening. There were no significant relationships between emotionality and respiratory rate for the whole REM period, respiratory rate during the last 6 min of the REM period, or any measure of respiratory variability. Respiratory variability in the last minute before awakening was negatively related to "involvement" of the subject in the dream.

Shapiro *et al.* (1964) found no significant relationship between REM period respiratory rate and whether a dreaming, thinking, or no content report was elicited on awakening, but they found that high respiratory irregularity was significantly related to the incidence of dream reporting. Hobson, Goldfrank, and Snyder (1965) related respiratory measures to a "total content rating," a combined estimate of physical activity, emotion, and vividness which should correlate highly with what we have called dreaminess. In their study, the relationship of the total content rating to respiratory variability fell short of significance, but there was a significant relationship between respiratory rate and total content rating both within REM and NREM sleep.

Although the reports on respiration and dream content in REM sleep represent a somewhat mixed bag of data, there are definite indications of a relationship between respiratory activity and what we have called dreaminess which is of theoretical significance. But the significance might be quite different from the traditional conception of a heightened autonomic response to an exciting mental content. Later we will find cause to question whether the respiration-content correlations might not be "secondary" to more fundamental relationships between respiration and certain "phasic" events of sleep.

VII. ELECTRODERMAL ACTIVITY

One of the favorite responses of psychophysiologists, electrodermal activity, does not show up very well as an indicator of mental activity during sleep. On the basis of stage-related changes in mental activity, one might expect a decrease in basal skin resistance and more spontaneous electrodermal changes in Stage REM than in NREM sleep. No such results have been reported. One early study of stage-related changes in skin resistance (Hawkins *et al.*, 1962) reported an increase in basal skin resistance during Stage REM over the level during the preceding NREM sleep, but subsequent studies have revealed no consistent relationship of basal electrodermal levels to sleep stages (Johnson, 1966; Koumans, Tursky, & Solomon, 1968; Tart, 1967). None of the above studies has shown any consistent skin resistance decline in Stage REM.

With respect to spontaneous electrodermal responses, several investigators have reported the initially surprising result that these responses were by far most frequent during Stages 3 and 4 (Asahina, 1962; Broughton, Poire, & Tassinari, 1965; Burch, 1965; Hauri, 1968; Johnson & Lubin, 1966; Lester, Burch, & Dossett, 1967). These electrodermal fluctuations are so vigorous during Stages 3 and 4 that they have been called "GSR storms" (Burch, 1965). Broughton *et al.* (1965) have suggested that the appearance of these storms ". . . when psychological activity is apparently least developed . . . would appear to be another reason for discarding the term 'psychogalvanic reflex'." Lester, Burch, and Dossett (1967) reported that nonspecific GSRs increased in all sleep stages on nights following daytime stress. Whether these GSR increments following stress are associated with distinctive mental activity during sleep, or whether they represent some delayed chemical response to stress that does not have immediate psychological correlates remains to be determined. Hauri and Rechtschaffen (1963) found no relationship between spontaneous or evoked skin potential changes and mental activity during NREM sleep. Verdone (1963) found no relationship between basal skin resistance and several content features of REM reports.

Hauri and Van de Castle (1970) did report one specific association between psychological and electrodermal activity during sleep. In a study of REM period reports, they found that skin potential activity during the last minute preceding the awakening was significantly related to the judged emotionality of the reported dream. Broughton *et al.* (1965) had noted that skin potential responses were relatively infrequent in Stage REM, but that when they did occur they tended to appear with bursts of rapid eye movements. Therefore, one has to question whether the skin potential changes associated with Stage REM emotionality might not depend upon the relationship of emotionality to other phasic changes during sleep. We will return to this issue later.

In general, there is not much evidence for a close association between electrodermal and mental activity during sleep. Broughton *et al.* and

Johnson and Lubin have suggested that the storms of electrodermal activity during Stages 3 and 4 might result from the liberation of electrodermal excitatory centers in the upper brain stem from the inhibiting influences of corticothalamic systems. Johnson and Lubin have suggested that the paucity of electrodermal activity in Stage REM might result from the activation of electrodermal inhibitory systems in the lower brain stem. These hypotheses suggest that major rearrangements of excitatory and inhibitory activity along the neuroaxis, such as occur with sleep, can alter the relationships between peripheral indicators and mental activity that obtain during wakefulness. As Johnson (1970) has pointed out "Instead of using our autonomic and EEG measures to define state, the reverse appears more appropriate. We must first determine the state before we can interpret our physiological measures." Furthermore, the data on GSR storms during NREM sleep indicate that the failure to observe usual waking relationships is not simply the result of a general depression of the response during sleep.

VIII. PENILE ERECTIONS

It has been well established that penile erections regularly accompany REM sleep. Fisher, Gross, and Zuch (1965) reported that full or partial erections were recorded in 95% of REM periods; 60% of REM periods showed full erections and 35% showed partial erections. Erections rarely occurred in NREM sleep. Similar results were reported by Karacan *et al.* (1966). They found that 80% of REM periods were accompanied by erections; 42% of REM periods had sustained erections which reached and maintained a maximal level, and 37% of REM periods had erections which had fluctuating amplitudes or were interrupted by detumescence. Only 19 erections were recorded during NREM sleep compared to 191 during REM sleep; thus the association of penile erections and REM sleep is quite specific. Of most immediate interest to us is the relationship of the erections to mental activity during sleep.

The data on the penile erections lend themselves to several different kinds of analyses. First, one can ask whether the regularly occurring erections of REM sleep are associated with sexual content. Here the answer is a clear "no," at least insofar as we deal with manifest content and with everyday definitions of what is sexual. If we were to predict sexual content on the basis of penile erections, we would have to predict that 80–95% of REM dreams should have the kind of manifest erotic content that is usually associated with erection—not just speaking with a member of the opposite sex, but engaging in expressly sexual physical contact or at least having explicit sexual fantasies. There is just not that much sexuality in dreams. For example, Hall and Van de Castle (1966) reported that sexual interactions occurred in only 12% of the dreams of their male subjects. The observation of most sleep researchers that nocturnal emissions are very rare in the laboratory is more consistent with the paucity of sexual content in dreams than with the frequency of penile erections. Fisher, Gross, and Zuch have reviewed the possible bases for the disassociation of erections and sexual content in dreams.

One could argue from a psychoanalytic orientation that there is something intrinsically sexual in all dream content, that is, the inferred libidinal energy which the dream theoretically is supposed to discharge in a disguised way so as to prevent awakening. But unless one specifies reliable empirical criteria for inferring sexuality, then the designation of all dreams as sexual is made a priori on a theoretical basis rather than on observable distinguishing features of the dream content.

Although the regularly appearing erections of REM sleep are not regularly accompanied by manifest sexual content, there are some indications of occasional specific associations between erection and sexual content within REM periods. Fisher (1966) was able to successfully postdict a sudden, sharp increase in tumescence in five of six instances mainly on the basis of highly erotic sexual content. In 17 episodes with no or partial erections, there were no indications of overtly sexual content, whereas in 30 episodes of full or moderate erection there were eight instances of overtly erotic content. There is also evidence from both Fisher and Karacan, et al. (1966) that the failure of erections to occur in REM sleep as well as detumescence in REM sleep are associated with dysphoric content, e.g., anxiety, aggression, etc.

To attempt a summary of these data, it appears that the very high frequency with which erections appear in REM sleep is not associated with a correspondingly high frequency of manifest sexual content. In this respect, the erections are not diagnostic of dream content. On the other hand, variations in tumescence during REM are somewhat diagnostic of variations in REM dream content. There has been no specific study reported on the relationship of NREM erections to the incidence of NREM dream reports. However, the very infrequent occurrence of NREM erections would at least suggest that most NREM dreams occur in the absence of erections.

Two additional relationships involving REM erections are of interest. Karacan et al. (1966) found that 95% of awakenings from REM periods with sustained erections produced recalled content as compared with 85% of awakenings from REM periods with no or interrupted erections. (The difference was statistically significant.) Karacan *et al.* (1966) also found that sustained erections were associated with greater amounts of eye movement activity.

IX. TEMPERATURE

One might guess that an increase in general systemic arousal as reflected in body temperature might be positively correlated with psychological arousal. It is well established, for example, that several different kinds of waking performance are at their best when body temperatures are relatively high (Kleitman, 1963). It turns out, however, that body temperature is negatively correlated with several types of psychological arousal in dream content. Verdone (1963) examined the relationships between rectal temperatures recorded during REM periods and several content parameters of the dreams reported on awakenings from the REM periods. Rectal temperature was negatively related to the subjects' ratings of goodness of recall, vividness, and emotionality of the dream. Once again, however, the possibility arises that these relationships might be secondary to a more intimate relationship between the psychological variables and phasic events. In Verdone's study, there was a significant negative relationship between rectal temperature and amount of eye movement activity, which, in turn, was positively related to goodness of recall, vividness, and emotionality. The relationship of eye movement activity to recall and vividness were stronger than the relationship of rectal temperature to those two variables.

There was one psychological variable to which rectal temperature related that eye movement activity did not. Lower rectal temperatures were associated with dream content that referred to life experiences from the subjects' more distant past. Neither eye movement activity nor rectal temperature were significantly related to the implausibility of the dream content.

Finger and forehead skin temperatures did not relate in any consistently convincing way to the psychological variables.

X. SYMPATHETIC AROUSAL

Of course, we have dealt with several indicators of sympathetic arousal throughout our review. There are, however, a few studies which deal with sympathetic arousal in a more general sense and therefore deserve special attention. There is one report on sympathetic arousal which is unfortunately brief but noteworthy for the clarity of its theoretical formulation and the significance of its findings. Hersch *et al.* (1970) hypothesized that

"... the level of autonomic activity is a precondition which determines how the sleeper interprets impinging stimuli and memories; i.e., if the sympathetic nervous system is reasonably quiescent, ongoing cognition may be experienced as thought, but it may be experienced as dreams if the sympathetic nervous system is comparatively active." This formulation suggests that it is the sympathetic arousal of REM sleep that is responsible for REM mentation being experienced as dreams. To test the hypothesis that it is sympathetic arousal which is responsible for NREM mentation being experienced as dreams, epinephrine was injected subdermally during Stage 4, and the subjects were awakened 10 min later for reports. These reports were compared with reports elicited on awakenings made 10 min after control injections of saline. The postepinephrine reports were rated significantly more vivid, emotional, and perceptual than the control reports. The postepinephrine reports also tended to be more bizarre.

The "activation" of NREM mentation by norepinephrine stands as an important empirical result. It is certainly consistent with the report of Hobson et al. (1965) that respiratory rate is positively related to emotionality and vividness of NREM reports. What seems to require more discussion, however, is the original hypothesis that it is the sympathetic arousal of REM sleep which is responsible for the high incidence of dreaming in that stage.

Several lines of evidence suggest that Stage REM is not characterized by markedly elevated levels of sympathetic arousal. Baust, Weidinger, and Kirchner (1968) reported that in the cat sympathetic tone, defined as the tonic discharge of pre- or postganglionic sympathetic neurons, is regularly decreased in REM sleep from the preceding NREM level. Of course, it may be dangerous to generalize from the cat to the human, so a review of sympathetic activity during sleep in the human seems indicated.

Snyder et al. (1964) studied the changes in respiration, heart rate, and systolic blood pressure during human sleep. They found that there were increases in each of these variables during REM periods as compared to the preceding NREM level, but the magnitudes of these increases were quite small: 6% for heart rate, 7% for respiratory rate, and 4% for systolic blood pressure. Kamiya (1965) obtained similarly low REM period increments in his study of heart and respiration rates. The reduction of electrodermal responses during REM periods noted earlier could be taken to indicate a decrease in sympathetic activity during REM sleep. Are the increases in autonomic level great enough to account for the marked shifts in mental activity with REM sleep? Probably not. For one thing, the data of Snyder et al. show that heart and respiratory rates tend to fall in successive REM periods of a night, which is inconsistent with the increase in dreamlike quality of REM periods later in the night. (Blood pressure did tend to increase in later REM periods.)

An even more compelling argument against the sympathetic arousal–dreaming hypothesis is the evidence reviewed earlier on the absence of a relationship of heart rate and respiratory rate to sleep mentation. In the case of respiration the results were mixed.

Overall, the results indicated better relationships of dreamlike quality to heart and respiration rate variability than to rate per se. Considering these results, one might expect marked increases in the variability of autonomic indicators in the passage from NREM to REM sleep. This is exactly the case. In contrast to the meager increases in autonomic level, Snyder *et al.* (1964) reported increases in a variability measure of 55, 55, and 50% for pulse, respiration, and blood pressure, respectively. Johnson (1966) has also reported minimal changes in baselevels of autonomic activity with Stage REM but massive changes in variability. Furthermore, in contrast to the decrease in heart rate in successive REM periods of a night, Snyder *et al.* (1964) showed substantial increases in heart rate variability in successive REM periods—just as one might expect on the basis of correlations of dreaming with time of night.

What does a relationship of autonomic variability to mental activity during REM periods mean for the sympathetic arousal hypothesis? The hypothesis of Hersch *et al.* (1970) is addressed to the issue of autonomic level, not autonomic variability. Further theoretical work on the relationship of autonomic variability to sleep mentation seems indicated.

Finally, we must consider whether the autonomic variability of REM sleep represents variability in sympathetic or parasympathetic activity. This question is again prompted by the work of Baust and his collaborators in the cat. Their findings are perhaps not generalizable to humans, but they represent the best available data on the issue. Baust, Bohmke, and Blossfeld (1971a) found that reflex discharges of the cervical sympathetic nerve in response to sciatic nerve stimulation were reduced during NREM sleep as compared to wakefulness, and then *further* reduced during REM sleep. These results left open the question of whether the reduction of sympathetic response might have resulted from reduced sensory input. Therefore, Baust, Bohmke, and Blossfeld (1971b) directly stimulated the reticular formation. Similar results were obtained; evoked sympathetic activity was reduced during NREM sleep and then further reduced during REM sleep. Evoked responses in the vagal nerve were reduced in NREM sleep as compared to wakefulness, but in contrast to the sympathetic responses, the vagal responses during REM sleep were increased over those of NREM sleep and approximated the waking responses.

Baust and Bohnert (1969) also studied the phasic changes in heart rate associated with bursts of eye movements in REM sleep. The usual pattern was for heart rate to increase from 1–2 sec prior to the REM burst. Then there was a decline in heart rate which began during or at the end of the REM burst, reached a maximum in 5–8 sec, and was absent after 10–15 sec. Sympathetic and parasympathetic contributions to this pattern were evaluated by various heart denervations. Baust and Bohnert concluded that the initial 1–2 sec rise was caused mostly by decreases in parasympathetic activity, and that the later brachycardia was produced by a combination of increased vagal and decreased sympathetic activity. Therefore, the cat data show that during REM sleep there is not only a decreased tonic sympathetic discharge, but also a decreased sympathetic response to stimulation as well as phasic decreases in sympathetic activity in conjunction with bursts of eye movement. It remains to be considered how much of the phasic autonomic activity during REM in humans is associated with eye movement activity. We will return to this issue later. In the meantime, the cat data should raise some caution about the interpretation of the autonomic changes during sleep in humans.

XI. EYE MOVEMENT ACTIVITY

There are two types of relationship between eye movements and mental activity during sleep to be considered. One is the content-specific relationship or the so-called scanning hypothesis which proposes that the eyes move in REM sleep as the dreamer scans the dream scene and follows the movements of objects in the scene. This hypothesis predicts that the amount of eye movement activity will be related to the amount of visual scanning and that the direction of recorded eye movements will correspond to the direction of scanning in the dream. The second major type of relationship may be called nonspecific. It has to do with how the eye movements may relate to the amount and quality of reported mental activity. Although scanning activity may enter into the determination of such relationships, it is not crucial to them. Nonspecific relationships could obtain because the eye movements are a peripheral expression of central events which are correlated with mental activity, that is, the eyes might move during certain types of brain activation even when they are not engaged in the scanning of the dream imagery.

The most specific evidence on the content-specific relationships is the data on the relationship between dream imagery and eye movement direction, but first we will review some of the other evidence which has been brought to bear on the question.

Dement and Wolpert (1958) classified REM dreams as "active" or "passive" without knowing the amount of eye movement activity which had been recorded polygraphically. Active dreams were those ". . . in which the dreamer was an active participant in the events of the dream," that is, where many eye movements might be expected. Passive dreams were ". . . those in which S was quietly reflecting upon an event, talking quietly to another person, or watching an event occur, often from a distance, in which he took no active part," that is, dreams in which relatively less eye movement activity might be expected. There was a very highly significant relationship of this active–passive dichotomization of dreams to the amount of eye movement activity independently judged from the polygraph records. These results have been replicated by Berger and Oswald (1962).

The above results are certainly consistent with the scanning hypothesis, but of themselves they are not very convincing in view of a reasonable alternative interpretation. As Aserinsky (1965) has suggested, the eye movements might reflect heightened activity in parts of the central nervous system which are also responsible for active dreams rather than reflect a response of the oculomotor system to the dream imagery. In other words, the correspondence of amount of dream activity and amount of eye movement activity could be an example of what we have called a nonspecific correspondence.

There is evidence which shows that the amplitude, density, velocity, stereotypy, predominant direction, sequential pattern, temporal distribution, or organization of eye movements during REM sleep is different from those of eye movements during wakefulness (e.g., Aserinsky, 1971; Fuchs & Ron, 1968; Gabersek & Scherrer, 1970; Jacobs, Feldman, & Bender, 1971; Jeannerod, Mouret, & Jouvet, 1965; Oswald, 1962; Spreng, Johnson, & Lubin, 1968). Such evidence of differences in waking and REM eye movements has been used to argue against the scanning hypothesis (Aserinsky, 1971; Moskowitz & Berger, 1969; Oswald, 1962). Certainly these data do not speak for the scanning hypothesis, but neither do they doom it. First, we must allow for the possibility that peculiarities in the way the succession of dream images unfolds and peculiarities of the images themselves might account for some of the features of REM period eye movements. Second, we must allow for the possibility that peculiarities of oculomotor organization during Stage REM account for some unique features in Stage REM eye movements, even though a scanning correspondence is maintained. (A subject with impaired extraocular muscles might have abnormal eye movements during wakefulness, even though those eye movements are in the service of scanning.) Third, there is certainly more than one type of eye movement during sleep (Jeannerod *et al.*, 1965). Perhaps some types of eye movement are related to scanning whereas others are not. For example, Jeannerod *et al.* (1965) distinguished between isolated or small groups of eye movements and dense bursts of eye movement in the cat during REM sleep. Total decortication caused almost complete disappearance of the isolated eye movements but an increase in the number of bursts. Frontal decortication caused an increase in the ratio of burst to isolated movement, whereas occipital decortication caused a decrease in the ratio. Isolated and small group movements appeared during wakefulness, whereas the dense bursts appeared only in REM sleep. Pompeiano and Morrison (1965) found that bilateral lesions of the medial and descending vestibular nuclei abolished the bursts of rapid eye movements in REM sleep, but the isolated eye movements persisted. These results suggest that the isolated eye movements might be involved in scanning, whereas the burst activity is not. But the particulars of which eye movements might be involved in scanning is not crucial at this point. The major issue is that the hypothesis that all the eye movements of REM sleep represent scanning activity is just one of several possible scanning hypotheses. In one sense it is an impossible hypothesis to study. The complexity of eye movements in REM sleep, the need to account for such factors as head movement and compensatory eye movements in the scanning process, and the viscissitudes of dream recall make it virtually certain that we would never be able to muster conclusive support for this scanning hypothesis even if it were true.

Another approach to the scanning hypothesis has been to observe whether eye movements are present during REM sleep in subjects who do not have scanning activity. One such group is the congenitally blind or people who have been blind for so long that they no longer have visual imagery during wakefulness or sleep. Offenkrantz and Wolpert (1963), in a study of a congenitally blind subject, reported only a single instance of eye movements during "emergent Stage 1," the cyclically appearing EEG pattern which is usually accompanied by eye movements. In other words, their subject appeared to have "REM periods" without eye movements. Awakenings from these emergent Stage 1 periods produced reports of dream imagery in all the nonvisual modalities. Offenkrantz and Wolpert interpreted these results ". . . as supporting the hypothesis that while Stage 1 EEG is a physiological concomitant of dreaming, REMs (rapid eye movements) only reflect visual activity in the manifest content of dreams." Berger, Olley, and Oswald (1962) found that three congenitally blind subjects and two subjects who were blind for many years and no longer experienced visual imagery showed no eye movements during emergent Stage 1. Three subjects who had become blind more recently and still had visual images showed normal eye movements in REM sleep. Although Berger *et al.* conceded that their results were consistent with the scanning hypothesis, they also suggested the possibility that ". . . owing to non-use, nervous pathways involved in the execution of conjugate eye-movements are poorly developed in those with life-long blindness, or, once established, suffer through disuse during prolonged blindness."

Very different results were observed in two other studies of blind subjects. Amadeo and Gomez (1966) studied eight subjects with lifelong blindness. Seven of the eight showed eye movements during REM sleep although the eye movements appeared less frequently and were smaller than in sighted subjects. Noting the "disorganized, often asynchronous EOG records" of their subjects, Amadeo and Gomez suggested that the eye movements ". . . could be interpreted as indicative of a lack of those maturational processes normally underlying the close association between dream imagery and REMs." Gross, Byrne, and Fisher (1965), who used a ceramic strain gauge transducer to record eye movements,[5] recorded eye movements in the REM periods of five subjects blind since birth. These authors proposed, however, that this result had no necessary bearing on the scanning hypothesis. They proposed that the eye movements of the blind and sighted subjects had a similar "physiologic substratum," but that in the sighted subjects the eye movements might have become coordinated with the visual imagery of dreams. By analogy, they reasoned that the presence of mouth movements in infants did not preclude a later specific coordination of mouth movements with speech.

It is obvious that the data on blind subjects does not resolve the issue of the scanning hypothesis. Not only are the data conflicting, but the various plausible interpretations render any result ambiguous. For

---

[5] The use of the ceramic strain gauges arises from a methodological problem. Gross, Byrne, and Fisher (1965) argued that the failure to record eye movements from the blind in some studies might result from the EOG (electrooculographic) method of recording eye movements. This method could fail to register eye movements when there is a diminished or absent corneofundal potential, which could be the case in many blind subjects. The ceramic strain gauge method (Baldridge, Whitman, & Kramer, 1963) detects the mechanical rotation of the eye and does not depend on a normal corneofundal potential. Berger (1967) countered that his blind subjects, who showed no eye movements by the EOG method during emergent Stage 1, showed good EOG potentials when they voluntarily moved their eyes during wakefulness. Berger suggested that the deflections recorded in emergent Stage 1 in blind subjects with the strain gauge technique might have represented eyelid blinks rather than eye movements. This issue could be resolved by direct observation of blind subjects sleeping with their eyelids taped open. Rechtschaffen and Foulkes (1965) were able to observe the eye movements of sighted subjects during Stage REM with this technique.

example, for the two studies that showed no eye movements in the blind, the authors of one interpreted their results as favorable for the scanning hypothesis, whereas the authors of the other were inclined against the hypothesis. In both studies which showed eye movements in the blind, the authors were inclined toward the scanning hypothesis.

A similar diversity of interpretations befalls other studies which demonstrate the presence of eye movements during emergent Stage 1 in subjects who are not likely to scan visual images. Moskowitz and Berger (1969) cited several studies which showed that rapid eye movements are present in the REM periods of neonates as casting doubt on the scanning hypothesis. However, we have already noted the argument that eye movements might occur as a purely physiological expression of Stage REM in the absence of visual imagery, but might become linked to the imagery with maturation. Berger (1967) has countered this argument by citing evidence of Stage REM period eye movements in decorticate cats and humans. He has proposed this evidence as indicating that if there is a maturation linkage of the eye movements and dream imagery, the linkage has not rendered the two phenomena mutually dependent. I suppose one could respond to this point by suggesting that decortication interferes with the mature linkage pattern.

The ambiguities reviewed above seem to result from the uncertainty of generalizing to eye movement–imaginary relationships in normal, sighted subjects from data on other kinds of subjects. To show how inconclusive all of the above arguments are, consider that they would all fall by the wayside if there were strong, replicable evidence that the direction of recorded eye movements corresponded to the direction expected from the reported imagery. This would be the most direct test of the scanning hypothesis because this is what is meant by scanning—moving the eyes in the direction required to inspect the visual environment.

Unfortunately, such direct tests of the scanning hypothesis have produced conflicting results. In the first "directional" test of the scanning hypothesis, Dement and Kleitman (1957) awakened subjects after 1 min of one of four predominant EOG patterns: (1) mainly vertical eye movements, (2) mainly horizontal movements, (3) both vertical and horizontal movements, (4) very little or no movement. Unfortunately, only three periods of purely vertical and only one period of purely horizontal movement were seen. In each of these four instances, the correspondence between the imagery and EOG direction was very good. Periods with little movement generally produced reports of less active dreams than periods of mixed movement, but such a difference might also be expected on the basis of nonspecific relationships.

Dement and Wolpert (1958) concentrated on the correspondence between the very last eye movement before awakening and the very last fixation reported in the dream. Only 23 of 39 reported dreams were clear enough to differentiate the last fixation in the dream. In 17 or 74% of these 23 cases the report and the eye movement corresponded—far beyond chance probability. These data appear as strong support for the scanning hypothesis. Unfortunately, there was little discussion of the criteria for rejecting reports as insufficiently detailed or of guarantees against bias in judging the correspondence of dream reports and eye movements.

Roffwarg *et al.* (1962) conducted an elaborate study in which an independent interrogator who was not aware of the recorded eye movements carefully questioned the subject upon awakening and then made a blind prediction of the pattern of eye movements recorded in the last 10–20 sec before awakening. Two judges then rated the correspondence between the predictions and the paired EOG records as good, fair, or poor. "Good correspondence" was judged for 75–80% of the pairs in which subjects had confidence in their recall of the dream. The problem with this study is that there may not have been a reliable operational definition of good correspondence. What these investigators called good correspondence might not have been called "good" by judges less friendly to the scanning hypothesis.

Moskowitz and Berger (1969) improved on the method of Roffwarg *et al.* (1962) by having a judge who was naive about the pairing of reports and EOG recordings try to match the two on the basis of the scanning hypothesis. In this way, the number of successful matchings of reports and eye movements could be evaluated against the probability of making successful matches by chance alone. Eighteen of 56 matches were correct, which was not significantly different from the 14 expected by chance. This improved methodology eliminates the effects of a bias for the scanning hypothesis. But prior to the actual matching procedure, a bias for the scanning hypothesis could help provide the fairest test of it. For example, the report of Moskowitz and Berger gives no indication of the kind of pretraining in recognizing waking scanning movements or of the kind of care in interviewing subjects that was exercised by Roffwarg *et al.* (1962). It might be productive to have investigators who are enthusiastic about the scanning hypothesis try to establish evidence for it by the rigorous methodology of Moskowitz and Berger.

Jacobs, Feldman, and Bender (1971) reported that recorded eye movements matched the dream action in only 18% of awakenings. However, the description of their methodology was very brief, and it is difficult to evaluate the study.

We have perhaps spent too many words in reviewing the data on the scanning issue. But the scanning hypothesis was one of the cornerstones on which modern psychophysiological dream research was built. Perhaps it requires a detailed review to demonstrate that the issue is still in doubt.

The evidence for nonspecific relationships between eye movements and mental activity during sleep indicates more dreamlike content associated with an abundance of eye movements. Verdone (1963, 1965) found that impressionistic ratings of amount of rapid eye movement activity in a REM period related significantly to the amount of recall, vividness, and emotionality of the awakening report. The implausibility or amount of bizarreness in a dream was not significantly related to judged amount of eye movement in the REM period, but the trend was in a positive direction. Hobson, Goldfrank, and Snyder (1965) found a highly significant relationship between amount of eye movement activity and their total content ratings, which combined estimates of physical activity, emotion, and vividness.

A recent series of experiments on the moment-to-moment relationships between eye movement activity and variations in dream quality will be considered in the next section on phasic events.

XII. PHASIC EVENTS

In the past few years, attention has been drawn to the "tonic–phasic model of sleep" (Grosser & Siegal, 1971). This model emphasizes the distinction between the long-lasting phenomena of sleep such as stages and the short-lasting discrete events such as eye movements. The model recognizes the inhomogeneity of the tonic periods and seeks to understand it in terms of phasic changes within the tonic periods. For the psychophysiologist, the model means greater attention to short-term covariations between mental experiences and phasic events. Of course, this kind of approach is not entirely new; it has been about 15 years since Dement and Wolpert tried to relate single eye movements to specific dream images. Apparently, enough of this kind of research has now transpired that it has earned the distinction of "model." The phasic–tonic model also suggests that similarities across different tonic periods might be understood in terms of similar phasic events in the different tonic periods. This is the kind of thing that Hobson, Goldfrank, and Snyder (1965) tried to do by relating respiratory activity to dreaminess both within REM and within NREM sleep.

To judge from the nonspecific relationships between eye movement activity and dream quality for the REM period as a whole, it is a reasonable hypothesis that moment-to-moment variations in dream quality might coincide with the presence or absence of eye movements. Aserinsky (1967) hypothesized such a relationship, and Molinari and Foulkes (1969) looked for it by having subjects describe their very last experience immediately prior to awakening. The experimenters then related the presence or absence of eye movements immediately prior to awakening to ratings of the report quality. REM period reports were evaluated for presence of "secondary cognitive elaboration," that is, cognitive activity such as thinking, interpreting, or comparing. Only 12% of reports from awakenings with eye movements contained secondary cognitive elaboration as compared to 80% of reports after intervals of ocular quiescence within the REM period. Secondary cognitive elaboration was about as frequent on Stage 2 awakenings as on awakenings after intervals of ocular quiescence during REM periods.

As Molinari and Foulkes pointed out, the results of their content classification required cross-validation ". . . since not all of the dimensions finally employed in that analysis were anticipated in advance of data collection." A cross-validation study was begun in Foulkes' laboratory by Medoff and Foulkes (1971). In two subjects intensively studied by them by the time of his preliminary report, there was no confirmation of the Molinari and Foulkes result. In contrast to the method of Molinari and Foulkes, in which secondary cognitive elaboration was judged from the reports, Medoff specifically asked his subjects about the presence of secondary cognitive elaborations. It is possible, therefore, that the failure of Molinari and Foulkes (1969) to obtain secondary cognitive elaboration on eye movement awakenings could have resulted from their occlusion in the reporting process by more salient features of the mental activity associated with eye movement activity. Evidence of such salient features will be noted later. Medoff also noted a tendency for a decrease in auditory imagery in association with eye movements as compared to awakenings from quiet intervals or intervals with sawtooth waves. Perhaps it was the relatively reduced auditory activity associated with eye movement awakenings that gave these reports the appearance of having less cognitive activity in the Molinari and Foulkes study.

Medoff also found a greater incidence of recall on sawtooth and eye movement awakenings than on quiet awakenings. In the one subject with enough data on the question, he did not find, as Molinari and Foulkes had, a greater incidence of visual imagery on eye movement than on quiet awakenings.

Moving to studies of phasic events during NREM sleep, Weisz (1971) investigated whether there were any psychological differences in reports elicited after K-complexes and those after sleep spindles. There were no significant differences on any of a large number of psychological variables, including recall, imagery, dreamlike fantasy, and secondary cognitive elaboration.

Pivik (1971) studied the association of phasic events in both REM and NREM sleep to the incidence and quality of recall of mental activity immediately preceding the awakening. For phasic events during REM sleep, Pivik used the eye movements. For phasic events during NREM sleep, Pivik used the phasic inhibition of the electrically induced spinal H reflex. In the major analysis (of a complex, multifactor study) there was no significant relationship of phasic activity to recall. From among a host of mental quality variables studied (including dreamlike fantasy, sexuality, orality, thought, emotion, etc.) only increased hostility and auditory imagery were significantly related to the phasic events.

The study of Pivik was notable for his deliberate attempt to examine, in both the NREM and REM sleep of humans, a peripheral manifestation of a cerebral event called the ponto–geniculate–occipital spike (PGO).

Bursts of high voltage (200–300 μV) monophasic potentials of about 100 msec duration were first reported to occur in the pons of the cat in conjunction with bursts of rapid eye movement during REM sleep (Jouvet, Michel, & Courjon, 1959). Shortly afterward, similar spikes were observed in the lateral geniculate nucleus (Mikiten, Niebyl, & Hendley, 1961) and then in the occipital cortex (Mouret, Jeannerod, & Jouvet, 1963). The spikes appear almost synchronously in the three structures and appear to originate from a common neural generator, probably in the pons. Their initial discovery in the three structures noted above accounts for the term ponto–geniculate–occipital spike. Later, the spikes were observed in several additional structures as well.

From almost the time they were discovered, the PGO spikes have been considered by many sleep researchers as excellent candidates for a very intimate correlate of dream activity for several reasons. Their prominent appearance in the visual system (Michel, *et al.*, 1964b) was consistent with dreams as very visual phenomena. The increase in unit firing rates in many areas of the brain in conjunction with spiking (see Hobson & McCarley, 1971) is consistent with expectations that the brain is probably very active during dreaming. The PGO spikes are most dense during REM sleep when dreaming is most reliably present. Within REM sleep, the spikes are closely, although not exclusively associated with eye movements—and we have already reviewed some evidence which indicates that amount of eye movement activity is positively related to the dreamlike quality of reports elicited on REM awakenings. (Most of the eye movement activity of REM sleep is accompanied by PGO spikes, but many spikes appear independent of eye movement. Usually, there is a build-up of spike activity for a second or two in advance of a burst of eye movements, and then the spikes continue through the burst. Frequently, isolated spiking appears without any correlated eye movement activity.) Although the spikes are most plentiful during REM sleep, where they occur at the rate of about 50–70/min, isolated or short bursts of spikes appear intermittently throughout NREM sleep, which allows for the possibility that they could correlate with mental activity in both REM and NREM sleep. Finally, PGO spikes are normally (except for special drug or surgically induced states) a phenomenon of sleep—just as dreaming normally is. Spike activity appears in the lateral geniculate nucleus during wakefulness in association with eye movements, but the waking spikes follow the eye movements, whereas the sleep spikes precede the eye movements (Delorme, Jeannerod, & Jouvet, 1965).

There has been no dearth of reasons for hypothesizing PGO spikes as correlates of dream activity. The problem has been one of recording some manifestation of PGO activity in the human which could then be correlated with reports of mental activity. The search for a PGO indicator in the human hinges on a willingness to extrapolate from correlates of PGO activity in cats. Pursuing this rationale, bursts of eye movement actvity during REM sleep in humans are almost certainly indicative of PGO spike activity, which explains Pivik's use of eye movements as phasic indicators in REM sleep. The problem with this indicator, however, is that it would miss the PGO spikes of Stage REM that occurred in the absence of eye movements. Nevertheless, the eye movements should constitute a partial PGO indicator, since there are many more spikes in association with the eye movements than without them.

The problem of a PGO indicator in NREM sleep is more acute. The use of sensitive measuring techniques, multielectrode dc electrooculography by Jacobs, Feldman, and Bender (1971) and the ceramic strain gauge technique by Rechtschaffen *et al.* (1970), has revealed the presence of small but definite rapid eye movements in NREM sleep. In our experience, however, these NREM eye movements are very infrequent and do not begin to approach the incidence of PGO spiking in feline NREM sleep.

The solution to the NREM–PGO problem selected by Pivik was the phasic suppression of a spinal reflex, because it had been shown that such phasic suppressions were highly correlated with the eye movement bursts of REM sleep in the cat and in the human (Baldissera, Broggi, & Mancia, 1966; Gassel, Marchiafava, & Pompeiano, 1964; Hodes & Dement, 1964; Shimizu *et al.*, 1966). Furthermore, Pivik and Dement (1970) found that in the human, phasic suppressions of the H-reflex were coincident with phasic inhibitions of the chin muscle during NREM sleep. In the cat, phasic inhibitions of the neck musculature are frequently coincident with PGO spikes in NREM sleep, although there are many more spikes than phasic inhibitions.

Our own approach to the problem of a PGO indicator in the human was to proceed from observations that spikes recorded from the electrodes in the extraocular muscles of the cat frequently coincide with both REM and NREM–PGO spikes recorded in the brain (Gadea-Ciria & Jouvet, 1971; Michel, Rechtschaffen, & Vimont-Vicary, 1964; Rechtschaffen, Michel, & Metz, 1971). We attempted to record from surface electrodes near the orbit of the human some manifestation of the electrical activity of the extraocular muscles (Rechtschaffen *et al.*, 1970). By using very high amplification and integrating the activity to "stretch" it out enough

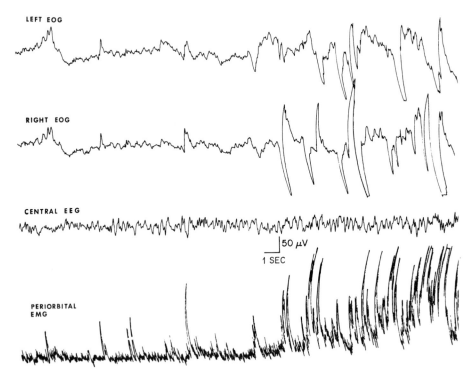

Fig. 5.3. Illustration of PIPs (in periorbital EMG tracing during Stage REM). Note the occurrence of PIPs both in the presence and absence of distinctive eye movements. In the latter part of the tracing there is a marked increase in tonic periorbital EMG activity along with the marked increase in PIP activity.

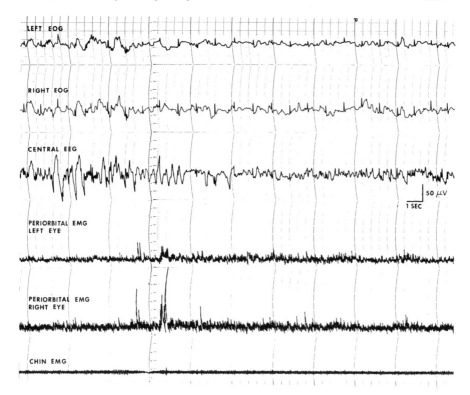

Fig. 5.4. Illustration of a short burst of PIP activity in the periorbital EMG tracing during Stage 2. Note the indication of a phasic suppression of the chin EMG about the time of the PIPs. Note the appearance of sawtooth waves in the EEG tracing at the time of the PIPs.

in time so that it could be monitored by the galvanometers, we recorded spike potentials which resembled those we had recorded from the extra-ocular muscles of the cat. These periorbital phasic integrated potentials (PIPs as we called them) regularly appear in conjunction with the rapid eye movements of REM sleep, but are also plentiful in REM sleep in the absence of eye movements (see Fig. 5.3). (Waking eye movements are generally accompanied by much smaller phasic potentials.) The PIPs also appear intermittently during NREM sleep, sometimes in conjunction with phasic inhibitions of the chin muscle and sawtooth waves (see Fig. 5.4).

We cannot be sure that the periorbital PIP signals originate in the extraocular muscles, because we have not recorded from electrodes directly in these muscles in the human. Many of the PIPs undoubtedly originate in the orbicularis muscles, and these probably represent false positive PGO spikes, since the orbicularis muscle of the cat sometimes shows spikes in the absence of PGO activity, but fortunately these orbicularis spikes are relatively rare. Most likely the periorbital PIPs do not originate in the masseter muscle. Spikes recorded from electrodes over the masseter muscle frequently accompany periorbital PIPs in NREM sleep, but in REM sleep the PIPs increase dramatically in frequency and amplitude, whereas the masseter spikes decrease in frequency and amplitude. Although we cannot be sure that the PIPs originate in the extraocular muscles, they do tend to be distributed in sleep like PGO spikes. Also, they have some functional properties of PGO spikes. Rechtschaffen and Chernik (1971) found that REM period deprivation increased the incidence of PIPs in NREM sleep, which parallels the increase in NREM PGO spikes after REM deprivation in the cat (Vimont-Vicary, 1965). Wyatt *et al.* (1971) found that the drug parachlorophenylalanine caused a redistribution of PIPs in human sleep similar to the effect of the drug on the distribution of PGO spikes in feline sleep.

If the PIPs do indeed arise from the extraocular muscles, then they probably reflect PGO activity in the pons more closely than the PGO spike activity in the lateral geniculate nucleus. Gadea-Ciria and Jouvet reported that every PGO spike in the pons was accompanied by a discharge in the lateral rectus muscle. We have observed that although most of the lateral geniculate spikes of REM sleep were accompanied by lateral rectus spikes, only about half of the NREM lateral geniculate spikes were accompanied by lateral rectus spikes. It appears that, at best, some false negative as well as false positive detection is involved in the use of periorbital PIPs as PGO spike indicators. Nevertheless, there appeared to be sufficient similarity between the two phenomena to venture studies of the relationship of PIPs to mental activity during sleep.

Two studies on the relationship of mental activity to PIPs have just been completed in our laboratory. The data analysis has just begun, and to date only the analyses on "distortion" (lack of correspondence to everyday life) have been completed. In the first study (Rechtschaffen, *et al.*; paper submitted for presentation at the 1972 annual meeting of the Association for the Psychophysiological Study of Sleep) we investigated the PIPs in NREM sleep. Ten subjects who slept in the laboratory for 10–22 nights each were awakened after 3–5 sec of PIP activity in Stage 2 and from control periods in Stage 2 without PIP activity. Subjects were asked to describe their experience just prior to awakening. PIP awakenings produced significantly more reports with distortion than control awakenings. The relationship was most pronounced for instances of "extreme distortion" as rated by independent judges. In this analysis, only 5% of control awakenings produced reports with extreme distortion. Awakenings from intervals with a mixture of PIPs and tonic periorbital activation produced extreme distortion in 27% of reports. Awakenings from intervals with PIP activity alone produced extreme distortion in 50% of the reports. Eye movement activity (recorded by the strain gauge technique) in association with the PIPs did not increase the incidence of distortion in the reports.

Watson (paper submitted for presentation to the 1972 meeting of the Association for the Psychophysiological Study of Sleep) followed-up this study with an investigation of PIP activity in the REM sleep of four subjects. Watson employed three kinds of awakenings: control awakenings— made after at least 15 sec of quiescence (no PIPs or eye movements); PIP awakenings—made after about 3–4 sec of PIPs in the absence of detectable eye movements; PIP–REM awakenings made after about 3–4 sec of PIPs accompanied by rapid eye movements. PIP and PIP–REM awakenings were preceded by at least 12 sec of quiescence. Both PIP and PIP–REM awakenings produced subjects' ratings of very bizarre or moderately bizarre for the last experience on 55% of reports as compared to 24% for control awakenings. Only 7% of control awakenings, as compared to 61% of PIP and 41% of PIP–REM awakenings produced reports of an increase in bizarreness from the next-to-last to the very last experience. Only 9% of control awakenings, compared to 34% of PIP and 37% of PIP–REM awakenings produced reports in which the very last experience did not fit into the context of the next-to-last experience.

Taking the two studies together, it appears that PIPs, with or without eye movements, are associated with bizarreness or unreality in the stream of sleep mentation. This association obtains within Stage 2 sleep, and within REM sleep. Considering the much greater frequency of PIPs in REM sleep, PIP activity is very likely related to many of the differences between REM and NREM mentation as well. It should be emphasized that PIPs do not appear responsible for dreaming per se. Rather, they are associated with the appearance of the bizarre in the dream. Whether this appearance results from the active intrusion of discordant mental engrams or from the loosening of associative connections remains to be determined.

Following are excerpts from two PIP awakening reports from Watson's study which illustrate the intrusion of bizarre content into the dream, presumably coincident with PIP onset.

In the next to the last experience, the dreamer, a female, was talking with an older woman who said, "If I could get you to work better." During the last experience, which the subject estimated as about 5 sec in duration, she suddenly felt she was both women: "There was two of me." She spoke a confused sentence to herself: "To keep those two days free, I'll probably surround the weekend." (PIPs started 6 sec before the awakening; there were no eye movements.)

In the next-to-the last experience, the dreamer was listening to his girl friend talk about a problem she was having and was feeling concerned and wondering what he could do for her. The girl was crying. At some point within the last 5 sec by the subjects' estimation, he noticed that her tears were running down in four straight vertical lines from each eye. (PIPs started 5 sec before awakening; there were no eye movements.)

XIII. PHASIC EVENTS AND OTHER PHYSIOLOGICAL VARIABLES

For several of the instances in which we have noted a relationship between a psychological and physiological variable, there was evidence that one or both of the variables were also related to eye movements (and by inference to PGO activity). Dreamlike mentation was related to low rectal temperature; both of these variables were related to amount of eye movement activity in the REM period. In fact, dreamlike quality tended toward stronger relationships with eye movements than with rectal temperature. There was some evidence of an association of skin potential activity in REM sleep to dream emotionality; other evidence indicated that the skin potential fluctuations of REM sleep tended to appear with bursts of rapid eye movement. Sustained erections in REM sleep were associated with more recall of content on awakening; sustained erections were also associated with more eye movement activity in the REM period—which in turn had been related to more recall in other studies. There are some indications that heart rate variability is related to dream emotionality, as well as suggestions from the work of Aserinsky (1965) and Baust and Bohnert (1969) that the heart rate tends to vary at the time of rapid eye movement bursts. Respiratory rate is related to dreaminess in Stage REM; in the same study (Hobson, Goldfrank, & Snyder, 1965) the correlation of dreaminess to eye movement activity was even greater, and Aserinsky has noted a stereotyped increase of respiratory rate in conjunction with eye movement bursts in REM sleep. Respiratory rate was also related to dreaminess of NREM mental activity; one can only wonder whether both these variables are related to undetected NREM phasic events.

What we are getting at is that the psychophysiology of sleep research is at the point where we should think about unconfounding our physiological variables in the search for the specific variables which are most intimately related to sleep mentation. Of course, we will also need to unconfound the psychological variables, but this seems to be the less pressing problem at the moment. Most recent psychophysiological studies of sleep have measured several dimensions of the mental activity—which at least permits a statement about the dimensions that do relate to a physiological variable and the dimensions that do not. (Where more than one psychological dimension has related to a physiological variable, there has not been much effort to determine the dependence of one dimension on another.) On the physiological side, the attempts at a multidimensional approach have been fewer. The difference is understandable. Once a verbal report has been elicited, it can be rated on a number of dimensions. By contrast, there are limits to the number of channels on a polygraph and the amount of gear that can be attached to a subject and still allow him to sleep comfortably. Furthermore, the amount of work in a study begins to escalate geometrically. I already regret having raised this issue.

Nevertheless, sleep researchers will have to proceed with some unconfounding. Partial correlation techniques may help. Making awakenings after different combinations of physiological activity is another tactic.

The confusion which seems most bothersome at the present is between the phasic events which reflect PGO activity and the systemic variables—mostly the autonomic measures. Are the correlations between autonomic variability and sleep mentation epiphenomenal to the correlations between phasic events and sleep mentation? Phrased another way, can we find autonomic-content correlations when there are no PGO indicators associated with the autonomic changes. Johnson and Karpan (1968) have reported that autonomic changes are regularly associated with K-complexes but not with isolated sleep spindles, whereas Weisz (1971) could find no psychological differences in reports after K-complexes and reports after sleep spindles.

Or perhaps, following a James–Lange approach, the phasic event–mental activity correlations are epiphenomenal. Are there any such correlations when autonomic changes do not accompany the phasic events?

Perhaps the phasic events and the autonomic changes are largely inseparable because they arise from a common generator. Morrison and Pompeiano (1970) have reported that the lesions of the medial and descending vestibular nuclei which abolish the bursts of rapid eye movement in the REM sleep of the cat also abolish many of the phasic vegetative variations of REM sleep. On the other hand, Spreng, Johnson, and Lubin (1968) have reported that autonomic variability in human REM sleep is not significantly related to the amount of eye movement burst activity.

But one then has to wonder about possible relationships to the phasic events which are not associated with eye movements.

Back to the laboratory!

The Discussion of Dr. Rechtschaffen's Paper

LED BY DR. DEAN FOSTER
Virginia Miltary Institute

Foster: As a direct result of the paper you have just heard, I know that you are all going to sleep better and for several reasons. One of them is that during the non-REM sleep that you enjoy this very night, a little spike may be occasionally firing, saying, "Never mind if I, with liquor or without it, upset my 'remming' tonight; I will make it up later."

Dr. Rechtschaffen did not tell you of the many hundreds of experiments he has conducted, or collaborated on, in the REM-deprivation work. Nor did he tell you about his investigations of presleep, postsleep mentation. I believe that there have not been nearly enough explorations of either the presleep (sometimes called the hypnogogic) state, nor of the postsleep stage. These two facets may turn out to be crucial to our eventual understanding of the process we call sleep.

Nor do we have sufficient effort addressed to the control of this hallucinatory behavior, meaning dreaming; you heard of some very pertinent work, such as the taped eyelid experiments, in which the eyes of the sleeper are kept open during sleep. This approach and others like it show us that sensations from the retina are not as significant an influence on sleep as we would have expected. The point is that we know too little about stimulation before or during sleep.

Nor do we know what happens when we give a waking subject maximum dosages of sensory stimulation. Jouvet studied this as have I in my own sensory bombardment laboratory: The results with his cats and our human subjects are the same. Overstimulation while it is actually going on induces sleepiness. Load on the stimulation to very high levels and the organism does not become more alert or more aroused. Instead, he wishes only to curl up and go to sleep.

In an attempt simply to understand more about the sleep–waking continuum, for no bizarre or quixotic reasons, Dr. Rechtschaffen has pursued the use of such tools as hypnosis and telepathy in an effort to get a better fix. In thinking about sleep we are all overly prone to be moved by the conventional semantics involved. Accordingly, we get caught up in a word or a concept such as "sleep," as with other concepts summarized today by Messrs. Black, Chapman, and Mulholland, and we are moved to view these concepts as if they were discrete entities.

In this context, let us remember the presleep and postsleep portions of the experience and let us try to think of these behaviors independently of the terms used. In the last analysis, we shall surely conclude that all of these areas of activity are closely related from a psychophysiological point of view. Finally, I find myself wishing that the four speakers we have heard here today, each giving major addresses on different areas of investigation, could work together for a while in the excellent laboratories that Dr. McGuigan has set up here. Together they might conjunctively and synergistically explore some of the highly similar questions that they have individually considered.

As Dr. Rechtschaffen spoke, I am sure that many of you thought about the influence of memory, and how we can't, as he apologized in the beginning, capture or recapture our dreams—our own, or dreams of other subjects. If only these mentations, or hallucinations, or whatever one elects to call them, could be projected in the more tangible form of a motion picture. Since we can't, we are always at the mercy of subject's reports, each with his fallible memory. Equally problematic, we are handicapped by the reporter's lack of communicative skill, his lack of descriptive ability, and all the while his body was undergoing changes in metabolic and related vegetative functions. In other words, while body processes are slowed, a subject is not at a proper state of alertness for any function; he is state-bound. Dr. Rechtschaffen and many others would love to have a more vivid, isomorphic translation of all too private an experience in a more reified form. We can not have such an ideal; but let us reflect on what memory has to do with it. Are we remembering a dream, since all of the dream contents, obviously, are from experience: Nothing novel ever seems to get into this particular form of thought; it is always a memory.

We hope that Dr. Rechtschaffen continues with the phasic, and that he amplifies this departure a great deal, as he has been, by turning the microscope so to speak on every bit. Laverne Johnson, the sleep researcher, has taught us that the various parts of the autonomic, or sympathetic nervous system, do not march in step. Dr. Rechtschaffen referred more than once to this lack of coordination in his talk, one key consequence of which is that one part of the musculature will be going into contraction, while another part is relaxing. This gives us a potential clue to the measurement or procession of rest. If only we could see the various ways in which the sympathetic nervous system, at one point, stops beating in rhythm with another part, and begins going off on its own, we should certainly be enlightened.

In outline form, three other areas need to be dealt with, as follows.

1. The need for classification of subjects in any systematic study of thinking, dreaming, hallucinating or any of the related "states" discussed at the symposium.

2. The need to define and better understand these so-called 'states" ranging from alert or aroused, schizophrenic, learning, reflective, hypnotic, drowsy-associative, REM or hypnagogic, visualizing or imaging, the various drug states, sleep, problem solving, etc., etc. All of these and others were repeatedly referred to as "states."

3. The need for experimental data to differentiate both the type of subjects and the "states" and the interaction between the two, i.e., subject–state interface. Some tests have successfully differentiated both. It is obvious to me that subjects are by no means equivalent and therefore must be classified. Nor are intrasubject variations to be forgotten. Roland Fischer's evidence on state-bound experience is certainly worth noting. Recall the recent alcohol-learning studies in which drunken subjects learned materials to criterion but could not recall what they had learned after sobering up. Later when again inebriated they performed well again. The point is that much of our experience is state-bound and these differences can be demonstrated experimentally. Once this is admitted, perhaps autogenically or otherwise, we could return to a desired dream or other state.

Open Discussion

Dr. Timothy J. Teyler (University of California at Irvine): Would you speculate on the generality of REM episodes across phylogeny and ontogeny?

Rechtschaffen: To summarize the major facts, REM sleep is present in the newborn where it comprises about half the total sleep as compared to about one-fourth or one-fifth of total sleep in the young adult. There are further but smaller declines in REM sleep in the human elderly. REM sleep has been observed in every mammal tested with the exception of the spiny anteater. Birds show REM periods of short duration. Below this phylogenetic level the picture gets quite confused because the brain wave patterns are not neatly comparable to those of mammals and the behavior is not so easily classifiable. In our studies of crocodilia, we often find it difficult to distinguish sleep and wakefulness.

Audience: Why does Stage 4 sleep decrease in elderly people?

Rechtschaffen: There is no factual answer to this question, but we would speculate that the death of neocortical cells in advanced age may be largely responsible for the Stage 4 loss. Several facts are consistent with this view. First, the occurrence of the high amplitude slow waves, which define Stage 4, seems to depend on the integrity of the neocortex. Apparently, the similar directional orientation of neocortical neurons firing synchronously permits the development of high amplitude, slow potentials on the surface of the brain. Second, the amount of slow-wave activity is also very small in the neonate where the cortex is not yet fully developed. Third, it is known that there is a considerable loss of cortical cells in the human aged. Finally, recent studies in our own laboratory have shown that in the rat, where there is minimal loss of cortical cells in old age, there is no decline in the amplitude of the sleep EEG with old age. Although the neocortex may be necessary for generating the slow waves of Stage 4, a number of other variables may contribute to the amount of slow-wave activity. One of these may be metabolism. For example, Kales and his associates have shown that there is a subnormal amount of Stage 4 in hypothyroid patients, and it is known that there is a decline in metabolic activity in the aged. Therefore, it is also possible that lowered activity could contribute to the decline of Stage 4 in the aged.

Dr. Tom Mulholland (Perception Laboratory, VA Hospital, Bedford, Massachusetts): Would you speculate on the significance of a dream, and about possible information processing in the dream?

Rechtschaffen: The evidence on the "P-hypothesis," which proposes that REM sleep is important for the processing of information gathered during the day, is still very mixed. Probably, about half the evidence is for the hypothesis and half the evidence against it (which might be the same ratio of investigators for and against the hypothesis).

As for the meaning of dreams, I really don't know; I do not have any firm ideas on this topic. Sometimes we seem to have such great wisdom about the psychological significance of the dream. I like good stories, so someone gives me a neat dream interpretation, and I say, "Gee, that makes sense." Then someone else takes the same dream and gives me another interpretation, and I say, "That makes sense, too." I just can't trust myself with dream interpretations. Also, if our postdictions (interpretations) were so right, it would imply that we had some knowledge of lawfulness between presleep events and dreams; and if we really had our finger on such lawfulness, we would be able to study a person's life circumstances and predict his dream. To the best of my knowledge, nobody has ever predicted a dream in any detail.

There has been considerable attention to the significance of REM sleep for psychological adjustment. Certainly, deprivation of REM sleep does not lead to psychosis as some of the earliest reports led us to believe. In fact, one is hard pressed to pick up any major psychological changes with REM deprivation. But the REM-deprivation experiments may not have been conducted in the best possible way for demonstrating psychological effects. Dement and co-workers have proposed that the PGO spike may be the most obligatory part of REM sleep. They found that if cats were awakened according to a schedule which blocked NREM spikes in addition to REM sleep, there was a much greater REM rebound during subsequent undisturbed sleep as compared to a deprivation schedule which prevented only REM sleep but not the PGO spikes in NREM sleep. Also, if cats were awakened by a very gentle procedure which permitted a great deal of NREM spiking but no REM sleep, there was little or no REM rebound. It is possible, therefore, that a more complete deprivation of PGO spiking may be required before unusual psychological effects are observed.

Dr. Charles Osgood (University of Illinois): You spoke about a wave of central inhibition that descends, in a sense, and inhibits movements of the gross musculature during sleep.

Rechtschaffen: Right. During REM sleep.

Osgood: I suppose this inhibition against overt movement functionally prevents the startle you sometimes get, that is, it prevents awakening. This suggests that the eye movements do not cause awakening. Now, exploring a little bit subjectively, consider the eye movements that occur when you close your eyes and when you posture your eyes in different places. Unless you were to think about it, you would not know where your eyes were postured; so perhaps proprioceptive feedback from eye muscles, as to their location and orientation, is determined by the visual input. In contrast, you can often tell exactly what position your hand is in.

Rechtschaffen: Right. With the eye, you can't tell where it is except by what you are seeing.

Osgood: The reason for so much eye movement in dreaming is that the eye (essentially) is the only body system which will not give sufficient feedback to produce waking.

Rechtschaffen: I don't think the eye movements of REM sleep occur simply because they would not awaken the sleeper. Biological events usually happen for better reasons than the fact that they do not have adverse effects. Therefore, let's separate this issue into two questions: Why do the eye movements occur? Why have they not been inhibited?

There is no definite answer to either of these questions, but we can consider the alternatives. As for the first question, why they occur, there have been a few theoretical positions. One, of course, is the scanning hypothesis, from which we would infer that the visual system engages in an apparently adaptive scanning of the visual environment because this environment has not been discriminated as "unreal." Another theory proposes a very specific adaptive role for the eye movements. Berger has proposed that they occur as part of a periodic restitutive adjustment which "tunes up" the mechanisms of binocular oculomotor coordination. Other approaches have treated the eye movements as if they were epiphenomenal byproducts of a more or less general cerebral excitation.

This last possibility brings us to the second question, which is really the focus of your remarks. Given that there is a more or less general excitation of the cerebral centers for motor discharge during REM sleep—perhaps in response to some "need" for such central excitation—it makes adaptive sense, for two reasons, to have simultaneous inhibition of peripheral motor output so that sleep may continue. On the one hand, the proprioceptive feedback from the muscles would not be available as sensory stimuli to awaken the sleeper. There are stretch receptors in the extraocular muscles, but they do not seem to produce the sensory experiences of movement and position that the stretch receptors in other muscles do. In this sense, your point is well taken. Inhibition of the eye muscles may not be necessary because they do not stimulate sensory experiences as other muscles do.

But this leaves us with a bit of a paradox. Why should proprioceptive feedback have such potency for disturbing sleep, whereas most of the very vivid imagery of dreams does not? Yet it is true that someone might sleep through a very exciting dream, whereas we would probably not have very much difficulty in awakening him by lifting his arm. Therefore, it is not the sensory value per se of proprioceptive feedback that is so threatening to sleep. At some level, "real" proprioceptive stimulation produces effects which the spontaneous imagery of the dream does not. Does the nervous system have a capacity for distinguishing dream and reality that is not reflected in our conscious discriminations?

The second adaptive feature of motor inhibition during REM sleep would be to prevent the physical consequences of unrestrained motor activity. Without such inhibition, we would either come into such massive physical contact with the environment as to cause awakenings, or we might stay asleep but get into an awful lot of trouble. From this perspective it also makes sense that inhibition of the eye muscles would not be necessary. These muscles do not "reach out" into the environment the way other striated muscles do. We could move our eye muscles every which way without increasing our confrontation with the environment, so it may not, for this reason, be necessary to inhibit their activation during sleep. Therefore, the idea that an inhibition of eye muscle activation may have been "selectively omitted" makes sense on two counts.

However, we should not make too much of the importance of motor inhibition for the maintenance of sleep. The motor inhibitory mechanisms of REM sleep are not entirely successful in blocking peripheral motor discharge; there is an abundance of fine movements of the extremities during REM sleep which does not cause awakening. Bruxism, or nocturnal teeth-grinding, can proceed with a vigor unattainable during wakefulness, and still not produce awakening. Of course there is sleep talking and sleepwalking. Even more pertinent is the fact that most of us sustain major movements of the head and/or trunk about fives times an hour without awakening. In summary, your idea about the eye muscles and sensory feedback does make sense, but the whole question seems much too complicated to permit a simple yes or no answer.

Audience: Let's go back to the cat. Have you taken a cat and congenitally blinded it at birth and looked at PGO spikes?

Rechtschaffen: Somebody has blinded a cat at birth and looked at eye movements, but I don't remember what he found.

Audience: Are PGOs related in any way to night terrors?

Rechtschaffen: Nobody knows, but they might be. "Night terrors" refers to those incidents where a subject awakens from sleep screaming in sheer fright, but with no recall of a dream. It is conceivable that such terrors might be generated by a brainstem activation, reflected in PGO activity, but without enough cortical arousal for dream elements to register in memory. We are waiting to record a night terror while we are simultaneously recording the periorbital EMG activity.

Mr. Adam Reeves (City College of New York): Night terrors seem to be related to previous life experiences, due to certain forces, or things that happen in life. If that's true, then night terrors constitute a more complicated phenomenon than can be accounted for by the brain stem; or the brain stem is more complicated than we think.

Audience: Do you think the spike is responsible for the NREM dream?

Rechtschaffen: Probably not. Our impression is that there is more dream activity in NREM sleep than there is spike activity. About all we can say now is that we have a correlate of the appearance of bizarre elements in the dream, and we do not have a very good idea of the nature of the correlation. Does the spike indicate the intrusion of a new mental engram into the stream of consciousness, or does the spike indicate a disruption of the ongoing stream, which then allows for a loosening of associative connections? Also, we must consider that the spikes represent very brief bursts of neural activity. It seems unlikely they could fully parallel the seemingly continuous dream stream. More likely, the spikes themselves are only very imperfect indicators of yet unknown, longer-lasting neural processes which are more intimate correlates of the dream activity. But even if we find very intimate neural correlates, or even neural determinants, of the dreaming process, we would still be faced with the enormous task of explaining the psychological organization of the dream. Dreams are not the kaliedoscopic jumbles of sensory images that one might expect from generalized activation of one brain area or another. They are organized sensory patterns arranged in temporally extended sequences which make thematic sense. Even if we find unique correlates of dreaming, we are still a long way from explaining the dream as an organized psychological experience. We can't even explain the dream imagery in terms of the recrudescence of old engrams. In a recent study we found that about half the content elements in dreams, including those which were not particularly bizarre, could not be identified by the dreamers as having appeared in their prior waking lives.

Rechtschaffen: I'm surprised nobody has asked whether waking hallucinations might not be related to PGO spiking. Dement has observed that cats who are chronically maintained on the drug parachlorophenylalanine show PGO spikes during wakefulness and, at the same time, behaviors which could be interpreted as responses to hallucinations. To date, we have tested only two hallucinating schizophrenics during wakefulness, one of whom was intact enough to tell us just when she was hallucinating. So far, we have seen no convincing evidence of waking periorbital spike activity in these patients which could not be attributed to eye blinks, or vigorous eye movements, or movement of the facial muscles. During sleep, periorbital spikes may be observed in the absence of such activity.

Dr. Richard Blanton (Vanderbilt): It's unlikely to find that anyway, since most of their hallucinations are auditory, and very few are visual. You might find such a relationship in alcoholics.

Rechtschaffen: During sleep, there is auditory imagery with the spiking, as well as visual; so that doesn't necessarily negate the relationship.

Dr. Richard Jennings (Walter Reed): Are you looking at heart rate in your current studies on phasic and tonic spiking?

Rechtschaffen: Not yet, but it is just a matter of time.

Dr. Louis Aarons (Department of Mental Health, Chicago): We heard today about operant conditioning of neural elements in the brain, about feedback cycles of alpha, and a very regulated series of 6/sec PGO spikes. Is it possible to operantly condition the PGO spike, in a feedback cycle, with some sort of stimulation?

Rechtschaffen: I don't know about the PGO spikes. The closest we have come to that is to attempt conditioning of the REM period, which might be tantamount to conditioning the PGO spike. There is a peculiar phenomenon whereby if you turn the cage lights off while rats are asleep, they tend to go into REM sleep. We paired a previously neutral sound stimulus with "lights off," but we had absolutely no luck in conditioning the REM period.

But why is this spike in REM sleep in the first place? In fact, it is a complete mystery why we sleep at all, because, if you look at sleep from a purely adaptive standpoint, while you are sleeping, you are not eating, you are not procreating, you are not defending yourself, etc. It is so blatantly maladaptive that you would think there must be some important function that sleep is serving to make us suffer the vulnerability of this particular state, and yet that function completely eludes us.

REFERENCES

Amadeo, M., & Gomez, E. Eye movements, attention and dreaming in subjects with lifelong blindness. *Canadian Psychiatric Association Journal,* 1966, **11**, 501–507.

Arkin, A. M., Toth, M. F., Baker, J., & Hastey, J. M. The degree of concordance between the content of sleep talking and mentation recalled in wakefulness. *Journal of Nervous and Mental Desease,* 1970, **151**, 375–393.

Asahina, K. Paradoxical phase and reverse paradoxical phase in human sleep. *Journal of the Physiology Society of Japan,* 1962, **24**, 443–450.

Aserinsky, E. Periodic respiratory pattern occuring in conjunction with eye movements during sleep. *Science,* 1965, **150**, 763–766.

Aserinsky, E. Rapid eye movement density and pattern in the sleep of normal young adults. *Psychophysiology,* 1971, **8**, 361–375.

Aserinsky, E., & Kleitman, N. Regularly occurring periods of eye motility, and concomitant phenomena, during sleep. *Science,* 1953, **118**, 273–274.

Baldissera, F., Broggi, G., & Mancia, M. Monosynaptic and polysynaptic spinal reflexes during physiological sleep and wakefulness. *Archives Italiennes de Biologie,* 1966, **104**, 112–133.

Baldridge, B. J., Whitman, R. M., & Kramer, M. A simplified method for detecting eye movements during dreaming. *Psychosomatic Medicine,* 1963, **25**, 78–82.

Baust, W., & Bohnert, J. The regulation of heart rate during sleep. *Experimental Brain Research,* 1969, **7**, 169–180.

Baust, W., Bohmke, J., & Blossfeld, U. Somato-sympathetic reflexes during natural sleep and wakefulness in unrestrained cats. *Experimental Brain Research,* 1971, **12**, 361–369. (a)

Baust, W., Bohmke, J., & Blossfeld, U. Reflex responses in the sympathetic and vagal nerve evoked by reticular stimulation during sleep and wakefulness. *Experimental Brain Research*, 1971, **12**, 370–378. (b)

Baust, W., Weidinger, H., & Kirchner, F. Sympathetic activity during natural sleep and arousal. *Archives Italiennes de Biologie*, 1968, **106**, 379–390.

Berger, R. J. Tonus of extrinsic laryngeal muscles during sleep and dreaming. *Science*, 1961, **134**, 840.

Berger, R. J. When is a dream is a dream is a dream? *Experimental Neurology, Suppl.* 1967, **4**, 15–28.

Berger, R. J., & Oswald, I. Eye movements during active and passive dreams. *Science*, 1962, **137**, 601.

Berger, R. J., Olley, P., & Oswald, I. The EEG, eye movements and dreams of the blind. *Quarterly Journal of Experimental Psychology*, 1962, **14**, 183–186.

Broughton, R. J., Poire, R., & Tassinari, C. A. The electrodermogram (Tarchanoff effect) during sleep. *Electroencephalography and Clinical Neurophysiology*, 1965, **18**, 691–708.

Burch, N. R. Data processing of psychophysiological recordings. In L. D. Proctor & W. R. Adey (Eds.), *Symposium on the analysis of central nervous system and cardiovascular data using computer methods*. Washington, D.C.: National Aeronautics and Space Administration, 1965. Pp. 165–180.

Delorme, F., Jeannerod, M., & Jouvet, M. Effects remarquables de la reserpine sur l'activite EEG phasique ponto-geniculo-occipitale. *Comptes Rendus des Seances de la Societe de Biologie*, 1965, **159**, 900–903.

Dement, W., & Kleitman, N. The relation of eye movements during sleep to dream activity: An objective method for the study of dreaming. *Journal of Experimental Psychology*, 1957, **53**, 339–346.

Dement, W., & Wolpert, E. A. The relation of eye movements, body motility, and external stimuli to dream content. *Journal of Experimental Psychology*, 1958, **55**, 543–553.

Fahrion, S. L., Davison, L., & Breger, L. The relationship of heart rate and dream content in heart-rate responders. Paper presented at the meeting of the Association for the Psychophysiological Study of Sleep, Santa Monica, California, April 1967.

Fisher, C. Dreaming and sexuality. In R. M. Lowenstein, L. M. Newman, M. Schur & A. J. Solnit (Eds.), *Psychoanalysis—a general psychology*. New York: International Universities Press, 1966. Pp. 537–569.

Fisher, C., Gross, J., & Zuch, J. Cycle of penile erection synchronous with dreaming (REM) sleep. *Archives of General Psychiatry*, 1965, **12**, 29–45.

Foulkes, D. Dream reports from different stages of sleep. Unpublished doctoral dissertation, University of Chicago, 1960.

Foulkes, D. *The psychology of sleep*. New York: Scribner, 1966.

Foulkes, D. Nonrapid eye movement mentation. *Experimental Neurology, Suppl.*, 1967, **4**, 28–38.

Foulkes, D., & Rechtschaffen, A. Presleep determinants of dream content: Effects of two films. *Perceptual and Motor Skills*, 1964, **19**, 983–1005.

Foulkes, W. D. Dream reports from different stages of sleep. *Journal of Abnormal and Social Psychology*, 1962, **65**, 14–25.

Fuchs, A. F., & Ron, S. An analysis of the rapid eye movements of sleep in the monkey. *Electroencephalography and Clinical Neurophysiology*, 1968, **25**, 244–251.

Gabersek, V., & Scherrer, J. Les mouvements oculaires pendant la phase pardoxale du sommeil. *Acta Neurologia Latinoamerica*, 1970, **14**, 40–50.

Gadea-Ciria, E., & Jouvet, M. Corticofugal control of pontine PGO activity in the cat. Paper presented at the meeting of the Association for the Psychophysiological Study of Sleep, Bruges, Belgium, June 1971.

Gassel, M. M., Marchiafava, P. L., & Pompeiano, O. Tonic and phasic inhibition of spinal reflexes during deep, desynchronized sleep in unrestrained cats. *Archives Italiennes de Biologie*, 1964, **102**, 471–499.

Goodenough, D. R., Shapiro, A., Holden, M., & Steinschriber, L. A comparison of "dreamers" and "nondreamers": Eye movements, electrocephalograms, and the recall of dreams. *Journal of Abnormal and Social Psychology*, 1959, **59**, 295–302.

Goodenough, D. R., Lewis, H. B., Shapiro, A., Jaret, L., & Sleser, I. Dream reporting following abrupt and gradual awakenings from different types of sleep. *Journal of Personality and Social Psychology*, 1965, **2**, 170–179.

Gross, J., Byrne, J., & Fisher, C. Eye movements during emergent stage 1 EEG in subjects with lifelong blindness. *Journal of Nervous and Mental Disease*, 1965, **141**, 365–370.

Grosser, G. S., & Siegal, A. W. Emergence of a tonic-phasic model for sleep and dreaming: Behavioral and physiological observations. *Psychological Bulletin*, 1971, **75**, 60–72.

Grossman, W., Gardner, R., Roffwarg, H., Fekete, A., Beers, L., & Weiner, H. Relations of dreamed to actual limb movement. Paper presented at the meeting of the Association for the Psychophysiological Study of Sleep, Bruges, Belgium, June 1971.

Hall, C. S., & Van de Castle, R. L. *The content analysis of dreams.* New York: Appleton, 1966.

Hauri, P. Effects of evening activity on early night sleep. *Psychophysiology*, 1968, **4**, 267–277.

Hauri, P., & Rechtschaffen, A. An unsuccessful attempt to find physiological correlates of NREM recall. Paper presented at the meeting of the Association for the Psychophysiological Study of Sleep, New York, March 1963.

Hauri, P. & Van de Castle, R. L. Dream content and physiological arousal during REMPs. Paper presented at the meeting of the Association for the Psychophysiological Study of Sleep, Santa Fe, March 1970.

Hauri, P., Sawyer, J., & Rechtschaffen, A. Dimensions of dreaming: A factored scale for rating dream reports. *Journal of Abnormal Psychology*, 1967, **72**, 16–22.

Hawkins, D. R., Puryear, H. B., Wallace, C. D., Deal, W. B., & Thomas, E. S. Basal skin resistance during sleep and "dreaming". *Science*, 1962, **136**, 321–322.

Hersch, R. G., Antrobus, J. S., Arkin, A. M., & Singer, J. L. Dreaming as a function of sympathetic arousal. *Psychophysiology*, 1970, **7**, 329–330.

Hobson, J. A., & McCarley, R. W. *Neuronal activity in sleep. An annotated bibliography.* Los Angeles: Brain Research Institute Publications Office, 1971.

Hobson, J. A., Goldfrank, F., & Snyder, F. Respiration and mental activity in sleep. *Journal of Psychiatric Research*, 1965, **3**, 79–90.

Hodes, R., & Dement, W. C. Depression of electrically induced reflexes ("H-reflexes") in man during low voltage EEG "sleep". *Electroencephalography and Clinical Neurophysiology*, 1964, **17**, 617–629.

Jacobs, L., Feldman, M., & Bender, M. B. Eye movements during sleep. I. The pattern in the normal human. *Archives of Neurology*, 1971, **25**, 151–159.

Jacobson, A., Kales, A., Lehmann, D., & Hoedemaker, F. S. Muscle tonus in human subjects during sleep and dreaming. *Experimental Neurology*, 1964, **10**, 418–424.

Jeannerod, M., Mouret, J., & Jouvet, M. Etude de la motricite oculaire au cours de la phase pardoxale du sommeil chez le chat. *Electroencephalography and Clinical Neurophysiology*, 1965, **18**, 554–566.

Johnson, L. C. Spontaneous and orienting responses during sleep. *Navy Medical Neuropsychiatric Research Unit Report* #66–9, 1966.

Johnson, L. C. A psychophsiology for all states. *Psychophysiology*, 1970, **6**, 501–516.

Johnson, L. C., & Karpan, W. E. Autonomic correlates of the spontaneous K-complex. *Psychophysiology*, 1968, 4, 444–452.

Johnson, L. C., & Lubin, A. Spontaneous electrodermal activity during waking and sleeping. *Psychophsiology*, 1966, 3, 8–17.

Jouvet, M. Neurophysiology of the states of sleep. *Physiological Review*, 1967, **47**, 117–177.

Jouvet, M., Michel, F., & Courjon, J. Sur un stade d'activite electrique cerebrale rapide au cours du sommeil physiologique. *Comptes Rendus des Seances de la Societe de Biologie*, 1959, **153**, 1024–1028.

Kamiya, J. Behavioral, subjective, and physiological aspects of drowsiness and sleep. In D. W. Fiske & S. R. Maddi (Eds.), *Functions of varied experience*. Homewood, Illinois: Dorsey Press, 1965. Pp. 145–174.

Karacan, I., Goodenough, D. R., Shapiro, A., & Starker, S. Erection cycle during sleep in relation to dream anxiety. *Archives of General Psychiatry*, 1966, **15**, 183–189.

Kleitman, N. *Sleep and wakefulness*. (2nd ed.) Chicago: University of Chicago Press, 1963.

Knopf, N. B. The study of heart and respiration rates during dreaming. Unpublished master's thesis, University of Chicago, 1962.

Koumans, A. J., Tursky, B., & Solomon, P. Electrodermal levels and fluctuations during normal sleep. *Psychophysiology*, 1968, **5**, 300–306.

Larson, J. D., & Foulkes, D. EMG suppression during sleep and dream activity. *Psychophysiology*, 1968, 4, 371.

Lester, B. K., Burch, N. R., & Dossett, R. C. Nocturnal EEG-GSR profiles: The influence of presleep states. *Psychophysiology*, 1967, 3, 238–248.

Max, L. W. An experimental study of the motor theory of consciousness: III. Action-current responses in deaf mutes during sleep, sensory stimulation and dreams. *Journal of Comparative Psychology*, 1935, **19**, 469–486.

McGuigan, F. J., & Tanner, R. G. Covert oral behavior during conversational and visual dreams. *Psychophysiology*, 1970, 7, 329.

Medoff, L., & Foulkes, D. "Microscopic" studies of mentation in stage REM: A preliminary report. Paper presented at the meeting of the Association of the Psychophysiological Study of Sleep, Bruges, Belgium, June 1971.

Michel, F., Jeannerod, M., Mouret, J., Rechtschaffen, A., & Jouvet, M. Sur le mecanismes de l'activite de pointes au niveau du systeme visuel au cours de la phase paradoxale du sommeil. *Comptes Rendus des Seances de la Societe de Biologie*, 1964, **158**, 103–106. (a)

Michel, F., Rechtschaffen, A., & Vimont-Vicary, P. Activite electrique des muscles oculaires extrinseques au cours du cycle veille-sommeil. *Comptes Rendus des Seances de la Societe de Biologie*, 1964, **158**, 106–109. (b)

Mikiten, T., Niebyl, P., & Hendley, C. EEG desynchronization during behavioral sleep associated with spike discharges from the thalamus of the cat. *Federation Proceedings*, 1961, **20**, 327.

Molinari, S., & Foulkes, D. Tonic and phasic events during sleep: Psychological correlates and implications. *Perceptual and Motor Skills*, 1969, **29**, 343–368.

Monroe, L. J., Rechtschaffen, A., Foulkes, D., & Jensen, J. Discriminability of REM and NREM reports. *Journal of Personality and Social Psychology*, 1965, **2**, 456–460.

Morrison, A. R., & Pompeiano, O. Vestibular influences during sleep. VI. Vestibular control of autonomic functions during the rapid eye movements of desynchronized sleep. *Archives Italiennes de Biologie*, 1970, **108**, 154–180.

Moskowitz, E., & Berger, R. J. Rapid eye movements and dream imagery: Are they related? *Nature*, 1969, **224**, 613–614.

Mouret, J., Jeannerod, M., & Jouvet, M. L'activite electrique du systeme visuel au cours de la phase paradoxale du sommeil chez le chat. *Journal de Physiologie*, 1963, **55**, 305–306.

Offenkrantz, W., & Wolpert, E. A. The detection of dreaming in a congenitally blind subject. *Journal of Nervous and Mental Disease*, 1963, **136**, 88–90.

Oswald, I. *Sleeping and waking. Physiology and psychology*. New York: Elsevier, 1962.

Pivik, R. T. Mental activity and phasic events during sleep. Unpublished doctoral dissertation, Stanford University, 1971.

Pivik, T., & Dement, W. C. Phasic changes in muscular and reflex activity during non-REM sleep. *Experimental Neurology*, 1970, **27**, 115–124.

Pivik, T., & Foulkes, D. NREM mentation: Relation to personality, orientation time, and time of night. *Journal of Consulting and Clinical Psychology*, 1968, **37**, 144–151.

Pompeiano, O., & Morrison, A. R. Vestibular influences during sleep. I. Abolition of the rapid eye movements of desynchronized sleep following vestibular lesions. *Archives Italiennes de Biologie*, 1965, **103**, 569–595.

Rechtschaffen, A., & Chernik, D. A. The effect of REM deprivation on periorbital spike activity in NREM sleep. Paper presented at the meeting of the Association for the Psychophysiological Study of Sleep, Bruges, Belgium, June 1971.

Rechtschaffen, A., & Foulkes, D. Effect of visual stimuli on dream content. *Perceptual and Motor Skills*, 1965, **20**, 1149–1160.

Rechtschaffen, A., Goodenough, D. R., & Shapiro, A. Patterns of sleep talking. *Archives of General Psychiatry*, 1962, **7**, 418–426.

Rechtschaffen, A., Hauri, P., & Zeitlin, M. Auditory awakening thresholds in REM and NREM sleep stages. *Perceptual and Motor Skills*, 1966, **22**, 927–942.

Rechtschaffen, A., Michel, F., & Metz, J. T. Relationship between extraocular and PGO activity in the cat. Paper presented at the meeting of the Association for the Psychophysiological Study of Sleep, Bruges, Belgium, June 1971.

Rechtschaffen, A., Verdone, P., & Wheaton, J. V. Reports of mental activity during sleep. *Canadian Psychiatric Association Journal*, 1963, **8**, 409–414.

Rechtschaffen, A., Vogel, G., & Shaikun, G. Interrelatedness of mental activity during sleep. *Archives of General Psychiatry*, 1963, **9**, 536–547.

Rechtschaffen, A., Molinari, S., Watson, R., & Wincor, M. Extraocular potentials: A possible indicator of PGO activity in the human. *Psychophysiology*, 1970, **7**, 336.

Roffwarg, H. P., Dement, W. C., Muzio, J. N., & Fisher, C. Dream imagery: Relationship to rapid eye movements of sleep. *Archives of General Psychiatry*, 1962, **7**, 235–238.

Shapiro, A., Goodenough, D. R., Biederman, I., & Sleser, I. Dream recall and the physiology of sleep. *Journal of Applied Physiology*, 1964, **19**, 778–783.

Shimizu, A., Yamada, Y. Yamamoto, J., Fujiki, A., & Kanedo, Z. Pathways of descending influence on H reflex during sleep. *Electroencephalography and Clinical Neurophysiology*, 1966, **20**, 337–347.

Snyder, F., Hobson, J. A., Morrison, D. F., & Goldfrank, F. Changes in respiration, heart rate, and systolic blood pressure in human sleep. *Journal of Applied Physiology,* 1964, **19,** 417–422.

Spreng, L. F., Johnson, L. C., & Lubin, A. Autonomic correlates of eye movement bursts during stage REM sleep. *Psychophysiology,* 1968, **4,** 311–323.

Stoyva, J. M. Finger electromyographic activity during sleep: Its relation to dreaming in deaf and normal subjects. *Journal of Abnormal Psychology,* 1965, **70,** 343–349.

Tart, C. T. Patterns of basal skin resistance during sleep. *Psychophysiology,* 1967, **4,** 35–39.

Verdone, P. Variables related to the temporal reference of manifest dream content. Unpublished doctoral dissertation, University of Chicago, 1963.

Verdone, P. Temporal reference of manifest dream content. *Perceptual and Motor Skills,* 1965, **20,** 1253–1268.

Vimont-Vicary, P. *La suppression des differents etats de sommeil: etude comportementale, EEG, et neuropharmacologique chez le chat.* Lyon, France: Imprimerie L.M.D., 1965.

Vogel, G. W., Barrowclough, B., & Giesler, D. D. Similarity of REM and sleep onset Stage 1 reports. Paper presented at the meeting of the Association for the Psychophysiological Study of Sleep, Santa Fe, New Mexico, March 1970.

Watson, R. Mental correlates of periorbital PIPs during REM sleep. Paper presented at the meeting of the Association for the Psychophysiological study of Sleep, Lake Minnewaska, New York, May 1972.

Weisz, R. Phenomenal correlates of discrete events in NREM sleep. Paper presented at the meeting of the Association for the Psychophysiological Study of Sleep, Bruges, Belgium, June 1971.

Wolpert, E. A. Studies in psychophysiology of dreams. II. An electromyographic study of dreaming. *Archives of General Psychiatry,* 1960, **2,** 231–241.

Wyatt, R. J., Gillin, J. C., Green, R., Horwitz, D., & Snyder, F. Measurement of phasic integrated potentials (PIP) during treatment with parachlorophenylalanine (PCPA). Paper presented at the meeting of the Association for the Psychophysiological Study of Sleep, Bruges, Belgium, June 1971.

EMPHASIS ON CENTRAL NERVOUS SYSTEM—PRIMARILY SURGICAL APPROACHES

CHAPTER SIX

Lateral Specialization of Cerebral Function in the Surgically Separated Hemispheres[1]

R. W. SPERRY

Division of Biology
California Institute of Technology

The main theme to emerge from the following is that there appear to be two modes of thinking, verbal and nonverbal, represented rather separately in left and right hemispheres, respectively, and that our educational system, as well as science in general, tends to neglect the nonverbal form of intellect. What it comes down to is that modern society discriminates against the right hemisphere.

The evidence for functional asymmetry in the cerebral hemispheres of man goes far back to the early observations of Dax and Broca in the 1800s (Critchley, 1961) regarding lateralization of speech and writing. Thinking has generally been correlated with language capacity, and hence the observed hemispheric lateralization of language could be considered as indicative of a corresponding lateralization in associated thinking processes. It is conceivable *a priori* that thinking must necessarily require the integrated action of both hemispheres, but we know in fact from hemispherectomy and commissurotomy studies that a single hemisphere can think independently in the complete absence of any assistance from the other. This is not to imply that the quality of thinking carried out in

[1] Work of the author and his laboratory is supported by Grant No. MH 03372 from the National Institute of Mental Health and the F. P. Hixon Fund of the California Institute of Technology.

one hemisphere is as good as when the two cooperate, only that the basic cerebral mechanisms requisite for conscious thinking can function effectively through a single hemisphere. We shall come back to this and related questions later.

Most of the evidence for hemispheric specialization in mental capacities comes historically from the differential symptoms produced by asymmetric cerebral damage. This evidence has been subject to the usual uncertainties and difficulties of assessing observations of clinical patient populations. As recently as 1962 (Mountcastle, 1961) the existence of true lateral differences in cerebral organization was still being questioned by the more cautious authorities, and the view that the two hemispheres of man are equal in functional potential at birth (Glees, 1967) continues to have wide acceptance.

The majority of studies in the past decade, however, including those on cerebral commissurectomy where direct comparisons can be made of the positive performance of each hemisphere on the same task in the same person, have come increasingly to reinforce support for a basic inherent specialization in hemispheric organization that, to a large extent, is innately predetermined. The last few years have produced a further burst of studies on normal subjects in which the utilization of a variety of lateralizing techniques including unilateral or competitive sensory input, differential reaction time latency, selective biofeedback techniques, and the like seem to confirm further the existence of qualitative lateral specialization of function in the normal intact hemispheres. Genetic models for the inheritance of cerebral dominance have been proposed, one of the most recent of which (Levy & Nagylaki, in press) postulates two genes, one determining which hemisphere is language dominant and the other determining whether hand control is contralateral or ipsilateral to the language hemisphere.

The following is restricted mainly to a brief review of some of the evidence for hemispheric specialization that has come from studies by a long line of research colleagues and myself on a group of some nine commissurotomy patients. The results, to forecast the outcome, seem to show that the surgically separated left hemisphere has its own mode of thinking that qualitatively is distinctly different from that used by the right hemisphere in the same individual. All are patients of Philip Vogel and Joseph Bogen, neurosurgeons at the White Memorial Medical Center in Los Angeles, and have undergone essentially the same rather special form of brain operation for treatment of intractable epileptic convulsions.

Put crudely, the operation consists of having the brain divided down the middle into right and left halves. More precisely, the surgery involves selective midline division of the main fiber systems that cross-connect the left and right hemispheres (Bogen, Fisher, & Vogel, 1965). The corpus callosum is sectioned in its entirety as is also the anterior commissure. The thin hippocampal commissure closely subjacent to the corpus callosum is not separately visualized, but is presumed to have been divided along with the callosum. The variable massa intermedia, as a potential bridge for seizure transmission, is also sectioned in those patients where it is observed to be present. All these sections are performed in a single operation to effect a rather complete anatomical and functional disconnection of the two cerebral hemispheres.

This kind of surgery is undertaken as a last resort measure for selected severe cases only; it constitutes a last ditch stand against advancing, life-threatening, epileptic convulsions that are not controlled by medication. The outcome with respect to seizure control has been remarkably good to date, but this is another story that we leave to our medical colleagues. Our own work is restricted to follow-up studies on the neurological and psychological effects of this surgical elimination of cross-talk between the hemispheres.

The behavioral symptoms produced by severance of these enormous systems of fiber cross-connections are found first of all to be surprisingly inconspicuous in ordinary behavior (Sperry, Gazzaniga, & Bogen, 1969). The hemispheres continue to function in the separated state at a fairly high level such that a person 2 years recovered and otherwise in good condition could easily go through a routine medical checkup without revealing that anything was particularly wrong—to someone unacquainted with his surgical history. This is what started our studies initially: The remarkable lack of any definite symptoms after section of the corpus callosum, or its congenital absence, was being used back in the 1940's and 1950s to support various far-out theories of how brains can operate at the upper levels without specific fiber connections.

Despite this deceptive normality of the cerebral commissurotomy patient to casual inspection and even in routine neurological tests, we are now able to demonstrate with controlled lateralized testing procedures a whole multitude of distinct neurological symptoms that reflect directly the lack of interhemispheric integration in nearly all mental activity. A long series of studies indicate that the two disconnected hemispheres function independently and in effect have each a separate mind of its own (Gazzaniga, 1965; Gazzaniga et al., 1967; Levy, 1969; Gordon & Sperry, 1969; Levy et al., 1971; Milner, & Taylor, 1971; Nebes, 1971;

Nebes & Sperry, 1971; Sperry, 1968c; Sperry *et al.*, 1969). Each of the separated hemispheres appears to have its own private sensations, perceptions, thoughts, feelings, and memories. Each hemisphere has its own inner visual world, each cut off from the conscious awareness of the other.

I turn now for present purposes to those observations in these same studies that relate to lateral differences in the cognitive properties of the two surgically separated hemispheres. Not being sure where perception stops and thinking begins in the brain, nor where thinking stops and motor expression starts, I will not attempt in the following to draw sharp distinctions along these lines. Very early in the postoperative examination of these subjects it became apparent that the disconnected left hemisphere processing information from the right hand and the right half visual field is the hemisphere that does essentially all the talking, reading, writing, and mathematical calculation in these right-handed subjects (Gazzaniga, Bogen, & Sperry, 1967). The disconnected right hemisphere on the other hand remains essentially mute, alexic, agraphic, and unable to carry out calculations beyond simple additions to sums under 20. In other words, thinking that deals with information processed through the left hand, the left half visual field, the right nostril or with any other information processed entirely within the right hemisphere, remains cut off from the centers for language and calculation located in the left hemisphere. These test results added up to a striking confirmation of hemispheric lateralization with respect to language in general.

With reference to thinking in the disconnected hemispheres, we can infer further that much of the thinking and reasoning that involved linguistic and numeric processes must also have been carried out in the left hemisphere. Those patients least afflicted with extracallosal damage have been able to carry on verbally in their school work and home life at a level where it was questionable in members of the immediate family whether abstract reasoning and symbolic thinking were at all affected beyond a weakening in mnemonic functions.

It was further apparent that the postoperative behavior of these patients was governed almost entirely from the more dominant, leading left hemisphere. Presumably it is the highly developed cognitive and expressive capacities of this dominant hemisphere and its tendency to take command of the motor system that are largely responsible for earlier impressions that no distinct symptoms result from complete section of the corpus callosum. There are reasons to think that the cognitive capacities of a single hemisphere are better inferred from the postoperative behavior of the commissurotomy patient than from that of the patient with a hemispherectomy.

The disconnected minor hemisphere, lacking language like the animal brain and thus unable to communicate what it is thinking or experiencing, is much less accessible to investigation, and accordingly the nature and quality of the inner mental life of the silent right hemisphere have remained relatively obscure. There is reluctance is some quarters to credit the minor hemisphere even with being conscious, the contention being that it is carried along in a reflex, trance-like state, with consciousness centered over in the dominant left hemisphere. The reasoning seems to be that the conscious self by nature has to be single and unified, as if the gates of heaven shall be opened only to one psyche per cranium.

Actually the evidence as we see it favors the view that the minor hemisphere is very conscious indeed, and further that both the separated left and the right hemispheres may be conscious simultaneously in different and even conflicting mental experiences that run along in parallel (Sperry, 1970a). From its nonverbal responses we infer that the minor hemisphere senses, perceives, thinks and feels all at a characteristically human level, and that it learns and remembers and has some reasoning capacity and considerable perceptual insight that is superior to that of the major hemisphere for certain things. Also that it may even do some silent reading of object names and some drawing, not to mention various things that we have not yet tested.

Much has been written and argued about the dependence of thinking upon language mechanisms—upon the implicit use of verbal symbols and the syntactical grammatic structure of language (Furth, 1971). In the performance of the surgically disconnected minor hemisphere we have an exceptional opportunity from which to gain added insight into the level and kind of thinking that can go on in the human brain without benefit of language. Remembering that in the great majority of tests, and in all tests where any linguistic processing is involved, it is the disconnected major left hemisphere that is superior and dominant, we can look now at some of the kinds of exceptional activities in which it is the disconnected minor hemisphere that excels.

It was found very early (Bogen & Gazzaniga, 1965; Bogen, 1969) that the minor hemisphere is superior in the construction of block designs and also in copying and drawing various test figures like a Necker cube, a swastika, Greek cross, etc. The results from these standard tests for visual constructional apraxia left it open as to whether the hemispheric differences involved praxis and motor expression primarily or more central cognitive processing.

Indirect evidence regarding lateralization of more complex central functions was obtained from studies of another patient, an "asymptomatic" case of congenital absence of the corpus callosum (Saul & Sperry, 1968; Sperry, 1968b, Sperry, 1970b). This agenesis patient performed easily most of the tests for hemispheric cross integration that the commissurotomy patients continued to fail even years after surgery. Her performance in more complex mental activities, however, indicated a consistent pattern of impairment. Verbal thinking and reasoning tasks showed normal or slightly above normal performance, like the verbal WAIS score of 112. By contrast, a whole array of nonverbal spatial activities were markedly subnormal, like geometry, geography, and drawing spatial representations.

Amytal tests indicated the presence in this agenesis patient of language in both hemispheres. This of course, precludes the typical division of labor in which the verbal and nonverbal functions are carried out in separate hemispheres. With both the verbal and the nonverbal perceptual functions necessarily forced to develop within the same hemisphere, the latter were apparently handicapped in favor of verbal development. The general observation that intellectual performance appears not to rise above mediocrity in such cases (about 17 asymptomatic cases of agenesis of the corpus callosum are recorded in medical history) suggests that the verbal as well as the nonverbal mode of thinking does not flourish when both are obliged to develop within the same hemisphere.

To better separate praxis from central processing in the commissurotomy subject Levy (1969a) devised a test that required only a very simple motor readout, manual pointing, but a rather complex understanding and manipulation of spatial relationships based on cross-modal spatial transformations. Thirteen sets of wooden blocks small enough to be grasped in the hand were constructed with three similar but different blocks in each set. Each block differed from the other two within a set either in shape or in the relationship of surface textures and markings. One of the three blocks was placed in the subject's left or right hand for identification by touch through the right or left hemisphere, respectively. The working hand and the test items were hidden from view behind a screen. The subject then looked at a card in free view with three patterns of what the blocks would look like if they were constructed of cardboard and unfolded into two dimensions. Both hemispheres saw the two-dimensional patterns but only the hemisphere holding the block knew the answer. The subject was asked to point to the pattern which represented the block which he was holding. The task required that the subject try to mentally fold up the visual pattern or unfold the tactual block, or otherwise reach a correct match between the tactual block and the visual form. The tabulated scores showed the minor hemisphere to be two to three times more proficient in this task than the verbal hemisphere. In addition to the quantitative superiority of the minor hemisphere, Levy also found a qualitative difference. When the left hand was feeling a block, responses tended to be quite rapid, direct, and silent. On the other hand, when the right hand was feeling a block, the subjects often took as much as 45 sec to respond; the responses were hesitant and the subjects tended to verbalize aloud with running comments on their logical approach to the task. It appeared that the two hemispheres were processing the same information in entirely different ways, the left thinking in verbal, symbolic, analytic terms while the right utilized simple visualization. Parts of the test that yielded the best scores for one hemisphere gave the worst scores for the other and conversely. From an analysis of the data, Levy inferred the presence of a mutual antagonism or interference between the two modes of mental processing and suggested that the evolution of cerebral dominance provides for the separation into separate hemispheres of these two different modes of thinking (Levy, 1969b).

The standard Ravens Progressive Matrices Test was modified for presentation to the commissurectomy subjects by Zaidel and myself (Zaidel & Sperry, 1971): In this test the subject examines in free vision a pattern matrix with a missing section and then feels with the left or right hand out of sight behind a screen for the correct missing section among a choice array of several raised Braille-like figures. This test, like the foregoing, involves a cross-modal matching between the visual figure and the tactual perception. The left hand–right hemisphere combination performed about twice as well as did the right hand–left hemisphere. As observed earlier by Levy, the thinking seemed very different depending on whether the subject worked with the left or with the right hand. The performance with the left hand was silent and rapid, while that with the right hand was drawn-out, and accompanied generally by a running, overt vocalization as the subjects talked and reasoned aloud to themselves, with comments like "two lines up, need three dots, spreads to the right," etc.

The special spatial aptitude of the minor hemisphere is not confined to the visual modality. Milner and Taylor (1971) used nondescript shapes made of bent wire to test for perception and memory of shape where both the recognition and the recall were based entirely upon touch with vision excluded. The results again revealed a striking superiority for the disconnected right hemisphere, and showed that in the purely tactual realm, complex patterned stimuli can be discriminated and remembered without verbal coding.

In a test devised by Nebes (1971) for the perception of part–whole relationships, the subject was given a part or segment of a whole circle to identify and then tries to select from a choice array the correct whole circle to match the sample segment. The sample and the choice array were presented in three ways: both through touch, or cross-modally from touch to vision, or from vision to touch. Whereas in control trials the direct matching of whole circles to whole circles, or of arc segments to arcs could be done well by either hemisphere, when it came to matching the parts to the whole, the right hemisphere was much better than the left. In another test used by Nebes (1971) the subject first examined an exploded or fragmented pattern and then felt behind a screen, using either the left or the right hand, for the correct one of three raised patterns which the fragmented pattern would form if put together. Again the right hemisphere–left hand proved much superior, with the scores for the left hemisphere hardly rising above chance. In other words, this task was almost too much for the verbal hemisphere.

In a modification of the Kasan–Haufmann Concept Formation Test used by Kumar (1971) the subjects were required to discover by trial and error, with controlled feedback from the examiner, the correct properties for sorting 16 items into 4 categories. The right hemisphere excelled in acquiring concepts that involved spatial qualities like height, size, shape, and the left excelled when the concepts involved familiar objects with distinctions that were easily verbalized.

Scanning movements of the eyes from the right to the left edge of an object being examined in free vision results in the formation of two complete perceptual images in the divided brain, one in each hemisphere (Sperry, 1970a). The well-known constancy of the visual image in the presence of eye movements must be taken into account. This right–left duplication is something that would logically occur also in the normal brain, not only for vision but for other senses as well. The cortical sensory map for the face is represented bilaterally in both hemispheres. We have often wondered what good may be served by so much redundant right–left doubling in the cerebral operation. If, as we now suspect, each hemisphere processes its sensory imput in distinctly different ways, then such a doubling begins to make sense. In the normal intact brain the right and left contributions to any given perceptual experience become fused, making it difficult or impossible to determine which hemisphere is contributing what.

In another procedure employed more recently in studies headed by Trevarthen and Levy (Levy, Trevarthen, & Sperry, 1972) different conflicting percepts are formed in the left and right sides. A left–right composite visual stimulus such as two separate half faces joined in the midline, is flashed at $\frac{1}{10}$ of a second with the subject's gaze held steady on a central fixation point. Each hemisphere by a process of illusory perceptual completion, gets the impression that it has seen a separate and different whole face. In other words, the two hemispheres are induced to see different things, faces or whatever, at the same point in space at the same time. This is something that the normal brain of course does not do. With the percept of each hemisphere set off in its own inner visual world, each cut off from awareness of the other, the commissurotomy subjects remain blandly unaware that there is anything peculiar about the appearance of these chimeric stimuli, even in the presence of leading questions such as "Did you notice anything strange about the stimulus?" The same principle has been used for presentation of geometric and nondescript figures, words, serial patterns, movement stimuli, colors, and combinations of these.

With this procedure we get two rival competing processes set up in the left and right hemispheres. The question then is which of these will dominate the response under different test conditions, that is, with different categories of test material, with different mental and motor sets, and with different forms of readout and central processing.

In general the results with this type of study conform with the earlier findings in that, if any linguistic processing is involved, the subjects' response is dominated by the left hemisphere. In other words, the right half of the stimulus is responded to rather than the left. However, in the perceptual discrimination of faces, and for any kind of direct visual–visual matching of shape or pattern, the right hemisphere dominates. This is especially true with nondescript shapes that resist verbal description. Even when no competing stimulus is involved the left hemisphere finds these to be exceedingly difficult to discriminate and handle. Special difficulty was also observed in attempts to associate names with faces; whereas the names themselves were easily learned or the faces easily discriminated, the subjects had great difficulty in associating the correct name with the proper face, presumably because the two were processed in separate hemispheres.

Even when words were used as stimuli presented in cursive script the minor hemisphere was found to dominate the verbal hemisphere provided that no interpretation of word meaning was involved and the readout required only a direct visual matching of the word pattern. Dominance promptly shifted to the opposite hemisphere when the task instructions were changed to demand a conceptual transformation involving the meaning of the word.

Although no direct perceptual or psychological conflict seems to be produced by these composite left–right stimuli, the subjects do show signs of secondary confusion as when one hemisphere sees or hears the other giving what the first hemisphere considers to be an erroneous response. This is something that we have to deal with all along in working with these people. When this happens, the correctly informed hemisphere tends to act disgusted with itself—the subject may give a negative shake of the head, or, if it is the verbal hemisphere, he may make remarks like "Now why did I do that? What made me do that?" We purposely do not dwell on these conflicts and pass along to the next trial.

This kind of annoyance, however, in the second hemisphere with what is a correct response for the first hemisphere, along with the occasional double correct responses in which first one and then the second hemisphere gives a different and correct response lends further support to our contention that each hemisphere is indeed having its own separate and different perceptual experience, with both being conscious simultaneously and in parallel.

The chimeric studies also reaffirm our earlier impressions that the left and right hemispheres perceive and apprehend things in ways that are qualitatively different. For example, in dealing with faces, the right hemisphere seems to respond to the whole face directly as a perceptual unit, whereas the left hemisphere seems to focus separately on salient features like the moustache, the eyes, the hair—to which verbal labels are easily attached. The disconnected right hemisphere is found in the tests to date to be the superior and dominant brain for perceptual recognition of faces and of nondescript figures as whole patterns, and for dealing with spatial and part–whole relationships, for noverbal thinking, and for direct perceptual transformation, but not conceptual or symbolic transformation. These latter are done better by the verbal, left brain, which appears to be the superior and dominant brain for verbal communication, linguistic and numeric processing, sequential and analytic thinking, for conceptual symbolic recoding, and for directing motor activity in general.

Another thing to come out of these studies is the demonstration that the minor hemisphere is quite capable of capturing and controlling the motor system under conditions in which it is in equal and free competition with the major hemisphere—where the sensory input is equated and the subject is quite free to use either the left or the right hand. We had not seen this so convincingly before. It suggests that in the normal intact brain the impetus for voluntary, willed movements need not be triggered entirely from the major, dominant leading hemisphere, but may be prompted in some activities directly from the minor hemisphere.

During thinking in the normal brain the two hemispheres cooperate presumably and complement each other, each contributing its respective specialty. A continuum of possibilities is conceivable for such cooperation. At one extreme one could have a distinct alternation of left and right functions performed separately. At the other one can picture a highly unified, bilateral process in which both hemispheres work as one, each contributing fractional elements to a unified whole. I would guess that an intimate interaction along the latter lines, mixing the spatial and the linguistic aspects of the thought sequence, is more typical than is a series of distinct alternations from one hemisphere to the other.

The extent to which thinking is dependent normally on right–left integration should be objectively deducible from the difference in the quality of thinking of these commissurotomy patients before and after their surgery. Unfortunately, precise measurements on logical ability or spatial creativity or the like, are not available and would be difficult to obtain. The majority of the patients already have extensive brain damage in addition to the commissurectomy. We, therefore, would base conclusions on the top performance among the few cases with least impairment. Thought deficits produced by the surgery seem to be sufficiently mild at best (as in L.B. or N.G.) that the patient's family report only an impression that there seems to be some impairment, as in capacity to handle mathematics in school. However, it is not so severe as to be blatantly obvious. Weakening of memory capacity for postsurgical events is the primary consistent complaint. What the foregoing means probably is not so much that few deficits are present, but only that the ordinary social encounter fails to reveal them. One continues to be amazed at what can pass for reasonable mentality under the conditions of ordinary social interaction.

The minor hemisphere of one patient scored better on Levy's spatial transformation test than did 31% of controls from university sophomores. Postoperative scores on the WAIS for these patients gathered by Levy (1969a) show several to be well above normal on the verbal scale. Tasks like comprehension and vocabulary, are relatively unaffected, as compared with performance tasks like digit symbol, block design and picture arrangement which are markedly impaired. The scores for picture completion are exceptional in being high though this last seems at first glance to be a more spatial than verbal task. This test is one, however, in which the minor hemisphere could be used for detecting and fixing on the missing answer, leaving the target of fixation to be named by the major hemisphere. We commonly see this kind of interhemispheric cooperation in the commissurectomy patients and presume that it prevails in the thinking of the intact brain.

It should be remembered that the postulated spatial–verbal antagonism or interference effect in hemispheric processing is not one of total incompatibility. Both functional modes can be carried out within the same hemisphere when conditions require it, as with congenital absence of the corpus callosum (Sperry, 1968b, 1970b), early hemispherectomy, or any extensive lateral brain damage, or in that small percentage of the population in which language develops bilaterally (Milner, Branch & Rasmussen, 1966; Jones, 1966). It is only that forced sharing of the same hemisphere by both modes appears to prevent top level performance for either.

Looking back over the evidence one sees an implication in the findings that strong cerebral dominance and specialization are good, whereas cerebral ambivalence is less so. If it be true that a hemisphere committed to language is thereby handicapped in the spatial, perceptual, nonverbal functions like geometry, drawing, sculptural and mechanical ingenuity, then this should show up statistically in a population of left-handers. This is because cerebral representation of language tends to be more bilateralized in left-handers, as determined from the way in which they recover from cerebral injuries. Silverman, Adevai, and McGough (1966) found left-handers to be inferior to right-handers in basic perceptual tests for "field dependency" and tactual localization. It was suggested that sinistrals have a lesser degree of hemispheric differentiation than do dextrals. Sinistrals have also been reported to do less well than dextrals on tests of spatial orientation and perceptual closure (James et al., 1967). Levy (1969a) compared a group of 10 left-handers with 15 right-handers, selected from graduate science students, and found that the left-handers showed three times a greater discrepancy between the verbal and performance scale on the WAIS. The performance score, reflecting right hemispheric function predominantly, was always lower as predicted. A similar discrepancy has been reported by Lansdell (1969) for persons who have developed right hemisphere speech as a result of early birth injury, etc. Furthermore, Nebes (1971) using his part–whole circle–arc test, found that Caltech left-handers as a group scored very significantly below right-handers, with hardly any overlap.

All of this fits the idea that the verbal and nonverbal perceptual faculties are antagonistic as inferred by Levy and do not do so well when they develop for one reason or another within the same hemisphere. The more common tendency, apparently, when this occurs, is for the nonverbal performance functions to be handicapped in favor of the verbal, though we presume the opposite may also occur. Left-handers who can align themselves with Leonardo da Vinci, Raphael, Michelangelo, and many other giants in history should remember that all of this is very statistical. Individual sinistral brains come in varied degrees and kinds of right–

left asymmetry. A complete mirror switch should leave no effect on cerebral performance—save for those little problems of getting along in a predominantly right-handed world. In any case it may be seen that differential balance and loading between these right and left hemispheric faculties in different individuals could make for quite a spectrum of individual variations in the structure of human intellect—from the mechanical or artistic geniuses on the one hand who can hardly express themselves in writing or speech, to the highly articulate individuals at the other extreme who think almost entirely in verbal terms.

Individual variations of this kind we believe to be hereditary, or at least innate, to a considerable degree, more than is perhaps commonly recognized. Left-handedness, for example, seems to be a familial trait for which genetic models are proposed. Anatomical asymmetries in the brain correlated with cerebral dominance (Geschwind, 1970) have been reported recently (Wada, 1970) to be demonstrable already at birth in the brains of stillborn infants. Dyslexia, a reading and language disability, is agreed to be congenital usually, and often shows a clear family history with a higher incidence among males and sinistrals. I should mention perhaps that one of the commissurotomy patients is a left-hander, and shows a reversal of lateral specialization with speech centered in the right hemisphere, but like left-handers in general no switch has occurred apparently in the specialized spatial perceptual capacities, so that both of these must compete within the right hemisphere.

Through forced training or through spontaneous imitation the genetic left-hander may come to learn to use the naturally subordinate hand for writing, etc., but this is said to invite difficulties, conflict, tensions, stammering, and other impediments to mental proficiency (Trembly, 1970). There is a remarkable account by Jones (1966) of four patients who had been stammerers from early childhood, were shown to have developed bilateral speech by the amytal test, and then all four lost the stammer in their speech as a result of brain operations performed for other reasons that apparently put out of action the speech mechanisms on one side.

The observed dichotomy between verbal and nonverbal mental capacities will suggest to some readers the possibility of looking for correlated male–female differences. We have not pursued this ourselves, as yet, but we note that males are said to be six times more frequently afflicted than females with congenital language disability, that in a world-wide application of the Porteus (1965) maze test in many different cultures girls scored significantly inferior to boys, that Smith (1967) claims females show a selective spatial disability (compensated presumably by extra verbal ability?)

that females lacking one X chromosome are average or above in verbal
abilities, but show a profound impairment in nonverbal preceptual performance (Alexander, Ehrhardt, & Money, 1966) and that genetic
females masculinized *in utero* by excess male hormone show an exceptionally
high incidence of very high IQ (Money, 1970). The common tendency
has been to write off observed mental differences between the sexes as a
product of social and cultural pressures. More and more the accumulating
evidence in psychology (Sperry, 1971) points to more basic biological
and evolutionary innate factors. According to Levy, (1971), "It is
hard to reject the notion that a spatial–perceptive deficit in women is
a sex-linked genetically-determined incapacity, an incapacity which possibly
results from hemispheres less well laterally specialized than that of males."
The evidence is such, however, that it would seem wise to reserve any
conclusions here until more facts become available.

The Discussion of Dr. Sperry's Paper

LED BY DR. PAUL J. WOODS
Hollins College

Woods: This is certainly exciting and fascinating work. It has been my
experience in talking with students, laymen, and professionals outside of
the area that when people first hear about Dr. Sperry's work they are
immediately interested in the research and impressed with psychology's
ability to discover such important aspects of brain functioning. It is a
sure-fire way to wake up a disinterested class, and it is excellent ammuni-
tion when one has to argue for the value of basic research.

Regarding some of the specific findings, it seems to me astounding that
the minor hemisphere is able to process verbal material without possessing
verbal ability. As you will recall, a word tachistoscopically flashed to
the minor hemisphere could be processed or recognized, as shown by
the fact that the left arm could retrieve a related object that was out of
sight. The retrieval can apparently be accomplished without the use of
language.

One question: What are the implications of the improvement manifested by the young boy? Is it not surprising that he is getting better?

He is certainly not having neural regeneration. Can it be that new functions are being learned by the minor hemisphere, and do your findings have relevance for the theory of equipotentiality?

Open Discussion

Sperry: One possibility to consider is that he is developing speech in the minor hemisphere. A certain fraction of the population does have bilateral speech. We find it in one patient who was accidentally discovered to be totally lacking in a callosum. This was a college sophomore with a C+ record. Another possibility is that the contralateral systems of the brain are being enriched and utilized in a way that they could not be used before. Both hands are represented in both hemispheres, predominantly in the contralateral, of course, but there is a crude representation also in each hemisphere, of the ipsilateral hand. It is possible that vision, also, has its ipsilateral representation. Thus far, we aren't able to select between these alternatives, but suspect some of both.

Dr. Allen Paivio (University of Western Ontario): I have a couple of questions that stem from my work and relate to your work with these patients: Is there anything different about your subjects in terms of their introspective awareness of themselves and their environment? Do they feel different after the operation than they did before? The other question is: Can you detect, by common-sense questions, the lack of contact between the systems? For example, consider the illustration that I gave this morning of asking a person to describe his living room. Can your subjects perform such a common-sense task which requires contact between a nonverbal representation and a verbal output of that information?

Sperry: The patients don't report anything to indicate they are aware that they are particularly different than they used to be. Some subjects report things like, "I don't get the message from the left hand" or, "The left hand is numb," during the early months after the surgery. In general, however, the general rule applies that brains seem to be oblivious of what they lack. Take out a whole hemisphere and the other hemisphere doesn't know it. It's like a blind spot in the visual field; you tend not to know it isn't there. In short, we have not seen anything to indicate that there is a difference.

As to the second point, we haven't pushed that thoroughly. I tried this last week, in the smallest boy—asking him to visualize former places where he had lived and been, and so on—and the things that came out were very discouraging, in terms of looking for a separation of the spatial engrams. Since his surgery, they have become pretty intermixed. We are still studying the matter.

Dr. Fred Gault (Western Michigan University): Could you just speak briefly about the effect of these procedures on the epilepsies? Does the individual still have to focus, and if he does, what does this tell us about why it is not expressed as a seizure?

Sperry: The answer in part is that I, by policy, don't know anything about epilepsy. For one patient, the epilepsy was building up, and she came into the hospital in a coma after having had more than 50 seizures the preceding 3 days. She has not had a seizure since recovering from the surgery, and even the EEG, which was abnormal before the surgery is reported by Dr. Bogen to have returned to a normal condition. The very first patient went 7 years without a generalized convulsion, but I'm afraid I would have to refer these and related questions to the medical people.

Dr. T. H. Bhatti (University of Virginia): A study conducted in Italy indicated that injection of sodium amytal in one hemisphere produced emotionally depressive reactions, whereas injection of the second hemisphere of the same individual on another day produced manic, or euphoric, responses. This finding was very consistent over a number of cases, but has not been corroborated by any of the other studies using sodium amytal injection. Have you had occasion to observe any difference between hemispheres in emotional responses?

Sperry: No, but we have not done enough work with emotion to exclude the possibility.

Dr. Allen Rechtschaffen (University of Chicago): I had a thought with respect to dreams. During the REM period of sleep, most of the areas of the brain tested show an increase in unit-firing. In the cat, at least, there is one area which shows a decrease in unit-firing, and that is the callosum. Now the thought occurred to me that perhaps dreams may be the way they are because, during the REM period, it may be that you would one time dream with one-half your brain, the other time with the other half of your brain, and one-half doesn't know what the other half is doing. I was thinking of the two examples I cited yesterday, where in one dream a person has a visual image of talking to an old lady, and then suddenly the phrase comes into mind, "I have got to surround the weekend." Maybe the talking part, with the visual image, is a right-sided dream, and then suddenly, an engram in the left brain takes over, and you get this discontinuity, and she starts to dream with the left side of the brain.

The other example: The subject was thinking about his girl friend's problems, and suddenly he sees the tears falling down her eyes in four straight vertical lines; that could be a shift over from a left- to a right-sided dream. This could possibly account for the very prevalent appearance of strangers in dreams; about 40% of the characters in dreams are strangers, people we don't recognize. They are not unusual in any other way; they are just people we have never seen before. Perhaps these are people we *have* seen before, but if we are having the dream in the right hemisphere, we don't recognize them with a verbal label. In the waking life of your subjects, do they show any discontinuities in spontaneous mentation that resembles our normal dreams?

Sperry: A good analysis of their speech, alone, as well as of their modes of thinking, is certainly called for, but it is a very difficult thing to do. You would expect their thinking and their speech, maybe, to be lacking in certain properties that normally are contributed by the other hemisphere. Even the simple things are hard enough, but we just haven't gotten to an analysis of this kind.

Rechtschaffen: We would not expect their dreams to be different from anyone else's dreams; but you might expect, if my idea has any merit at all, that in waking life, they have sudden dramatic shifts in the stream of consciousness, depending on which kinds of engrams were prepotent in this spontaneous consciousness. And you wouldn't necessarily find evidence of such shifts from conversations with them, because while you are conversing with them, the left hemisphere would necessarily be predominating.

Sperry: That's the trouble. The left hemisphere predominates nearly all, if not all, of the time under ordinary conditions, and if you don't get this kind of information though their conversation, how can you get it? It wouldn't be easy.

Dr. Larry Thompson (Duke University): Have you looked at slow potential changes over the left and right brains of these patients?

Sperry: Not ourselves, and I know of nothing striking to come out of such recording.

Dr. Ralph Hefferline (Columbia University): Does your statement that each hemisphere has motor control, and can initiate action, imply anything about the moment-to-moment muscular status of the body in terms of postural readiness, and so on? Wouldn't there be a tendency toward rather intense conflicts and spastic conditions?

Sperry: There is a whole series of unifying factors that tend to keep motor behavior together, like the double representation of the motor system for the axial body, face, neck, and so on. Whichever hemisphere is running the show, it thus runs it in a unified way.

Audience: Is there a shift back and forth with one side or the other being dominant at any given instant, or does each hemisphere always have partial control?

Sperry: Under testing conditions, you can force the minor hemisphere to retrieve items and do other things; but, under ordinary conditions, the major hemisphere seems to dominate most of the time. It appears that, for the first several months after surgery, the subjects are really alert and conscious only in the major hemisphere, and not in the minor. The minor seems to be more severely depressed, as if it is more subject to cerebral (surgical) shock.

Bhatti: In reference to the coordination of movements, particularly on the two sides, it may be relevant to note that in an encephalic child that is born without any of the forebrain structures, if you hold the child so that his toes touch the table, he will make walking attempts; and if you put him in the water, he will make swimming movements. These apparently are coordinated at the midbrain, or brain stem, level. The basic pattern of these movements is present, and can be initiated by either one, or both, of the hemispheres.

Dr. Peter MacNeilage (University of Texas at Austin): Three brief questions: First, have any of your patients been typists, and if so, have they had problems with typing? How does the right hemisphere perform on visually presented spatial prepositions, like "up," "down," "left," "right," "back," and so on? And third, can the right hemisphere assimilate visual–verbal information? Like, what is the perceptual span, and does a following masking visual stimulus have as much effect as in normal subjects?

Sperry: Our subjects have not been typists. But, some cases of Akelaitis with extensive section of the callosum, apparently, continued typing; and one of them continued to play the piano with both hands, as does one of these present cases at a very simple level.

With regard to spatial prepositions: When we flashed words like "up," "down," and so on, to the minor hemisphere, the responses were pretty nil except in the youngest subject who by now has reached the point where he often can report things flashed for the left-half field. How he does it, we don't yet know. There is a big difference here as to whether such surgery was performed at the age of ten or so, before losing the plasticity of development. The congenital case showed the extreme of this kind of compensation. With her, we can go through all of the tests and discover practically no symptoms at all. It is only in complex mental functions that symptoms show up.

The third question, about how good and how fast is the perceptual capacity of the right hemisphere to assimilate letter information: quicker than the left, I suppose. There is no problem as far as receiving detailed perceptual information. You mean refined details, don't you?

MacNeilage: Yes. I mean how many letters can the subjects perceive in, say, a 12-msec flash; or how much are they affected by a following visual masking stimulus?

Sperry: We haven't measured this, but they perceive four- and five-letter words, flashed at a tenth of a second, or less. There are difficulties with peripheral vision as well as timing.

Audience: In the new learning of new words, are there any differences in the fact that pitch is taken in one hemisphere, and rythm by another?

Sperry: No such differences have been noted after surgery. Rythm is in both.

Audience: Has anyone had occasion to learn a new language since their operation?

Sperry: We have not taken on the problem of new language learning. Some subjects have been bilingual, but we haven't noticed any differences between the original and the second language. Both seem to be lateralized similarly.

Audience: If the left hemisphere is active, can the right hemisphere be independently active? For instance, can you have someone reading with one side, and simultaneously do arithmetic with the other? If so, what is the mechanism?

Sperry: When one hemisphere takes command of the motor system of the brain stem and cord, it tends to prevent the other hemisphere from getting into that system. Now, if there is a common motor set throughout the whole body so that one hemisphere doesn't conflict with, or mutually exclude, the other, two behaviors may be carried out by right and left hemispheres without conflict—in this case, you can get the two hemispheres working in parallel.

Audience: Can one hemisphere read and speak what was read, while the other performs a tactual task?

Sperry: We sometimes deliberately put the right hand to a task, like doing a tic-tac-toe, or sketching, or rolling balls, just to get it out of the picture so that we can get at the minor hemisphere; some such routine tasks can apparently be performed without disrupting the activity of the minor hemisphere expressed through the left hand.

REFERENCES

Alexander, D., Ehrhardt, A. A., & Money, J. Defective figure drawing, geometric and human in Turner's syndrome. *Journal Nervous and Mental Disease*, 1966, **142**, 161–167.

Bogen, J. E. The other side of the brain. I: Dysgraphia and dyscopia following cerebral commissurotomy. *Bulletin L.A. Neurol. Society*, April 1969, **39**, 73–105.

Bogen, J. E., & Gazzaniga, M. S. Cerebral commissurotomy in man. Minor hemisphere dominance for certain visouspatial functions. *Journal of Neurosurgery*, 1965, **23**, 394–399.

Bogen, J. E., Fisher, E. D. & Vogel, P. J. Cerebral commissurotomy: A second case report. *Journal of the American Medical Association*, 1965, **194**, 1328–1329.

Critchley, MacD. Speech and speech-loss in relation to the duality of the brain. In V. B. Mountcastle (Ed.), *Interhemispheric relations and cerebral dominance*. Baltimore, Maryland: Johns Hopkins Press, 1961. Pp. 208–213.

Furth, H. G. Linguistic deficiency and thinking: Research with deaf subjects, 1964–1967. *Psychological Bulletin*, 1971, **76** (1), 58–72.

Gazzaniga, M. S. Some effects of cerebral commissurotomy on monkey and man. Unpublished Ph.D. thesis, California Institute of Technology, 1965.

Gazzaniga, M. S., Bogen, J. E., & Sperry, R. W. Dyspraxia following division of the cerebral commissures. *Journal of Nervous and Mental Disease*, 1967, **16**, 606–612.

Geschwind, N. The organization of language and the brain. *Science*, 1970, **170**, 940–944.

Glees, P. Are both sides of our central nervous system of equal value? *Triangle, The Sandoc Journal of Medical Science*, 1967, **8**(3), 101–108.

Gordon, H. W., & Sperry, R. W. Lateralization of olfactory perception in the surgically separated hemispheres in man. *Neuropsychologia*, 1969, **7**, 111–120.

James, W. E., Mefford, R. B., Jr., & Wieland, B. Repetitive psychometric measures: Handedness and performance. *Perceptual and Motor Skills*, 1967, **25**, 209–212.

Jones, R. K. Observations on stammering after localized cerebral injury. *Journal of Neurology, Neurosurgery and Psychiatry*, 1966, **29**, 192–195.

Kumar, S. Lateralization of concept formation in human cerebral hemispheres, *Biol. Ann. Rept.* California Institute of Technology, 1971, No. 136, 118.

Lansdell, H. Verbal and nonverbal factors in right-hemisphere speech: Relation to early neurological history. *Journal of Comparative and Physiological Psychology*, 1969, **69**, 734–738.

Levy, J. Information processing and higher psychological functions in the disconnected hemispheres of human commissurotomy patients. Unpublished Thesis, California Institute of Technology, 1969. (a)

Levy, J. Possible basis for the evolution of lateral specialization of the human brain. *Nature*, 1969, **224**, 614–615. (b)

Levy, J. Lateral specialization of the human brain: Behavioral manifestations and possible evolutionary basis. 32nd Annual Biology Colloquium on the Biology of Behavior, April 13–14, 1971. Oregon State University, Corvallis, Oregon.

Levy, J., & Nagylaki, T. A model for the genetics of handedness, (in press).

Levy, J., Trevarthen, C., & Sperry, R. W. Perception of bilateral chimeric figures following hemisphere deconnection. *Brain*, 1972, **95**, 61–78.

Milner, B., & Taylor, L. Right hemisphere superiority in tactile pattern-recognition after cerebral commissurotomy: Evidence for nonverbal memory. *Neuropsychologia*, 1971, **9**, 1–15.

Milner, B., Branch, C., & Rasmussen, T. Evidence for bilateral speech representation in some non-right-handers. *Transcriptions of the American Neurological Association*, 1966, **91**, 306–308.

Money, J. Sexual dimorphism and homosexual gender identity. *Psychological Bulletin*, 1970, **74**, 425–440.

Mountcastle, V. B. (Ed.) *Interhemispheric relations and cerebral dominance*. Baltimore, Maryland: Johns Hopkins Press, 1961.

Nebes, R. D. Investigation on lateralization of function in the disconnected hemispheres of man. Unpublished Thesis, California Institute of Technology, 1971.

Nebes, R. D. Superiority of the minor hemisphere in commissurectomized man for perception of part-whole relations. *Cortex*, 1972, **7**, 333–349.

Nebes, R. D., & Sperry, R. W. Hemispheric deconnection with cerebral birth injury in the dominant arm area. *Neuropsychologia*, 1971, **9**, 247–259.

Porteus, S. D. *Porteus maze tests: Fifty years application.* Pacific Books, 1965.

Saul, R., & Sperry, R. W. Absence of commissurotomy symptoms with agenesis of the corpus callosum. *Neurology*, 1968, **18**, 307.

Silverman, A. J., Adevai, G., & McGough, E. W. Some relationships between handedness and perception. *Journal of Psychometric Research*, 1966, **10**(2), 151–158.

Smith, I. M. *Spatial ability.* San Diego: Robert R. Knapp, 1967.

Sperry, R. W. Mental unity following surgical disconnection of the cerebral hemispheres. *The Harvey lectures*, Ser. 62. New York: Academic Press, 1968. Pp. 293–323. (a)

Sperry, R. W. Plasticity of neural maturation. *Developmental Biology*, Supplement 2, 27th Symposium. New York: Academic Press, 1968. Pp. 306–327. (b)

Sperry, R. W. Hemisphere deconnection and unity in conscious awareness. *American Psychologist*, 1968, **23**(10), 723–733. (c)

Sperry, R. W. Perception in the absence of the neocortical commissures. *The Association for Research in Nervous & Mental Disease.* 1970, **48**, Ch. VII. (a)

Sperry, R. W. Cerebral dominance in perception. In F. A. Young and D. B. Lindsley (Eds.), *Early experience in visual information processing in perceptual and reading disorders.* Washington, D.C.: National Academy of Science, 1970. Pp. 167–178. (b)

Sperry, R. W. How a developing brain gets itself properly wired for adaptive function. In E. Tobach, E. Shaw, and L. R. Aronson (Eds.), *The biopsychology of development.* New York: Academic Press, 1971. Pp. 27–44.

Sperry, R. W., Gazzaniga, M. S., & Bogen, J. E. Interhemispheric relationships: The neocortical commissures; syndromes of hemisphere disconnection. In P. J. Vinken and G. W. Bruyn (Eds.), *Handbook of Clinical Neurology*, Vol. 4. Amsterdam: North Holland, 1969. Pp. 273–290.

Trembly, D. Should your child write with the left hand? In J. I. Arena (Ed.), Building Handwriting Skills in Dyslexic Children. San Rafael, California: Academic Therapy Publications, 1970. Pp. 107–113.

Wada, J. Paper presented at 9th International Congress of Neurology, New York, 1969. Cited by Geschwind: *Science*, 1970, **170**, 944.

Zaidel, D., & Sperry, R. W. Performance by the left and right hemispheres on the Raven's colored progressive matrices. *Biology Annual Report*, California Institute of Technology, 1971, No. **130**, 115.

EMPHASIS ON PERIPHERAL MEASURES—PRIMARILY
AUTONOMIC BEHAVIOR

CHAPTER SEVEN

The Role of Consciousness and Cognition in Autonomic Behavior Change

WILLIAM W. GRINGS

University of Southern California

This paper deals with some of the ways that research on autonomically mediated behavior interacts with research on higher mental processes in humans. It emphasizes psychophysiological responses of the type associated with emotional experience and, particularly, the role that conscious verbal processes play in determining learning and unlearning of such physiological responses in emotion. The topic might be called the study of relations between cognitive thought processes and the conditioning of internal physiological reactions.

Research on verbal reports as they relate to the psychophysiology of emotional behavior has focused upon a few crucial questions. One concentrates on gross relations between cognitive experience and physiological reaction during emotional states. A typical question with such an orientation would be "Does autonomic behavior correlate with subjective experience and with verbal reports of such experience?" There is a long history of affirmative answers (McCurdy, 1950) suggesting that reports of intense experiences accompany strong autonomic reactions. On the other hand, work pursuing the question by means of correlations between subjective reports and amplitudes of autonomic response (Mandler, Mandler, & Uviller, 1958; Mandler & Kremen, 1958) supports only the conclusion that a positive relation does exist but that it is small and observable more through secondary variables of task performance than through direct correlation of physiological changes and conscious experience.

Views about conscious reactions to internal responses as providing vital ingredients to emotional behavior have persisted since the earliest days

233

of the James–Lange theory (Wenger, 1950). During the past decade, work on this type of question has been given quite a boost by the use of novel experimental arrangements which manipulate as independent variables one or the other aspects of the pair (i.e., cognition or physiological reaction). An approach made well-known by Schachter and his colleagues (Schachter & Singer, 1962) produces bodily changes pharmacologically and also manipulates the subject's need for explanation (or cognitive labeling) of his internal sensation. Those investigations have provided convincing evidence of a strong relation between emotions and the perception and labeling of bodily changes. A summary of much of this work has been presented recently by Valins (1970).

Faced with a weak direct verbal link between autonomic responses and their subjectively reported experiences, yet a potent relation between cognitive perceptions or labeling of bodily reactions and their correlated emotional behavior, the research domain has become even more complex lately by an emphasis upon a third general research proposition which stresses voluntary behavior. Stated as a question, it becomes "Can a subject voluntarily change an autonomic state by consciously willing it to change?" The past few years have seen a surprising number of instances where people are being told to "think about speeding up their heart" or to try to produce alpha waves. With the refinement of these procedures has grown an emphasis on new-sounding old concepts like "bio-feedback."

I mention most of the preceding research questions more to exclude them than to discuss them, for I wish to proceed to still another focus of research interest on verbal processes as they relate to autonomic behavior. This time the link is through an emphasis on Pavlovian conditioning and paired or sequential stimulation situations. Stated differently my central question becomes, how do conscious cognitive processes affect human autonomic behavior in the paired stimulation paradigm which characterizes classical conditioning.

Before proceeding further it might be desirable to express a few attitudes about the basic fields of emotion, psychophysiology, and thinking. For example, if one tries to incorporate the facts of autonomic conditioning into both a traditional theory of learning and a theory of thinking, there is not much integrative work to build on. In a decade or more of concern for these problems, I have come up with a collection of interrelated concepts which serve as gross working propositions. I would like to call them a theory for explaining relations between conscious thought processes and autonomic conditioning. However, I do not feel that they are sufficiently organized to provide more than some loosely developed constructs which I can try to present.

From the standpoint of "thinking" and cognition I am most comfortable with some kind of information-processing model. Perhaps the conception of Simon (1967) comes close when he treats the central nervous system as a serial information processor that is viewed as serving an organism which has multiple needs and lives in an environment that presents unpredictable threats and opportunities. He emphasized two mechanisms, the first of which is a goal-terminating mechanism, and the other is an interruption mechanism which he feels has the properties ascribed to emotion. His task at hand becomes that of elaborating these mechanisms to show how they control or direct attention and activity in an information processing theory of human cognition.

Closely similar are notions of Pribram (1967) who suggests that emotion expresses the relationship between perception and action. It involves a variety of processes engaged in changing states of equilibrium and in developing types of control to meet specific stimulus circumstances. Amount of arousal or amount of activation (e.g., autonomic activity) is seen as dependent upon a concept of certainty and thus upon the sequence of information being received by the organism. Pribram further elaborates the notion that internal adjustments for uncertainty are accomplished by increasing or decreasing the rate of handling information. Other investigators have emphasized the importance of information input control in emotion and have emphasized a variety of concepts. For example, Lacey (1967) refers to the organism's "transaction with his environment" and tendencies to take in or reject stimuli. Others have emphasized individual subject differences among input "augmenters" and "reducers" (Spilker & Callaway, 1969; Buchsbaum & Silverman, 1968).

My preference has been to view the situation as one of modulation of arousal and to use the electrodermal responses as the index of arousal. Arousal phenomena fall along a continuum ranging from mild reactions characteristic of states of alerting or attention, to strong reactions characteristic of defensive adjustment to the environment. In between lie reactions of normal adaptation to situations of only moderate and nonthreatening demands upon the organism. Different stimuli are assumed to possess different capabilities for eliciting different classes or responses, like those which are primarily orienting (ORs), those which anticipate or prepare the organism for succeeding stimuli (ARs), as well as those that involve defensive reactions to strong or significant stimuli (DRs). The response classification is similar to that proposed by Sokolov (1963).

The conditioning process or experience may be viewed as a stimulational sequence involving gradations in arousal requirements. The CS is initially adequate to elicit orienting behavior and the UCS adequate to elicit stronger (defensive) reactions. Experience with the sequence produces changes in the arousal properties of elicited behavior. The CSs take on informational properties of signaling the occurrence and characteristics of the strong events.

In summary, a conditioning sequence is viewed as a longitudinal event showing changes through learning of modulation of arousal by the subject. When cognitive thought processes are emphasized the central questions become how conscious awareness and verbalizations affect the nature and course of development of this modulation of arousal.

The associations between stimuli and responses or between stimuli and stimuli occupy an important position in all theories about human behavior. It is easy to cite well-known scholars who would say that thinking is essentially such conditioned associations (Guthrie, 1935; Thorndike, 1932), with language being the most potent eventual source of conditioned stimuli. Pavlov subscribed to this with his notion of the second signal system in conditioning. Interesting explanations of the relations between conditioning and verbal behavior have been made, like identifying structures in language (the sentence) with the simple conditioning paradigm (Mowrer, 1954). At the same time, many people are concerned about the possible overuse of the classical conditioning paradigm as an empirical–theoretical building block for the study of higher mental processes. They would emphasize other forms of learning like reception strategy (Bruner, 1956); plans (Miller, Galanter, & Pribram, 1960); skill learning (Bartlett, 1958); and concept formation (Hunt, 1962) among others.

In the background of many of these differences among points of emphasis and research approaches is a central methodological question about how much we can generalize explanatory principles across species. Classical conditioning is a viable empirical–theoretical concept. Yet when pushed far enough with human subjects it reduces to certain operations of temporal pairing of stimulus events. When applied to lower species, the interpretation of what determines the observable behavior changes can be fairly well identified. That is, independent and dependent variables can be identified within the framework of the conditioning paradigm.

As one proceeds up the phylogenetic ladder, it is not the ability of the animal to use language and to think that causes the first problem. Instead the problem appears to be that of identifying the stimulus. Some decision has to be made about what the environmental event is to which the organism is responding, what his primitive unit of perception is, and how stimulus complexes develop. The volume of literature devoted to the continuity–discontinuity controversy attests to the historical importance of this question. A decade and a half of sporadic research on the question of stimulus compounding in the electrodermal conditioning context have led me (Grings, 1972) to the conclusion that verbal conscious processes dominate with human subjects and that the most defensible theoretical position is an evolutionary one like that emphasized by Razran (1971).

After the question of perception of stimuli comes the question of relations among stimuli. In classical conditioning with humans, the development of a perception of sequences of stimuli is important, as Woodworth (1947) among others has suggested. If one assumes this to be the essence of human conditioning, conditioning becomes primarily a matter of thinking, for human conditioning becomes symbol manipulation and associations of "signs" and "significates."

One form in which this research problem is very manifest is the study of "awareness" in human autonomic conditioning. It starts with the question of whether autonomic "CRs" can be set up by verbal association of CS and UCS and asks whether awareness of CS–UCS relations is a necessary conditioning for learning to take place. At least two alternate conclusions prevail today. One is that autonomic change does not occur without awareness, the other is that there is a range of degrees in which higher order (i.e., cognitive–verbal–conscious) processes dominate over others and that the research task is to isolate and investigate determiners of events along this range. My own identity is with the latter view and my perception of the state of theory is that it is not very adequate.

With the time that I have at my disposal I would like to explore just a few of the problems encountered in devising empirical tests of some of these questions. As the autonomic response, I will emphasize electrodermal behavior. The experimental situation will be fairly standard—the presentation of sequences of stimuli to human subjects for periods of an hour or so. Two classes of stimuli will be used—strong ones capable of eliciting what I will call defensive GSRs, and weak ones which elicit what will be called orienting responses. A clear set of criteria for differentiating between these two classes of electrodermal reactions is difficult to present, and it will be assumed that such a presentation is not completely necessary here in order for the discussion to proceed.

As a background, consider the general situation of about a decade ago. People had shown that electrodermal reactions to a signal stimulus (like a light or a tone) could be produced reliably by telling subjects that a signal would be followed by a noxious event (Cook & Harris, 1937). Follow-up studies had shown the response to the signal (threat of the event) to be greater than to the event itself at times. Sparked by a general interest in autonomic indications of perception and recognition (e.g., subception) the question of conscious awareness came under scrutiny (Adams, 1957; Eriksen, 1960). When this research was extended to the classical conditioning paradigm, it was concluded that so-called GSR conditioning was merely verbal expectancy learning (i.e., that response change resulted from awareness of temporal contingencies among stimuli).

Along with these studies which attributed to verbal processes the essence of the S–R and S–S associations, there were many researchers who emphasized the role of verbal variables as determining performance rather than learning or association. Here the emphasis was upon notions of verbally induced response sets which inhibit or facilitate responding (Hill, 1967; Dawson & Reardon, 1969) and the observation that "no more shock" instructions facilitated the reduction of response which occurs with extinction trails (Silverman, 1960; Wickens, Allen, & Hill, 1963; Grings & Lockhart, 1963).

However, proving that conscious awareness of CS–UCS relations is necessary for autonomic modification to occur turns out to be a very difficult task. It rests upon the demonstration of an absence of conditioning when there is an absence of awareness. If an absence of conditioning is observed under circumstances that are assumed to be "unaware," there is always the possibility that other necessary conditions for learning have not been met. Examples of this difficulty can be seen by an experiment

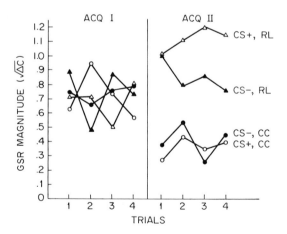

Fig. 7.1. Differential reinforcement (CS + vs. CS −) with a masking task (acq. I) and without a masking task (acq. II). In acq. II half are instructed (RL) and half are not (CC). [From Dawson, M. E. & Grings, W. W. Comparison of classical conditioning and relational learning. *Journal of Experimental Psychology*, 1968, **76**, 227–231. Copyright 1968 by the American Psychological Association, and reproduced by permission.]

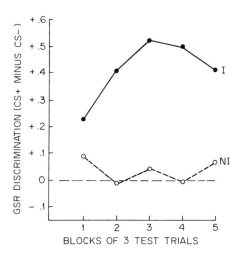

Fig. 7.2. Effects of instructions (I) upon discrimination scores. [From Dawson, M. E. Cognition and conditioning: Effects of masking the CS-UCS contingency on human GSR classical conditioning. *Journal of Experimental Psychology*, 1970, **85,** 389–396. Copyright 1970 by the American Psychological Association, and reproduced by permission.]

(Dawson & Grings, 1968) which used a masking task to disguise CS–UCS relations and observed no differential response to reinforced and nonreinforced stimuli until subjects were instructed of stimulus relations. However, only relatively few trials had been used and there was a distinct possibility that subjects were distracted to a degree that might keep them from perceiving stimuli. Dawson (1970) has endeavored to cope with such difficulties by devising a masking task in which the subject makes discriminative judgments among members of a series of tone stimuli while reinforcement circumstances are introduced by pairing a UCS with only one of the tones.

The most commonly used experimental procedure for evaluating the "conscious-awareness" question has separated subjects into aware and unaware groups on the basis of some criteria, usually as applied to post-experimental interviews (Diven, 1937; Lacey, Smith, & Green, 1955). Even though the difficulties in this procedure are almost impossible to overcome it continues to be used. The fact that the information is collected at the end of the experiment makes it possible that learning could occur first and then produce awareness. As with any interview procedure, difficulties arise from potential bias and social interaction of the subject with the demand characteristics of the situation.

One procedure which has been used a few times employs intertrial reports by subjects and endeavors to verify the proposition that learning occurs on the trial on which awareness occurs. While this procedure has apparently been used successfully in studies of awareness as related to verbal conditioning (DeNike, 1964) its use with electrodermal conditioning has run into various complications so that the reports of the study

(Fuhrer & Baer, 1965; Shean, 1968) have been forced to rely upon post-experimental reports in arguing their case. Recent studies of awareness employing a masking task during conditioning have shown that the masking technique does not completely eliminate awareness as compared to groups who undergo conventional conditioning (Mandel & Bridger, 1967; Fuhrer & Baer, 1969).

Another research problem which has been introduced in this context has been termed the problem of levels of conditioning. It faced the possibility that conditioning can operate at different levels of awareness. One level would be that of conscious awareness of stimulus relations, the situation which has been so frequently demonstrated with human subjects. The other level would be an unconscious, relatively mechanistic form of learning similar to that which is assumed to operate with lower animals. This issue of levels, perhaps more than any other, emphasizes the relations between conditioning and thinking.

A series of assumptions about the role of verbal–conceptual behavior in conditioning led me to make some observations of conditioning performance of human subjects as low as we could observe on the conceptual intelligence continuum. For those of you who are not familiar with this research (Grings, Lockhart, & Dameron, 1962) we selected from among institutionalized mentally deficient adolescents subgroups who were assumed to differ in their capability for verbalization, ranging down to the

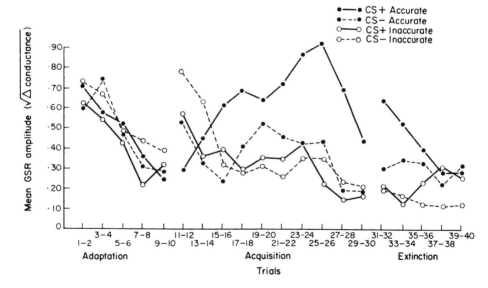

Fig. 7.3. Discrimination as a function of accuracy of postexperimental reports of awareness. [From Shean, 1968.]

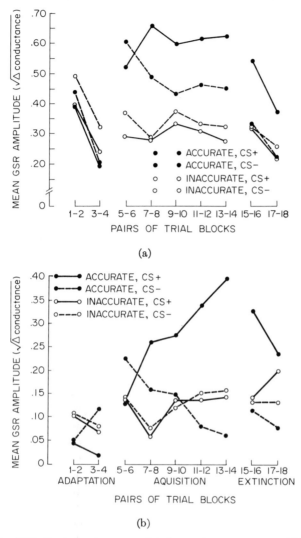

Fig. 7.4. The GSR discrimination over trials for an Accurate group which correctly verbalized the stimulus contingencies during an interview after conditioning and an Inaccurate group which did not; (a) responses during the delay interval, (b) UCS-omission responses. [From Fuhrer, M. J. & Baer, P. E. Differential classical conditioning: Verbalization of stimulus contingencies. *Science*, 1965, **150**, 1479–1481, Fig. 1. Copyright 1965 by the American Association for the Advancement of Science.]

lowest levels. We found that conditioning of electrodermal behavior proceeded without handicap in the absence of verbal–perceptual skills. Rather than being cited as an example of learning without thinking the research may be used better as an example of the complexities in arriving at adequate definitions of concepts like awareness and levels of conditioning.

A closer look should be taken at other efforts to substantiate what might be called different levels of learning applied to autonomic phenomena and to differentiate them on the basis of the extent to which they involve verbal conscious variables.

The notion that learning may occur at more than one level has been discussed on several occasions by Razran (1955, 1965, 1971). In the earliest reference he spoke of the desirability of separating situations involving conditioning with perception, and situations involving conditioning without perception. Thus he clearly subscribed to a notion of conditioning without awareness. In fact, on one occasion (1961), he discussed such unaware conditioning as an important contributor to unconscious behavior processes. In developing notions of conditioning with perception, he recommended differentiation among classes of perception, particularly those involving perception of stimuli and those involving perception of relations between stimuli.

Some of the followers of Pavlov have subscribed to similar notions without using the same terminology. They spoke instead in terms of an interaction of first and second signal systems (Skorunskaia, 1958). Conscious verbal processes are viewed as exerting an inhibitory role over first signal

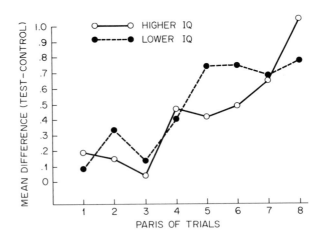

Fig. 7.5. Discrimination performance curves plotted as the difference between test and control responses for the higher and lower IQ groups. [From Grings, W., Lockhart, R., & Dameron, L. Conditioning autonomic responses of mentally subnormal individuals. *Psychological Monographs*, 1962, **76**, 39 (Whole No. 558). Copyright 1962 by the American Psychological Association, and reproduced by permission.]

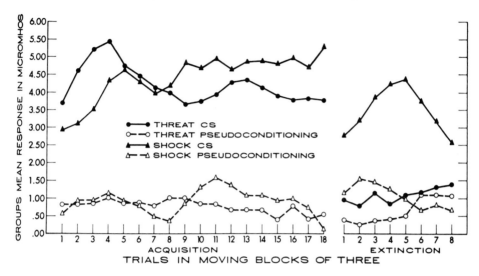

Fig. 7.6. Effect of extinction instructions upon responses established by shock and shock threat. [From Bridger & Mandel, 1964.]

system conditioning in the normal human adult. Unaware, or unconscious conditioning could be viewed as having small significance in adult human behavior under normal circumstances although it could become quite important where intensity of experience is very high (e.g., as in trauma).

Apparently a number of American workers have felt otherwise and have sought to demonstrate that differences between levels of learning may occur in the typical GSR or electrodermal conditioning situation. For example, Bridger and Mandel (1964) measured electrodermal behavior of two groups of subjects both of whom wore electrodes for receiving an electric shock. Both groups were told that a shock would occur after a particular stimulus. However, only one of the two groups was given the shock, the other having only the threat of shock. Yet both groups gave GSRs to the signal stimulus that were greater than those given by a pseudoconditioning control group. Both groups were then told that there would be no more shocks and a series of signal-alone trials was given. The group which had been threatened extinguished rapidly whereas the group that had received the shock did not. These investigators interpreted that difference as evidence that two types of learning had occurred, one due to verbal factors and the other due to the actual experiences associating the signal and shock.

From this first study, they proceeded to elaborate the capability of instruction manipulation to separate different levels of learning. In one experiment (Bridger & Mandel, 1965), instructions to the effect that no more shock would occur led to the abolition of a partial reinforcement extinction effect, as compared to the retention of the effect for subjects who had not been so informed. To quote their interpretation of this difference, they asserted "these components may be categorized as a simple versus a mediated CS–UCS relationship. In the simple CR, the CS directly signals or is a surrogate for the UCS. In a mediated CR, the CS signals an anticipation (e.g., fear) of the reinforcement [p. 481]." In other words, extinction instructions and removal of the shock electrodes were assumed to eliminate the mediated conditioned response, leaving only the more basic or simple conditioned response. The comparison group, not so informed, was assumed to continue to possess both mediated and simple behavior.

More recently the same authors (Mandel & Bridger, 1967) manipulated interstimulus interval and instructions with six groups of subjects. All were informed that the experiment would contain a period when responses to a light alone would be recorded, a period in which light would be associated with electric shock, and finally a period during which the responses to the light alone would be recorded again. Then, at the beginning of the third or extinction period, half of each of three interstimulus interval subgroups was interrupted by the experimenter who removed the shock electrodes and told the subject that there would be no more shock. For

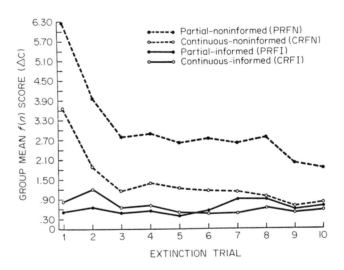

Fig. 7.7. Information instructions and the partial reinforcement extinction effect. [From Bridger, M. H. & Mandel, I. J. Abolition of the PRE by instructions in GSR conditioning. *Journal of Experimental Psychology,* 1965, **69,** 476–482. Copyright 1965 by the American Psychological Association, and reproduced by permission.]

the other half of each of the three interstimulus interval groups, the experiment continued without interruption.

The main dependent variable was the difference between a reinforced and a nonreinforced stimulus during the extinction period. Under the circumstances of no information, the long interstimulus interval group demonstrated a larger differential response during extinction than did the short-interval group (.5 sec.). On the other hand, under the informed condition the half-second groups had a larger differential response during extinction than did the 5-sec groups. Because both forward interstimulus interval groups demonstrated persistence of a differential response when compared with pseudoconditioning control groups, the authors concluded that both the groups demonstrated conditioned responding which was contrary to their cognitive expectancies. They interpreted their results as "evidence for a level of GSR conditioning analogous to Mowrer's (1938) concept of true learning."

The strategy of this research is to hold a factor of cognitive assessment of stimulus relations constant by informing subjects of the three phases of stimulation. This is assumed to provide an opportunity for both kinds of conditioning to occur, that based on conscious and cognitive expectancies, and that based on simple repetitive stimulation. Then, by dividing the subjects for administration of different extinction instructions it is assumed that one of the two types of learning (i.e., the cognitive) can be removed by verbal information. The role of conscious learning is inferred from differences in amount of extinction under different instructions and existence of nonconscious or "true" conditioning is inferred from the fact that differential responding persisted in spite of cognition.

I am unable to accept this interpretation of the results. That changes in autonomic performance have occurred as a result of changes in cognitive expectation appears to be a quite reasonable interpretation. The second conclusion, however, that unaware learning has been demonstrated is fraught with difficulty. In order to infer from a lack of evidence for extinction that the observed behavior is due to some noncognitive unconscious process requires the investigators to assume that the subjects do not have cognitive expectations. In an effort to allow for this possibility they eliminated about 37% of their sample of informed subjects on the basis of a postexperimental interview in which there was some indication of belief in the fact that they would or would not be shocked. It is always reasonable that human experimental subjects remain suspicious of experimental operations and the postexperimental interview procedure is conducive to their reporting what they think is expected of them. Put in other terms, they may be asking their subjects to report that the experimenter told them a falsehood. Subjects might have really expected the shock but have said that they did not because that was what they had been told.

A question which remains about this type of research is whether or not it conclusively demonstrates the existence of two different types of learning, one based on conscious cognitive expectancies, and the other based on noncognitive or unconscious processes. Results, to date appear more clear in their indication of the fact that cognitive variables produce differences in autonomic behavior than they are in support of the conclusion that conscious and unconscious learning proceed simultaneously. The possibility, however, that learning may occur independently of or contrary to verbal processes remains important and continues to be investigated.

At least one laboratory argues that they are demonstrating the existence of different levels of conditioning. In this instance, a masking task was used and the conclusion was drawn that cognitive factors produce differences in response topography from that of simple conditioning. Fuhrer and Baer (1969) had groups conditioned with and without a masking task and further separated subjects according to awareness. They found that in their masking task group both the aware and the unaware subjects showed significant discrimination with that component of the response which is tied to the signal but that only the aware subjects showed such discrimination for the response which occurs just prior to the onset of the noxious event (the anticipatory response). They conclude that they have demonstrated unaware conditioning and state

Razran's terminology serves to highlight a potentially important distinction between first and second interval GSR differentiation. While first interval discrimination may be learned in conjunction with both conditioning and relational learning, second interval discrimination appears to be exclusively a correlate of relational learning. This formulation is consistent with the view that second interval GSRs are emitted as concomitance of a preparatory set in anticipation of the UCS. It is probable that this set is under covert verbal control, particularly with respect to time estimation of the CS–UCS interval. On the other hand, first interval GSRs may be viewed as conditioned orienting responses which are more under stimulus control and potentially more independent of verbal processes [p. 178].

The direction that some other research on this problem has taken can be illustrated by a recent study from our laboratory. Before doing so, however, note will be made of an experimental arrangement which was employed by Wilson (1968) to argue against the Mandel and Bridger interpretations. As an alternative to the "no more shock" extinction instructions for evaluating contributions of simple and cognitive learning, he employed a form of reversal learning. Using a discrimination paradigm, and a short interstimulus interval, he instructed subjects prior to acquisition and again prior to extinction. At the beginning of extinction he told them that a reversal would occur in the sense that the stimulus which had previously been followed by shock would not be followed by shock whereas the stimulus previously not followed by shock would be shocked. He then administered stimuli without shock and observed a sudden reversal of the differential conditioning (i.e., GSRs of greater magnitude were elicited by the previous CS–). He concluded, and I quote "The study finds no evidence to support the contention that some part of a conditioned autonomic response is 'simple' in the sense that it is not mediated by the subject's perception of stimulus contingencies."

We decided to employ the reversal procedure in a situation which extended upon Wilson's observation in the following ways. First, a group was added whose members were explicitly instructed of a lack of pairing of stimuli and shock during the initial learning phase. This permitted the comparison of discrimination performance for a group which had to reverse their cognitive expectancies and a group who shifted from a noncontingency to an expectancy situation. In addition, provision was made for observing the effect of a long and a short interstimulus interval under the assumption that conscious cognitive processes would be more effective with the long interval than with the short interval.

The results demonstrated a clear dominance of cognitive variables, with significant discrimination occurring on the first trial for all groups

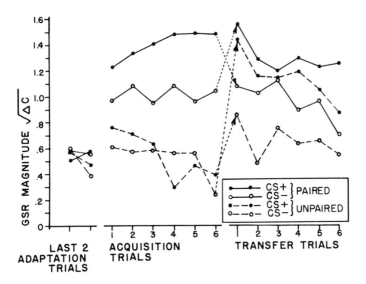

Fig. 7.8. Reversal study. Half-second interstimulus interval. [From Grings, Schell, & Carey, 1973.]

during the last performance phase. With the long interstimulus interval such discrimination was evident in all three response categories observed; namely the orienting response, the anticipatory response, and the UCS-omission response. The data also show some clear evidences for sensitization. For example, with the short interstimulus interval groups, the transition from the first series to the second series led to no significant elevation in response levels for the group who had had contingent experience previously but did lead to a significant elevation in level for the group which had not previously encountered contingent stimulation experience. This same effect is evident in the long-interval groups for the orienting response and the UCS-omission response.

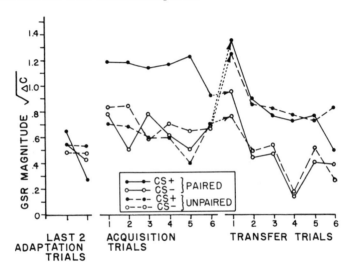

Fig. 7.9. Reversal study. Long ISI. OR or CS-response. [From Grings, Schell, & Carey, 1973.]

In summary, the results of the data just presented suggest a strong capability for verbally instituted expectation to determine autonomic behavior in the direction of the verbalized expectancy. It also shows that the responses elicited by the stimuli are greater for the class to which significance is given by virtue of their contingent relation to subsequent stimuli as compared to those which are not so associated. The absence of differences between performance of groups reversing their expectancies and groups experiencing contingencies for the first time argues against the existence of a persevering "simple" conditioning effect.

Several other experimental arrangements have been employed which

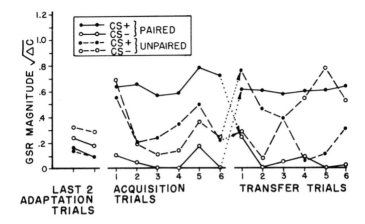

Fig. 7.10. Reversal study. Long ISI. Anticipatory or pre-UCS response. [From Grings, Schell, & Carey, 1973.]

lead to the same conclusion; namely that the cognitive perception of the subject determines the direction and magnitude of the electrodermal response. For example, Colgan (1970) made the receipt of a shock predictable to his subjects by instructing them about stimuli. He had three distinctive stimuli each of which was followed equally often by shock during an initial acquisition period. Then half of the subjects were instructed that two of the stimuli would no longer be shocked but one would, and the other group was informed that they would have a second series like

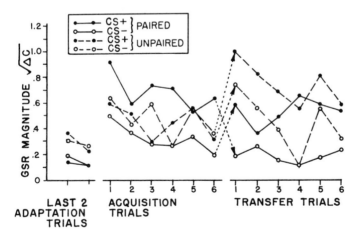

Fig. 7.11. Reversal study. Long ISI. UCS-omission response. [From Grings, Schell, & Carey, 1973.]

the first one. The electrodermal response in anticipation of the shock for the instructed group remained high for the critical stimulus and dropped sharply for the other stimuli whereas the responses for the second subgroup produced no between-stimulus differences.

A somewhat analogous situation can be observed where a motor avoidance task is involved and the GSR during the performance of that task is used as an index of anticipatory response. On one such occasion, Grings and Lockhart (1966) had persons operate a four-position switch in response to four distinctive visual signals. One signal was always followed by shock, another signal was never followed by shock and two of the signals were associated with switch positions which were capable of avoiding the shock. Instructions were also manipulated to vary the amount of awareness of contingencies which the subject possessed. The general results showed progressively better avoidance learning with increased awareness and showed a sudden decrease in magnitude of anticipatory electrodermal response at the point of learning an avoidance contingency for the stimuli signaling such contingency.

There continues to be a variety of explorations of this general problem. None of them appears to have conclusively demonstrated that with human subjects some primitive mechanistic form of conditioning is operating at the same time that higher order cognitively dominated changes are being produced. On the other hand, none of the studies has been adequate to

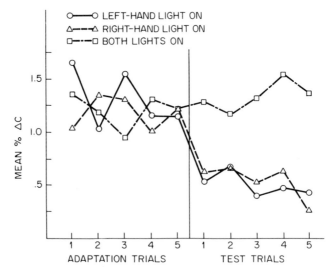

Fig. 7.12. Effect of instructions changing stimulus expectancy. [From Colgan, D. M. Effects of instructions upon the skin resistance response. *Journal of Experimental Psychology*, 1970, **86,** 108–112. Copyright 1970 by the American Psychological Association, and reproduced by permission.]

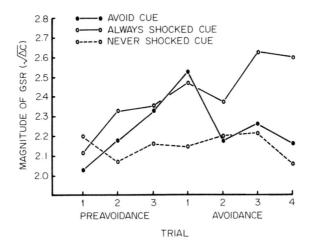

Fig. 7.13. Anticipatory galvanic skin responses (GSRs) on trials preceding and after point of motor avoidance learning. [From Grings, W. & Lockhart, R. Galvanic skin response during avoidance learning. *Psychophysiology*, 1966, **3**, 29–34. Copyright 1966 by the Williams & Wilkins Co., Baltimore.]

argue that there is no such primitive learning occurring. Instead, the conclusion appears to be that cognitive expectancies are dominant in this situation, and that greater research ingenuity will be required if inferences about autonomic conditioning in the absence of cognitive processes are to be made conclusively.

Perhaps one further attempt at this problem should be mentioned for it explored an approach which is theoretically significant. In all of the work previously mentioned, the learned stimuli were exteroceptive—they were presented to the main sense channels associated with conscious awareness. There has long been a persistent notion that (in the field of emotion particularly) unconscious behavior may be dominated by stimuli whose end organs are within the body, namely the interoceptors. Russian workers (Bykov, 1957) and others (Adam, 1967) have demonstrated that conditioning does occur to stimuli introduced to internal organs. For obvious reasons, most of this work has been done with animals and it is not possible to employ verbal reports to assess the subject's awareness of the internal stimuli.

Uno (1970) compared electrodermal conditioning to exteroceptively presented CS + s and CS − s (tones) and interoceptive stimuli obtained by having human subjects swallow a balloon to a point midway in the esophagus and then filling the balloon with water of different temperatures (0° and 50° C) as differential signals for a UCS (shock). He emphasized two kinds of awareness observations; one was the ability of the subject to report differences between stimuli, and the other was the subject's learned

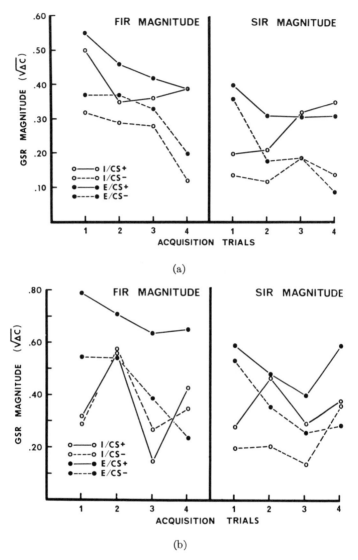

Fig. 7.14. Awareness group comparisons of interoceptive (I) and exteroceptive (E) conditioning. Unaware group (U) above and aware group (A) below. [From Uno, T. The effects of awareness and successive inhibition on interoceptive and exteroceptive conditioning of the galvanic skin response. *Psychophysiology*, 1970, **7**, 27–43.]

awareness of the contingency between a signal and the UCS. Differential conditioning was obtained to both interoceptive and exteroceptive stimuli. When he analyzed subgroups, in terms of their awareness of stimulus differences and their awareness of CS–UCS relations, he found that unawareness of the stimulus differences or unawareness of reinforcement contingencies tended to eliminate the conditioned response occurring during the delay interval (the anticipatory response) but it did not eliminate the conditioning of the conditioned response occurring on trials where the UCS is omitted (or what has been termed the CS–omission response). Unfortunately only one response was measured during the delay interval so that it is not possible to compare his conclusions with those of workers endeavoring to separate orienting behavior from anticipatory behavior. One of his general conclusions from the study was that cognitive awareness does appear to be a potent relevant variable even for interoceptively delivered stimuli with human subjects.

Thus far we have seen a great deal of empirical information without much consistent basis for explanation other than the fact that conscious awareness somehow determines autonomic behavior. What appears to be important is that a stimulus serves as a signal for a noxious or otherwise motivationally significant event, and that knowledge of the impending occurrence of this event somehow brings about autonomic changes in advance of the event and perhaps concomitant with it. The concept that appears in various forms is that of cognitive expectancy, anticipation, or preparation. I have preferred and elaborated upon a combined anticipatory–preparatory perceptual concept rather than a simple anticipatory concept. This is largely because the effects observed persist into the period of the signaled event. In other words the response to the signaled event is different than it would be if it were not signaled or were improperly signaled.

In the preliminary discussions of these problems, (Grings, 1969) a general anticipatory–preparatory concept was emphasized, suggesting that a series of related phenomena should be identifiable and capable of manipulation as cognitive phenomena. These include, first, modification of orienting or attention behavior; second, changes in the responses occurring after the signal and in anticipation of the signaled event; and finally, changes in the nature of perception and response to the signaled event. Such a point of view poses empirical–theoretical problems that are too lengthy to examine here. However, I would like to point out a few directions which such research takes.

In conclusion, I will mention two or three studies which are based on elaboration of the previous notions. The experiments go back to the previously stated assumption that the essence of the expectation process is a transmission of information or a processing of sequential information. The signal (CS) is viewed as providing information about the succeeding event. One type of such information may be termed *certainty*, by which is meant information basic to accurate prediction of the second event. Certainty may be manipulated empirically in various ways. For example, one may define a concept of event certainty by providing subjects with different rates of association of two events. Another is a time certainty defined by providing the individual with different degrees of regularity in time of receipt of the second event. Similarly, quality certainty can be defined by manipulating predictability of properties (like intensity) of the signaled events.

One recent study will be cited as an example of manipulation of event certainty (Grings & Sukoneck, 1971). Subjects were presented with a task involving four distinctive light cues. Each light cue was associated with a different probability of being followed with a strong stimulus (shock). These were 0, 25, 75, and 100%. The task was presented as a probability guessing task with the subject asked to press buttons on a board to designate his prediction of likelihood that the cue presented visually will be followed by a shock. He was also asked to press a second device to indicate the certainty of his judgment about the probability. The interval between the signal and the receipt of shock was long enough to permit definition of several responses: that tied to the onset of the signal and called the CS response or OR; that which anticipates the onset of the UCS and is termed an anticipatory response (or AR); and the two classes of responses associated with the signaled event, namely the response to the UCS itself, and the response when the UCS does not occur (the UCS-omission response).

The results demonstrate clear relations between event certainty and the different responses. Anticipatory responding shows an increase with higher certainty whereas the response to the shock itself shows a decrease with greater certainty. There are certain methodological difficulties associated with interpretation of these relative magnitude changes because the response components are not independent, and care needs to be taken to separate associative from nonassociative determiners.

To pursue further just one of the phenomena evident in this study, it will be recalled that a reduction in magnitude of the UCR has been observed to occur when the UCS is signaled, as compared to when it is not signaled—the phenomenon referred to as UCR diminution (Kimmel, 1966; Grings & Schell, 1971).

Given the existence of an empirical phenomena of UCR diminution, we are faced with a couple of problems. One is to separate associative from nonassociative determiners of the results. I would like to ignore this for the moment even though I have written about it (Grings & Schell, 1969). The other problem is to develop an explanation for why a response reduction should occur.

Several explanations have been put forth. One suggests that some form of inhibition becomes conditioned to the signal and holds down the response to the UCS. A second explanation assumes that the signal elicits a pre-

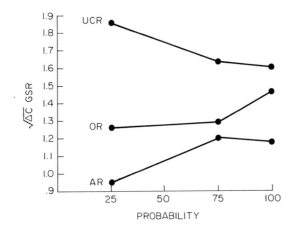

Fig. 7.15. Effect of reinforcement probability upon different components of response. [From Grings, W. & Sukonek, H. Prediction probability as a determiner of anticipatory and preparatory behavior. *Journal of Experimental Psychology*, 1971, **91**, 310–317. Copyright (1971) by the American Psychological Association, and reproduced by permission.]

paratory response which "sets" the *S* for receipt of the shock. Closely linked to the last explanation is one which introduces a concept termed *preception*. It postulates a mechanism for amplifying or attenuating the subjective intensity of predictable stimuli. In elaborating the concept, Lykken (1962, 1968) has suggested that it could operate to either enhance perceived intensity of a second signal stimulus (positive preception) or to decrease such intensity (negative preception). The basis is assumed to be neural activity in input channels. The phenomenon has been shown to occur with evoked EEGs as well as with electrodermal reactions.

To explore these propositions Schell and Grings (1971) measured subjective intensity of noise UCSs by loudness-matching procedures, and compared values when the UCS was signaled and when it was not signaled. The signaled stimulus was judged less intense than an unsignaled stimulus, and was also accompanied by a smaller GSR. Other recent investigations using different rating procedures have found different results (Kimmel, 1967; Furedy & Doob, 1971).

Situations leading to enhancement rather than diminution had been obtained previously in our laboratory suggesting that improperly signaled events would be responded to more intensely than properly signaled events. The differences between responses to properly and improperly signaled events was termed a *disparity response*. Early studies (Grings, 1960) predicted such disparity to influence response magnitudes in one direction only.

More recent studies have suggested that whether diminution or enhancement occurs may depend upon the nature of the information signaled.
A brief experiment may suffice to illustrate this last point. A series of
loud noises was generated which varied in five intensity steps. Each
presentation of a loud noise was preceded by a statement verbally introduced through the same channel as the noise and told the subject which
level of noise was to occur. After a series of such properly signaled noises,
test trials were introduced in which the intermediate level signal was
given but one of the extreme intensities was presented. If the signaling
process influences reception of the signaled stimulus there should be a
difference in response when properly signaled and when improperly signaled.
Such was the case. The response to the noises was determined, in part,
by the information provided by the signal. A loud noise signaled to be
softer is reacted to less; whereas a soft noise signaled to be louder is reacted
to as if it were louder.

The previous research endeavors to tease out some of the subtleties of
relations between conscious, judgmental processes and autonomic behavior.
Hopefully, what we will learn is more about how organisms process significant informational inputs, and particularly how we learn to modulate
the intensity or arousal aspects of such sequences of experiences. It is
assumed that there is an ultimate utility of such observations in the field
of emotion. For example, it is assumed that there is relevance for thought-
disorder types of psychopathology, like information and arousal modulation theories of schizophrenia (Epstein, 1970).

In summary, then, this rather long review of empirical investigations
tries to bring out ways in which study of autonomic behavior interacts
with the study of higher order processes of thinking and cognition. The
foundations of the work are in some form of information processing by
the organism which determines the intensity of the reaction made to the
environmental stimuli received. The goal is to relate thinking and emotion,
to find better means for bridging the gap between the higher mental
processes as we see them in the human subject, and the subtleties of
internal organismic behavior such as that mediated by the autonomic
nervous system.

The Discussion of Dr. Grings's Paper

LED BY DR. ROBERT CHAPMAN
Eye Research Foundation of Bethesda

Chapman: It is really a pleasure to hear some of these issues brought up, for several reasons. We tend not to hear as much about classical conditioning these days and it is nice to hear a presentation that primarily involves it. I think it is instructive to also see that the issues that have concerned people for a good many years are basically similar to the issues that are coming up today under new guises, especially "biofeedback." The classical conditioning paradigm generally begins with a conditional stimulus, followed by an unconditional stimulus which produces some response (Fig. 7.16). The simple notion is that the pairing of these two stimuli leads to a change—one of the simplest notions is that the change to the conditional stimulus comes to produce the conditioned response. But we have heard today about some data which suggest that the process is not quite as simple as that because it isn't always the unconditional

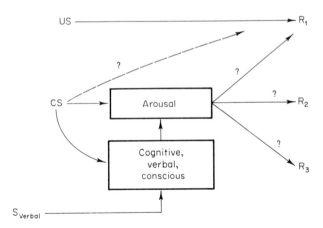

Fig. 7.16. Classical conditioning paradigm with additional concepts based on Grings's paper. The US is unconditional stimulus which leads to response R_1. The CS is conditional stimulus which when paired with US produces conditioning. Under various conditions the CS may produce various responses, R_1, R_2, or R_3. This is modeled by interposing additional constructs between stimulus and response, namely Arousal and Cognitive, Verbal, Conscious processes with which Grings was especially concerned. Grings demonstrated that verbal instructions could dramatically alter responses.

response that is produced. The conditioned response is similar to the unconditional response but is in some respects different. And we have heard a discussion about response topography today.

Another basic question raised was whether or not the two stimuli are interchangeable, in some sense. For whatever we use for a CS, can we substitute a particular kind of auditory stimulus, a particular kind of visual stimulus, or what have you? Can we, with impunity, substitute different kinds of stimuli, and still get the same kind of new response, or same response?

If the response to the conditional stimulus varies, then there is not a straight line, neurally speaking from the conditioned stimulus to the response—something must intervene. Dr. Grings has indicated the intervening something concerns verbal processes. He has manipulated those verbal processes by presenting additional stimuli, as indicated by "verbal stimulus" in Fig. 7.16. That "verbal box" of Fig. 7.16 represents the relationship that the CS leads to the US. Another verbal stimulus may modify that relationship to say that CS will not lead to US. Dr. Grings has studied the rapidity, amplitude, and topographies of these changes, and supported the hypothesis that verbal conscious processes dominate autonomic behavior.

Similar issues are also raised for biofeedback and operant conditioning and thus are not unique to classical conditioning. For one, the previous question of interchangeability of stimuli raises the question of whether or not there are groupings of stimuli that are related to groupings of responses—do we have stimulus–response systems that are organized such that some stimulus–response connections are more efficient than others? That question is very much alive. If you are interested in practical procedures to produce responses quickly, which stimuli do you want to deal with?

One experimental paradigm not reported on would be to manipulate a generalization paradigm: as the CS, visually present "ONE," and then test with "1", or "WON," or even "TWO." The degree of generalization among such would suggest something about the relevant kinds of internal verbal processes.

Open Discussion

Grings: Relevant to your comments are some fascinating old experiments that established differences in transfer among homonyms and synonyms, and current work on problems of semantic generalization. Another verification of the relevance of what you said is in the work of David Grant on chains of intervening verbal processes.

Dr. F. J. McGuigan (Hollins College): Could you comment on biofeedback studies using GSR?

Grings: You open up a very extensive matter. In one published example, extinction was facilitated by providing subjects with information about their responses during extinction. Unfortunately, a lot of other studies were not successful. A few years ago I used a fancy circuit for delivering either true or false autonomic feedback to subjects with all sorts of resulting complications. I now think the reason we failed was that the subjects got into an interactive pose with us, or with the gadgets that provided the feedback. Hence, they tried to control the GSR meter, rather than simply getting information that could be used to change their behavior; this is a problem for all feedback situations.

REFERENCES

Adam, G. *Interoception and behavior.* Hungarian Academy of Science, 1967.

Adams, J. K. Laboratory studies of behavior without awareness. *Psychological Bulletin,* 1957, **54**, 383–405.

Bartlett, F. C. *Thinking.* London: Allen & Unwin, 1958.

Bridger, W. H., & Mandel, I. J. A comparison of GSR fear responses produced by threat and electric shock. *Journal of Psychiatric Research*, 1964, **2**, 31–40.

Bridger, W. H., & Mandel, I. J. Abolition of the PRE by instructions in GSR conditioning. *Journal of Experimental Psychology*, 1965, **69**, 476–482.

Bruner, J. S., Goodnow, J. J., & Austin, G. A. *A study of thinking.* New York: Wiley, 1956.

Buchsbaum, M., & Silverman, J. Stimulus intensity control and the cortical response. *Psychosomatic Medicine*, 1968, **30**, 12–22.

Bykov, K. M. *The cerebral cortex and the internal organs.* (Trans. W. H. Gantt). New York: Chemical Publishing Co., 1957.

Carey, C., Schell, A., & Grings, W. Effect of ISI and reversal manipulations on cognitive control of the conditioned GSR. Paper presented to Society for Psychophysiological Research, October, 1971.

Colgan, D. M. Effects of instructions upon the skin resistance response. *Journal of of Experimental Psychology*, 1970, **86**, 108–112.

Cook, S. W., & Harris, R. E. The verbal conditioning of the galvanic skin reflex. *Journal of Experimental Psychology*, 1937, **21**, 202–210.

Dawson, M. E. Cognition and conditioning: Effects of masking the CS–UCS contingency on human GSR classical conditioning. *Journal of Experimental Psychology*, 1970, **85**, 389–396.

Dawson, M. E., & Grings, W. W. Comparison of classical conditioning and relational learning. *Journal of Experimental Psychology*, 1968, **76**, 227–231.

Dawson, M. E., & Reardon, P. Effects of facilitory and inhibitory sets on GSR conditioning and extinction. *Journal of Experimental Psychology*, 1969, **82**, 462–466.

DeNike, L. D. The temporal relaxationship between awareness and performance in verbal conditioning. *Journal of Experimental Psychology*, 1964, **68**, 521–529.

Diven, K. Certain determinants in the conditioning of anxiety reaction. *Journal of Psychology*, 1937, **3**, 291–308.

Epstein, S., & Coleman, M. Drive theories of schizophrenia. *Psychosomatic Medicine*, 1970, **32**, 113–140.

Eriksen, C. W. Discrimination and learning without awareness. *Psychological Review*, 1960, **67**, 279–300.

Fuhrer, M. J., & Baer, P. E. Differential classical conditioning: Verbalization of stimulus contingencies. *Science*, 1965, **150**, 1479–1481.

Fuhrer, M. J., & Baer, P. E. Cognitive processes in differential GSR conditioning: Effects of a masking task. *American Journal of Psychology*, 1969, **82**, 168–180.

Furedy, J. J., & Doob, A. N. Autonomic responses and verbal reports in further tests of the preparatory-adaptive-response interpretation of reinforcement. *Journal of Experimental Psychology*, 1971, **89**, 258–264.

Grings, W. W. Preparatory set variables related to classical conditioning of autonomic responses. *Psychological Review*, 1960, **67**, 243–252.

Grings, W. W. Verbal-perceptual factors in the conditioning of autonomic responses. In W. F. Prokasy (Ed.), *Classical conditioning*. New York: Appleton, 1965.

Grings, W. W. Anticipatory and preparatory electrodermal behavior in paired stimulation situations. *Psychophysiology*, 1969, **5**, 597–611.

Grings, W. W. Compounds stimulus transfer in human classical conditioning. In A. H. Black and W. F. Prokasy (Eds.), *Classical conditioning II*. New York: Appleton, 1972.

Grings, W., & Lockhart, R. Effects of "anxiety lessening" instructions and differential set development on the extinction of the GSR. *Journal of Experimental Psychology*, 1963, **66**, 292–299.

Grings, W., & Lockhart, R. Galvanic skin response during avoidance learning. *Psychophysiology*, 1966, **3**, 29–34.

Grings, W., & Schell, A. Magnitude of electrodermal response to a standard stimulus as a function of intensity and proximity of a prior stimulus. *Journal of Comparative and Physiological Psychology*, 1969, **67**, 77–82.

Grings, W., & Schell, A. The effects of trace versus delay conditioning, ISI variability, and instructions on UCR diminution. *Journal of Experimental Psychology*, 1971, **90**, 136–140.

Grings, W., & Sukoneck, H. Prediction probability as a determiner of anticipatory and preparatory behavior. *Journal of Experimental Psychology*. 1971, **91**, 310–317.

Grings, W., Lockhart, R., & Dameron, L. Conditioning autonomic responses of mentally subnormal individuals. *Psychological Monograph*, 1962, **76**, 39 (Whole no. 558).

Grings, W., Schell, A., & Carey, C. Verbal control of an autonomic response in a cue reversal situation. *Journal of Experimental Psychology*, 1973 (in press).

Guthrie, E. R. *The psychology of learning*. New York: Harper, 1935.

Hill, F. A. Effects of instructions and subject's need for approval on the conditioned galvanic skin response. *Journal of Experimental Psychology*, 1967, **73**, 461–467.

Hunt, E. B. *Concept learning: An information processing problem*. New York: Wiley, 1962.

Kimmel, E. Judgments of UCS intensity and diminution of the UCR in classical GSR conditioning. *Journal of Experimental Psychology*, 1967, **73**, 532–543.

Kimmel, H. D. Inhibition of the unconditioned response in classical conditioning. *Psychological Review*, 1966, **73**, 232–240.

Lacey, J. I. Somatic response patterning and stress. In M. Appley & R. Trumbull (Eds.) *Psychological Stress.* New York: Appleton, 1967.

Lacey, J. I., Smith, R. L., & Green, A. Use of conditioned autonomic responses in the study of anxiety. *Psychosomatic Medicine,* 1955, **17,** 208–217.

Lykken, D. T. Preception in the rat: Autonomic response to shock as function of length of warning interval. *Science,* 1962, **136,** 665–666.

Lykken, D. T. Neuropsychology and psychophysiology in personality research. In Borgatta and Lambert (Eds.), *Handbook of personality theory and research.* New York: Rand McNally, 1968.

Mandel, I. J., & Bridger, W. H. Interaction between instructions and ISI in conditioning and extinction of the GSR. *Journal of Experimental Psychology,* 1967, **74,** 36–43.

Mandler, G., & Kremen, I. Autonomic feedback: A correlational study. *Journal of Personality,* 1958, **26,** 388–399.

Mandler, G., Mandler, J. M., & Uviller, E. I. Autonomic feedback: The perception of autonomic activity. *Journal of Abnormal and Social Psychology,* 1958, **56,** 367–374.

McCurdy, H. G. Consciousness and the galvanometer. *Psychological Review,* 1950, **57,** 322–327.

Miller, G. A., Galanter, E., & Pribram, K. *Plans and the structure of behavior.* New York: Holt, 1960.

Mowrer, O. H. Preparatory set. *Psychological Review,* 1938, **45,** 62–91.

Mowrer, O. H. A psychologist looks at language. *American Psychologist,* 1954, **9,** 660–694.

Pribram, K. The new neurology and the biology of emotion: a structural approach. *American Psychologist,* 1967, **22,** 830–838.

Razran, G. Conditioning and perception. *Psychological Review,* 1955, **62,** 83–95.

Razran, G. The observable unconscious and inferable conscious in current Soviet psychophysiology: Interoceptive conditioning, semantic conditioning, and the orienting reflex. *Psychological Review,* 1961, **68,** 81–147.

Razran, G. Evolutionary psychology: Levels of learning and perception and thinking. In B. Wolman (Ed.), *Scientific Psychology,* Ch. 13. New York: Basic Books, 1965.

Razran, G. H. *Mind in evolution.* Boston, Massachusetts: Houghton, 1971.

Schachter, S., & Singer, J. Cognitive, social and physiological determinants of emotional state. *Psychological Review,* 1962, **5,** 379–399.

Schell, A. M., & Grings, W. W. Judgments of UCS intensity and diminution of the unconditioned GSR. *Psychophysiology,* 1971, **8,** 427–432.

Shean, G. D. The relationship between ability to verbalize stimulus contingencies and GSR conditioning. *Journal of Psychosomatic Research,* 1968, **12,** 245–249.

Silverman, R. E. Eliminating a conditioned GSR by the reduction of experimental anxiety. *Journal of Experimental Psychology,* 1960, **59,** 122–125.

Simon, H. A. Motivational and emotional controls of cognition. *Psychological Review* 1967, **74,** 29–39.

Skorunskaia, T. N. Interaction of signal systems during simultaneous presentation of direct and verbal stimuli of opposite significance. *Pavlov Journal of Higher Nervous Activity,* 1958, **8,** 327–332.

Sokolov, Y. N. *Perception and the conditioned reflex.* New York: Macmillan, 1963.

Spilker, B., & Callaway, E. "Augmenting" and "reducing" in averaged visual evoked responses to sine wave light. *Psychophysiology,* 1969, **6,** 49–57.

Thorndike, E. L. *The fundamentals of learning.* New York: Teachers College, 1932.

Uno, T. The effects of awareness and successive inhibition on interoceptive and exteroceptive conditioning of the galvanic skin response. *Psychophysiology,* 1970, **7,** 27–43.

Valins, S. The perception and labeling of bodily changes as determinants of emotional behavior. In P. Black (Ed.), *Physiological correlates of emotion*. New York: Academic Press, 1970.

Wenger, M. A. Emotion as visceral action: An extension of Lange's theory. In M. L. Reymert (Ed.), *Feelings and emotions*. New York: McGraw-Hill, 1950.

Wickens, D. D., Allen, C. K., & Hill, F. A. Effects of instruction on extinction of the conditioned GSR. *Journal of Experimental Psychology*, 1963, **66**, 235–240.

Wilson, G. D. Reversal of differential GSR conditioning by instructions. *Journal of Experimental Psychology*, 1968, **76**, 491–493.

Woodworth, R. S. Reinforcement of perception. *American Journal of Psychology*, 1947, **60**, 119–124.

CHAPTER EIGHT

Psychophysiological Correlates of Imagery[1]

ALLAN PAIVIO

University of Western Ontario

Recent behavioral studies have shown clearly that nonverbal imagery is a major factor affecting memory, language, and thought (Paivio, 1971). The studies also have gone a long way toward revealing the functional characteristics that distinguish imagery from verbal symbolic processes. Some neuropsychological research, such as the work on the functional asymmetries of the cerebral hemispheres (Kimura, 1966; Milner & Teuber, 1968; Sperry, 1968, 1971), has contributed to this differentiation by demonstrating that the mechanisms subserving verbal and nonverbal processes are, to a considerable degree, distinct anatomically as well as functionally. Psychophysiological studies have provided further support for the validity of the imagery construct but such studies have generally lagged behind behavioral research in their contribution to theoretical understanding in this area. This paper reviews some of the attempts to

[1] Preparation of this paper and the author's research reported in it were supported by grants from the National Research Council of Canada (APA-0087) and the University of Western Ontario Research Fund.

find theoretically useful psychophysiological correlates of imagery, with particular emphasis on our own work on pupillary reactions. To provide a framework for the discussion, I will first describe our theoretical and empirical approaches to the concept of imagery, and briefly outline some of the distinctions between imaginal and verbal processes as revealed to date by behavioral research.

I. THEORETICAL DEFINITION OF IMAGERY

Like any inferential construct, imagery can be understood only by comparing and contrasting it with other processes that have distinct theoretical and empirical properties. In our research, we have distinguished between imaginal and verbal processes. The underlying mechanisms are viewed as independent but interconnected systems for the storage, manipulation, and retrieval of stimulus information. The imagery system is presumably specialized for dealing with information concerning relatively concrete objects and events. The verbal system is also useful for dealing with concrete information, and in addition it surpasses imagery for the representation and manipulation of abstract information. A further distinctive feature of *visual* imagery is in the way units of information are organized. Visual imagery, like visual perception, is apparently specialized for parallel processing—the information in visual images is organized spatially thereby permitting simultaneous access to its components. Verbal processing, on the other hand, is sequential—units of information are organized sequentially into higher-order units, although parallel processing also occurs in the operational sense that verbal units can be processed to some extent independently of each other. A third distinction is that imagery is a dynamic process, capable of rapid transformations, whereas the verbal system may be relatively less proficient in transformational thinking. This is exactly the reverse of the traditional view that images are static portraits and of such contemporary views as Bruner's (Bruner, Olver, & Greenfield, 1966), according to which imagery is relatively sluggish and untransformable whereas the verbal system is swift and flexible in its functioning. Nevertheless, it is the direction in which theory seems to be moving at present (see Berlyne, 1965; Paivio, 1971).

1. Empirical Distinctions

Obviously these theoretical distinctions can be useful only to the extent that imaginal and verbal processes can be operationally distinguished as well. During the introspective era of psychology, researchers distinguished between the two processes on the basis of introspective evidence related to vividness of quasi-perceptual experience related to different sensory modalities. Thus concrete nonverbal visual imagery was distinguished from auditory or kinesthetic speech imagery, and so on. The emphasis on subjective vividness as a defining attribute of the imagery construct is still dominant among some researchers (Richardson, 1969; Sheehan, 1966). Unfortunately, however, reported vividness of imagery has been relatively unsuccessful as a predictive variable, both in the early history of imagery research as well as more recently, so we have relied mainly on other approaches while recognizing that introspective reports can sometimes be a useful adjunct.

We have used three major classes of independent variables: stimulus attributes, experimental manipulations, and individual differences in symbolic habits and skills. In the stimulus approach, imagery is defined in terms of the image-evoking value of the stimulus as measured by subjects' ratings or reaction time data. For example, a large sample of nouns has been scaled on the ease with which they arouse images (Paivio, Yuille, & Madigan, 1968). This approach extends to pictures and objects at the high imagery end, and to larger verbal units such as phrases and sentences at the linguistic level (Begg & Paivio, 1969). The experimental approaches have included manipulations designed to increase or decrease the probability that imagery or verbal processes will be effectively used in a particular task. This has been done by instructing subjects to use imagery in the task (Paivio & Foth, 1970; Yuille & Paivio, 1968), or by varying the rate of presentation of items (Paivio & Csapo, 1969), and so on. The third approach involves measurement of individual differences using spatial manipulation tests as well as questionnaires to define imagery ability (Ernest & Paivio, 1969). The differential availability of such processes also can be inferred from sensory deficits such as blindness or deafness (Bugelski, 1970; Paivio & Okovita, 1971).

2. Functional Characteristics of Imaginal and Verbal Processes

Some of the theoretical distinctions between imagery and verbal processes, as inferred from empirical evidence, will now be summarized. It is in regard to these points in particular that the psychophysiological findings will be evaluated later on.

Functional independence of the underlying systems. First, the two symbolic systems are assumed to be functionally independent. Evidence from memory research involving manipulation of relevant item attributes and experimental manipulations provides compelling support for this generalization (Paivio, 1971). For example, the verbal code can be made functionally unavailable using pictorial stimuli presented at such a fast rate that they cannot be implicitly labeled, yet they can be recalled or recognized, apparently on the basis of stored visual images alone (Paivio & Csapo, 1969). Pictures are recalled better than words, however, at slower rates when both codes presumably are available, suggesting that they are additive in their effects on recall—two independent codes for the same target memory are better than one. Functional independence is also supported by neuropsychological findings concerning functional asymmetries of the cerebral hemispheres in perception and memory for verbal and nonverbal material (Kimura, 1966; Milner & Teuber, 1968; Sperry, 1971). For example, lesions in the left hemisphere can result in selective impairment of memory for verbal material without impairing memory for nonverbal material, and vice versa for lesions in the right hemisphere.

Interconnectedness of the two systems. A second important generalization is that, although independent, the two systems become functionally interconnected through associative experience involving language and concrete events. This means that words can be transformed into images, nonverbal stimuli can be labeled, and transformations can occur cognitively from images to implicit speech and vice versa. Introspective evidence is particularly compelling on this point. Suppose I ask you to describe your living room. The input is verbal and your description verbal, but the mediating memory is likely to involve a nonverbal visual representation of the layout of your living room. I believe that it is in fact always such a memory, except among blind people who must make use of other modalities in the task. The example illustrates interconnectedness because it involves transformations from verbal input, to memory image, to verbal output. The introspective evidence is amply supported by research involving, for example, mnemonic techniques that apparently require such transformations, and by memory studies involving verbal recall of pictures, or pictures as mediators of verbal recall (see Paivio, 1971; Reese, 1970).

Task concreteness and availability of the symbolic processes. Still another generalization is that the arousal and functional usefulness of imagery varies directly with the concreteness of the stimulus situation and task. The verbal system is not similarly dependent on concreteness. This simply means that concrete objects and events or their linguistic descriptions readily evoke nonverbal images, whereas abstract concepts, relations, and tasks do so less readily if at all. Verbal processes, however, are readily evoked by abstract as well as by concrete stimuli. This implies that the relative advantage of verbal processes should increase as the stimulus situation and task increase in abstractness. This generalization is overwhelmingly supported by reaction time studies which have shown that images are aroused much more quickly by concrete than by abstract words or phrases, whereas the speed of verbal associative reactions is not similarly affected by abstractness. The results of learning and memory studies involving such stimuli are also consistent with this view (Paivio, 1971). Findings from some of the pupillary research that I will review later bear directly on this point.

Parallel versus sequential processing. A fourth point is that the two systems differ most clearly in their relative capacity for parallel and sequential information processing. In particular, the information contained in visual images is apparently organized spatially, so that the components can be processed synchronously. Imagery is relatively inefficient, however, for sequential processing of discrete item information. Conversely, the verbal system is specialized for sequential organization, presumably because of its auditory motor nature, but spatial organization is probably difficult in verbal terms alone. The superiority of the verbal system for sequential processing was demonstrated in a study (Paivio & Csapo, 1969) which showed that recall of pictures was inferior to recall of words in a sequential memory task, such as immediate memory span, when the rate of presentation was too fast to permit implicit labeling of the pictures, but not at a slower rate where such labeling could occur during input. However, pictures did not suffer when the tasks did not require memory for item order.

The postulated superiority of imagery for spatial organization is intuitively compelling and is supported by some experimental findings as well. For example, the finding from tachistoscopic recognition studies (Bryden, 1960) that verbal stimuli are reported more accurately from left to right than from right to left, whereas arrays of nonverbal stimuli are reported equally accurately in either direction from the immediate memory image is consistent with the generalization. So, too, is the finding that paired associate learning of pairs of concrete nouns, such as *elephant–ambulance*, is facilitated by presenting pictures of the objects in some kind of interactive relationship (Epstein, Rock, & Zuckerman, 1960; Wollen, 1969), or by instructing subjects to form mental images of such relationships (Bower, 1970), but not if the depicted objects are separated. Some relevant neuropsychological evidence on functional distinctions between the cerebral hemispheres is also available (see Kimura, in press; Sperry, 1971), but I am aware of no psychophysiological studies that bear on the issue.

Independence of symbolic systems and sensory modalities. The final theoretical point that deserves mention here is that the distinction between verbal and nonverbal symbolic processes is conceptually distinct from differences in sensory modality. This means simply that both verbal and nonverbal stimulus information can be visual, or auditory, or haptic, or some combination of these. The idea that symbolic and sensory modalities are orthogonal has important implications for memory research (see Paivio, 1971, Chap. 7), and it is an area where psychophysiological studies should be particularly valuable although no relevant information appears to be available at present.

Other theoretical distinctions can be made, but the ones I have summarized are best supported by available evidence from behavioral research. We will now consider in more detail what, if anything, has been revealed about such distinctions by psychophysiological studies, and what contributions such research might make in the future to the understanding of the processes underlying the various phenomena that behavioral studies have revealed or supported. The review begins with a brief discussion of EEG recordings and eye movements as possible correlates of imagery, and then deals at greater length with our attempts to relate pupillary reactions to imagery activity.

II. ELECTROENCEPHALOGRAPHIC STUDIES

In 1943, Golla, Hutton, and Walter initiated a line of investigation that has continued at least sporadically up to the present time. The research has focused on the relationship between EEG patterns and modes of thought, in the hope that individuals could be classified into different cognitive types on the basis of a purely objective, physiological measure. For example, Golla et al. (1943) reasoned that people classified as habitual visualizers should show an absence of alpha rhythm, whereas habitual verbalizers should show unusually persistent alpha. The underlying assumptions were that visual imagery, like visual perception, involves activity in the occipital cortex and that the occipital alpha rhythm therefore will be absent or attenuated among those whose habitual mode of thinking is visual–imaginal, whereas verbal thinking is mainly auditory–kinesthetic in nature and should be associated with persistent occipital alpha. Results purporting to support such distinctions were obtained by Golla, Hutton, and Walter as well as by a number of subsequent investigators (Short, 1953; Short & Walter, 1954; Slatter, 1960). However, other studies reviewed by Oswald in 1957 and more recently by Richardson (1969) failed completely to find differences in EEG patterns as a function of imagery type. One problem with the early research was that many investigators used unspecified or ad hoc methods of assessing imagery types. In addition, the scoring of a subject's EEG and the assessment of imagery type usually were not done independently, thus introducing potential experimenter bias. In 1956, Barratt manipulated the mode of thinking experimentally rather than in terms of individual differences alone. He presented his subjects with mental problems that required either visual imagery or verbal thought for their solution. He concluded from his results that suppression of the alpha rhythm was not associated reliably with visual imagery as defined by the experimental task.

Simpson, Paivio, and Rogers (1967) further investigated the relation between EEG activity and imagery using Barratt's experimental tasks and correcting for some of the shortcomings of the earlier research involving individual differences. Specifically, rather than using an ad hoc method of assessing imagery types, we used an objective spatial manipulation test (The Minnesota Paper Form Board), along with rating scale measures to assess the subject's visual imagery ability. Second, the EEG records were scored independently by an experimenter who had no involvement in the experimental task. We obtained significant results that contradicted those reported in previous investigations of the relation between EEG and imagery. Whereas Golla *et al.* (1943) reported that visual imagers had little or no resting alpha, we found that high imagers had greater EEG amplitude than low imagers during a control condition involving resting alpha. Moreover, we found lower alpha amplitude during the verbal task than during the visual task, which goes contrary to the hypothesis that greater occipital activity, hence greater desynchronization of occipital EEG activity, is involved in the visual than in the verbal problem. The results, however, can be interpreted in terms of general activation or arousal related to task difficulty. When an independent sample of subjects completed both the verbal and the visual problems, we found that the visual task was correctly answered by many more subjects than the verbal task, suggesting that the latter was the more difficult. Thus the greater alpha attenuation during the verbal as compared to the visual task could be due simply to greater cognitive arousal associated with the former. Be that as it may, our findings and the results of other studies on the problem are generally inconclusive in that there seems to be no firm evidence that imagery can be differentiated from verbal thought in terms of alpha blocking.

Perhaps Kamiya's recent work (cited in Stoyva & Kamiya, 1968, pp. 201–203) on the operant control of the EEG alpha rhythm will be a more fruitful approach to the general problem. The most relevant point in the present context is that when alpha was "on" Kamiya's subjects reported that they felt relaxed and were not experiencing any visual imagery. During periods of alpha suppression, on the other hand, the subjects reported "seeing" things. However, alpha was also suppressed if they reported exerting mental effort of some kind, suggesting that the physiological correlates may not be specific to imagery. They may be related instead to verbal processes, general cognitive arousal, or simply to asymmetrical lateral movements of the eyes, which Bakan and Svorad (1969) found to be negatively correlated with EEG alpha activity when a subject is engaged in a reflective mental task. Obviously the problem is complex and it will probably be some time before the various contributing factors are teased apart.

Whereas the conclusions from the study of general EEG wave patterns are somewhat discouraging, research involving average evoked potentials appears to be a more promising approach to the study of physiological correlates of the symbolic processes. Particularly interesting is John's (1967) discussion of the relation between meaning and the shape of evoked potentials recorded from the brain. John, Herrington, and Sutton (1967) had demonstrated that different geometrical patterns, such as a square and a circle, elicit evoked potentials differing in shape. John refers to further unpublished work (pp. 410–411) which showed that wave shapes resembling those normally evoked by a particular geometric form can be obtained in response to illumination of an empty visual field if the subject merely imagines that the same form is present in the field. Different reactions were also obtained to the printed words *square* and *circle*, which were equated for area. John raises the interesting question of whether subsequent research can demonstrate an invariant aspect to the wave shape of responses evoked in the same region by presentation of a geometric form and the name of the form. Such demonstrations would be extraordinarily interesting in relation to the kinds of problems I have been discussing, especially in that they might reveal something about the specific content of imagery aroused by stimulus words, but I will curb my enthusiasm until the hard data are in.

III. EYE MOVEMENTS AND IMAGERY

I turn to a brief discussion of the relationship between eye movements and imagery. The issue is especially interesting because it implies that imagery involves a motor component that gives it a dynamic quality quite different from the static quality attributed to images by the ancient wax tablet model and the more recent photograph analogy. Thus, such diverse theorists as Hebb, Skinner, and Piaget have assumed that motor processes are important in imagery, although they do not insist that such processes need be manifested in peripheral motor reactions. Hebb (1968) suggested that eye movements, or imagined movements, facilitate the formation of a clear image. Skinner (1953) discussed imagery in terms of both "conditioned seeing" and "operant seeing." In the case of the latter, the private events include implicit motor activity comparable to that involved in the perception and manipulation of objects. Piaget (Piaget & Inhelder, 1966) defines imagery as internalized imitation, paralleling the motoricity involved in perceptual exploration, in which movements "imitate" the contours of a perceived figure.

Relevant evidence has been provided by studies that investigated the relationship between eye movement patterns and imagery as inferred from subjects' reports. Perhaps the most dramatic demonstration of a positive relationship is the study by Roffwarg, Dement, Muzio, and Fisher (1962), in which an interrogator, working only with the dream narrative, was able to predict with remarkable accuracy the number, direction, and timing of rapid eye movements that occurred during the dream sequence. Increased eye movements have also been reported during periods of imagery activity among awake subjects by Lorens and Darrow (1962), and Antrobus, Antrobus, and Singer (1964). A study by Deckert (1964) is particularly interesting because it appeared to provide rather unequivocal evidence of the perceptual nature of imagery. His subjects first observed a beating pendulum and then were asked to imagine the movement. Deckert reported that the subjects developed smooth pursuit movement of a frequency comparable to that of the previously visualized pendulum, rather than saccadic movements, which would be normally expected with eye movements in the absence of a moving object.

However, the observed correlations between eye movements and imagery can be interpreted in several ways. One possibility is that the eye movements reflect the scanning of an experienced image. Thus Roffwarg and his colleagues suggested that the rapid eye movements constitute the physical representation of the dreamer's "watching" of the visual imagery of the dream. Lorens and Darrow proposed similarly that increased eye movements in their study reflected scanning of visual images during mental multiplication. Deckert suggested that the necessary prerequisite for the pursuit eye movements in his experiment was the development of an appropriate cerebral image. His finding appears to support an "outflow" theory of eye movement control, in which that control presumably is initiated by the central activity (imagery). More recently, however, Graham (1970) reported that he failed to obtain a similar correspondence between eye movements during actual observation of a moving pendulum and movements recorded during the imagination of such activity. Deckert's particular interpretation in terms of an outflow theory must therefore be regarded as questionable at this time. The internal scanning interpretation of rapid eye movements during dreaming also fails to be supported by recent evidence (Rechtschaffen, 1971).

Another possibility is that the eye movements, rather than reflecting implicit scanning activity, are involved in the generation, or regeneration, of imagery by proprioceptive feedback cues. Suggestive evidence of such a process can be found in Ivo Kohler's (1964) research. The relevant finding was that negative afterimages resulting from the prolonged wearing of colored filters occurred subsequently in response to eye movements, apparently as a result of sensory conditioning in which motor feedback from eye movements functioned as the CS for the negative afterimage. The evidence at least makes it plausible that a similar mechanism might operate in relation to visual mental images as well. Hefferline and Perera's (1963) finding that the auditory image of a tone could be conditioned to a thumb twitch can be similarly interpreted to mean that one function of the motor component of an image is to provide feedback stimulation that would trigger a further sensory response, and so on, in an imagery chain.

The interpretations I have suggested and other possible ones encounter the problem that eye movements are sometimes absent during imagery. As early as 1910, Perky reported that eye movements did not occur during images of imagination, although they accompanied memory images. More recently, Singer (1966) reported that eye movements did not occur during daydreamlike thought. Perhaps the best experimental evidence on the issue has been presented recently by Hale and Simpson (1971). They required their subjects to generate images to noun pairs under instructions to make eye movements, to think about making eye movements, or to do neither. The latency and rated vividness of mediating images were the dependent variables, and eye movements were continuously monitored by means of electrooculograms. They found no significant effect of the eye movement conditions on either latency or vividness of images. Moreover, the rate of occurrence of eye movements was unrelated to image latency and vividness. Thus we are faced with negative evidence concerning both the internal scanning and the proprioceptive cuing hypotheses of the relationship between eye movements and imagery. What, then, is the precise role of eye movement tendencies and other motor processes in the control or modulation of imagery? Obviously we need more data before that question can be answered. Thus far, then, neither EEG recordings nor eye movement have been found to correlate consistently with imagery if we accept subjective reports and reaction times under imagery instructions as valid indicators of imagery. In the remainder of the paper, I shall consider where studies of pupillary reactions have taken us in the search for such correlates.

IV. PUPILLARY REACTIONS DURING IMAGERY TASKS

My interest in pupilography began naively with the hope that pupillary reactions might reflect specific characteristics of memory images. Jaensch (cited in Klüver, 1932) reported that children classified as having eidetic imagery showed pupillary constriction when asked to imagine bright objects, and dilation when asked to imagine dark objects. This observation, if reliable, has remarkable implications concerning cognitive influences on an autonomic response. I shall return to these. First, let us consider the more modest possibility that pupillary dilation might at least correlate in a reliable way with the act of imaging, if not with specific attributes of images.

1. Effects of Imaging to Concrete and Abstract Words on Pupillary Dilation

It has long been known that the pupil dilates when a person engages in almost any kind of mental activity (Hess & Polt, 1964; Lowenstein & Loewenfeld, 1962). That is, the pupil gets bigger when we think about something or attempt to solve a problem mentally. Moreover, it dilates more when the cognitive task is more difficult than when it is simple (Beatty & Kahneman, 1966; Hess & Polt, 1964). The research I did in collaboration with Drs. Herb Simpson and Frank Colman, and subsequently pursued by them, was concerned with the effect of an imagery task on the magnitude and latency of dilation. Earlier research had established that it is more difficult to generate images to concrete than to abstract words, as measured by ratings of ease of imagery (Paivio, 1965) and imagery reaction times (Paivio, 1966). We reasoned that these differences would also be reflected in pupillary dilation.

We investigated the problem in a series of experiments involving the following procedure. The subject sat at a box with a goggle-like opening at one end which supported his face while he looked into the box. The other end of the box contained a ground-glass screen in the center of which was a small plus (+) sign on which the subject fixated. So positioned, the subject was required to generate images to stimulus words while one of his eyes was continuously photographed in order to record changes in pupil size. The stimulus words were either concrete nouns such as *coffee,* *house,* and *pencil,* or abstract nouns like *fate, moment,* and *opinion.* In some experiments the words were presented visually one at a time on the ground-glass screen. In others, they were presented auditorily by a tape recorder. The pupil was photographed with a movie camera at a rate of two frames per second using infrared film. The task sequence always included a control period beginning, for example, with the instruction that the subject was to relax, then an experimental period preceded by instructions to generate an image to the stimulus word presented to him. In different experimental conditions the subject indicated that he had an image by pressing a key, or by saying that he had one, or no overt response at all was required. As will be seen presently, the nature of the response that indicated task fulfillment turned out to be critically important.

The consistent general findings from the various experiments can be quickly summarized. The pupil dilates during the imagery task, and the magnitude of the dilation is greater and reaches its maximum later when the stimulus words are abstract rather than when they are concrete. The effects on size but not on latency to maximum dilation are qualified by the nature of the response that indicates task fulfillment. These effects are illustrated by the following series of figures. Figure 8.1 shows one of our earliest experiments (Paivio & Simpson, 1966) in which subjects pressed a key when they thought they had generated an image. You can see that dilation is greater under the experimental than under the control condition, and that pupil size is generally larger when the words were abstract

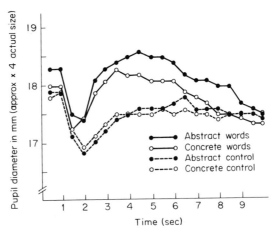

Fig. 8.1. Mean pupil size for subjects viewing abstract and concrete words under instructions to generate images to the words, and when viewing blank control slides. [Based on Fig. 1 in Paivio and Simpson, 1966.]

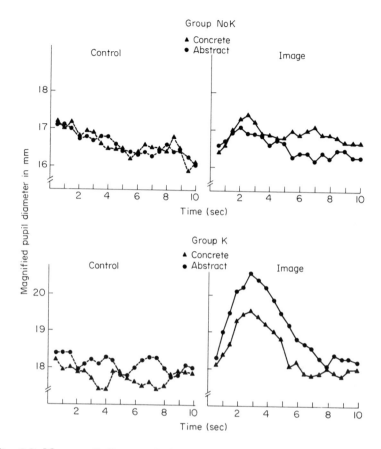

Fig. 8.2. Mean pupil diameter during control periods and while subjects were attempting to generate images to abstract and concrete words, for subjects not required to respond overtly (upper panels) and for subjects required to press a key (lower panels) when they had an image. [Based on Fig. 1 in Simpson and Paivio, 1968.]

than when they were concrete. Figure 8.2 shows the results of one pair of conditions in a later experiment by Simpson and Paivio (1968). It can be seen that, when a key press was the indicator of image arousal the results were essentially the same as in Fig. 8.1, but when the subject was not required to press a key, the pupillary reaction did not differ from the control period. The increase in pupil size and the concrete–abstract difference occurred also when task fulfillment was indicated by verbalization rather than by a key press.

Although the size effect was attenuated by the absence of an overt response, the difference in latency of the response was not. Figure 8.3,

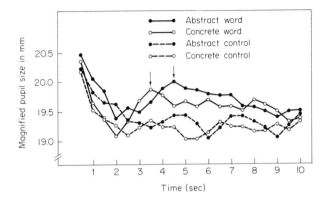

Fig. 8.3. Pupillary response curves over time while subjects were imaging to concrete and abstract words and during control conditions. Arrows indicate points of maximal dilation. [From Paivio and Simpson, 1968.]

shows the results of an experiment by Paivio and Simpson (1968) in which the subjects were not required to press a key or verbalize during the imagery task. It can be seen that the pupil nevertheless reached a maximum sooner when the words were concrete than when they were abstract.

Alternative interpretations of the pupillary findings. What do these results mean? In general they can be interpreted as an arousal or activation effect associated with the cognitive task rather than as a specific indicator of imagery per se. In this respect the findings are consistent with a large body of earlier literature showing that the pupil dilates during cognitive activity and that the degree of dilation is related to the difficulty of such activity. However, the results also extend the previous findings by showing unequivocally that the pupillary response is enhanced when an overt motor response is required to indicate task fulfillment. It becomes important, therefore, to understand precisely why the motor response has this potentiating effect.

Simpson and Paivio (1968) considered a number of alternative possibilities. One is that making an overt response required the subject to decide explicitly whether the appropriate mental state (the image) is present or absent, and such a decision increases arousal level. A related possibility, suggested also by Hakerem and Sutton (1966), is that increased activation results from motor feedback associated with the *anticipation* of making the overt response. A third alternative is that feedback from the motor response itself contributes directly to the level of activation (cf. Nunnally, Knott, Duchnowski, & Parker, 1967). Finally, the subject's arousal level may be increased because the overt response (e.g., the description of an image) is publicly observable and, therefore, exposes the subject to evaluation by the experimenter as audience. There are various difficulties with each of these interpretations but none of them could be ruled out on the basis of the evidence that we were aware of at that time.

Simpson subsequently set out to investigate the effects of some of the variables we had considered. In one experiment (Simpson, 1969) he compared the effects of a key-press response that was either related or unrelated to the preceding cognitive task, which involved pitch discrimination. The results showed a much more pronounced dilation effect when the response was relevant to the task than when the same response was irrelevant. In another experiment, Simpson and Climan (1971) measured pupillary as well as electromyographic changes during an imagery task and were able to conclude that pupillary dilation during the task could not be explained in terms of muscle activity in the effectors involved in making the response that indicated task fulfillment. These experiments suggest that feedback from the motor response itself is not an adequate explanation of the potentiating effect of that response on pupil size. In a further experiment, Simpson and Molloy (1971) used subjects who scored either high or low on a measure of proneness to audience anxiety, reasoning that this might reveal any effects attributable to apprehension about verbalizing or otherwise responding overtly in the task situation. They indeed found that high-anxiety subjects showed greater pupil size than low-anxiety subjects but the effect was specific to the time immediately preceding the subject's response. Apparently, anticipation of the verbal report was somewhat anxiety-arousing for the high audience anxious group and it resulted in a maintenance of pupil dilation for these subjects. Nevertheless, both groups showed similar pupillary dilation to the cognitive task itself, so the emotional factor was not sufficient in itself to account for the changes in pupil size that accompany mental activity.

The results of these various experiments leave decision processes as the most likely explanation of that effect. That is, before the subject can respond overtly, he must decide whether the appropriate mental state, in this case an image, has occurred, and such a decision increases arousal level and pupillary dilation. Consistent with this interpretation, Simpson and Hale (1969) found greater pupillary dilation among subjects that were required to decide in which direction a lever was to be moved than among yoked controls who were told in which direction to move the lever. The term *decision* in this context could be interpreted to mean the motor command that initiates the overt response, but this is a matter for further research.

Contribution of the pupillary data to the operational definition of imagery.

The potentiating effect of the motor response on pupil size is interesting in its own right and worth pursuing because it may be relevant to such general issues as the motor theory of thought. But have the pupillary data contributed anything specifically to the conceptualization or imagery as a mode of thinking? The answer is "yes" in at least one respect—they provide further support for the validity of a particular operational definition of the concept of imagery. I said earlier that subjects' ratings and reaction time data have indicated that concrete and abstract words differ in the ease with which they evoke sensory images. The pupillary data are completely consistent with this conclusion. That is, we can infer that the pupil dilates more and takes longer to reach maximum size with abstract than with concrete words as stimuli because it is more difficult to generate images to abstract terms. Note that this inference is justifiable despite the potentiating effect of the overt response on pupil size because the subjects responded similarly to both classes of words. Thus whatever the factors involved in making that response, it is difficult to see how they would account for the differences in the magnitude of dilation to concrete and abstract stimuli.

The time to maximal dilation provides even better validation of the word imagery concept inasmuch as maximum size was reached sooner in the case of concrete words even when no overt response was required on the part of the subject, and the magnitude of the pupillary response did not differ significantly for the two classes of words. Indeed, Simpson, Molloy, Hale, and Climan (1968) showed for three levels of word concreteness that the latency of dilation was a more reliable index than magnitude. Moreover, Colman and Paivio (1969) found that latency of dilation was a more reliable indicator of word concreteness than was another autonomic measure, the GSR. Thus the latency of the pupillary reaction seems to be particularly sensitive to the difficulty of the act of generating images to words and could be especially valuable in a variety of cognitive tasks. Thus it might be useful to combine this index with EMG recordings in the way that McGuigan (1970, 1971) has done in his investigations of covert speech. It is possible that differences in the latency of the pupillary response would correlate with covert activity in the speech muscles although no overt response is required of the subject in the imagery task. Such implicit speech activity might be picked up by EMG recordings from the speech muscles. If they are not, it would strengthen the argument that the imagery task indeed involves nonverbal cognitive activity, although it would not be an argument against a motor theory of thought. In fact, the occurrence of pupillary reactions during cognitive activity appears superficially to be perfectly consistent with the motor theory of thought. There is one difficulty, however—the ciliary muscles lack receptors to provide sensory feedback after a pupillary response. This has some interesting implications to which I will return later.

2. Imaginal versus Verbal Processes and Pupillary Dilation

The preceding discussion raises a question: Might the pupillary reactions somehow differentiate between imaginal and verbal cognition? There is no good reason why the pupillary response itself should reveal such differences, although it might supplement other behavioral indicators in a particular situation. In any case, too little has been done on the problem to suggest any firm answer. In one study, Steeves, Paivio, and Simpson (1967) investigated pupillary reactions to both the imagery task and a comparable task in which subjects were asked to generate verbal associates mentally to the same stimulus words. The study included other variables which resulted in complex interactions that are irrelevant here. The relevant point is that pupillary dilation occurred to a similar degree during both the imagery and the verbal associative tasks.

In another experiment, Colman and Paivio (1970) monitored pupillary activity during a paired-associate learning task involving nouns as items. The abstractness–concreteness of the nouns was varied and the subjects were asked to learn the pairs under standard paired-associate learning instructions, or using imagery or verbal mediators. In the case of the imagery mediation condition, the subjects were told to try to associate each pair by generating a compound image that incorporates the objects or events suggested by the nouns, and in the verbal mediation condition they were told to form phrases or sentences that linked the two nouns. The performance data showed that learning was better under the two mediation conditions than under the standard paired-associate learning instructions, at least when the stimulus nouns were concrete. This is generally consistent with earlier research on mediated learning (see Paivio, 1971). The most interesting feature of the data for present purposes is that the pupillary reaction differed for the different conditions over trials. The mean pupillary diameter is shown in Fig. 8.4 for each of four recall trials, during which the subjects were presented each of the stimulus words in turn and were asked to recall the responses. The figure shows that pupil size decreased systematically over trials for both the imagery and verbal mediation subjects, but remained at a high level over trials for the subjects who were not given the mediation instructions. These results are consistent with the view that the task was more difficult and the pupil, therefore, dilated more under the condition that involved no mediators as associative aids. I should mention also that the different groups performed equally well by the fourth trial, so the differences in pupil size are not simply correlated with learning performance. They suggest that

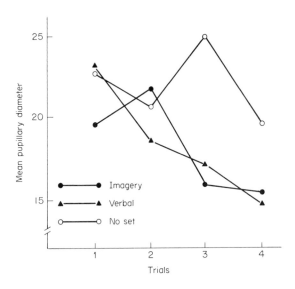

Fig. 8.4. Mean pupillary diameter in millimeters (magnified approximately ×4) during four paired-associate recall trials, for subjects learning under imagery, verbal, and no mediation instructions. [From Colman and Paivio, 1970.]

the subjects had to work harder throughout the task when learning under standard conditions than when they had a specific mediational set to follow. In this respect, the physiological measure appears to be more sensitive than the performance measure to the cognitive demands of the learning task. In addition, larger pupil size was associated with word pairs with abstract stimulus members. This also is consistent with the performance data, which showed that such pairs are more difficult to learn than ones with concrete stimulus members.

Up to this point, then, it can be concluded that the pupillary response can be an informative addition in cognitive tasks, but in our hands at least it has not permitted us to differentiate clearly between verbal cognitive processes and nonverbal imagery. The possibility remains that some of the findings in fact represent effects mediated specifically by imagery and that our procedures were simply too insensitive to detect when this was the case. The final section of this paper deals with our attempts to find more more sensitive procedures.

3. Pupillary Reactions and the Content of Imagery

The pupillary studies to be discussed in this section directly investigated the possibility that pupillary reactions might reveal something specific concerning the nature of imagery. Earlier I mentioned a comment by Jaensch to the effect that eidetic children showed differential pupillary reactions when imaging bright and dark objects. This observation, if reliable, has remarkable implications. It implies either that appropriate pupillary reactions can be directly conditioned to verbal stimuli as a result of their association with bright and dark objects, or that imagery (itself perhaps a product of conditioning) is a central mediator of the reaction. The direct conditioning interpretation runs into the problem that pupillary conditioning has been difficult to demonstrate with changes in light intensity as the unconditioned stimulus (Young, 1958, 1965). In addition, Loewenfeld (1966) has recently argued that "all psychologic and sensory stimuli, with the exception of light, dilate the pupil and none of them contract it [p. 294]." Such problems raise doubts concerning the reliability of the phenomenon reported by Jaensch unless a mechanism other than conditioning is postulated. However, successful pupillary conditioning with light as the UCS has been reported in recent studies in the Soviet Union (see Hartman, 1965, p. 100; Sokolov, 1963), so the occurrence of appropriate conditioned reactions to words denoting bright and dark objects could not be entirely ruled out; or so it seemed to us at the time that we became interested in the problem. Alternatively, the possibility that conditioned reactions could be mediated by some central process such as imagery has been suggested by a number of investigators (Beritoff, 1965, p. 7; Mowrer, 1960, p. 171; Sheffield, 1965, p. 315), and such mediation may be the basis of the phenomenon described by Jaensch.

In any case, Paivio and Simpson (1967) investigated the general reliability of Jaensch's observation, with a view to exploring the alternative hypotheses in later studies if the effect could be obtained. Rather than using eidetic children, we used university students who differed in their imagery ability according to scores on spatial manipulation tests and questionnaires. Their task was to attempt to generate memory images of pictures of black or white objects to which they had previously been exposed. Their pupils were continuously photographed during the task. The task also included control periods during which the subjects presumably were not imaging. The specific sequence of events was as follows. A black or white picture was shown for 10 sec. This was followed by a 10-sec control period during which the subject fixated on an X on the screen while attempting to keep his mind a blank. Then the printed letter R was shown, which was the cue for the subject to try to generate a mental picture of the photograph he had just seen. We also included a small control group that were not given the recall instructions.

The results showed no effect attributable to the imagery ability variable, but they did suggest that differential dilation occurred during the imagery task. The findings are shown in Fig. 8.5. The left panel of the figure shows the results for the control period for the experimental group while the right-hand side shows the results for the recall period for that group. The lower two curves represent the pupillary reactions of the control subjects not given the recall instructions. The upper two curves in each case are the results for the experimental subjects. The control subjects essentially showed no differential effects, simply a decrease in pupil size during the periods corresponding to the control and recall intervals for the experimental subjects. During the first part of the control interval, the experimental subjects showed slightly greater pupil size after viewing the black stimuli than after white stimuli, which simply reflects a carry-over effect of the stimulus itself. By the end of the control period at time blocks C and D in the figure, the pupil size did not differ for the two stimulus conditions. During the recall period, shown in the upper two curves at the right of the figure, pupil size stayed at a high level throughout the recall period when the subject was recalling black objects, whereas a significant reduction in size occurred when they were recalling white objects. Thus, although the results did not show constriction relative to a neutral base

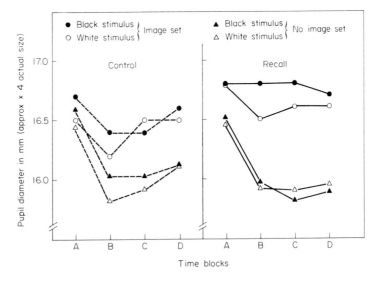

Fig. 8.5. Mean pupil size over time blocks for (a) an image-set group ($N = 36$) under control conditions and while attempting to recall black and white stimuli, and (b) for a group ($N = 6$) not given the recall instructions. [From Fig. 3 in Paivio and Simpson, 1967.]

line, they did show differential amounts of dilation which in general appeared to be consistent with Jaensch's observation. The fact that absolute constriction did not occur during recall of white pictures might simply mean that the pupillary response reflected a tendency toward constriction superimposed on general dilation associated with the difficulty of the imagery task.

An alternative possibility is that the results were an artifact of our procedure. It is known that pupillary reactions to changes in illumination are elicited most readily when the stimulus falls on a very small area of the retina including the macula. In the case of our experiment, during the recall of black pictures the subject's attention may have been somehow directed to black portions of the slide (e.g., the letter R which cued his attempt to generate images) whereas during recall of white pictures he attended to white parts of the slide (cf. Loewenfeld, 1966; Woodmansee, 1966). Such differences in attention could result from implicit verbalizations during attempts to recall the stimuli. For example, when trying to recall a black stimulus a subject may say to himself "black square" and this could mediate his attending to a black part on the recall slide. Such a possibility as well as other problems could be better controlled by the use of auditory rather than visual cues during control and recall periods while maintaining constant, homogeneous illumination of the visual field. This is precisely what Simpson and I did in another experiment, with the result that we failed completely to replicate our finding from the first experiment. We were forced to conclude, therefore, that differential pupillary reactions do not occur reliably when subjects imagine white or black objects.

It could be argued of course that we failed to demonstrate the phenomenon reported by Jaensch simply because we did not use eidetic children as subjects. While our sample included people with high-imagery ability according to certain measures, they were not tested for eidetic imagery according to the criteria suggested by Haber and his associates (Haber & Haber, 1964; Leask, Haber, & Haber, 1969). The imagery that eidetikers report apparently differs qualitatively from that reported by noneidetikers, particularly in regard to its vividness and its perceptlike localization "out there" rather than within the individual, and it may be that the qualitative differences are necessary in order to demonstrate pupillary constriction under instructions to image bright objects. Thus the question remains open in a strict sense, although I must confess that I am skeptical about the possibility of obtaining positive findings in this area. This view is reinforced by the fact that Barber (1971) recently reported a failure to get differential pupillary reactions to hypnotically induced images of bright and dark objects.

If such pupillary reactions were in fact demonstrated, it would implicate classical conditioning as the mechanism responsible for the effect. It is relevant, therefore, as well as interesting in its own right, to consider experimental attempts to condition pupillary constriction with light as the UCS. Recall my earlier statement that successful conditioning has been reported in Soviet literature, but the best-controlled studies in the United States (Young, 1965) have failed to do so. Again, however, certain methodological differences left the issue open. The American studies have generally used sound as the condition stimulus, whereas Sokolov (1963) reported positive results with temporal duration as the CS. Specifically, Sokolov presented his subjects with alternating periods comprised of 4 sec of darkness interspersed with periods of light. After repeating the cycle a number of times, the dark period was unexpectedly increased to 10 sec. Under these conditions the one subject for whom Sokolov reported data showed an anticipatory constriction of the pupil approximately at the point where the light had previously occurred, namely, 4 sec after dark onset.

Without having any idea why differences in the CS should be crucial, Frank Colman and I attempted to replicate Sokolov, following his procedure as precisely as we could, and using a larger number of subjects. Without burdening you with all the details, I can report that the results were unequivocally negative. Thus the results of the imagery research as well as our conditioning experiment are completely in agreement with Loewenfeld's (1966) assertion that psychologic stimuli can only dilate the pupil, they do not contract it. Why this should be the case is an interesting puzzle that challenges conditioning theories in particular. Young (1965) suggested that pupillary reactions cannot be classically conditioned with changes in illumination as the UCS because sensory feedback from the response is essential for conditioning to occur and the ciliary muscles that control pupil size lack sensory receptors that could produce such feedback. This seems to be an argument against a central (S–S) interpretation of sensory preconditioning and centralist interpretations of thought, both of which assume that at least some associations can be formed within the central nervous system without any motor feedback. I mention this just to indicate that the kind of research I have been discussing raises some fundamental issues concerning the mechanisms of learning and thinking, but I am unable to add anything that would clarify those issues on the basis of the research reported.

The Discussion of Dr. Paivio's Paper

LED BY DR. CHARLES OSGOOD
University of Illinois

Osgood: Both Dr. Paivio and myself are a couple of molars in what seems like a sea of moleculars. Our concerns have been to try to get help from psychophysiology—and in my case from psychophysiologists, like Dr. McGuigan—in trying to resolve some of our own problems; it is not so much to just extend knowledge of psychobiology, or psychophysiology, per se.

Yesterday, we had some interesting discussion about how psychophysiologists were reviving some of the unidimensional mentalistic concepts, e.g., attention, arousal, etc. It seems to me that Dr. Paivio, and I in my own talk later, will be going even further back to concepts of imagery, meaning, and even William James' ideomotor action, i.e., images of action. This is old stuff, but, like some kinds of bourbon, it does not seem to lose its flavor.

As most of you who have read the work know, Dr. Paivio's revival, in contemporary psychology, of the role of imagery—in learning, in memory, and in many other fields—is one of the more impressive sets of programmatic researches of our present psychological generation. He has, at the behavioral level, clearly put imagery back into contention as a significant function, in many of the processes where we would have never even thought of it before.

Dr. Paivio and I have had, over the last couple of years, a rather voluminous interchange of correspondence about our agreements and disagreements with regard to theory. I just want to point out a couple of things which raise questions.

The first one concerns Dr. Paivio's statement, or assertion, that imagery is essentially a simultaneous, parallel kind of processing of information; whereas verbal behavior, or linguistic processing, is essentially sequential. I would like to point out that imagery, itself, can well be a sequential process. And certainly, when you look at one of the fundamental defining characteristics of human languages at both phonemic and semantic levels, you have simultaneous bundles of components, i.e., phonetic and semantic components, which are in parallel; literally, these are simultaneously excited and are operating as a whole pattern. I'll come to this later myself.

The interesting thing is that these simultaneous processes have a clear, coded componential nature, i.e., they function like a set of components, at both the phonemic and the semantic levels; this is an extraordinarily efficient system. I would suggest that one of the main *differences* between imagery and meaning is the componential nature of the verbal semantic system, as compared with imagery.

This leads to very interesting problems. Dr. Paivio talked about (and the evidence certainly supports him) the role of imagery in recall; somehow images must be stored. There is a great deal of evidence about storage in terms of meaning. In fact, most of the recent evidence makes it clear that storage in long-term memory is itself, to a large extent, a function of the very efficient componential kind of system I have just noted. But I find it awfully hard to imagine just how images are "stored." My argument would be that images are not stored; rather, at some point, perhaps in delayed processing, they are put into a componential coding system, which is probably the same as that used for meanings. There is good evidence that perceptual and linguistic *signs* share the same representational (semantic) systems. Then those processes can, in turn, recreate the image, on a reduced cue, feedback basis—thus an image is a redintegrated perception (to use another ancient notion).

There is, I think, a real problem in Paivio's theory and I do not think, in my reading of his work, that it has been touched on yet. If you do really have independent systems of imagery and meaning, at higher levels of the nervous system, and if they are completely independent in terms of not only the mediating activity but also in terms of memory and storage, then the problem is, how can images as wholes be stored? Images, as far as I can see, do not have any comparable componential kind of character, efficiently broken down into features which can be distinctively combined, etc. This is an interesting problem, Dr. Paivio, and you might like to comment on it.

Another problem I find most puzzling is how imagery and meaning are interrelated. As Dr. Paivio clearly indicates, he believes that they *are* interrelated. Now I will take an extremely strong position—one that I probably do not exactly believe, but, just for the sake of argument, I will assert it for the moment. This argument would be that you always have coded (semantic) central storage and that imagery is always a dependent event, centrally innervated *from* stored meaningful material. It is one kind of re-creation, if you will, of something very much perceptionlike, but from central innervation, rather than from externally initiated perceptual integration; we call it *perception* when it is externally excited, but *imagery* when it is centrally excited. That is the strong case.

This leads to yet another problem—the relation between perception and image. Usually, if the perceptual integrative process is clearly dependent upon external stimulation, e.g., looking at an object or a picture, we do not call it *image*—we call it *perception*. But then we have the problem of the initiation of imagery: what is it that initiates images, as in dreaming, or as when asked to imagine what your living room looks like? Clearly, the input here may be external, but it still requires the central contribution—the meaning of your living room, etc., in order to somehow initiate the imagery. In fact, the very early study of Perky (1910) that Paivio referred to showed that, if you had subjects striving to create a central image of a banana on a screen, and a very *faint* input picture of a banana was projected, the subjects would typically say, "Oh, I have a marvelously clear image." Apparently, it is very difficult—subjectively at least—to distinguish between what is a very faint, externally excited, perceptual integration, which we call perception, and what normally would be considered a very clear and sharp image. So I am suggesting that, really, imagery and perception involve the same basic level or system—perceptual integration—the difference being initiation, whether through the external projection system or via feedback from the more central system.

Open Discussion

Paivio: With regard to sequential versus parallel processing, the language code (words, or their subunits, and how they are organized) is a sequential operation. The process, which Dr. Osgood considers to be simultaneous bundles, is aroused as simultaneous bundles by the verbal input. The bundles are in the same class as images, in this sense: the subject first sees the word, and the word matches some kind of internal representation in the speech center; other processes are then aroused which are the semantic, emotional, Osgood's EPA components, and imagery as well. Imagery differs from language in that imagery is a parallel rather than a sequential processing operation: Think of the phrase, "white horse." Now imagine the referent—the "white" and the "horse" are together as one, but the two words are sequential. In contrast, consider another pair of units that are, like white horse, associatively linked: "basic theory." You can't unitize basic theory into a simultaneous image, as you can white horse. Basic theory function as two units. The difference is related to the imagery characteristics of the items. So one pair creates a parallel, simultaneous representation of some kind, and the other does not. I strongly agree that imagery and perceptual processes are similar, probably involving the same channels. With regard to imagery and meaning, our differences are a matter of how one views meaning. "Meaning" is a multimeaning word, and I see imagery as one kind of meaning reaction.

Audience: Could you elaborate on the tests of spatial manipulations which you used to classify people as vivid imagers?

Paivio: Of course they are not measures of vividness, but measures of spatial manipulation skills, e.g., The Minnesota Paper Form Board, Spatial Relations, Thurstone's Flags Test, items from Guilford's classification of figural and transformational abilities in his work on the structure of the intellect.

Audience: Have you used the Betts test of vividness?

Paivio: Somewhat. It is a vividness test, patterned after Galton's original "breakfast table" questionnaire. It hasn't paid off well, in Sheehan's research in Australia, nor in our attempts. The objective ability tests seem to be better predictors in some situations than the vividness tests.

Dr. Richard Blanton (Vanderbilt University): Regarding Dr. Osgood's statement about the regeneration (recovery) problem, and with regard to both imagery and perception, Hebb once said that quite often when you ask people to verbally reconstruct their living room, they will do it from a standpoint from which they do not ordinarily perceive it. This suggests that the reconstitutional process often produces a different product than the original perception, and raises the old question of the relationship between relaxation and the vividness of the imagery. Relevant here is Dr. Foster's statement, yesterday, that we have done very little with hypnogogic states and with reproduction of imagery under various kinds of elicitation conditions. Have you some thoughts on that?

Paivio: We have more generally been concerned with the functions of our postulated system in relation to behavior than in making the fine distinctions among different types of imagery. Perhaps qualitative differences in images can be made, perhaps there are none, or perhaps they are simply defined by the time and kind of situation in which they occur. There are images of memory, where you reconstruct something you know, that occur in dreams (very bizarre forms) and in waking. But objectively, we know very little, or almost nothing, of those images; and you cite merely Hebb's introspection about it. I have anecdotes similar to Hebb's; for example, when I imagined my kitchen, I had the startling experience of realizing that I looked through the house from the kitchen, through the living room, into the garage on the other side. This is bizarre, but I do not believe it is given by anything but my sensory experiences associated with the various components of my home.

Audience: It suggests, though, the reconstitution of a recreative kind of process, rather than a template, a picture.

Paivio: To be sure. Many people have said such things, but I don't believe they really understood the distinction between static and constructive–dynamic images. Surely today we must get away from the idea of a static memory of a still picture of a situation. Memory is a dynamic and constructive process, but we don't know how images are stored. We don't know how words are stored, either. I am absolutely sure that we store information about nonverbal situations; you can be convinced by remembering familiar things—such memories aren't verbal, but there is a linkage. This is one of the most interesting questions to which the psychophysiologist could address himself, viz., how does the interrelationship between verbal and nonverbal memories occur? I believe that they can be independent, since you can affect one without the other being involved. We can also show experimentally that they are interconnected because of the kinds of transformations that I was talking about. Even the introspective evidence is compelling on the point. But we haven't got the vaguest idea of the way that information is stored, and still less than none about the verbal–nonverbal interconnections, other than they perhaps go through the corpus callosum. How the information is coded and stored is a complete mystery.

Dr. Rechtschaffen, yesterday, talked about the lack of information concerning the nature of dreams. Dreams, images, and thoughts generally are unexplained by any current theories. Here lies an enormous challenge for psychology, psychophysiology, and neuropsychology.

Dr. Michael Seitz (University of Pittsburgh): You mentioned that your work focused on one eye. Have you done a study with both eyes?

Paivio: No, not with the pupillary response.

Seitz: My question, perhaps, anticipates Dr. Sperry's talk: If you gave verbal input instead of visual, would there be a differential dilation between the right eye and the left eye, versus the right hemisphere and left hemisphere?

Paivio: I doubt that would happen. You get consensual dilation, for example, with the stimulation of one eye only; the other eye, depending on the stimulus, will respond similarly. I would be surprised if you get differences, unless there is some kind of neurological damage.

Dr. Louis Aarons (Department of Mental Health, Chicago): Do you really believe that language and image systems differ as far as sequential and parallel processing are concerned?

Paivio: Well, it is not a matter of belief; it is a working hypothesis.

Aarons: Yes, but there is evidence on both sides that, by varying the dimensions and instructions, you can make pairs of words unified, e.g., "cruel–kindness" is unified to me.

Paivio: "Cruel–kindness?" Abstract phrases like that have been studied and the fact is that they function like two units in memory. With regard to parallel versus sequential processing, Dr. Osgood mentioned that images are sequential. I think we have to distinguish here between the way information is organized in the system—in memory, e.g., and the *total processing* of it; there could be serial aspects of processing during input to output. Most processing of visual information is serial at the perceptual level, because of the limitations of the output channels. So if I describe what is in my visual field, I fixate on different points, but the output, of course, will be one at a time in the description. This serial output occurs even though the information exists in parallel, in the sense that it's all simultaneously available to my retina; and how I process the information serially in outputting it depends on what I attend to. And that is a problem of set, or motivation, or some other factor than the layout of that information.

Audience: What about the image of, "Jack jumped over the candlestick?"

Paivio: There *are* sequential images, provided that you have learned the sequence of activity related to it; so that "Jack jumped over the candlestick" involves a learned series. I am not saying that imagery can't go on continuously, but that this probably is created by a motor aspect to which the imagery is linked; and the perceptual aspects and information, at any point in time, are synchronous, so that "Jack jumping over the candlestick" is more synchronous than the words, "Jack . . . jumped . . . over . . .," etc. If you compress it in time, it seems to be more or less simultaneous in the language aspect. You can get effects in imagery which behave like sequential information if they are tied to a verbal sequence, as in the use of the "one, bun; two, shoe; . . ." technique; but the sequence here is created by the verbal aspect to which the imagery is tied. "One, bun" creates the image of "bun, two, shoe." The rhyme and the numerical sequence is sequential; the images themselves are not. And we have shown, using our pictorial materials, that discrete items of information, with no natural action sequence, are not remembered sequentially, unless there is some kind of motor or verbal component. Discrete verbal units, however, *are* well-ordered sequentially, even if they don't have a natural high transitional probability between them.

Dr. Paul Woods (Hollins College): Would you outline again the theoretical implications of the fact that the pupillary response is greater to abstract than to concrete words?

Paivio: The interpretation is in terms of activation or arousal—it is more difficult to generate images to abstract words, because the interconnection between an image and a verbal system is either weak or absent.

Dr. David Johnson (Sweetbriar College): In one of your studies, using a paired associate task, you had three groups of subjects: One group was told to use an imagery type of mediator; another group, the verbal mediator; and the third group was given no set at all. Were the data obtained for recall performance?

Paivio: Yes.

Johnson: They are typical unloading functions.

Paivio: Yes. The unloading occurs more easily for the mediation group, as shown by the decrease of the pupil size.

Johnson: But what assurance did you have that the no-set group learned as well as the other two?

Paivio: They didn't; but by the fourth trial, the learning differences between groups were minimal. In studies like this, you typically get a convergence over trials for the mediation and control groups, so that after three or four trials, there really is minimal difference. Regarding the unloading hypothesis, while the performance of all groups improved dramatically over four trials, the pupillary data reflected the improvement only in the case of the mediation-set group.

Johnson: That's what was puzzling to me, but I certainly wouldn't argue that the mediation would help in the learning rate. However, given that the three groups had learned at the same level, it is hard for me to see how the mediator helps to unload.

Paivio: I think you can learn at the same level with greater or lesser effort. You can really learn to use imagery devices—mnemonic pegs, e.g., with consummate ease, to remember enormous amounts of information. Using rote repetition to learn the same amount of information in a larger time period does not seem as easy. This is subjective, because nobody has systematically asked people about the ease of the experience; anecdotally, this is the way it seems, and I think that the pupillary data are interesting in this respect.

REFERENCES

Antrobus, J. S., Antrobus, J. S., & Singer, J. L. Eye movements accompanying daydreaming, visual imagery, and thought suppression. *Journal of Abnormal and Social Psychology,* 1964, **69,** 244–252.

Bakan, P., & Svorad, D. Resting EEG alpha and asymmetry of reflective lateral eye movements. *Nature*, 1969, **223**, 975–976.

Barber, T. X. Imagery and hallucinations: Effects of LSD contrasted with the effects of "hypnotic" suggestions. In S. J. Segal (Ed.), *The adaptive function of imagery*. New York: Academic Press, 1971.

Barratt, P. E. Use of EEG in the study of imagery. *British Journal of Psychology*, 1956, **47**, 101–114.

Beatty, J., & Kahneman, D. Pupillary changes in two memory tasks. *Psychonomic Science*, 1966, **5**, 371–372.

Begg, I., & Paivio, A. Concreteness and imagery in sentence meaning. *Journal of Verbal Learning and Verbal Behavior*, 1969, **8**, 821–827.

Beritoff, J. S. *Neural mechanisms of higher vertebrate behavior*. (Translated and edited by W. T. Liberson.) Boston: Little, Brown, 1965.

Berlyne, D. E. *Structure and direction in thinking*. New York: Wiley, 1965.

Bower, G. H. Imagery as a relational organizer in associative learning. *Journal of Verbal Learning and Verbal Behavior*, 1970, **9**, 529–533.

Bruner, J. S., Olver, R. R., & Greenfield, P. M. *Studies in congnitive growth*. New York: Wiley, 1966.

Bryden, M. P. Tachistoscopic recognition of non-alphabetic material. *Canadian Journal of Psychology*, 1960, **14**, 78–86.

Bugelski, B. R. Words and things and images. *American Psychologist*, 1970, **25**, 1002–1012.

Colman, F. D., & Paivio, A. Pupillary response and galvanic skin response during an imagery task. *Psychonomic Science*, 1969, **16**, 296–297.

Colman, F., & Paivio, A. Pupillary dilation and mediation processes during paired-associate learning. *Canadian Journal of Psychology*, 1970, **24**, 261–270.

Deckert, G. H. Pursuit eye movements in the absence of a moving visual stimulus. *Science*, 1964, **143**, 1192–1193.

Epstein, W., Rock, I., & Zuckerman, C. B. Meaning and familiarity in associative learning. *Psychological Monographs*, 1960, **74**, (4, Whole No. 491).

Ernest, C. H., & Paivio, A. Imagery ability in paired-associate and incidental learning. Psychonomic Science, 1969, **15**, 181–182.

Golla, F. L., Hutton, E. L., & Walter, W. G. The objective study of mental imagery. *Journal of Mental Science*, 1943, **89**, 216–223.

Graham, K. R. Eye movements during visual mental imagery. Paper presented to the Eastern Psychological Association, Atlantic City, April, 1970.

Haber, R. N., & Haber, R. B. Eidetic imagery: I. Frequency. *Perceptual and Motor Skills*, 1964, **19**, 131–138.

Hakerem, G., & Sutton, S. Pupillary response at visual threshold. *Nature*, 1966, 485–486.

Hale, S. M., & Simpson, H. M. Effects of eye movements on the rate of discovery and the vividness of visual images. *Perception and Psychophysics*, 1971, **9**, 242–246.

Hartman, T. F. Dynamic transmission, elective generalization, and semantic conditioning. In W. F. Prokasy (Ed.), *Classical conditioning*. New York: Appleton, 1965.

Hebb, D. O. Concerning imagery. *Psychological Review*, 1968, **75**, 466–477.

Hefferline, R. F., & Perera, T. B. Proprioceptive discrimination of a covert operant without its observation by the subject. *Science*, 1963, **139**, 834–835.

Hess, E. H., & Polt, J. M. Pupil size in relation to mental activity during simple problem solving. *Science*, 1964, **143**, 1190–1192.

John, E. R. *Mechanisms of memory*. New York: Academic Press, 1967.

John, E. R., Herrington, R. N., & Sutton, S. Effects of visual form on the evoked response. *Science*, 1967, **155**, 1439–1442.

Kimura, D. Dual functional asymmetry of the brain in visual perception. *Neuropsychologia*, 1966, **4**, 275–285.

Kimura, D. Asymmetries in perception related to hemispheric differentiation of function. In M. Kinsbourne (Ed.), *Hemispheric asymmetry of function*. London: Tavistock, in press.

Klüver, H. Eidetic phenomena. *Psychological Bulletin*, 1932, **29**, 181–203.

Kohler, I. (Translated by H. Fiss). The formation and transformation of the perceptual world. *Psychological Issues*, 1964, **3**, (12, Whole No. 4).

Leask, J., Haber, R. N., & Haber, R. B. Eidetic imagery in children: II. Longitudinal and experimental results. *Psychonomic Monograph Supplements*, 1969, **3** (3, Whole No. 35).

Loewenfeld, I. E. Comment on Hess' findings. *Survey of Ophthalmology*, 1966, **11**, 291–294.

Lorens, S. A. Jr., & Darrow, C. W. Eye movements, EEG, GSR, and EKG during mental multiplication. *Electroencephalography and Clinical Neurophysiology*, 1962, **14**, 739–746.

Lowenstein, O., & Loewenfeld, I. E. The pupil. In H. Davson (Ed.), *The eye*. Vol. III. New York: Academic Press, 1962.

McGuigan, F. J. Covert oral behavior during the silent performance of language tasks. *Psychological Bulletin*, 1970, **74**, 409–326.

McGuigan, F. J. Electrical measurement of covert processes as an explication of "higher mental processes." Conference on psychophysiology of thinking. Hollins College, Roanoke, Virginia, 1971.

Milner, B., & Teuber, H. L. Alteration of perception and memory in man: reflections on methods. In L. Weiskrantz (Ed.), *Analysis of behavioral change*. New York: Harper, 1968.

Mowrer, O. H. *Learning theory and the symbolic processes*. New York: Wiley, 1960.

Nunnally, J. C., Knott, P. D., Duchnowski, A., & Parker, R. Pupillary response as a general measure of activation. *Perception and Psychophysics*, 1967, **2**, 149–155.

Oswald, I. The EEG, visual imagery and attention. *The Quarterly Journal of Experimental Psychology*, 1957, **9**, 113–118.

Paivio, A. Abstractness, imagery, and meaningfulness in paired-associate learning. *Journal of Verbal Learning and Verbal Behavior*, 1965, **4**, 32–38.

Paivio, A. Latency of verbal associations and imagery to noun stimuli as a function of abstractness and generality. *Canadian Journal of Psychology*, 1966, **20**, 378–387.

Paivio, A. *Imagery and verbal processes*. New York: Holt, 1971.

Paivio, A., & Csapo, K. Concrete-image and verbal memory codes. *Journal of Experimental Psychology*, 1969, **80**, 279–285.

Paivio, A., & Foth, D. Imaginal and verbal mediators and noun concreteness in paired-associate learning: The elusive interaction. *Journal of Verbal Learning and Verbal Behavior*, 1970, **9**, 384–390.

Paivio, A., & Okovita, H. W. Word imagery modalities and associative learning in blind and sighted subjects. *Journal of Verbal Learning and Verbal Behavior*, 1971, **10**, 506–510.

Paivio, A., & Simpson, H. M. The effect of word abstractness and pleasantness on pupil size during an imagery task. *Psychonomic Science*, 1966, **5**, 55–56.

Paivio, A., & Simpson, H. M. Pupillary responses during imagery tasks as a function of stimulus characteristics and imagery ability. *Research Bulletin* No. 45, Department of Psychology, University of Western Ontario, 1967.

Paivio, A., & Simpson, H. M. Magnitude and latency of the pupillary response during an imagery task as a function of stimulus abstractness and imagery ability. *Psychonomic Science*, 1968, **12**, 45–46.

Paivio, A., Yuille, J. C., & Madigan, S. Concreteness, imagery and meaningfulness values for 925 nouns. *Journal of Experimental Psychology Monograph Supplement*, 1968, **76**, (1, Pt. 2).

Perky, C. W. An experimental study of imagination. *American Journal of Psychology* 1910, **21**, 422–452.

Piaget, J., & Inhelder, B. *L'image mentale chez l'enfant*. Paris: Presses Universitaires de France, 1966.

Rechtschaffen, A. The psychophysiology of mental activity during sleep. Conference on psychophysiology of thinking. Hollins College, Roanoke, Virginina, 1971.

Reese, H. W. Imagery and contextual meaning. In H. W. Reese (Chm.), Imagery in children's learning: A symposium. *Psychological Bulletin*, 1970, **73**, 404–414.

Richardson, A. *Mental imagery*. New York: Springer Publ., 1969.

Roffwarg, H. P., Dement, W. C., Muzio, J. N., & Fisher, C. Dream imagery: Relationship to rapid eye movements of sleep. *Archives of General Psychiatry*, 1962, **7**, 235–258.

Sheehan, P. W. Functional similarity of imaging to perceiving: Individual differences in vividness of imagery. *Perceptual and Motor Skills*, 1966, **23**, 1011–1033.

Sheffield, F. D. Relation between classical conditioning and instrumental learning. In W. F. Prokasy (Ed.), *Classical conditioning*. New York: Appleton, 1965.

Short, P. L. The objective study of mental imagery. *British Journal of Psychology*, 1953, **44**, 38–51.

Short, P. L., & Walter, W. G. The relationship between physiological variables and stereognosis. *Electroencephalography and Clinical Neurophysiology*, 1954, **6**, 29–44.

Simpson, H. M. Effects of a task-relevant response on pupil size. *Psychophysiology*, 1969, **6**, 115–121.

Simpson, H. M., & Climan, M. H. Pupillary and electromyographic changes during an imagery task. *Psychophysiology*, 1971, **8**, 483–490.

Simpson, H. M., & Hale, S. M. Pupillary changes during a decision-making task. *Perceptual and Motor Skills*, 1969, **29**, 495–498.

Simpson, H. M., & Molloy, F. M. Effects of audience anxiety on pupil size. *Psychophysiology*, 1971, **8**, 491–496.

Simpson, H. M., & Paivio, A. Effects on pupil size of manual and verbal indicators of cognitive task fulfillment. *Perception and Psychophysics*, 1968, **3**, 185–190.

Simpson, H. M., Paivio, A., & Rogers, T. B. Occipital alpha activity of high and low visual imagers during problem solving. *Psychonomic Science*, 1967, **7**, 49–50.

Simpson, H. M., Molloy, F. M., Hale, S. M., & Climan, M. H. Latency and magnitude of the pupillary response during an imagery task. *Psychonomic Science*, 1968, **13**, 293–294.

Singer, J. L. *Daydreaming: An introduction to the experimental study of inner experience*. New York: Random House, 1966.

Skinner, B. F. *Science and human behavior*. New York: MacMillan, 1953.

Slatter, K. H. Alpha rhythms and mental imagery. *Electroencephalography and Clinical Neurophysiology*, 1960, **12**, 851–859.

Sokolov, E. N. *Perception and the conditioned reflex*. New York: MacMillan, 1963.

Sperry, R. W. Hemisphere deconnection and unity in conscious awareness. *American Psychologist*, 1968, **23**, 723–733.

Sperry, R. W. Lateralization of function in the surgically separated hemispheres. Conference on psychophysiology of thinking. Hollins College, Roanoke, Virginia, 1971.

Steeves, R., Paivio, A., & Simpson, H. M. Effects of personal values and stimulus word attributes on pupil size during imagery and verbal association tasks. Research Bulletin No. 46, Department of Psychology, University of Western Ontario, 1967.

Stoyva, J., & Kamiya, J. Electrophysiological studies of dreaming as the prototype of a new strategy in the study of consciousness. *Psychological Review*, 1968, **75**, 192–205.

Wollen, K. A. Variables that determine the effectiveness of picture mediators in paired-associate learning. Paper presented at the meeting of the Psychonomic Society. St. Louis, November, 1969.

Woodmansee, J. J. Methodological problems in pupillographic experiments. *Proceedings of the American Psychological Association*, 1966, **1**, 133–134.

Young, F. A. Studies of pupillary conditioning. *Journal of Experimental Psychology*, 1958, **55**, 97–110.

Young, F. A. Classical conditioning of autonomic functions. In W. F. Prokasy (Ed.), *Classical conditioning*. New York: Appleton, 1965. Pp. 358–377.

Yuille, J. C., & Paivio, A. Imagery and verbal mediation instructions in paired-associate learning. *Journal of Experimental Psychology*, 1968, **78**, 436–441.

EMPHASIS ON PERIPHERAL MEASURES—PRIMARILY ELECTROMYOGRAM

CHAPTER NINE

Hallucinations: An Experimental Approach[1]

RALPH F. HEFFERLINE, LOUIS J. J. BRUNO, AND JANET A. CAMP

Columbia University

There are few among us who cannot offer a passable definition for the term *hallucination*, a word that has been a part of the English language for the past four centuries. Many in fact might agree to its original definition—a mistaken condition of the mind characterized by imaginings of ghosts, noises, visions, and forewarnings (Sarbin & Juhasz, 1967). For our own part, we prefer the less vivid but more precise definition now current in the medical literature. By this definition, hallucinations are reports of sensory perceptions in the absence of adequate external stimuli (cf. Fischer, 1969). The current definition, couched in the phenomenological language of the behavioral sciences, improves upon the original by opening the way for an experimental approach to the hallucinatory report.

The new, phenomenological definition has not, however, succeeded in changing word usage: The attribution of hallucinations to an individual continues to imply a negative evaluation. Although its definition makes

[1] Preparation of this paper was supported by Grant MH-13890 from the National Institute of Mental Health to R. F. Hefferline and L. J. J. Bruno.

no such demand, the term hallucination is typically used only to describe the behavior of psychopathologic persons (Sarbin, 1967). In fact, one of the criteria for concluding that an individual suffers certain forms of pathology is the presence of hallucinatory behavior. Of course, as Sarbin and Juhasz point out, this usage is misleadingly circular—we judge a man insane because he hallucinates and then proceed to explain that he hallucinates because he is insane. But the familiar circularity of current psychiatric usage is not our immediate concern. Our concern instead is with the fact that current usage, apart from current definition, relegates hallucinations to the realm of the abnormal and pathological. Usage would make it appear that some "reports of sensory perception in the absence of adequate external stimuli" are abnormal and diagnostic of pathology—these are called hallucinations—and other reports, such as those obtained under laboratory conditions, are normal and hence deserve a less pejorative name.

The question arises: Why not adopt a definition or set of definitions more consistent with usage? Here the temptation is strong to accede to usage, following the example of textbook writers who have "differentiated hallucinations from errors of perception through the simple expedient of locating them in different chapters [Sarbin & Juhasz, 1967, p. 353]." To give in to this temptation, however, would be to ignore a fundamental strength of the current definition. By failing to distinguish between normal and abnormal hallucinations, it directs our attention to the possibility that all hallucinations share a common psychological mechanism. In other words, the definition suggests that the occurrence of hallucinations is not restricted to pathologic individuals, but rather may be observed in all segments of the population under opportune conditions. Our task as experimentalists, then, is to define and specify those conditions under which experimental hallucinations may be produced in the hope that this will lead us to understand how hallucinations are generated outside of the laboratory.

I. HYPNOTICALLY INDUCED HALLUCINATIONS

The experimental condition, or manipulation, that has generated the largest amount of literature and also the largest number of hallucinations is that of hypnosis. The typical experiment on hypnotic hallucinations involves hypnotizing persons who have previously been determined to be highly susceptible. While these persons are in the trance state, they are told either that they will experience sensory stimuli that are not present—positive hallucinations—or that they will not experience stimuli that are present—negative hallucinations. If the person then reports that he experiences what the experimenter suggested, he is considered to be hallucinating. Typically, a second test, based on the suggestions of the experimenter, is also included in the experimental design. For example, Rosenthal and Mele (1952) presented hypnotized subjects with gray cards, suggesting however that the cards were blue, red, yellow, green, or orange. After staring at the first gray card for a minute, subjects were then presented with a second gray card and asked to describe what they saw. The hypothesis was that if the subjects had experienced the suggested color of the first card, they would now see the negative afterimage of that color on the second card. All four subjects tested reported appropriate negative afterimages, indicating that they had, in fact, hallucinated colors on the first cards. Using a somewhat more sophisticated design, Underwood (1960) tested the ability of hypnotized subjects either to hallucinate positively the presence of background fields for illusion figures or to hallucinate negatively the absence of these fields. Of the three illusion figures used, two yielded insignificant results with respect to the hallucinated fields. The results for the third illusion were that subjects in the *very* deep trance group—but not those in the deep trance group—gave, as a result of positively hallucinating the background field, a significantly higher number of correct illusion reports than did the control subjects. Experiments like those of Rosenthal and Mele, and of Underwood lead to the conclusion that hypnosis is an effective means of obtaining hallucinations in normal subjects.

Unfortunately, this conclusion is weakened by the fact that most studies seeking to demonstrate that hypnosis can be used to generate hallucinations are flawed by two major design problems. First, for practical reasons, hypnotic subjects in the experimental groups are usually a highly select group of individuals: Subjects are first pretested as to their susceptibility to hypnosis—one of the tests occasionally being the ability to hallucinate—and are often given preexperimental training in reporting their trance experiences. Consequently, in addition to constituting a group whose characteristics specifically include one of the features of the experimental design and hypothesis, these subjects have also been trained to give precisely the type of report the experimenter is interested in obtaining (cf. Barber & Calverley, 1964b; also, Sutcliffe, 1961). In contrast, control subjects are either selected at random or are the rejects from the experimental group. To add to this obvious confusion of subjects and treatment (cf. Thorne, 1967), experimental and control groups have typically received different sets of instructions, the nature of which is to clearly load the die in favor of the experimental group. For example, while the experimental hypnotic group is told in the trance state that it *will* perceive the stimuli in question, the control group is often told to respond "as if" it perceived those same stimuli (cf. Underwood, 1960; Sarbin & Andersen, 1963). With these two biases in favor of the experimental hypnotic group, it is not hard to see why the experimental groups tend to report hallucinations significantly more often than do the control groups.

One wonders, then, what results would be obtained if the biases against the control group subjects were removed or equalized. How necessary is the hypnotic trance to the induction of hallucinatory reports? A number of studies have been conducted with just this question in mind.

The prototypical experiment involves selecting a group of subjects, randomly distributing them among experimental and control groups, giving all groups the same instructions, and then comparing the number and/or vividness of the resulting hallucinations across groups. Using a design of this sort, Barber and Calverley (1964a) told all their subjects to "hear" a recording of a song and to "see" a cat sitting in their laps. When subsequently asked to rate the vividness and reality of their experiences, half of the subjects reported that they had heard, and a third of them reported that they had seen the suggested items. The group was then randomly divided into three subgroups, which received either (1) hypnotic induction during which subjects were told that they would have unusual experiences, (2) motivating instructions in which subjects were told that they had not tried hard enough and that everyone could do this if he tried, or (3) no further instructions (control group). Subjects were then given a second test similar to the first. The results showed that while subjects in the control group rated the vividness and reality of their experiences to the same degree as they had during the first test, subjects in both the hypnotic induction and the motivating instructions groups now rated their experiences as more vivid and more real. Although both groups were reliably different from the control group, there were no significant differences between the two experimental groups. Apparently the hallucinatory behavior observed under trance conditions is not a result of hypnosis per se, but is rather an effect produced by the motivating nature of the instructions typically given while the subject happens to be in the trance state. Thorne (1967), like most of the others who questioned the necessity of hypnosis, came to the same conclusion, but Thorne's design was interestingly different. He selected susceptible subjects for both his experimental (hypnotic induction) and control (motivating instructions) groups. He found no difference between the two groups in their ability to hallucinate a song as evidenced by the song's interference with the learning of paired associates.

At point in studies like those of Barber and Calverley, and of Thorne is not whether the hypnotic trance can help generate hallucinatory reports— it can—but rather whether the same reports can be as easily obtained by sufficiently motivating subjects via instructions. On this point it may be worthwhile to examine an experiment performed by Sarbin and Andersen (1963) whose intent was to replicate without hypnosis the study carried out by Underwood (1960). The design was basically identical to that used by Underwood, except that instead of carefully selecting experimental group subjects for their high susceptibility to hypnosis and suggestion, Sarbin and Andersen used 120 subjects selected completely at random. Subjects were first given instructions designed to generate interest and cooperation, and then were told to either see or not see the background fields from the Underwood illusions. After the data on the number of correct illusion responses had been collected, Sarbin and Andersen merely selected the "best" 11 subjects and compared their data to that of the remaining 109 subjects. When portrayed graphically, these two sets of data were extraordinarily similar to those obtained from Underwood's very deep trance and control groups, respectively. As a demonstration study, this experiment clearly made its point: The hallucinatory behavior which Underwood could obtain only with 3% of all the subjects he tested—only 3% could achieve the very deep trance condition and only subjects in this condition gave a significantly high number of hallucinatory responses— Sarbin and Andersen were able to find in 9% of the population, without recourse to hypnosis. The conclusion here is obvious: The hypnotic trance is clearly not a necessary condition for obtaining hallucinatory behavior and it is probably the case that when hypnotized subjects do hallucinate, the trance state is simply a superfluous accessory to the motivating instructions given during it.

What we have seen, then, is that normal individuals operating under a set of strongly motivating instructions do give hallucinatory reports. Unfortunately, such instructions elevate the demand characteristics of the experiment to a rather high level. Subjects told that they definitely will experience certain phenomena are likely to report that they do experience them, if only to please the experimenter or to do what they presume is expected of them. That this tends to be the case was shown in a study by Bowers (1967). Part one of his experiment was basically a replication of Barber and Calverley's 1964(a) study in which subjects were asked to hear a song and to see a cat in their laps. In part two, half the subjects were given motivating instructions as in the original study, and were then retested by asking them to hear a different song and to see a dog rather than a cat. The rest of the subjects were told by the experimenter of part one to be as honest as possible with a second experimenter who then made his appearance to continue the experiment. The second experimenter told the subjects that not everyone was in fact capable of seeing and hearing things that were not present, and that they should simply be as honest as possible in their reports. The second experimenter then gave the song–dog retest to this group. When the retest ratings for vividness and reality for the two groups were compiled, it was found that the first group (motivation) had significantly higher retest than pretest ratings, but the ratings of the second (honesty) group remained the same. Although these results cannot be directed to the question of how hallucinations are generated, they do point up the fact that strong suggestions and highly motivating instructions are capable of increasing subjective reports of the reality of hallucinations.

In summary, hypnosis and/or motivating instructions, when used as adjuncts to verbal suggestion, seem to provide conditions sufficient for eliciting hallucinatory reports. Still further evidence is needed, however, to determine the mechanisms responsible for the production of hallucinatory behavior. What we are looking for is not simply a means for generating hallucinations—the method of verbal suggestion serves admirably in this respect. Rather, we would like to know how normal subjects can be brought to make hallucinatory reports when they have not been specifically told that they are to experience stimuli that are not present. In other words, do nonverbal means exist for instructing the subject to hallucinate?

II. CONDITIONED HALLUCINATIONS

A. Looking at the Literature

The search for a nonverbal means of training hallucinations leads naturally to the conditioning laboratory. Here, among the procedures of classical conditioning, lies hope not only for a generalized technique for producing experimental hallucinations, but hope also of finding an explanatory principle applicable to a broad range of hallucinatory phenomena. From the conditioning laboratory come studies of three types: studies combining conditioning with hypnosis, studies that test for hallucinatory reports after passive CS–UCS pairings, and studies that train the hallucinatory report as a conditioned response.

The studies combining conditioning with hypnosis constitute a fairly direct analog to the studies reviewed earlier that combined suggestion with hypnosis. In both sets of studies the subjects were instructed, either by suggestion or by conditioning, during the hypnotic trance; in both they were tested for hallucinatory reports when in the posthypnotic waking state. The earliest of the studies to combine conditioning and hypnosis was performed by Scott (1930), who exposed ten hypnotized subjects to buzzer–shock pairings administered under a classical delayed conditioning paradigm. After an average of 14.2 trials, each of his subjects had produced a finger-withdrawal response to the buzzer when it was presented without shock in the trance state. After waking from the trance, each subject continued to give conditional finger-withdrawal responses to the buzzer alone. Two subjects spontaneously reported shock sensations while being settled into the apparatus for the posthypnotic tests (both claimed amnesia for the events that took place during the trance); other subjects volunteered that the buzzer produced pain or fear sensations.

Scott's data, although scarcely striking or sophisticated, are useful in the present context because they point up the interesting possibility of working with nonverbal hallucinations. The possibility, of course, is inherent in our definition of hallucinations—reports of sensory perception in the absence of adequate external stimuli—since the definition does not demand that the hallucinatory reports be verbal. In Scott's data, the possibility is manifest in the fact that each of his subjects, in the absence of the adequate external stimulus—the shock—made finger-withdrawal responses to the buzzer. It might be argued, then, that all of Scott's subjects hallucinated the shock manually, although only a few also hallucinated it verbally. On theoretical grounds, the argument is both tenable and didactic; at the least, it suggests that hallucinations are at root no more exotic than any other particularized subclass of the general class of conditioned behavior. On practical grounds, however, we must reject the argument with respect to Scott's data because it broadens beyond management the class of reports that we intend to legitimize as hallucinations. We are ready to accept as hallucinations nonverbal reports that for the hallucinator and for his audience are equivalent to verbal reports of sensory perception, that is, we will accept a key press made in lieu of saying "I saw it," but we are not ready, for the present purposes, to accept as hallucinations any and all of the responses that can be made to occur in the absence of adequate external stimuli.[2]

After restricting our consideration of hallucinations to those based on verbal or equivalent reports, Scott's data become unconvincing. Only two

---

[2] It should be noted that we have been careful not to imply that the conditional finger-withdrawal responses should be excluded from the class of hallucinatory reports on the grounds that they are classically rather than instrumentally conditioned responses. Our care in this matter reflects our views on the traditional distinction between respondents and operants (cf. Hefferline, Bruno, & Davidowitz, 1971).

of his ten subjects hallucinated the shock spontaneously. However, the paucity of hallucinations in Scott's experiment may simply reflect the fact that Scott was not looking for hallucinations and consequently recorded them only when they were volunteered by his subjects. Leuba (1940), who asked his subjects "to report at once . . . anything . . . besides the usual direct effects [p. 345]" of the test stimuli, was far more successful. In a series of informal experiments using a variety of different stimuli for the CS and UCS—the sound of a clicker was a typical CS, a pinprick a typical UCS—Leuba succeeded in eliciting waking-state hallucinatory reports from 14 of the 16 subjects who underwent trance-state delayed classical conditioning. Although their posthypnotic amnesia seemed otherwise complete, Leuba's subjects reported seeing, hearing, smelling, or feeling the appropriate UCS when stimulated in the waking state by the previously associated CS.

Leuba's informal experiments have recently been corroborated in a more rigorous way by Graham's work (1969) with a similar procedure. Graham told each of his subjects that whenever the buzzer sounded he was to examine the stimulus card in front of him and describe it by saying whether or not he saw circles. After instructing his subjects, Graham hypnotized them and gave them ten conditioning trials during which the sound of the buzzer was paired for 5 sec with a white stimulus card displaying two black circles, one centered on each half of the card. Graham then aroused his subjects from hypnosis and tested them with ten trials on which a blank card was presented while the buzzer sounded. Only 2 of the 26 subjects treated to Graham's procedure failed to hallucinate two black circles on the blank test card. Graham's work then, taken together with the earlier reports of Leuba and Scott, suggests that hallucinatory verbal reports can be obtained from normal individuals trained under hypnosis with one of several classical conditioning procedures. And this in turn suggests the familiar question: Is hypnosis necessary?

Two of the studies (Fishkin, 1969; Kelly, 1934) pertinent to this question used a design similar to Leuba's, but omitted the hypnotic trance: Training trials consisted of exposing the subject to paired presentations of the CS and UCS; test trials were carried out by giving the CS alone and asking the subject to report verbally on whether he also experienced the UCS. Kelly's study (1934) was an attempt to condition chromesthesia by pairing under a simultaneous, classical conditioning paradigm each of the eight notes of the C-major scale "with the color occupying the same relative position in the spectral series as the note occupies in the musical scale [p. 324]." The experiment, carried out in group sittings over a period of 7 weeks, involved 13 subjects, each of whom knew the purpose of the study.

Five of the subjects completed the experiment and were exposed to 2000 pairings. The only training instructions given were to "look at the colors and listen to the tones [p. 327]." Test trials, during which each of the eight notes was given alone five times in random order, were conducted after each weekly session. The subjects were asked to write down on each trial whether (1) "a real image or sensation" of color was experienced, or (2) in the absence of an image, the name of the color that goes with the tone, or (3) a guess of the appropriate color. Astoundingly, none of Kelly's subjects ever hallucinated a color. Separate experiments in which five subjects were exposed to 1000 pairings of a single note with a single color also produced completely negative results.

Although it would be surprising to find another report of results as spectacularly negative as Kelly's—Kelly even failed to obtain conditioned chromesthesia when he dosed several subjects with mescal before testing them—it was not surprising to find that the only other study of conditioned sensations (hallucinations) to use a design like Kelly's was also somewhat less than successful. Fishkin (1969), taking off from Agathon and Lelord's one-page report (1963) that they had conditioned the spiral aftereffect in 43% of the subjects tested, used four groups of 16 subjects each in an attempt to replicate these results. Fishkin's subjects all watched a rotating spiral in an illuminated box for 14.8 sec at the start of each of 25 training trials. Subjects in the control group completed each training trial by watching the spiral stop (it took about 1 sec after the motor was turned off) and then looking at the stationary spiral for 3.4 sec more, after which the lights in the viewing box were extinguished. Subjects in the long-tone group had identical trials except that a tone came on just after the start of a trial and went off just before the end. Subjects in the short-tone group heard the same tone but it did not come on until 1.2 sec after the spiral motor was shut off. Subjects in the last group, called light-out, were treated like the short-tone subjects except that the lights in the viewing box went off when the spiral motor was shut off. Subjects in all of the groups were "not required to respond in any way during the training period [p. 133]."

Fishkin gave 20 test trials to each of his subjects. On each trial, the lights in the viewing box were lit for about 5 sec, revealing a stationary spiral for half the subjects or a stationary circle for the other half. The training tone was presented along with the lighted spiral or circle on alternate test trials. The subjects were told to press a key "if the spiral (circle) seems either to get bigger or come towards you [p. 133]." The results were that *all* of Fishkin's subjects pressed the key on at least 45% of the test trials, no matter which test figure they viewed (spiral or circle), no matter whether the tone was present or absent, and no matter which training group they belonged to. In one sense, then, Fishkin was quite successful: Whenever he showed a stationary spiral or circle to a subject who had witnessed spiral rotation, he elicited reports of figure movement. In the conditioning sense, however, Fishkin was but mildly successful: Only the light-out group pressed the key sufficiently more often during tone than no-tone test trials (6.2 tone vs 4.5 no-tone presses) for the tone/no-tone difference in key presses to be significantly larger (.025 level) than the difference generated by control group subjects. In short, neither Kelly nor Fishkin was particularly successful in using classical conditioning without hypnosis to instruct his subjects to give hallucinatory reports.[3]

Kelly's failure and Fishkin's limited success do not, however, tell the whole story about attempts to condition hallucinations without hypnosis. Neither Seashore (1895) nor Ellson (1941a, b) used hypnosis, but their attempts to condition hallucinations met with more generous measures of success. Seashore, in a number of separate experiments, obtained hallucinations in 60–100% of his subjects. Ellson found that 80% of the subjects in one study and 53% in another gave hallucinatory reports. Both Seashore and Ellson, unlike Kelly and Fishkin, used variations on the classical paradigm termed *anticipatory instructed conditioning* (Grant, 1964, pp. 3–8)—a paradigm that trains the hallucinatory report as a conditional response.

Seashore conducted a number of simple experiments during which he collected hallucinatory reports of warmth, light, sound, touch, taste, smell, and shock. In most of his experiments, a training trial consisted of giving one stimulus as a ready signal (CS) and following it within a few seconds by another stimulus (UCS) to which the subject was required to make either a manual or verbal response (UCR). Test trials, during which the CS was presented without the UCS, were generally interspersed among training trials in the ratio of one test to ten training trials, although in some cases test and training trials were alternated, and in a few instances a number of test trials were presented in succession. Although most of his experiments used the procedure just described, some used a form of the temporal conditioning procedure. Here the UCS was presented at regular intervals and the subject was required to report each occurrence of the UCS, or every fifth or tenth occurrence. Tests for hallucinations were carried out by omitting one or more of the scheduled UCS presentations. In both types of experiments, the UCS was typically a near-threshold

---

[3] Fishkin's over-all success in generating reports of perceived figure movement is of no interest to us here because it cannot be attributed to any single aspect of his procedure.

stimulus whose appearance the subject was asked to report as quickly or accurately as possible. This allowed Seashore to represent the experiments to his subjects as tests of their discriminative abilities. To maintain the misrepresentation, Seashore generally concluded his test trials by presenting the otherwise omitted UCS when the subject failed to hallucinate it.

As noted earlier, Seashore succeeded in obtaining hallucinatory reports from most of his subjects on most of their test trials. Seashore's success in teaching subjects to report a missing UCS prompted Ellson to incorporate many of the features of Seashore's experiments into the studies he reported nearly a half-century later (Ellson, 1941a, b). Like Seashore, Ellson misrepresented the purpose of the experiment to the subject by telling him that he wanted "to determine how faint a tone you can hear [p. 350]." Ellson's training trials (60 were given) were also similar to Seashore's. On each trial, a light given as a ready signal (CS) was turned on simultaneously with a subthreshold tone (UCS). The intensity of the tone was increased at the rate of 2 dB/sec until the subject pressed a key to indicate that he could hear the tone. The threshold intensity of the tone was maintained for 2 sec, after which tone intensity was decreased 2 dB for each second that the subject held the key closed. When the subject released the key, reporting that the tone had become inaudible, both the tone and the light were turned off. Ellson's ten test trials were also patterned after Seashore's. On these trials, given after the training trials, the tone onset was delayed for 30 sec after the light onset if no key press occurred, but was turned on and rapidly increased to an intensity just above threshold whenever a key press was made during the delay interval. On test trials, the tone intensity began decreasing 2 sec after its presentation, and both the tone and the light ended when the subject released the key.

With the procedure just outlined, Ellson (1941a) obtained one or more auditory hallucinations from 80% of the 40 subjects in his experimental group. In contrast, hallucinations were obtained from 57% of the 30 subjects in a control group given the test but no training trials, from 53% of the 30 control subjects given ten training trials before the test trials, and from only 20% of the 60 subjects in another control group who received no training trials and whose test trials omitted the tone entirely. Ellson elaborated these results by demonstrating the remarkable persistence of the hallucinatory report (1941b): Subjects given 60 training trials followed by 20 test trials during which the tone was never presented did not show any diminution in the tendency to hallucinate until explicitly informed, prior to ten additional test trials, that the tone would definitely not be presented.

Ellson's results, considered together with Seashore's, clearly indicate that classical conditioning applied without hypnosis can be used to train normal subjects to hallucinate. Since the indications from Ellson's and Seashore's set of experiments are inconsistent with those stemming from the set reported by Kelly and by Fishkin, it would seem worthwhile to examine both sets of studies with an eye toward locating a determining difference. Two areas of difference appear, one having to do with instructions to the subject, the other relating to the schedule of classical conditioning. With regard to instructions, Kelly, who failed entirely in his attempts to condition chromesthesia, stands alone among those who sought to train hallucinations: Kelly is the only experimenter who explained the purpose of his study to his subjects; the others systematically misinformed their subjects or, at the least, left them uninformed. Unfortunately, in the absence of specific evidence concerning the effects of informing, misinforming, or not informing the subject, we can neither attribute Kelly's failure to the fact that he informed his subjects nor offer advice on this topic more recent than Seashore's. Seashore (1895) reported "If an observer begins an experiment warned against illusion and determined not to be deluded, this . . . may be overcome by repetition of the real stimulus . . . as if he had been unwarned [p. 45]."

With regard to the second area of difference between the sets of studies, that is, the schedule of classical conditioning, firmer conclusions may be drawn. Both Kelly and Fishkin paired the CS and UCS during training trials without requiring the observer to respond overtly to the UCS. Their common rationale, we presume, was that the paired CS–UCS presentations would render the CS capable of eliciting a significant subset of the unspecified set of responses or events—call it an "image"—originally elicited only by the UCS. Under this rationale, an observer presented with the CS alone during a test trial might be expected to report, as an hallucination of the UCS, the image conditioned to the CS. In fact, hallucinatory reports might well be generated in this fashion if the subset of events conditioned to the CS happens to overlap sufficiently with the set of events that ordinarily determines reports of experiencing the UCS. But Kelly and Fishkin did nothing to insure that the events conditioned to the CS were a subset of those that determine reports of the UCS. In contrast, Seashore and Ellson did; by requiring that the observer report the UCS on each training trial they arranged to condition to the CS not only the unspecified set of events elicited by the UCS—the image—but also the set that, in the context of the experiment, determined a report of the UCS. Our point is made clearer by shifting our attention from the events conditioned to the CS to those antecedent to and presumably determinant of a report of the UCS. In Kelly's and Fishkin's experiments an hallucinatory report of the UCS would occur if by happenstance the events determining UCS reports outside of the laboratory overlapped with those evoked in the laboratory by presenting the CS alone after the training trials. In Seashore's and Ellson's experiments, however, the events antecedent to a UCS report made during a training trial were (1) those evoked by the UCS, (2) those regularly occurring during the CS–UCS interval, and (3) those evoked by the CS. On a test trial, then, although (1) would be absent, both (2) and (3) would presumably occur. This appears a more favorable set of circumstances for generating hallucinations than the happenstance offered by the procedures of Kelly and of Fishkin.

B. INTRODUCING A COVERT CS

Our approach to hallucinations began with a definition that attempted to characterize a set of phenomena of general clinical interest. From there we turned to the experimental laboratory to find ways of creating "model" hallucinations that would meet our starting definition. Our reasoning was that knowledge of the means for creating the models would contribute to our understanding of the conditions that generate the clinically observed phenomena. In the laboratory we found that verbal suggestion combined with hypnosis and/or motivating instructions led easily to the production of model hallucinations. However, this method of inducing hallucinations was deemed unsatisfactory both on clinical grounds—it implies, to put it ironically, that the psychotic's hallucinations are the result of his therapist's suggestions—and on experimental grounds because verbal suggestion appears too complex and too loosely specified to do duty as an explanatory principle. What we were looking for was a simple, nonverbal means of instructing our subjects to produce model hallucinations. What we found was that classical conditioning, under a reasonably limited set of circumstances, provides a method powerful enough to generate model hallucinations of convincing persistence, but simple enough to serve as an explanatory principle for the mechanistically minded scientist.

The classical conditioning studies we have examined up to this point would suggest that an hallucination is a (verbal) report of sensory perception made in the absence of the adequate external stimulus (UCS) but in the presence of another external stimulus (CS) that in the past has occurred in close temporal contiguity to the UCS and probably to its accompanying report. As it stands, this account is clearly no better than the account that could be given based on verbal suggestion as an explanatory principle. Although some of its defects can easily be corrected by reference to the well-established laws of reinforcement and of stimulus control, its chief defect is one that it shares with the verbal suggestion account, namely, a reliance on external agents. To think of hallucinations as reports conditioned to an external CS may be adequate as an explanation for experimentally produced hallucinations, and, some may argue, also for hallucinations occurring in the absence of prearranged conditions (cf. Skinner, 1953), but we question the likelihood that the specific conditions of the classical conditioning paradigm (cf. Jones, 1962) are met often enough adventitiously to allow hallucinations based on external CS–external UCS pairings to develop and persist. Consequently, it may be more profitable to search for the antecedents of hallucinations within the organism itself. Our question then is whether covert events can serve as conditional stimuli which can be discriminated by the organism and can come to elicit hallucinatory reports in the absence of the external stimuli.

The notion that covert events can serve as conditional stimuli is not without clinical evidence. McGuigan (1966), and Inouye and Shimizu (1970) have reported that verbal hallucinations in some schizophrenic patients are closely correlated with electromyographic (EMG) activity in their own speech musculature. The suggestion implicit in these studies is that the patient discriminates his EMG activity (CS) and then reports "hearing" it as the vocal activity (UCS) of another, external individual. The suggestion gains credence when one considers that everyday conversation might well provide the context within which a conditional relation between the CS and UCS might be elaborated. However, correlational data like those of McGuigan, and of Inouye and Shimizu, although useful and suggestive, are nevertheless open to other interpretations. Our question of whether covert events can come to elicit hallucinatory reports still stands.

A preliminary answer to this question was attempted in our laboratory several years ago (Hefferline & Perera, 1963). The broad aim of this study was to determine whether a covert muscular response can function as a discriminative stimulus for other behavior. We expected to accomplish this aim by teaching the subject to report a covert response (functioning as a discriminative stimulus or CS) as if it were a tone (UCS), that is, to hallucinate.

> Our plan was to train the subject, although he might remain otherwise unresponsive to an occasional twitch in the muscle of his left thumb (abductor pollicis brevis), nevertheless to "report" its occurrence within 2 sec by pressing a key with his right index finger. In order to circumvent the problems of "self-instruction," we disguised the purpose of the experiment by representing it to the subject as a reaction-time task. After the first session, during which the subject had only to sit back and relax for the duration of the hour, he was informed that his task in each succeeding session was to press the key with his right index

finger whenever he heard the moderately loud tone (1000 Hz; .5 sec) which we would occasionally superimpose on the constant, random masking-noise. He was told that each correct key press would advance his score, as shown on a digital display, and would be worth two cents at the end of the session. What the subject was not told was that our aim was gradually to transfer discriminative control of the overt key press from the tone to the covert thumb twitch.

Throughout the experiment we monitored electromyographically both the thumb twitch and the covert activity in a muscle associated with key pressing (extensor carpi radialis brevis). The twitch and the covert key press, or the "sub-key press" as we termed it, appeared on separate traces of our dual-beam oscilloscope as sinusoidal deflections of less than 75 μV amplitude, peak-to-peak. Our purpose in recording the sub-key press was twofold: since it represents a fractional version of the response that we intended to bring under the control of the thumb twitch, we hoped (1) by training the sub-key press to occur within 2 sec after a twitch (see later), to have "partially" trained its overt counterpart, and (2) by measuring the sub-key press, to obtain a "covert" index of the course of the discrimination (cf. Fink and Davis, 1951).

In fact, two discrimination indices were computed: "detected thumb twitches" (those followed within 2 sec by sub-key presses) and "correct sub-key presses" (those occurring within 2 sec after a thumb twitch). The indices summarize the conditional relations between the thumb twitch and the sub-key press, each of which occurred about 600 times per hour throughout the experiment. Evidence for the formation of a discrimination required a concurrent increase in both indices—that is, since the absolute rates of the thumb twitch and the sub-key press remained stable over sessions, we required that most twitches should come to be detected and that most sub-key presses should come to "report" twitches.

As shown by the first point on each curve in Fig. 9.1, the relative frequency of detected twitches and of correct sub-key presses was approximately .15 in the first session, when no contingency was imposed (the curve for detected thumb twitches has been displaced upward by .2). The subsequent break in each curve indicates that relative frequencies could not be gathered in Session 2. In this session, as indicated by the schedule of contingencies in Fig. 9.1, we triggered the tone as quickly after each thumb twitch as was manually possible [Hefferline, Bruno, & Davidowitz, 1971, pp. 260–262].

Our aim in Session 2 was to establish a conditional relation between the thumb twitch and the tone. To accomplish this we trained the subject under a reaction-time version of the anticipatory instructed paradigm of classical conditioning—the paradigm that Seashore and Ellson had successfully applied in their experiments to generate conditioned hallucinations. In our reaction-time version, the discriminable or "stimulus" aspects of the twitch played the role of the warning signal (CS), the tone functioned as the reaction stimulus (UCS), and the subject's key press telling us he heard the tone constituted the reaction-time response (UCR). The twitch-tone interval, or foreperiod, was of course variable in our version because its length was determined by the time it took for the experimenter to

manually present the tone once he had recognized a twitch on his oscilloscope. Our hope was that by repeatedly pairing the tone with the twitch,
the twitch would come to elicit a fractional or covert replica of the key-
press response made to the tone. Our expectations in this regard were
based on Davis' finding (1940) that covert key presses, or, as we termed
them, sub-key presses do, in fact, develop during the foreperiod of a
reaction-time experiment using an exteroceptive CS.

In Sessions 3–6 we switched from a classical to an instrumental conditioning paradigm in an attempt to strengthen whatever tendency existed
for the twitch to elicit a sub-key press. As shown in Fig. 9.1,

> . . . we modified our reaction-time paradigm to *require* that sub-key presses
> occur during the foreperiod: the tone was presented only after those thumb
> twitches which were followed within 2 sec by a sub-key press . . . The effect was
> an unmistakable increase during Session 3 in both detected thumb twitches
> and in correct sub-key presses (cf. Fig. 9.1), and this was maintained with only
> slight additional increases in Sessions 4–6 [Hefferline *et al.*, 1971, pp. 262–263].

Our interpretation of the results obtained in Sessions 3–6 was that they
achieved the broad aim of our experiment, namely to demonstrate that
a covert muscular response (the twitch) can function as a discriminative
stimulus for other behavior (the sub-key press). For the present pur-

DISCRIMINATION OF A COVERT RESPONSE

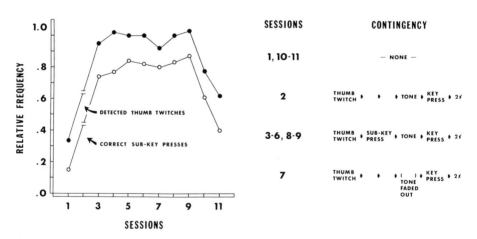

Fig. 9.1. Procedure and results for a subject trained to report covert twitches of
the left thumb by pressing a key with his right index finger. Results are for covert sub-
key presses except in Session 7 where they are for overt presses. The curve for detected
thumb twitches has been displaced upward by .2. Both curves computed from raw
data reported by Hefferline and Perera (1963).

poses, however, our interpretation of the results is of less interest than the prediction that can be made from them based on our earlier analysis of the Seashore and Ellson studies. The crux of that analysis was the suggestion that both experimenters were successful in generating hallucinatory reports of the UCS because each had arranged his training trials so that veridical reports of the UCS were preceded not only by the events evoked by the UCS, but also by the events occurring regularly during the CS–UCS interval and by the events evoked by the CS. This arrangement, we argued, made it likely that presentation of the CS alone on a test trial would call forth enough of the events ordinarily antecedent to a UCS report to call out the UCS report itself. With this analysis in mind, then, let us look again at the data of Sessions 3–6. During those sessions, each key press (UCS report) was preceded not only by those events evoked by the tone (UCS), but also by the sub-key press, an event that occurred regularly during the twitch-tone (CS–UCS) interval and by the events evoked by the twitch (CS). Moreover we know from the indices plotted in Fig. 9.1 that a strong conditional relation existed between the sub-key press and the events evoked by the twitch: During the sixth session, 80% of the twitches were followed in 2 sec by a sub-key press, and 82% of the sub-key presses occurred within 2 sec after a twitch. Given this conditional relation and the fact that the sub-key press is a fractional version of the key press, our analysis suggests that if a test were made by removing the tone, the twitch, when it occurred, would be likely to evoke the sub-key press and in turn the key press, which would be, in effect, an hallucinatory report of the tone. We made this test in the next session.

In Session 7, each time the twitch and sub-key press occurred together the tone was reduced in intensity, so that after 20 presentations it was completely gone. Of course, as the tone became faint, the subject complained over the intercom that it was "getting hard to hear"; he was told to continue to respond to those tones he did hear. Our hope was that by fading out the exteroceptive stimulus we could . . . [facilitate transfer of the] discriminative control of the overt key press from the tone to the twitch (cf. Terrace, 1963) . . . . Fading out the tone was marked by small reductions in both indices of the discrimination, although this was not observed in other subjects. What is remarkable, however, is that the curves for Session 7 were computed using overt key presses, and not sub-key presses as in all other sessions: with the tone faded out, 72% of the thumb twitches were followed within 2 sec by an overt key press, and 80% of the key presses "reported" the occurrences of thumb twitches [Hefferline *et al.*, 1971, p. 263].

At the manual or key-pressing level at least we had succeeded in teaching our subject to report his twitches as tones, that is, to hallucinate. Interestingly, the subject's manual hallucinations were accompanied by verbal hallucinations as well. "When questioned at the end of the experiment the subject said that he still heard the tone [Hefferline *et al.*, 1971, p. 263]." That both manual and verbal hallucinations were obtained seems reasonable

> . . . when we recall that our instructions to the subject had explicitly equated, at least within the experimental context, the status of two responses—the overt key press, and the verbal report "I heard it." We had, in effect, told the subject to report with a key press the same events which ordinarily he would report by saying "I heard the tone." If we assume, with Schoenfeld and Cumming (1963), that what is reported is the occurrence of a mediating event, and not the occurrence of the stimulus per se, then it makes sense to presume that the effect of our procedures was to enable the thumb twitch to enter significantly into the control of those events originally evoked primarily by the tone, with the result that the twitch, via the mediating events, acquired discriminative control of *both* the key press *and* the verbal report . . . .
>
> Our analysis is in keeping with the results of the final sessions of the experiment. In Sessions 8 and 9, we reinstated the tone after joint occurrences of the twitch and the sub-key press. Although this had little effect on the discrimination indices, we found that the subject responded to this thumb twitch with a key press that came faster than our reaction time in presenting the tone. The subject claimed that he sometimes heard the tone twice in rapid succession. Apparently the events evoked by the twitch and those evoked by the tone were not appreciably different; indeed, they both gave rise to the same verbal report. In the last two sessions, both the tone and the payoff were withheld, and the discrimination indices decreased toward their baseline values. Here again, the key press and the verbal report showed evidence of being jointly controlled: the subject pressed the key, and later reported that he had heard the tone, not more than four or five times in each of the last sessions [Hefferline *et al.*, 1971, pp. 263–264].

Our results clearly indicate that a covert muscular response—an event that ordinarily goes unobserved both by its maker and by the social community at large—can be made by conditioning procedures to evoke hallucinatory reports of a stimulus once present in the laboratory environment. Although the results are necessarily encouraging to those who would consider a conditioning account of the genesis of hallucinations, they offer no more than the beginnings of an account that still needs much elaboration.

C. Work in Progress

Although our 1963 study (Hefferline and Perera) contributed an important new element to the experimental account of hallucinations, it did so at the expense of adding two new parameters to the conditioning procedures previously used to generate "model" hallucinations. Earlier studies had used training regimens in which the sequence of events was (1) warning stimulus or CS followed by (2) reaction stimulus or UCS, leading to (3) an overt reporting response or UCR. Our study lengthened this sequence by two events. The first of these was the sub-key press, or as we shall call it from now on, the subpress: A response that in earlier studies may well have been present as a CR during the CS–UCS interval was, in our study, required during that interval. The second new event was the monetary reinforcer that we delivered in token form after each "correct" reporting response. Whereas earlier studies may have provided implicit or intrinsic payoff for the reporting response, in our study payoff was explicit.

Presumably, our additions to the experimental sequence of events helped us to answer a worthwhile question about conditioned hallucinations, but the additions themselves now pose new questions about the nature of hallucinations. We wonder whether the payoff used in our study could be supplanted by motivating instructions. That is, was the action of payoff specific and necessary either to the acquisition or to the maintenance of hallucinations, or was it nonspecific and emotionalizing? Suppose it was specific in effect. Would the introduction of a payoff matrix providing weighted gains and losses for correct key presses (hits), incorrect key presses (false alarms), and unreported twitches (misses) have changed the likelihood of hallucinatory reports and/or would it have made the hallucinations more or less "vivid"? With respect to payoff, these are some of the questions with which the work now in progress in our laboratory attempts to deal.

As regards the subpress, the second element added by our study to the experimental sequence, the questions raised are perhaps less obvious than those related to the use of explicit payoff, but their potential relevance may be broader. To develop these questions we must consider the general relation of covert muscular responses to the intervening variable called the "stimulus-as-coded" by Lawrence (1963), and to the not unrelated variable termed "efferent readiness" by Festinger (Festinger, Burnham, Ono, & Bamber, 1967).

In papers that appeared back-to-back in Vol. 5 of *Psychology: A study of a science*, Lawrence (1963), and Schoenfeld and Cumming (1963) adopted the position that overt perceptual responses do not report the occurrence of an exteroceptive stimulus per se but rather report the occurrence of a mediating event evoked by the stimulus—an event that might, however, (1) occur in the absence of the usual stimulus (leading to an hallucinatory report), (2) occur in the presence of part of the usual stimulus (redintegration), or (3) which might come to be evoked by other stimuli (mediated generalization). Lawrence described the mediating event as an "implicit response" which should "be thought of as a form of instrumental behavior." Similarly, Schoenfeld and Cumming talked about the mediating event as a

"covert response" that they were inclined to refer to the musculature, although they were in fact wary of trying to locate "the perceptual needle
in the motor haystack." For Lawrence, then, and for Schoenfeld and
Cumming, perception involves a three-term paradigm, stimulus → mediating event → response, whose middle term is a (possibly motor) response
that functions to code or represent the exteroceptive stimulus.

Recently, a related although not identical view of perception was expressed by Festinger *et al.* (1967; but see also Rock, 1966; Taylor, 1962)
who elaborated Sperry's (1952) notion that "perception is basically an
implicit preparation to respond." Festinger suggested that perception is
determined by the preprogrammed sets of efferent instructions that the
stimulus input activates into a state of readiness for immediate use. Both
Sperry and Festinger advocate a motor theory of perception in the sense
that both assume that the perceptual report is mediated by what the
observer is prepared to do about the exteroceptive stimulus. Both, however, make it clear that they are dealing with central rather than peripheral
preparations of readiness: Sperry says that his ". . . emphasis on the motor
approach . . . should definitely not be taken to imply that subjective experience resides within any motor reaction or within the motor system";
Festinger's readiness is a readiness to issue efferent instructions from the
central nervous system.

Although we have done little more than to point to the accounts of
perception given by Lawrence, and by Schoenfeld and Cumming on the
one hand, and by Sperry and by Festinger, on the other, it is, nonetheless,
clear that the coding notion, which has its roots in modern behaviorism,
and the readiness notion, which is the product of a more cognitive–neurophysiological camp, are both notions that find a motor-related event
mediating the perceptual response to stimulation. To be sure, they are
complementary notions: The coding account emphasizes the processing of
stimuli into categories and the fact that the perceptual report depends on
the occurrence of the category and not necessarily on the occurrence of the
stimulus ordinarily sorted into that category; the readiness account tells
us that the categories are not stimulus representations but rather efferent
preparations or sets from which particular behaviors may emerge. Both
accounts are, incidentally, somewhat vague about the origin of the mediating categories, but, significantly, they agree that the categories may be
learned and, in any case, are certainly subject to modification through
learning experiences.

For present purposes, the important difference between the coding and
readiness accounts lies in the locus assigned to the mediating categories.
The coding account suggests a peripheral locus, but is not adamant on

this point. The readiness account opts for a central locus, but does not deny the possibility of peripheral reflections. Our own inclination is to avoid another resurrection of the central–peripheral issue and to assume instead that mediating categories are cortically located (cf. John, Shimokochi, & Bartlett, 1969; Pribram, Spinelli, & Kamback, 1967) but may be peripherally reflected (cf. Blough, 1959; Davis, 1952).

We have introduced both the coding and the readiness accounts of perception because together they seem to provide a fairly complete description of the role of the subpress in our 1963 study. The results of that study made it necessary to account for two facts: (1) that the subject pressed the key after thumb twitches when the tone had been withdrawn, i.e., he hallucinated manually; (2) that he claimed that he pressed the key during no-tone sessions because he "heard the tone," i.e., he hallucinated verbally. In trying to deal with these facts earlier, we noted the equivalence, for the purposes of our experiment, of the key press and the verbal report "I heard it." The equivalence came about, we said, because the subject had been instructed to report with a key press those events that ordinarily he would report verbally by saying "I heard it." We assumed that he honored those instructions. We assumed further—here following the coding account of perception—that the events reported were not occurrences of the tone per se, but rather events evoked by the tone, events that also came to be evoked by the thumb twitch. And now—following here the readiness account—we suggest that the subpress, which literally represents a partial preparation for key pressing, was in part a peripheral reflection of the events, that is, of the efferent readiness, that determined both key pressing and the equivalent response "I heard it." By making presentations of the tone contingent on subpresses that followed twitches within 2 sec (Sessions 3–6), we set up the situation under which twitches would evoke subpresses. Thus, to the extent that subpresses reflect the readiness determining key presses and reports of hearing tones, we would expect, when the tone was withdrawn, to find thumb twitches evoking this readiness and consequently being reported "as if they were tones." This is what seems to have happened.

Jointly considered, then, the coding and readiness notions suggest that the subpress was crucial to the generation of hallucinatory reports. This suggestion, of course, is simple to test: We can repeat the 1963 study without requiring subpresses. If the coding-readiness account is correct we would expect hallucinations only if subpresses appear as CRs during the twitch-tone interval. But there are other tests too: We can present the tone only when a twitch has *not* been followed within 2 sec by a subpress; or we can require both that subpresses not occur and that fractional versions of another, unrelated response do occur. Here, presumably, hallucinations would not be generated if the subpress functions as indicated by the coding-readiness account.

In summary, our earlier study of conditioned hallucinations (Hefferline & Perera, 1963) introduced two new elements—payoff and the subpress—to the procedures used to produce experimental hallucinations. Our current and future studies have been designed to establish whether these elements are necessary, and if they are, how they contribute to the acquisition and maintenance of hallucinatory reports. Although the studies now in progress are the conceptual offspring of the earlier study, they have been schooled under new methods of data collection and analysis. To illustrate the approach we are now using—and to show some of the pitfalls of "automating" a study that was originally run by hand—we have decided to conclude this presentation by describing the first of our new studies, an unsuccessful attempt to repeat the original experiment.

1. Method

The new study was a preliminary or pilot effort that sought to generalize the results of the 1963 paper by the process of systematic replication (cf. Sidman, 1960). It differed from the earlier experiment in two important ways. First, the replication was entirely automated, eliminating the need for the experimenter to make complex decisions "on-line," removing the temporal variability introduced by the experimenter's reaction time, and, hopefully, decreasing the possibility of experimenter bias. Second, the replication worked with different responses: The twitch was no longer a thumb twitch, but rather a twitch of the muscle active during extension of the middle finger of the left hand; the subpress had also been redefined so that it was based on low-level activity in the muscles of the right hand that move the little finger outward (abduction).

Figure 9.2 depicts the electrode placement that was used to record twitches in the new study. The placement was selected by palpation and visual observation so that the recording (distal) and indifferent (2 cm proximal) electrodes straddled the longitudinal axis of that portion of extensor digitorum participating in extension of the middle finger. Figure 9.3 shows the electrode pair for the subpress channel of EMG, and shows, applied to the anterior aspect of the wrist, the ground electrode that was common to both the twitch and subpress channels. The subpress placement was chosen so that the recording electrode rested on the belly of the hypothenar eminence, a muscle group active during abduction (outward movement) of the little finger. The indifferent electrode was placed, 3 cm proximal to the recording, at the palpated base of the hypothenar muscle group.

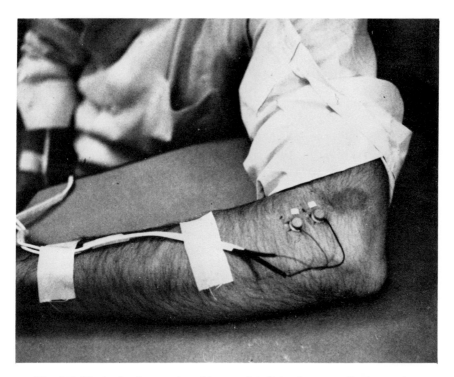

Fig. 9.2. Electrode placement used to record twitches in our replication study.

The electrodes for both placements were Beckman miniature skin electrodes consisting of silver silver-chloride pellets encapsulated in plastic. The standard electrodes were modified by the addition of shielded leads. Before applying the electrodes, we cleaned the recording sites with a commercial towelette saturated with skin conditioner, then abraded the sites with a motor-driven ink eraser, and finally pricked the skin with a lancet. Disinfected electrodes were then filled with Beckman recording paste and attached to the subject with adhesive collars. Interelectrode resistances were measured using an Airborne Instruments Model 152 tissue resistance meter. If the resistances were too high or unbalanced, the electrodes were reapplied.

After outfitting the subject with a full complement of electrodes, we seated him in a reclining chair within a shielded booth. During a session, the subject sat upright, but comfortably, in the chair with his right hand resting palm down on a padded board that was placed over the arm of the chair. The board contained a relatively sensitive microswitch—it operated with the application of about 20 g of static pressure—whose lever arm had been modified to allow the subject to close the switch by abducting the little finger.

The subject's booth was shielded with a double-layer of copper screen, sound-deadened with acoustical tile, and equipped with temperature controls. During a session, the booth was dark except for the light emitted by a 30-V dc pilot lamp and by a digital feedback display that kept track of the subject's earnings.

Figure 9.4 shows in schematic form the recording and control system used in our replication. The left-hand portion of the figure contains the inputs to our system derived from the subject—the twitch and subpress EMGs, the overt key press, and his verbal productions—and the outputs from our system to him, namely, communications from the experimenter, noise and tone stimuli, and points on the feedback counter. The right-hand portion of the figure gives the general configuration of the apparatus.

Let us look first at that portion of the system concerned with processing the EMG inputs. As indicated by the schematic, each channel was initially amplified by a factor of 10,000 using two cascaded Tektronix 122 preamplifiers set for a passband of 8–1000 Hz. The amplified EMGs were then displayed on an oscilloscope (Tektronix 565) and stored for later analysis using an FM magnetic tape recorder (Technical Measurements 700) whose frequency response was flat from dc to 600 Hz. Each channel

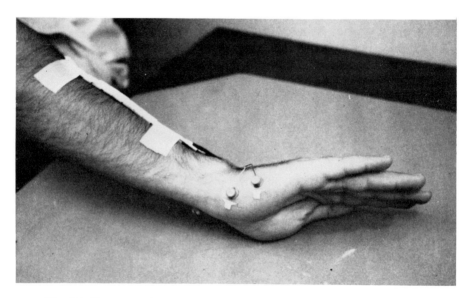

Fig. 9.3. Placement of the ground electrode (on the wrist) and the electrodes used to record subpresses.

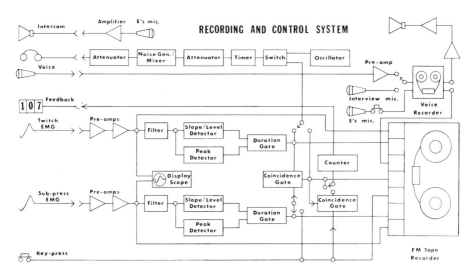

Fig. 9.4. Schematic of the recording and control apparatus for our replication study.

of EMG was also led, after amplification, to one of two identical networks designed to discriminate EMG waveforms from each other on the basis of their amplitude and duration characteristics. The inputs to these networks passed in each case through a filter (Krohn–Hite 3750) set for a passband of 6–200 Hz, attenuating frequencies outside of the band at the rate of 24 dB per octave. The networks each consisted of a slope and level detector (oscilloscope trigger) that operated on the initial negative-going troughs of either the twitch or the subpress waveforms, of a peak detector (Technical Measurements 607) operating on the subsequent positive-going peaks, and of a transistorized duration gate that operated on the trough-to-peak intervals. The networks, whose operation is described more fully later on, had as their outputs pulses representing automatically defined twitches (from one network) and subpresses (from the other). These pulses, which we will refer to as twitches and subpresses, were laid down for storage on FM tape and were also led to a coincidence gate that opened for 2 sec with each twitch. (The gate stayed open continuously when the intertwitch interval was less than 2 sec.) The first subpress to occur when the gate was open had two effects: It closed the gate, and it produced an output that we will call a coincidence—meaning the temporal coincidence of a subpress following a twitch within 2 sec. Coincidences were recorded on tape, and were simultaneously used to trigger a Grason–Stadler switch (Model 829E) and timer (Model 471), provided that they had not been triggered within the last 500 msec. As indicated schematically by the switch placed at the input to the switch and timer, these units could also be triggered by twitches alone instead of by coincidences. The switch and timer gated the output of a Hewlett–Packard 202D oscillator, and the gated output was fed to a Grason–Stadler 901B noise generator and mixer, and from there presented to the subject binaurally over Telephonics TDH-39 earphones. This network allowed us to drive the earphones continuously with speech-band noise at 70 dB and, at appropriate times, to superimpose on the noise a 1000-Hz, 200-msec, 70-dB tone (25 msec rise and decay). Hewlett–Packard 350D attenuators inserted in the network provided for independent control of the intensity of the tone, and the intensity of the tone plus noise outputs.

A second coincidence gate, shown in the lower right-hand portion of Fig. 9.4, was used to pay off the subject with points whenever he pressed the response key within 500 msec of the onset of a tone. All key presses, of course, were recorded on tape. Those that got through the second coincidence gate advanced the counter control circuitry and the subject's feedback counter. As indicated in the schematics by the two-position switches, the solid state logic network could also be set to deliver a point to the subject for the first key press made within 2 sec after a twitch.

The upper right-hand corner of Fig. 9.4 depicts a two-channel voice recorder. One channel was used for recording the experimenter's remarks; a duplicate channel recorded both the pre- and postsession interviews and the subject's comments during a session. This channel was monitored continuously in the control room via a loudspeaker.

With the overview of the recording and control system now completed, it remains to consider the functions performed by the networks used to define twitch and subpress responses. Figure 9.5 shows how one of these networks operated on the waveforms recorded from the twitch channel of EMG. (The network placed in the subpress channel functioned in similar fashion, but its time and voltage parameters were, of course, set differently.) The response definition network made use of the earlier finding from our laboratory (Bruno, Davidowitz, & Hefferline, 1970) that the action potentials generated by an individual muscle can be identified in the raw EMG by the trough-to-peak duration of their waveforms. Accordingly, the network measured not only waveform amplitude, but also waveform duration.

As shown in Fig. 9.5, a response epoch opened when a waveform crossed the -30 μV level in a negative-going direction. The crossing generated a 1-msec slope and level detection pulse that, within a few microseconds, initiated the response epoch, rendering without effect further crossings at any time during the epoch. The first portion of the response epoch consisted of the duration window delay. For the twitch channel, this was a

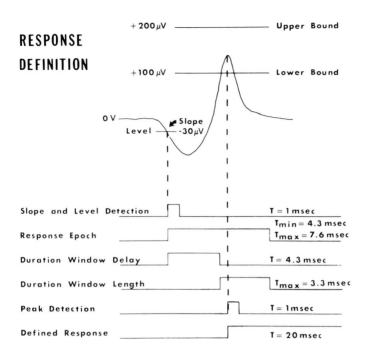

Fig. 9.5. Operation of the logic network used to define twitches based on parameters of the EMG waveforms recorded from the twitch placement shown in Fig. 9.2.

4.3-msec delay during which a peak detection pulse could terminate the response epoch but would have no further effect. At the end of the duration window delay, the duration window itself opened and remained open for 3.3 msec or until a peak detection pulse occurred. The closing of the duration window, either with or without the occurrence of a peak detection pulse, thus terminated those response epochs that had extended beyond the duration window delay. When the duration window was open a peak (inflection point) occurring between the upper and lower bounds of the amplitude window (for twitches the bounds were $+100$ to $+200$ μV) would pass through and close the duration window and, more importantly, generate the output of the network—a 20-msec pulse identifying a defined response. As mentioned previously, the network used to define subpresses differed from that presented in Fig. 9.5 only in the values chosen for its parameters. The subpress network opened a response epoch with a -16 μV negative crossing; it produced a defined subpress pulse when the positive peak occurred both between $+16$ to $+32$ μV and within 4.3–6.5 msec after the initiation of the epoch.

The operation of the response definition network outlined in Fig. 9.5 is illustrated by the waveform data presented in Fig. 9.6. The waveforms portrayed in the latter figure were collected from the twitch channel during the first half-hour of the first session, when we were working with a twitch whose positive peak fell within a $+30$ to $+70$ μV window. In that session, a tone was delivered within 2 msec after the start of the defined twitch pulse, and the subject was paid one cent for each tone he responded to by pressing the key within 500 msec of its onset. Panel A in Fig. 9.6 shows 200 waveforms superimposed by photographing the face of an oscilloscope whose sweep was triggered whenever a waveform crossed the -30 μV level in a negative-going direction. Although there was initially

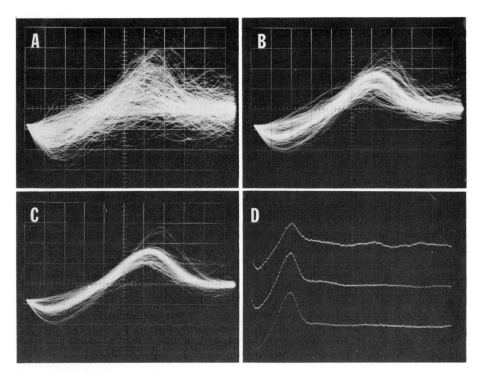

Fig. 9.6. Waveforms collected from the forearm muscle controlling the middle finger of the left hand during the first (A), second (B), and third (C) 5-min periods of the initial training session. Panels A–C show 200 photographically superimposed waveforms sampled when our oscilloscope triggered a sweep whenever waveform amplitude exceeded -30 μV in a negative-going direction. Calibration is 50 μV/div vertically and 1 msec/div horizontally. Panel D shows the same sets of 200 waveforms after computer averaging. The top trace corresponds to panel A, the middle to B, the bottom to C. Calibration is 50 μV/div vertically, and 3.12 msec/div horizontally.

a great deal of variability in both the amplitude and duration of the recorded waveforms, 5 min later, shown in panel B, the waveforms of inappropriate durations (originating in the "wrong" muscles) had dropped out and there was a narrowing of the range of amplitude variability. Five minutes later again, panel C, the variability in amplitude had decreased to nearly its final level, with 85–90% of the available waveforms falling within both the amplitude and duration windows of the response definition network. For comparison purposes, panel D of the figure displays the three computer-averaged tracings made simultaneously with the multiple-sweep photographs in panels A–C. The upper trace in D is for panel A, the middle for B, the bottom for C. In the absence of a variance readout, we infer that variability decreased during the session from the fact that the three successive averages grow slightly larger in amplitude and each appears to delimit the twitch with increasingly smooth traces.

2. Procedure

As was previously indicated, the study now being described was tentative and preliminary in nature. Every few sessions brought modifications and revisions in the details of our apparatus and procedures. Consequently we have chosen to exemplify our replication efforts by dealing with four sessions—numbers 13–16—during which there were no provisional changes in the parameters of the study. These sessions were obtained from George, a pilot subject who served a total of 21 1-hr sessions in all.

Figure 9.7 lists on the left the numbers of the four sessions with which we are concerned and on the right the contingencies in effect during those sessions. As the figure shows, during Sessions 13 and 14 we presented a tone—with a minimum intertone interval of 500 msec—whenever a twitch was followed within 2 sec by a subpress. If the subject responded to the tone with an overt key press within 500 msec, his feedback counter

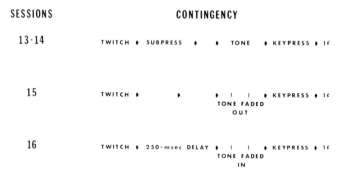

Fig. 9.7. Schedule of the experimental contingencies in effect during Sessions 13–16.

advanced one point, earning him one cent. The subject, of course, was not informed of the effective contingency. He was told only that we were interested in monitoring his bodily processes (hence the electrodes) while he earned money by key pressing within .5 sec after the start of each tone. Unfortunately, by Session 13 the subject was no longer totally naive with respect to the true contingencies. After his eighth session he had volunteered that "the machine was trying to trick me," by presenting tones whenever he moved his left arm. George had tried to solve that problem by tricking the machine: He rhythmically clenched and unclenched his left fist thus generating a steady stream of twitches. This was, of course, quite effective during earlier sessions when the subpress was not part of the contingency. The effectiveness of this strategy diminished, however, when the subpress requirement was added. Although by Session 13 George had by and large given up trying to outwit the machine, his superstition occasionally returned to haunt us.

As shown in Fig. 9.7, we changed contingencies during Session 15. Midway through this session we faded out the tone over a 10-min period and provided pennies for each twitch followed within 2 sec by an overt key press. George, like subjects in the earlier study, complained that he couldn't "hear the tones too well." We told him to do the best he could.

At the start of Session 16, we briefly reinstated the tone consequent on twitch–subpress coincidences, then faded it out again, meanwhile telling the subject that we thought we had "repaired the problem with the tone generator" but we were not sure and enjoining him to "listen hard" and to make sure he heard a tone before pressing the key. Midway through the session, as indicated in the figure, we faded the tone back in, presenting it consequent upon twitches but after a 250-msec delay. The assumption here was that if George were "hearing" his twitches as tones, he would presumably report hearing two tones—"his" first, and then "ours"—as did the subjects in the study we had set out to replicate.

3. Results

Figure 9.8 shows, via computer averages, the twitch and subpress waveforms that met the criteria imposed by the response defining networks during Sessions 13–16. In the figure, averaged twitches are displayed on the left, averaged subpresses on the right. Listed down the center of the figure are the session numbers, with the prefix A denoting an average taken during the first, and B during the second half-hour of a session. Each trace is the average of 200 tape-recorded waveforms sampled by triggering the summating computer with the defined twitch or subpress pulses previously recorded. The figure indicates that the average trough-to-peak

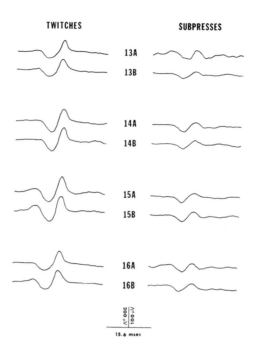

Fig. 9.8. Computer-averaged traces for twitch and subpress waveforms sampled during the first (A) and second (B) halves of Sessions 13–16. Each trace is the average of 200 waveforms. Here the computer was triggered by tape-recorded pulses generated whenever a waveform met the criteria of the response-defining network schematized in Fig. 9.5.

durations and amplitudes were acceptably constant both within and over sessions, although the level of background noise did vary.

Figure 9.9 summarizes by half-sessions the results obtained during Sessions 13–16 based on the response waveforms displayed in Fig. 9.8. Each graph in Fig. 9.9 has been divided into two parts by a vertical line. To the left of the line are displayed the data gathered when tones were being presented consequent on twitch–subpress coincidences. To the right of the line are data taken from half-sessions during which the tone was largely absent. The two graphs at the top of the figure show that the subject produced twitches and subpresses both when the tone was present and when it was absent, with the respective rates bearing no apparent relations to the contingencies in effect. Our suspicion is that the rate fluctuations reflect the comings and goings of George's fist-clenching superstition. However, fluctuations aside, it is relevant to note that we are dealing here with relatively high rates—the average twitch rate over Sessions 13–16 was 220/min, the rate of subpresses was 110/min—compared to the rates obtained in the 1963 study, which were about 10/min for both twitches and subpresses. In fact, as shown by the third graph from the top, in this study the average rate of coincidences—67/min—was higher than either the twitch or subpress rates previously obtained. (It should be

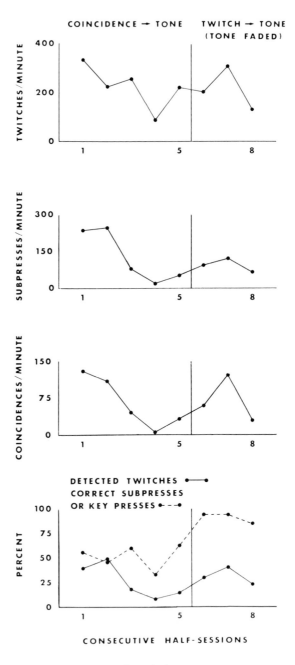

See legend on facing page.

noted with respect to the graph of coincidence rate that data points lying to the left of the vertical line, that is, points taken when tones were present, were computed using twitch–subpress coincidences; points to the right of the line, taken when the tone was absent, are based on twitch–*key press* coincidences.)

The bottom graph in the figure depicts the percentages of detected twitches and correct subpresses or key presses by half-sessions. The percentage of detected twitches was obtained by dividing the coincidence rate (third panel) by the twitch rate (top panel). Similarly, percentage of correct subpresses is coincidence rate (third panel, left of line) divided by subpress rate (second panel, left of line) and percentage of correct key presses is coincidence rate (third panel, right of line) divided by key press rate (not shown here). Note that in this replication the percentages of detected twitches and correct subpresses or key presses are not, as in the earlier study, uniformly high nor are they nearly equal (cf. Fig. 9.1). Instead, the percentage of detected twitches remained low and in fact never exceeded 49%. In contrast to this trend for detected twitches are the uniformly higher percentages of correct subpresses when the tone was present, averaging 51%, and the nearly optimal percentages of correct key presses—averaging 91%—when the tone had been faded out.

In short, many points of difference emerged when the present results were compared to the former, but the present high percentage of correct key presses suggested that we had at least taught George to report twitches with a key press, and perhaps, if we asked we would find he also would report hearing tones when none were present.

After the half-session during which the tone was first faded out, George said, "It's fantastic," presumably referring to his earnings of $17.10 for the first half-hour. And then he said, quite spontaneously, "I didn't hear a thing!" When questioned about this (not hearing tones) he told us that he "didn't have to." He could "sense, feel" when to respond. There were "patterns" of responding he had noticed before and those continued to work for him.

After the next half-session and after admonitions to make sure he heard the tone before pressing the key, George had this to say "Same old problem ... I couldn't resist the temptation ... I didn't hear a thing, but I kept on, and the thing [the feedback counter] kept on going."

Fig. 9.9. The top three panels give, by half-sessions, the twitch rates (top), subpress rates (second down), and coincidence rates (third down) observed during Sessions 13–16 under the contingencies listed in Fig. 9.7. The discrimination indices introduced in Fig. 9.1 were computed for the data graphed in the top three panels and are displayed in the bottom panel.

At this point, just before the second half of Session 16, we appealed to our subject's better nature and asked him to help us find the "problem" with our tone generator which we told him he could do if he would "listen real carefully" and follow the golden rule—"Don't press the key unless you've heard something." As it turned out, George did follow our instructions exactly. He pressed only when he heard *something.* But he was quite explicit about stating that he did not hear any tones until midway through the half-hour—when in fact the tone was reinstated. Needless to say, George also did not hear double tones.

In short, we were not successful in generating verbal hallucinations, but it still seemed possible, based on the high percentage of correct key presses, to assume that we had taught George to hallucinate manually. Although this assumption violates the verbal–manual equivalency on which we based our analysis of the earlier, successful study, it nevertheless appeared tenable when we examined the distributions of twitch to key-press latencies taken in the present study when the tone had been entirely removed. Figure 9.10, by way of example, shows the relative frequency distribution of twitch–key-press latencies measured for a 10-min period during Session 16. As indicated in the upper right-hand legend, 2043 latencies (N) made up this distribution, eight of which (D) were longer

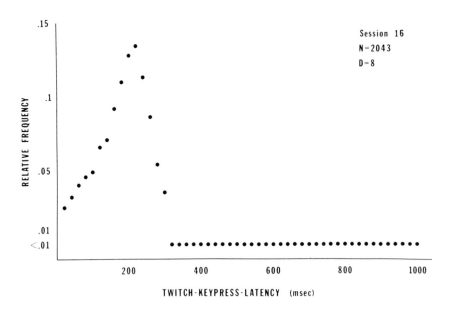

Fig. 9.10. Relative frequency distribution of twitch to key-press latencies taken during a 10-min period after the tone had been faded out in Session 16.

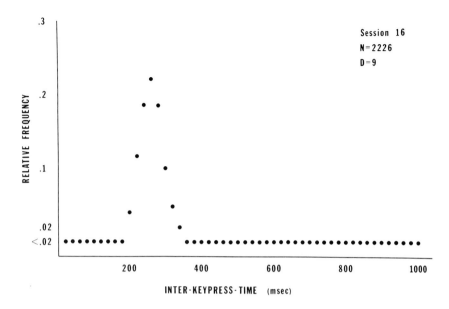

Fig. 9.11. Relative frequency distribution of inter-key-press intervals sampling during the 10-min period used for Fig. 9.10.

than our 1-sec analysis epoch and so are not graphed. Notice that this distribution, whose mode occurs at 220 msec, resembles a conventional latency distribution taken with an exteroceptive stimulus—except in its short latency tail. Here there are an uncommonly large number of short latencies or premature reactions. Yet this phenomenon would not be unwarranted since there was no penalty for short latencies and there might be a tendency for twitches and key presses to synchronize. Unfortunately, the explanation seems to lie elsewhere—namely in the distributions of inter-key press and intertwitch times.

Figure 9.11 shows the relative frequency distribution of inter-key-press times taken during Session 16 over the same 10-min period as the twitch–key-press latency distributions graphed in Fig. 9.10. Note that the modal inter-key-press time is 260 msec, or 40 msec longer than the modal twitch–key-press latency.

Figure 9.12 gives the relevant distributions of intertwitch times sampled here over a 500-msec computer analysis epoch. Its mode occurs at 40 msec. (There are no intertwitch times during the first 20 msec because the response-defining network excluded twitches with interresponse times shorter than 20 msec.)

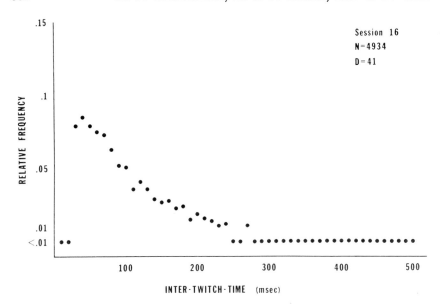

Fig. 9.12. Relative frequency distribution of intertwitch intervals sampled during the 10-min period used for Fig. 9.10.

Is it simply a matter of coincidence that the modal intertwitch time equals the difference between the modal inter-key-press time and the modal twitch–key-press latency? Apparently it is not. Rather it would seem that the twitch–key-press latency distribution does not portray the stimulus control of key presses by twitches, but instead shows what happens when the waiting time from a twitch to the next key press is determined, given, first, that the twitch and key-press rates are independent of each other, and then, that the modal intertwitch time is shorter than the modal inter-key-press time.

Consider what happens when we compute twitch–key-press latencies. Each computation ends with the occurrence of a key press—a key press which also marks the start of a new inter-key-press interval—and the next computation begins with the first twitch to occur in the new inter-key-press interval. Since the modal inter-key-press interval is 260 msec long and the modal intertwitch time is only 40 msec, on the average 260/40 or 6.5 twitches will occur during the new inter-key-press interval, and the time from the first twitch in the new interval to the key press that terminates it will approximate 6.5 minus the first or 5.5 intertwitch times, that is, 5.5 times 40 msec equals 220 msec. In other words, the modal twitch–key-press latency will equal, as happens in our data, the modal inter-key-press time less the modal intertwitch time. But, of course, some of the inter-key-press times are shorter than the modal time and some of the intertwitch times exceed the modal time for that distribution. This means that some of the twitch–key-press latencies will in fact be considerably shorter than the shortest inter-key-press time. As Fig. 9.10 shows, this in fact happened.

Now what about the case of a new inter-key-press interval coming from the long end of its distribution while the first twitch comes from the short end of its intertwitch time distribution? Well, this would generate long twitch–key-press latencies, but if there are no intertwitch times longer than the longest inter-key-press interval—as it happened there were not—then the longest twitch–key-press latency will be shorter than the longest inter-key-press time. This, too, is true of our data.

To put this in other terms, it appears that our twitch–key-press latency distributions represent nothing more than the multiplicative product of two independent distributions, namely the intertwitch time cross-multiplied with the inter-key-press time distribution. As Fig. 9.13 shows this conclusion was not weakened when we looked backward in time from the key press to examine the relative frequency of key press to twitch times. Here, had the twitch entered significantly into the stimulus control of the

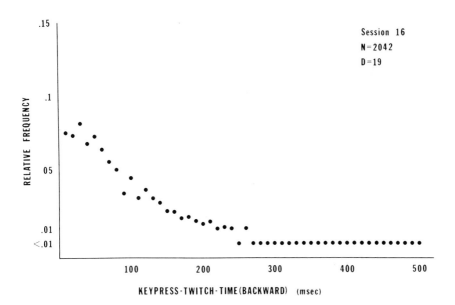

Fig. 9.13. Relative frequency distribution of key press to twitch latencies sampled during the 10-min period used for Fig. 9.10. The latencies were computed by measuring *backward* in time from a key press to the first antecedent twitch.

key press, we would have expected to find key press–twitch times clustered about the modal value of the twitch–key-press latency distribution. This is clearly not the case here, nor was it the case when we averaged all twitches occurring within a period that began 2 sec prior to and ended with the overt key press. Instead the backward distribution of key press–twitch times is virtually a replica of the intertwitch time distribution—the result we would expect to generate by cross-multiplying the nearly Gaussian inter-key-press time distribution with the intertwitch time distribution.

The analysis for a comparable 10-min interval during Session 15 gave similar results. The twitch–key-press latency distribution had its mode at 420 msec. This value was within 10 msec of the value that would be predicted by subtracting the modal intertwitch time (70 msec) from the modal inter-key-press time (480 msec). And for Session 15, too, the shape of the key press–twitch-time distribution taken by sampling backward in time from the key press was again quite similar to the shape of the inter-twitch-time distribution.

In sum, we were not successful in generating verbal hallucinations, nor were we successful in teaching George to hallucinate manually. George's high percentage of correct key presses in the absence of the tone was not attributable to the discriminative control of key presses by twitches but simply to the fact that George twitched rapidly and key pressed rapidly so that 91% of his key presses followed a twitch within 2 sec. Our analysis of the earlier study still holds: As evidence for the formation of a discrimination we must require that most key presses (or subpresses) be correct *and* most twitches be detected.

In closing, a word or two is in order regarding the fact that the twitch and subpress rates observed in the replication exceeded by an order of magnitude the rates reported in the original experiment. As might be suspected, the rate differences cannot be attributed to subject differences or to differences arising from the particular muscle groups chosen for each study. This leaves us to account for the rate differences by differences in response detection and/or by differences in payoff schedule. But these factors come down to the same thing: *automatic* versus *manual* response detection and payoff. Although our automated control system was designed to do exactly what the experimenter said he did in the earlier study, it not only did it faster—detection and payoff were accomplished in tens of microseconds rather than hundreds of milliseconds—but it did it continuously rather than in fits and starts. A burst of muscular activity that previously gave the experimenter occasion to pause and wait posed no problems for our transistorized logic networks. They simply continued to sort criterion from noncriterion waveforms, to calculate coincidences, to deliver tones, and to pay off correct key presses. The experimenter in the earlier study, then, differentially paid off low rates of twitches and subpresses because (1) he could not keep up with high rates, and (2) he could not sort criterion from noncriterion responses when they occurred together. In contrast, the apparatus of the present study provided, within limits, higher payoff densities for higher response rates.

Our suggestion then is that the rate differences between the studies resulted from differences in payoff density. Ironically, the differences in payoff density occurred because we automated the experimenter's criteria and functions but neglected to automate his limitations. The irony, of course, is that our oversight in translating from man to machine is likely the factor responsible for our unsuccessful replication. Our oversight produced tonic twitching rather than phasic and presumably discriminable twitches.

The Discussion of Dr. Hefferline's Paper

LED BY DR. RANDALL FLORY
Hollins College

Flory: My particular interest is going to be biased, because my research is in the area of animal behavior, and it is of an operant nature. For this reason, I find Dr. Hefferline's latter experiment particularly interesting, even though he did not confirm the 1963 experiment, i.e., stimulus control was not established so that the twitch did not produce a discriminative stimulus for conditioned hallucinations or for the key press. At the same time, perhaps accidentally or as a function of the more sophisticated apparatus he was using, some very interesting results have emerged. One might look at this from an operant standpoint as complex patterning behavior; the two behaviors being intertwitch time (a 40-msec modal intertwitch time), essentially a paced schedule between twitches, and the other schedule being the inter-key-press time of something around 260 msec. Now if these are truly independent, then one does have concurrent scheduling, and one might apply to these patterns some of the techniques and some of the mathematical equations that have been derived from pigeon research.

From what Dr. Hefferline mentioned about the control of this high-rate twitch behavior, the utilization of a pacing schedule, such as differential reinforcement of low rate whereby twitches occur with an intertwitch time of less than x milliseconds, would not result in presentation of a tone or of a reinforcer. Eventually, however, such a contingency would result in an intertwitch time that was more similar to that of key pressing.

Also, experimental analysts of behavior are very interested in this kind of research, because it does generalize work from animal research to a very molecular response, and to a response which is typically involved in human behavior.

The signal detection approach, mentioned by Dr. Hefferline, offers another way of isolating twitches, that of using penalties; the penalty might be not getting reinforced, or certain other penalties, such as delay of reinforcement.

My final comment is that perhaps the superstitious behavior that was developed (the pattern of responding that developed in the second experiment) might have been due to the type of apparatus that was used, as compared to that of the first experiment. If you remember, in the Hefferline and Perera (1963) study, the times for the presentation of tone were determined by the experimenter; necessarily, reaction times are going to vary. An operant conditioner might look at this as a variable-interval schedule, whereas, in the latter experiment, the times were fixed by the apparatus; and, in one case, there was a 250-msec delay (Session 16). Knowing something about superstitious behavior on these two types of schedules might give us some insight into the superstitious behavior that developed in the second experiment.

Open Discussion

Audience: The crux of the problem is in trying to find an independent measure of hallucination; you depended on the temporal relationship between the muscle twitch and the overt response, and there might be a brain process in between. Have you considered the possibility of recording evoked potentials from the temporal lobe when auditory stimuli are produced? I know there is a very tenuous relationship between EEG-evoked potentials and any sensory experience, but maybe this approach would increase the frequency of reports of hearing the tone.

Hefferline: We have done some evoked potential work on movement, but we have some equipment limitations. Nevertheless, thank you for the idea.

Dr. Tom Mulholland (Perception Laboratory, VA Hospital, Bedford, Massachusetts): I was very interested in that beautiful slide you showed in which the response topography changed as a function of turning on the tone. Originally you got a wide variance; then there was a selection of the waveform that was very apparent, even in the unaveraged slide. How do you think this is accomplished? What's happening in the muscles?

Hefferline: Well, it is not a change in topography. Our topography stays the same. It is simply that the noise (waveforms which are not interesting) tends to drop out. I suppose that the subject is settling down. If you show a person his response on the scope and say, "Hey, look at that waveform right there; I want you to clean everything else off the scope," he watches, and after awhile he cleans it up. What we were doing was to reinforce a particular, very specific wave form.

Mulholland: His settling down is the real interesting concept here.

Hefferline: Yes, but there has to be a little bit of activity going on. There may be electrical silence at the level that we are working with, and the subject gets too relaxed. When he has a task though, like watching the scope, he maintains sufficient tone throughout the body, so that there is enough going on for our purposes.

Dr. Richard Jennings (Walter Reed): Did that settling-down process break apart under the so-called hallucination conditions when the tone was omitted? Did the variability increase somewhat then?

Hefferline: We don't have any continuous recording of variability. I simply showed you a demonstration slide, reproducing what we have on tape. It would be very nice to have a continuous readout of variability, but that won't be possible until someone comes up with a technological improvement.

Dr. Allan Rechtschaffen (University of Chicago): The really important question about hallucinations is evident in the difference between your 1963 experiment and this one. In the first experiment you obtained a verbal report of hallucinatory activity (it is a report, and we are not sure to what extent the hallucination actually is there); but the subject did not report hallucinations in the replication. Consider Pavlov's situation: First, the dog gets food and salivates; then later a bell alone is rung, and he salivates. It is necessary to assume that he is "hallucinating the food" when he salivates in response to the bell. Pavlov's experiment is like your first one, viz., you *do* get a report that they are "hallucinating the food," or in your case, that they hear a tone. But no positive report in your second experiment? The difference between the two experiments is that in the second experiment the stimulus is so sharpened that the response can be made very reliably to it. Therefore, there is no need, if I may speak anthropomorphically for a moment, for the subject to search for another stimulus. Maybe the generation of imagery, or hallucination, has to do with uncertainties in the stimulus situation. In other words, the reported hearing of the tone in the first experiment has to do with the search for what the effective stimulus might have been—what the appropriate stimulus for getting the reinforcement might have been. In the second situation, the subject may not have known what the stimulus was. Nevertheless, there was no need to search any further for a stimulus.

Hefferline: I think you are right on many points there. Actually, though, most of our research is done without the subject being able to specify the contingencies. None of the subjects in the 1963 study ever knew anything about a thumb twitch; they simply heard tones. They also had no knowledge about the sub-key press. In this recent situation, I think it was partly that we had a very intelligent young Columbia college man who was hungry for money. He explored, he experimented, and he found that if he made certain movements, it had a bearing on the reinforcement. You could also say this: The motivation variable is involved in that he got what he wanted (the pay) without having to hallucinate.

We are, however, better off when the subject has to wait until he says, "Well, I thought I heard it again," and *then* responds, than when we merely have people say, "I heard the tone." In the latter case, we only have a verbal report, which we can't directly check any more than when somebody offers an excuse that he has a terrible headache. The conditioning paradigm is such that, with the instruction, "Press the key when you hear the tone," that sequence gets very deeply ingrained; there develops a leaning toward actually hearing something. Dr. Grings, a number of years ago, worked on a study using Skinner's verbal summator, in which people listen to meaningless, empty sound patterns. People came to the conclusion that the "man" on the record actually says something and they become quite convinced of it. Since the subjects did get into arguments as to what the man was saying, they were thought to be hallucinating, in a sense, putting in their own meaning; but even after he knew that the man on the verbal summator record was producing only empty sound patterns, he still heard the man saying something, even if he was administering the test to someone else. We thus get into very formidable problems of the verbal report, and of the relevance of instructions to the subject.

Dr. Louis Aarons (Department of Mental Health, Chicago): Have you any plans to get at the receptor organ? I think the ear muscles internally give responses to sound; perhaps by placing electrodes in there you could correlate adjustment of the ear muscles with the (hallucinated) report of the sounds, providing a further check.

Hefferline: Where are you going to get me some middle ear muscles that are expendable?

Aarons: There are different ways of recording from the ear.

Audience: An acoustic impedance instrument, put in the ear, could do this.

REFERENCES

Agathon, M., & Lelord, G. F. Conditioning of the spiral aftereffect. *Perceptual and Motor Skills*, 1963, **17**, 302.

Barber, T. X., & Calverley, D. S. An experimental study of "hypnotic" (auditory and visual) hallucinations. *Journal of Abnormal and Social Psychology*, 1964, **68**, 13–20. (a)

Barber, T. X., & Calverley, D. S. Toward a theory of "hypnotic" behavior. *Archives of General Psychiatry*, 1964, **10**, 137–144. (b)

Blough, D. S. Delayed matching in the pigeon. *Journal of the Experimental Analysis of Behavior*, 1959, **2**, 151–160.

Bowers, K. S. The effect of demands for honesty on resports of visual and auditory hallucinations. *International Journal of Clinical and Experimental Hypnosis*, 1967, **15**, 31–36.

Bruno, L. J. J., Davidowitz, J., & Hefferline, R. F. EMG waveform duration: A validation method for the surface electromyogram. *Behavior Research Methods and Instrumentation*, 1970, **2**, 211–219.

Davis, R. C. Set and muscular tension. *Indiana University Science Series*, No. 10. Bloomington, Indiana: Indiana University Press, 1940.

Davis, R. C. The stimulus trace in effectors and its relation to judgment responses. *Journal of Experimental Psychology*, 1952, **44**, 377–390.

Ellson, D. G. Hallucinations produced by sensory conditioning. *Journal of Experimental Psychology*, 1941, **28**, 1–20. (a)

Ellson, D. G. Experimental extinction of an hallucination produced by sensory conditioning. *Journal of Experimental Psychology*, 1941, **28**, 350–361. (b)

Festinger, L., Burnham, C. A., Ono, H., & Bamber, D. Efference and the conscious experience of perception. *Journal of Experimental Psychology Monograph*, 1967, **74**, (2, Whole No. 637).

Fink, J. B., & Davis, R. C. Generalization of a muscle action potential response to tonal duration. *Journal of Experimental Psychology*, 1951, **42**, 403–408.

Fischer, R. The perception-hallucination continuum. *Diseases of the Nervous System*, 1969, **30**, 161–171.

Fishkin, S. M. Conditioning the spiral aftereffect. *Perceptual and Motor Skills*, 1969, **29**, 131–138.

Graham, K. R. Brightness contrast by hypnotic hallucination. *International Journal of Clinical and Experimental Hypnosis*, 1969, **17**, 62–73.

Grant, D. A. Classical and instrumental conditioning. In A. W. Melton (Ed.), *Categories of human learning*. New York: Academic Press, 1964.

Hefferline, R. F., & Perera, T. B. Proprioceptive discrimination of a covert operant without its observation by the subject. *Science*, 1963, **139**, 834–835.

Hefferline, R. F., Bruno, L. J. J., & Davidowitz, J. Feedback control of covert behaviour. In K. J. Connolly (Ed.), *Mechanisms of motor skill development*. New York: Academic Press, 1971. Pp. 245–278.

Inouye, T., & Shimizu, A. The electromyographic study of verbal hallucination. *The Journal of Nervous and Mental Disease*, 1970, **151**, 415–422.

John, E. R., Shimokochi, M., & Bartlett, F. Neural readout from memory during generalization. *Science*, 1969, **164**, 1534–1536.

Jones, J. E. Contiguity and reinforcement in relation to CS-UCS intervals in classical aversive conditioning. *Psychological Review*, 1962, **69**, 176–186.

Kelly, E. L. An attempt to produce artificial chromaesthesia by the technique of the conditioned response. *Journal of Experimental Psychology*, 1934, **17**, 315–341.

Lawrence, D. H. The nature of a stimulus: Some relations between learning and perception. In S. Koch (Ed.), *Psychology: A study of a science*. Vol. 5. New York: McGraw-Hill, 1963. Pp. 179–212.

Leuba, C. Images as conditioned sensations. *Journal of Experimental Psychology*, 1940, **26**, 345–351.

McGuigan, F. J. Covert oral behavior and auditory hallucinations. *Psychophysiology*, 1966, **3**, 73–80.

Pribram, K. H., Spinelli, D. N., & Kamback, M. C. Electrocortical correlates of stimulus response and reinforcement. *Science*, 1967, **157**, 94–96.

Rock, I. *The nature of perceptual adaptation*. New York: Basic Books, 1966.

Rosenthal, B. G., & Mele, H. The validity of hypnotically induced color hallucinations. *Journal of Abnormal and Social Psychology*, 1952, **47**, 700–704.

Sarbin, T. R. The concept of hallucination. *Journal of Personality*, 1967, **35**, 359–380.

Sarbin, T. R., & Andersen, M. L. Base-rate expectancies and perceptual alterations in hypnosis. *British Journal of Social and Clinical Psychology*, 1963, **2**, 112–121.

Sarbin, T. R., & Juhasz, J. B. The historical background of the concept of hallucination. *Journal of the History of Behavioral Science*, 1967, **3**, 339–358.

Schoenfeld, W. N., & Cumming, W. W. Behavior and perception. In S. Koch (Ed.), *Psychology: A study of a science*. Vol. 5. New York: McGraw-Hill, 1963. Pp. 213–252.

Scott, H. D. Hypnosis and the conditioned reflex. *Journal of General Psychology*, 1930, **4**, 113–130.

Seashore, C. E. Measurements of illusions and hallucinations in normal life. *Studies of the Yale Psychology Laboratory*, 1895, **3**, 1–67.

Sidman, M. *Tactics of scientific research*. New York: Basic Books, 1960.

Skinner, B. F. *Science and human behavior*. New York: Macmillan, 1953.

Sperry, R. W. Neurology and the mind-brain problem. *American Scientist*, 1952, **40**, 291–312.

Sutcliffe, J. P. "Credulous" and "skeptical" views of hypnotic phenomena: Experiments on esthesia, hallucination, and delusion. *Journal of Abnormal and Social Psychology*, 1961, **62**, 189–200.

Taylor, J. G. *The behavioral basis of perception*. New Haven, Connecticut: Yale Univ. Press, 1962.

Terrace, H. S. Errorless transfer of a discrimination across two continua. *Journal of the Experimental Analysis of Behavior*, 1963, **6**, 223–232.

Thorne, D. E. Is the hypnotic trance necessary for performance of hypnotic phenomena? *Journal of Abnormal Psychology*, 1967, **72**, 233–239.

Underwood, H. W. The validity of hypnotically induced visual hallucinations. *Journal of Abnormal and Social Psychology*, 1960, **61**, 39–46.

CHAPTER TEN

Electrical Measurement of Covert Processes as an Explication of "Higher Mental Events"

F. J. McGUIGAN
Hollins College

I. ON THE GENESIS OF THE PROBLEM OF "MIND," AND OF A NATURAL SCIENCE APPROACH TO "MENTAL PROCESSES"

Man's early use of language undoubtedly included terms that were supposed to refer to unobservable phenomena. One can, for example, imagine primitive man dreaming of the dead, and later referring to those "visited" in the dream as "spirits." When strange, important events occurred in his life, he postulated the existence of mystical "gods" as the

343

causal factors. And feelings of "self-awareness" and processes of silently "talking to himself" led to notions about immaterial events and phenomena, using words like "consciousness," "mind," "thoughts" and "ideas." Later, such incorporeal notions were more formally developed by the Mental Philosophers.

The 17th and 18th centuries witnessed the flowering of science, an influence that guided some mental philosophers toward the empirical study of mind; the result was the empiricism of the British Associationists. This observational approach to mental phenomena by philosophers was joined in the 19th century by members of two other professions: Physicists were forced to take into account the role of sense receptors as part of their observational apparatus as they studied the nonliving world; and physiologists asked questions about sensation, perception, and mind itself, particularly when they sought to understand vision, hearing, and the like. These common endeavors were indicative of the *zeitgeist* that led to the founding of a science specialized for the study of mental phenomena—Wundt founded psychology, the science of consciousness.

Decades of vigorous introspective investigations followed, and in a sense the Structuralists wrote their own death warrant as they and their colleagues accumulated evidence of the sterility of the introspective approach. The death blow was wielded none too gently by the early behaviorists, as psychology ceased to be the study of "one's-self" and was proclaimed to be the study of "the other one." Yet, it is important to emphasize that the early behaviorists maintained some of the older "mentalistic terms"; they merely rejected the Introspectionists' definitions in terms of "nonmaterial stuff." Hence, "mental" phenomena were redefined according to natural science principles, so that, for example, "emotion" ceased to be a matter of "affective quality" and became primarily a visceral response. Consciousness now referred to the objectively observable behavior of a man naming his world both inside and out, essentially the behavior indicated, respectively, by Skinner's (1957) terms of "internal" and "external tacts." And "thinking" became primarily a matter of laryngeal ("language habit") responding, with associated nonoral behavior.

Two points thus emerge from this brief history: how the notion of mind arose in the first place, and how we laboriously arrived at a natural science approach to "mental processes." The stage thus was set in the early part of the 20th century for a (scientific) explication of mind—the behaviorists showed us in principle how to explicate "the higher mental processes," how to replace vaguely defined mentalistic terms with precise, objective definitions.

II. DEVELOPMENT OF EXPERIMENTAL TECHNIQUES

In the early 1900s experimenters enthusiastically and creatively attempted to directly measure "implicit language habits," thus providing objective evidence relevant to the behavioristic theory of thinking. Among the variety of techniques that were developed to record covert activity of the speech mechanism during thinking were such devices as inflated balloons and flattened wine glasses placed on or about the tongue, with mechanical connections from such "sensors" to systems of tambours and kymographs. The culmination of this mechanical measurement trend was Thorson's (1925) device which magnified tongue movements by about ×4.5 (Fig. 10.1). It is apparent that adequate technological "know-how"

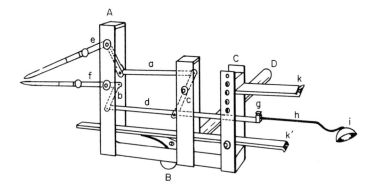

Fig. 10.1. Thorson's experimental apparatus (×.5) ABC: rigid frame supported in adjustable clamp by the rod, BD. *i*: metal suction cup for attachment to tongue. *a*: aluminum bar, attached to suction cup by the aluminum wire, *h*, adjustable by the set screw, *g*, and transmitting movements through the links and bell cranks, *b*, *c*, *d*, and *e*, to the writing points. The writing points are adjustable horizontally by thumb screws, *m*, acting against light bronze springs.

during the first quarter of this century was simply lacking, and one might be amazed that these early experimenters reported successful measurements of such small-scale events as covert processes. The needed technological breakthrough came in the 1920s with the pioneering electrical measurements of covert behavioral events by Jacobson (1927), and of brain events by Berger (1929). As a consequence, the experimental techniques for carrying out the behaviorist's theoretical strategy became clear: We have sought to measure electrically those events that occur within a person when he thinks.

III. LANGUAGE STIMULI AS AN INDICATOR OF THINKING

But now the question is, how do we know when someone is thinking—what are the relevant objectively observable conditions present that may be used to indicate the existence of "thought processes"?

A wide-variety of different definitions of thinking have been offered by various authorities, but *linguistic* processes have been universally implicated. While there well may be nonverbal thought, it is safe to assume that linguistic thinking is predominant—it seems clear that man's amazing capacity to control his world has come about by internally manipulating linguistic symbols. Language *must* hold a central position in the study of thought processes, and we give it the highest priority. There may thus be several *indicators* [in Kaplan's (1954) sense] of thinking; but we shall consider the *major* (priority) definitional indicator as *the composite of bodily activities that necessarily occur following the presentation of a language stimulus*. This definition has the added advantage that it also places the traditional problem of mental processes within the more contemporary framework of information processing.

IV. INTERNAL INFORMATION PROCESSING

Figure 10.2 represents an attempt to diagram the sequences of physiological, psychological, and psychophysiological events that occur when a meaningful stimulus impinges on a person. At least some of these covert events are critical during information processing consequent to the stimulus. We may, thus, use Fig. 10.2 to develop a primitive classification of these potentially important internal, covert processes.

Covert processes, defined as those small-scale events that can only be directly observed through psychophysiological techniques, include two general, nonoverlapping classes: (1) central nervous system events, and (2) response (i.e., muscular and glandular) events. For the study of thinking, or internal information processing, the most interesting subclasses of covert events in Fig. 10.2 are those uniquely evoked by linguistic stimuli; perhaps they consist of events in the speech (language) regions of the brain, and of conditional linguistic responses. (We shall not, however, ignore the overt effector events that are the primary data of the classical behaviorists, particularly when those overt responses are verbal.) The dark boxes of Fig. 10.2 specify these covert events of greatest interest as central nervous system events and two classes of effector events: (1) those responses that are antecedent to, and perhaps determiners of, overt behaviors; and (2) those not followed by overt responses.

The psychophysiological techniques currently in greatest use for directly measuring these covert events as a function of external linguistic stimuli

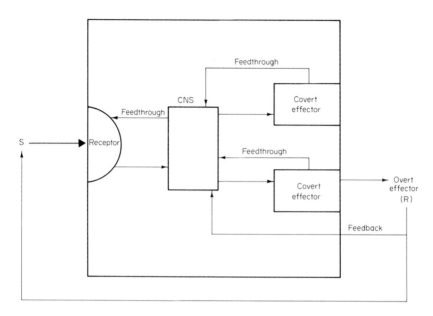

Fig. 10.2. Representation of potentially critical events during internal information processing. Covert processes in the brain (measured by EEG) and in the effectors (measured by EMG, GSR, etc.) provide clues as to the nature of the hypothesized loops within a person.

are (1) electroencephalography for central nervous system events; (2) electromyography for skeletal responses; and (3) autonomic activity measures (pupillometry, electrocardiography, and the like). (I think there is little direct measure of the receptor events of Fig. 10.2 as a function of linguistic stimuli.)

When we report on the covert neural and behavioral events of Fig. 10.2, it is important not to let ourselves lapse into the notion that these are temporally discrete, isolated phenomena. Rather, we use these measured events as cues of the nature of the extremely complex and rapid feedthrough systems depicted. The fact simply is that at this stage of psychophysiology, we cannot directly record all of the continuous activity in feedthrough loops between and among say, the auditory regions of the brain, the tongue, the eye, and the muscles of the ear.

I am, incidentally, using the neutral term feedthrough in preference to feedback because feedback implies that we know what organ in a loop is in control. Even with the brain, there may be some question. It may be that so-called "brain wave conditioning," for instance, is mediated by muscular responses and is, in fact, *muscular* conditioning. The theorizing of Knott (1939) and others over three decades ago to the effect that the muscles drive the brain may not turn out to be so absurd.

In short, a general strategy for studying these loops (one used in our laboratory) is to simultaneously place a number of sensors at selected bodily locations while the subjects engage in various linguistic tasks. The hope is to record critical internal events as a function of the input, and to form these events into reliable patterns of covert processes. Relationships among the components of these patterns should provide hints about the nature of internal information processing.

The literature contains some very impressive findings using electro-encephalography, like the contingent negative variation and evoked potentials as a function of language stimulus input; similarly impressive is the work on verbal aspects of autonomic behavior. Both areas are providing important cues as to the place of CNS and autonomic events in the feedthrough loops that we study. The major concentration of my research, however, has been on the electromyographic study of responses. Guided by the impressive historical background of "internal speech," dating from Plato through Bain (cf. Langfeld, 1933), and Watson (1930), our initial emphasis was on covert oral activity of the speech musculature. We shall first summarize results of efforts to determine whether or not the covert oral response *does* reliably occur under a variety of linguistic conditions; the next step will be a summary of research directed toward a specification of conditions under which covert oral behavior changes—by specifying the environmental and subject variables with which covert oral behavior systematically varies, some insight into its function should be gained.

V. MEASUREMENT OF COVERT ORAL BEHAVIOR

A. AUDITORY HALLUCINATIONS

Our earliest work was, actually, under a linguistic condition where the experimenter and subject disagreed as to whether or not there *were* external language stimuli, viz., research on auditory hallucinations. Following Watson's theory of thinking, and the very imaginative work of Gould (1950), the notion was that the voices "heard" during hallucinations might be produced by covert activity of the hallucinator's own speech mechanism. In particular, we finally got a schizophrenic subject to relax and successfully depress a button each time that he (apparently) heard voices. The subject was asked to report the content of ten auditory hallucinations and to remain silent after the other 15 hallucinations. It was found that chin EMG and breathing amplitude significantly increased during the (apparent) hallucinatory experience, with no noticeable change in EMG of the nonactive arm (Fig. 10.3). Slight whisperings were also detected significantly often during the (apparent) hallucinations. In two instances, the whisperings were sufficiently clear that they could be identified as part of the content of the overt reports of the hallucinations. These findings thus quantitatively confirmed those of Gould (1950), and also were in accordance with some unpublished findings of Malmo (cf. McGuigan, 1970a). It seems that heightened covert oral behavior significantly often coincided with auditory hallucinations. We might reason that covert speech and the resulting proprioceptive activity internally creates, or leads to, voices. One is reminded of Hefferline and Perera's (1963) conditioning of proprioceptive activity to experimentally produce hallucinations.

B. READING AND MEMORIZATION

Apparently, the first EMG measures of covert oral behavior during silent reading were made by Faaborg-Andersen and Edfeldt (1958),

Fig. 10.3. A sample tracing of the report of an hallucination. The 2-sec intervals before and after the report are marked on the event line at the top. Next in order are the pneumogram, arm EMG, chin EMG, tongue EMG, and the sound record. [From McGuigan (1966) by permission of The Williams & Wilkins Co., Baltimore.]

though Jacobson and Kraft in 1942 had studied a nonoral measure (leg EMG) during silent reading. Faaborg-Andersen and Edfeldt (using needle electrodes) concluded that the silent speech of adults during silent reading specifically involved an increase (from rest) in electrical activity in the vocal and mylohyoid muscle, but a decrease in the posterior crico-arytenoid. Edfeldt (1960) recorded mylohyoid EMG with needle electrodes from Swedish college subjects and concluded ". . . that silent speech occurs in the reading of all persons [p. 154]." McGuigan, Keller, and Stanton (1964) measured surface lip and chin EMG in children and college students, and found that these measures of covert oral behavior significantly increased over rest during silent reading in both kinds of subjects. Mean numbers of subvocalizations per minute (studied through high audio amplification) during silent reading for two samples of children were 1.53 and .43, but .00 for the college students. Respiration rate (possibly a measure of covert oral behavior) also significantly increased during silent reading. These general findings are summarized in Fig. 10.4. Mc-

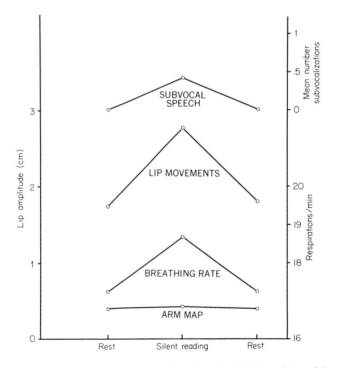

Fig. 10.4. During silent reading, subvocalization, lip EMG, and breathing rate increases in children, while nonpreferred arm EMG changes little.

Guigan and Rodier (1968) confirmed these findings of increased covert oral behavior (tongue and chin EMG), and increased respiration rate during silent reading, relative to rest. Sokolov (1969) reported increased speech muscle activity during a variety of linguistic tasks, including silent reading. McGuigan and Bailey (1969a) found that college students significantly increased amplitude of chin and tongue EMG during silent reading (and also during memorization of prose) over baseline level, and that these increases were significantly greater than under two nonlinguistic conditions (listening to music, and attentively listening to a blank tape on a tape recorder). Additionally, respiration rate and preferred arm EMG significantly increased during silent reading (these two measures also increased during two other linguistic conditions, viz., memorizing, and listening to prose); these increases were, furthermore, greater than under the two nonlinguistic conditions of listening to music and to nothing. Finally, increases in covert oral behavior during silent reading were not accompanied by increases in a sample of nonspeech regions of the body (cf. McGuigan, 1970a). Locke and Fehr (1970), following some of the reasoning of Blumenthal (1959) had adult subjects perform a serial learning task using visually presented disyllabic words characterized by the presence or absence of letters representing labial phonemes. Mean peak amplitude of lip EMG was significantly greater for labial than for nonlabial words during presentation and rehearsal periods, supporting the hypothesis that subvocalization during learning is actually a form of speech.

The results thus indicate that covert oral behavior typically increases during silent reading and during "memorization," relative to a resting baseline condition. Additionally, there is some evidence that the increased level of covert oral responding during silent reading was greater than during a sample of nonlinguistic tasks; and, that behavioral increase appears to be localized in the speech mechanism. In short, relatively localized covert responses seem to occur in the oral regions; and they seem to be uniquely associated with silent reading (and similar linguistic tasks); apparently, this phenomena is quite general among language-proficient people.

C. HANDWRITING

Lepley (1952) said that after "approximately seven hours at intensive hurried, writing tasks . . . he was clearly aware of a marked 'stiffness' and soreness in the reacting mechanisms involved in speech; and this particularly in the region of the larynx [p. 597]." On the basis of this observation, Lepley conducted an experiment in which he found that subjects who said that they subvocalized had poorer handwriting than those who said that they did not subvocalize. Stimulated by Lepley's work, we conducted a series of experiments in which amplitude of covert oral behavior was measured while college students wrote words, and also while they engaged in two comparable nonlinguistic tasks. It was found (see Fig. 10.5) that heightened tongue and chin EMG occurred during cursive writing, and the increased covert oral behavior was significantly larger than during the performance of the nonlinguistic comparison tasks (McGuigan, 1970b).

D. DREAMS

Since covert oral behavior increases during the waking performance of linguistic activities, increases in covert oral behavior might also occur

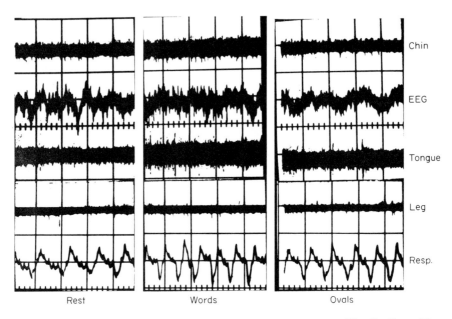

Rest   Words   Ovals

Fig. 10.5. Chin and tongue EMG increase from rest more while silently writing words than for comparison task (e.g., drawing ovals). Leg EMG changed but little.

during dreams that consist primarily of conversational content. We thus measured changes in amplitude of covert oral behavior during conversational dreams, and during visual nonlinguistic dreams for comparison purposes (McGuigan & Tanner, 1971). Four subjects reported a total of eight dreams that were classified as visual in content and five as conversational in content. It was found that covert oral behavior (lip and chin electromyograms) was significantly higher during rapid eye movement (REM) periods in which there were conversational dreams than during nonrapid eye movement (NREM) periods. On the other hand, there were

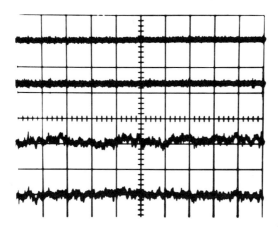

Fig. 10.6. Illustration of signals during NREM periods. Reading from top down, signals are lip EMG, chin EMG, from horizontal eye placement, and frontal EEG. Amplitude for the top three traces is 50 μV/division, and 100 μV/division for EEG. Time is 1/sec/division. [From McGuigan & Tanner (1971) by permission of *Psychonomic Science.*]

only minor and nonsignificant changes in covert oral behavior during REM periods for the visual dreams, relative to the NREM periods. Little change occurred for neck responses, suggesting that behavioral changes were not generalized throughout the body and perhaps localized in the speech region. These findings are thus consistent with those obtained from waking subjects and suggest that covert oral behavior may serve a linguistic function during conversational dreams, too (see Figs. 10.6–10.8).

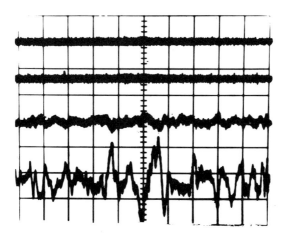

Fig. 10.7. Illustration of signals during a visual dream, as in Fig. 10.6. [From McGuigan & Tanner (1971) by permission of *Psychonomic Science.*]

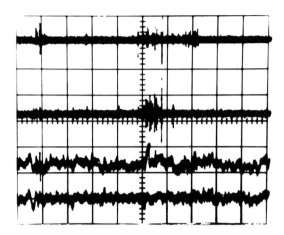

Fig. 10.8. Illustration of signals during a conversational dream, as in Fig. 10.6. [From McGuigan & Tanner (1971) by permission of *Psychonomic Science.*]

In some preliminary work, Claudia Albright, Bettsie Adamson, and I induced three kinds of dreams into college students through hypnotic techniques: "oral dreams" (silent recitation of "The Lord's Prayer"); "leg dreams" (riding a bicycle); and "relaxation dreams" (doing nothing). It is not meant that the hypnotic dream is a duplicate of the night dream, though they are perhaps related—the hypnotic dream is a phenomenon of interest in its own right and has all of the relative research advantages of experimentation versus systematic observation. The results were generally as hypothesized, as illustrated in Figs. 10.9 and 10.10. The third trace from the top is tongue EMG, the response measure of greatest interest here, and it can be seen how dramatically that measure increased from a resting state under hypnosis (Fig. 10.9) to the silent recitation dream (Fig. 10.10). In neither of the nonoral dreams was there an apparent increase in covert oral activity. As in the night linguistic dream, it seems that the oral mechanism is covertly active during the linguistic hypnotic dream too.

E. Listening to Speech

Activity in the listener's speech apparatus has long been implicated in the process of speech perception as in Wyczoikowski's (1913) statement that

> . . . Every word pronounced aloud acts upon the ear and the tongue of the hearer in a way similar to that in which a vibrating tuning-fork acts upon another fork. . . . The ear and the tongue of the hearer enter into . . . sympathetic vibration with those of the speaker. . . . Only when the stimulus coming from the voice of person A incites mechanically the same coordinate movements of the organ of speech of person B is the latter able to understand the word spoken

and heard. This means, however, that one does not completely understand the word that is spoken to him until it is repeated by his own organ of speech. . . . Conscious understanding follows upon these intraorganic processes. . . .

She also elaborates interesting anatomical connections between the ear and the tongue that might serve speech perception functions, as well as to explain why some people report that they "hear words while thinking."

While not directly conducted for this purpose, studies by Smith, Malmo, and Shagass (1954), by Bartoshuk (1956), and by Wallerstein (1954) give some hint of heightened speech muscle EMGs during speech perception; however, other factors, such as the subjects straining to hear the unclear speech, obscure the relevance of the results for the present purposes. Novikova (1961) reported EMG traces from the tongue that showed heightened activity while the subjects were listening to instructions. But, except for the possibility of a correlation between auditory perceptual clarification and heightened tongue EMG in the Gilbert and Sullivan study by McGuigan, Hadley, and Osgood, as reported in Chap. 13, there apparently are no really convincing direct measurements of heightened covert oral behavior during the auditory reception of language. McGuigan

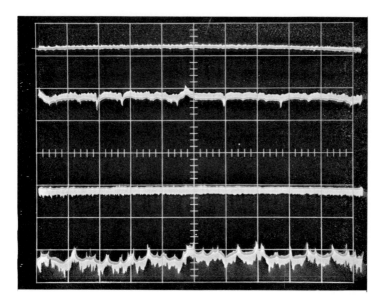

Fig. 10.9. Sample tracings typical of six college students while resting when hypnotized. From top down: left arm EMG, horizontal eye, tongue EMG, and frontal EEG. Horizontal scale is 1 sec/division; vertical scale is 100 μV/division for EMG and 50 μV/division for EEG.

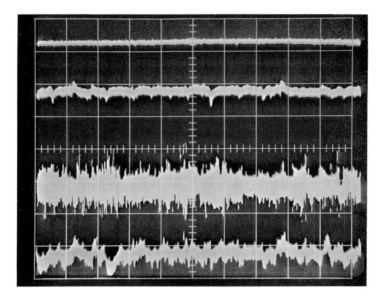

Fig. 10.10. Sample tracings during induced hypnotic verbal dream, as in Fig. 10.9.

and Bailey (1969a) did not find a significant increase in oral EMG when their subjects listened to a story, but interestingly enough while listening there *was* a significant increase from the preferred arm, as if the subjects were making covert linguistic (writing) responses.

F. Imagination

Jacobson's (1932) work in which he found that highly localized covert responses occur as a function of the particular kind of stimulus for "imagination" and in the part of the body that one would use should the response have been overtly made, has received some empirical verification from others [e.g., Blumenthal (1959)]. This work is so classical and well-known that we shall not further dwell on it.

G. Problem Solving by Normal Subjects

Heightened covert oral behavior (tongue EMG, lip EMG, etc.) has been recorded when normal subjects engage in a wide-variety of verbal and mathematical (mental) problems, as in the work of Jacobson (1932), and Bassin and Bein (1961).

H. Problem Solving by Deaf Subjects

In his classical work, Max (1937) hypothesized that the activity of the linguistic mechanisms in the fingers of deaf subjects would increase during the solution of "thought problems." He found that abstract thought problems elicited action-current responses more frequently and to a greater extent in the arms than in the legs and concluded: ". . . these manual responses in the deaf are more than adventitious effects of irradiated tensions . . . and . . . have some specific connection with the thinking process itself . . . our results thus lend some support to the behavioristic form of the motor theory of consciousness [Max, 1937, pp. 336–337]." Max's work received some confirmation from Novikova (1961). We replicated a portion of Max's research using six deaf subjects proficient in manual speech, and who were learning oral speech (McGuigan, 1971a). It was found (Fig. 10.11) that mean amplitude of left arm and lip significantly increased over baseline during problem solving. Left arm EMG increased significantly more during problem solving than during a nonverbal control task; integrated EEG from the left motor area decreased significantly more during problem solving. No significant changes occurred for leg EMG, but respiration rate increased significantly during all tasks. In conformity with the findings of Max and Novikova, it was concluded that the manual and oral regions were covertly functioning as a common linguistic system during thinking.

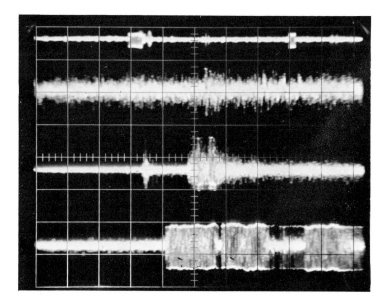

Fig. 10.11. Sample traces from a deaf subject while engaged in problem solving. The two events in top trace indicate presentation of the problem and subject's report of its solution. Increases in EMG can be noted from top down from lips, left arm, and right arm. Horizontal scale is 2 sec/division, and vertical scale is 100 μV/division.

I. Verbal Mediation

Using a paradigm based on that of Tracy Kendler, McGuigan, Culver, and Kendler (1971) studied children under three conditions: (1) during verbal oral mediation; (2) during nonoral (i.e., leg and arm) mediation based on the concepts of right and left; and (3) a no-mediation control condition. It was found that amplitude of tongue EMG significantly increased from before training to the mediation phase, only for the Verbal Mediation Group; that increase, furthermore, was significantly greater than for the other two (control) groups (Fig. 10.12). The arms were possible loci of mediational behavior for the Nonoral Mediation Group, and it was in fact, found that arm EMG was relatively large under this directional, nonoral mediation condition. Eye movements, also possible indicators of right and left mediational activity, were greater under the nonoral mediation condition, too. These psychophysiological measures of covert behavior during mediation are thus consistent with verbal mediational theory that has been based on the study of overt behavior. More particularly, the relatively heightened tongue EMG for the Verbal Oral Mediation Group may have been a direct measure of, or at least an indicator of, the verbal mediational response.

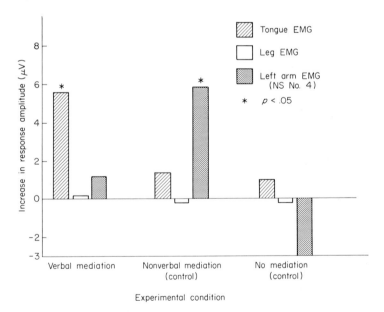

Fig. 10.12. Tongue EMG increased significantly more for an oral–verbal mediation group than for two control groups. Limb activity was greatest for the directional (right vs left) nonverbal mediation group, as illustrated by reaction to one mediational symbol (Nonsense symbol No. 4).

VI. SUMMARY

We have in this section summarized research in which heightened covert oral behavior has been recorded during a variety of linguistic activities. These activities are of two kinds: (1) where the response is correlated with external linguistic stimuli; and (2) where the activity is not directly controlled by external linguistic stimuli but is, presumably, a direct function of internal stimulus processing. In the vernacular, the activities in the first class are referred to by such words as "imagination," "problem-solving," "cursive writing," "memorization," and "verbal mediation," and in the second class by "hallucinations," and "night dreams."

The general conclusion, then, is that heightened covert oral behavior is intimately associated with the performance of linguistic activities in normal language-proficient humans (and that heightened covert dactylic behavior similarly occurs for deaf individuals). We shall now turn to the second major phase of this section, as previously specified, viz., a study of *changes* in covert oral behavior, and of the variables of which those changes are a function.

VII. SYSTEMATIC CHANGES IN THE AMPLITUDE OF COVERT ORAL BEHAVIOR

Two categories of variables will be considered—subject characteristics, and environmental variables. Two subclasses of subject variables are changes in covert oral behavior (1) as a function of characteristics as they are *selected* in subjects, and (2) as a function of experimentally produced changes in subjects. Concentration here will be on the linguistic task of silent reading, an activity particularly appropriate for this research.

A. Subject Variables

Amplitude of covert oral behavior during silent reading as a function of selected characteristics of subjects was studied by Faaborg-Anderson and Edfeldt (1958). These researchers selected Danish subjects who were accustomed to reading a foreign language (Swedish), and subjects who could read Swedish but were not accustomed to it. They found that silent speech (vocal and mylohyoid EMG) was substantially greater for those who were unaccustomed to reading the foreign language.

Adults selected on the basis of their poor reading proficiency emit larger amplitudes of covert oral behavior during silent reading than do adults who are proficient readers (Edfeldt, 1960). Amplitude of covert oral behavior is also inversely related to handwriting proficiency (McGuigan, 1970b). Similarly, more covert oral behavior occurs in children while reading than in adults, who were (obviously) the more proficient readers

(McGuigan *et al.*, 1964; McGuigan & Pinkney, 1971). Children selected on the basis of especially high levels of covert oral behavior while silently reading, naturally decreased their covert oral response amplitude over the years, as reading proficiency improved, but response amplitude stabilized at about the normal adult level (McGuigan & Bailey, 1969b); furthermore, audible subvocalizations were prominent in the first test but none were detected after 3 years (see Fig. 10.13).

These data thus indicate that amplitude of covert oral behavior is inversely related to linguistic proficiency of *selected* subjects.

Two possible *experimental* strategies for studying subject variables to decide whether the covert oral response is beneficial or detrimental, are to (1) increase reading proficiency and note any consequences on covert oral behavior, and (2) manipulate amplitude of covert oral behavior, and note consequences on reading proficiency. If increased reading proficiency results in reduced amplitude of covert oral behavior, the response is probably detrimental; an increase (or perhaps no change) in response amplitude would suggest that the response is beneficial (Strategy 1). By Strategy 2, should reduction in response amplitude result in decreased reading proficiency, one could conclude that the response was beneficial; an in-

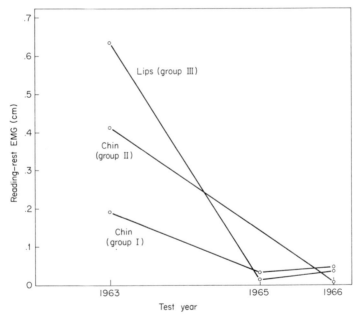

Fig. 10.13. Amplitude of covert oral behavior during silent reading over a 3-yr period. [From McGuigan & Bailey (1969) by permission of *Perceptual and Motor Skills*.]

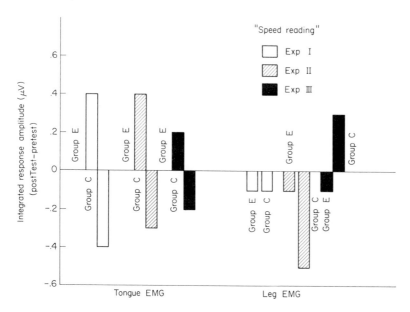

Fig. 10.14. Selected results from three experiments on the psychophysiological effects of increasing reading rate. In all three experiments tongue EMG increased for those who took the reading course, but decreased for those who did not (probably due to habituation to the laboratory).

crease in reading proficiency would suggest that the response is detrimental.

When mean adult reading rates were experimentally improved (by 149 wpm) the amplitude of one measure of oral behavior (tongue EMG) significantly increased (see Fig. 10.14); a similar increase in tongue EMG occurred in children, as a result of increased rate (increases of 172 wpm and 220 wpm in two experiments). However, the measured effect was not as pronounced for the children as it was for the adults, perhaps because amplitude of the covert oral behavior for the children was relatively large at the start of the experiment. Tongue EMG, incidentally, decreased for all three control groups in these three experiments; other oral measures were, however, not so systematic. The increased reading rate was confirmed by systematic changes in electrically measured eye movements (Fig. 10.15; McGuigan & Pinkney, 1971). Similar results occurred in a remedial reading case (McGuigan & Shepperson, 1971), i.e., a child's reading proficiency was increased from the 5.6 grade level to the 7.3 grade level, as measured by a standardized test. Tongue and chin EMG also sizeably increased from before to after the remedial work (Fig. 10.16). These behavioral consequences of improving reading proficiency thus seem to be

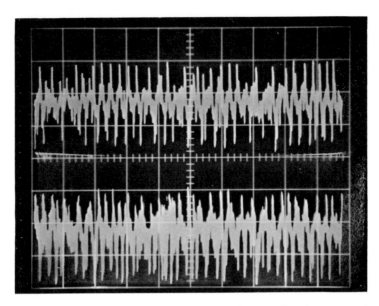

Fig. 10.15. Sample record of eye activity during silent reading for an experimental subject who took the reading improvement course. Pretest record is upper trace and posttest record is lower trace. The large spikes indicate movement of the eye from the end of a line of prose to the start of the next line. Each horizontal division is 4 sec. Number of end-of-line eye movements decreased per unit line read as a consequence of the reading improvement course.

more consonant with the theory that covert oral behavior facilitates reading proficiency.

For the second strategy, external feedback techniques *have* successfully reduced amplitude of covert oral behavior during silent reading (cf. Hardyck, Petrinovich, & Ellsworth, 1966; McGuigan, 1967; Hardyck & Petrinovich, 1969). The only study in which reduced amplitude was shown to affect reading proficiency was that by Hardyck and Petrinovich (1970); these experimenters reduced laryngeal EMG (surface electrodes) through external feedback while college subjects read easy and difficult passages. Relative to two other groups who did not receive laryngeal feedback, Hardyck and Petrinovich found that "the laryngeal feedback group did significantly less well on comprehension of the difficult material [p. 647]," leading them to conclude that "... subvocal speech ... is a useful stimulus input capable of mediating a cognitive response [p. 651]." The problems entailed by this second strategy are, however, quite complex. For instance, the *statements* of Hardyck et al. (1966, 1969) that the reduction is rapidly accomplished, and permanent conflict with the empirical findings of McGuigan (1971b) that reduced amplitude of covert oral behavior is temporary and dependent on the presence of the feedback signal (see Figs. 10.17–10.19).

In conclusion for the second strategy, there is some evidence that reduced covert oral behavior decreases reading proficiency; but the complexity of the methodological problems and the crudeness of measures of reading proficiency as rate in words per minute, and comprehension as a percentage indicate that this is going to be a particularly difficult research problem to solve to any degree of satisfaction.

To summarize research on the purposive manipulation of subject variables, increasing reading rate seems to increase amplitude of covert oral behavior; more clearly, we can say that amplitude does not decrease. Furthermore, there is some limited evidence that experimental reduction of oral response amplitude decreases reading proficiency.

B. ENVIRONMENTAL VARIABLES

A variety of external stimulus variables affect amplitude of covert oral behavior, e.g., amplitude is increased by increasing the level of difficulty of the prose being read, and by increasing the blurriness of the letters (Edfeldt, 1960). Increasing the difficulty of other verbal tasks, like problem solving, also increases amplitude of covert oral behavior (e.g., Bassin &

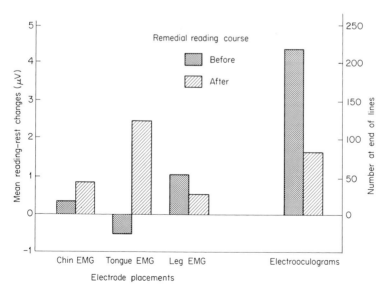

Fig. 10.16. Two covert oral measures increased after successful remedial reading course for a child, in contrast to a nonoral measure (leg EMG). [From McGuigan & Shepperson (1971) by permission of *The Journal of Clinical Psychology.*]

Bein, 1961; Sokolov, 1969). While their subjects were silently reading, McGuigan and Rodier (1968) systematically introduced white noise, auditory prose different from that being read, and the auditory prose played backward. They found that presentation of prose and of backward prose led to a significantly greater amplitude of covert oral behavior than while reading during silence, but white noise did not have that effect. The conclusion was that the subjects needed to enhance amplitude of covert oral behavior as a function of condition—that the response facilitated the reading process.

These results on environmental variables thus indicate that amplitude of covert oral behavior becomes exaggerated as the prose and environmental conditions become more demanding.

VIII. SUMMARY AND PRELIMINARY INTERPRETATION

In summary of this section on systematic changes, the findings indicate that amplitude of covert oral behavior is inversely related to reading proficiency of selected subjects, and is a direct function of the degree of the textual and environmental demands. In experimental manipulation of reading rate and of amplitude of covert oral behavior, it seems that amplitude of covert oral behavior and reading proficiency are directly related. As a start in interpreting these empirical conclusions, let us consider

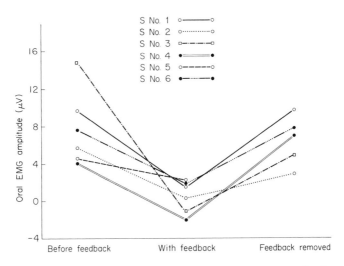

Fig. 10.17. Effect of external auditory feedback presentation and subsequent withdrawal on the triggering covert oral behavior during silent reading. Feedback was from the chin of *S*s 1, 3, 4, and 5, and from the lips for *S*s 2 and 6. [From McGuigan (1971) by permission of *Psychonomic Science.*]

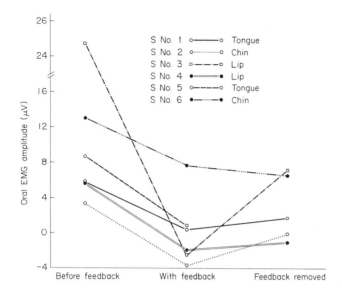

Fig. 10.18. External feedback also typically reduces activity of speech muscles other than the one controlling the tone. [From McGuigan (1971) by permission of *Psychonomic Science*.]

the developmental process of responding to linguistic stimuli. We shall concentrate on reading, with the hope that our considerations will more broadly apply to the other mental processes described above.

During the visual reception of language stimuli (reading), one orally responds to those linguistic components (the words that constitute the prose being read). In first learning to read, the child makes large (and inefficient) articulatory movements when he attempts to pronounce the written word. As with any skill, when proficiency increases, the gross amount of muscular activity becomes reduced and efficiency increases— as one learns to read, swim, or ride a bicycle, initial large-scale and erratic movements become woven into smooth, highly coordinated response chains. And, these response chains may most efficiently be run off at the covert level. Hence, the covert oral behavior that persists in the adult continues to function during the performance of linguistic activities. However, those who are relatively less proficient in performing a linguistic task must exaggerate their oral behavior in order to bring their comprehension "up to par." Casual observation suggests that this exaggeration mechanism is quite common in the elderly. Similarly, under demanding conditions, normal people enhance their reading proficiency by exaggerating the amplitude of covert oral behavior; sometimes we even read aloud for this purpose.

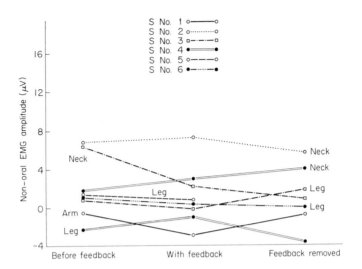

Fig. 10.19. There is no systematic change in amplitude of nonoral response measures during feedback and subsequent nonfeedback reading sessions. [From McGuigan (1971) by permission of *Psychonomic Science.*]

In short, poor adult readers, children, or normal readers who are reading under distracting conditions (like on a subway), must emit relatively pronounced covert oral responses. Similarly, when one's reading rate is suddenly increased, as in a speed reading course, there are demands for increased amplitude of covert oral behavior; presumably, as one continues to practice at the faster rate, amplitude of response will decrease, just as it naturally does with children.

In short, on the basis of findings of heightened covert oral behavior during a wide-variety of linguistic conditions, and on the basis of systematic increases of amplitude as a function of selected characteristics of subjects and of experimental manipulations, we may conclude that the covert oral response is beneficial during the performance of linguistic tasks. As a basis for considering just how covert oral behavior functions in processing information contained in (external and internal) linguistic stimuli, let us turn to a schema for summarizing the covert processes recorded during various mental events.

IX. STUDY OF PATTERNS OF COVERT PROCESSES

In Table 10-1, we have started to summarize patterns of covert processes as they occur "naturally" (i.e., nonexperimentally produced). Recall the major division of covert processes into behavioral and neurological events, and note that the two subdivisions within the behavioral events are oral (having to do with the speech region) and nonoral. In addition to EMG measures of oral activity, we include rate and amplitude of pneumograms, because the breathing apparatus is so intimately involved in speech production. Leg EMG is the most prominent nonoral control measure for generalized bodily activity. Because the preferred arm is apparently a locus of covert linguistic activity, (e.g., McGuigan & Bailey, 1969a) as may be the nonpreferred arm through bilateral transfer, EMGs from the arms are

TABLE 10-1

Patterns of Covert Processes during "Mental Events"

Vernacular name (stimulus condition)	Covert oral			Covert nonoral				Neurological processes	
	EMG	Pneumo.		Leg EMG	Arm EMG		Autonomic	EEG	
		Rate	Amp.		Pref.	Non-pref.		Amp.	Other
S_L [a]									
Silent reading	+	+		0	+	0			
Memorization	+	+			+				
Silent writing	+	+		0		0			–
Problem solving									
Verbal	+								
Other									
Mediation									
Verbal	+			0				0	
Directional	0			0	+	+		0	
Imagination									
Oral	+			0					
Nonoral				+	+	+			
Perception									
Speech	?	+			+				
Other		+							
s_L [b]									
Hallucinations									
Auditory	+		+	0					
Other									
Dreams									
Conversational	+								
Visual	0								

[a] S_L—External Language Stimuli.
[b] s_L—Internal Language Stimuli.

not good control indices for assessing arousal states. A single column for Autonomic Behavior is obviously gross injustice, as is the abbreviated classification for nervous system events.

A plus in the columns indicates that there is evidence that the measure increases during the linguistic activities loosely specified by these terms from everyday language. A zero indicates that the measure does not change significantly, and a negative sign marks a decrease. First, there are far too many blanks that need to be filled in—some of these can be completed merely by further study of the literature, but most are indicative of priority research needs. Second, the rows suggest a program for objectively defining these mental events—by extensively measuring covert processes, we should be able to form common psychophysiological patterns among linguistic activities, for example, perhaps similar information processing events occur during reading and writing; similarly we may be able to empirically differentiate among classes of linguistic activities. Completion of this program would constitute a successful explication (in Carnap's sense) of "the higher mental processes." However, once these various classes of mental activities are explicated, as the work of R. C. Davis (1957) suggests, I think it makes little difference to us whether we continue using the common sense terms, or refer to each psychophysiological pattern with a neutral symbol like a Greek letter.

The final summary point, and obviously a major one for this paper, emerges more clearly than before: The covert oral response is especially prominent among the linguistic activities. Let us turn to a more specific reason for its prominence among covert patterns.

While Table 10-1 is a useful model for summarizing covert patterns, it merely shows us whether or not certain events occur under various linguistic conditions. To advance beyond this mere categorization of events re-

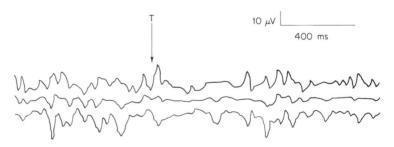

Fig. 10.20. Average tongue EMG (middle trace) during 32 presentations of the word "mind" (randomly alternated with five other stimuli). Two outer traces are for ±1 SD from the mean. The reduced variability and relatively stable mean after the stimulus (vertical arrow) occurred in the speech musculature of several subjects.

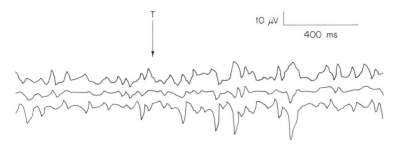

Fig. 10.21. As in Fig. 10.20 except stimulus was white noise.

quires considerably more sensitive quantification techniques that would yield highly refined parameters with which to more effectively specify psychophysiological patterns. In this way, we may eventually be able to make some truly sensible inferences as to the critical events in the numerous feedback loops.

We have employed two such approaches in efforts to identify critical covert events during linguistic processing. The first relied on signal averaging. We sought changes in neural and response measures as a function of type of input (linguistic vs nonlinguistic, class of speech sound, etc.). As is common in evoked potential research, no really general findings emerged in this work with Ron Hietala and with Suzanne Hadley, but certain aspects of the techniques are promising. Two illustrative tracings are presented in Figs. 10.20 and 10.21. One of the problems with research in which you keep repeating the same meaningful stimuli, we suspect, is that verbal satiation sets in, in which case there would be no constant internal signal to average. I present these figures as much as anything to illustrate how we have employed variability measures for evoked potentials, relevant to the important question that Dr. Mulholland raised in his discussion of Dr. Chapman's paper.

The second approach in which the effort was to specify relatively refined covert patterns has been more successful (McGuigan & Pavek, 1972). In this work people were asked a series of questions (a language stimulus) and instructed to silently think the answer to each (his covert reaction to the stimulus). The subject then pressed a button that indicated whether his answer was "yes" or "no."

We had a computer define and search for covert reactions during the period of the subject's silent answer. It then printed out the negative latency, duration, and amplitude for each reaction. Negative latency, the time *before* overt button pressing, was of greatest interest, and allowed us to study the temporal relationships among the response and neural events.

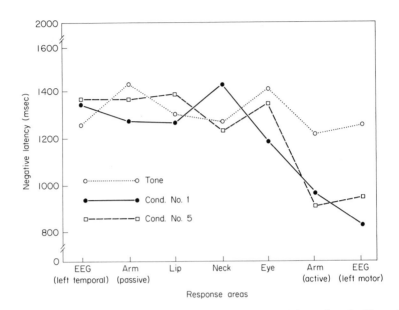

Fig. 10.22. Relative mean latencies of responses identified in various bodily regions. (The higher the data point on the vertical scale, the earlier the response followed stimulus termination.) [From McGuigan, F. J., & Pavek, G. V. On the psychophysiological identification of covert nonoral language processes. *Journal of Experimental Psychology,* 1972, **92,** 237–245. Copyright 1972 by the American Psychological Association, and reproduced by permission.]

Mean results for eight subjects are presented in Fig. 10.22. The earliest detected reaction after the question is plotted on the vertical axis for each of a variety of measures. For simplicity, focus on condition No. 1 in which the subjects answered the questions affirmatively. Reactions were detected (on the average) in the temporal cortex, passive arm, lip, neck, and eyes at approximately the same time following the question (about 1300 msec prior to the overt report of his answer—that is, prior to his button press); reactions in the active arm and motor cortex occurred some 400 msec later. The passive arm responded significantly earlier than did the active arm; the mean latency of events in the temporal cortex were significantly earlier than in the motor cortex.

The data now allow us to speculate more specifically about linguistic patterns and loops. We can presume that a complex pattern occurred during the perception of the question, but perceptual events, of course, occurred prior to those in Fig. 10.22 and were actually not studied in this experiment—the events in Fig. 10.22 are presumably those during the "thought period." More particularly, perhaps the reactions in the temporal cortex, passive arm, lips, neck, and eye are components of a complex pattern while answering the question—maybe we have measured events in feedthrough loops that function to integrate the speech musculature (lips) with the speech (temporal) regions of the brain, and with the eye, related perhaps to a covert nod or shake of the head (indicated by the response in the neck region). (Incidentally, differential linguistic patterns should be identifiable at this instant; and we did, in fact, find that the duration of the eye response is significantly longer when the subject is thinking "yes" than when he thinks "no.") Concomitant with this hypothesized peripheral–central integration in which a yes–no decision is reached, and part of the almost simultaneous running-off of these loops, a "command" may be issued to the passive arm that is inhibitory in nature— perhaps the active arm can only overtly respond once the passive arm is commanded to "not respond"; hence, the significantly earlier response in the passive arm, relative to that in the active arm. Such an inhibitory response, involving as it does the skeletal musculature, might be the behavioral counterpart of inhibitory neural activity, as reported by Hernandez-Peon, Scherrer, and Jouvet (1956).

Finally, continuing this line of speculation, after the complex decision (yes or no) was made, the dominant motor cortex was uniquely activated, commanding the overt response to be made in the active arm.

Regardless of the ultimate outcome of these speculations, the point here is that the strategy of studying temporal relations among patterns of events, illustrated by Fig. 10.22 should, in the long run, be valuable— particularly as we improve experimental techniques and develop more refined analysis procedures.

It should be clear that, while in our early work we concentrated on the study of the covert oral response, I am really interested in relatively widespread patterns of covert processes and loops among them. The problem is to specify the critical function of the speech mechanism during thought, particularly how the covert oral response relates to other components of the pattern.

One of the reasons that we have used silent reading so much is that one's thought processes during that linguistic activity are controlled by the language stimuli that constitute the words being read. Hence, the experimenter knows *what* the thinker is thinking. What is happening, a guess is, is that the impinging linguistic stimuli (the prose) evoke conditional covert responses in the speech mechanism (during prolonged chains of mental processes those conditional speech responses may be evoked directly by internal linguistic stimuli). This kind of interpretation is also supported by research like that of Locke and Fehr (1970) who found greater lip EMG while subjects learned labial than nonlabial words, leading them to conclude that subvocalization during learning is actually

a form of speech. It may be that the speech muscle activity generates a
linguistic code that is carried to the brain (cf. McGuigan, 1970a) and as
Sokolov (1969) has suggested, these afferent neural impulses may help
integrate the various verbal regions of the brain. Consonant with a principle of behavioral efficiency, under normal circumstances, the accomplished
reader (thinker) typically generates the minimal amount of afferently
carried verbal information in his oral region that is necessary for understanding. But the poor reader, or the good reader under distracting conditions, requires a greater amount of verbal information, perhaps needs
to send a redundancy of information to his brain, as well as, of course,
to other bodily regions that constitute the covert linguistic pattern.
Even Thorson (1925) found that tasks like thinking when a file was being
scraped, or silently reciting the multiplication tables while singing "ah"
and tapping the table with one's finger, led to increased tongue movement—who would not require an increased amount of verbal coding under
such conditions?

But what is the nature of such a code? Everyone knows that the brain
has about ten billion neurons, but few ponder the richness of the speech
musculature. In contrast to grosser bodily regions, the speech region is
extremely fine in the sense that each motor neuron there typically "con-
nects" to only several muscle fibers. The kinds of computations between
input-throughout and output units that McCulloch (1951) made in his
article entitled, "Why the Mind is in the Head" may help guide us toward
an understanding of such a code, particularly by establishing some constraints. I think I disagree with his conclusion, but his reasoning processes
provide us with an excellent model. For example, one of the reasons that
he put the mind in the head is that, in effect, he said that information
delivered through the nervous systems cannot be adequately transferred
to the muscles, due to limitations of the muscles. As he put it, part of the
corruption ("loss of information") is "referable to the coupling of our
nervous system to our muscles . . . so that the rate at which impulses can
come over the nerve is wasted by the inability of muscle to follow. In us a
nerve of a thousand axons can be in 2^{1000} possible states, whereas the muscle,
because it can only add tensions, has only a thousand possible states. 1000
is about 2^{10}; so the corruption in passing from nerve to brawn is 100 to
1 [1951, p. 45]."

I don't think that this is true. According to Basmajian (1962), in man
there are from two or three to 2000 or so muscle fibers in each motor unit,
i.e., many muscle fibers may be activated by each efferent neuron. Furthermore, a muscle fiber takes about 1 or 2 msec to fire, and in strong contractions, fires as rapidly as about 50/sec which "seems to be the upper physi-

ological limit for the frequency of propagation of axonal impulses [p. 8]."
In other words, McCulloch's argument seems to be in the reverse—activity
of muscle fibers may be limited by the ability of the nervous system to
transmit information. This matter of transferring information from one
system to another is, obviously, extremely complicated, but I think we
have no reason to suppose that the speech musculature may not be sufficiently rich to generate the required verbal code. Perhaps further anatomical
and functional study may lead us eventually to conclude something like
this: A brief discrete linguistic stimulus like a word, a phoneme, or whatever
evokes a conditional response pattern that consists of the contraction of
an extremely complex and widespread pattern of muscle fibers, with
major concentration in the speech musculature. Since the muscle fiber
obeys the all-or-none law, a basic binary spatially distributed pattern is
thus generated. Now, add a temporal dimension to the spatial coding of
the linguistic stimulus in the speech musculature, and consider the signals
generated by this complex "set of on–off switches": The afferent proprioceptive impulses can vary in such dimensions as latency, rate, probability
of firing, changes in rate, etc. Some kind of mechanism like this may
work. To study it further, we must more closely examine what we have
been talking about by the covert oral response. More particularly, we must
examine what is meant by "increased amplitude of covert oral behavior."
For, the basic assumption here is that what we have been measuring and
referring to by this phrase is hypothesized to be the generator of a verbal
code.

First, it is obvious that increases in the electromyographic measures of
covert oral behavior do not mean that the muscle fibers per se increase in
amplitude. It must, rather, mean that as those fibers contract, they either
fire more rapidly or the number firing per unit of time increases. Hence,
where we concluded that increased amplitude of covert oral behavior
facilitates the thought process, what was happening was that there was
an increase in the rate with which oral muscle fibers were firing and/or
there was an increase in the number firing per unit time. In short, by this
hypothesis, increased amplitude of covert oral behavior means that there
is an increase in information generated in the speech musculature, and
this increase in the amount of verbal coding is what facilitates the thought
processes.

One final comment about this possible muscular–neural encoding process.
Watson got himself in trouble with *brief* phrases like "thinking is subvocalizing," because people then didn't pay attention to his more complete
sentences that included nonoral activity, too. We have some good evidence
that covert oral behavior is intimately linked with covert nonoral

responses (McGuigan, 1970a) and these patterns develop, as Novikova (1961) put it, into a "single functional system within the motor speech analyzer." That is, we can well expect that a linguistic stimulus becomes conditioned to widespread responses through the body, including autonomic, as well as skeletal responses. The running-off of these complex, interacting covert processes is what Watson meant by the phrase that "we think with our whole bodies." And I believe that we do, when one considers the massive amount of evidence that implicates the eyes, arms, GSR, heart, etc., in thought processes.

X. MEDIATIONAL PROCESSES

Our concentration in this paper has been, so to speak, to directly measure those events that occur within a person as he thinks. The classical approach of the behaviorist has, however, been to indirectly study "thought processes" by postulating logical constructs on the basis of external stimuli and overt responses. Hull's (1952) r_G, Kendler and Kendler's (1969) *mediational response*, Osgood's (1953) *mediating reaction*, Schoenfeld and Cumming's (1963) *perceptual response*, and the *implicit associative response* of Bousfield, Whitmarsh, and Danick (1958) and adopted by Underwood (1965), are a few examples. Hence, the goals pursued in the development of hypothetical constructs and in the measurement of psychophysiological variables are somewhat similar. That is, the purposes of these hypothetical constructs and of the direct recording of electromyograms, electroencephalograms, galvanic skin responses, and so forth have both been (largely) to specify events between the (external) S and the (overt) R. Consequently, progress in the areas of psychophysiology and in theoretical behaviorism should both be enhanced if we could relate the hypothetical constructs of the theoretician with the directly measured empirical events of the psychophysiologist's laboratory. One study that we previously cited *was* an attempt to obtain data relevant to the direct measurement of the mediating response (McGuigan *et al.*, 1971). There should, though, be some heuristic value in speculating more generally about the direct measurement of hypothetical constructs. Consider, for example, the paradigm of the "question–answer experiment" discussed previously (McGuigan & Pavek, 1972). During the presentation of the question we may expect to directly measure a complex psychophysiological pattern that constitutes linguistic *perception*; such a pattern might be the motor-speech perceptual activity postulated by the Haskins group; it could be the construct called "the perceptual response" by Schoenfeld and Cummings (1963), or, by Bousfield *et al.* (1958), and by Underwood (1965) the "Representational Response," the response of perceiving a verbal unit. The Perceptual or

Representational Response then evokes a second, the Implicit Associative Response, which may be the complex pattern represented by the values of Fig. 10.22. Chains of these implicit associative responses may continue indefinitely until, perhaps, they are terminated by an overt language response. We have previously represented chains of such interacting patterns of covert oral and nonoral responses as in Fig. 10.23.

In addition to relating our work to the topic of mediating reactions, these considerations also allow us to elaborate on our previous definition of thinking, i.e., those events that necessarily occur after the reception of language stimuli. It is obvious that this ensuing chain of events may be very short, or it may be quite lengthy. For example, this definition of thinking forces us to include: (1) a brief sequence of loops that constitute speech perception itself (e.g., the representational response); (2) somewhat longer response chains set off by linguistic stimuli of the nature "How much is 33 × 99?"; and (3) such lengthy chains as run off by Archimedes culminating in his "Eureka" episode.

XI. CONCLUDING STATEMENT

The central–peripheralist issue, of course, never was solved, and it may be wise now to just drop these terms. On the other hand, perhaps it *would* be fruitful, or perhaps we have at least a scholarly responsibility, to relate present data to this ancient issue. The classical statement of

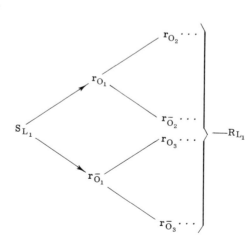

Fig. 10.23. An arbitrary behavioral unit which is commenced when an external language stimulus (S_{L_1}) evokes a covert oral (r_{O_1}) and a covert nonoral ($r_{\bar{O}_1}$) response. (It is hypothesized that each covert oral and nonoral response results in an additional covert oral and nonoral response, and that the sequence may continue indefinitely. The unit is arbitrarily said to be terminated when an overt language response (R_{L_1}) occurs; R_{L_1} may be the report of a solution to a problem posed by S_{L_1}, a tact of an internal event like an hallucination, etc.) [From McGuigan, F. J. Covert oral behavior during the silent performance of language tasks. *Psychological Bulletin*, 1970, **74**, 309–326. Copyright 1970 by the American Psychological Association, and reproduced by permission.]

the peripheralist's theory is to the effect that the peripheral components of the feedthrough loops are critical for thinking—that the efferent neural impulses, the responses, and the afferent neural impulses are necessary components of the thought processes. I grant that a "Donovan's Brain Theory" *is* possible—that a brain kept alive in a fishbowl might be able to think. However, I don't see, in any sense, how it could think very well. It might run-off intracerebral loops, but all of those very important loops involving other bodily organs would be missing, including, of course, the hypothesized loops in which verbal codes are generated by the speech musculature. Even Hebb grants that feedback from responses facilitates thinking.

In conclusion, I think the data *do* indicate that humans, in their most effective thinking, use widespread feedback loops, including responses. Earlier I mentioned McCulloch's (1951) good paper entitled, "Why the Mind is in the Head." With apologies to him, perhaps mine should have been entitled, "Why only Part of the Mind is in the Head."

The Discussion of Dr. McGuigan's Paper

LED BY DR. PETER MacNEILAGE
University of Texas at Austin

MacNeilage: I am very impressed with the paper, with the amount of good data that we have been shown, and with the amount of moderation in theoretical statements. I think that—certainly for the purposes of this discussion—we should revive for a moment the centralist–peripheralist issue and point out that Dr. McGuigan has put himself, to a certain extent, fairly squarely on the peripheralist's side with some of the statements that he has made. I agree with him that it can be still a very useful way of talking about things at this stage.

As you know, one of the main things that Watson believed—and that a lot of the peripheralists since Watson have believed—is that things are organized in terms of response chains, whereby the stimulus from a previous response evokes the next one. And, in fact, Lashley in his 1951 paper described the verbal report of one behaviorist who said that when he got up to give a speech, he just turned his mouth loose and went to sleep. I find it hard to believe that we have just had a demonstration of that kind of organization. I think this speaker deserves much more credit.

It seems that we have looked at a wide-variety of phenomena here—a wide-variety of different kinds of tasks and performances—and so it is dangerous to make very general statements about all of these different things. But let me try and do so anyway, because it might help the discussion, and it might have a grain of truth in it. I am skeptical that peripheral output is actually beneficial over all of these tasks, though it may be in a small number of them. The best candidate for it being beneficial is in learning lists of syllables—the Locke and Fehr situation—where you subvocally rehearse each item. Another good candidate is the McGuigan and Rodier situation where you read with noise present, and amplify the linguistic material at your disposal, somehow, by activating the peripheral system.

I don't know what you can say about the hallucination data, except that the hallucinatory experience is correlated with peripheral action. A major problem—that the speaker acknowledged—is that of cause-and-effect, the problem of which comes first.

In tasks like reading, I am more convinced that the covert response does not necessarily have to be beneficial. Consider the most recent study by Hardyck and Petrinovich, where they have shown that reduction of the level of laryngeal EMG while reading impairs reading. Perhaps the act that you inhibited was beneficial to reading, but it can also be that when one manipulates the same system that is used for another purpose, the operation for the first purpose is impaired—you try to do two things with the system, and that is difficult.

Lack of positive data while listening constitutes another problem for interpretation that peripheral output is beneficial. If we assume that the covert response is *speech related*, why should we get more EMG during reading than during listening? Reading is less related to *speech* organization than is the input of oral speech.

Another point is about the chaining model: The evidence is fairly negative for the operation of feedback loops in overt speech production. In particular, nerve-block studies have produced rather minimal effects on speech production. So I would argue that if we use feedback very little in the production process in an S–R manner—out to the periphery and back—then is it reasonable that we use it a lot in input processes that are supposedly capitalizing on our general organization capacity for language? I suspect the answer is no.

The EMG patterns do not indicate a series of discrete events—discrete in the sense that there is some input and then some output that can be defined in short spaces of time. I have some EMG data from various speech muscles during reading, and the predominant impression is that there is an increase in tonic level of activity, with little in the way of quick phasic changes. It is just as if the system "comes up" a little bit.

Hence, a lot of the data might be accounted for by some kind of overflow model, as Lashley suggested—with the proviso that the overflow has to be regional. That is, there are very clear data presented here that when you perform linguistic tasks, you get increased activity in the linguistic apparatus, but not in the leg and other places, whereas the opposite is true (in some cases) for nonlinguistic tasks. The increase is thus regional, but it might, nevertheless, be inessential overflow, with the two exceptions that I feel very clear about (cited previously).

One illustration of this problem is one of Dr. McGuigan's slides in which a problem was posed to the subject, but after the problem was solved, the EMG stayed up at the same level as during solution. Now, if EMG information is so specific, and if it is sufficiently specific to have a controlling role over details of mental events, then it should not act in such a tonic manner—it should not continue after solution of the problem at the same fairly high level. (See a comment on this point on p. 26—Ed.).

Several people have reported an increase in rate of respiration during silent reading. This is strange because rate of respiration decreases during speech. That's just a little puzzle, but it reinforces the point that we need to examine such variables in a very detailed way.

To return to the report by Locke and Fehr that activity of the musculature during rote-learning has a sensible relation to what was being learned, that is, that lip EMG is relatively heightened when learning words that contain bilabial stop-consonants: this is a good approach, and should be followed up. Thus, we should ask: "What kind of pattern do we expect down here in these peripheral indices?" and then see whether or not we get them.

I conducted a very small experiment on this, but unfortunately it had negative results. Of the intrinsic muscles, only the posterior cricoarytenoid muscle is an abductor of the vocal cords—it should be expected to work during voiceless consonants. The prediction was that amount of activity in the posterior cricoarytenoid during silent reading would increase for words with voiceless consonants. With only one subject we found the opposite was the case—little activity in the posterior cricoarytenoid while reading a high frequency voiceless list of words, and somewhat more activity while reading a list with few voiceless sounds. (This experiment was conducted in Dr. Thomas Shipp's laboratory.)

Another problem: the variability of the data, both within subjects and between subjects. Does an individual show high levels of activity only for one kind of task, or does he do it across the board? One might suspect something like a general motor-activation factor, one that people have to different degrees.

Looking at these data in detail, to me is kind of a frightening thing, because I have been working for a long time in overt speech production. Most recently, I have studied the jaw where we know the anatomy very well and know what muscles should be working. We have quite often found no activity in those muscles at all—leaving us at our more extreme moments to consider that the jaw opens by gravity and closes by elastic recoil. Luckily, logic allows us to say that we can't have both of those things operating at the same time. It's hard enough to figure out the patterns during overt production, so we have a lot of work ahead of us in looking at covert patterns.

The one question that has bothered me about the chain model, for a long time, is—What is the form of the information that goes back to the CNS? If there is necessary information to perform these tasks, what is it "down there" that we need? I am at a loss to answer that question. It is clearer in overt speech production where you can argue that sensory information about what the articulator is doing enables you to make sure it gets to its target, and doesn't overshoot or undershoot. That function would not be of much importance in a general chaining model implicating peripheral processes as beneficial to the control of these very high events. So what else is provided from the periphery, if indeed anything is? This is to me a really puzzling question.

The other question is a related one. What is the time constant of these loops? We read fairly quickly, so it seems unlikely that before we would assimilate a letter—to take an extreme example—we go out to the periphery and we get a little event that helps us. If things don't happen that quickly—and I don't think they do—then we are forced into time constants of larger size; and we are forced into suggesting that what is being assisted is the organization of higher-order units of some kind—not the letter. It seems to me that the more higher order you push the role of this feedback—in terms of what part of the message it is supposed to have something to do with—then the more difficult it is to understand how the information from "out there" could be of any use.

Open Discussion

Dr. Donald Mankin (Lehigh University): Concerning the function of subvocal speech, assume, for the sake of argument, that the medium for short-term memory is acoustic or auditory; might one of the functions of subvocal speech be to perform this transformation of visual stimuli into this acoustic, or auditory, medium? If so, then it will answer the question that Dr. MacNeilage had as to why reading results in more covert activity than listening.

McGuigan: Such, of course, is possible. Also, subvocal speech may function in speech perception, but we haven't really successfully measured it yet. The earliest explicit form of a motor theory of speech perception, that I am aware of, was that of Anna Wyczoikowska (1913), in which she points out neural connections between the inner ear and the tongue. It is relevant here, since she stated that those connections explain why some people say they hear sounds when they think words that are visually presented. Perhaps a loop is run off peripherally, before the auditory information ever gets into the brain.

Mankin: The verbal hypothesis is a fairly common hypothesis in talking about short-term memory, and might be an obvious function for subvocal speech.

McGuigan: It makes sense.

Dr. Abe Black (McMaster University): I hate to bring this up, but if these loops, going out to the periphery and back, are really important in the processing of information, then any interference with the loop really ought to interfere with the efficiency of information processing. Here, you will recall, are the curare studies, going back to the Smith, Brown, Toman, and Goodman (1947), where Smith reports that, when he was curarized, he could process information very well; all the experiments on animals show that learning, under curare, is often as good, or even better than in normal conditions. I am curious as to how you would deal with this information.

McGuigan: That one is easy to deal with. The Smith *et al.* article is a great pioneering work, and it is nice in principle. So now we should do the experiment properly, as I suggested (McGuigan, 1966), e.g., curare *supposedly* knocks out the skeletal musculature; I would like to see EMG tracings monitoring the subject at that time.

Black: We have those data in the animal studies.

McGuigan: All right, then, suppose that you prove that you have knocked out the skeletal musculature. What are you going to do with the rest of the body? I am not asking this facetiously, for loops elsewhere can function—the brain to smooth musculature, for example. The heart is intimately involved in cognitive functions; the whole autonomic system is involved. And those were not knocked out in your work, or in Solomon's.

Black: Some of them are. Let me put it this way then: If something is important in function, then interference ought to have a terribly profound effect.

McGuigan: Except that we are such wonderfully developed, evolved organisms, in some ways, and have many redundancies built into us. One of the reasons we have survived so far is because when one loses his larynx, for example, he still has other linguistic loops that he can run off. This is why the information that we get, with regard to the writing arm, is interesting. When you talk to me, why do I covertly activate my arm? And it is my right arm, not my left! My writing arm is helping me somehow. If you knock our right-arm feedback, I may rely on some other, redundant, peripheral–central loop. This may be a wild assumption, but the principle is important.

Audience: There are two possible things that are happening here, at least: (1) feedback from the muscular system is necessary in some sort of facilitative, or activating, way to make the thought process possible; and (2) it provides specific coding information. Have you anything that can discriminate between these two possibilities?

McGuigan: We try by taking multiple measures, those that involve linguistic regions and those for arousal measures. The data suggest that the reason that the response does facilitate thinking is because it does provide verbal coding.

Audience: How do we go about testing that?

McGuigan: It is complicated, obviously, and I feel that this is what we are trying to do in this whole conference. We should be thinking about it and try to develop some strategies. It might help, for a moment, to use an analogy with the computer. You run the computer with a series of off–on events by inserting a message—the computer does not work unless you put in some coding. The muscles employ a binary system and fire all-or-none in the same way, sending information into the brain, and back out again.

Audience: What is the unit of linguistic coding in this system?

McGuigan: I gave you about five possible parameters, but there must be more. Rate of firing would be an example.

Audience: The firing of what?

McGuigan: The firing of a muscle fiber and consequent afferent neural impulses.

Audience: Is the external linguistic unit words or phrases, or intonation patterns?

McGuigan: That is why we have people here like Osgood. I suggested words, phonemes, etc. Osgood and MacNeilage should speculate about this. (Osgood later suggested "the humble word."—Ed.).

Dr. Louis Aarons (Department of Mental Health, Chicago): I agree and disagree with the comments made by both you and Dr. MacNeilage. First, Edfeldt says quite plainly and strongly that reading proficiency is

not inhibited by subvocalization, period. My work with subvocal EMG
feedback agrees that the effect does persist, but I used a different muscle
than both you and Hardyck and Petrinovich. And Dr. MacNeilage's point
about the intrinsic laryngeal muscle is very good, because there is a difference in the abductor and adductor; the picture gets more complicated
because that laryngeal EMG is related to respiration as well as silent
reading.

Dr. MacNeilage talked about feedback, and you talked about feedthrough to get away from feedback; P. Schmidt, the physicist, talks
about feedahead that does not have to fire out into the muscles. The
pattern of ordering of muscles, in speech, is so complex that it has to be
somehow programmed in the neural structure before it hits the periphery—
the programming probably has to do with memory, and is possibly related
to an echoic memory of the sensory buffer. Therefore, you do get a change
in reading proficiency if you change whatever is taken up in this central
process that alludes to analog linguistic material; you do get an increasing
reading proficiency, if the motor apparatus is working, when the material
gets more difficult.

Rena Namey (Allegheny College): I knew a woman once who, when
cutting out material, would make up-and-down movements with her
mouth; they were not like articulatory movements. She was not conscious
that she was doing this. Is this related to what you are saying about a
feedback loop, or is it just some kind of motor overflow?

Osgood: I suggest that there is common meaning to the two responses.

Namey: It seemed like, if she was not doing it, she was having a harder
time cutting the material.

McGuigan: I believe it.

Dr. Lawrence Pinneo (Stanford Research Institute): How would both
you and Dr. MacNeilage handle the question of Helen Keller?

McGuigan: I would be interested in knowing how Dr. MacNeilage
handles it.

MacNeilage: I do not think it is any problem for me.

McGuigan: Dr. MacNeilage has made some good points, as have the
rest of you. I hope, though, that I have focused attention on how the
muscles may serve some kind of function in thinking. As I suggested
earlier, if we put all our measures together, we will know how the whole
organism thinks; we cannot forget that some parts are very important.

REFERENCES

Bartoshuk, A. K. Electromyographic gradients and electroencephalographic amplitude
during motivated listening. *Canadian Journal of Psychology*, 1956, **10**, 156–164.

Basmajian, J. V. *Muscles alive.* Baltimore, Maryland: Williams & Wilkins, 1962.

Bassin, F. V., & Bein, E. S. Application of electromyography to the study of speech. In N. O'Connor (Ed.), *Recent soviet psychology.* New York: Liveright Publishing Corp., 1961.

Berger, H. Ueber das Elektrenkephalogram des Menschen. *Archiv für Psychiatrie Nervenkrankheiten,* 1929, **87,** 527–570.

Blumenthal, M. Lingual myographic responses during directed thinking. An abstract of a dissertation presented to the faculty of the Graduate College, University of Denver, 1959.

Bousfield, W. A., Whitmarsh, G. A., & Danick, J. J. Partial response identities in verbal generalization. *Psychological Reports,* 1958, **8,** 703–713.

Davis, R. C. Response patterns. *Transactions of the New York Academy of Sciences,* Ser. II, 1957, **19,** 8, 731–739.

Edfeldt, A. W. *Silent speech and silent reading.* Chicago: University of Chicago Press, 1960.

Faaborg-Andersen, K., & Edfeldt, A. W. Electromyography of intrinsic and extrinsic laryngeal muscles during silent speech: Correlation with reading activity. *Acta Oto-Laryngology,* 1958, **49,** 478–482.

Gould, L. N. Verbal hallucinations as automatic speech. *American Journal of Psychiatry,* 1950, **107,** 110–119.

Hardyck, C. D., & Petrinovich, L. F. Treatment of subvocal speech during reading. *Journal of Reading,* 1969, **12,** 361–368, 419–422.

Hardyck, C. D., & Petrinovich, L. F. Subvocal speech and comprehension level as a function of the difficulty level of reading material. *Journal of Verbal Learning and Verbal Behavior,* 1970, **9,** 647–652.

Hardyck, C. D., Petrinovich, L. F., & Ellsworth, D. W. Feedback of speech muscle activity during silent reading: Rapid extinction. *Science,* 1966, **154,** 1467–1468.

Hefferline, R. F., & Perera, T. B. Proprioceptive discrimination of a covert operant without its observation by the subject. *Science,* 1963, **139,** 834–835.

Hernandez-Peon, R., Scherrer, H., & Jouvet, M. Modification of electric activity in cochlear nucleus during "attention" in unanaesthetized cats. *Science,* 1956, **123,** 331–332.

Hull, C. L. *A behavior system.* New Haven, Connecticut: Yale University Press, 1952.

Jacobson, E. Action currents from muscular contractions during conscious processes. *Science,* 1927, **66,** 403.

Jacobson, E. Electrophysiology of mental activities. *American Journal of Psychology,* 1932, **44,** 677–694.

Jacobson, E., & Kraft, F. L. Contraction potentials in man during reading. *American Journal of Psyhiology,* 1942, **137,** 1–5.

Kaplan, A. *The conduct of inquiry.* San Francisco: Chandler Publishing Co., 1954.

Kendler, H. H., & Kendler, T. S. Reversal-shift behavior: Some basic issues. *Psychological Bulletin,* 1969, **72,** 229–232.

Knott, J. R. Some effects of "mental set" upon the electrophysiological processes of the human cerebral cortex. *Journal of Experimental Psychology,* 1939, **24,** 384–405.

Langfeld, H. S. The historical development of response psychology. *Science,* 1933, **77,** 243–250.

Lepley, W. M. The participation of implicit speech in acts of writing. *American Journal of Psychology,* 1952, **4,** 597–599.

Locke, J. L., & Fehr, F. S. Subvocal rehearsal as a form of speech. *Journal of Verbal Learning and Verbal Behavior,* 1970, **9,** 495–498.

Max, L. W. Experimental study of the motor theory of consciousness: IV. Action-current responses in the deaf during awakening, kinesthetic imagery and abstract thinking. *Journal of Comparative Psychology*, 1937, **24**, 301–344.

McCulloch, W. W. Why the mind is in the head. In L. A. Jeffress (Ed.), *Cerebral mechanisms in behavior; the Hickson Symposium*. New York: Wiley, 1951.

McGuigan, F. J. *Thinking: Studies of covert language processes*. New York: Appleton, 1966.

McGuigan, F. J. Feedback of speech muscle activity during silent reading. *Science*, 1967, **157**, 579–580.

McGuigan, F. J. Covert oral behavior during the silent performance of language tasks. *Psychological Bulletin*, 1970, **74**, 309–326. (a)

McGuigan, F. J. Covert oral behavior as a function of quality of handwriting. *The American Journal of Psychology*, 1970, **83**, 337–388. (b)

McGuigan, F. J. Covert linguistic behavior in deaf subjects during thinking. *Journal of Comparative and Physiological Psychology*, 1971, **75**, 417–420. (a)

McGuigan, F. J. External auditory feedback from covert oral behavior during silent reading. *Psychonomic Science*, 1971, **25**, 212–214. (b)

McGuigan, F. J., & Bailey, S. C. Covert response patterns during the processing of language stimuli. *Interamerican Journal of Psychology*, 1969, **3**, 289–299. (a)

McGuigan, F. J., & Bailey, S. C. Longitudinal study of covert oral behavior during silent reading. *Perceptual and Motor Skills* 1969, **28**, 170. (b)

McGuigan, F. J., & Pavek, G. V. On the psychophysiological identification of covert nonoral language processes. *Journal of Experimental Psychology*, 1972, **92**, 237–245.

McGuigan, F. J., & Pinkney, K. B. Effects of increased reading rate on covert processes. Paper read at the XIIIth Interamerican Congress of Psychology, Panama City, December 1971.

McGuigan, F. J., & Rodier, W. I., III. Effects of auditory stimulation on covert oral behavior during silent reading. *Journal of Experimental Psychology*, 1968, **76**, 649–655.

McGuigan, F. J., & Shepperson, M. H. The effect of remedial reading on covert oral behavior. *Journal of Clinical Psychology*, 1971, **27**, 541–543.

McGuigan, F. J., & Tanner, R. G. Covert oral behavior during conversational and visual dreams. *Psychonomic Science*, 1971, **23**, 263–264.

McGuigan, F. J., Culver, V. I., & Kendler, T. S. Covert behavior as a direct electromyographic measure of mediating responses. *Conditional Reflex*, 1971, **6**, 145–152.

McGuigan, F. J., Keller, B., & Stanton, E. Covert language responses during silent reading. *Journal of Educational Psychology*, 1964, **55**, 339–343.

Novikova, L. A. Electrophysiological investigation of speech. In N. O'Connor (Ed.), *Recent Soviet psychology*. New York: Liveright Publ., 1961.

Osgood, C. E. *Method and theory in experimental psychology*. New York: Oxford Univ. Press, 1953.

Schoenfeld, W. N., & Cumming, W. W. Behavior and perception. In S. Koch (Ed.), *Psychology; A study of a science*. New York: McGraw-Hill, 1963.

Skinner, B. F. *Verbal behavior*. New York: Appleton, 1957.

Smith, A. A., Malmo, R. B., & Shagass, C. An electromyographic study of listening and talking. *Canadian Journal of Psychology*, 1954, **8**, 219–227. (Abstracted in *American Journal of Psychology*, 1953, **8**, 437–438).

Smith, S. M., Brown, H. O., Toman, J. E. P., & Goodman, L. S. The lack of cerebral effects of d-tubocurarine. *Anesthesiology*, 1947, **8**, 1–14.

Sokolov, A. N. Studies of the speech mechanisms of thinking. In M. Cole & I. Maltzman (Eds.), *A handbook of contemporary Soviet psychology*. New York: Basic Books, 1969.

Thorson, A. M. The relation of tongue movements to internal speech. *Journal of Experimental Psychology*, 1925, **8**, 1–32.

Underwood, B. J. False recognition produced by implicit verbal responses. *Journal of Experimental Psychology*, 1965, **70**, 122–129.

Wallerstein, H. An electromyographic study of attentive listening. *Canadian Journal of Psychology*, 1954, **8**, 228–238.

Watson, J. B. *Behaviorism.* (Rev. ed.) New York: Norton, 1930.

Wyczoikowski, A. Theoretical and experimental studies in the mechanism of speech. *Psychological Review*, 1913, **20**, 448–458.

CHAPTER ELEVEN

Biofeedback Techniques and the Conditions for Hallucinatory Activity[1]

JOHANN STOYVA

University of Colorado Medical Center

Psychophysiology, as the name implies, involves both physiological and psychological observations. If we grant that psychology can be divided into a behavioral component and an experiential one, then, psychophysiology may be thought to embrace three levels of observation—the physiological, the behavioral, and the experiential—the latter indexed by verbal report.

One's first reaction might be to view such an approach as a strategy designed to produce a maximum of confusion. But we think this is not

[1] Supported by Grant Number MH-15596, National Institute of Mental Health; Research Scientist Development Award No. K01-MH-43361-01, National Institute of Mental Health; and Bioengineering Neurosciences Grant NS-08511, National Institute of Health (for development work by the University of Colorado Medical Center Bioengineering Department on the instrumentation system described in this paper).

the case—or at least not necessarily! The thesis advanced here is that the combined use of physiological and psychological data can be a fruitful method of experimental inquiry—useful both as a means of gathering evidence about psychological phenomena, and as a method for discovering new relationships. Further, with the addition of the information feedback principle, a new dimension is grafted to psychophysiological methodology. The emerging technique of feedback psychophysiology can, we believe, be valuable not only in exploring a variety of mental processes, but also in teaching individuals to produce certain psychological states at will.

In developing the argument of this paper, we will first examine recent electrophysiological research on dreaming as a method of studying the mental activity which occurs during sleep. We will then consider biofeedback techniques in the exploration of waking mental activity, particularly in the induction of low arousal, twilight states.[2] Finally, it will be argued that biofeedback techniques can be useful in helping to specify some of the conditions under which "naturally occurring" hallucinatory experiences are likely to arise (including the hallucinatory experiences of dreams, sleep-onset, sensory isolation, and hypnosis, but excluding those produced by drugs or surgical intervention).

I. INFERENCES ABOUT CONSCIOUSNESS

A striking feature of contemporary psychological research is how the study of dreaming suddenly became much more scientifically respectable after the discovery that bursts of rapid eye movements (REMs) during sleep were closely associated with vivid visual dreaming (Aserinsky & Kleitman, 1953; Dement & Kleitman, 1957). Was the new enthusiasm for the study of dream processes as a fit topic for scientific inquiry well-justified, or were the supposed benefits largely illusory?

In the author's opinion there was good reason for the rekindled enthusiasm. The use of physiological indicators, such as REMs, in combina-

---

[2] By "twilight states" we refer to psychophysiological events occurring at the border between sleep and waking. In terms of EEG patterns these states are mainly indexed by alpha rhythms, or theta rhythms, or incipient Stage 2 "spindling" sleep. Their experiential attributes are discussed later in this paper. We refer to them in the plural since they seem to exist in some variety.

By "low arousal" we refer to a condition in which the major indicators of arousal are at reduced levels compared to when the individual is alert and active. Typically, muscle tension is reduced; autonomic activity such as heart rate and respiration are diminished; and cortical activity has shifted from low amplitude–fast activity to the slower brain wave frequencies characteristic of sleep onset.

tion with verbal reports of dreaming amounted to a methodological innovation. This innovation was *both* a method of proof, *and* a technique for discovering new relationships between physiological events and psychological events, such as dreaming (see Stoyva & Kamiya, 1968; Stoyva, 1970).

As an example of the new method, let us consider the association between REMs and dreaming. If a subject is awakened during a REM period, there is about an 80% probability that he will report a dream. On the basis of this observation, there are at least three different hypotheses which could be proposed:

1. Verbal reports of dreaming from REM sleep reflect recall of a genuine dream experience which was in progress just prior to the awakening.

2. The dream which the subject reports from his REM awakening did not actually occur, but is a fabrication.

3. The subject is remembering a genuine dream, but it occurred earlier during the night. This dream has nothing to do with the presence of REMs.

Experiments carried out early in the history of the REM sleep era demonstrated that Hypotheses 2 and 3 could be rejected, leaving Hypothesis 1 as the interpretation offering the best fit to the data. For example, Dement and Kleitman (1957) noted a positive correlation between the subjectively estimated length of a dream and the amount of REM sleep which had elapsed just prior to an awakening; Berger and Oswald (1962) found that REM density was related to the amount of physical activity in the dream narrative; Lewis *et al.* (1966) observed a positive correlation between REM period density and the dream's bizzareness.[3]

Once the validity of the REM indicator of dreaming had been established, a cluster of new findings was brought to light. The effects on dreaming of presleep experiences were examined, as were the effects of sensory stimulation of various kinds during sleep. Processes of dream recall were investigated, as was the relationship of REM dreams to personality attributes. Characteristic quality of mental activity at various stages of the sleep cycle was explored—in REM sleep, in non-REM sleep, and in the hypnagogic or sleep-onset state (see Foulkes, 1966).

---

[3] Dement and Kleitman (1957), and later Roffwarg, Dement, Muzio, and Fisher (1962) reported a close relationship between the recorded direction of eye movement activity and the visual activity in the dream narrative—e.g., imagery involving horizontal eye movements was associated with predominately horizontal eye movements on the chart paper. This observation, frequently cited in support of a scanning hypothesis of dreaming, has recently been challenged by the negative findings of Berger and Moskowitz (1970).

The methodological innovation employed in these studies—combined use of physiological measures and verbal reports of dreaming—was a technique involving a particular experimental logic. This logic, which has rarely been made explicit, is basically a method of excluded hypotheses. It has been ably described by Platt (1964) in his paper, "Strong Inference."

Platt states that in strong inference the researcher postulates the alternative hypotheses which could account for a given experimental result. He then systematically puts these hypotheses to empirical test and determines which can be destroyed. Then, with the hypothesis which has survived, he makes further inferences which in turn are tested. So there is a kind of creative destruction, involving the natural selection of the fittest hypotheses!

In the author's opinion this method of excluded hypotheses, or strong inference, should be used more extensively and more explicitly in psychological experimentation. In part, the reason is that we end up using it anyway, but often in an inefficient manner—usually, after a crossfire of colleague and editorial criticism! Also, its deliberate use encourages the experimenter to focus on experiments which affirm or deny a hypothesis, rather than to do work which is simply piling up additional data. (For an elegant example of this method, involving a series of experiments of the operant conditioning of hippocampal theta rhythm, see Black, 1971.)

To summarize the argument of this section: The events of consciousness can be scientifically studied to the extent that we can make testable inferences about them. One area which has made use of testable inferences about consciousness is contemporary dream research. The basic approach has involved the combined use of physiological measures and verbal report. In the remainder of this paper, we shall attempt to show that this approach can be usefully extended to some types of waking mental activity—particularly the thinking which occurs in association with low arousal, sleep onset conditions.

A. Linking the Physiological and the Experiential—The Feedback Loop

The combined use of physiological measures and verbal report, as described above, need not be confined to the study of dreaming, but can be employed in the study of certain waking mental activity as well. In particular, with the addition of the feedback loop, a new dimension is added to the basic technique.

1. Alpha Control

The first to seize on the implications of information feedback techniques in the study of conscious events was Kamiya (1969). In the late 1950s he asked himself whether a subject would be able to discriminate the presence or absence of his own alpha rhythm—as detected by conventional EEG recording techniques. Some individuals proved highly skillful at learning this task—if they were told on a trial-by-trial basis whether their response had been right or wrong.

Kamiya next shifted to a technique which gave the subject continuous information as to whether he was in *alpha* or in *non-alpha*. A tone indicated alpha, no-tone the absence of it—the subject was now in a closed feedback loop. Many individuals, over the course of four to ten training sessions learned to stay in alpha a high proportion of the time.

Perhaps the most salient feature of alpha's attractiveness was its association with characteristic mental states, at least on an individual subject basis. Alpha was frequently described as a condition in which visual imagery was dampened or absent, a state of "blank mind," letting go," or of "relaxation." Another characteristic pertained to *willing*: If a subject tried hard to produce alpha, he was sure not to succeed. The act of striving was inimical to the production of alpha.[4]

2. EMG Feedback Techniques

In our Colorado laboratory, we also became interested in feedback techniques, but instead of pursuing alpha, we turned our attention to electromyographic (EMG) feedback. A main reason for this focus was the evidence from Jacobson's (1938, 1970) progressive relaxation, from behavior therapy, and from autogenic training which indicated the clinical usefulness of muscle relaxation.

Instrumentation. Once the formidable task of developing a high-performance instrument had been accomplished by my associate, Dr. Thomas Budzynski (see Fig. 11.1 for functional diagram), we tested it to see whether EMG feedback worked better than no-feedback or irrelevant feedback in producing deep muscle relaxation. The feedback condition proved clearly superior (Budzynski and Stoyva, 1969).

---

[4] There has been much controversy about the origin of the alpha rhythm. Some have dismissed it as an artifact (Kennedy, 1959; Lippold, 1970). More convincingly, Mulholland (1968) has linked it to the operation of the oculomotor system. But regardless of exactly how it originates, alpha remains of value to those interested in producing the experiential state associated with it.

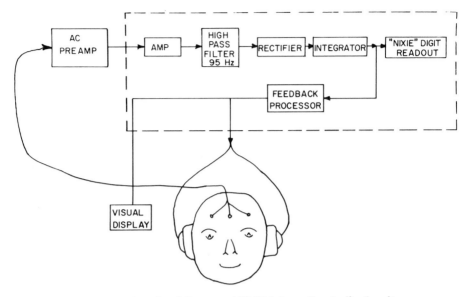

Fig. 11.1. Functional diagram of EMG information feedback unit.

Recently Dr. Budzynski has developed an exceedingly useful and versatile instrumentation system. It can be best thought of as a *biofeedback polygraph*, and it now used routinely with all our experimental subjects. The system has feedback capability for EMG activity, for alpha rhythms (8–12 Hz), and for theta rhythms (4–7 Hz). Additionally, it provides continuous quantification of six physiological parameters on a minute-by-minute basis.

The heart of the system is a constant reset level integrator (also known as a Drohocki integrator or resetting integrator). There is one resetting integrator for each parameter to be quantified, such as theta, forearm EMG, etc. The integrators allow electrical energy to build up to a predetermined point. When this point is reached, a pulse fires, and the integrator resets to zero. Each integrator, therefore, generates a train of digital pulses. These pulses perform three tasks: (1) They provide auditory feedback to the subject—a series of variable-rate clicks which he hears through his headphones (see Fig. 11.1). (2) They provide a moment-to-moment printout on the chart paper—a series of digital pulses is obtained for each parameter (see Fig. 11.2). (3) They drive the quantification apparatus. Each digital pulse adds one increment to the Nixie-tube readout which, essentially, is a device for counting pulses. At the end of every 1-min trial the experimenter notes the accumulated pulse count for each parameter and then resets each Nixie-tube counter back to zero.

The foregoing instrumentation system should prove useful in many areas of psychophysiological research since it not only gives feedback information on several parameters, but also provides precise quantification of measures which generally have been laboriously and often inaccurately handscored, e.g., EMG activity.

Applications. For the past several years, our main research emphasis has been strongly applied. We have been interested in teaching individuals to reach low arousal conditions, and in making clinical use of this ability. In this endeavor, we were greatly encouraged by the work of Jacobson (1938) and by the research on autogenic training (Schultz & Luthe, 1959), both of which attest to the clinically valuable properties of the ability

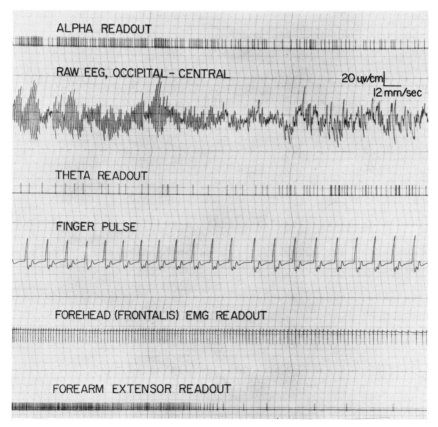

Fig. 11.2. Digital readout and quantification system for EEG and EMG.

to voluntarily reach low arousal levels. The technique of feedback-induced relaxation has been applied to the treatment of tension headache (Budzynski, Stoyva, & Adler, 1970), in the desensitization process in behavior therapy, and in the treatment of several cases of sleep-onset insomnia.

Despite our strongly applied emphasis, however, we have noticed that the subject who shifts to a low arousal condition experiences changes in the nature of his thinking, changes which are difficult to ignore.

As with alpha, the condition of feedback-induced muscle relaxation is associated with an alteration in the quality of thinking, and involves a departure from the thought processes of alert, reality-oriented wakefulness to the imagery and sensations characteristic of the twilight states bordering on sleep. In deep relaxation, sensations of heaviness and warmth are common—probably related to a shift toward parasympathetic dominance in the autonomic nervous system. Distortions or changes of body image are likewise common—feelings of floating, of turning, of a limb moving, or disappearing. Vivid visual images, often of a hallucinatory intensity, frequently appear. These images occur spontaneously, and seem related to "nonstriving mode of experiencing" in which the subject finds himself.

B. Some Principles and Properties of Biofeedback Training

Although the area is still new, certain principles and continuities in biofeedback research seem regular enough to be worth noting, and will probably figure prominently in future investigations.

1. The Active–Passive Dimension

As already noted, if the subject strives hard to produce alpha, he fails to attain it. The same observation holds for muscle relaxation. A person who strives hard to relax—and this is especially likely to be the beginner or the anxious patient—finds instead that he is tensing up.

It is necessary for the learner to abandon the "active-willing mode" appropriate to accomplishing tasks in the external world. Instead, if he follows the guidance of the feedback signal, he finds himself shifting to another kind of orientation characterized by a lack of striving, a "letting go" quality.

That this dimension of passive, as opposed to active concentration, has emerged so clearly in biofeedback work is in striking confirmation of independent observations from related disciplines. For example, in Zen literature, a recurring theme (and one puzzling to Westerners) is that the best way to attain satori, or a state of enlightenment, is to stop trying to reach it. Similarly, in autogenic training (Schultz & Luthe, 1959), great emphasis is placed on the cultivation of "passive concentration" as opposed to "active concentration." A related emphasis may be found in Jacobson's progressive relaxation (1938, 1970).

2. Testing Hypotheses of Association

Biofeedback techniques can be useful in demonstrating an association between a physiological event and an experiential one, and in determining whether the association is strong or weak. Specifically, are the two events closely enough linked so that changing one member of the paired events produces a simultaneous change in the other member? For example, if we wish to show that the 4–7 Hz theta rhythm and the experience of drowsiness are related, then the subject can be provided with feedback of his theta rhythms. When he succeeds in producing more extended periods of theta, he should report more extended periods of drowsiness.

Certain other events occurring during drowsiness could be expected to show an association of a weaker nature, e.g., the slow rolling eye movements which occur during sleep onset (see Foulkes, 1966). If a subject voluntarily produces slow rolling eye movements, would it make him drowsy? Probably not. In any case, the question would be open to empirical test.

If the linkage between the physiological event and the experiential event is tight, then the approach should be reversible. Thus, a subject could deliberately attempt to make himself drowsy without the aid of external feedback. If he succeeded, we would expect that the more drowsy he became, the more theta would be in evidence.

This reversed technique would not involve the use of an external feedback loop. Its efficacy would, however, hinge on the ability of the subject to detect internal sensations associated with the response he wishes to control, for example, the sensations of drowsiness associated with theta. Even though external feedback would not be present, the subject would be receiving self-generated internal feedback, or "proprioceptive cues"— which are crucial in maintaining the feedback-acquired response after termination of training.

3. Biofeedback Training and Introspection

Can biofeedback training sharpen an individual's ability at introspection? It probably can, at least in some respects (see Stoyva & Kamiya, 1968). For example, if we provide a subject with alpha feedback, he can learn to identify those private events associated with "tone on," for example, a feeling of letting go, a dampening or absence of visual imagery, or relaxation. We could also train him to identify the sensations accompanying the theta rhythm, the beta rhythm, muscle tensing, or muscle relaxing. After a subject had been taught to perceive accurately one or several kinds of internal events, perhaps this enhanced ability would transfer readily to other kinds of internal events.

With the advent of the feedback technology, this speculation can now be framed as a testable proposition. For example, if we first trained subjects to detect the presence of their own alpha rhythms, would they subsequently be better at discriminating the presence or absence of their own theta rhythms than if they had not been given any previous training in alpha?

A relevant observation is provided by Kamiya (1969), who suggests that practiced meditators—people with ample experience in attending to internal cues—are likely to be skilled at acquiring feedback control of alpha. Similarly, we might expect actors and poets, in view of their training and inclinations, to be abler than most at detecting internal events.

As Ferster (1963, p. 335) has maintained, probably the fundamental reason we are poor at discriminating private events is that the reinforcement contingencies for such events are extremely variable. Out of the shifting flood of internal cues, we do not know which are the right ones, for example, those associated with the production of alpha as opposed to those associated with theta. In many instances, biofeedback techniques should be able to tell us which are the correct cues.

Another question concerning introspective ability is whether such a skill is associated with certain personality characteristics. Are some people better than others either at detecting internal events or at learning to control them? For example, are introverts better at perceiving private events than are extraverts? On the basis of Jung's writings, we would expect this to be the case.

A dissertation project, conducted in our laboratory by Mr. Irwin Matus, is addressed to this and related questions. Subjects are initially assessed on introversion–extraversion scores by Eysenck's Maudsley Personality Inventory and Cattell's 16 PF test, on Witkin's rod-and-frame test of field-dependence versus field-independence, and on their ability to estimate varying levels of muscle tension within themselves. Muscle tension is measured by our EMG quantification equipment. The experiment, still in progress, falls into four phases: (1) Personality assessment, (2) subject's ability to estimate muscle tension levels prior to training, (3) subject's ability to learn the muscle relaxation task with EMG feedback training, and (4) subject's ability to estimate his muscle tension levels after training.

An interesting relationship which has emerged is that accuracy on the Witkin test and accuracy at estimating levels of forearm muscle tension are significantly associated ($r = +.43$, $p < .05$). Subjects who are good at the Witkin test are said to be those who rely on internal bodily cues in estimating the luminous rod's departure from the true vertical; these same subjects might also be expected to be skilled at estimating the cues associated with muscle tension.

4. Biofeedback Training and Alterations in Thought Processes

Practically since their inception, there has been speculation that bio-feedback techniques could be useful in altering thought processes. This seems often to be the case, although a great deal remains to be learned.

Feedback training in alpha and in muscle relaxation generally result in a shift away from the thinking of ordinary wakefulness—the subject is more immersed in his internal world, feels relaxed, is in a nonstriving, letting go mode. During muscle relaxation, a number of bodily sensations may be experienced—heaviness, warmth, drowsiness, hovering. When profound relaxation occurs, thought processes shift from action and decision-oriented thinking to a fleeting, visual imagery over which the individual has diminishing voluntary control as he drifts off to sleep.

Also occurring under low arousal conditions is the 4–7 Hz theta rhythm. This rhythm occurs just prior to the onset of Stage 2 spindling sleep, and is associated with drowsiness and, we believe, with muscle relaxation. It is also associated with imagery, mostly visual in nature. The imagery is of an involuntary, emergent type—if the subject tries to produce it, he fails; rather, he must let it happen.

Foulkes (1966) has likened hypnagogic or sleep-onset imagery to a series of disconnected photographic "stills," which is also an apt description for much of theta imagery. Frequently, though, theta images are vivid enough to acquire an hallucinatory intensity, i.e., they seem real. In these instances, the imagery can be better likened to a succession of unrelated film clips, each clip focused on a single scene. Some examples: A handful of old coins sliding off a green velvet cloth; a garden implement; a ship being launched; a stooped figure in a dark overcoat hurrying down a country road; a forest meadow with a freshly dug grave in the middle of it—overhead, a V-formation of geese flying south; someone jumping over a little freshet of water caused by the sudden melting of snow.

The group which has worked most extensively with theta feedback has been Green, Green, and Walters (1970) at the Menninger Foundation. They, too, find that theta is associated with vivid imagery. A major interest of this group is to explore the role of hypnagogic reverie in creativity.

C. SOME BIOFEEDBACK EXPERIMENTS

An attractive feature of theta training is that, at least for many individuals, it offers a means of putting the subject into a condition in which he will experience imagery of hallucinatory intensity. There is a major practical problem, however. When a subject is in theta he seems dissociated from his surroundings, and we are still uncertain whether a subject in this condition will continue to pay any attention to the feedback signal—although this may be a skill which improves with practice.

A matter of first importance is how best to teach subjects to produce theta. One approach is to begin immediately with theta feedback. However, it may be better to conduct the training in two phases—an initial phase of muscle relaxation training, followed by a second phase in which training is shifted to direct feedback of theta. The aim of this second approach is to break the training into two easier-to-master stages. Learning to produce theta is a subtle task; and the base operant level of the rhythm is generally low—often too low to generate a usable feedback signal. But a condition of muscle relaxation is associated with an increase in theta EEG frequencies. Thus, if the subject first attains a deeply relaxed condition as a prelude to theta training, he will have something to work with when he later begins the task of acquiring feedback control of theta. Experiments to test this two-step training are currently being conducted in our laboratory as part of the doctoral dissertation by Miss Pola Sittenfeld.

The foregoing two-phase technique could be considered part of a more general approach aimed at the shaping of low arousal conditions (suggested by Dr. Budzynski). Thus, beginning his training from a point of alert wakefulness, the subject would be gradually led in the direction of sleep. Over several sessions, he would first train in the production of alpha, next in producing mixed alpha and theta frequencies, then in the production of theta frequencies. Later in his training the subject would attempt to produce a particular low arousal condition in the absence of any feedback. An objective criterion for his ability to attain a given low arousal condition could be assessed electroencephalographically, e.g., how readily is he able to produce theta, and how does his performance compare with that of untrained subjects?

Another facet of the research would involve sampling the mental activity associated with alpha, with mixed alpha and theta rhythms, and with theta frequencies. The data would be examined for regularities across subjects. Within-subject regularities would also be investigated since Foulkes (1966) has stated that individual differences are a prominent feature of sleep-onset imagery.

It seems likely that feedback techniques could be profitably employed to increase imagery retrieval from twilight states. Ordinarily, when a subject is roused from a sleep-onset condition and asked to report his thoughts, he frequently finds it difficult to return to a drowsy state. Feedback training, especially in muscle relaxation and in producing theta, can assist the subject in knowing what he must do to return to the drowsy condition in which imagery is likely to occur.

Subjects can also be allowed to signal when they are experiencing imagery, for example, by using a finger switch. By this means, we have found that subjects will press the "imagery switch" 8–12 times in the course of a 20-min session of theta training (although these subjects were not asked to report any details until after the end of the session).

A useful technique for increasing hypnagogic recall has been described by Tart (1969). The subject lies on his back, but keeps one arm in a vertical position, balanced on the elbow. As the subject drifts into sleep, muscle tonus drops, and his arm falls. This awakens him, thereby allowing him to take note of whatever imagery or thinking was in progress. A refinement of this technique has been developed by Green *et al.* (1970) who use a tilt detector consisting of a mercury switch finger ring. Whenever a subjects' hand deviates from the vertical, the mercury switch circuit closes and a chime is sounded.

With theta training it seems likely that we could produce some different-from-normal conditions. For example, we could explore the experiential consequences of hovering for extended periods in the theta zone. Under everyday circumstances, such as falling asleep, we drop through our sleep-onset phase in a matter of seconds or a few minutes. What if subjects were kept in theta for a long period of time, for example, 30–50 min? Perhaps the imagery would reveal new properties, for example, become more intense or more dreamlike. A possible means of keeping someone in theta for extended periods would be to provide him with a feedback signal whenever he began drifting out of the theta band. Give him a high-pitched tone if he slipped in the direction of sleep, a low-pitched tone if he moved toward normal wakefulness.

II. BETWEEN SLEEP AND WAKEFULNESS

Biofeedback training in alpha control and particularly in muscle relaxation have a quieting effect on the individual; they lower his arousal level and nudge him into a condition close to sleep. This borderland between wakefulness and sleep seems to be especially propitious for evoking alterations in consciousness—an observation which deserves more attention than has so far been bestowed on it in the Anglo-American literature. For example, in hypnotic induction there is much emphasis on relaxation, on quieting oneself, on listening only to the hypnotist's voice. And, as Gill and Brenman (1961, pp. 57–58) have emphasized:

> . . . we see a significant departure from normal, *waking* modes of thought: instead of relatively stable, logical kind of thought—which for the most part employs words as its material—we see the emergence of fluid, archaic forms which often employ visual images and symbols as material, forms which do not follow the ordinary rules of logic, and which moreover are not bound to realistic limitations of time and space.

In autogenic training, a technique which has been extensively used in treating stress-related disorders, emphasis is placed on attaining the "autogenic shift" or *Umschaltung*—a condition for which passive concentration is held to be absolutely essential. In its physiological aspects, this condition involves a shift to parasympathetic predominance in the autonomic nervous system—as evidenced by muscle relaxation, slowed heart rate and respiration, increased skin temperature. Experientially, sensations of flowing warmth are often reported, as is a light quality in the visual field (eyes are closed). Luthe (1965) and others, however, point out that the autogenic shift is not characterized by drowsiness.

Koestler (1964), in his stimulating book, emphasizes that reverie states (which probably occur in the border zone between waking and sleep) figure prominently in literature about creative thinking. For example, Kekulé's conception of the benzene ring originated in a drowsy, reverie state—it was a warm summer's evening, and the famous chemist dozed as his omnibus made its way through the streets of London. The German psychiatrist, Kretschmer (quoted in Koestler, 1964, p. 325), has emphasized that:

> . . . creative products of the artistic imagination tend to emerge from a psychic twilight, a state of lessened consciousness and diminished attentivity to external stimuli. Further, the condition is one of "absent-mindedness" with hypnoidal overconcentration on a single focus, providing an entirely passive experience, frequently of a visual character, divorced from the categories of space and time, and reason and will.

A. HYPNAGOGIC IMAGERY

A valuable contribution of recent sleep research has been the finding that hypnagogic or sleep-onset experiences are surprisingly common. In fact, they are an everyday occurrence. Generally, though, we fail to notice them, or forget them.

Some of the earliest research on hypnagogic imagery was conducted by Silberer (1951) shortly after the turn of the century. He described his approach as a "Method of evoking and observing certain symbolic hallucinatory phenomena." Silberer, a German philosopher, could not have been lacking in old-fashioned will-power, for he would force himself to try to solve problems while in a drowsy condition. Then he would rouse himself and note the images which had slipped into consciousness. Silberer maintained that in this drowsy condition there is a transformation in the thought process—from mental activity of an intellectual character to thinking of a visual, symbolic type. Drawing from his self-observations, Silberer (1951, p. 202–204) provided many instances of this transformation.

> Example 1. My thought is: I am to improve a halting passage in an essay.
> Symbol: I see myself planing a piece of wood.
> Example 7. In opposition to the Kantian view, I am attempting to conceive of time as a "concept."
> Symbol: I am pressing a Jack-in-the-Box into the box. But every time I take my hand away it bounces out gaily on its spiral spring.[5]

Contemporary electrophysiological studies of sleep-onset by Foulkes, Rechtschaffen, and their associates have established that sleep-onset imagery, like dreaming, is an everyday occurrence. Thus, Foulkes and Vogel (1965) found that when their subjects were "awakened" close to sleep-onset they recalled some specific mental experience over 90% of the time.

Pilot research by these investigators had suggested that there was an orderly sequence of different types of mental activity with progressive stages of sleep-onset—fragmentary visual material passed into more extended and self-involved "dreamlets" as the EEG shifted from alpha rhythm to spindling sleep. This hint was confirmed in a detailed study of hypnagogic imagery (Foulkes & Vogel, 1965) in which subjects were awakened from each of four sleep-onset EEG patterns: (1) Alpha EEG with rapid eye movements (REMs), (2) alpha rhythm with slow rolling eye movements (SEMs), (3) descending stage 1 sleep (predominance of theta rhythms), and (4) descending Stage 2 sleep (13–16 Hz spindle bursts prominent). As a group, the subjects showed a clear progression

---

[5] Later investigators have generally failed to find such a continuity between problem-oriented thinking and the hypnagogic imagery immediately succeeding it. This continuity may have resulted from the unusual nature of Silberer's approach, in which he forced himself to solve problems while in a drowsy condition rather than permitting himself a free flow of imagery.

toward increasingly hallucinatory material as they drifted toward sleep. Distribution of hallucinatory dreamlike experiences was as follows:

Alpha REM reports	29%
Alpha SEM reports	47%
Descending Stage 1 reports	74%
Descending Stage 2 reports	80%

Recent research suggests that this sleep-onset zone may provide clues as to the necessary conditions for dreaming. A vexatious observation in sleep research has been the finding that dreams are not confined to REM sleep, but are sometimes reported from non-REM sleep as well (see Foulkes, 1966). Why? An experiment by Zimmerman (1970) may help provide an answer. In this study there were two extreme groups—a *light sleeper group*, subjects easily awakened by an auditory signal; and a *deep sleeper group*, subjects who needed much more intense auditory stimulation to wake up. When awakened from non-REM sleep, the light sleeper group showed a far higher incidence of dreamlike recall than did their opposite numbers (71% compared to 21%). Subjects in the light sleeper group were also more aroused physiologically as measured by heart rate, respiration, body temperature levels, spontaneous awakenings, and gross body movements while asleep (Zimmerman, 1967).

Zimmerman's conclusion was that a moderate level of physiological arousal may be necessary in order for dreaming to occur. Consequently, dreamlike experiences could be expected to occur both at sleep-onset and during those epochs of non-REM sleep in which a moderate level of physiological arousal is present. Support for this position comes from an intriguing study by Hersch *et al.* (1970) in which arousal level during non-REM sleep was deliberately increased by chemical means. Catheterized subjects, serving as their own controls, were given intravenous norepinephrine injections during non-REM sleep. An equal number of saline control injections were made, also during non-REM sleep. Awakenings after the norepinephrine injections yielded a significantly greater proportion of dreamlike reports—as assessed by degree of emotionality, type of imagery, etc.

III. ON THE CONDITIONS FOR HALLUCINATORY ACTIVITY

West's theory. Why should imagery and hallucinations blossom so readily in this twilight terrain between waking and sleep? A theory addressed to this question has been advanced by West (1962). He begins with the observation that in a variety of altered states of consciousness—hypnosis, hypnagogic imagery, dreaming, Zen and Yoga meditation, sensory isolation experiences—certain common conditions are present. West postulates that a major predisposing condition for hallucinatory activity is a reduction in the level or variety of external sensory input to the brain. As the sensory isolation literature in particular has emphasized (Bexton, Heron, & Scott, 1954), ordinary levels of sensory input exercise an organizing and inhibiting effect on consciousness. When sensory input is substantially reduced or made extremely monotonous, it loses its customary organizing effect on the processes of consciousness.

A second requirement for the evocation of hallucinatory activity is the maintenance of an arousal level sufficient to permit awareness. West characterizes this condition as one of "residual awareness." Self-awareness is still present; there is some appreciation of one's own thoughts, feelings, and sensations, but there is a disengagement from one's surroundings— the reality moorings have been severed. Though hard to define operationally, residual awareness is associated with the conditions pertaining to sleep onset, rather than with the comparatively high arousal of active wakefulness or with the low arousal and minimal mental activity of Stage 3 and Stage 4 sleep.

The basic tenet of the theory is that a reduction or impairment of sensory input together with an arousal level sufficient to permit residual awareness is a condition likely to produce hallucinatory experiences. According to West (1968, p. 268) ". . . when the usual information input level no longer suffices completely to inhibit their emergence, the perceptual traces may be 'released' and reexperienced in familiar or new combinations." [6]

Similar conclusions were reached by Zimmerman (1970) with respect to when the experience of dreaming is likely to occur. As already mentioned, Zimmerman maintains that what is essential for the experience we call dreaming is not the presence of REM sleep, but a given (moderate) level of arousal in the absence of reality contact. Thus, dreaming could be expected to occur in non-REM sleep if arousal level were sufficiently high—a hypothesis confirmed by the abovementioned experiment of Hersch *et al.* (1970).

Some additions to West's theory. We believe that West's theory underscores some major determinants of naturally occurring hallucinatory experiences, i.e., those hallucinations which can be made to occur without

---

[6] Whether the basic mechanism is an active release process as West maintains, or simply a passive slowing down, is difficult to test at this point. So the question will be left open.

drugs or surgical intervention. We also believe that on the basis of recent work, particularly in the biofeedback area, the theory can be made more specific and given greater explanatory power in terms of generating testable propositions. In our opinion, the following additional postulates serve to define further those proposed by West:

1. In the production of hallucinatory experiences it is important to reduce not only external sensory input but to reduce internal or proprioceptive input as well. As mentioned earlier, we have found muscular relaxation, with its accompanying reduction of CNS input (see Gellhorn, 1964), conducive to the evocation of hypnagogic material.

It will be remembered that relaxation of the musculature also plays an important role in autogenic training, and in the induction of hypnosis. Conversely, tensing up the musculature acts to eliminate a low arousal condition and the associated alterations in consciousness. For example, a person may tense his muscles to keep from dozing off in a lecture.

2. A second additional postulate is that the ability to shift to a condition of "passive volition" is critical for the attainment of those twilight states in which imagery and hallucinatory activity are likely to occur. This passive volition characteristic, as Green *et al.* (1970) have termed it, has been noted in several types of biofeedback training, e.g., in work with alpha, theta, and EMG activity. In autogenic training it has been termed passive concentration. As Deikman (1971) has recently emphasized, this ability is required for what he terms the "receptive mode of consciousness"—a mode he regards as essential to the attainment of contemplative states.[7]

3. Also important in the induction of twilight states is a change in autonomic function, a shift from sympathetic predominance to one of parasympathetic predominance. Gellhorn (1964) maintains that the mechanism of this shift is a resetting of hypothalamic balance. A reduction in proprioceptive input, as produced by muscular relaxation, causes hypothalamic balance to change to a parasympathetic pattern.

---

[7] Deikman conceives of two fundamental ways in which waking consciousness operates, (a) an "active" mode—the striving, adaptive, goal-oriented, consciousness of everyday life, and (b) a "receptive" mode, characterized by a lack of striving, a "letting go," calmness, and a quiet receptiveness. This receptive mode has been little emphasized in Western cultures, and most people seem only vaguely aware of it. But writings of the Eastern mystical disciplines suggest that the receptive mode of consciousness could be cultivated and made voluntarily accessible to those willing to do the training.

Whether the condition of passive volition is required for *all* biofeedback learning, or only for acquiring feedback control over those responses characteristic of low arousal (e.g., alpha, theta, muscle relaxation), is not yet known.

As the subject moves from alert wakefulness toward sleep, respiration and heart rate decline, skin temperature increases, muscle tension diminishes, and EEG patterns display a change toward slower frequencies. This physiological shift seems to be intimately linked with the altered quality of thinking which occurs in the twilight or sleep-onset state, a point emphasized in the autogenic training literature (Schultz & Luthe, 1959; Stokvis & Wiesenhütter, 1961).

A related point is that the magnitude of the physiological shift seems important. That is to say, the changes in consciousness are greater if a subject goes from high arousal to low arousal than if he merely goes from a moderate level of arousal to a low arousal condition. Why this should be, we are uncertain. Perhaps it is a contrast effect; or possibly there is a greater build-up of some active inhibitory or disinhibitory neural process if the change in arousal level is great; perhaps a large shift generates more internal stimuli. Lest too much stress be put on this observation, its preliminary nature should be emphasized—however, it should be readily open to empirical test.

Also worth noting is that the shift to parasympathetic predominance seems also to be associated with both a change in affect, and a broadening of the range of consciousness. As Koestler (1964) has perceptively remarked, sympathetic predominance is linked to emotions in which the range of awareness is restricted—anger and fear, for example. Parasympathetic functioning he states is associated with subtler emotions— wonder, religious and esthetic experiences, contemplation—emotions characterized by a broader range of awareness.

IV. SUMMARY OF ARGUMENT

The events of consciousness can be scientifically studied to the extent that we are able to make testable inferences about them. One area which has made use of testable inferences about consciousness is contemporary dream research. The basic approach has involved the *combined* use of physiological measures and verbal report—as, for example, in the research which has explored mental activity during the various phases of sleep.

It is argued here that the combined use of verbal report and physiological measures can be profitably extended to the study of certain waking mental activity as well—particularly with the addition of the information feedback principle, which adds a new dimension to the basic methodology. The emerging technique of feedback psychophysiology can be valuable both in exploring mental activity and in teaching individuals to produce some psychological states at will.

Biofeedback techniques have been useful in producing the low arousal state bordering on sleep. In this low arousal state there are characteristic changes in the nature of the thought process—reality-oriented thinking is supplanted by imagery, often of an hallucinatory intensity.

It is argued that the conditions conducive to such low arousal, sleep-onset experiences have broader implications in helping to specify the circumstances under which naturally occurring hallucinatory experiences are likely to arise (phenomena such as dreams, hypnagogic imagery, the hallucinations of hypnosis, and sensory isolation). The major predisposing conditions are (1) a reduction in sensory input, to the brain—both external and internal (proprioceptive) input are important, (2) a shift to a non-striving, passive volitional mode of consciousness, (3) a shift to a low arousal condition characterized by a predominately parasympathetic response pattern in the autonomic nervous system.

The Discussion of Dr. Stoyva's Paper

LED BY DR. ABE BLACK
McMaster University

Black: Whenever I finish a talk and a discussant gets up on the stage, and I start to hear many compliments, I become very anxious and my heart sinks because, as we all know, "more compliments at the beginning, more criticisms at the end." So I am going to inhibit myself from talking too much about the contributions and the excellence of Dr. Stoyva's talk in order to prevent him from becoming anxious except to say that I am sure that all of you found it as interesting as I did. The demonstration of the control that one can achieve by operantly conditioning EMG, and of the effects of such control on related internal states is truly impressive.

Some additional comments: On the problem mentioned by Dr. Stoyva of whether we should call this operant conditioning or biofeedback, I am embarrassed to talk about this as the name isn't very important—except that, in this case, it may be useful in that it will help direct research in a productive way.

Let me begin by talking about what we do in operant conditioning. I will focus on the response and on stimulus events that are made contingent on the response. There are two dimensions of the stimulus event that one can look at. One is an "information about response state" dimension. Suppose I am interested in the response of lifting and lowering an arm. I could hook up a tone, such that the intensity or the pitch of the tone would increase if my arm went up, and decrease if it went down. Such information about the response is information that is added to that provided by proprioceptive feedback.

Now, the second dimension that operant conditioners talk about is something like "payoff"; the stimulus that follows the response, in operant conditioning situations, is a valuable one. It may be food for a hungry organism, or avoidance of shock. These two dimensions are represented in Fig. 11.3.

What particular set of points, in this two-dimensional space, produces learning? What is it that increases the probability of the response? Suppose you eliminate all the payoff and just work on the baseline, i.e., just provide information about response state. That will not work with an animal for most types of stimuli that we use.

In our research, for example, you can produce a click each time a theta wave occurs; the dog sits there for 24 days, and the probability of theta waves will not change any more that it would have, had you left the click out. Therefore, in operant conditioning situations, moving along the horizontal (information) dimension alone is not sufficient for learning. On the other hand, if you are working on the vertical dimension, where

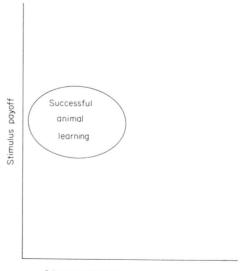

Fig. 11.3. Two functions of stimuli contingent on responses plotted in a two-dimensional space. Animal learning does not require much positive distance on the horizontal axis.

you have an effective payoff (there is food as well as a click), then the dog learns. Somehow this notion of payoff is essential for the reinforcement. What happens when you are reinforcing EEG potentials in humans? Dr. Stoyva feels that since we really don't know what the reinforcement could be, we ought to use the term biofeedback, which emphasizes the information dimension. I disagree with that. Instead of trying to avoid the problem, you should find out where you are in this two-dimensional space—what are the payoffs in these human situations? Is simply achieving success in the situation in itself reinforcing for a human? Is it cooperating with the experimenter, as Orne has suggested? Changing the name to biofeedback turns us away from a really important problem. If you need payoff, then it would be a shame to ignore that dimension in the control of behavior.

The second question concerns the states associated with the reinforced (biofeedback) event—the theta wave, or the alpha wave, or whatever. As Dr. Rechtschaffen very clearly demonstrated on Monday, studying the relationship between EEG patterns and various types of behavioral indices is really a very difficult task—it requires a lot of careful, analytic experiments. So the question for Dr. Stoyva is this: How far have we gone along that road? Consider the alpha wave and its relation to serene, relaxed, meditative states; it seems to me that in the last year or two there has been much less certainty about that relationship than before.

I hope Dr. Stoyva will comment on those two issues.

Open Discussion

Stoyva: Dr. Black has raised some very important questions, indicating the need for some primary studies, e.g., testing out various kinds of feedback, or simultaneously studying various bodily systems while a given muscle group is getting feedback. On the question of the nature of reinforcement, there is little systematic work—among the subjects' motives in these experiments is a desire to do well and to develop a feeling of mastery.

As to the question of which physiological and experiential parameters go together, and which can be pulled apart, we know little. When subjects get into this low arousal condition, as indicated by muscle amplitude, there is also evidence of a slowing of autonomic functions.

Our initial orientation was a fairly strongly applied one. We said, "Let's induce muscle relaxation in our behavior therapy for tension headaches," so we haven't done very much with the questions that Dr. Black raised. Regarding one of his questions, Barbara Brown reported about a year ago that theta is associated with problem-solving activity. This is apparently the only report that associates theta with problem-solving. Perhaps there was something special in the conditions of Brown's experiment, e.g., her subjects were students close to examinations, or the problem was especially presented to them as an intellectual task, i.e., the subject learned to turn on three different lights by various brain waves. You might have a red light for alpha, a blue light for theta frequencies, and a green one for the higher beta frequencies. The task was to identify what was happening when your EEG turned on each of the different colors, and this made it seem like rather an intellectual task.

Dr. Thomas Mulholland (VA Hospital, Bedford, Massachusetts): Most of the criticism of the biofeedback studies has been directed against the alpha studies, whereas muscle feedback work is on much better footing.

Regarding this complication of the reinforcement during the alpha training, we found that a subject can go through a couple of stages. We had a man (somewhat obsessive–compulsive) who was hardworking and who was a survivor of open-heart surgery. When he went back to his job, which was heading up his own law firm, the old tensions of the job built up. Could we teach him how to relax? We said we didn't know, but he could try as part of an experimental program. Now here is an intelligent man, educated, and he knows that psychologists are out to fool you and to play tricks on you. In the first part of alpha training he was able to produce lots of tones right away, but reported: "I can't see any difference between when the tone is on and off." We explored this, and it came out to mean, "I know that you guys are trying to trick me into giving a tone without any alpha, and you are not going to fool me." After we worked with theta for about 2 weeks, and got to know each other, he described his alpha state as a pleasant relaxing hour—he was able to reproduce mainly alpha and be relaxed. But by the third or fourth week, his life-style began to enter into the experiment, so that he became dissatisfied with his achievement of getting the tone on about 60% of the time, and he wished to do more. Now this man happened to have a lot more alpha on one side than the other, so when we hooked the tone onto the side which produced lots of alpha, he had a relaxing hour; but when we connected the tone to the other side, he would recognize that he was getting quite a bit less tone, yet his over-all alpha was about the same. He reported that this was bad, and by the end of the fifth week in this situation, he decided that he had gotten what he could out of it, and that was that.

Now I didn't present this to illustrate how we go about relaxation training, because we obviously failed. I want to bring out the problem of the interaction between the meaning of the tone for the subject and the information feedback, since the tone conveys both.

Dr. Richard Jennings (Walter Reed): Regarding the reinforcement question, and the relevance of monetary reward, there may be something akin to escape learning, i.e., nonalpha is unpleasant and alpha is pleasant; or, even more clearly in EMG work, tension headaches are obviously unpleasant, and during the training a pleasant state is achieved.

Stoyva: We did not use monetary reward with people who had tension headaches, feeling that their motivation would be to get rid of the headaches.

Mulholland: The reinforcement for students who try alpha training is that they always report it as fun to turn it on or turn it off. The problem is that the reinforcement of getting control is confounded with the information feedback. That is the issue.

Stoyva: Perhaps we could get some leverage on that by using subjects who produce large amounts of alpha, vs others who produce less, and then getting both to a high degree of control with a great sense of mastery.

Black: The problem of confounding of those two dimensions is much more difficult for humans than for animals; so it's easy for those of us who work on infrahumans to moralize.

Audience: Regarding theta conditioning and problem-solving, there are a fair number of anecdotal and introspective reports about creative problem-solving during these hypnagogic states. There has been some suggestion that theta conditioning might facilitate problem-solving.

Stoyva: I think one question we can work on is the empirical one of whether subjects can, in fact, acquire some degree of voluntary control over theta learning. Actually, this is rather elusive; when most people are showing theta, they are in a kind of disconnected state. When Foulkes's subjects were falling asleep, they became disconnected from the external reality of the place they were in, and they tended to stop paying attention to the experiment.

Audience: In one study, the feedback tone was used to get the subject out of the theta state, so that he could immediately report on what was experienced during the theta state.

Stoyva: Yes. A device was used in that case, whereby a switch closed when the subject began to fall asleep, and a signal woke them up. Then they would report on the imagery.

Dr. Fritz Klein (Duke University): Could you briefly indicate the electrode preparation and frequency settings used in your experiment? If you are trying to record EMG's from the frontalis, wouldn't you also be picking up a lot of EEG there also?

Stoyva: Yes, there are technical problems there. Originally, we used a band-pass of about 30–100 Hz; but we changed that to 95–1000 Hz when we found EEG signals creeping in on the recordings. The EEG frequencies are, of course, fairly easily eliminated. Surprisingly, though, there is a problem of the heart rate getting into the signal at times. Even though the heart rate is a slow signal, it has components with a very sharp rise time.

After training, our subjects typically got down to about 2 or 3 μV signals, mean levels peak-to-peak, on the frontalis. Our amplification was around 1×10^6. The electrodes were placed 4 in. apart, 1 in. over the eyebrows. Rather than an abrading drill, as Dr. Hefferline used, we employed an abrasive cream, which removed some of the epidermis and assured good contacts for the electrodes.

Dr. Richard Carney (Eastern Kentucky University): Would you comment on the relative effectiveness of the feedback techniques, and alternate techniques, in producing the outcome that you got? You mentioned controls, and I am not quite sure what kind of relaxation techniques were used with these controls.

Stoyva: In the experimental studies, characteristically, we gave the subjects written instructions; the experimentals received the feedback—a continuous, monotonous, low tone—and the controls were merely instructed to relax, without the contingent feedback. We would like to develop a system that combines feedback-induced muscle relaxation training with Dr. Jacobson's approaches. It is important to give the subject cues that will later help him recapture the condition of relaxation. Sensations of heaviness and warmth, for example, are very useful. Feedback can aid in a person reinstating those internal cues, and consequently the relaxed state.

Dr. Larry Thompson (Duke University): I have a question about that very issue. Very early in this type of training, subjects report using all sorts of imageries and fantasies to help them modify physiological states to conform to whatever the experimenter wants, whether it is an increased heart rate, decreased heart rate, changes in vasomotor reactivity, etc. As training goes on, the use of these aids drops out, and they seem to be able to slip very quickly into the states on command from the experimenter. Apparently this is fairly reliable. Do you have any comments about how this comes about? I have heard this compared to the development of a motor skill, that is, intially attention to the imagery is very important, but with practice it becomes unnecessary.

Stoyva: Let me say two things: First, I think these associated cues or images may vary quite a lot from person to person, and they would probably vary with the parameter on which you are trying to feedback train. Secondly, we have found it important to have the subject practice relaxation at home without feedback. With declining frequency of headaches, it seemed as if these tension headache subjects were going through stages in their control over the muscle relaxation response. In the first phase of training, some reported they were becoming more sensitive to the headaches. There was a second phase in which the subjects became aware of the muscle tension cues, and then would lie down to relax—a very deliberate response. Finally, many got to a stage where the rising tension cue was able to initiate relaxation on the part of the subject, sometimes automatically, or without awareness.

Black: The point you made that this goes on in motor learning is an important one—this narrowing down of the response into a more efficient one is seen in practically every type of operant conditioning.

Dr. Allan Rechtschaffen (University of Chicago): The real appeal of this technique is that people can direct their attention by means of mediating operants that we don't ordinarily consider. The appealing thing about biofeedback will not turn out to be in the nature of the reinforcement—that is an age-old question. And I don't feel the signal value of the biofeedback is vital, either. We are using a biological event that is correlated with a feeling state. I can't believe that the electrical signal is a better indication of how we feel than *how we feel.* It is not the pure signal value that is important here; what *is* important is that it points to a mediating state and process of control. Bioelectrical feedback allows the individual to focus on the mediating processes, and lets him perform the mediating operants which will alter a feeling state. Now what the exact nature of those mediating operants is we don't know. But that's what is new about this technique.

Black: Let me just comment on the first part of your point. I wasn't suggesting that biofeedback researchers ought to spend their time on that chase for the essence of reinforcement. One of the things they are interested in is the efficacy of training. My point is that you should think of this in a way that is analogous to training a bar press—you should look at both dimensions, if you are interested in that problem of improving efficiency of training. You can, thus, discover the controlling variables. Also, my worry about the switch in name was because it moved the attention of the researcher away from the reinforcement dimension, which is obviously important for this practical problem.

Stoyva: The feedback enables you to pick out clusters of cues which can be used to later reinstate a particular condition by yourself. This is clinically useful, as in muscle relaxation, and the feedback is useful in telling a person which cues are associated with the relaxation.

REFERENCES

Aserinsky, E., & Kleitman, N. Regularly occurring periods of eye motility and concomitant phenomena during sleep. *Science*, 1953, **118**, 274–284.

Bexton, W. H., Heron, W., & Scott, T. H. Effects of decreased variation in sensory environment. *Canadian Journal of Psychology*, 1954, **8**, 70–76.

Berger, R. J., & Moskowitz, E. Failure to confirm a directional relationship between rapid eye movement and dream imagery. *Psychophysiology*, 1970, **6**, 640–641. (Abstract)

Berger, R. J., & Oswald, I. Eye movements during active and passive dreams. *Science*, 1962, **137**, 601.

Black, A. H. The direct control of neural processes by reward and punishment. *American Scientist*, 1971, **59**, 236–245.

Budzynski, T. H., & Stoyva, J. M. An instrument for producing deep muscle relaxation by means of analog information feedback. *Journal of Applied Behavior Analysis*, 1969, **2**, 231–237.

Budzynski, T. H., Stoyva, J. M., & Adler, C. S. Feedback-induced muscle relaxation: Application to tension headache. *Behavior Theory and Experimental Psychiatry*, 1970, **1**, 205–211.

Deikman, A. J. Bimodal consciousness. *Archives of General Psychiatry*, 1971, **25**, 481–489.

Dement, W., & Kleitman, N. The relation of eye movements during sleep to dream activity: An objective method for the study of dreaming. *Journal of Experimental Psychology*, 1957, **53**, 339–346.

Ferster, C. B. Essentials of a science of behavior. In J. T. Nurnburger, C. B. Ferster, & J. P. Brady (Eds.), *An introduction to the science of human behavior.* New York: Appleton, 1963, Pp. 197–345.

Foulkes, D. *The psychology of sleep.* New York: Scribner, 1966.

Foulkes, D., & Vogel, G. Mental activity at sleep onset. *Journal of Abnormal Psychology*, 1965, **70**, 231–243.

Gellhorn, E. Motion and emotion: The role of proprioception in the physiology and pathology of the emotions. *Psychological Review*, 1964, **71**, 457–472.

Gill, M. M., & Brenman, M. *Hypnosis and related states.* New York: International Universities Press, 1961.

Green, E., Green, A., & Walters, D. Voluntary control of internal states: Psychological and physiological. *Journal of Transpersonal Psychology*, 1970, **1**, 1–26.

Hersch, R. G., Antrobus, J. S., Arkin, A. M., & Singer, J. L. Dreaming as a function of sympathetic arousal. *Psychophysiology*, 1970, **7**, 329–330. (Abstract)

Jacobson, E. *Progressive relaxation.* (2nd ed.) Chicago: Univ. of Chicago Press, 1938.

Jacobson, E. *Modern treatment of tense patients.* Springfield, Illinois: Thomas, 1970.

Kamiya, J. Operant control of the EEG alpha rhythm and some of its reported effects on consciousness. In C. T. Tart (Ed.), *Altered state of consciousness.* New York: Wiley, 1969. Pp. 507–517.

Kennedy, J. L. A possible artifact in electroencephalography. *Psychological Review*, 1959, **66**, 347–352.

Koestler, A. *The act of creation.* New York: Macmillan, 1964.

Lewis, H. B., Goodenough, D. R., Shapiro, A., & Sleser, I. Individual differences in dream recall. *Journal of Abnormal Psychology*, 1966, **71**, 52.

Lippold, O. Origin of the alpha rhythm. *Nature*, 1970, **226**, 616–618.

Luthe, W. (Ed.) *Autogenic training: Correlationes psychosomaticae.* New York: Grune & Stratton, 1965.

Mulholland, T. Feedback electroencephalography. *Activitas Nervosa Superior (Praha),* 1968, **10,** 410–438.

Platt, J. R. Strong inference. *Science,* 1964, **146,** 347–353.

Roffwarg, H. P., Dement, W. C., Muzio, J. N., & Fisher, C. Dream imagery: Relationship to rapid eye movements of sleep. *Archives of General Psychiatry,* 1962, **7,** 235–258.

Schultz, J. H., & Luthe, W. *Autogenic training: A psychophysiological approach in psychotherapy.* New York: Grune & Stratton, 1959.

Silberer, H. Report on a method of eliciting and observing certain symbolic hallucination-phenomena. In D. Rapaport (Ed.), *Organization and pathology of thought.* New York: Columbia Univ. Press, 1951. Pp. 195–207.

Stokvis, E., & Wiesenhütter, E. *Der Mensche in der Entspannung,* (2 Auflage). Stuttgart: Hippokrates Verlag, 1961.

Stoyva, J. M. The public (scientific) study of private events. In E. Hartmann (Ed.), *Sleep and dreaming.* Boston: Little, Brown, 1970. Pp. 353–368. (Republished in T. X. Barber, L. V. DiCara, J. Kamiya, N. E. Miller, D. Shapiro, J. Stoyva (Eds.), *Biofeedback and self-control, 1970; An Aldine annual on the regulation of bodily processes and consciousness.* Chicago: Aldine Publishing Co., 1971.)

Stoyva, J. M., & Kamiya, J. Electrophysiological studies of dreaming as the prototype of a new strategy in the study of consciousness. *Psychological Review,* 1968, **75,** 192–205.

Tart, C. T. (Ed.) *Altered states of consciousness.* New York: Wiley, 1969.

West, L. J. A general theory of hallucinations and dreams. In L. J. West (Ed.), *Hallucinations.* New York: Grune & Stratton, 1962. Pp. 275–291.

West, L. J. Hallucinations. In J. G. Howells (Ed.), *Modern perspectives in world psychiatry.* Edinburgh: Oliver & Boyd, 1968. Pp. 265–287.

Zimmerman, W. B. Psychological and physiological differences between "light" and "deep" sleepers. Unpublished doctoral dissertation, University of Chicago, 1967.

Zimmerman, W. B. Sleep mentation and auditory awakening thresholds. *Psychophysiology,* 1970, 1970, **6,** 540–549.

INTEGRATIVE APPROACHES

CHAPTER TWELVE

Central Processes Controlling Speech Production during Sleep and Waking

PETER F. MacNEILAGE

and

LINDA A. MacNEILAGE

University of Texas at Austin

This paper is primarily concerned with questions raised by Lashley in 1951 in his classic paper "The Problem of Serial Order in Behavior." Central to the paper was the claim that "language presents in the most striking form the integrative functions that are characteristic of the cerebral cortex and that reach their highest development in human thought

417

ʃʃprocesses." The purpose of this paper is to attempt to characterize some aspects of the central integrative processes underlying speech production both in the waking and the sleeping states, beginning with the waking state.

I. LASHLEY'S VIEWS ON SERIAL ORDER IN BEHAVIOR

The problem of serial order as posed by Lashley was by what mechanisms do we produce smooth temporally ordered sequences of action? Lashley considered this problem to be the most important and the most neglected problem in cerebral physiology. One of the principal theses of part of this paper devoted to waking speech is that Lashley showed a remarkable prescience in formulating hypotheses applicable to the speech production process in particular, hypotheses which remain most appropriate in the light of present knowledge.

Lashley pointed out that "not only speech but all skilled acts seem to involve the same problems of serial ordering even down to the temporal coordination of muscular contraction in such a movement as reaching and grasping." However, the most outstanding thing about language to Lashley was that it was so obvious that it consisted of predetermined (planned or rule-governed) *sequences* of action. And although Lashley did not comment on this directly, the reason that sequencing is so obvious in language is because, contrary to most other behavior, we can identify specific units (such as words, syllables, vowels, and consonants) which makes us more able to precisely define the term sequence by saying what is being serially ordered.

In order to establish our thesis that Lashley's views on these matters remain appropriate, it is first necessary to outline the hypotheses Lashley put forward about the serial ordering process. Lashley contrasted his view at a number of points with the view of serial ordering from Watsonian behaviorism, namely that sequences are produced by associative chains in which the performance of each element of a series provides the stimulus for the performance of the next. One argument against associative chain theories was that the same motor element can occur in a number of different positions in sentences. Thus, elements have no intrinsic associative bonds to other elements (they are context-free) and therefore, the order in which they occur on a given occasion must be determined by some mechanism other than association. As an example, he cites the rule of the word pronounced /raɪt/ in the sentence "The millwright on my right thinks it's right that some conventional rite should symbolize the right of every man to write as he pleases." He also pointed out that the two words "right" and "tire" could be considered to be composed of the same units but in reverse order. Lashley conceived of this mechanism specifying the position of units rather vaguely as the idea, or the intention, to act.

Lashley then argued that in addition to the intention, and the units to be activated, there is a third conceptual entity which is responsible for the serial activation of the units in accordance with the intention. Evidence for this includes typing errors such as "lokk" for "look" and "thses" for "these," where the dynamics of the letter repetition procedure are dissociated from the identity of the units and, of course, from the intention to produce "look" and "these." Lashley also points out that there is evidence from speech errors where parts of an utterance up to five or six words apart are transposed by mistake in a spoonerism (e.g., ake is indisposed with a stomach ike) that prior to output a number of units are simultaneously activated though obviously without total inherent constraints on their potential temporal ordering, hence the errors.

In considering coordinated patterns of movement, Lashley advanced a further objection to associative chain theories in the course of concluding that sensory factors (produced by responses) play a very minor role. This was the well-known argument that skilled response sequences occurred too fast (e.g., 16 strokes/sec in piano playing) to permit stimuli arising from a response to control the next response. This reasoning was based on reaction times of about 125 msec to tactile stimulation.

A further argument against serial ordering being the result of associative chains of movements, and one that we consider crucial, is that the control principles governing movement can be shown to be independent of the precise pattern of movements in the subsequent act. This is shown by the fact that in some movement sequences the necessary movements may be "transferred directly to other motor systems than the ones practiced. In such transfer, as to the left hand for writing, an analysis of the movements shows that there is not a reduplication of the muscular patterns on the two sides, but a reproduction of movements in relation to the space coordinates of the body. Try upside down mirror writing with the left hand and with eyes closed as evidence for this. The associative linkage is not of specific movements but of directions of movement."

Lashley attaches a great deal of importance to space coordinate systems in producing temporal sequences of movements in a spatial pattern. He gives a number of examples of space coordinate systems, including the postural system, the system whereby we retain our "sense of direction" while walking, even though continually changing our orientation by turning, and the system which enables some of us to voluntarily reverse spatial relations while playing chess blindfolded from alternate sides of the board. He points out that influences of space coordinate systems "pervade the motor system so that every gross movement of limbs or body is made with reference to the space system."

Lashley also points to the existance of numerous timing mechanisms in the central nervous system and emphasizes their importance for organizing sequential output. Examples here range from rhythms governing the movement of the dorsal fin of fishes, through rhythms in music, to the fact that rhythms are so compelling that we tend to fall in step with externally imposed rhythms.

Finally, Lashley finds language to be typical of cerebral activity in general in possessing a series of hierarchies of organization, citing "the order of vocal movements in pronouncing a word, the order of words in the sentence, the order of sentences in the paragraph, (and) the rational order of paragraphs in a discourse."

I have spent some time summarizing Lashley's hypotheses because all the points he raises remain relevant to the theory of speech production today, and, in our opinion, neglect of these points has almost always resulted in faulty models of the production process. However, this summary does not begin to do justice to the scope of Lashley's paper so that any appearance from this exposition that his theoretical offering is somewhat meager is due to the compression necessary in this context, and is easily corrected by reading the original paper.

II. PHONEME-BASED MODELS OF SPEECH PRODUCTION

The first theories of speech production we wish to consider in relation to Lashley's hypotheses are a rather similar group put forward by workers in the field of speech communication in the early 1960s. The most prominent proponents of these theories were members of the Haskins Laboratory group (Liberman et al., 1962, 1967a, and b), a number of writers from M.I.T. who shared similar views (Stevens & House, 1963; Stevens & Halle, 1967; Henke, 1967), and Lindblom and Öhman from the Royal Institute of Technology in Stockholm (Lindblom, 1963; Öhman, 1966).

Almost all of these theories considered the phoneme to be the main functional unit, at least on the level at which language manifested itself in spoken form. The process of serial ordering of speech was conceived primarily as the output of sequences of phoneme commands according to the phonotactic rules of the language. The main question they concerned themselves with was given that the phonotactic decisions have already been made, what is the form of the phoneme commands which result in the movements of speech? These theories hoped to establish that there was only a relatively small number of phoneme commands, perhaps, in English for example, not much in excess of the 30–50 postulated by linguists to be the phonemes of the language. The main apparent objection to this small total was the fact that if one looked at the movements and positions of the speech apparatus and their acoustic correlates, it was, for the most part, impossible to find any invariant property of the manifestation of a particular phoneme. Output associated with a phoneme was found to vary with the identity of adjacent phonemes, with the nature and the position of application of stress, and with speaking rate. However, this peripheral variability was not taken to invalidate the possibility that the production process was based on a limited number of discrete invariant phoneme commands. It was thought to be due to three factors: (1) The mass and consequent inertia of the organs made them incapable of the rapid discrete movements being called for; (2) there were also limitations in the possible speed of response of the neuromuscular control system, and (3) time intervals between successive commands were often insufficient to allow a command to be realized before the next one was called for. How successful are these attempts to solve or evade the one-to-many relation between phonemes and their manifestations, and how consistent are these models with Lashley's hypotheses? To answer these questions, it is necessary to evaluate separately two types of hypotheses as to the nature of the invariant phoneme commands. The first one to be evaluated is that invariance lies in the "motor commands" activating the vocal organs. The second view is that the invariance lies in the central specification of certain vocal tract configurations or "targets."

III. THE "MOTOR COMMAND" HYPOTHESIS

The "motor command" hypothesis was put forward primarily by the Haskins Laboratory group and they initiated a series of electromyographic studies to determine whether the pattern of muscle contraction accompanying various manifestations of a phoneme showed invariant features. Some initial studies did show that interference patterns associated with a given phoneme remained similar in their time and amplitude characteristics when the phoneme was placed in various phonological contexts. However, the phonological environments chosen for these studies were such that the muscles being recorded from were, for the most part, not required to be operative for the adjacent phonemes. And even in these environments most favorable to the invariance hypothesis, there were some instances of departure of the EMG pattern from invariance. In a number of subsequent studies, sampling many more phonemes and phonological environments, including environments in which the muscle being recorded from was also required to contract, a very large number of departures from invariance have been noted. A number of studies have also shown that the pattern of muscle contraction and articulator movement for a given phoneme often varies depending on the *following* phonemes (e.g., MacNeilage & DeClerk, 1969). In fact, it has become clear that the one-to-many relation between a phoneme and its manifestations which was previously observed at the acoustic level, and at the level of vocal tract shapes and movements is also true of the level of muscle contraction.

This conclusion may not come as a surprise to many people. It seems quite clear a priori that the amount of muscle contraction required to move an articulator to a given approximate position for a phoneme will at least differ according to the articulator's previous position and different preceding phonemes require different previous positions. The Haskins group acknowledged the possibility that some variation in motor control could occur, but attributed this variability to lower order, and, by implication, relatively unimportant mechanisms, and asserted that there would nevertheless remain a "core" of invariance. However, there appears to be no objective test of the hypothesis that there is a core of invariance in the motor command, and no reason to believe that the mechanisms producing the variability are of less significance in the serial ordering process than any hypothetical invariant component.

IV. THE "TARGET" HYPOTHESIS

It is clear that rather than there being an invariant pattern of muscle contraction for a given phoneme, there is more likely to be a ubiquity of variability in motor correlates of a phoneme. The thing that manifestations of a phoneme have in common then is not the means by which the articulators are activated, but the fact that the articulators tend to reach a similar end point for a phoneme. Recognition of the fact that manifestations of a given phoneme tended toward a similar end gave rise to the second type of hypothesis as to the nature of invariant phoneme commands, the hypothesis that the invariance lay in a central specification of targets, or vocal tract configurations. This hypothesis is not damaged by the fact that motor correlates of phonemes are so variable and thus is preferable to the motor command hypothesis, at least on one count. The main problem with the target hypothesis as initially formulated (Lindblom, 1963; Stevens & House, 1963) was that the term target was used primarily as a summary term, or a descriptive convention to designate the tendency for an articulator to approach an invariant end point for a given phoneme. In the absence of evidence that targets have some reality status in the brain of the speaker, the target notion is considerably hampered by metaphysical connotations. In an earlier paper (MacNeilage, 1970), I attempted to remove these connotations by providing evidence, which I will summarize here, that the internal specification of targets is indeed a possible function of the speech production apparatus. One of the most obvious sources of support for this notion is Lashley's evidence of the existence of space coordinate systems controlling movement. A target can be regarded as a specification of a point within a space coordinate system. Lashley himself did not specifically conceptualize the speech act in terms of the action of space coordinate systems, saying only that all *gross* bodily movements are governed by space coordinate systems. But it is just a short step to apply the idea of control by space coordinate systems to speech movements, and it is not inconsistent with the variability in the motor patterns used to approximate targets if one postulates, as I did in a previous paper (1970), a subsequent motor control mechanism which actively generates motor patterns on the basis of paired sets of target specifications contiguous in time. Further indirect evidence of the appropriateness of the target notion arises from Hebb's 1949 analysis of the analogous problem of visual motor coordination, known in psychology as the motor equivalence problem, the problem of accounting for "a variability of specific muscular responses with circumstance in such a way as to produce a single result [Hebb, 1949]." Hebb's contention was that the success of an animal's repeated and varied attempts to get food from a goal box depends on the concomitance during learning of information from visual and tactile perception about the goal (target), and motor activity, and its sensory consequences. With learning, the perceptual information becomes internalized (perhaps in a space coordinate system), and can then be used together with information about present position of the body to control target attainment. As Lashley said, the stimulus (or target) is *"there,* in a definite place; it has a definite relation to the position of the body."

It is perhaps more obvious that internalized targets and space coordinate systems exist in a visual motor coordination rather than in speech production, because we can *see* the targets and we can reach some targets even when blindfolded. Most of us have little consciousness of what happens in the vocal tract when we speak. I thought, until after finishing my Ph.D., that muteness followed the loss of the tongue (the

Ph.D. was not in speech research). However, space coordinate systems and targets can exist without our being conscious of them. There is some relatively direct evidence that space coordinate systems do exist for the control of the speech musculature. The most simple form of evidence consists of our ability to move our tongue into various positions in the mouth in response to verbal command. Our ability to specify the form of three-dimensional objects placed in the mouth is another form of evidence. More evidence comes from a recent case study of a 17-year-old patient whose speech was almost totally unintelligible, apparently as a result of a generalized deficit in somesthetic perception, as no other aspects of normal functioning seemed to be directly impaired (MacNeilage, Rootes, & Chase, 1967). Finally, the immediate "spontaneous" reorganization of movement patterns required to produce the virtually normal speech still possible when a person speaks with his teeth clenched, strongly suggests, in accordance with Lashley, that what is involved is not specific movements, but directions of movement in relation to goals or targets specified within space coordinate systems. Lindblom and Sundberg (1971) have shown that these adjustments are in fact immediate by showing that the formant patterns produced on first attempts to make certain vowels are virtually identical to the normal patterns.

V. THE ROLE OF SENSORY FEEDBACK

An issue which arises when considering spontaneous reorganization of sequences of speech movements, and unique movement patterns used by an animal to achieve a goal, is that of the extent of a closed loop or a feedback control of movements. In this discussion we consider only feedback from peripheral sensory receptors, and exclude the question of feedback control systems entirely within the nervous system. A basic proposition in this regard is that the *need* for peripheral sensory feedback can be thought of as inversely proportional to the ability of the central nervous system to predictively determine, without sensory information, every essential aspect of following acts. Lashley's most important point in this regard was that because units could occur in various orders, the sensory consequences of a given unit could not determine associatively the *identity* of the next unit, contrary to the claims of associative chain theorists. This argument is equally applicable regardless of what the neural consequences of production of a unit are, and whether they are manifested centrally or at the periphery. The fact, pointed out by many writers (e.g., McGuigan, 1970) that feedback can operate with loop times much faster than the 125 msec noted by Lashley does not invalidate this point, it just opens up the possibility that feedback could be of some use in controlling details of the following acts, the identity of which has already been determined. There are two main possibilities here: (1) that feedback could *trigger* the delivery of subsequent units, that is, provide timing information without having any influence on the *form* of the unit; (2) that feedback could provide information on the extent to which parameters of articulator dynamics were exhibiting values discrepant with intended ones, the information being used for corrections. We do not wish to discuss the first possibility which seems to us to be remote. With regard to the second possibility, one salient fact is the enormous body of information that multiple sources of potential sensory information seem to provide according to studies of animals other than man. The information is in terms of the variety of receptor types and in terms of the multiple loop circuits to which they belong. One way of evaluating these possibilities is to consider, as suggested earlier, the need for feedback in achieving the correct form of speech movements. One place where there appears to be an inescapable need for sensory feedback in order to achieve correct speech movements is in the initiation of speech. The articulators can be involved in a number of maneuvers between utterances (chewing, sucking, "doodling," laughing, yawning, inspecting the teeth with the tongue) and the control mechanism has no way of predicting what position they will be in when initiation of speech is required. It must, therefore, use feedback information because the initial movement it makes to reach a fixed speech position is contingent on prespeech position. The fact that initial movement is contingent on prespeech position has been shown for the jaw by MacNeilage, Krones, and Hanson (1969).

It would also appear that there is an inescapable need for sensory feedback in order to speak successfully with clenched teeth, because the unique movement patterns produced are contingent on prior articulator positions. Furthermore, as one can talk at normal rates with clenched teeth, it is possible that the feedback control is achieved within the average interphoneme time of 70 msec, a much shorter time than is available at speech initiation. Another possibility is that feedback occurs but without any elegant temporal properties because all that may be necessary is a constant sensory input indicating the constant position of the jaw. On the other hand, feedback may not be required. It may be that as soon as a constant jaw position is adopted, a new constant jaw target is assigned in the relevant space coordinate system. Jaw targets would then become as predictable as any other required targets, thus allowing the motor control mechanism to generate movements, as usual, on the basis of target specifications, and without sensory assistance. We do not know enough about the control mechanism at present to choose between these possibilities.

As this analysis suggests, there is a limit to the extent to which we can assess the needs of the speech generation system which is at present rather rapidly reached. Let us now consider the capabilities of sensory feedback systems. The gamma loop to the muscle spindles has often been suggested as a possible means of closed loop control of speech as it appears to be a means whereby a muscle can be adjusted to a given length independent of its prior length. Both Bowman (1971), and Sussman (1971) have recently reviewed anatomical and physiological evidence suggesting a spectacular capacity of muscle spindles in the tongue for provision of sensory information about tongue movement. Dewhurst (1967) has shown that the loop can be brought under human voluntary control by showing latencies of about 20 msec in muscle contraction in response to changes in load on the biceps muscle while in an isometric contraction situation. Sears and Newsom Davis have shown that in response to an unexpected increase in resistance to air flow during phonation, there is an increase in contraction of the muscle generating the air flow with a latency of about 50 msec, only slightly longer than would be expected from the gamma loop. This is of interest because Euler (1966) has shown that an analogous response in cats is due to gamma control. Smith (1969) has temporarily blocked gamma input to elbow extensors by anesthetizing the radial nerve, capitalizing on the slower recovery times of the smaller diameter gamma fibers from an anesthetic. She found a reduction in acceleration of extension movements, relative to normal values, and an inability to appropriately arrest movements initiated by these elbow flexors.

Results of recent attempts to show that the gamma loop actually operates during speech have varying implications. Abbs and Netsell (1970) have produced, by means similar to those used by Smith, a selective block of gamma efferent fibers leading to the muscles of the mandible. They found decreases in acceleration and velocity of the mandible, and a decrease in efficiency of coordination of the mandible with other simultaneously operating articulators. According to Abbs (personal communication), the speech produced by his two subjects sounded normal. The similarity of the results of Smith, and Abbs and Netsell with respect to acceleration decreases is notable. However, there are some problems in interpreting the results of Abbs and Netsell. First, very little information about jaw movement under other adverse conditions is available. Is it possible that acceleration would also decrease with administration of high levels of white noise during production? Second, the authors did not present detailed evidence on the ability of the mandible to achieve targets in the block condition. Neither did they present data on acceleration rates during nonspeech jaw movements where target achievement was not required. They reported that the experiments were done when the ability of the jaw to apply force had returned to 90% of preblock levels. Could the reduced acceleration be due to reduced efficiency of smaller diameter alpha motor neurons?

Smith and Lee (1971) were unsuccessful in an attempt to show that an unexpected increase in resistance to lip closure during production of bilabial stop consonants is followed, in a few milliseconds, by an increase in muscle contraction. On the contrary, they actually observed inhibition in many instances.

There is some indirect contrary evidence to the hypothesis that the gamma loop is operative during speech, which can be summed up by the statement that muscles do not always assume equal lengths for different manifestations of a phoneme, and these deviations cannot be accounted for by mechanical constraints. MacNeilage and DeClerk reported, in 1969, that the amount of elevation of the hyoid bone (and therefore, the lengths of muscles controlling the hyoid) differed by several millimeters in the production of final /k/ depending on the identity of the preceding vowel. Furthermore, those differences were in a direction opposite to that which would occur as a result of mechanical limitations on the peripheral control system; that is, hyoid elevation was greater after lower vowels. In addition, Nooteboom (1970) and Lindblom (1971) have pointed out that the ability of the central system to reach targets in the clenched teeth situation requires more than the gamma loop mechanism because in this situation, muscle lengths associated with targets must often be different than in the normal case.

Finally, cases of anticipation in which movement of an articulator begins before the segment in which it is required violate the equal muscle length hypothesis in the segments in which the anticipation occurs.

The balance of this evidence is not particularly favorable to the possibility of gamma loop control of speech production. As to other means of sensory control, Scott (1970) has recently conducted a nerve block study in order to test the influence of somesthetic feedback on speech production. Using a local anesthetic, she was able to block sensation from surface receptors in the tongue, palate, lips, teeth, and oral mucosa. Although this treatment had minimal effects on speech intelligibility, naturalness of speech was clearly impaired. Detailed analysis of articulation revealed a complex of effects: "1. less close sibilant production, 2. retracted place of articulation during stops and fricatives, 3. changes in the release characteristics of voiceless stops, and 4. nonretroflexion of /r/ and delabialization of normally rounded phonemes [Scott, 1970]."

Although we require much more evidence about the role of closed loop control of ongoing speech, present evidence suggests that it does not play a major role, and that the very fast loop times (less than 70 msec) have not yet been shown to be a factor in speech control. Sensory nerve block studies do produce articulatory changes, and the specificity of these changes in Scott's case implies specific use of sensory information for at least some purposes. But the changes that have been observed are relatively minor in relation to the over-all transmission of articulatory information during speech. This may be because the sensory input being interfered with has a comparatively insignificant role in control of ongoing movement. Or it may be that the well-known redundancy in central nervous system control mechanisms (Rosner, 1970) enables open loop control to compensate effectively for loss of normal operation of closed loop control circuits.

These conclusions would not have been particularly uncongenial to Lashley. He considered that sensory factors play a "minor role" in the regulation of movement. If one wished to counter this argument by saying that much sensory control is normally involved but its elimination is compensated for by reorganization of response capabilities under nerve block conditions, he would be providing support for Lashley's contention that the executive apparatus is independent of the control mechanism.

VI. THE MULTIPLICITY OF FUNCTIONAL UNITS

In this paper so far we have discussed two candidates for the functional unit of speech production, the phoneme, and the target. Insofar as there may be more than one target per phoneme, the notion of target is similar in scope to the concept of "distinctive feature" which refers to some aspect of the total articulatory or perceptual complex that is capable of producing a minimal distinction between one phoneme and another. In the past, many papers have been written with the intention of establishing which is *the* functional unit of speech output, with the implication that there is only one. In this paper, we have argued that the target is preferable to the phonemic motor command in accounting for a number of facts about serial ordering. This should not be taken to mean that we prefer the distinctive feature to the phoneme as *the* functional unit of speech output. One of Lashley's main points about the speech production process is that it is organized in an hierarchical fashion, and it seems clear that, as he asserted, this hierarchy is associated with a hierarchy of functional units rather than just one functional unit. The most general question to be asked about the serial ordering of speech production is, how many different levels must be postulated for the hierarchy, and how are these levels and their associated units related to each other in performance?

VII. THE IMPLICATIONS OF SPEECH ERRORS

Lashley pointed out that a most useful source of information about this question is the study of speech errors. Since 1951, a number of extremely informative studies of speech errors have been done (Cohen, 1966; Hockett, 1967; Boomer & Laver, 1968; Nooteboom, 1969; MacKay, 1970; Fromkin, 1971), in which the main error type has been the spoonerism, or the transposition of two adjacent segments. I will now attempt to summarize some of the main points arising from these studies.

Practically every unit of speech that has been postulated by linguists or others seems to have behavioral reality in the speech production process in that they can be substituted, transposed, omitted, or added as a unit in an otherwise correct sequence. The distinctive feature, the phoneme, the syllable, the morpheme, and the word all have a claim to reality in this sense.

Speech errors also serve to improve our definition of some of these concepts. For instance, one does not observe diphthongs or affricates splitting into two components, one of which participates in an ordering error, thus suggesting that they are single phonemic units rather than closely associated pairs of units. On the other hand, individual consonants in a consonant cluster sometimes act independently in an ordering error, suggesting that clusters are best regarded as groupings of individual phonemes. Similarly, postulated distinctive features can be evaluated by noting whether or not their physical correlates are independently variable in an otherwise stable sequence of speech output.

One of the senses in which units larger than the distinctive feature and phoneme can be said to have reality is that they place strong constraints on the positional privileges governing phoneme or feature errors. Prevocalic consonants, vocalic nuclei (vowels), and postvocalic consonants rarely occur erroneously other than in the same syllable positions that they originated in.

VIII. AN HIERARCHICAL SCHEMA FOR
SPEECH PRODUCTION

A schematic view of the speech production process incorporating these facts as well as a number of other implications of speech errors, and the conclusions reached earlier about the motor control process, is shown in

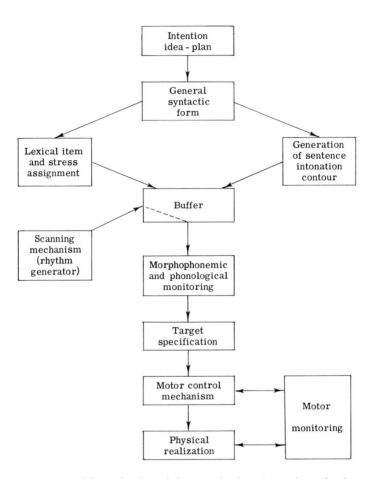

Fig. 12.1. Schematic view of the organization of speech production.

Fig. 12.1. The three boxes at the bottom require little further explanation. The penultimate pair represent the necessary separation between target and the motor control levels discussed earlier. The final box represents the operation of the final motor pathways. Similarly, the box at the top requires little discussion. It recognizes as did Lashley the necessity of an initial idea, plan, or intention which is preverbal and is typically, though not always, "satisfied" by production of a particular sentence. The parts of the model most dependent on speech error data are the remaining parts intermediate between initial conception and verbalization.

The intention must include some semantic information to be made more specific in the formation of a sentence. The next step may be to decide on the general syntactic form of the utterance, at least to a point sufficient to allow the generation of the over-all form of the sentence intonation contour. For example, a choice may be made of "I'll have a *steak*" and not "A *steak* for me," so that the main sentence stress is assigned to the last word in the sentence. Following this, we have suggested two parallel operations, the generation of the sentence intonation contour, and the selection of appropriate lexical items with their associated stress patterns. Some characteristics of the lexical selection process are indicated by speech errors. One possibility is a "semantic" error, e.g., "hate" for "like," which appears to involve selection of the wrong value for a semantic feature and a following look-up at a wrong lexical address (Fromkin, 1971). A second class of error, e.g., "pressure" for "present," appears to involve selection of a wrong lexical item "near" the correct one in the lexical storage system (Fromkin, 1971).

Following lexical selection, the items are fed into a buffer into which is also fed the sentence intonation contour to which the items are eventually matched.

It is at this point that speech error data begin to provide some obvious constraints on the form of the model, and at this stage that the motivation for some aspects of the model we have already outlined may become clear. It is necessary to have a temporary storage in which a number of lexical items and a sentence intonation contour can coexist for a number of reasons. First, it is necessary to have a number of words available simultaneously to account for transposition of words, as Lashley pointed out. In one of Fromkin's examples a "computer in our own laboratory" becomes "a laboratory in our own computer." Second, it is necessary for these transpositions to take place before the assignment of the sentence intonation contour, as evidenced by the fact that whereas in the previous example the correct version would have a major sentence stress on the *first* syllable of "laboratory," the transposed version received major sentence stress on the *second* syllable of "computer." Blends may be accounted for by a selection of parts of two lexical items which were simultaneously available, in temporary store, probably because a definite choice could not be made between them at the time, to fill one lexical slot. "Grisp" where the blend was derived from "grip" and "grasp" is a recent example one of us produced. The items in this store must have their lexical stress patterns already assigned, otherwise it would not be possible for the sentence stress to fall on the appropriate, most highly stressed syllable of the lexical item, as we observed in "computer." For stress to be assigned, syllable structure must also have been specified prior to that point, as the syllable is the domain of stress. At this point too, we suggest that although lexical items are specified here as units, there remains some "fluidity" in the linkages within lexical items, such that syllables, phonemes, and distinctive features are in some sense separately available for selection, thus allowing the transposition of syllables, phonemes, and distinctive features which takes place in speech errors.

We postulate that the next step is the serially ordered removal of items from the buffer by a scanning mechanism proposed by Lashley, a mechanism which probably provides timing information. This results in the transfer of the items to the stage where their appropriate target values are assigned after passing through an intermediate store of morphophonemic and phonological monitoring. We know that the scanning mechanism is susceptible to being "confused" in its serial selection both by stress values assigned to syllables and by segmental properties, and these variables seem to be the main source of serial ordering errors at the phonetic level (MacKay, 1970). Segment or feature reversals typically involve similar segments and the reversed pair are often preceded or followed by an identical phoneme which seems to have a "triggering" role. Components of stressed syllables are especially likely to participate in reversals, which suggests that the components being advanced in the order are in some way especially salient to the scanning mechanism. One reason Lashley postulated a finite buffer was to account for the inclusion of the delayed component in the spoonerism. It remains available for selection by the scanner when it comes to the point when it requires the unit that has already been advanced. This in turn suggests that degree of stress is positively related to prominence of representation in the nervous system prior to production.

It is necessary to postulate the morphophonemic and phonological monitoring stage after the serialization produced by the scanning mechanism, because there are available numerous instances that suggest that *after* a transposition has occurred, morphophonemic and phonotactic rules renormalize the sequence. It is very rare that even an erroneous output sequence violates either of these two types of rules. As an example of morphophonemic rule operation, consider: "a kice ream cone" for "an ice cream cone," where the form of the indefinite article in the erroneous phrase is changed, obviously to fit the form of the new initial segment of the next word.

In "ƒlay the pictor" for "play the victor," a phonotactic rule apparently devoices the transposed /v/ (giving /f/) after the transposition, as /vl/ is not a permissable sequence in English.

The last three stages in the model have already been discussed. All ordering errors are deemed to occur before the operation of the target specification mechanism. They certainly occur before the motor control mechanism, because it apparently operates efficiently to produce the movements appropriate to the sequencing of the units, showing that the sequencing, although wrong, is fully specified before the motor control mechanism is activated (the specification of the appropriate movements for a segment must *follow* the ordering decision, otherwise the production of movements for a segment appropriate to its old context would seldom result in its acceptable production). The motor monitoring mechanism at this stage is called for by the fact that we sometimes stop entirely during an attempt to produce a word containing an ordering error with the feeling that some insurmountable motor barrier has been reached. Errors that reach this stage are missed by the earlier monitor.

IX. A CONTEMPORARY ASSOCIATIVE CHAIN MODEL

Despite Lashley's criticisms of associative chain models, such a model, though more sophisticated than its forebears, has again been put forward quite recently as an alternative explanation of the serial ordering process, this time with special reference to speech (Wicklegren, 1969). The part of this paper on speech production during waking concludes with a discussion of this alternative model.

Wicklegren's associative chain model appears to be primarily a response to Lashley's contention that as the same unit could occur in a variety of orders of output, its occurrence could not be determined simply by associative links with its neighbors, but must be determined by some separate nonassociative controlling influence. Wicklegren's response was that this problem could be avoided by postulating as basic units, stored allophones which are context-sensitive in that they fit only one prior and post context. For example, Wicklegren points out, with Lashley, that if the units composing the words "struck" and "crust" (namely /ʌ/, /r/, /s/, /k/, and /t/) are context-free, then associative links between them could not be responsible for *both* of the orderings occurring in the two words. But if units were specified for context—for example, if the initial /s/ in "struck" was represented by a unit $_*S_+$, the following /t/ by "$_{st_r}$" and so on—then Wicklegren claims that the activation of some representation of the word required to be produced will in turn activate the unordered set of context-sensitive allophones: "then all that is needed to achieve full activation of the set in the correct order is the well-learned association from the internal representation of 'begin' to the set of emr representatives $_*X_z$. In the case of /struk/ (sic), this will cause $_*S_+$ to be the most strongly activated emr, at first. Then "$_st_r$" will be most strongly associated to $_*S_+$ among all the partially activated emr's composing the word, so "$_st_r$" will be the next to be most strongly activated, and so on."

This model has provoked a number of criticisms since its formulation (Halwes & Jenkins, 1971; Lenneberg, 1971; MacKay, 1970; MacNeilage, 1970; Whitaker, 1970). In our opinion, the most damaging criticism arises from a point made by Lashley in 1951. This was the point that speech output like other serially ordered behavior requires a model in which the control principles are independent from the actual movements themselves, not in a 1:1 relation with them as Wicklegren proposes. Wicklegren attempts to avoid this criticism by dubbing speech "noncreative" behavior, in which the movements made for a given allophone are much the same each time and can therefore be produced by a finite (though literally incredibly large) number of stored units. Now it might appear at first sight that speech articulation is noncreative. We have pointed out that in speech the targets of movement have a basically constant, obligatory, and therefore, predictable spatial relation to the articulators which achieve them. Why not then have a stored movement representation for every possible target-to-target movement? However, the present contention is that these movements are generated afresh each time they are required by a mechanism which, even though it does not always reveal it, has a *potential* for creativity. This potential is revealed when one voluntarily modifies the operation of one's own speech apparatus. These modifications cannot be accounted for in terms of sets of stored output patterns because they require the creative generation of new patterns, which, being new, could not have any associative relations to adjacent patterns which could account for their special ordering. The ability to speak with teeth clenched is the best example of this. Others enumerated by Halwes and Jenkins (1971) are "the ability of children to acquire and employ a variety of 'pig Latins' "; (as Lashley noted) the ability to imitate an "accent," a dialect, or a lisp; the ability to modify articulatory behavior in order to talk while performing other acts with the mouth such as eating, chewing gum, holding a pencil in the mouth, or smoking; the ability to whisper, to shout, to speak rapidly, or slowly; the ability of the ventriloquist to speak a modified version of the speech code; and so on." One may argue that these performances involve learning to various degrees, and to that extent could depend on task-specific storage of sets of emr's. But it is difficult to avoid the conclusion that a good deal of spontaneity, and therefore, creativity is involved in many of them.

If this conclusion is adopted, then Wicklegren's model, on these grounds alone, cannot be considered a viable alternative to the type of model suggested by Lashley.

X. SPEECH PRODUCTION DURING SLEEP

The remainder of this paper is devoted to the question of central control of language output during sleep. Here, the question is not so much how is language produced during sleep but, what insight does language production during sleep cast on the more general issue of cerebral and mental organization during sleep. Our aim here is considerably more modest than in the section on waking speech, namely to summarize and discuss primarily our own work in this area (MacNeilage, 1971; MacNeilage & MacNeilage, 1972).

XI. SUBVOCAL ACTIVITY DURING SLEEP

About 18 months ago, we began doing experimental work on sleep by asking the question of whether subvocal activity (i.e., linguistically motivated activity of the speech musculature), as judged from electromyograms from the speech apparatus, occurred during sleep. We were encouraged by evidence that subvocal activity occurs during waking, that a good deal of motor activity of other parts of the bodily musculature occurs during sleep, and that sleep talking occasionally occurs. Also, we had just heard of the preliminary finding of McGuigan and Tanner (1970) that lip and chin EMG activity were higher during REM periods containing conversational dreams, than during either NREM periods or REM periods containing predominately visual dreams. Being new to the area of sleep research, we were even naive enough to hope that subvocal activity might provide an objective index of neurological and mental organization during sleep comparable in power to the REMs themselves. Although this hope was not realized, we did find out some things about linguistic function in general during sleep which we think are of theoretical interest, and suggest that a good deal of further study of this topic would be very rewarding.

To do an effective study of subvocal activity during sleep, it is very useful to have a criterion for deciding what activity of the speech apparatus was initiated by linguistic processes, and what by nonlinguistic factors, for example, swallowing and chewing, or less organized nonspeech movements of the vocal apparatus. The criterion decided on was that the pattern of EMG activity be analogous to that found during overt waking speech, but typically lower in amplitude. In waking speech there is almost continuous activity of moderate levels on all channels, but the level of activity on any given channel fluctuates rapidly, and these level fluctuations are typically out of phase with fluctuations on other channels. In addition to these EMG characteristics, overt speech is typically accompanied by very little muscle artifact in EEG and EOG channels.

Five male university students who indicated on a questionnaire that they recalled dreams frequently and sleep talked at least occasionally were studied during sleep over a period of 6 nights each. In addition to EEG, EOGs, and audio recording, electromyograms were recorded from four locations in the speech musculature. Electrodes were placed on the lips, the chin, and peripheral to the thyroid cartilage (larynx). A bipolar thin hooked wire electrode was inserted into the tongue from a position inferior to the mandible. The subject's first night's sleep which was uninterrupted was not analyzed. The second and third night's sleep which were also uninterrupted were analyzed to determine the frequency of occurrence of subvocal activity in the various sleep stages.

Approximately 4.5% of the sleep time, or approximately 20 min per night, were accompanied by activity of the speech musculature lasting more than 1 sec, and occurring simultaneously on all EMG channels. The pattern of distribution of this activity across sleep stages was broadly similar to that reported for other bodily musculature (Dement & Kleitman, 1957). Periods of activity were more frequent though shorter in duration in Stage 1 (REM and NREM) than in Stages 3 and 4, with Stage 2 showing intermediate values. The EMG peak amplitudes were smallest within the REM periods, larger during Stages 1 (NREM) and 2, and largest during Stages 3 and 4.

Very few periods of motor activity satisfied our preordained criteria for subvocal activity. Only 13% of the episodes had peak EMG amplitudes which were less than $\frac{2}{3}$ rds of the subjects' comparable waking speech levels, and 76% of EMG peak levels in the EEG channel equaled or exceeded comparable levels during waking speech. Furthermore, the pattern of EMG activity was typically quite unlike that observed during waking speech. Relatively long bursts of activity, synchronous on all channels, were typical during sleep, though never observed during waking speech.

These findings would have made us conclude that there is very little subvocal activity during sleep, but for one thing. Occasionally, in the midst of most unspeechlike-looking EMG activity, a subject would produce a sleep talking episode. This occasional event suggests that although patterns of activity of the speech musculature during sleep may not look like those of waking speech, they may nevertheless, to some extent, be linguistically motivated. Our somewhat misplaced confidence about the power of our criterion of subvocal activity resulted in our neither recording from control electrodes not in the speech musculature, nor gathering any evidence of the movement of the speech apparatus associated with EMG activity, both of which may have made more clear the proportion of linguistic and nonlinguistic contribution to the observed EMG patterns.

XII. PHYSIOLOGICAL CORRELATES OF SLEEP TALKING

As well as having the implications just stated for subvocal activity, this study also has implications for the phenomenon of sleep talking. The implications arise from a rather serendipitous result which certainly requires replicating, but which nevertheless appears worthy of comment at the present time. Although all five experimental subjects had claimed that they sleep talked at least occasionally, during the last 5 nights of the experiment only three of the five subjects accounted for all 28 sleep-talking episodes (apart from a single episode recorded for the fourth subject). In addition, the three subjects who produced all but one of the speechlike utterances also produced many more vocalizations of a non-speechlike nature than did the other two subjects. This difference was paralleled by a number of other differences in activity of the speech musculature during the 2 nights of sleep in which it was measured. The sleep-talking subgroup produced 60% more episodes of this activity. There was no overlap in frequency of these episodes between members of the two subgroups. This difference is a good deal greater than can be accounted for merely in terms of the vocalizations produced by the sleep-talking subgroup. The difference was spread over all sleep stages. Average duration of episodes of activity was also about $1\frac{1}{2}$ sec greater, averaged over all stages, in the sleep-talking subgroup, and this difference was reflected in each sleep stage. Finally, there was a different pattern of distribution of peak EMG amplitudes over the various sleep stages. Average peak amplitudes were lower for the non-sleep talkers in the REM period, and higher in Stage 2, and Stages 3 and 4.

We have tentatively concluded from these results that the propensity to sleep talk is to some extent the result of a relatively high propensity for motor activation during sleep. We have speculated that in sleep talkers, this motor activation might sometimes serve to "project" verbal components of concurrent sleep mentation to the periphery. This interpretation has some problems. One is the difficulty in explicating the neurophysiological connotations of the term project. The second is that if coincidences between motor activation and concurrent verbal mentation were all that was involved, then we would expect some sleep-talking episodes from the non-sleep-talking group. They did produce an average of 70 periods of motor activity per night. Furthermore, data derived from the second 3 days of the experiment when dream reports were obtained showed that the two subgroups recalled sleep mentation with approximately equal frequency, the frequency being roughly comparable to that found in other studies of good recallers. The two subgroups were also approximately equal in the frequency with which verbal components of sleep mentation were recalled.

Although it is clear that we do not yet have a satisfactory interpretation of our preliminary findings regarding sleep talking, we do plan to attempt to replicate the findings, and we have made one further step toward substantiating the hypothesis. One clear implication of the "projection" hypothesis is that there should be a positive relation between propensity to sleep talk, and frequency of verbal mentation in dreams, for the simple reason that what does not occur cannot be projected. Our investigation of this relation was based on the assumptions that dream reports are a relatively accurate reflection of dream mentation and that amount of verbal mentation in dreams is proportional to amount of dreaming. We investigated, by the somewhat indirect method of questionnaire, the relation between propensity to sleep talk and frequency of dream recall (MacNeilage, Cohen, & MacNeilage, 1972). We found in three separate studies that there was a highly significant relation between indicated propensity to sleep talk, and indicated frequency of dream recall.

XIII. LANGUAGE BEHAVIOR DURING SLEEP: FURTHER QUESTIONS

Our justification for burdening this audience with a mass of preliminary results from pilot studies, and speculations, and inadequately supported assumptions, is not so much that we believe it all ourselves, which may simply be an index of our naivety in this field, but because we consider the question of language formation during sleep to be a very neglected area, and we wish to stimulate more work in the area by identifying some questions which are of theoretical interest.

The two questions we have been attempting to answer here relate to the nature of subvocal activity during sleep, and to the explanation for sleep talking, particularly the fact of individual differences in sleep talking. I conclude this paper by raising some other questions about language behavior during sleep.

XIV. THE VERBAL COMPONENT OF DREAM CONTENT

It is surprising to us that so little work has been done on the question of verbal aspects of dream content, as it is a salient and easily definable subarea of dream content. In a search of the literature, the only statement that we could find about the frequency of verbal components of dream mentation was in Hall and Van DeCastle's book (1966). They report 511 instances of verbal activity in 1000 morning reports of dreams.

We have been unable to find an unequivocal statement about the co-variation of any aspect of verbal sleep mentation with the REM–NREM distinction. Verbal characteristics do not figure in attempts to define differences between REM and NREM mentation. Using the 85 dream reports of the second part of our study, we made a small-scale analysis of the frequency of verbal aspects of mentation reported after REM and NREM mentation. We used a number of subcategories of verbal content, but as the number of dreams we analyzed was so small, only the most all-encompassing category will be reported on here. This category was "The subject reports that some verbal output did occur." (He was always questioned on this point specifically if he did not otherwise cover it in his report.) In terms of this category, 70% of dreams during the REM period included verbal components, and 38% of NREM dreams did. These figures may simply reflect the over-all tendency of dream reports from REM periods to be much more likely to be coherent and explicit than dream reports from Stage 2, and so, therefore, may not be indicating that, relative to other indices of dreaming, there is more verbalization in the REM period.

XV. SPEECH ERRORS IN SLEEP-TALKING EPISODES

A final question is related to the theme of the first part of the paper. Is it possible that an analysis of what one can call errors in the content of sleep-talking episodes may reveal something of importance about the organization of the brain related to language which adds to our understanding of both speech production and sleep states? Arkin has made an extensive study of the content of sleep-talking episodes (Arkin, 1966, 1970). He finds them to be in general more coherent in the REM period

than in NREM sleep. He also finds many instances of errors by both de-
ducing them from the content, and by observing the sleeper's own attempts to correct them. We intend to make a collection of these errors
and compare them to errors of waking speech. In this we intend to confine
ourselves largely to errors in the sound pattern of speech, rather than to
consider semantic aspects of the speeches. We conclude this paper with
an example of a sleep-talking error and its analysis. Early this year at a
convention, a colleague of mine, at 3 a.m., produced the utterance "cones
after goans after gowns after gowns." I wrote it down and when I taxed
him with it in the morning, he said that it must have been motivated by
a lecture on formal systems that he had attended 2 days before, in which
the lecturer used the example of "cones within cones" to illustrate his
point. This is an example that might have been interesting to Freud for
semantic reasons. However, from the phonetic point of view, it can easily
be interpreted in terms of two sound changes, the first simply a change in
the voicing feature of the velar stop consonant, the second a change to a
very similar vowel, perhaps partly motivated by the existence of gowns
but not goans in English. This can be construed as evidence for the behavioral reality of the distinctive feature and/or the phoneme in linguistic
organization during sleep, and, more broadly, hints that Lashley's suggestion of an approach to analysis of serial ordering through speech errors
may have utility in the understanding of sleep states as well as waking
states.

ACKNOWLEDGMENT

Preparation of this paper was supported in part by Grants GU-1598 and GS-3218
from the National Science Foundation and Grant MH-19513-01 from the National
Institute of Mental Health, U.S. Public Health Service.

The Discussion of Dr. MacNeilage's Paper

LED BY DR. RONALD WEBSTER
Hollins College

Webster: I am really delighted to have this opportunity to discuss the
paper that was presented by "Meter PacNeilage." I enjoyed it. I am in a
strange position at this conference. In my own work, I try to restrict

myself to the use of a minimal number of constructs which require any sort of extension into the realm of the unknown; therefore, I am rarely involved in theorizing about central nervous system functions. But, here I am looking at the conceptual nervous system and enjoying it.

Dr. MacNeilage's development of Lashley's views is indeed interesting and quite well done, given the time restrictions here. He also gives us a creditable model of speech production, and his discussion of deficiencies in the associative chaining approach was cogent. The concept of the space coordinate system in speech guidance is a good one; at least in conception, it efficiently accounts for the phenomena we have observed. The model resembles an inertial guidance system, much like that of the ICBMs, in that the system always knows where it is; and, because it knows where it started from it can always tell you, at a given point in time, exactly where it is to within a few thousandths of 1% accuracy.

In developing his model, with respect to speech control, Dr. MacNeilage doesn't care much for sensory feedback; that disturbs me a little bit, because the phenomena I deal with are intimately involved with sensory feedback. For example, in discussing sensory feedback, Dr. MacNeilage gave us some options: First, sensory feedback might provide timing information in speech guidance; secondly, it may provide information on articulatory gestures which can be compared with the internalized program controlling the gestures. This too abruptly dismisses sensory feedback, and a few things that need to be said. One is that when you break into the auditory feedback loop by delaying auditory feedback, marked changes are produced in the output properties of speech, viz., a decrease in speech rate, changes in voice quality, and often marked deficiencies in articulatory performance. Even more interesting than delayed feedback is the kind of intervention into the auditory feedback loop, where accelerated air-conducted feedback accelerates the rate of speech production, as it was done by Peters in 1954, and by Davidson in 1959.

Our work with stutterers indicated that stuttering is fundamentally a problem involving the faulty release of speech sounds, probably resulting from aberrations in the auditory feedback loop which are produced by the faulty action of the middle ear muscles, relative to the initiation of vocal fold action. This suggests to me the importance of the auditory feedback component in timing speech performance. A stutterer with a rhythmic cuing stimulus speaking in time—a metronome or a flashing light—proceeds fluently, suggesting that the external cuing stimulus realigns the timing functions in speech. So sensory feedback may well temporally control behavior.

Dr. MacNeilage raised a second point, the error detection role of sensory feedback, which would be essential for any sort of inertial guidance system that we know of, and which has some real world properties to it; he discussed the role of a local anesthetic in producing slight deterioration in articulation. But, does the anesthetic really take out the critical sensory feedback channels? Or, does it merely lead to a shift form one kind of sensory feedback channel to another? We have shown that normally fluent speakers can shift the reliance in speech guidance away from the auditory feedback signal, and toward what apparently are motor feedback cues. Thus, at least in some instances, it is possible to switch from one kind of monitoring feedback channel to another. Sensory feedback is clearly present, and it is hard to believe that it is not important in the ongoing control of behavior.

Taub, and Berman and Taub, in their work on deafferentiation in monkeys, give evidence of some sort of central planning, but the deafferented animals are terribly inefficient behavers. Sensory feedback seems to be necessary to give ongoing behavior any real precision in either space and/or time.

Dr. MacNeilage's sensitivity to the concept of the variety of functional units in speech production leads to an increased precision of thinking about speech production, an important need. Once I got over my acute discomfort with the conceptual nervous system, I found that I liked Dr. MacNeilage's model of speech assembly and production. It seems to be consistent with the speech–error data that Dr. MacNeilage described, and the sequence of acts in assembly is particularly insightful. When Dr. McGuigan was talking, some people, including Dr. MacNeilage, seemed to think that possibly Dr. McGuigan had a periphery with no center. I sort of feel that Dr. MacNeilage has a center with no periphery. I am full of questions about how you test this model. What are the experiments? And how might one develop the model further?

How would you relate your model to Dr. Sperry's finding that spatial functions are represented primarily in the minor hemisphere, and verbal functions in the major hemisphere?

Open Discussion

Dr. MacNeilage: Those are very good points. I do not want to prejudge the sensory issue, or the function of the auditory channel. Regarding delayed auditory feedback (DAF), the DAF not only interferes with the auditory feedback, but it also provides a systematically confusing feedback which we do not really understand. The worst effect occurs with 2 sec delay, but apparently nobody knows why.

On the question of what experiments to do, I am planning some on the role of sensory feedback in which we produce "blocks" and observe consequences for rate of articulation and single motor unit activity; we could thus see what the motor command system is actually doing, and whether it systematically changes in ways that related to sensory feedback. Furthermore, I want to work along the lines of the H-reflex paradigm, where you put a little electrical stimulation into the system while it is in operation, and then see what the gain in the loop is at various times. These things are almost entirely related to the question of what the sensory–motor organization is doing. Also, I want to collect more speech errors.

Dr. Larry Rust (State University of New York at Potsdam): Given the always monitored buffer, and given random access memories, could you please speak to the issue of Chomsky's model of the uniqueness of all possible English sentences, in fact, all possible sentences in all languages? And would you address the problem of priming, or precursing, or anticipation? This is something potentially unique that the organism does as he deciphers sentences, especially in terms of Lashley's more famous sentence, "Rapid righting with his uninjured hand saved from loss the contents of the capsized canoe."

MacNeilage: I think we do a little anticipation of that kind; it is my guess that it is not nearly as elegant as Chomsky argues. We need to pay much more attention to the information that is coming in, and less attention to a grand predictive mechanism.

Rust: I have a feeling that Lashley's sentence can never be said, that it can only be written.

MacNeilage: You just said it.

Rust: I read it, having had it written; but I have never heard a speaker come out with that kind of juxtaposition.

MacNeilage: There are various degrees of uniqueness, and the idea that every sentence is unique, period, is one that is not very satisfying to me. I have to admit that I do not know much about linguistic theory; what I am putting forward is an incompetence model. I am not in the competence business.

Dr. Paul Woods (Hollins College): In your search for speech errors, you might use children; they are a wonderful source of errors.

MacNeilage: We need tons of such data, collected systematically. Errors do not happen very often, but they do happen a lot more often than we think. If in 1956 I had had Fromkin's insight, I would now have thousands and thousands of errors. She showed that if you merely write out the errors that you hear in everyday life, you can collect a large number very quickly.

Dr. Adam Reeves (City College of New York): In your model you have replaced sensory feedback with motor monitoring, at least at the peripheral level. Suppose you have an ongoing series of motor commands, one following another, and you get to one of these commands and make a mistake; I do not understand how a motor system can decide it has made a mistake. It seems to me that it is only through resulting sensory feedback that you know that you have made a mistake, whether it is over a phrase, or over a phoneme. It seems to me that is exactly where sensory feedback comes in. Can you make a distinction between the two?

MacNeilage: Not really! "Monitoring of the act, while you are doing it" may be an ill-chosen phrase. Such monitoring *would* have to be on the basis of sensory information, and probably of a considerable amount.

Reeves: You did say at one point that sensory feedback only played a small role in your process; from your model, that is not true. It plays an intimate role.

MacNeilage: We make more speech errors than we realize, but very few per hour.

Reeves: That indicates a highly efficient sensory feedback mechanism, proving that sensory feedback is very important.

MacNeilage: No, because there are limits to where the correction can take place.

Dr. Michael Seitz (University of Pittsburgh): You suggested the phoneme, or some small unit, as the basic element. Do the phonemes come in a sequential manner, or is there parallel processing from the buffer? Consonants tend to shape larger units.

MacNeilage: There are data suggesting that you can anticipate the rounding, in a rounded vowel, four phonemes back from where it occurred. If you assume 70 msec per phoneme, you can anticipate by about 280 msec, not an enormous amount of time. The target's information is provided, a few targets in advance, to the motor control mechanism. And the mechanism has rules that enable it to put in that anticipation; that is, the knowledge of what is soon going to happen, within a few phonemes.

Seitz: That 280-msec lag is also very close to the primary DAF error element in time, i.e., .2 sec. Can you make anything out of that?

MacNeilage: Not really, because that example of 280 msec is really an extreme example. Most anticipations are more like 100 msec.

Dr. Charles Osgood (University of Illinois): The basic notion of central motor programming should particularly relate to syllabic units. I am also a collector of spoonerisms, of my own production and of others, and I have never found a single case where the substitutions, (the things that are changed) are not syllabic changes; there was never production of a non-English syllable. This suggests that there is a programming in the motor integration areas, of at least syllabic units. Now notice something else interesting: On the perception side of language, one does get mixed up in the recall (short-term memory) of words, like mixing up "stress" and "pitch"; but you never get something like "hist my mister." So I am suggesting that the output level, based upon the programmed unit, is not phonemic—it is syllabic. Our error evidence is consistent.

Audience: Note that the .2 sec for an optimal DAF effect is also the approximate duration of one syllable; this relates to timing mechanisms.

Osgood: Precisely.

MacNeilage: On that last point, there are relevant data that bother me. In one study between two groups, one group of subjects had syllables of short duration, the other of long duration; and the critical delay interval did not shift as a function of the average syllable duration. That is a bit bothersome to the .2-sec notion that you cite.

The other point you made is quite congenial to me. You have got to say that the phoneme to be spoken in the future did play some organizational role; but the syllable organization is probably the primary timing organization.

Osgood: Precisely. And you mentioned that the memory storage is quite sufficient; the actual number of syllables in languages, like English, are not terribly large.

MacNeilage: Right. Would you know how to define these syllables, though?

Osgood: Well, that is hard. Also, the interactions around the boundaries are very interesting. But that, I think, still can be handled with your kind of theory, added to a syllabic-unit theory.

Audience: What about Abercrombie's theory about two types of language? This would be syllable time and stress time; in a stress-timed language, the units are larger than a syllable.

MacNeilage: It is not that the unit is larger than a syllable-unit, but that a stress factor is superimposed on the syllabic unit.

Osgood: But the stresses are always on syllables, interestingly enough.

MacNeilage: Right.

Audience: But the time in between, like in a polysyllabic word, is such that you can get two or more syllables within the same period of time.

Rust: Regarding Dr. Osgood's comment, Chinese Mandarin is a language in which all the units are in syllables; that language might be used to support, or to refute, Dr. Osgood's argument.

MacNeilage: You mean all words are monosyllabic?
Rust: Right.
MacNeilage: Well, that will not affect his argument; they are still all syllables.
Rust: No, I believe it would support his argument. Anything that was kicked out of memory would have to be in terms of any juxtaposition of letters, as in English, which is a highly serial type of function.
MacNeilage: That is kind of cheating; you have taken an example where Osgood's model has the most going for it, in that the syllable corresponds to another unit as well. If it works out, it may be because the syllable is also a word.

REFERENCES

Abbs, J. H. and Netsell, R. The inferential role of the gamma loop in speech production: A new application of an old technique. Paper presented at the annual convention of the American Speech and Hearing Association, New York City, November 1970.

Arkin, A. M. Sleeptalking: A review. *Journal of Nervous and Mental Disease*, 1966, **143**, 101–122.

Arkin, A. M. Qualitative observations on sleep utterance in the laboratory. In *Proceedings of the International Symposium on the Psychophysiology of Sleep and Dreams.* Editrice Vita e Pensiero: Milan, 1970.

Boomer, D. S. and Laver, J. D. M. Slips of the tongue. *British Journal of Disorders of Communication*, 1968, **3**, 1–12.

Bowman, J. P. *The muscle spindle and neutral control of the tongue.* Springfield: Charles C. Thomas, 1971.

Cohen, A. Errors of speech and their implication for understanding the strategy of the language user. *Proceedings of the 18th International Congress of Psychology.* Moscow, 1966.

Dement, W. and Kleitman, N. Cyclic variations in EEG during sleep and their relation to eye movements, body motility, and dreaming. *Electroencephalography and Clinical Neurophysiology*, 1957, **9**, 673–690.

Dewhurst, D. J. Neuromuscular control system. *IEEE Transactions of Biomedical Engineering*, 1967, **14**, 167–171.

Euler, C. V. Proprioceptive control in respiration. In R. Granit (Ed.), *Muscular afferents and motor control.* New York: Wiley, 1966.

Fromkin, V. A. The nonanomalous nature of anomalous utterances. *Language*, 1971, **47**, 27–52.

Hall, C. S. and Van De Castle, R. L. *The content analysis of dreams.* New York: Appleton-Century-Crofts, 1966.

Halwes, T. and Jenkins, J. J. Problem of serial order in behavior is not resolved by context-sensitive associative memory models. *Psychological Review*, 1971, **78**, 122–129.

Hebb, D. O. *The organization of behavior.* New York: Wiley, 1949.

Henke, W. Preliminaries to speech synthesis based on an articulatory model. Preprints of the Conference on Speech Communication and Processing, Cambridge, Massachusetts, November 1967.

Hockett, C. F. Where the tongue slips, there slip I. In, *To Honor Roman Jakobson, Vol. 2,* Janua Linguarum, Series Major XXXII. The Hague: Mouton, 1967.

Lashley, K. S. The problem of serial order in behavior. In L. A. Jeffress (Ed.), *Cerebral mechanisms in behavior* (the Hixon symposium). New York: Wiley, 1951.

Lenneberg, E. H. The importance of temporal factors in behavior. In Horton, D. L. and Jenkins, J. J. (Eds.), *The Perception of Language.* Columbus, Ohio: Charles E. Merrill Publishing Co., 1971.

Liberman, A. M., Cooper, F. S. Harris, K. S., and MacNeilage, P. F. A motor theory of speech perception. In, *Proceedings of the speech communication seminar.* Stockholm: Royal Institute of Technology, 1962.

Liberman, A. M., Cooper, F. S., Harris, K. S., MacNeilage, P. F., and Studdert-Kennedy, M. G. Some observations on a model for speech perception. In W. Wathen-Dunn (Ed.), *Models for the perception of speech and visual form.* Cambridge, Massachusetts: M.I.T. Press, 1967(a).

Liberman, A. M., Cooper, F. S., Shankweiler, D. P., and Studdert-Kennedy, M. G. Perception of the speech code. *Psychological Review,* 1967(b), **74,** 431–461.

Lindblom, B. E. F. Spectrographic study of vowel reduction. *Journal of the Acoustical Society of America,* 1963, **35,** 1773–1781.

Lindblom, B. E. F. Numerical models in the study of speech production and speech perception: Some phonological implications. Paper presented at the VIIth International Congress of Phonetic Sciences, Montreal, August 1971.

Lindblom, B. E. F. and Sundberg, J. Neurophysiological representation of speech sounds. Paper presented at the XVth World Congress of Logopedics and Phoniatrics, Buenos Aires, Argentina, August 1971.

MacKay, D. G. Spoonerisms: The structure of errors in the serial ordering of speech. *Neuropsychologia,* 1970, **8,** 323–350.

MacNeilage, L. A. Activity of the speech apparatus during sleep and its relation to dream reports. Unpublished Ph.D. dissertation, Columbia University, 1971.

MacNeilage, L. A. and MacNeilage, P. F. Activity of the speech musculature during sleep. *Psychophysiology,* 1972, **9,** 130 (A).

MacNeilage, P. F. Motor control of serial ordering of speech. *Psychological Review,* 1970, **77,** 182–196.

MacNeilage, P. F., Cohen, D. B. and MacNeilage, L. A. Subject's estimation of sleep-talking propensity and dream recall frequency. *Journal of Consulting and Clinical Psychology,* 1972, **39,** 341.

MacNeilage, P. F. and DeClerk, J. L. On the motor control of coarticulation in CVC monosyllables. *Journal of the Acoustical Society of America,* 1969, **45,** 1217–1233.

MacNeilage, P. F., Krones, R. and Hanson, R. Closed-loop control of the initiation of jaw movement for speech. Paper presented at the meeting of the Acoustical Society of America, San Diego, November 1969.

MacNeilage, P. F., Rootes, T. P., and Chase, R. A. Speech production and perception in a patient with severe impairment of somesthetic perception and motor control. *Journal of Speech and Hearing Research,* 1967, **10,** 449–467.

McGuigan, F. J. Covert oral behavior during the silent performance of language tasks. *Psychological Bulletin,* 1970, **74,** 309–326.

McGuigan, F. J. and Tanner, R. Covert oral behavior during conversational and visual dreams. Paper presented at the meeting of the Association for the Psychophysiological Study of Sleep, Santa Fe, 1970.

Nooteboom, S. G. *The tongue slips into patterns. Nomen: Leyden studies in linguistics and phonetics.* A. G. Sciarone *et al.* (Eds.). The Hague: Mouton, 1969.

Nooteboom, S. G. The target theory of speech production. *IPO Annual Progress Report*, 1970, **5**, 51–55.

Öhman, S. E. G. Coarticulation in VCV utterances: Spectrographic measurements. *Journal of the Acoustical Society of America*, 1966, **39**, 151–168.

Rosner, B. S. Brain functions. In P. H. Mussen and M. R. Rosenweig, *Annual Review of Psychology*, 1970, **21**, 555–594.

Scott, C. M. A phonetic analysis of the effects of sensory deprivation. Unpublished Ph.D. dissertation, Purdue University, 1970.

Smith, J. L. Fusimotor neuron block and voluntary arm movement in man. Unpublished doctoral dissertation, University of Wisconsin, 1969.

Smith, T. S. and Lee, C. Y. Peripheral feedback mechanisms in speech production models? Paper presented at the VIIth International Congress of Phonetic Sciences, Montreal, August 1971.

Stevens, K. N. and Halle, M. Remarks on analysis by synthesis and distinctive features. In W. Wathen-Dunn (Ed.) Models for the perception of speech and visual form. Cambridge, Massachusetts: M.I.T. Press, 1967.

Stevens, K. N. and House, A. S. Perturbation of vowel articulation by consonantal context: An acoustical study. *Journal of Speech and Hearing Research*, 1963, **6**, 111–128.

Sussman, H. M. What the tongue tells the brain. *Psychological Bulletin*, 1971, **77**, 262–272.

Wicklegren, W. A. Context-sensitive coding, associative memory and serial order in (speech) behavior. *Psychological Review*, 1969, **76**, 1–15.

Whitaker, H. A. Some constraints on speech production models. In Tatham, M. A. A. (Ed.), Essex Symposium on Models of Speech Production. Occasional papers 9. University of Essex, Colchester, England.

CHAPTER THIRTEEN

Psychophysiological Correlates of Meaning: Essences or Tracers?

CHARLES E. OSGOOD[1]

University of Illinois

and

F. J. McGUIGAN

Hollins College

The past decade has witnessed a major revolution in linguistics, identified particularly with Noam Chomsky's (1957, 1965) development of the notion of a universal generative grammar. This development has had direct impact upon psycholinguistics, in the form of critiques of the adequacy of contemporary behavior theory for explaining, or even describing, language performance. These critiques also have serious implications for neobehaviorism in general—even though most psychologists seem blissfully unaware of it. Since no one in psycholinguistics, regardless of his biases, makes the claim that his theory is sufficient *in detail*, the arguments and counterarguments during this decade of controversy have been over the sufficiency *in principle* of competing theories.

---

[1] The first author presented this paper orally at Hollins College; hence, the first person singular throughout is used.

449

One of the claims of the Chomskian psycholinguists has been that human language behavior is, in its most interesting aspects, *innately determined* and therefore, any associationistic theory is inadequate in principle (cf. Chomsky, *Language and Mind*, 1968; McNeill, 1970). Behavior theory (in contrast to learning theory per se) includes the notion of innate propensities for language, but its counterclaims are that these propensities are *not species-specific* (see Gardners' intriguing description of sign language in a chimpanzee, 1969, and Roger Brown's thoughtful commentary, 1970), and that these propensities are *not language-specific*, as detailed in a paper by Osgood (1971) titled "Where Do Sentences Come From?"

As to the need for learning principles in any complete theory of language performance, it is sufficient to point out that the phonological rules, the syntactic rules (particularly for transformations from deep to surface structures), and the semantic rules of reference for *particular* languages must be learned. A child does not "mature" to speak English, Japanese, or Turkish. Generative grammars include no learning rules—nor should they, since they are static, post hoc descriptions of competence. But, more importantly, the Chomskian psycholinguists have so far failed to formulate any general, well-motivated set of learning principles for language (however, cf. Bever, 1970, on what he calls "perceptual strategies"). This is why—for psychology as contrasted with linguistics—the impact of Chomsky's work has not been a full-blown scientific revolution in Thomas Kuhn's (1964) terms; there has been no competing paradigm to substitute for learning theory.

It, therefore, behooves us to reconsider the potentialities and possible limitations (in principle) of psychological learning theory as applied to language behavior. It must be realized at the outset that not all learning theories are the same, except for their common utilization of association principles; there is a significant difference between the Skinnerian "single-stage" model and, for example, Osgood's "three-stage" model, which includes both *representational mediation processes* (S–R type principles), and *sensory and motor integration processes* (S–S and R–R type principles).

It was out of a common interest in providing psychophysiological evidence relevant to "higher mental processes" that the collaboration between F. J. McGuigan and myself began about 2 years ago. I think we constitute a reasonably well-balanced team for such research; although we are both behaviorists (and materialistic monists!), McGuigan leans toward a Peripheralist view and I toward a Centralist position. However, our collaboration has been over the long distance between Hollins and Illinois, and herein lies some apologia: Due in part to the occasionalness of our face-to-face contacts, in part to my having been out of the country for nearly 10 of the past 15 months on my cross-cultural research on affective meaning systems, and in part to Joe McGuigan having many other things to do in his fine lab than our joint work, my presentation must be more programmatic than data-based. But this, of course, has its advantages— where could we get more sophisticated advice than from the participants in this conference?

I. TWO-STAGE (REPRESENTATIONAL) NEOBEHAVIORISM

Let me begin with a brief description of the representational level— which for me came first in time and was a rather straightforward generalization from Hull's (1943) notions about anticipatory goal responses to behavior in general.

Representational mediation theory is the only learning approach that has seriously attempted to incorporate the symbolic processes in general, and meaning in particular, within an S–R associationistic model. My own version of neobehaviorism, as it has come to be called, has made explicit the origins of mediating (symbolic) processes in nonlinguistic, perceptuomotor behaviors—I refer you to my 1957 paper on perception and language as cognitive phenomena for details. Significates (referents or things signified) are simply those patterns of stimulation, including previously learned signs, which regularly and reliably produce distinctive patterns of behavior. The primary postulate of this theory of meaning is given in S–R terms as the upper part of Fig. 13.1 and may be verbalized as follows: *a stimulus pattern* (S) *which is not the same physical event as the thing signified* (S) *will become a sign of that significate when it becomes conditioned to a mediation process, this process* (a) *being some distinctive representation of the total behavior* (R_T) *produced by the significate and* (b) *serving to mediate overt behaviors* (R_x) *to the sign which are appropriate to* ("take account of") *the significate.* Although this provides only the crudest beginning for a semantic system, it is a beginning that is anchored, at least potentially, to observables.

By the time LAD (popular acronym for "Language Acquisition Device") is launching himself into linguistic sign learning, perceptual signs of most of the entities in his familiar environment (utensils, food objects, pets, toys, faces that smile and faces that frown) have been meaningfully differentiated in terms of distinctive mediators. Not only can such prelinguistic processes serve as "prefabricated" mediators in the subsequent learning of linguistic signs, but even more importantly many of the distinctive features of meaning have already been established.

There are two central issues that are relevant for us here—the nature of mediation processes and their source. But first a note on S–R symbolism: As shown in Fig. 13.1, I *now* use the subscript cap M to symbolize the *total* representational mediation process elicited by a sign, and the subscript lowercase m to symbolize the mediator *components*, or semantic features, into which total M can be analyzed. Failure to make this distinction clear caused no end of confusion in my debates with Jerry Fodor (Fodor, 1965, 1966; Osgood, 1966, 1971).

With regard to the *nature* of mediation processes in behavior, r_M's (both caps and lowers) have the theoretical status of *hypothetical constructs* (with presumed existential properties) rather than intervening variables (convenient summarizing fictions). I assume that in the adult human language-user, certainly, these mediating events have become cortical

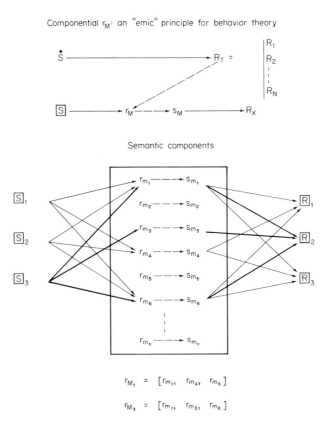

Fig. 13.1. Componential r_M: an "emic" principle for behavior theory.

processes—processes whose neurological nature and locus will remain obscure for a very long time. The r_M's and their automatic consequents s_M's are defined *functionally* in S–R terms in order to incorporate mediation processes within the larger body of learning theory and facilitate transfer of such broadly applicable single-stage principles as habit strength, generalization and inhibition to the two-stage model. We can thus say that both big total $_M$s and little componential $_m$s have responselike functions as dependent events (in semantic decoding or sentence understanding) and stimuluslike functions as antecedent events (in semantic encoding, or sentence creating).

The lower portion of Fig. 13.1 illustrates the critical assumption that representational mediation processes are *componential* in nature. A relatively small number of independent r_m components, by virtue of their combination in diverse simultaneous patterns, can serve to differentiate the meanings of a very large number of distinctive total r_M's, each related to its source behavior (R_T) uniquely—but uniquely as a whole, not in terms of unique components. This is what I have referred to elsewhere as the "emic" principle of behavior (Osgood, 1970). Like the *phoneme* (or, more properly, the *sememe*) in linguistic theory, the total r_M in neobehaviorism (1) *renders functionally equivalent classes of different behavioral events,* either signs having the same significance (like signs 1 and 2 in Fig. 13.1) or behaviors expressing the same intention (like behaviors 1 and 3 with respect to intention r_{M1}), (2) *is an abstract entity,* presently unobserved itself but necessary for interpretation of what is observed, and (3) *is resolvable into a "simultaneous bundle" of distinctive features or components* which serve to differentiate among meanings (thus, as shown in Fig. 13.1, the meanings of signs 1 and 3 are distinguished by the presence of components 4 versus 3, respectively). The continuous and bipolar nature of semantic components is not shown here for the sake of simplicity but is assumed in the general theory.

With regard to the *source* of representational mediators, it is true that the theory postulates—for the historical origins of semantic features—derivation of r_m's from R_T's (overt behaviors to the things signified). It is important to emphasize that r_m's are representations of those aspects of R_T's which have made a difference in appropriateness of behaving with respect to the things signified by signs and have therefore been differentially reinforced. Thus the locomotor movements by which an organism moves from place A to place B (walking, running, swimming, etc.) may be nondistinctive with respect to avoiding signs of danger at A, or approaching signs of safety at B, but the common *affective features* of the diverse ways of avoiding versus approaching will be differentially reinforced and become components of the signs of A versus B. Nevertheless, the most deep-set resistance to this neobehaviorist account of meaning, I think, is to its anchoring of r_m's to R_T's—having semantic distinctions originate in differences in the *behaviors* to Things rather than in the *perceptions* of Things. This "metaphysical repugnance" persists even when it is understood that this anchoring is *historical* and not contemporary for the adult speaker.

Meeting this repugnance with some hard psychophysiological data on the development (and possible centralization) of representational processes will be one of our prime research tasks. From a behavioristic point of view, the anchoring of meanings to subsequent, as well as antecedent, observables serves at least two functions: (1) It eliminates, in principle, the sheer circularity of defining semantic features in terms of perceptible distinctions—which *would* erase all but terminological differences between mentalistic and behavioristic positions. (2) It places rather severe constraints upon *what* differences that are perceptibly discriminable will actually come to make a difference in meaning. The human sensory systems are capable of quantities of discriminations that are literally incredible; any psycholinguistic theory must be able to account for the relatively small number (and nature) of those discriminations which will acquire the status of semantic features. Without such constraints, representational mediation theory would indeed become a universal Turing Machine—like God's Will, capable of explaining anything but patently incapable of disproof. By providing a behavioral rationale for such constraints on the proliferation of semantic features, the present theory enhances the prospect of discovering, and even predicting the nature of, those that are universal in human language.

II. UNIVERSALS OF AFFECTIVE MEANING

A little over 20 years ago—without exactly expecting it to turn out that way—I began working on the quantification of certain features of affective or emotional meaning. First using ordinary native speakers of American English (college sophomores taking introductory psychology, of course), we found that when samples of such subjects were given samples of diverse concepts to judge against samples of diverse 7-step scales, defined by adjectival polar opposites, and factor analysis was applied to the "cubes" of data thus generated, we kept obtaining evidence for three gross factors. These factors defined themselves, in terms of the scales loading highest on them, as Evaluation (e.g., *good–bad, pleasant–un-*

pleasant, *kind–cruel*, etc.), Potency (e.g., *strong–weak*, *hard–soft*, *big–little*, etc.), and Activity (*active–passive*, *quick–slow*, *lively–dull*, etc.)—henceforth E, P, and A. Was it possible that this system was somehow peculiar to American culture or to the English language? During the past 10 years we have gradually extended the semantic differential technique (SD) to some 25 human communities around the world varying in both language and culture. We have minimized reliance upon translation and have maximized the opportunity for each community to generate its own modes of qualifying (most productive adjectival dimensions) and its own ways of relating them (dominant factors). Without a single exception, E, P, and A have appeared as dominant factors; in other words, this underlying structure of affective meaning is a human universal (see Osgood, 1971b, for details).

But *why* the universality of E, P, and A? I believe it has to do with the importance of emotion in human affairs. It was M. Brewster Smith who first pointed out to me the close similarity of our E–P–A to Wundt's *dimensions of feeling*. Apparently, what is important to us now, as it was in the Age of the Neanderthal—Chomsky and the rationalists to the contrary—is the *good* or *bad* for us of the things signified by signs, the *strength* or *weakness* of these things with respect to ourselves, and their *activeness* or *passiveness* (is it a saber-toothed tiger or merely a pool of quicksand, which I can simply walk around?).

But why does the SD (semantic differential) technique yield these massive affective factors rather than the equally ubiquitous denotative features, like Abstract/Concrete and Human/Nonhuman, which linguists, philosophers, and lexicographers are wont to exercise? The answer, in a nutshell, is that the SD technique literally forces the metaphorical usage of adjectival qualifiers, *and shared affective appears to be the common coin of metaphor*. With subjects instructed to check every item, they must deal somehow with *hot defeat* versus *cold defeat, hard power* versus *soft power* and *sweet mother-in-law* versus *sour mother-in-law*; the fact that they do deal with many such items—and in very consistent ways—is the fact to conjure with. Since multivariate analysis runs factors through bundles of closely related scales, and since most scales must be used most of the time in affectively metaphorical rather than in denotative ways, out come booming old E, P, and A.

I have been accused—by some of my close associates as well as by some of my dissociates—of being schizophrenic as far as my SD measurement model and my representational mediation theory of meaning are concerned. There is, they claim, no obvious relation between loadings on factors and little r_m's.

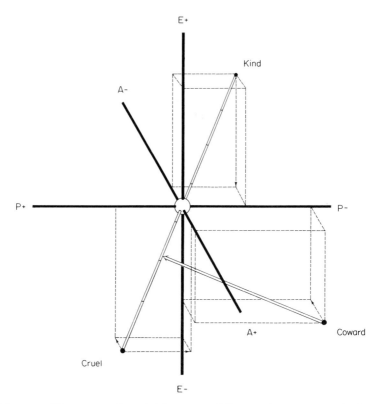

Fig. 13.2. The common factorial (componential) space for concepts and skill terms in semantic differential analysis.

As shown in Fig. 13.2, application of the factor-analytic measurement model provides a framework of underlying dimensions *which is common to both concept-meanings and scale-meanings* and in terms of which both can be described in relation to each other. These underlying dimensions thus have the functional properties of *semantic features*. We refer to scales as having *loadings* on these underlying factors; the scale *kind–cruel*, for example, has loadings of +.70 on E, −.35 on P (that is, *cruel* is more Potent than *kind*), and −.15 on A. From these loadings we can assign *kind* and *cruel* their reciprocal locations in the space. We can characterize *kind* as being Very Good, Quite Weak, and Slightly Passive affectively, and *cruel* as being Very Bad, Quite Strong, and Slightly Active. We refer to concepts as having *scores* on the same underlying factors; if the concept COWARD, for example, had scores of −.50 on E, −.70 on P and +.20 on A, its affectivity paraphrase would be *A COWARD is Quite Bad, Very*

Weak, and Slightly Active. Making the projection from the COWARD point to the *kind–cruel* line in the three-factor space, we predict that COWARD will be rated as "slightly cruel" on the *kind–cruel* scale.

How does representational mediation theory relate to this spatial measurement model? (1) The r_M is componential in nature; (2) the components (r_m's) which do become part of the total mediation process, or meaning, of a sign represent those aspects of the total behavior to things which have made a difference in adjustment toward these things and hence have been differentially reinforced; and (3) it will be recalled that, although I presume representational mediators to be entirely central (cortical) events, in theory they retain the functional properties of "responses" as subsequent events, and of "stimuli" as antecedent events. Several theoretically relevant properties of mediation processes flow from this: (1) Since the overt reaction systems which central mediators represent are organized on a reciprocally antagonistic basis, as Sherrington and many others have shown—for example, the muscles which contract in making a fist are inhibited in making an open hand, and vice versa—it follows that *the r_m components derived from such systems will also function in reciprocally antagonistic fashion.* (2) Since overt reaction systems vary in the intensity with which they respond to various stimuli (here, intensity of motor contraction, etc.), *so should their central representations vary in intensity* (here, presumably rate of neural activation). And (3) since the same reaction system cannot assume reciprocally antagonistic "postures" at the same time, but rather must display compromise between excitatory and inhibitory tendencies, it follows that *simultaneous tendencies toward antagonistic r_m's* (e.g., toward $+P$ and $-P$) *must cancel each other toward neutrality or meaninglessness.* This last property of representational mediation processes is the entrée of behavior theory into cognitive dynamics generally and into semantic anomaly specifically.

I identify the underlying semantic factors or features derived in the measurement model with the affective components (r_m's) *of representational mediation processes.* That such features are characteristically bipolar in nature is consistent with the reciprocally antagonistic nature of the reaction systems from which such mediator components arise. That semantic factors should be ordered in productivity (frequency and diversity of usage as aspects of meaning) is consistent with the behavioristic notion of differential reinforcement of those mediating behaviors which make a difference in adjustment. Thus, in the affective meaning system Evaluation (the Good versus the Bad of things) has more weight than Activity, just as Sex (The Masculine versus Feminine of things) has more weight than Maritality in the semantics of kinship. *I identify the points in the measure-*

ment space which represent the meanings of concepts (whether they be nominals like COWARD, or adjectivals like *kind* and *cruel*) *with the total and unique mediation processes* (r_M's) *presumed in theory to be elicited by signs.* Such total representational processes, however, are analysable into simultaneous bundles of mediator components which vary in polarity and intensity (the directions and length of vectors in Fig. 13.2). But, these components are *not* unique to particular signs; thus COWARD, *kind* and *cruel* all include in their r_M's the E, P, and A component r_m's, but with varying signs and intensities.

The characterization I have just given of representational mediation processes has certain implications for the use of EEG and EMG recording in tracking either the "essences" or "tracers" of r_M's, whichever may turn out to be the case. Since total r_M's involve a reasonably large number of components, it seems infeasible to even attempt to record them in toto—although there is at least the possibility of distinctive EEG patterns, *if* we knew where and how to look. I certainly wish we could get differential readings on E, P, and A, because here we have a very good handle on their overt psycholinguistic manifestations. However, it should be feasible to tap r_m components—again, either of "real" semantic features or of "artificial" ones we build into the subject—with appropriate EMG recordings. But in this case, since the theory says such meaning components are based on the reciprocally antagonistic activations *of the same reaction systems*, we must be able to either use the *same* electrode placement to differentially record excitation versus inhibition of the same muscle (e.g., as excited in lip flattening, and inhibited in lip pursing), or use electrodes placed in different locations to record separately from the different muscles that are reciprocally innervated (e.g., one for the lip-flattener, and one for the lip-purser).

III. THREE-STAGE (INTEGRATIONAL) NEOBEHAVIORISM

Even the crudest observation of behavior reveals that certain patterns and sequences of stimuli have perceptual priority over others (e.g., word-forms over nonword letter strings) and that certain patterns and sequences of responses are more readily executed than others (e.g., familiar multisyllabic words like *representational* (!) over unfamiliar ones like *platyhelminthean*, as said in characterizing a species of flatworm). The phenomena of *perceptual organization*, long the stronghold of gestalt psychology and the waterloo of behaviorism, and of *motor organization*, as emphasized as long ago as 1951 by Lashley, are clearly part of total behavior, including language behavior, and must somehow be accounted for. Without having exactly these things in mind, Donald Hebb in 1949 put his finger on a general property of certain central nervous system tissues that may underly the formation of such perceptual and motor skills: *whenever the more central correlates of signals at the termini of projection systems are caused to be simultaneously active and are in fibrous contact, either directly or mediately, an increased dependence of each upon the other results.* Note that such integrative processes must occur more centrally than the projection systems, since "what leads to what" in the latter is essentially isomorphic and unmodifiable by experience. By virtue of these properties, however, excitation patterns at the termini of the projection systems do provide a faithful "mirror of what is" for the organism.

What kind of functional psychological principle seems to be embodied here? I would phrase it this way, fully appreciating the oversimplification of the statement: *The greater the frequency with which stimulus events* (S–S) *or response events* (R–R) *have co-occurred in the input or output experience of the organism, the greater will be the tendency for their postprojectional* (s–s) *or preprojectional* (r–r) *central neural correlates to activate each other.* In essence this Integration Principle says that redundancies in either the sensory input or the motor output of an organism will come to be mirrored by evocative (high frequency) or merely predictive (lower frequency) dependencies in its central nervous system—perhaps in what have been called "the sensory and motor association areas?" This might be termed a predictive "mirror of what ought to be." (And while talking about how organisms reflect the environment in their nervous systems, the mediation processes I discussed earlier might be termed a representational "mirror of what is signified"—involving, unlike sensory and motor integrations, past contingencies of behaviors with differential reinforcements.) Note that this Integration Principle, in contrast to gestalt theory, is an associative *learning* principle; however, it asserts the formation of associations *among* input events (s–s), and *among* output events (r–r), rather than *between* input and output events (s–r), as is the behaviorist's wont (see Osgood, 1957a and b).

On the sensory side this principle leads to prediction of "closure," or central completion, of familiar perceptions on the basis of sketchy input information and, with lower frequencies of input pairing, to the preparatory "tuning up" of certain perceptions as against others—as when hearing part of a familiar tune facilitates hearing the remainder of it even when drowned in noise. On the motor side, this principle predicts the formation of tightly welded skill components (the syllabic skills of language, the pincing, grasping, and typing skills of manipulation, and so on) which run themselves off as wholes on the basis of exactly the kind of central programming that I think Lashley was talking about; with lower frequencies of output pairing, we have the stabilizing effects of correctly executed prior acts upon performance of other acts that are often subsequent—even to embarrassing sequencing, as when one blows out the match that someone has just used to politely light his cigarette first!

Before leaving the realm of pure (or impure, as the case may be) theorizing, I must say something about the humble *word*, and about *feedback* between representational levels in this model. They turn out to be critical matters in the McGuigan–Osgood research program. The word is the most familiar and easily identified unit of language for ordinary native speakers, yet it has defied ready definition by linguists, lurking somewhere between the morpheme and the sentence. The word also has duality of function in my model (Osgood, 1963). I assume it to be the *largest* unit at the integration level; it is typically the largest unit which meets the criteria of brevity of temporal duration, frequency of occurrence, and redundancy as a whole necessary for formation of evocative integrations. As Greenberg (1957) has demonstrated, it is at the boundaries of words (rather than of morphemes within words) that there is practically unlimited possibility of insertion, and hence the production of an almost infinite variety of sentences; therefore, larger units rarely have high enough frequencies of occurrence *as wholes*. On the other hand, I assume the word to be the *smallest* unit at the representational or meaningful level; although non-word morphemes may signal aspects of meaning (i.e., r_m components), it appears to be words that are associated with simultaneous bundles of semantic features (i.e., total r_M).

There are three types of feedback within this behavior model that are of particular concern to Joe McGuigan and myself. The first is long-loop proprioceptive feedback from the peripheral speech musculature to the other sensory integration systems (particularly hearing and vision); this is McGuigan's prime candidate for explaining certain (perceptual) phenomena we are studying. The second is short-loop, purely central feedback from the representational (meaning) level into the integrational (perceptual) level; this, of course, is Osgood's prime candidate for explanation of the same phenomena. The third is perhaps better described as "short circuiting" than as "feedback"; it is the centralizing process itself, the pulling back up into the representational level of processes that (I assume) begin as overt reactions in muscles and glands, lose their overtness as they gain programming in the motor integration system, and finally become directly elicitable as meaningful r_M's by signs as stimuli (Watson referred to this possibility as a "recession" into the central nervous system).

Some such centralizing process is implicitly assumed in my interpretation of other (semantic) phenomena we are studying. I should also mention a similar type of short-circuiting proposed recently by Anthony Greenwald (1970) in his rejuvenation of William James's notion of ideo-motor action—the principle that the perceptual image or idea of an action initiates execution of that action. In Greenwald's behavioristic transcription of this notion, it is proposed that the peripheral feedbacks (visual, etc., as well as proprioceptive) of actions, thus *images of actions*, become conditioned to sign-produced input stimuli and thereby can become anticipatory to and serve to initiate the very actions from which they were derived. It should be noted that this proposal explicitly involves the formation of s–s associations. I shall return to these conceptions in appropriate contexts.

IV. CENTRAL VERSUS PERIPHERAL FACILITATION OF PERCEPTION

The idea behind one of our joint studies came from a phenomenon I once observed while listening to a recording of a Gilbert and Sullivan operetta with my wife. She was following the printed libretto. In the midst of a many-voiced male chorus—which I found completely unintelligible—I happened to glance down to where her finger was tracing the music. I also started following the text, and suddenly the words became perfectly intelligible. It was not simply that I now "understood" what was auditorily fuzzy; the words being sung *sounded* clear. Repeated tests gave the same subjective effect. I have since checked with other people, and many report the same observation. The first question was whether this Gilbert-and-Sullivan Effect (as we have come to call it) can be demonstrated under controlled laboratory conditions. If so, then we face the question of the basis of the phenomenon: Is the enhancement of hearing by seeing mediated by proprioceptive feedback from the speech musculature, covertly activated in silent reading (the McGuigan hypothesis)? Or is it mediated by feedback from the representational (meaning) processes elicited by the unambiguous printed text (the Osgood hypothesis)? And here we find ourselves right back in the middle of the classic controversy between Periphalists and Centralists over the nature of thought and consciousness. But first, and briefly, some irrelevant data—"irrelevant" because they have nothing to do with electropsychological measurements, although they are clearly relevant to my own general theory.

I have already discussed the dual status of the humble word—typically the largest unit at the level of meaningless sensory integration, and the smallest unit at the level of meaningful representation. Over the past year Mr. Rumjahn Hoosain and myself have been running a series of experiments designed to demonstrate the salience of the word in tachistoscopic perception as compared with either smaller or larger linguistic units. The first experiment compared both guessing thresholds (where the first guess, word or nonword, correct or incorrect, is counted as the threshold estimate) and the usual recognition thresholds of (1) nonword morphemes (like -*voke*) versus words that include them (like *provoke*), (2) nonword morphemes versus real words matched for general shape (like *poke*), and (3) nonword combinations of morphemes (like *lossate*) versus matched multisyllabic real words (like *lobster*). In all cases, the real words were selected so as to have *lower* frequencies of usage than the minimal estimates of the frequencies of the morphemes (which occur in many words, of course).

Table 13-1 gives the data for nonword morphemes versus words including them. The first column gives the estimated frequencies of usage; as you see, in all cases they are higher for nonwords than for words. Columns two and three give the mean guessing and mean recognition thresholds, respectively; here the sign tests for correlated data (subjects as their own controls) for recognition thresholds were significant at the .001 level but those for guessing thresholds were not. The last column gives the most frequent misperceptions (guesses); you will notice that they are usually, but not always, words—and, more importantly, they are *always* of the same general shape as the correct form, indicating that the guessing itself is being driven by the partial sensory integration. Table 13-2 presents parallel data for nonword morphemes versus matched monosyllabic words. Here, although the item means for guessing thresholds do not indicate it, the correlated sign tests across subjects as their own controls (using means for all items of a given type) are significant for both guessing ($p = .02$), and recognition thresholds ($p = .001$). Again you will note that estimated frequencies of usage for words are always less than the minimal estimates for nonword morphemes, and usually by considerable amounts. Table 13-3 presents parallel data for multisyllabic nonwords versus matched words. No estimated frequency of usage is given for *grobion*—this being a flub on our part, since *grob* is not a morpheme—but you will note again the extreme differences between most of the other nonwords and words in usage frequency. As you can see by comparing the second and third columns for nonwords and words, in this multisyllabic condition both guessing and recognition thresholds are much lower for the words than the morpheme combinations, significance being greater than the .001 level in both cases.

It seems clear that words have a higher salience in language perception

TABLE 13-1

Morphemes versus Words

	Monosyllabic nonword morphemes				Words containing the morphemes				
	Freq./ million	Means, guesses	Means, recog.	Most freq. mispercept.		Freq./ million	Means, guesses	Means, recog.	Most freq. mispercept.
ment	130	14[a]	19[a]	mant (3)[b]	mental	41	13[a]	15[a]	menial (4)[b]
mani	17	15	20	male (3)	manifest	17	12	14	—
fide	76	13	17	tide (5)	fidelity	6	15	16	finally (2)
para	29	13	19	pars (6)	paradox	3	14	17	pardon (2)
voke	18	14	18	voice (3)	provoke	15	13	17	provide (6)
sist	129	14	18	mist (3)	resist	33	18	18	—
cuse	76	16	20	curse (4)	accuse	28	16	17	—
sult	407	12	19	suit (7)	insult	21	13	14	—

[a] Times in milliseconds.
[b] Frequencies in parentheses.

TABLE 13-2
Morphemes versus Words

	Monosyllabic nonword morphemes					Monosyllabic words			
	Freq./million	Means, guesses	Means, recog.	Most freq. mispercept.		Freq./million	Means, guesss	Means, recog.	Most freq. mispercept.
ment	130	14[a]	19[a]	mant (3)[b]	mend	49	14[a]	18[a]	hand mand (3)[b]
mani	17	15	20	male (3)	mane	10	14	19	name (5)
fide	76	13	17	tide (5)	pile	50	13	16	pills (3)
para	29	13	19	pars (6)	pave	14	13	16	prove (3)
voke	18	14	18	voice (3)	poke	12	14	16	pose (3)
sist	129	14	18	mist (3)	seat	124	13	20	nest (4)
cuse	76	16	20	curse (4)	fuse	7	14	14	—
sult	407	12	19	suit (7)	salt	100	13	14	—

[a] Times in milliseconds.
[b] Frequencies in parentheses.

TABLE 13-3

Morphemes versus Words

	Multisyllabic nonword morpheme combinations					Multisyllabic words			
	Freq./ million	Means, guesses	Means, recog.	Most freq. mispercept.		Freq./ million	Means, guesses	Means, recog.	Most freq. mispercept.
famness	135	25[a]	45[a]	famous (9)[b]	dashing	3	15[a]	16[a]	—
roofism	63	24	35	—	sublime	8	13	16	—
planial	194	20	23	—	plaster	16	13	14	plastic (3)[b]
framive	179	13	44	famine (2)	frantic	12	14	16	frontier (3)
artover	606	18	21	actover (3)	article	153	13	14	artistic (3)
grobion	—	25	35	question (4)	problem	178	13	16	—
lossate	86	22	48	—	lobster	7	14	15	luster (3)
henette	36	22	36	benette (2)	harmony	23	13	13	—

[a] Times in milliseconds.
[b] Frequencies in parentheses.

465

than more frequent nonword morphemes, but what about larger units than the word? Hoosain has recently completed analyzing the data from what we have dubbed "the peanut butter experiment." We chose nominal compounds like *peanut butter* as the larger units to compare with the words composing them because they function linguistically more like units than any other combinations of words (e.g., *happy man*, or *run fast*) and because there are semantic constraints on the co-occurrence of their parts (e.g., *stumbling block* is something quite different in meaning from either *stumbling* or *block*, unlike, say, *purple mushroom*). Again both guessing and recognition thresholds were compared for 13 such compounds and the 26 words which make them up, half of the subjects having the compounds first, and the other half the individual words first. It was expected, of course, that prior presentation of the words would lower thresholds for the compounds, and vice versa, so we would compare compounds versus words, when both are given first (but to different sets of subjects), and then the *shifts* in threshold for compounds and words between being prior and being subsequent in order of presentation. Figure 13.3 presents the primary data for recognition thresholds. First you will note that, when each type is presented first in order, compounds have much higher thresholds than the words that compose them; comparing the means for the 15 subjects getting the compounds first with the means of the other 15 subjects getting the single words first (26 word/compound pairs), compounds had higher thresholds in 24 cases and single words in only two cases.

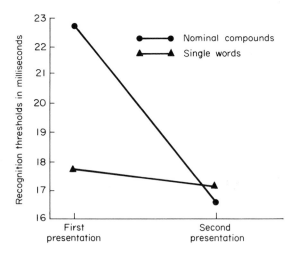

Fig. 13.3. Effects upon recognition thresholds of prior exposure to words upon their compounds and vice versa.

Second, you will note the most interesting fact that whereas recognition of compounds is markedly and significantly facilitated by having seen the component words first, prior presentation of compounds has practically no facilitative effect upon the thresholds for single words.

If this is not some inverse kind of "ceiling effect"—which must be checked by comparing the facilitative effect of prior presentation of the 26 single words upon subsequent recognition of *the same words* (which should be considerable, judging from the literature)[1]—then it would appear that words tend to lose their identity in compounds and thereby the facilitation of "repetition," even in reducing alternatives. The "identity" lost can only be in terms of *meaning*—both *stumbling* and *block* having quite different r_M's independently than when in the compound *stumbling block*. Since the s_M producing facilitative feedback upon the perceptual integration of *stumbling* is that appropriate to the meaning of this single word, and not that appropriate to the meaning of the compound, prior recognition of the compound has little effect upon subsequent recognition of its component words. But this will *not* be the case for effects of prior recognition of single words upon subsequent recognition of their compounds. Why? Because representational "tuning up" of *either* word in the subsequently tested nominal compound will—given the semantic constraints—serve to lower the recognition threshold of the whole. The same type of interpretation may hold for the perceptual salience of words as compared with morphemes. Since only *total* s_M's are *uniquely* associated with facilitation of particular words via feedback, whereas *componential* s_m's (e.g., +Sex or −Potency) are associated with whole classes of words, it follows that at the borderline of near-recognition of a form the specific feedback for words will be more likely to make them leap into perceptual clarity than the generalized feedback from single semantic features.

Which is not to say that single features cannot have any effects under any conditions, and this leads me to one more "irrelevant" experiment. Rona Roydes and I (1972) wanted to find out if a *grammatical set* for Noun versus Verb could have differential facilitative effects upon the tachistoscopic perceptual integration of words in the same way that semantic sets (e.g., for animal words, for food words, for success versus failure words, etc.) have been shown to have. To keep the stimulus (and hence sensory integration) characteristics of the words constant, we used 20 test words that can function as *either* Noun or Verb in English, but 10 were HiNoun, used as nouns 90%, and as verbs 10% of the time (e.g., *ship, box, fire, head*), and 10 were HiVerb by the same criterion (e.g.,

---

[1] Since the writing of this chaper, this has been checked experimentally, and it is not a ceiling effect.

look, can, move, call). Half of the subjects were given a Noun set and half a Verb set—by being given lists of 20 *unambiguous* nouns or verbs and asked to look for the part of speech the words all had in common. Although there were no significant main effects for either set or grammatical class—and it was predicted that there would be none—the *interaction* of set with dominant form class was significant at the .05 level. As predicted, subjects set for Noun had recognition thresholds lower than controls for HiNouns, and higher than controls for HiVerbs—despite the fact that identical word forms were being presented. Not only do these results suggest that grammatical features are in at least some respects like semantic features, but for present purposes it is further evidence for feedback from representational to integrational systems.

Let us now return to the Gilbert-and-Sullivan Effect (henceforth, G-S). It has been amply demonstrated that perception in one modality may be facilitated by increasing stimulation in another (Hartman, 1933; Kekcheev, Kravkov, & Shvarts, 1954; Zwosta & Zenhausern, 1969). However, these are all cases of generalized, noninformational facilitation. The only studies we have been able to locate in which specific facilitation across auditory and visual modalities is investigated are reported by W. M. Smith (1965a, b). Smith found that near-synchronous presentation of auditory verbal stimuli facilitates tachistoscopic recognition of the "same" verbal stimuli in the visual mode. Only the thresholds for matched, not mismatched, three-syllable words showed this effect. According to Smith (1965b), the fact that the effect occurs when another's voice (the experimenter's) is heard synchronously with the visual display, as well as when the subject himself speaks the words (repeating the experimenter), eliminates feedback from the speech musculature as an explanation. However, the possibility that the subjects were subvocalizing while listening to the experimenter is not eliminated.[2] Therefore, Smith's results offer another instance of the G-S effect (albeit in reverse, hearing upon reading), but they do not help to differentiate between covert oral and representational sources of facilitation.

There seems to be no question but that covert oral responses do increase measurably during the silent performance of linguistic tasks. Restricting ourselves to those EMG studies which meet three methodological criteria (McGuigan, 1970a)—that the covert oral EMG increase significantly during silent linguistic performance, that it does so independently of simultaneous measures at other loci, and that it not occur under non-

---

[2] The fact that the effect peters out progressively as the visual exposure is moved toward the *end* of the auditory stimulation seems to rule out the obvious response bias explanation pretty effectively (personal communication to F. J. McGuigan).

linguistic performance conditions—we may note Jacobson's (1932) positive evidence for tasks like "imagine counting" and "recall a poem," McGuigan and Rodier's (1968) positive evidence for enhanced covert oral behavior during silent reading (due to simultaneous listening to prose), and McGuigan's (1970b) positive evidence during writing words versus nonlinguistic tasks. Furthermore, it has been concluded by many investigators (Schilling, 1929; Edfeldt, 1960; McGuigan, 1970a; Sokolov, 1969) that covert oral behavior has beneficial effects upon the performance of linguistic tasks. McGuigan (1970a) hypothesized the covert oral response to be a critical event in extremely rapid and complex feedback loops among the speech regions of the brain, the vocal musculature, the inner ears, the eyes, and so on—all involved interactively, for example, in reading out loud and presumably in reading silently as well. More particularly, he suggests that covert oral responses generate verbal codes, these codes being carried in afferent neural impulses, performing an integrative function among the linguistic regions of the body, and serving to amplify code distinctions in these other regions (see Chapter 10).

In short, the two theoretical issues are:

1. Is such demonstrable covert oral activity *necessary* for linguistic processing? This was the original question posed by Jacobson (1932), and Max (1935), and in related EMG studies. It is conceivable that subvocal activity is nothing more than excitatory overflow along those pathways ordinarily involved in overt execution—and like the noise of an engine, not essential to its functioning. A compromise view would be that while peripheral involvement is necessary for the *development* of language, including both phonological and semantic codes, it is no longer necessary for adult linguistic performance (cf. Osgood, 1953, pp. 653–655).

2. Is such demonstrable covert oral activity *sufficient* for linguistic processing? If proprioceptive feedback from the vocal musculature were to provide anything more than a generalized tonic effect upon language perception or meaning, it would have to display precisely particularized relationships to the auditory linguistic stimuli. This is certainly true for *overt* speech, but it must be shown to hold as well for *covert* speech.

Although it is not required that covert speech be a miniature of overt speech—resemble it in every way except amplitude—there is some evidence for a reasonably close resemblance. For example, heightened covert oral EMG during silent reading and during auditory hallucination may be accompanied by slight "whispering" that can be understood as English words by the experimenter (Gould, 1949, 1950; McGuigan *et al.*, 1964; McGuigan, 1966). Locke and Fehr (1970) had adult subjects perform a serial learning task using visually presented disyllabic words characterized by the presence or absence of letters representing labial phonemes; mean peak amplitudes of lip EMG were significantly greater for labial than for non-labial words during both presentation and rehearsal. To the extent that this issue can be resolved affirmatively, then an affirmative answer to issue (1) becomes much more likely.

To summarize, McGuigan's "peripheral" theory would explain the Gilbert-Sullivan effect in terms of enhancement of the auditory signals by feedback from the vocal musculature, the feedback being produced by covert reading of the clear visual signals. Osgood's "central" theory would explain the G-S effect in terms of representational-level feedback from the meanings (s_M) of the words which are normally near-synchronous with clear hearing, but here are produced by "synonymous" and clear visual signs.

We planned a series of four experiments to get at the "truth" of the matter. Experiment I, using Gilbert and Sullivan choral materials, was designed to demonstrate the empirical validity of the phenomenon, but it does not allow choice among the alternative interpretations. Experiment II would use Finnish linguistic materials—a language which, though easily and fluently pronounceable after surface training, would be *still* meaningless to the subjects; if the G-S effect still appears with r_m removed, a peripheral interpretation is favored and a central one disfavored. Experiment III would use the operetta materials again, but with oral proprioceptive feedback damped; if the G-S effect still appears, the central interpretation is favored as against the peripheral one. And Experiment IV would again use the Finnish materials but also with damping of proprioceptive feedback; if the G-S effect still appears, then we must obviously look elsewhere for an explanation. Unfortunately, only the first of these planned experiments has been completed, though we are making some progress in other relevant collaborative studies (see later).

Eight volunteer undergraduates at Hollins College served as subjects in Experiment I.[3] They were introduced into the laboratory (see McGuigan & Rodier, 1968, for details on apparatus and general procedures) and the usual assurances that they would be harmed in no way were given by the experimenter. Surface electrodes were placed on the chin, lip, tongue, and right calf for recording electromyograms. The subjects were told that they would listen to several pieces of choral music, and would simultaneously be viewing several slides containing the printed passages, that sometimes the printed words would help them understand the words being sung and

---

[3] Many thanks to Suzanne Hadley, who was the experimenter and coauthor of this research.

sometimes not, but that they were to pay attention to the music, pressing a button during periods when they felt they could clearly hear and understand the words *being sung* and releasing the button when they could not clearly hear and understand. This is our measure of *subjective understanding* of the auditory materials.

A panel of three independent judges had previously listened to various male chorus sections of several Gilbert and Sullivan operettas, being instructed simply to write "yes" or "no" next to the selection numbers to indicate when they "could clearly hear and understand" a majority of the words, and when they could not. Passages judged *unanimously* "yes" were selected as highly intelligible (HiI), and those judged unanimously "no" as of low intelligibility (LoI) for the experiment.

Five musical selections of 40-sec duration were presented to each subject: two were HiI, two were LoI, and one selection was purely instrumental music. Each subject served as her own control, with the order of the four choral selections being counterbalanced across subjects. The musical selection was last in all cases. The order of slides during each selection was 10 sec blank slide, 10 sec matching *or* nonmatching visual slide, 10 sec blank slide, and 10 sec matching *or* nonmatching slide; the order of matching and nonmatching slides in slots two and four was randomized. After each 40-sec selection the subject was given a recognition test containing 10–12 phrases from the actual choral passage, three or four items from the nonmatching (visually presented) passage, and ten extraneous phrases from other operettas. For all except the purely instrumental selection (where they were to check items *seen*), subjects were instructed to "check those items which you recognize as having been *sung.*" These recognition scores are our measure of *objective understanding*. There were periods of relaxation (monitored by the EMG levels) prior to the first selection, and after each following selection.

Turning now to the results, we may note first that the subjects *did* reliably report the subjective G-S effect: they signaled understanding of the LoI choral material during 60% of its presentation time when the accompanying slides matched the sung words, as against 11% of the time when nonmatching slides accompanied the music ($t = 4.11$, $p < .05$; $\alpha = .05$ throughout) and as against 17% of the time for the LoI/Blank-slide condition ($p < .05$). That the subject were signaling understanding of the words actually being *sung*, as instructed, is shown by the fact that they not only signaled understanding for HiI 86% of the time for matching slides, but also 84% of the time for nonmatching slides.

Recognition scores were computed as the percentage of items from the actual choral passages that were correctly identified. Over-all veracity of the *subjective* reports of understanding is indicated by the fact that *objective* recognition scores were higher for choral passages signaled "understood" (48% correct) than for those signaled "not understood" (22% correct); this difference is also significant at the .05 level.

A more stringent test of the G-S effect is provided by the data shown in Table 13-4. Recognition scores for the LoI/Matching-Slide Understood condition (54%) were significantly higher ($p < .05$) than for LoI/Blank-slide/Not-understood condition (10%), the subjects thus reporting that relatively unintelligible passages become perceptually clear in the *auditory* modality when the same words are being seen in the visual modality.[4] Testifying to the validity of the judges' classifications of selections as to their intelligibility, we note that for both Matching-slide and Blank-slide conditions (whether Understood or Not) HiI selections get higher recognition scores than LoI selections; this does not hold for the Nonmatching-slide condition, but two of the cells have N's of only 2.

The strange recognition scores for the Blank-slide condition—only 26% for HiI/Understood but 47% for HiI/*Not*-understood—are probably due to the fact that one Blank-slide condition was always first in order for each selection (and hence could not benefit from any perseveration effects), and the fact that the other Blank-slide condition followed *either* a Matching-slide (conducive to subjective understanding) *or* a Nonmatching slide (not conducive) condition. To check this out, as shown in Table 13-5, we compared

TABLE 13–4

Recognition Scores for G-S Choral Music (Percentage of Items Correct) as Functions of Visual Conditions and Subject Reports

Report of subject	Matching slide (%)	Nonmatching slide (%)	Blank slide (%)
Understood			
HiI selections	69 ($n = 8$)	46 ($n = 8$)	26 ($n = 8$)
LoI selections	54 ($n = 8$)	50 ($n = 2$)	20 ($n = 6$)
Not understood			
HiI selections	67 ($n = 3$)	00 ($n = 2$)	47 ($n = 8$)
LoI selections	44 ($n = 6$)	10 ($n = 8$)	10 ($n = 8$)

[4] The surprisingly high recognition score for LoI/Nonmatching/Understood (50%) is based on only two subjects, one of whom scored 100% and the other 00%!

TABLE 13-5

Signaled Understanding and Recognition Scores for Blank-Slide Periods, the Second Following Either Matching or Nonmatching Visual Materials

	First blank-slide period	Second Blank-Slide period Following matched/following non-matched visual material	
	% Time signaled	% Time signaled	% Time signaled
Understood			
HiI selections	55	64	54
LoI selections	2	64	2
Recognition scores			
HiI selections	28	44	50
LoI selections	12	12	00

subjective understanding and objective recognition scores for the first and second blank-slide periods separately, the latter being differentiated in terms of whether the immediately *preceding* slide had matched or had not matched the auditory material. First, note that for the first Blank-slide condition, without benefit of any warm-up, both signaled understanding, and recognition scores are typically low, relative to values for the second blank-slide period. Second, note that, for the second Blank-slide condition, signaled understanding of the LoI choral music (64%) was significantly higher than recognition scores (12%) *when a matching slide had just preceded*; when a nonmatching slide had preceded, however, there was practically no subjective understanding (2%) and absolutely no recognition. Apparently, when subjects have really been understanding the music (with the aid of a matching slide) and a blank slide comes on, *they persevere in an illusion of understanding* even though they do not (without the aid of a matching slide), as the recognition scores indicate.

There is, of course,[5] an alternative explanation that must be countered before we can accept the validity of the G-S phenomenon. This is the possibility that our subjects were not really following instructions *to attend to the sung words* but were attending to what really was clear, viz., the visual words—they may have reported subjective understanding in a

---

[5] However, this had to be pointed out to one of us (F. J. M.) by Ben Underwood!

self-deceiving fashion when the two inputs happened to match. There are several lines of evidence against this explanation: (1) As already noted, subjects signaled understanding of the HiI/nonmatching-slide choruses nearly as often (84%) as for the HiI/Matched-slide choruses (86%), whereas they signaled much less understanding for the LoI conditions— if the subjects *were* reading instead of listening, these values for HiI and LoI conditions would be about equal. (2) Recognition scores *on items from the visually presented materials* for the purely instrumental music conditions were much higher (74%) than for the Nonmatching slide/LoI/ Nonunderstood conditions (12%); if the subjects *had* been attending to the nonmatching slide materials in the latter case, why were their recognition scores for these materials not higher? (3) If the subjects were *not* paying attention to the sung words, why was the recognition for the choral (auditory) material as high as it was (46% correct) under the Nonmatching-slide condition? (4) As is clearly evident from Table 13-6, the over-all recognition scores *for the visually presented materials* (three or four items on the recognition tests for choral selections) are extremely low: for both HiI and LoI choral selections, not a single subject got a single item correct when the Nonmatching-slide condition was first in order (after the initial blank slide); when the Nonmatching-slide condition came

TABLE 13-6

Recognition Scores for Materials Presented Visually on Nonmatching Slides During HiI and LoI Choral Music

Subject No.	HiI selections When		LoI selections When	
	first	second	first	second
	In presentation		In presentation	
1	00%	00%	00%	00%
2	00%	66% (2/3 items)	00%	00%
3	00%	00%	00%	00%
4	00%	00%	00%	75% (3/4 items)
5	00%	00%	00%	00%
6	00%	33% (1/3 items)	00%	00%
7	00%	00%	00%	25% (1/4 items)
8	00%	00%	00%	00%
Means	00%	08% (3/24 items)	00%	12% (4/32 items)

TABLE 13-7

Mean Ratios of Covert Response Amplitudes for LoI Selections as Functions of Slide
Conditions and Understanding of Choral Materials

Measures	Matching slide Understood	Blank slide Not understood	t
Tongue EMG	.63	.44	2.48*
Chin EMG	.50	.46	0.49
Lip EMG	.40	.31	1.14
Leg EMG	.26	.18	0.90

second, there was only an average of 8% (3/24 possible) correct recognitions of visually presented material for HiI selections, and only 12% (4/32 possible) correct for LoI selections. If subjects were simply reading the slides, then they certainly did not retain much of what they had read.

The final question for this experiment concerns the EMG measurements made from tongue, chin, lip, and leg locations. One hypothesis, it will be recalled, is that heightened covert oral behavior should occur during perceptual clarification—the G-S Effect. The required comparison would be for oral behavior during the G-S Effect, relative to one in which there was lack of understanding, but with controls for general activation due to slide changing, etc. Consequently, means for each subject were computed for two conditions: (1) that in which LoI singing was accompanied by a matching slide and understanding was reported; and (2) that in which LoI singing was accompanied by a blank slide and no understanding was reported. These values were then used to compute a ratio that corrects for individual differences, based on the work of Lykken, *et al.* (1966). The larger the ratio, the greater the response amplitude. The results are presented in Table 13-7. There it may be noted that amplitude of tongue EMG (typically the most sensitive measure of covert oral behavior) was significantly higher under the condition in which the integration effect occurred (viz., .63 versus .44, $p < .05$). Since the nonoral measure (leg EMG) was relatively low in amplitude, and since the difference here between the two experimental conditions did not approach significance, it seems likely that the behavioral change was localized in the speech region. We, therefore, have some reason to believe that covert oral activity (in the tongue, where one would most expect it) does occur with higher amplitudes when the G-S effect is present than when it is absent.

The result of this first experiment in our planned series of four thus give us reasonable confidence that the Gilbert-and-Sullivan effect is a valid phenomenon—that presentation of synonymous material in one communication modality can clarify perception in another modality. But at this point both peripheral (covert oral) and central (meaningful) feedback mechanisms remain as possible explanations.

V. ON THE NATURE AND NURTURE OF TRACERS OF M

There are certain general agreements about the nature of semantic features, regardless of one's metaphysics: that they are typically bipolar (whether discrete or continuous), that they are ordered in generality, and therefore, frequency of utilization (whether hierarchically or paradigmatically), and that they combine componentially as simultaneous "bundles" in the differentiation of meanings. If meanings are indeed "mental" events (in the sense of mental/physical dualism), then there is nothing that objective science can do with them, and certainly it cannot make a determination as to their ultimate nature.

If we consider it more fruitful to assume that meanings are physical events in material bodies (brains, muscles, etc.), then we are right back in the Central/Peripheral issue again. If meanings are purely central events, then EMG correlates of them would be mere "tracers" in the sense that tracers are only indices of meanings. On the other hand, if meanings include peripheral events, in the sense that behavioral concomitants are necessary components, then the EMG's recorded [e.g., by Jacobson (1932) from the oral muscles while subjects did "mental" problems, and by Max (1935) from the fingers while deaf-mutes were thinking and dreaming] are not tracers but "essences." In either case, meanings must be either innately given distinctions that human bodily systems make, or they must be based upon some kind of sensory–perceptual learning; in the former case, meanings would not originate in behavior toward Things and, as I noted earlier, there would be no obvious constraints upon the proliferation of semantic features. If a compromise view should be closest to the truth of the matter—that meanings begin dependent on peripheral events, probably involving all of the organism's behavior systems, and then shift gradually to dependence on central *representations* of these events—then one should be able to use EMG's to record the peripheral establishment of meanings and perhaps EEG's as well to trace the centralization process. Ideally, we would like to know something about the "when" (in the course of semantic development), the "how" (what short-circuiting mechanisms operate), and the "where" (in the CNS) of centralization—if, indeed, it can be shown to occur. This compromise view would also postdict certain well-documented facts, for example, that immature humans typically have greater amplitudes of EMG than mature ones,[6] that less intelligent humans typically have greater EMG amplitude than more intelligent, and (as McGuigan, 1970b, has shown) writers with poor penmanship yield higher covert *oral* EMG's than writers with excellent penmanship. In this connection, we might note the general rule that there is decreasing dependence upon overt representing mechanisms (e.g., in making delayed reactions) as we go up the phylogenetic scale (cf. Osgood, 1953, pp. 655–666).

Let us now consider some more irrelevant data—again, irrelevant in the sense that they do not bear directly on psychophysiological measurements. First, with regard to the affective features of Evaluation, Potency, and Activity (E–P–A)—which I hope you will agree have been well-established psycholinguistically—Delos Wickens (1970) has demonstrated marked "release from proactive inhibition" in short-term memory when there is a sudden shift from presenting E+, P+, or A+ triads of words to presentation of E−, P−, or A−, or vice versa, of course. Interestingly enough, shifts in the physical or even grammatical characteristics of words had little effect. Working along related lines in our own laboratory, Meredith Richards and I have been able to show that the insertion of simple little function words *and* or *but* in simple little conjoined predicative sentences, like *X is sweet_____kind* versus *X is beautiful_____dumb* is predictable to an extraordinarily precise degree by the congruence or incongruence of the two adjectives conjoined—as indexed by their E–P–A feature loadings. And Rumjahn Hoosain has followed this up by demonstrating that, not only does increasing the number of negatives in a sentence (e.g., *Mary is sweet_____kind* versus *Mary is sweet_____not kind* versus *Mary is not sweet_____not kind*) increase the latency of inserting *and* or *but*, but in otherwise equivalent sentences those requiring *but* for regaining congruence take significantly longer than those which accept *and*.

However, E–P–A features yielded by the semantic differential technique are insufficient characterizations of meaning—as would be true for any subset of features, for that matter—and in recent years, we have been working with what I call "semantic interaction technique." So far it has only been applied to limited domains, the meanings of interpersonal verbs (with Kenneth Forster, cf. Osgood, 1970) and the meanings of emotion nouns (with Marilyn Wilkins). Very briefly, this technique utilizes the rules of usage of words *in systematically varied syntactic combinations* (phrases or sentences) as a means of inferring the minimum number and

---

[6] But see McGuigan (in press) for an alternative explanation, viz., that linguistic performance develops like motor skills so that initially the large scale responses that occur during reading, or riding a bicycle, dimish in amplitude with increasing proficiency, but still persist.

intuitive nature of features necessary to account, in componential combination, for exactly those rules of usage. For example, from arrays of linguistic facts—like *sudden surprise* being judged "apposite" or fitting by native English speakers, *sudden melancholy* being judged strange or "anomalous," and *sudden excitement* being judged at least "acceptable"— we are able to infer a semantic feature that might be dubbed Terminal/ Interminal. We find this same feature operating for interpersonal verbs as well, as witness *He met her suddenly* versus *He consoled her suddenly*, and also for other noun domains, as witness the acceptability of *sudden movement* versus the oddness of *sudden infinity*.

We are now working busily on the psycholinguistic validation of the semantic features inferred in this fashion. One experimental technique, reported in a recent doctoral thesis by Sara Smith (1971), utilizes a "word-finding" task, in which a *target word* (interpersonal verb of "known" feature composition) is presented with missing letters, for example,

$$\_X\_LO\_T,$$

either *alone* (control condition), along with *one cue word* (BULLY), along with *two cue words* having *redundant* semantic information with respect to the target word (BULLY and PERSECUTE), or along with two cue words having *nonredundant* information about the target (BULLY and IMPOSE ON). The *number* of features by which the target differed from the cue words in each set varied—one, two, three, or four of the six clearest features inferred for interpersonal verbs. The results, in a nutshell, were these: (1) the less the semantic distance in terms of these features between cue and target, the shorter the time for word-finding; (2) redundant double cues were better than single cues, but showed the same linear relation to number of shared features; nonredundant cues, however— cues which give *different* semantic component information about the target—facilitated word-finding more than redundant cues, and there was no simple linear relation to number of shared features in this case. Sara's husband, William R. Smith, has yet to face his final orals, but the data from his doctoral thesis are analysed. He used the "false recognition" technique—in which, after a certain point in a long list of words, some words presented are "old words" (previously shown) and others are "new"—and he also varied the number of semantic features by which the new words (also interpersonal verbs with "known" codings) differed from previously presented words. In this case, again, the probability of false recognition increased with the number of shared features.

I have offered these irrelevant data because I think that such reasonably sure psycholinguistic data on the nature and functioning of semantic features give McGuigan and myself better "external handles" on the setting up of experiments designed to determine the psychophysiological nature of little r_m's and trace their fates in the development of meaning. So, finally, let me offer what—given the present status of our collaborative work—might best be called "fragments of a research program on the nature and nurture of tracers." The essential steps in the program, as we see it, are (1) developing a technology of tracers, (2) using tracers in the study of meaning in mature language users, and (3) extending the technology to the study of the development of meaning in immature language users—where the most critical tests of peripheral versus compromise (centralization) versus central theories can be made.

1. Developing a Technology of Tracers

McGuigan and Childress (unpublished research) have already made encouraging progress on developing the technology of tracers. From some preliminary work, it seems possible to condition a single motor unit (SMUT), following Basmajian (1963), in the right abductor pollicis brevis (muscle in the thumb) to presentation of the word CLICK on a slide. The "conditioning" procedure uses auditory biofeedback to allow the subject to monitor his covert movement; the subject then demonstrates control over the covert response by making it only to CLICK slides and not blank ones. This is certainly not the way mediating reactions would be conditioned during language acquisition in children. Is such a deliberate process necessary or merely speedier with adult subjects? Particularly encouraging in this experiment, however, were the facts that there were no EMG differences between "intentional" thumbings, and "unintentional" thumbings (presumably) when lists of words, including "click," were merely read when the experiment was supposed to be over, and that the thumbing sometimes seemed to generalize to "click-like" words ("bang," "pop," "crack") during the same unintentional period.

However, as I have already pointed out, if my conception of representational mediator components (r_m's) is correct, our EMG recordings must tap *single reciprocally innervated reaction systems* in order to catch the bipolar character of semantic features. The technology of doing this—either from single motor units or from more massive reciprocal systems and either via dual EMGs types from a single electrode placement (reflecting excitation versus inhibition of the same muscle) or dual EMGs from double electrode placement on the antagonistic muscles—remains to be explored. This methodological problem arises whether, depending upon the conceptual thrust of a particular experiment, we are dealing with arbitrary reactions conditioned to artificial semantic features or with nonarbitrary, "natural" reactions presumably mediating "real" semantic features.

2. Research with Mature Language Users

One approach here is *to attach "artificial" (arbitrary) tracers to "old" (already developed) semantic features*. In a pilot study run by McGuigan and Anna Rose Childress (and delightfully titled "Double SMUT"), subjects were conditioned to react covertly by the biofeedback procedures described previously, with the *right* thumb to the word "future," and with the *left* thumb to the word "past." Then, having been told that in many cultures people relate the upward direction with the future, and the downward direction with the past, they were shown randomized slides with bars at the top, with bars at the bottom, or blank slides; instructions were to demonstrate their "control" over implicit thumbing. Following this (successful) conditioning procedure, lists of words (including future-oriented words like *tomorrow* and *up*, past-oriented words like *yesterday* and *down*, and neutral words like *century* and *click*) were read by the experimenter and repeated by the subject, and finally the experimenter quietly discussed the experiment and other matters with the subject (electrodes still attached) deliberately introducing time-oriented words.

There are a number of encouraging things about the results of this pilot study: (1) EMGs in right and left thumbs were more frequent ($p < .10$) for time-related words than neutral words, as well as for bars—up-or-down slides versus blank slides; (2) EMGs appeared in right thumbs significantly more frequently to future stimuli than to past (41/6), and in left thumbs more frequently to past than to future (28/8), ($p < .05$); (3) the concept *century* yielded either right *or* left thumbing from different subjects, apparently reflecting the inherent ambiguity of time-orientation for this concept. But, although these differential thumbings are now tracing a semantic feature, it is clearly the old Future/Past r_m component that is mediating the new reaction system—and we are still lacking measures in reciprocally antagonistic reaction systems.

An Artificial Language experiment that is still in the planning phase would also fall in this category. Here, three semantic features, known to differentiate among both emotion nouns and interpersonal verbs—Terminal/Interminal, Future/Past, and Dynamic/Insipid, the last a fusion of affective Potency and Activity—will be represented by synesthetic visual signs (the artificial language) and by emotion nouns, and interpersonal verbs (the natural language). The motor tracers attached to these already existing semantic features, although in a sense arbitrary, are designed to be gesturally symbolic, in the same way that the natural signing of deaf-mutes is. Thus, right-palm-vertical-with-chopping versus right-palm-down-horizontal-with-stroking for Terminal/Interminal; left-palm-down-index-pointing-forward   versus   left-palm-up-index-pointing-backward (over shoulder) for Future/Past; right-foot-tensed-upward versus right-foot-relaxed-downward (from neutral position) for Dynamic/Insipid. The visual "language" presented on slides would be abrupt-small-square versus elongated-oval for Terminal/Interminal, located in upper-right versus lower-left for Future/Past, and being either solid-form or thin-outline-form for Dynamic/Insipid. The parallel verbal language for which we have feature codings (also presented on slides) would be SURPRISE and THANK versus CONTENTMENT and SERVE for Terminal/Interminal, HOPE and PROMISE versus PRIDE and APOLOGIZE for Future/Past, and RAGE and ATTACK versus AWE and APPEASE for Dynamic/Insipid. Using these materials for the conditioning phase, with either visual *or* verbal stimuli, two types of experimental tests would be made: (1) of *transfer* from the visual to the verbal sign modality, or vice versa, of the tracer reactions; (2) of *generalization* of appropriate combinations and relative intensities of the tracer reactions to *novel combinations* of the signs, e.g., a neutral gray elongated oval in the middle of the slide *or* words like EXCITEMENT, ADORATION, MANIPULATE, and EVADE—again following either visual or verbal training. All this remains to be done, of course.

Another approach would be *to use natural tracers of new meanings*, and the main purpose here would be to trace the process of centralization of representational processes, if indeed centralization occurs (this obviously cannot be done with old mediators presumably centralized in the early history of the individual). But the problem here is *what* new semantic features? Features that are overt in some languages but not in English (e.g., gender tags in Romance languages, shape affixes on verbs for Navajo) do not help, because English also utilizes such features, even if not explicitly. However, possible semantic features like Tighten/Loosen (screwing-in versus screwing-out rotation with right hand), Collect/Discard (pincing-together versus separating-apart movements of the left hand) and perhaps Oriental/Occidental (eye squinting versus eye widening!) to a variety of both visual and verbal sign materials. In this case, it would be necessary to "shape" and then differentially reinforce these motor reactions in the process of reacting to the visual or verbal training materials, then produce semantic generalization and discrimination by the use of differential reinforcement with appropriate signs, and then test with novel stimulus materials in a completely relaxed state. Tests for centralization would require correct *verbal* reactions to novel sign combinations at various stages in the "conditioning" process while demonstrating that the amplitudes of the *tracer* reactions decrease—to the point where they can be damped out entirely.

A third approach with adults would be to check predictions from existing psycholinguistic data upon EMGs of tracers. One of our collaborative studies of this type has already been piloted in the McGuigan laboratory (with special thanks to Kathy Blake Pinkney and to Reggie Schoonover) using ambiguous sentence materials. The sentence *they are cooking apples* is ambiguous without indication of stress; in *they are cooking APPLES*, the pronoun *they* is usually coded +Human ("people") and *cooking* is coded as a Verb, but in *they are COOKING apples, they* is coded as −Human ("things") and *cooking* is coded as an Adjective. Other examples of such ambiguous sentences would be *they are coloring books*, and *they are riding horses*. On the other hand, there are many *unambiguous* sentences of this same surface form, for example, *they are washing clothes* and *they are taking tests* (must be "people" and Verb) versus *they are hitching posts* and *they are working clothes* (must be "things" and Adjective).

With Grass electrodes for EMG recording placed on the right forearm, left forearm, right leg, lip, and horizontal eye, and medial electroencephalogram (EEG) recorded as well, an attempt was made to condition both a "natural" tracer (lip-flattening in saying *ADJ*ective versus lip-pursing in saying *V*erb) and an "artificial" tracer (right-palm-down for Adjective versus right-palm-up for Verb). The sequence of events was as follows: (1) unambiguous adjectives and verbs were presented as single words in randomized orders, with subjects instructed to make the right-hand movement while saying adjective or verb, (2) *unambiguous* Verb or Adjective sentences of the above surface form were presented, with the key word repeated and the subject instructed to say either adjective or verb and make the correct movement; (3) to establish differential sets, Experimental Group I was shown four *unambiguous Adjective* sentences and Experimental Group II four *unambiguous Verb* sentences,[7] but now with the instruction to simply relax (no overt "saying" or "hand moving") and decide whether the *they* in each sentence referred to "people" or to "things" and, on delayed signal, say either "people" or "things"; (4) then four *ambiguous* sentences were presented, with no additional instructions; (5) step (3) above was repeated for each group, to reestablish the Adjective or Verb set; finally (6) four sentences *unambiguously opposed to* their set (Verbs if they were set for Adjectives, and vice versa) were presented, again with no additional instructions or break in the procedures.

The critical phases in the above design, of course, are (4) and (6). Since the coding of *they* as people or things must be congruent with interpretation of the *-ing* word as Verb or Adjective, respectively, we must predict

---

[7] A control group was given the same materials throughout, but with instructions to identify which letter of the key words occurred first in the alphabet and lift the toes of the right foot!

that during (4), particularly at the beginning, Group I subjects will *covertly* signal Adjective and the Group II subjects Verb, with both lip and right-arm EMGs *and hopefully without awareness*. Similarly, during step (6), where their sets are incompatible with the *un*ambiguous sentences, we must predict covert evidence of initial conflict in the lip (flattening versus pursing) and arm (opposed rotation tendencies), as indicated by "freezing" or rapid alternation.

Although at the time of this writing only two to three subjects have been run in each group, and individual EMGs are too variable to permit any firm conclusions, we nevertheless offer this type of research as a paradigm for further development of behavioral psycholinguistics.

3. Research with Immature Language Users

Research with young children, say, 3–6 years of age, will necessarily wait upon refinements in tracer technology and upon information obtained with adult subjects. We are also well aware of the difficulties associated with taking electrophysiological and electropsychological measures with very young children as subjects. Nevertheless, it is with immature language users that we would expect to obtain the clearest evidence for the central-ization (or lack thereof) of representational processes. There is now con-siderable evidence in the literature bearing on the approximate ages at which certain semantic features of adult language become established, for example, of Negation, of Possession, of Time-orientation, and the like. We do not, of course, know what behavioral processes are "naturally" associated with such features, but we may be able to take our cues from the gestural language of deaf-mutes. In any case, you can see that we are only in the very beginnings of this research program, but we are both excited by the possibilities it holds.

The Discussion of Dr. Osgood's Paper

LED BY DR. ALLAN PAIVIO
University of Western Ontario

Paivio: Well, I am delighted to start off the discussion of the paper, and agreeing and disagreeing with Dr. Osgood's comments.

The agreements are much more substantial than the disagreements, in that I agree that a theoretical approach, using a mediational model, is required. The controversy between Osgood and McGuigan is probably irrelevant for mediational constructs.

One thing quite important in psycholinguistics is Dr. Osgood's consistent emphasis on the primacy of the semantic, rather than the syntactic, component in language processing generally. The emphasis in Chomskian linguistics has been the other way around—that syntax somehow comes first, and then semantics, or meaning, afterward. I have tremendous respect for Dr. Osgood's steadfast maintenance of this position: that meaning is primary and syntax builds on it. Recently, even the transformationists have been coming around to Osgood's viewpoint; for example, McCauley's work, where they reject, or think they don't need, the deep structure level—that what you really have is mappings of meanings on surface structure; if that kind of approach becomes primary amongst the transformationists, it's a vindication of Dr. Osgood, even by that linguistic group.

Dr. Osgood emphasizes the necessity of some kind of learning theory to explain language behavior, meaning, and syntax. I think that this can be taken for granted. We may not agree about the kind of learning theory that is necessary, but the nativistic approach is bound to be sterile for psycholinguists who are interested in performance.

The semantic differential, and the theory behind it, has been a revolution in conceptual and operational approaches to meaning. It was a very important and obviously influential development, and we should be grateful for that. I like also the new emphasis—I know that it was there in the original version as well, but it is clearer now, and I think it has become more explicit in Dr. Osgood's thinking, too. The new emphasis is on meaning as a simultaneous bundle of distinctive features. I thought at one time the model had limitations in that it was linear (sequential)—where you went from the stimulus to r_m to the self-stimulation of the s_m to the overt mediated response. Well, this looked like a linear mediational chain, no different from implicit verbal chaining. But with the unit being a simultaneous bundle of distinctive features, many processes may occur in parallel rather than just straight-through, sequentially.

Perhaps my most important disagreement is the relative neglect of denotative meaning. Dr. Osgood has said that the semantic differential approach has been largely concerned with universal dimensions of affective meaning. That they come out universally may be a function of the particular use of the semantic differential, and the referential, or denotative, area of meaning is thus effectively excluded. Perhaps this is because the scales that are used to rate the concept interact in some way, and their combination may tend to force the rater into the metaphorical mode that Dr. Osgood emphasized here. Hence, you show that an enormous chunk of the variance is accounted for by the evaluative scale and decreasingly less by the other two; but if you put some denotative scales into the instrument, you can pull out a big factor, such as concreteness or abstractness. The items I have put into it are pertinent to imagery. In one-factor analytic study, I included concrete–abstract, tangible–intangible, and high imagery–low imagery items among a series of semantic differential-type scales, and the concepts to be rated varied in terms of their "thingness." Imagery–concreteness came out as the strongest factor, accounting for most of the variance. We gave short shrift to the affective dimensions, because we didn't put enough relevant scales in, and the usual affective factors failed to emerge clearly. The point is simply that you can get different results, depending on what scales you put in, and what kinds of concepts are being rated; what kind of meaning dimensions you get are probably going to be affected by an interaction of the scales that you use and the type of concepts involved. Whether you use the scales metaphorically or not may depend on just the combination of scales and concepts that you have used.

Now this is a very fundamental point in terms of what one considers meaning to be. For example, Dr. Osgood stated that it is important for an organism to know whether something is good or bad, strong or weak, and so on—is it a saber-toothed tiger or a cute, Neanderthal girl? This is certainly important; but note that prior to that kind of judgment, you must have identified the objects as saber-toothed tiger or cute girl. In other words, I cannot see the evaluation being made before you have had proper referents—a proper categorization at a referential or denotative level of the item. Now that's at the "thing" level, and Dr. Osgood is concerned with words. At the word level, consider rating some object, or some person that is absent, or perhaps not alive, like Einstein. On what basis would you rate him on affective scales? Will it be on the basis of the meaning of that word, independent of what it refers to? You must have a memory for that referent; and the first thing that word must do is call up that referent before you can identify its affective characteristics. I know that Dr. Osgood recognizes this, and we both know the work of Staats, where denotative meaning has been looked at by the use of semantic differential type scales, so that, in fact, it would be easy to extend the measuring instruments (and the model) to take into account the distinction in the two types of meaning, if they are two types. Maybe you, Dr. Osgood, chose the one and didn't emphasize the referent, because emphasizing the referent forces one to think of images, and you had a behavioristic hangover at the time you wrote your 1953 book and were reluctant to use that concept. "Image" certainly was forbidden then, and the ghost hadn't yet visited us again. Maybe somebody is going to come around and exorcise the ghost again.

All this doesn't affect the psychophysiological measurement of essences or tracers directly, but I have commented on a central feature of your talk, and of your whole approach; namely, the problem of meaning. There are two issues with regard to the McGuigan–Osgood controversy. There is a Peripheralist–Centralist controversy, but in addition, there is an integrational versus representational controversy. You see, Dr. Osgood emphasized a feedback effect from what he calls the representational level; that is, the affective meaning level, or the componential level of hypothetical internal reactions. His representational level is centralist, and he is contrasting it with a peripheralist interpretation; and the integrational level gets into the periphery as well. Dr. Osgood's integrational level, with which he contrasts the representational level, could also be central. So you may not be making the kind of distinction that you want in your experiments, if your intention is to distinguish between an integrational and a representational interpretation of where meaning lies.

The evidence from those studies clearly enables us to say that the word is a fundamental, integrated unit in some sense, but it does not in any way force us to interpret the effect in terms of feedback from an affective meaning system to the integrational level. That is one possible interpretation; another is that there is some kind of effect from within the integrational level. The whole tachistoscopic recognition situation is very complex, and many people have been caught with issues of teasing apart the effects of the structure of the word, the length of the word, and what the subject tends to pick out first (i.e., whether he picks out the first few items when he doesn't recognize the whole thing, or whether he picks out the entire word pattern, or only the last part of the word). These are just some of the enormous number of complexities, and the chain of inference required to tease out affective feedback effects from effects purely at a phonological or structural–visual level is very complicated indeed. We have done enough work with these things that I can appreciate the complexities.

My bet is that most of the effects in the Gilbert and Sullivan study are going to turn out to be of a structural nature; maybe this will support Dr. McGuigan. The reason is that in our work on threshold studies, we have found that higher order meaning does not really affect the perception of a word. What does affect it is the integration of the word into a unit, as determined by frequency of experience with it—not necessarily with the visual pattern or its spoken sound, but with the pronunciation, or some kind of overt reaction. So if it's at the integrational level, in Osgood's terms, then perhaps both the S–S and the R–R are involved; but in any case, an attribute that will affect perceptual thresholds consistently is frequency or familiarity of the item. Meaning attributes of words, when controlled for familiarity, do not have a consistent effect, either in auditory perception or in visual perception. This cannot be attributed simply to some general weakness in higher order meaning attributes, like concreteness or associative meaningfulness, inasmuch as concreteness at least has very big effects in memory studies, but none in perception where memory factors and familiarity have been controlled.

Open Discussion

Osgood: I have a few reactions. First, I don't think Dr. McGuigan and myself disagree about the existence of mediation; I think we agree that both integrational mediation processes (as witnessed in the ordinary clear hearing of something) and representational mediation processes are involved. What we disagree on is the *nature* of this second, representational process. Does it require peripheral feedback in the fluent adult language user, particularly from the oral muscles? Or, as my theory would say, no—at least with mature speakers, for I hold that representational feedback has become centralized. Peripheral feedback is thus no longer either necessary or sufficient for the adult. That is the issue between Dr. McGuigan and myself, not about the *existence* of representational processes, etc.

Now, with regard to the semantic differential and metaphor: The technique requires a subject to judge every item presented to him. He thus must rate concepts like "tornado" as *fair* or *unfair*. Obviously, sentences like "tornados are very unfair" don't occur when speaking English correctly, since tornados can be neither *fair* nor *unfair*; only something coded "human" can be *fair* or *unfair*—not even dogs, I guess, can be *fair* or *unfair*. Yet subjects make such judgments, and they agree, among themselves, that tornados are absolutely unfair! They have to judge "defeat" as *hot* or *cold*, and it is usually *cold*. Other examples of metaphorical scale usage are *hard* or *soft* "power," or *sweet* or *sour* "mother-in-law." The thing to conjure with here is the lawfulness with which native speakers do utilize metaphor. For any particular scale—be it *hot–cold*, or *sweet–sour*—in any random sample of, say a hundred concepts, there will be less than 10 out of the hundred, for which *hot* or *cold* is denotatively relevant. Except for such items as "fire" or "snow," there are very few concepts that are denotatively relevant to any particular scale. Therefore, for most concepts, most of the time, most of the scales must be used metaphorically.

Now, the point is that it is apparently the shared affect (or shared feeling) that is the common coin of metaphor; it is this which makes a jagged red line feel like the word "agitated," and so forth. This affective agreement—this very primitive, deep aspect of meaning—is apparently the basis of metaphor. Therefore, for most concepts, *sweet–sour* will rotate toward and be used, primarily, as a metaphor for *good–bad*; *hard–soft*, for most concepts, will be used as a pure potency kind of metaphor, like *hard* rather than *soft* "power." This being the case—and with factor analysis running its factors through the clusters of highest correlations—the highest correlations will be based on shared affect (because most of the scales, most of the time, are being used metaphorically), and the dominance of Evaluation, Potency, and Activity is thus explained.

Regarding integration, feedback, etc., the *theory* is not restricted to affective meaning; rather, we empirically obtain these massive affective factors by the semantic differential technique. The theory is completely general, and includes denotative features as well. I assume that in the case of the Gilbert-and-Sullivan phenomenon very complex meaningful feedback is involved, probably very little affective meaning and much more of the denotative sort. In ordinary listening and reading there is a total pattern of simultaneous semantic components which are regularly elicited; hence, their self-stimulation effects are feeding back every time you hear or read a word. Of course, heard and seen words are as close to synonyms as you can get, having nearly identical meanings. Therefore, the meaning one gets through one modality, in reading *or* hearing, is available as a *total* r_M process for "tuning up" perceptual integrations, not just affective feedback.

Finally, because of the limitation to E, P, and A of the semantic differential technique (by forcing metaphors), we have been developing a completely different technique which I call the semantic interaction technique. I feel this is particularly relevant to Dr. McGuigan's and my work on tracers. The semantic interaction technique utilizes the rules of usage of words in combination with other words, i.e., in phrases, sentences, etc. Some phrases sound apposite (fitting), others are merely permissible, but other combinations of words are semantically anomalous. The semantic interaction technique is designed to tease out the minimal set of features which will account for such complex patterns of rules of usage. We have applied this technique to emotion nouns and interpersonal verbs. Consider the phrase "sudden surprise": subjects say that this is apposite, fitting; "sudden surprise" feels right. But what about "sudden melancholy"? This seems very strange, indeed. Now, from such facts, we tease out, for emotion nouns, a Terminal–Interminal feature: "sudden" and "surprise" share + Terminal, whereas "melancholy" is coded − Terminal (i.e., interminable, prolonged). Thus, "sudden melancholy" is anomalous; you can't represent + and − Terminal both at once. When you drive the same representational component (r_m) in opposed directions at the same time (e.g., both terminably, by "sudden," and interminably, by "melancholy") you get "freezing" and the judgment of semantic anomaly: ". . . it sounds strange." We can use these facts to tease out much richer, more denotative features of meaning.

Dr. Peter MacNeilage (University of Texas at Austin): I have a suspicion about your associative principle for motor integration; that is, the principle that stimuli that go together tend to get evoked together, or tend to evoke each other—

Osgood: Or a response for a response; this is S–S and R–R really.

MacNeilage: —(continued)—With regard to the actual serial ordering process, when you make a typing error, there is no tendency for the letter that comes in to produce a more frequent digraph with the previous letter, than the digraph that it would have been had the error not occurred.

Osgood: My own personal favorite typing error occurs when I try to type "ratio"; unless I literally stop, I type "ration." Would that be a counterexample of what you are saying? What you are saying is that, when you actually study all types of errors, my type is not the dominant one.

MacNeilage: Right. In fact, when you look at the error and the previous letter, more often than not it is not even a digraph sequence that occurs in the English language. Two variables are at work. One is the difficulty of hitting various keys, and that is predictive to some extent. Second, as in the phenomenon of spoonerisms, something comes later that potentiates an error.

Similarly, if you take a good look at spoonerisms, you find that when something gets advanced and tacked onto something else, it is probably not because of the frequency of that pair, as such; it is probably more because of the potentiating effects.

Osgood: I take it from yesterday's discussion of your paper that you would agree that syllabic units do tend to occur in simultaneous bundles, more centrally than the motor projection system.

MacNeilage: Right. As long as we have a unit that contains subunits, the associative notion may explain why they cohere. But then, when you are asking how the two units get put together, the associative principle is not so pertinent.

Osgood: We still agree that word-units in speech perception and (probably) syllabic units in speech production tend to be integrated centrally because of their high frequency, redundancy, etc. The spoonerism phenomenon occurs when there is formal relation *between* such units. In the latter case, I agree absolutely that the picture is much more muddled—it is not a simple association mechanism, but probably involves motivational effects as well—a tendency of items of focal interest to the speaker to move ahead and become anticipatory.

REFERENCES

Basmajian, J. V. Control and training of individual motor units. *Science*, 1963, **141,** 3579, 440–441.

Bever, T. A. The cognitive basis for linguistic structures. In J. R. Hayes (Ed.), *Cognition and the development of language.* New York: Wiley, 1970

Brown, R. *Psycholinguistics: Selected papers.* New York: Free Press, 1970.

Chomsky, N. *Syntactic structures.* The Hague: Mouton & Co., 1957.

Chomsky, N. *Aspects of the theory of syntax.* Cambridge, Massachusetts: MIT Press, 1965.

Chomsky, N. *Language and mind.* New York: Harcourt, 1968.

Edfeldt, A. W. *Silent speech and silent reading.* Chicago: University of Chicago Press, 1960, Viii 164.

Fodor, J. A. Can meaning be an r_m? *Journal of Verbal Learning and Verbal Behavior,* 1965, **4,** 73–81.

Fodor, J. A. More about mediators: A reply to Berlyne and Osgood. *Journal of Verbal Learning and Verbal Behavior,* 1966, **5,** 412–415.

Gardner, R. A., & Gardner, B. T. Teaching sign language to a chimpanzee. *Science,* 1969, **165,** 664–674.

Gould, L. N. Auditory hallucinations and subvocal speech. *Journal of Nervous and Mental Disease,* 1949, **109,** 418–427.

Gould, L. N. Verbal hallucinations as automatic speech. *American Journal of Psychiatry,* 1950, **107,** 110–119.

Greenberg, J. H. The definition of linguistic units. *Essays in Linguistics.* Chicago: University of Chicago Press, 1957.

Greenwald, A. G. Sensory feedback mechanisms in performance control: With special reference to the ideo-motor mechanism. *Psychological Review,* 1970, **77,** 73–99.

Hartman, G. W. II. Changes in visual acuity through simultaneous stimulation of other sense organs. *Journal of Experimental Psychology,* 1933, **16,** 393–407.

Hebb, D. O. *Organization of behavior.* New York: Wiley, 1949.

Hull, C. L. *Principles of behavior.* New York: Appleton, 1943.

Jacobson, E. Electrophysiology of mental activities. *American Journal of Psychology,* 1932, **44,** 677–694.

Kekcheev, K. K., Kravkov, S. V., & Shvarts, L. A. On factors reducing the activity of the visual and auditory organs. In I. D. London, (Ed.) Research on sensory interaction in the Soviet Union. *Psychological Bulletin,* 1954, **51,** 531–568.

Kuhn, T. S. *The structure of scientific revolutions*. Chicago: University of Chicago Press, 1964.

Lashley, K. S. The problem of serial order in behavior. In L. A. Jeffress (Ed.), *Cerebral mechanisms in behavior*. New York: Wiley, 1951.

Locke, J. L., & Fehr, F. S. Subvocal rehearsal as a form of speech. *Journal of Verbal Learning and Verbal Behavior*, 1970, **9**, 495–498.

Lykken, D. T., Rose, R., Luther, B., & Maley, M. Correcting psychophysiological measures for individual differences in range. *Psychological Bulletin*, 1966, **66**, 481–484.

Max, L. W. An experimental study of the motor theory of consciousness. III Action-current responses of deaf mutes during sleep. *Journal of Comparative Psychology*, 1935, **19**, 469–486.

McGuigan, F. J. Covert oral behavior and auditory hallucinations. *Psychophysiology*, 1966, **3**, 73–80.

McGuigan, F. J. Covert oral behavior during the silent performance of language tasks. *Psychological Bulletin*, 1970, **74**, 309–326. (a)

McGuigan, F. J. Covert oral behavior as a function of quality of hand-writing. *American Journal of Psychology*, 1970, **74**, 309–326. (b)

McGuigan, F. J. The function of covert oral behavior ("silent speech") during silent reading. *International Journal of Psycholinguistics*, in press.

McGuigan, F. J., & Rodier, W. I. III. Effects of auditory stimulation on covert oral behavior during silent reading. *Journal of Experimental Psychology*, 1968, **76**, 649–655.

McGuigan, F. J., Keller, B., & Stanton, E. Covert language responses during silent reading. *Journal of Educational Psychology*, 1964, **55**, 339–343.

McNeill, D. *The acquisition of language*. New York: Harper, 1970.

Osgood, C. E. *Method and theory in experimental psychology*. New York: Oxford Univ. Press, 1953.

Osgood, C. E. A behavioral analysis of perception and language as cognitive phenomena. In J. S. Bruner (Ed.), *Contemporary approaches to cognition*. Cambridge, Massachusetts: Harvard University Press, 1957. (a).

Osgood, C. E. Motivational dynamics of language behavior. In M. R. Jones (Ed.), *Nebraska symposium on motivation*. Lincoln, Nebraska: Univ. of Nebraska Press, 1957. (b)

Osgood, C. E. On understanding and creating sentences. *American Psychologist*, 1963, **18**, 735–751.

Osgood, C. E. Meaning cannot be an r_m? *Journal of Verbal Learning and Verbal Behavior*, 1966, **5**, 402–407.

Osgood, C. E. Interpersonal verbs and interpersonal behavior. In J. L. Cowan (Ed.), *Studies in language and thought*. Tucson, Arizona: University of Arizona Press, 1970.

Osgood, C. E. Where do sentences come from? In D. Steinberg and L. Jakobovits (Eds.), *Semantics*. New York: Cambridge University Press, 1971. (a)

Osgood, C. E. Exploration in semantic space: A personal diary. *Journal of Social Issues*, 1971, **27**, 5–64. (b)

Osgood, C. E., & Richards, M. M. From Yang and Yin to *and* or *but*. *Language*, 1973 (in press).

Roydes, R., & Osgood, C. E. Effects of grammatical form-class set upon perception of grammatically ambiguous English words. *Journal of Psycholinguistic Research*, 1972, **1**, 165–174.

Schilling, R. *Zeitschrift für Psychologie,* 1929, **111,** 204–46. In G. Humphrey (Ed.), *Thinking, an introduction to its experimental psychology.* New York: Wiley, 1951.

Smith, S. W. Word-finding in the presence of semantically related cues. Doctoral dissertation, University of Illinois, 1971.

Smith, W. M. Visual recognition: Facilitation of seeing by saying. *Psychonomic Science,* 1965, **2,** 57–58. (a)

Smith, W. M. Visual recognition: Facilitation of seeing by hearing. *Psychonomic Science,* 1965, **2,** 157–158. (b)

Smith, W. R. *Influence of semantic feature similarity on false recognition of interpersonal verbs.* Doctoral dissertation in process, University of Illinois, 1971.

Sokolov, A. N. Studies of the speech mechanisms of thinking. In M. Cole and I. Maltzman (Eds.), *A handbook of contemporary Soviet psychology.* New York: Basic Books, 1969.

Wickenś, D. D. Encoding categories of words: An empirical approach to meaning. *Psychological Review,* 1970, **77,** 1–15.

Zwosta, M., & Zenhausern, R. Application of signal detection theory to subliminal and supraliminal accessory stimulation. *Perceptual and Motor Skills,* 1969, **28,** 699–704.

CHAPTER FOURTEEN

Final Open Discussion

This period was for open discussion on an individual basis.

Dr. F. J. McGuigan (Hollins College): There were several themes running throughout the conference that deserve particular comment. First was the frequency and variety with which different speakers used motor concepts, both experimentally and theoretically, though I realize that this could be selective perception on my part. For example, Dr. Black reported a correlation between theta and overt responding, Dr. Mulholland studied the visual oculomotor system during attention, Dr. Rechtschaffen reported an eye (muscle) response prior to dreams, and Paivio's response to memory and organizing motor components.

Second, though the word "mediation" may mean a number of different things, mediational concepts ran through essentially all presentations.

A third common concept was Dr. Black's "concomitant measures," or the term "patterns of covert processes" that I used. The frequent occurrence of such a concept indicates an increasing sophistication in psychophysiology, in that we understand the necessity for making multiple measurements as a function of our independent variables.

A general commentary on contemporary psychology is the contrast with a decade or two ago in that we are now not afraid to use "mentalistic" terms, and I think we are finding out what they mean empirically. Whether or not such terms turn out to be useful is another matter; I strongly suspect that they won't be.

One final comment is why we are in trouble if an alternative to "peripheralism" is true. Suppose that thought (consciousness) really is the running off of a phase sequence, and that there is no corresponding lawful efferent activity. Now, if that is what thought is, how are we going to get into the brain and measure it? Even evoked potentials and the CNV are too crude for this purpose. But if some kind of neo-Watsonian position is

493

true, there are critical peripheral phenomena that we can get at and measure. Otherwise, we must hope that Hebb at least is right—that the central process is critical, but an "overflow" response is linked in a one-to-one fashion with each cell assembly. Hence, by measuring the response, whether it be overt or covert, we can get a handle on the critical central event. In short, if the motor event does not function in an isomorphic fashion with the central event, psychologists might as well quit in this area. For, I cannot see how you can ever get into the intact human and measure such central events. So my real hope and strategy is to concentrate on events that we can realistically measure. Let us hope that we can measure thinking by measuring peripheral events, with, of course, the contribution of evoked potentials, CNVs, etc.

Dr. T. H. Bhatti (University of Virginia): This Peripheralist–Centralist controversy that has been discussed here these past 3 days is a very relevant issue; I do not know how I would classify myself. As I was listening to Dr. McGuigan, one of the thoughts that occurred to me was a story I heard in Pakistan while I was a small boy. In a small village, where there was no electricity, someone found a guy looking around on the ground under a streetlamp. And someone asked him, "Hey, Joe, what are you doing down there?" He answered, "I am looking for a needle I lost." "Well," the man asked, "where did you lose it?" The man on the ground answered, "I lost it in my house; I dropped it while putting a button on my shirt." "Then why are you looking here?" "Because I don't have any light at home, so this was the only place I could look."

It is quite difficult, as Dr. McGuigan noted, to go into the central structures and identify the various processes going on. For example, if you take a human infant, a few weeks old, and you put him on a rope, strung from ceiling to ground, his behavior is something like this: he clutches the rope, he hangs there, he kicks his leg, and he cries. Now, if you study this from the input and response point of view—trying to figure out what is going on in the central mechanisms—you are going to come up with a theory that this child perceives danger, experiences a sense of helplessness, and is crying for help. Now you will find exactly the same behavior in infants whose forebrain structures are missing, aside from the thalamus and hypothalamus. As far as behavior is concerned, you cannot tell the difference by means of basic physical reflexes—temperature control, or what have you; the same behavior is manifested whether or not the forebrain structures are missing. So there is a deficiency in drawing conclusions about what is happening in the central nervous system without having direct recourse to measures.

There is probably some truth in both the Centralist and Peripheralist.

A small example from the results of a study that compared the sexual responses of two cats. (Psychologists are stuck with rats, and physiologists are stuck with cats.) Standard sexual behavior occurred in Cat A when the genital area was stimulated. In Cat B, with the same stimulation, there was a different response: at times Cat B exhibited the usual sexual response, and at other times, it turned around and bit the experimenter. The experimenter further investigated this by removing the ovaries of Cat A, and by injecting hormones (estrogen) into Cat B. Now, with no hormone levels at all, Cat A continued to respond as before; Cat B, also responded consistently in the standard fashion as long as the estrogen level was maintained.

This was not a personality difference in the two cats, as one might be tempted to assume. Previously, Cat A had a lesion around the midbrain. Such a midbrain cat responds to a peripheral stimulus in a very consistent, predictable way. In Cat B, the lesion was made so the forebrain structures were removed and only the hypothalamus was intact. In Cat B, you find that the basic neuronal reflex pattern of behavior, which was actually being elicited, is now modified by the intrinsic state of the animal, which in this case is a hormonal state. So, if you want to define instinct as a pattern of behavior that originates in, or is modified by the intrinsic state of the animal, you can say that Cat A has a reflex sexual behavior, and Cat B has an instinctive sexual behavior.

In essence, then, basic behavior patterns can be produced by the so-called lower brain structures; and as you go higher up, other structures control the initiation of basic response patterns. The main idea is that we have evidence that you can elicit similar responses from the lower centers and from the higher centers. Now, in this particular case, if we did not know about the lesions, would we be saying that Cat A is having "dirty thoughts" all the time? If we define thought as a neurological function, where an input comes in, is sensed or perceived, and something generates a response, then you could say there are two levels of thinking going on in these animals.

A similar difference has been noted in the speech of human subjects for whom there is a huge infarct in the speech areas in the frontal and parietal lobes, leading to global aphasia—the patient is thus unable to respond verbally to any input. He cannot perceive speech; he cannot say anything about it; he cannot have any spontaneous output. When these patients get extremely mad and frustrated, they *can* say a couple of words, like basic swearing phrases, and crying, and laughing. Some people believe that there may be a basic, evolutionary, speech mechanism located in the midbrain in addition to the more recent regions in the cortex.

Dr. Peter MacNeilage (University of Texas at Austin): A point about different uses of biofeedback techniques is based on a paper by Harvey Sussman, working in our laboratory. He placed a transducer on the tongue, and translated the signal generated by the tongue's movement into a tone that went into the subject's ear. The subject was provided with a target stimulus in the same modality, e.g., another tone in the other ear, and the subject's task was to track this target tone. The most interesting thing was that normal subjects track better if you put the tone that they themselves generate in their right ear, hence feeding to the left hemisphere (the standard tone goes to the left ear). The reason is that the left hemisphere has a specialized mechanism for sensory–motor integration that has been developed for use in speech and language. This kind of technique can be used as a measure of the integrity, or the lack of integrity, of various sensory–motor systems involved in language behavior—auditory or visual stimuli can be used to manipulate the hemispheric effects. We can also make the larynx a transducer, so that as it opens and closes, it can generate signals. In this way, we can test in clinical patients of various kinds, which combinations show up their deficiency, in relation to normal subjects. Such diagnostic uses have not been brought up at this conference, and they could be very significant. Additionally, we may be able to use this as a training technique in some cases of articulatory difficulty, where we provide discrete and continuous information about what the articulator is doing.

Dr. Tom Mulholland (Perception Laboratory, VA Hospital, Bedford, Massachusetts): One way EEG measures can be used to study some features of thinking: First, I would like to point out that attention is to the visual, as a question is to the verbal—attention is a request for information. If you get the information, you do not pay attention in the same way you did originally, e.g., when a stimulus is repeated, the alpha reaction decreases. If you habituate to one stimulus, and then change it slightly, the orienting response is reinstated. So, perhaps you could do an experiment like this: present a word that fits into a particular region of Dr. Osgood's semantic space, and habituate that word. Then test with a second word to see if you could reinstate the attentional response; if reinstated, you would know that that particular word belonged to a different class. For example, suppose you habituated to "hot," and tested with "warm" and "cold." Which one would have the greater probability of reinstating the attentional response?

Another method would be to habituate a whole class of words—the closer words are together in meaning, the more rapidly habituation should occur. The trick is to get a large-scale electroencephalographic effect of small changes in the psychological dimension.

Dr. Louis Aarons (*Department of Mental Health, Chicago*)*:* The conference was very enjoyable, though I am not starting out complimentary in order to dig anyone. I have heard many theories entertained by the different speakers. We have heard about elephants on elephants, and we have heard about sexing and unsexing cats, but I was surprised not to hear anything about chimps—chimps might provide an opportunity to get at some mechanisms similar to the humans at a different phylogenetic level. There also was an omission of Skinner's work, in an indirect way. Although we talked about operant conditioning, I was surprised that Dr. MacNeilage didn't discuss Skinner's consideration of errors in which he goes into intraverbal connectives; these have to be considered when you study speech errors. And I would remind people that Meehl really clarified Chomsky's analysis or misanalysis of Skinner, on a methodological level. There also should be more work on developmental aspects, which everyone seems to take for granted, like Dr. McGuigan's work that shows that as the child grows up, the motor movements in the mouth progressively decrease.

As a final statement, I would like to remind you of something that was said in many different ways here: language is not equal to thinking.

Dr. Richard Carney (*Eastern Kentucky University*)*:* Dr. Paivio's statement that denotative meaning is necessary for categorization for connotative meaning has gone unchallenged to date. I believe we have a great deal of psychophysiological evidence that this is not necessarily true. The GSR reaction time data from operated animals, and maybe even in the split-brain human, indicate that autonomic arousal occurs prior to the specific recognition, or classification, in the denotative sense of the concept being presented (and even prior in information processing sequence). There may indeed be functionally separate systems, and as Dr. Osgood suggested, the denotative system is primary and primitive. Even Bhatti's example on cats could be taken as an instance of this.

More generally, I want to defend chimps. We have had enough evidence on the thought processes and the genetic makeup of chimps to see that they are probably overlapping humans on both counts, about 99%. I would like to plead that we treat them like people, and not chop them up indiscriminately. Second, throughout the conference, was the recognition of great individual differences. But the reaction was to systematically distribute individual differences equally over conditions, or in order to eliminate individual differences from our data by using the same individual as his own control. I would like to plead that this source of variation not be treated as error, but treated as information; this is particularly critical when we are trying to understand thought, especially in dream states, and in twilight areas. Unless we take into account those variables that make people behave differently, we are going to have a great deal of difficulty getting comparability across our studies. Instead of treating individual differences as error, we ought to systematically investigate them. Until we do this, we are going to have noise that we cannot eliminate, and we are going to have incomparability in our studies.

Dr. Alec Dale (Allegheny College): There are differences in our connotative meaning of the Centralist–Peripheralist concepts, in contrast to the objective definition that Dr. McGuigan provided for us. An example of this would be jokes about thinking in the throat, and letting our head fall asleep, and talking. Using the terms in the jokes makes the whole area fuzzy. If we used the terms that Dr. McGuigan suggested and realized the importance of these concepts, then the area would be much more clarified.

I also want to reinforce the study of individual differences, as just mentioned. Unfortunately, in my own work on autonomic variables, the dimension of perceptual styles has not led to the discovery of very significant differences between individuals.

Author Index

Numbers in italics refer to the pages on which the complete references are listed.

499

Subject Index